Embodied Selves

Embodied Selves

AN ANTHOLOGY OF PSYCHOLOGICAL TEXTS 1830–1890

Edited by

Jenny Bourne Taylor

and

Sally Shuttleworth

CLARENDON PRESS · OXFORD

This book has been printed digitally and produced in a standard specification
in order to ensure its continuing availability

OXFORD
UNIVERSITY PRESS

Great Clarendon Street, Oxford OX2 6DP

Oxford University Press is a department of the University of Oxford.
It furthers the University's objective of excellence in research, scholarship,
and education by publishing worldwide in

Oxford New York

Auckland Bangkok Buenos Aires Cape Town Chennai
Dar es Salaam Delhi Hong Kong Istanbul Karachi Kolkata
Kuala Lumpur Madrid Melbourne Mexico City Mumbai Nairobi
São Paulo Shanghai Taipei Tokyo Toronto

Oxford is a registered trade mark of Oxford University Press
in the UK and in certain other countries

Published in the United States
by Oxford University Press Inc., New York

ISBN 0-19-871042-9

Printed in Great Britain by

Antony Rowe Ltd., Eastbourne

Acknowledgements

We would like to thank the Leverhulme Trust for awarding us Research Fellowships which enabled us substantially to complete this research, the Wellcome Institute for the History of Medicine Library, the London Library, the Leeds Library, and the Leeds City Reference Library. We are grateful to Professor François Lafitte for permission to publish the extract from H. Havelock Ellis's *The Criminal*. Thanks also to Joe Bearn of the Royal Society of Medicine, Tony Inglis, Elaine Showalter, and Roger Smith for their help and advice at various stages of the project, and to John Christie and Patrick Parrinder for their support throughout.

Contents

CONTENTS

Introduction

> In truth this 'we', which looks so simple and definite, is a nebulous and inde-
> finable aggregation of many component parts which war not a little among
> themselves, our perception of our existence at all being perhaps due to this
> very clash of warfare, as our sense of sound and light is due to the clashing
> of vibrations.
>
> Samuel Butler, *Life and Habit* (1877)

Embodied Selves makes available some of the wide range of writing on identity in the growing area of mental science that emerged between 1830 and 1890. Our aim here is not to provide a comprehensive history of psychology as we now understand it as a discipline, but to bring together primary sources which give a sense of how some of the crucial questions about the shaping of social identity were discussed at this time. These concerns included the complex relationship between the mind and the body; the workings of individual consciousness; the power of unconscious processes and the limits of self control; the problematic boundary between normal and aberrant states of mind, and the connections between the individual life and the long-term genealogy of which it is part. Together they formed an intricate, varied, and at times contradictory discourse that permeated Victorian intellectual culture.

Cultural critics now acknowledge how profoundly the broad concerns of nineteenth-century science—above all the perceptions and methods of evolu-tionary theory—shaped contemporary thought, providing crucial narrative models of social and organic change that were actively adapted and used by nineteenth-century novelists, but as yet there has been little work done on the close connections between Victorian narrative and the wider concerns of the emerging materialist science of the self. We are beginning to recognize how much concepts that now seem characteristically 'modern'—above all the 'dis-covery' of the unconscious and the development of psychoanalysis at the begin-ning of the twentieth century—drew on ideas that had been developing throughout the nineteenth century; but there is still a tendency to read explo-rations of the unconscious in Victorian fiction in the light of later theory rather than in the discursive context of their own time. Michel Foucault has drawn attention to the ways in which particular discourses and institutional practices, particularly relating to madness and crime, operated as regimes of disciplinary surveillance and forms of power. He has exploded the myth of the 'repressed' Victorians by showing the ways in which the endless discussion of a sexualized identity was central to the formation of a 'deep' self during this time. This varied work has knocked down many over-simple assumptions, yet some stubbornly remain intact; it is still often assumed, for instance, that the Victorians firmly believed in a unified, stable ego, that the English concept of the unconscious was of a crude physical reflex, or that medical and psychiatric discourses represented a monolithic, almost conspiratorial desire to construct and police dominant notions of gender. This anthology aims to give some indication of the range and subtlety of Victorian debates on identity, debates which expressed a profoundly ambivalent sense of self, even while they helped to mould dominant cultural perceptions, meanings, and power relations.

Our focus here is on the various forms of a materialist science of the self which rejected the dualistic division between mind and body, conceiving both the body and the mind in diverse and complex ways, and which was at once fascinated and perturbed by those hidden inner regions that remained beyond conscious control. 'Mental science' or 'mental physiology' was consolidated during the nineteenth century as a growing intellectual discipline and an important branch of the medical profession. Questions about the nature of consciousness and cognition, about the significance and workings of memory, and about the limits of self-knowledge and the will, had formed some of the central problems of philosophy, and they continued to be crucial to the philosophy of mind throughout the nineteenth century. Mental physiology, however, aimed to wrest these issues away from the abstract realm of metaphysics, and to subject them to empirical criteria and practical application based on the study of physiology. At the same time, the study of mental disease had been gaining respectability as a legitimate branch of medicine with the reforms in the treatment of insanity in both Britain and France, and their findings drew on and fed into wider psychological discussions. The development of the state asylum system, the newly respectable private practices, and the increasing specialization of medicine as a whole fostered a growing band of highly successful professional men whose careers stretched through the century, including many of the writers who appear here, such as John Conolly, Forbes Winslow, Henry Holland, Henry Maudsley, and James Crichton-Browne. The materialist study of the individual mind which centred, in the early nineteenth century, on phrenology, gave way by mid-century to the evolutionary study of the self as an aspect of a wider science of the organic world. Psychology contributed to an organic social theory in which the whole body, not just the brain, was seen as a collection of conscious and unconscious processes, linking the individual life to a collective narrative of change. These conceptual shifts can be charted in the various specific areas explored in this collection, such as the ways in which the mind is expressed through physical signs, the analysis of dreams and the divided self; the nature of insanity and the limits of moral responsibility; and forms of sexual and racial difference, the significance of memory, and the development of consciousness.

Although psychiatry was becoming more specialized it had not yet developed a 'scientific' language. Professional journals, such as the *Asylum Journal*, which became the *Journal of Mental Science*, the *Journal of Psychological Medicine and Mental Pathology*, the *Medical Critic and Psychological Journal*, *Mind*, and *The Brain*, were all started during the nineteenth century, but many of the ideas that they discussed were not only reported but developed in articles aimed at a wider readership. These included serious journals, such *Blackwood's Edinburgh Magazine*, the *Quarterly Review*, the *Fortnightly Review*, the *Westminster Review*, and more popular magazines aimed at a middle-class family readership, such as *Household Words* and *Macmillan's Magazine*. Popular textbooks in the tradition of 'self-help' works had great appeal; at the same time well-established writers aimed to reach an audience of well-informed contemporaries, and often responded to points raised by their readers and incorporated them into their work. Nineteenth-century culture did not share our sense of disciplinary divisions between 'arts' and 'science', 'theoretical' and 'practical' knowledge, and while these boundaries were beginning to emerge towards the end of the century, they had yet to harden. As many of these extracts show, psychological writers often developed their points through numerous literary allusions and tropes, and often, indeed, cited cases from novels as well as real life to illustrate particular arguments. The issues they debated formed a crucial aspect of the cultural landscape, permeating the work of contemporary novelists, poets, and cultural critics.

In choosing these extracts, we have had to be ruthlessly selective, and can offer only a glimpse of the debates that were taking place.[1] We have organized the material into five broad sections which reflect the wide range of interests and issues discussed, but they continually overlap and merge into each other. 'Reading the mind' focuses on how, particularly during the first part of the century, the body could be read as the map of the mind, providing clues to the working of the hidden self. Both the older aesthetically based practice of physiognomy and the science of phrenology claimed to hold the key to interpreting the inner mind through the outward signs of the body, but their methods and their cultural and political meanings, their sense of the individual's ability to control or develop their physical predispositions, were very different. The development

---

[1] There are several useful anthologies of specific developments in psychiatry and debates on insanity, the most extensive being Richard Hunter and Ida MacAlpine, (eds), *Three Hundred Years of Psychiatry: 1535–1860*, (London: Oxford University Press, 1963). Other useful collections include Vieda Skultans, (ed.), *Madness and Morals: Ideas on Insanity in the Nineteenth Century* (London: Routledge and Kegan Paul, 1975); Charles E. Goshen, (ed.), *A Documentary History of Psychiatry: A Source Book on Historical Principles* (London: Vision Press, 1967); Thomas E. Szasz, (ed.), *The Age of Madness: The History of Voluntary Mental Hospitalisation Presented in Selected Texts* (London: Routledge and Kegan Paul, 1975); Roy Porter, (ed.), *The Faber Book of Madness* (London: Faber, 1991). On nineteenth-century concepts of womanhood, see Pat Jalland and John Hooper, (eds), *Women from Birth to Death: The Female Life-Cycle in Britain 1830–1914* (Brighton: Harvester, 1985); for late nineteenth-century documents on class, poverty, and criminality, see Peter Keating, (ed.), *Into Unknown England: The Social Explorers 1866–1813* (London: Fontana, 1976).

of phrenology during the early part of the century was closely bound up with debates around mesmerism or animal magnetism, and we have included examples of these here. However, the concerns about the working of the hidden mind raised by both mesmerism and the later practice of hypnotism are explored more fully in the second section on the unconscious. The notion of latent thought, active and dynamic but beyond the threshold of consciousness, was absolutely central to mid-Victorian notions of the self, and to notions of the limits of individual self-control. The concept of 'latent mental modification' was an important part of the associationist tradition which was developed and reinterpreted through the middle of the century in the expanding field of physiological psychology. The changing interpretations of various manifestations of unconscious mental processes through the second half of the century are explored in the passages on dreams, double consciousness, and memory in this section; these intersect with each other, and with the passages on mesmerism.

Section III places specific writings on reproduction and sexuality, particularly in the growing field of gynaecology, within this wider context. Here we include discussions of both male and female sexuality, and the profound ambivalence that each in their different ways induced. William Acton's well-known pronouncements on female 'passionlessness' are set alongside the dominant notion that women were prisoners of their physiology and reproductive functions. The opening section on 'defining womanhood' illustrates the many contradictions which entered into medical attempts to articulate the female body. We trace the crucial role afforded to menstruation in the 'uterine economy' and the development of theories of hysteria, showing clearly the emergence of notions of sexual repression. Female 'vulnerability', many commentators observed, was heightened by the limitations of women's life-styles, by the 'unnatural' culture of femininity. Concern about masculine sexuality focused mainly on the evils of masturbation, the threat of impotence, and that anxiety-provoking disorder, spermatorrhoea. We also incorporate some dissenting voices in discussions on the pathology of the sexual body; both those that dispute the role of the uterus as the defining element of womanhood, and those which call for greater openness and freedom in sexual relations.

The fourth section on insanity and nervous disorders puts these specific anxieties about the potentially pathological nature of the sexual body into the wider framework of discussions on the nature of insanity, its various forms, and the possibility of its prevention and cure. There are close connections between these debates and those on phrenology and mesmerism and the unconscious and memory. Many of the specific arguments about how the mind worked were developed in treatises on insanity, and various kinds of deranged states—artificial somnambulism, and forms of trance, for example—were considered to provide vital clues to identity and consciousness in general. We trace the shift through the century from the utopian early hopes of the lunacy reform movement, through mid-century discourses on moral management, to the more pessimistic, deterministic notions of madness by the end of the 1860s, although this collection also suggests that these distinctions were never clear cut. The notion that insanity contained a strong inherited physiological component did not emerge for the first time in the second part of the century—it can be found throughout the century, even in the most optimistic discussions of madness. However, by the late nineteenth century inherited organic predispositions have become the predominant factor and they form part of widespread discourses on heredity and degeneration, which are explored in the final section. Here specifically psychological issues contribute to post-Darwinian debates on inheritance and descent; these formed part of the political, social, and cultural turmoil at the end of the century, shaping concepts of class, criminality, childhood, race, and sexual difference.

We have drawn these extracts from different sources, including general theoretical studies, medical and psychological textbooks, self-help manuals, and articles on aspects of contemporary psychology in serious and more popular journals. We hope that *Embodied Selves* will prove a rich resource for students of various aspects of nineteenth-century culture: in social and cultural history, literary studies, gender studies. In particular, these debates were taken up, developed, modified, and resisted in diverse ways by nineteenth-century novelists, poets, and cultural critics. This might be a case of direct and conscious influence: both George Eliot and Thomas Hardy, for example, drew on precise areas of physiological psychology and theories of descent in their writing. But there is also a much broader sense in which contemporary psychological discussions—particularly on insanity and sexuality—so pervaded contemporary life through popular newspaper reporting, advertising, and domestic manuals, that it would have been almost impossible for any writer to have remained untouched. Popular sensation writers such as Wilkie Collins and Mary Elizabeth Braddon, as well as Charles Dickens, Charlotte Brontë, Elizabeth Gaskell, and Robert Browning (amongst others), took up and reworked the widespread current interest in the slippery definition of madness, the mutability of the self, and the problematic nature of memory; while the various kinds of rational explanation of the supernatural provided a crucial source of narrative tension, testing and expanding the boundaries of realism. Specific and often contradictory concepts of inheritance, descent, and degeneration were debated, assimilated, and questioned in late nineteenth-century fiction, which thus participated in and extended the scope of contemporary social theory. A central part of Victorian culture, these discourses provided modes of perceiving and exploring consciousness and identity which are put to work in intricate and varied ways in the multiple strands of nineteenth-century narrative.

The collection spans 1830 to 1890, and while we have incorporated some pieces that fall outside this time-frame, we have not included debates that did not fully emerge until the 1890s, such as discussions of sexual inversion and the concept of the homosexual. We have also confined ourselves to British works, but as the biographical notes show, both Scottish and English writers had often studied in France and Germany and were familiar with both European and American debates. We have therefore included some pieces which were immediately translated and had a significant impact on discussions in Britain, and which in turn influenced developments in other European countries. There have been several studies of the significance of various aspects of nineteenth-century theories of the self in recent years, but the primary material itself is not always easily available, and in reproducing a small sample of these texts we hope *Embodied Selves* will stimulate further interest in this broad and fascinating field.[2]

[2] In the collection, authors' footnotes are cued by asterisks, editorial footnotes are cued by numbers.

List of Illustrations

Section I
Reading the Mind

Reading the Mind

There's no art
To find the mind's construction in the face

(Shakespeare, *Macbeth*,I. iv. 7)

When you observe the visible man with your eyes,
what do you look for? The hidden man.

Taine, *History of English Literature* (1863)

As Shakespeare's lines testify, the quest to find 'the mind's construction in the face' has a long cultural lineage. For the Victorians this age-old quest was invested with a new importance and specificity. Physiognomy, mesmerism, and phrenology, as they fed into Victorian culture, all offered different forms of reading the 'hidden man'. Although each of these movements had very different social and political origins, they were united in their attempts to penetrate external defences to disclose a concealed domain of inner selfhood. Accounts of people going 'masked through the streets' in order to avoid surveillance when the physiognomical 'epidemic' was at its height may well be apocryphal, but they clearly illustrate the ways in which these practices were embroiled for the Victorians in issues of power.[1] Arising in the turbulent years at the end of the eighteenth century, each of these practices offered a challenge to established forms of social classification and control.

The renewed interest in physiognomy in the last decades of the eighteenth century was due in large part to the work of a Swiss pastor, John Caspar Lavater, whose four-volume work, *Physiognomical Fragments, for the Promotion of the Knowledge and Love of Mankind* (1775 – 8) was reduced in 1783 to the volume which formed the basis of the numerous editions of *Essays on Physiognomy* published in England from the 1780s onwards. German Romanticism combined with theology in Lavater's work. Drawing on organicist philosophy, he stressed the unity of body and mind, that each fragment of the body expressed the whole. This spirit of the whole could be read in the details of external form since God had inscribed a language on the face of nature for all to read. Lavater was at pains to stress, however, the difficulty of physiognomical reading: the seeming democratic spirit of his work was belied by his scathing comments on the 'herd' of literal readers who tried to understand external form without reference to the inner animating spirit.

[1] See John Graham, 'Lavater's *Physiognomy* in England', *Journal of the History of Ideas*, 22 (1961), 562.

Lavater's work was immensely popular in England: by 1810 there were more than twenty different versions available, and the work continued to be reprinted throughout the nineteenth century.[2] The cultural impact of physiognomy in England was diffuse; generally, the idealist underpinnings of Lavater's philosophy were ignored in favour of a more materialist interpretation of the importance of external form. One can trace in the novel, from the Romantic period onwards, a new focus on the details of physical form: vague references to a handsome or unprepossessing countenance are replaced by precise delineations of facial contours. In the emerging practice of psychiatric medicine, physiognomy also played a crucial role: Conolly's work featured here, and Alexander Morison's *Physiognomy of Mental Diseases* (1838) in Section IV, form part of a wider concern with the decoding of the external signs of insanity. Like Lavater, these professionals were keen to insist on the skills needed to practise their art; they unveiled, however, not the inner spirit, but rather forms of latent insanity which might go undetected by the layman's eye.

The science of phrenology which evolved from the work of Franz Joseph Gall in the 1790s shared with physiognomy an interest in deciphering external signs, but it was defiantly materialist. Gall's lectures in Vienna, indeed, were proscribed in 1802 by Emperor Francis I on the grounds that they led to materialism and undermined morality and religion. Gall's primary aim was to create a physiology of the brain. The brain, he insisted, was the organ of the mind, and the mind itself was divided into different faculties each located in a different organ in the mind. The link with physiognomy lay in Gall's belief that the strength of a particular organ was indicated by its size, and this could be detected by analysis of the contours of the skull.

Phrenology was first popularized in England by Johann Gaspar Spurzheim, who had worked with Gall since 1800, first as pupil and then as collaborator. Spurzheim's *The Physiognomical System of Drs Gall and Spurzheim; Founded on an Anatomical and Physiological Examination of the Nervous System in General and of the Brain in Particular* (1815) was energetically publicized by the author on the lecture circuit (he was also to adopt the name of phrenology, following his friend, Thomas Forster's suggestion, that year). In 1816 George Combe attended a dissection of the brain and a course of lectures on phrenology in Edinburgh by Spurzheim. He was profoundly influenced, and, although not a medical man, became from henceforth the primary popularizer of phrenological doctrine in Great Britain, founding the Edinburgh Phrenological Society, the first of a whole network of such societies across the British Isles, and publishing in 1829 *The Constitution of Man Considered in Relation to External Objects*. By 1851 this work had sold 90,000 copies and, according to Harriet Martineau, was outstripped in alltime readership only by the Bible, *Pilgrim's Progress*, and *Robinson Crusoe*.

[2] See John Graham, 'Lavater's *Physiognomy* in England', *Journal of the History of Ideas*, 22 (1961), 562.

The impact of Gall's work and the subsequent phenological movement fall into three areas. First, Gall laid the foundations for later work on physiological psychology, and the anatomy of the brain. Although Gall's ideas were not embraced by the medical establishment initially, by mid-century his theory that the brain was the organ of the mind had gained widespread acceptance. Secondly, phrenology had a profound impact on the development of psychiatric practice in the first half of the century since it provided a framework within which alienists (the term employed for psychiatrists or mad-doctors) could diagnose localized, or restricted, forms of insanity, and prescribe forms of moral treatment, suitable to each case. Thirdly, it had, primarily through the writings of George Combe, a tremendous popular impact. Here the appeal lay not simply in the possibility of choosing a friend or servant through a reading of their cranial 'bumps', but rather in the whole social philosophy which Combe appended to phrenology. Although Gall had held to a relatively static conception of the faculties, Combe believed there was no end to human advancement once man had grasped the principles of phrenology. Faculty endowment might be given by birth, but each individual was free to combat their weaknesses and develop their strengths by vigorous exercise of the appropriate faculties. In Combe's hands, phrenology became a scientific authorization of the tenets of self-help. As the extracts from *The Constitution of Man* reveal, however, Combe and his followers also used the phrenological platform to campaign for changes in criminal legislation and penal institutions, educational practices, and industrial employment; any practices, indeed, which were deemed to stand in the way of an individual's full realization of their potential. This is not to suggest, however, that phrenology as a social movement was entirely uniform. Phrenology was used, by some writers, to argue for a traditional social positioning of women in accordance with their 'natural' propensities;[3] but, more radically, as the extract from Andrew Combe reveals, it could also offer grounds for a thoroughgoing attack on the meagre education offered to women. On George Combe's death the *English Woman's Journal* recorded its thanks to one whose counsels had penetrated and reformed the nation's nurseries and schools. Without his teachings, 'numbers of us might otherwise have come to an untimely end, or vegetated in ill health and nonentity'.[4] From its inception, phrenology also had a racial aspect, as the extract from the *Phrenological Journal* suggests. Although this element was not dominant, it helped establish the practice of using cranial measurements to define racial characteristics, and thus laid the foundations for the later practice of craniology which fuelled the racial debates in the latter part of the century (see Section V).

Mesmerism owes its origins to the work of Anton Mesmer, whose *Mémoire sur*

[3] See, for example, 'On the female character', *Phrenological Journal*, 2 (Aug. 1824–Oct. 1825), 275–88.

[4] 'George Combe', *English Woman's Journal*, 2 (1858–9), 55.

la découverte du magnétisme animal (1779) set in train the fashionable preoccupation with animal magnetism in pre-revolutionary Paris. In the hands of Mesmer's radical followers, this theory that there existed an invisible magnetic fluid which could be stored up, concentrated, and communicated at a distance to restore an individual's mental and bodily harmony, became a justification of Enlightenment belief in the reciprocal relations between physical and moral order.[5] The king set up a commission to inquire into animal magnetism, and as a result of its findings, in 1785, Mesmer was driven out of Paris.

Mesmerism did not have a major impact in England until the 1830s and 1840s. Its most prominent supporter was the eminent John Elliotson, Professor of Medicine at University College, London. Elliotson, a follower of phrenology, had founded the London Phrenological Society in 1824, and in 1843 founded the *Zoist: A Journal of Cerebral Physiology and Mesmerism*. Elliotson, like many other followers, saw fruitful connections between phrenology and mesmerism in the opportunities they offered for exploring and developing the hidden powers of the mind. Mesmerism, however, gained even less support amid the medical establishment than phrenology. Elliotson's experiments with mesmeric therapy on his patients at the University College Hospital were brought to an abrupt halt in 1838 when virulent attacks on his methods were published in the *Lancet*, and he was forced to resign his post. Mesmerism was too much associated with charlatanism and the supernatural ever to gain medical respectability. In 1843, however, James Braid published *Neurypnology; or, The Rationale of Nervous Sleep, Considered in Relation with Animal Magnetism* in which he sought to separate what he termed 'hypnotism' from animal magnetism. Hypnotism from henceforth attracted widespread medical attention, particularly in Europe, where Charcot's use of hypnotism to treat hysteria at his clinic in Paris influenced the development of Freud's theories of psychoanalysis.

Although mesmerism aroused hostility in both the medical and general press, even the most determined opponents were reluctant to conclude that it was all a matter of illusion. Many commentators dissented from any suggestion of prevision or clairvoyance, but were willing to acknowledge that mesmerism had probably discovered a new form of invisible force which was yet to be identified, and unveiled new potentialities of the mind. At the heart of the debates was the question of power. For the Reverend Townshend, 'the price to be paid for the increase of the mental powers and of sensitive capabilities, which attends upon the state of mesmeric sleepwalking, is a certain forfeiture of the will'. In his work he celebrated this loss, and the gains to be made from the union of minds of mesmerizer and subject. For a culture dominated by ideological projections of the forceful, directive will, such a proposed forfeiture was generally perceived as

---

[5] For an exploration of the social and political role of mesmerism in France see Robert Darnton, *Mesmerism and the End of the Enlightenment in France* (Cambridge, Mass.: Harvard University Press, 1968).

deeply threatening. The threat was intensified by the issue of sexuality: women were considered to be more impressionable and were most commonly used as subjects, arousing all sorts of claims about debauchery and sexual slavery.

In the common culture mesmerism made a lasting impact, providing a set of terms and language with which to speak of the powers of one mind over another, and the forces of sexual attraction. References to the 'magnetic gaze' or 'mesmeric attraction' abound in the fiction of the era. Mesmerism also provided a whole way of thinking about the unseen operations of the mind which was attractive to novelists and poets. Charles Dickens, a personal friend of both Elliotson and Townshend, used the concepts and language of mesmerism extensively in his novels, as did Wilkie Collins. Tennyson, another convert, actively practised mesmerism, whilst Harriet Martineau, who believed herself to have been miraculously cured by mesmerism, published extensively on its wonderful powers, thereby creating uproar in the periodical and medical press. As a renowned rationalist, Martineau did not fit into the usual stereotype of female victim; her claims were therefore, of necessity, hotly debated. Most of the literary élite of London in the mid-century engaged at some level with mesmerism, and even when sceptical, as G. H. Lewes or George Eliot, for example, still accepted that it offered significant insights into the hidden powers of the mind. Mesmerism fed into the growing interest in the operations of the unconscious mind. Later in the century it was taken up by members of the spiritualist movement, a development which rationalist supporters like Martineau thoroughly deplored.

1. Physiognomy

ON PHYSIOGNOMY

John Caspar Lavater, *Essays on Physiognomy*, trans. T. Holcroft (1789), 9th edn. (London: William Tegg, 1855), 6–7, 9–10, 54–5, 64–5, 339–40, 379–84, 400–3.

Although Lavater's work spawned numerous imitators, this work remained the crucial text on physiognomy for the general reader through the nineteenth century. The extracts highlight the religious base of Lavater's theories, and the skills he deemed necessary for physiognomical analysis. We include guidelines for interpreting those two crucial physiognomical features, the forehead and eyes, and Lavater's reflections on the relationship between race, sex, and physiognomy.

ON THE NATURE OF MAN, WHICH IS THE FOUNDATION OF THE SCIENCE OF PHYSIOGNOMY

Man [. . .] is in himself the most worthy subject of observation, as he likewise is himself the most worthy observer. Under whatever point of view he may be considered, what is more worthy of contemplation than himself? In him each species of life is conspicuous; yet never can his properties be wholly known, except by the aid of his external form, his body, his superficies. How spiritual, how incorporeal soever, his internal essence may be, still is he only visible and conceivable from the harmony of his constituent parts. From these he is inseparable. He exists and moves in the body he inhabits, as in his element. This material man must become the subject of observation. All the knowledge we can obtain of man must be gained through the medium of our senses. [. . .]

The moral life of man, particularly, reveals itself in the lines, marks, and transitions of the countenance. His moral powers and desires, his irritability, sympathy, and antipathy; his facility of attracting or repelling the objects that surround him; these are all summed up in, and painted upon, his countenance when at rest. When any passion is called into action, such passion is depicted by the motion of the muscles, and these motions are accompanied by a strong palpitation of the heart. If the countenance be tranquil, it always denotes tranquillity in the region of the heart and breast.

This threefold life of man, so intimately interwoven through his frame, is still capable of being studied in its different appropriate parts; and did we live in a less depraved world we should find sufficient data for the science of physiognomy.

The animal life, the lowest and most earthly, would discover itself from the rim of the belly to the organs of generation, which would become its central or focal point. The middle or moral life would be seated in the breast, and the heart would be its central point. The intellectual life, which of the three is supreme, would reside in the head, and have the eye for its centre. If we take the countenance as the representative and epitome of the three divisions, then will the forehead, to the eye-brows, be the mirror, or image, of the understanding; the nose and cheeks the image of the moral and sensitive life; and the mouth and chin the image of the animal life; while the eye will be to the whole as its summary and centre. I may also add that the closed mouth at the moment of most perfect tranquillity is the central point of the radii of the countenance. It cannot, however, too often be repeated that these three lives, by their intimate connexion with each other, are all, and each, expressed in every part of the body. [. . .]

How often does it happen that the seat of character is so hidden, so enveloped, so masked, that it can only be caught in certain, and, perhaps, uncommon positions of the countenance, which will again be changed, and the signs all disappear, before they have made any durable impression! Or, supposing the impression made, these distinguishing traits may be so difficult to seize, that it shall be impossible to paint, much less to engrave, or describe them by language.

This may likewise happen to the most fixed, determinate, and decisive marks. Numberless of these can neither be described nor imitated. How many, even, are not to be retained by the imagination! How many, that are rather felt than seen! Who shall describe, who delineate, the cheering, the enlightening ray; who the look of love; who the soft benignant vibration of the benevolent eye; who the twilight, and the day, of hope; who the internal strong efforts of a mind, wrapt in gentleness and humility, to effect good, to diminish evil, and to increase present and eternal happiness; who all the secret impulses and powers, collected in the aspect of the defender, or enemy, of truth; of the bold friend, or the subtle foe, of wisdom; who 'the poet's eye, in a fine phrenzy rolling, glancing from heaven to earth, from earth to heaven, while imagination bodies forth the forms of things unknown;'[1] who shall all this delineate, or describe? Can charcoal paint fire, chalk light, or can colours live and breathe?

---

[1] Shakespeare, *A Midsummer Night's Dream*, V. i, 12–15. The quotation is inaccurate: 'glancing' should read 'Doth glance' and 'while' should read 'and, as'.)

It is with physiognomy as with all other objects of taste, literal, or figurative, of sense, or of spirit. We can feel, but cannot explain. The essence of every organized body is, in itself, an invisible power. It is mind. Without this incomprehensible principle of life, there is neither intelligence, action, nor power. 'The world seeth not, knoweth not, the spirit.'[2] Oh! how potent is this truth, whether in declamation it be expressed with insipidity or enthusiasm, from the Holy Spirit, that in person inspired the apostles and evangelists of the Lord, to the spirit of the most insignificant being! The world seeth it not, and knoweth it not. This is the most general proposition possible. The herd satiate themselves with words without meaning, externals without power, body without mind, and figure without essence. Overlooked as it has been by mere literal readers, who are incapable of exalting themselves to the great general sense of the word of God, and who have applied the text to some few particular cases, though it be the key to nature and revelation, though it be itself the revelation of revelation, the very soul of knowledge, and the secret of secrets. 'It is the spirit that maketh alive, the flesh profiteth nothing.' [. . .][3]

What then is required of the physiognomist? What should his inclinations, talents, qualities, and capabilities be?

His first of requisites, as has, in part, already been remarked, should be a body well proportioned, and finely organized: accuracy of sensation, capable of receiving the most minute outward impressions, and easily transmitting them faithfully to memory; or, as I ought rather to say, impressing them upon the imagination, and the fibres of the brain. His eye, in particular, must be excellent, clear, acute, rapid, and firm.

Precision in observation is the very soul of physiognomy. The physiognomist must possess a most delicate, swift, certain, most extensive spirit of observation. To observe is to be attentive, so as to fix the mind on a particular object, which it selects, or may select, for consideration, from a number of surrounding objects. To be attentive is to consider some one particular object, exclusively of all others, and to analyze, consequently, to distinguish, its peculiarities. To observe, to be attentive, to distinguish what is similar, what dissimilar, to discover proportion, and disproportion, is the office of the understanding.

Without an accurate, superior, and extended understanding, the physiognomist will neither be able rightly to observe nor to compare and class his observations; much less to draw the necessary conclusions. Physiognomy is the highest exercise of the understanding, the logic of corporeal varieties.

The true physiognomist unites to the clearest and profoundest understanding the most lively, strong, comprehensive imagination, and a fine and rapid wit. Imagination is necessary to impress the traits with exactness, so that they may be renewed at pleasure; and to range the pictures in the mind as perfectly as if they still were visible, and with all possible order. [. . .]

[2] St John, 14, 17.   [3] St John, VI, 63.

NATIONAL PHYSIOGNOMY

MY OWN REMARKS

That there is national physiognomy, as well as national character, is undeniable. Whoever doubts of this can never have observed men of different nations, nor have compared the inhabitants of the extreme confines of any two. Compare a Negro and an Englishman, a native of Lapland and an Italian, a Frenchman and an inhabitant of Terra del Fuego. Examine their forms, countenances, characters, and minds. Their difference will be easily seen, though it will, sometimes, be very difficult to describe scientifically.

It is probable we shall discover what is national in the countenance better from the sight of an individual, at first, than of a whole people; at least, so I imagine, from my own experience. Individual countenances discover more the characteristics of a whole nation, than a whole nation does that which is national in individuals. The following, infinitely little, is what I have hitherto observed, from the foreigners with whom I have conversed, and whom I have noticed, concerning national character.

The French I am least able to characterize.—They have no traits so bold as the English, nor so minute as the Germans. I know them chiefly by their teeth, and their laugh. The Italians I discover by the nose, small eyes, and projecting chin. The English, by their foreheads, and eyebrows. The Dutch, by the rotundity of the head, and the weakness of the hair. The Germans, by the angles and wrinkles round the eyes, and in the cheeks. The Russians, by the snub nose, and their light-coloured, or black hair. I shall now say a word concerning Englishmen, in particular. Englishmen have the shortest, and best arched foreheads; that is to say, they are arched only upwards; and, towards the eyebrows, either gently decline, or are rectilinear. They very seldom have pointed, but often round, full, medullary noses; the Quakers and Moravians excepted, who, wherever they are found, are generally thin-lipped. Englishmen have large, well-defined, beautifully curved lips; they have also a round, full chin; but they are peculiarly distinguished by the eyebrows and eyes, which are strong, open, liberal, and steadfast. The outline of their countenances is, in general, great, and they never have those numerous, infinitely minute, traits, angles, and wrinkles, by which the Germans are so especially distinguished. Their complexion is fairer than that of the Germans.

All English women whom I have known personally, or by portrait, appear to be composed of marrow and nerve. They are inclined to be tall, slender, soft, and as distant from all that is harsh, rigorous, or stubborn, as heaven is from earth. [. . .]

ON CERTAIN INDIVIDUAL PARTS OF THE HUMAN BODY

THE FOREHEAD

The following are my own remarks on foreheads.

The form, height, arching, proportion, obliquity, and position of the skull, or bone of the forehead, show the propensity, degree of power, thought, and sensibility of man. The covering, or skin, of the forehead, its position, colour, wrinkles, and tension, denote the passions and present state of the mind.—The bones give the internal quantity, and their covering the application of power.

The forehead bones remain unaltered, though the skin be wrinkled, but this wrinkling varies according to the various forms of the bones. A certain degree of flatness produces certain wrinkles; a certain arching is attended by certain other wrinkles, so that the wrinkles, seperately considered, will give the arching of the forehead, and this, *vice versâ*, will give the wrinkles. Certain foreheads can only have perpendicular, others horizontal, others curved, and others mixed and confused wrinkles. Cup-formed (smooth), cornerless foreheads, when they are in motion, commonly have the simplest, and least perplexed wrinkles.

But leaving wrinkles, I hold the peculiar delineation of the outline and position of the forehead, which has been left unattempted by ancient and modern physiognomists, to be the most important of all the things presented to physiognomonical observation. We may divide foreheads, considered in profile, in three principal classes, the retreating, the perpendicular, and the projecting. Each of these classes has a multitude of variations, which may easily again be classed, and the chief of which are, 1, rectilinear; 2, half round, half rectilinear, flowing into each other; 3, half round, half rectilinear, interrupted; 4, curve lined, simple; 5, the curve lined double and triple. The latter is exemplified in the following 6 instances.

FIG. 1. The forehead

I shall add some more particular remarks:

1. The longer the forehead, the more comprehension, *cæteris paribus*, and less activity.

2. The more compressed, short, and firm the forehead, the more compression, firmness, and less volatility, in the man.

3. The more curved and cornerless the outline, the more tender and flexible the character; the more rectilinear, the more pertinacity and severity.

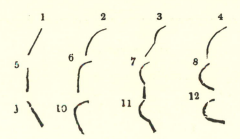

FIG. 2. The forehead

4. Perfect perpendicularity, from the hair to the eyebrows, want of understanding.

5. Perfect perpendicularity, gently arched at the top, like 6, denotes excellent propensities of cold, tranquil, profound, thinking.

6. Projecting like 9, 10, 11, 12, imbecility, immaturity, weakness, stupidity.

7. Retreating, like 1, 2, 3, 4, in general, denotes superiority of imagination, wit and acuteness.

8. The round and prominent forehead above, straight lined below, and on the whole, perpendicular, partly like 7, shows much understanding, life, sensibility, vehemence, and—icy coldness.

9. The oblique, rectilinear, forehead is also very vehement, and vigorous.

10. Arched foreheads, like 5,* appear, properly, to be feminine. Five denotes perspicuity (I reluctantly apply the word thoughtful to women. Those who have the most understanding think little, or not at all. They see and arrange images, but trouble themselves little concerning abstract signs). Eight is insupportably stupid. Twelve the *ne plus ultra* of stupidity, and imbecility.

11. A happy union of straight and curved lines, with a happy position of the forehead, express the most perfect character of wisdom. By happy union, I mean when the lines insensibly flow into each other, and by happy position, when the forehead is neither too perpendicular nor too retreating, in nearly the position of 2.

12. I might almost establish it as an axiom that right lines, considered as such, and curves, considered as such, are related as power and weakness, obstinacy and flexibility, understanding and sensation.

13. I have seen no man, hitherto, with sharp, projecting eyebones, who had not great propensity to an acute exercise of the understanding, and to wise plans.

14. Yet there are many excellent heads which have not this sharpness, and which have the more solidity if the forehead, like a perpendicular wall, sinks upon the horizontal eyebrows, and be gently rounded on each side towards the temples.

* Here is some mistake; perhaps it should be 4, or it may be that the six examples, page 380, which follow the number 5, are meant.—T. (See Fig. 1.)

15. Perpendicular foreheads, projecting so as not immediately to rest upon the nose, which are small, wrinkly, short, and shining, are certain signs of weakness, little understanding, little imagination, little sensation.

16. Foreheads with many angular, knotty, protuberances, ever denote much vigorous, firm, harsh, oppressive, ardent, activity and perseverance.

17. It is a sure sign of a clear, sound understanding, and a good temperament, when the profile of the forehead has two proportionate arches, the lower of which projects.

18. Eyebones with defined, marking, easily delineated, firm arches, I never saw but in noble, and in great men. All the ideal antiques have these arches.

19. Square foreheads, that is to say, with extensive temples, and firm eyebones, show circumspection and certainty of character.

20. Perpendicular wrinkles, if natural to the forehead, denote application and power: horizontal wrinkles, and those broken in the middle, or at the extremities, in general, negligence and want of power.

21. Perpendicular, deep indentings, in the bones of the forehead, between the eyebrows, I never met with but in men of sound understanding, and free and noble minds, unless there were some positively contradictory feature.

22. A blue vena frontalis, in the form of a Y, when in an open, smooth, well arched, forehead, I have only found in men of extraordinary talents, and of an ardent and generous character.

23. The following are the most indubitable signs of an excellent, a perfectly beautiful and significant, intelligent and noble forehead.

a. An exact proportion to the other parts of the countenance. It must equal the nose or the under part of the face in length (*i.e.* one third).

b. In breadth, it must either be oval at the top (like the foreheads of most of the great men of England), or nearly square.

c. A freedom from unevenness, and wrinkles; yet with the power of wrinkling, when deep in thought, afflicted by pain, or from just indignation.

d. Above it must retreat; below, project.

e. The eyebones must be simple, horizontal; and, if seen from above, must present a pure curve.

f. There should be a small cavity in the centre, from above to below, and traversing the forehead, so as to separate it into four divisions, which can only be perceptible by a clear, descending light.

g. The skin must be more clear in the forehead than in the other parts of the countenance.

h. The forehead must every where be composed of such outlines as, if the section of one third only be viewed, it can scarcely be determined whether the lines are straight or circular.

24. Short, wrinkled, knotty, regular, pressed in on one side, and sawcut foreheads, with intersecting wrinkles, are incapable of durable friendship.

25. Be not discouraged so long as a friend, an enemy, a child, or a brother, though a transgressor, has a good, well-proportioned, open forehead; there is still much certainty of improvement, much cause of hope.

We shall defer more accurate and copious definition till we come to speak of physiognomonical lines.

THE EYES

Blue eyes are, generally, more significant of weakness, effeminacy, and yielding, than brown and black. True it is there are many powerful men with blue eyes, but I find more strength, manhood, and thought, combined with brown than with blue. Wherefore does it happen that the Chinese, or the people of the Phillippine islands are very seldom blue eyed, and that Europeans only, or the descendants of Europeans, have blue eyes in those countries? This is the more worthy inquiry, because there are no people more effeminate, luxurious, peaceable, or indolent than the Chinese.

Choleric men have eyes of every colour, but more brown, and inclined to green, than blue. This propensity to green is almost a decisive token of ardour, fire, and courage.

I have never met with clear blue eyes in the melancholic; seldom in the choleric; but most in the phlegmatic temperament, which, however, had much activity.

When the under arch described by the upper eyelid is perfectly circular, it always denotes goodness and tenderness, but also fear, timidity and weakness.

The open eye, not compressed, forming a long acute angle with the nose, I have but seldom seen, except in acute and understanding persons.

Hitherto I have seen no eye, where the eyelid formed a horizontal line over the pupil, that did not appertain to a very acute, able, subtle man; be it understood I have met with this eye in many worthy men, but men of great penetration, and simulation.

Wide, open, eyes, with the white seen under the apple, I have observed in the timid and phlegmatic; and, also, in the courageous and rash. When compared, however, the fiery and the feeble, the determined and the undetermined, will easily be distinguished. The former are more firm, more strongly delineated, have less obliquity, have thicker, better cut, but less skinny, eyelids. [. . .]

MALE AND FEMALE

In general (for I neither can nor will state any thing but what is most known,) how much more pure, tender, delicate, irritable, affectionate, flexible, and patient, is woman than man.

The primary matter of which they are constituted appears to be more flexible, irritable, and elastic than that of man.

They are formed to maternal mildness and affection; all their organs are tender, yielding, easily wounded, sensible, and receptible.

Among a thousand females there is scarcely one without the generic feminine signs; the flexible, the circular, and the irritable.

They are the counterpart of man, taken out of man, to be subject to man; to comfort him like angels, and to lighten his cares. 'She shall be saved in child-bearing, if they continue in faith, and charity, and holiness, with sobriety.'— 1 *Tim.* ii. 15.

This tenderness, this sensibility, this light texture of their fibres and organs, this volatility of feeling render them so easy to conduct and to tempt; so ready of submission to the enterprize and power of the man; but more powerful through the aid of their charms than man, with all his strength. The man was not first tempted, but the woman, afterwards the man by the woman.

But, not only easily to be tempted, she is capable of being formed to the purest, noblest, most seraphic virtue; to every thing which can deserve praise or affection.

Highly sensible of purity, beauty, and symmetry, she does not always take time to reflect on internal life, internal death, internal corruption. 'The woman saw that the tree was good for food, and that it was pleasant to the eyes, and a tree to be desired to make one wise, and she took of the fruit thereof.'—*Gen.* iii. 6.

The female thinks not profoundly; profound thought is the power of the man.

Women feel more. Sensibility is the power of woman.

They often rule more effectually, more sovereignly, than man. They rule with tender looks, tears, and sighs; but not with passion and threats; for if, or when they so rule, they are no longer women, but abortions.

They are capable of the sweetest sensibility, the most profound emotion, the utmost humility, and the excess of enthusiasm.

In their countenances are the signs of sanctity and inviolability, which every feeling man honours, and the effects of which are often miraculous.

Therefore, by the irritability of their nerves, their incapacity for deep inquiry and firm decision, they may easily, from their extreme sensibility, become the most irreclaimable, the most rapturous enthusiasts.

Their love, strong and rooted as it is, is very changeable; their hatred almost incurable, and only to be effaced by continued and artful flattery. Men are most profound; women are more sublime.

Men most embrace the whole; women remark individually, and take more delight in selecting the minutiæ which form the whole. Man hears the bursting thunder, views the destructive bolt with serene aspect, and stands erect amidst the fearful majesty of the streaming clouds.

Woman trembles at the lightning, and the voice of distant thunder; and shrinks into herself, or sinks into the arms of man.

Man receives a ray of light single, woman delights to view it through a prism, in all its dazzling colours. She contemplates the rainbow as the promise of peace; he extends his inquiring eye over the whole horizon.

Woman laughs, man smiles; woman weeps, man remains silent. Woman is in anguish when man weeps, and in despair when man is in anguish; yet has she often more faith than man.

Man without religion is a diseased creature, who would persuade himself he is well, and needs not a physician; but woman without religion is raging and monstrous.

A woman with a beard is not so disgusting as a woman who acts the freethinker; her sex is formed to piety and religion: to them Christ first appeared; but he was obliged to prevent them from too ardently, and too hastily, embracing him—'Touch me not.' They are prompt to receive and seize novelty, and become its enthusiasts.

The whole world is forgotten in the emotion caused by the presence and proximity of him they love.

They sink into the most incurable melancholy, as they also rise to the most enraptured heights.

The feelings of the man are more imagination; those of the female more heart.

When communicative, they are more communicative than man; when secret, more secret.

In general they are more patient, long suffering, credulous, benevolent, and modest.

Woman is not a foundation on which to build. She is the gold, silver, precious stones, wood, hay, stubble (1 *Cor*. iii. 12.); the materials for building on the male foundation. She is the leaven, or, more expressively, the oil to the vinegar of man; the second part of the book of man.

Man singly, is but half a man; at least but half human.—A king without a kingdom. Woman, who feels properly what she is, whether still or in motion, rests upon the man; nor is man what he may and ought to be but in conjunction with woman. Therefore 'It is not good that man should be alone, but that he should leave father and mother and cleave to his wife, and they two shall be one flesh.'

A WORD ON THE PHYSIOGNOMONICAL RELATION OF THE SEXES

Man is the most firm—woman the most flexible.
Man is the straightest—woman the most bending.
Man stands steadfast—woman gently trips.
Man surveys and observes—woman glances and feels.

Man is serious—woman is gay.

Man is the tallest and broadest—woman less and taper.

Man is rough and hard—woman smooth and soft.

Man is brown—woman is fair.

Man is wrinkly—woman less so.

The hair of man is more strong and short—of woman more long and pliant.

The eyebrows of man are compressed—of woman less frowning.

Man has most convex lines—woman most concave.

Man has most straight lines—woman most curved.

The countenance of man, taken in profile, is more seldom perpendicular than that of the woman.

Man is most angular—woman most round.

THE PHYSIOGNOMY OF INSANITY

John Conolly, 'The physiognomy of insanity', *Medical Times and Gazette*, 16 NS (2 Jan. 1858), 3–4, 14.

Conolly published a series of thirteen articles on this topic in the Medical Times and Gazette *1858–9, illustrated by lithographs taken from the photographs of Hugh W. Diamond, Superintendent of the Surrey County Lunatic Asylum, Springfield, between 1848 and 1858. Conolly acknowledges his debt to the French physician, J. E. D. Esquirol, who published the first atlas of the insane as an appendage to his* Des maladies mentales *(1838), and to Diamond's predecessor at the Surrey asylum, Alexander Morison, whose work* The Physiognomy of Mental Diseases *(1838) was the first British treatment of this subject. With the invention of photography, Conolly notes, the lengthy, and very expensive, process of commissioning engravings of his inmates was now superseded; photography also had the added bonus of being able to catch the fleeting expressions of the insane.*

See also, Section IV, Alexander Morison, The Physiognomy of Mental Diseases.

There is so singular a fidelity in a well-executed photograph that the impression of very recent muscular agitation in the face seems to be caught by the process, which the engraver's art can scarcely preserve. This peculiarity seems to produce part of the discontent often expressed when people see the photographic portraits of their friends or of themselves. It gives, however, peculiar value when, as

FIG. 3. Religious melancholy

in the portraits of the insane, the object is to give the singular expression arising from morbid movements of the mind; and thus, instead of giving pictures which are merely looked at with idle curiosity, furnishes such as may be studied with advantage; helping the observation of the Medical student, illustrating the lectures of a teacher, and suggesting some not unproductive reflections to all who examine them.

When we contemplate such portraitures of the human face, strained or disfigured by the mysterious workings of a disordered brain, some desire naturally arises in us to inquire into the causes, physical or moral, of states so distressing; and our efforts, by every individual and social exertion, to lessen the weight of trial and of grief on those around us can scarcely fail to be stimulated. We are reminded of the havoc ever making—by evil thoughts, evil habits, or evil passions—or by want and distracting care; and seeing how all the beauty of man is worn away by his frailties or his struggles, we become more acutely sensible that all repose of heart has also been wrecked, and the better part of our nature becomes perhaps, even thus reflecting, finely touched, and 'to fine issues.'[1]

The engraving presented to the reader in this number is from a photographic portrait of a young woman labouring under religious melancholy. In this form of

[1] Shakespeare, *Measure For Measure*, I, i, 36–7.

19

melancholy there is no mere worldly despondency, nor thought of common calamities or vulgar ruin; but a deeper horror: a fixed belief, against which all arguments are powerless, and all consolation vain; a belief of having displeased the Great Creator, and of being hopelessly shut out from mercy and from heaven. This portrait, therefore, does not reflect the figure of patients so often recognised in asylums, sitting on benches by the lonely walls, the hands clasped on the bosom, the leaden eye bent on the ground, and the unvarying gloom excluding variety of reflection. It represents an affliction more defined. We discern the outward marks of a mind which, seemingly, after long wandering in the mazes of religious doubt, and struggling with spiritual niceties too perplexing for human solution, is now overshadowed by despair. The high and wide forehead, generally indicative of intelligence and imagination; the slightly bent head, leaning disconsolately on the hand; the absence from that collapsed cheek of every trace of gaiety; the mouth inexpressive of any varied emotion; the deep orbits and the long characteristic eyebrows; all seem painfully to indicate the present mood and general temperament of the patient. The black hair is heedlessly pressed back; the dress, though neat, has a conventual plainness; the sacred emblem worn round the neck is not worn for ornament. The lips are well-formed, and compressed; the angle of the jaw is rather large; the ear seems well-shaped; force of character appears to be thus indicated, as well as a capacity of energetic expression; whilst the womanly figure, the somewhat ample chest and pelvis (less expressed in the engraving than in the photograph) belong to a general constitution out of which, in health and vigour, may have grown up some self-accusing thoughts in an innocent and devout, but passionate heart. For this perverting malady makes even the natural instincts appear sinful; and the sufferer forgets that God implanted them. But the conflict in the case before us is chiefly intellectual. The meditations of that large brain are not employed on worldly cares, nor even on affections chilled, nor temporal hopes broken. They are engaged in religious scruples, far too perplexing for its power to overcome. In the meantime all the ordinary affections, from which consolation might be derived, are shut out. Soon, perhaps, the scruples themselves will appear crimes. To escape future punishment, bodily mortifications must be endured; severe fasts, or some self-inflicted pain. Under these, the bodily strength, usually impaired in the commencement of the attack, becomes further impaired. The digestion becomes feeble, and even the sparest meals occasion suffering. Emaciation takes place; often proceeding to an extreme degree. The uterine functions (for the subjects of this form of malady are usually women), are suppressed. Paroxysms of excitement may occur, with sudden activity in the prosecution of schemes of vaguest import; but with these futile efforts misgivings become mingled. The thought of suicide, often suggested, becomes fixed; and such varied and ingenious efforts are made to carry it into effect as to demand incessant vigilance. Yet, even in this state there may be days in which the mind is tranquilised, and needle-work is resumed, or the music of happier times is played once more. But these gleams are transient. The mind loses its energy; debility invades every function; [. . .] and the wretched patient is only relieved by death.

The subjects of this kind of affliction are often highly intellectual, and this seems to endow them with greater latitude of terrible delusions, and with an eloquence in describing them that cannot always be listened to without emotion; seconded as it is by an expression of countenance full of real horror, and significant of the state of utter spiritual abandonment and degradation into which the patient asserts herself to be plunged, without hope of relief on earth or pardon in heaven.

The medical treatment of religious melancholy is often of more import than that which enthusiastic and very well-meaning persons are too much inclined to resort to. Remonstrances, and the perusal of sermons, and of the tracts scattered over too many drawing-room tables, and showered with mischievous, although well-intentioned, activity among the poor,—nay, even the exclusive reading of the Bible and Prayer-book,—must often be refrained from or forbidden. There are states of mind in which the medical man must have courage to exclude these as poisons. The mind must be diverted to more common and more varied subjects, and the bodily health must have the most careful consideration.

These observations apply to all religious sects. The subject of this photograph had left the Protestant faith, and become what is commonly called a Roman Catholic. Her education had not been such as to enable her to reason well on either side, and she became merely wavering and unsettled in her belief. Attention to ordinary matters was neglected; she sate in the attitude shown in the engraving for a long time together; she was negligent of her dress, and occasionally destructive of it. Often she cried out that she was a brute, and had no soul to be saved. Now and then she had a desire to see some minister of religion, either Catholic or Protestant; and soon afterward would refuse to see either, declaring that neither could be useful to her. All this seems to be expressed in the photograph. The medal she wears was given to her by a gentleman connected with the Catholic establishment.

It is unnecessary to say that her case was managed in the asylum with the most prudent caution. She was encouraged to more bodily exertion; and her mental perplexities, not being aggravated by reasonings unadapted to her, gradually died away. She soon began to occupy herself, and became useful in the laundry of the establishment. She was strengthened by quinine. The inactivity of the digestive canal, so common, or so constant in cases of melancholia, was counteracted by combining the decoctum aloes compositum with a tonic; and shower-baths, of half a minute's duration, contributed to restore general bodily energy. Such attacks never yield at once. They come on gradually, and depart slowly. After a residence of ten months in the asylum, this patient became well.

21

It is gratifying to know that she remains well, having now left the institution seven months since.

The change presented by the countenance after recovery from severe mental disturbance is generally remarkable, and sometimes even surprising. In case of acute mania it is singularly marked; and in the particular form of religious melancholy the cheerful smile that supplants the dismal and anxious look of the patient is almost magical. In the case now referred to, whatever there was of a meditative or intellectual cast in the face during the period of melancholy, was almost wholly lost when the attack went off. The ample forehead, of course, remained, and the deep orbits; but the eyes, when open, were small and inexpressive, and the mouth seemed to have become common-place. Her whole appearance was, indeed, so simply that of an uneducated Irish girl, that the very neat gown, cloak, and bonnet, in which she was dressed by the kindness of those about her, seemed incongruous and peculiar. A second photograph, taken at that time, possesses, therefore, little interest. In some other instances the metamorphoses effected by malady and recovery may be usefully, and even instructively represented.

OUR NEXT-DOOR NEIGHBOUR

Charles Dickens, *Sketches by Boz: Illustrations of Every-Day Life and Every-Day People* (London: Chapman and Hall, n.d. [1836]), 58–9.

Dickens's sketches were first published between 1834 and 1836 in the Morning Chronicle *during his time as a reporter there. We include this satirical piece to show the hold already exerted on the public imagination by the various ideas of physiognomy, phrenology, and mesmerism. Dickens's comedy assumes an audience thoroughly conversant with such notions. Dickens's own passionate interest in phrenology and mesmerism dates from a couple of years later in 1838, when his friendship with John Elliotson developed.*

We are very fond of speculating as we walk through a street, on the character and pursuits of the people who inhabit it; and nothing so materially assists us in these speculations as the appearance of the house doors. The various expressions of the human countenance afford a beautiful and interesting study; but there is something in the physiognomy of street-door knockers, almost as characteristic, and nearly as infallible. Whenever we visit a man for the first time, we contemplate the features of his knocker with the greatest curiosity, for we well know, that between the man and his knocker, there will inevitably be a greater or less degree of resemblance and sympathy.

For instance, there is one description of knocker that used to be common enough, but which is fast passing away—a large round one, with the jolly face of a convivial lion smiling blandly at you, as you twist the sides of your hair into a curl or pull up your shirt-collar while you are waiting for the door to be opened; we never saw that knocker on the door of a churlish man—so far as our experience is concerned, it invariably bespoke hospitality and another bottle.

No man ever saw this knocker on the door of a small attorney or bill-broker; they always patronise the other lion; a heavy ferocious-looking fellow, with a countenance expressive of savage stupidity—a sort of grand master among the knockers, and a great favourite with the selfish and brutal.

Then there is a little pert Egyptian knocker, with a long thin face, a pinched-up nose, and a very sharp chin; he is most in vogue with your government-office people, in light drabs and starched cravats; little spare, priggish men, who are perfectly satisfied with their own opinions, and consider themselves of paramount importance.

We were greatly troubled a few years ago, by the innovation of a new kind of knocker, without any face at all, composed of a wreath depending from a hand or small truncheon. A little trouble and attention, however, enabled us to overcome this difficulty, and to reconcile the new system to our favourite theory. You will invariably find this knocker on the doors of cold and formal people, who always ask you why you *don't* come, and never say *do*.

Everybody knows the brass knocker is common to suburban villas, and extensive boarding-schools; and having noticed this genus we have recapitulated all the most prominent and strongly-defined species.

Some phrenologists affirm, that the agitation of a man's brain by different passions, produces corresponding developments in the form of his skull. Do not let us be understood as pushing our theory to the full length of asserting, that any alteration in a man's disposition would produce a visible effect on the feature of his knocker. Our position merely is, that in such a case, the magnetism which must exist between a man and his knocker, would induce the man to remove, and seek some knocker more congenial to his altered feelings. If you ever find a man changing his habitation without any reasonable pretext, depend upon it, that; although he may not be aware of the fact himself, it is because he and his knocker are at variance. This is a new theory, but we venture to launch it, nevertheless, as being quite as ingenious and infallible as many thousands of the learned speculations which are daily broached for public good and private fortune-making.

FIG. 4. George Cruikshank, *Our Next-Door Neighbour*

2. Phrenology

ON THE FUNCTIONS OF THE BRAIN

Franz Joseph Gall, *On the Functions of the Brain* (1822–5), trans. Winslow Lewis, 6 vols. (Boston: Marsh, Capen, and Lyon, 1835), ii. 42–44, v. 261–2, 263–5, vi. 307, 309–10.

The ideas of Gall and his disciple J. G. Spurzheim were already thoroughly disseminated in England when this English translation was published. It remains, however, the most authoritative statement of the theories of the founder of phrenology. The extracts illustrate Gall's hostility to Lavater's physiognomy and his own endorsement of a materialist theory of the brain as the organ of the mind. They also reveal the proselytizing fervour of the nineteenth-century scientist, convinced that the foundations for social and moral progress lay in the acquisition of material, empirical knowledge.

The physiology of the brain makes us acquainted with our entire dependence on the primitive laws of the creation; the source of moral good and evil; the cause of the diversity and of the opposition of our propensities; of the strength or weakness of our understanding; the internal motives of our will and of our actions. Instructors, moralists, legislators, and judges, cannot, with impunity, neglect the influence of the organization over our propensities, passions, and talents. It proves to them, that there is no certain quantum, either of the power of doing good, or of avoiding evil, or of the degree of moral liberty with which each individual is endowed. It therefore possesses a general interest for all intelligent classes of society.

It explains to us the modifications of our propensities and faculties at different ages, their successive and gradual development, their stationary state, their gradual decline down to the imbecility of old age; and thus it shows us to what degree, and under what conditions, we are capable of apprehending the lessons of education and experience.

It explains to us not only the diversity of the moral and intellectual character of individuals, but it also gives us a reason for these differences in the two sexes, and in different nations: it indicates the source of their customs, of their manners, of their legislation, their mode of judging of what is virtuous and what is vicious or criminal, of their religion, of their barbarism or their civilization, of their institutions: thus it shows us how a uniform system of education, rewards, punishments, laws, &c., would be little in conformity with nature, whether as it regards different individuals, or different nations; finally, it fixes our ideas, irrevocably, as to the unity of the human species.

Study the different developments of our cerebral parts, and you will no longer be deceived as to the prime motives which determine your tastes, and your actions; you will judge exactly of your merit and your demerit; you will know the reason, why it does not depend on yourself, that you have such and such a predominant propensity or talent, to become a mathematician, a mechanic, a musician, a poet, or an orator; you will comprehend why you excel, without effort, so to speak, in one thing, whilst in another you are inevitably doomed to mediocrity; you will see, why he who is brilliant in a particular station, must necessarily be eclipsed in another. Finally, you will explain the double man within you, and the reason why your propensities and your intellect, or your propensities and your reason, are so often opposed to each other. [. . .]

The study of the functions of the brain overthrows an infinity of physiological and philosophical error, and terminates those endless and tedious discussions. It assigns to each organ, whether of automatic or animal life, its proper function. We no longer regard the external senses as the origin of our faculties. It is the brain, which receives their impressions and operates upon them, according to the nature and the degree of its inherent force. It is no longer the *signs* so much talked of by modern philosophers, which develop our understanding. Signs have no value in regard to infants, to idiots, or to worn-out organs.—Signs, the language of speech, writing, the language of gesture or action, are creations of the brain, and are only understood, in proportion as they are addressed to pre-existing faculties. This is the reason why language changes from one individual to another, from nation to nation, from time to time, according as the internal conceptions change. Sooner or later there will be established an unbroken harmony between the internal man and his external products, between things and their expressions. Ere long it will no more be the physical which acts upon the moral, nor the moral which acts upon the physical; the result will be that certain affections will act either on the brain itself, or on other parts. Your understanding, your volition, your free will, your affection, your judgment, instinct, &c., will be no longer personified beings: they will be cerebral functions. You will no longer demand, what is the origin of the arts, sciences, war, civil institutions, religion, morality: God has revealed it all to you by means of your cerebral organization; and, finally, you will abandon to another tribunal, all questions in regard to the nature and seat of the soul, its reunion with the body, the mutual influence of spirit and matter, the unity of self &c. &c. In a word, the philosophical physician and the physiologist, instead of sounding his course amid the straits of speculation, will march confidently along the route of observation. [. . .]

OF PHYSIOGNOMY, OR THE TALENT OF KNOWING THE INTERIOR OF MAN BY HIS EXTERIOR

We understand by the expression *physiognomy*, the art of knowing the moral and intellectual character of man, by the sole external conformation, not of his face alone, but of all the other parts of the body, without these parts being put in action.

Not only the vulgar, but even philosophers, give to this art the preference, over the physiology of the brain. Others imagine, that my researches on the functions of the individual cerebral parts, and on the inferences to be drawn from a certain form of head, are of the same nature as those of the physiognomists. There is, however, absolutely, no relation between the two. A physiognomist, Lavater for example, is not at all guided by the knowledge of anatomy and of physiology; the laws of the organization of the nervous system in general, and of the brain in particular, are unknown to them; they have no idea of the different composition of the brain in different species of animals; they take no account of the different results of the different development of the cerebral parts. They know not the influence, which the brain exerts on the form of the head; they have no notion of the changes, which the encephalon and the cranium undergo in the different ages of life, in different diseases, in mania, &c.

I have proved, that the brain is exclusively the organ of the soul. There is then only the form of the brain or that of the osseous box, as far as it is determined by the form of the brain, which can enable us to judge of the qualities or faculties. There can exist no relation whatever between any other part, and the qualities or faculties. There is not, either in the nose, or in the teeth, or in the lips, in the jaws, hand, or knee, any thing, which can determine the existence of a quality or a faculty; these parts, therefore, cannot furnish any indication relative to the moral or intellectual character. [. . .]

In general, the physiognomists have recourse to more than one gratuitous hypothesis. They go so far as to say, that it is the soul, which builds itself its external envelope, and, consequently, that this last must necessarily bear the impress of the qualities and faculties of the former.

1st. This assertion is proved by nothing.

2nd. It supposes that the cause of the difference of the qualities and faculties of the soul depends on the soul itself, and not on the material organs.

3d. Experience proves, that, both in man and in woman, the virtues and the faculties are not proportional to the beauty of the different parts of their body, or, of the harmony which reigns among them. [. . .]

In all my researches, my object has been to find out the laws of organization, and the functions of the nervous system in general, and of the brain in particular. [. . .]

The moral and intellectual dispositions are innate; their manifestation depends on organization; the brain is exclusively the organ of the mind; the brain is composed of as many particular and independent organs, as there are fundamental powers of the mind;—these four incontestable principles form the basis of the whole physiology of the brain.

These principles having been thoroughly established, it was necessary to inquire, how far the inspection of the form of the head, or cranium, presents a means of ascertaining the existence or absence, and the degree of development, of certain cerebral parts; and consequently the presence or absence, the weakness or energy of certain functions. It was necessary to indicate the means for ascertaining the functions of particular cerebral parts, or the seat of the organs, and finally, it was indispensable, to distinguish the primitive fundamental qualities and faculties, from their general attributes.

After that I was enabled to introduce my readers into the sanctuary of the soul and the brain, and give the history of the discovery of each primitive moral and intellectual power, its natural history in a state of health and of disease, and numerous observations in support of the seat of its organ.

An examination of the forms of heads of different nations, a demonstration of the futility of physiognomy, a theory of natural language, or pathognomy,[1] added new weight to preceding truths.

The thorough development of the physiology of the brain, has unveiled the defects of the theories of philosophers, on the moral and intellectual powers of man, and has given rise to a philosophy of man founded on his organization, and consequently, the only one in harmony with nature.

Finally, I have discussed four propositions equally interesting to history and philosophy, concerning the motives of our actions, the origin of the arts and sciences, the perfectibility of the human species, and the capacity of the world of each living being, and I have shown, that the solution of all these questions, hitherto problematical, springs directly from the physiology of the brain. [. . .]

The physiology of the brain is entirely founded on observations, experiments, and researches for the thousandth time repeated, on man and brute animals. Here, reasoning has had nothing more to do with it, than to seize the results, and deduce the principles that flow from the facts; and therefore it is, that the numerous propositions, though often subversive of commonly received notions, are never opposed to or inconsistent with one another. All is connected and harmo-

---

[1] The knowledge or study of the passions or emotions, or of the signs or expressions of them.

nious; every thing is mutually illustrated and confirmed. The explanation of the most abstruse phenomena of the moral and intellectual life of man and brutes is no longer the sport of baseless theories; the most secret causes of the difference in the character of species, nations, sexes, and ages, from birth to decrepitude, are unfolded; mental derangement is no longer connected with a spiritualism that nothing can reach; man, finally, that inextricable being, is made known; organology composes and decomposes, piece by piece, his propensities and talents; it has fixed our ideas of his destiny, and the sphere of his activity; and it has become a fruitful source of the most important applications to medicine, philosophy, jurisprudence, education, history, &c. Surely, these are so many guarantees of the truth of the physiology of the brain—so many titles of gratitude to HIM, who has made them known to me!

A SYSTEM OF PHRENOLOGY

George Combe, *A System of Phrenology*, 3rd edn. (Edinburgh: John Anderson, 1830), frontispiece.

This chart was the basic model for phrenological analysis in England. Gall had only designated twenty-seven organs, but Spurzheim had increased the number to thirty-five, as illustrated here.

See Fig. 5.

THE CONSTITUTION OF MAN

George Combe, *The Constitution of Man Considered in Relation to External Objects* (1828), 5th edn. (Edinburgh: John Anderson, 1835), 45–9, 50–2, 140–1, 218–19, 220–1, 235–6.

This extraordinarily popular work gave its readers both the principles of phrenological analysis, and also Combe's moral and social philosophy of individual and social progress founded on the scientific principles of phrenology.

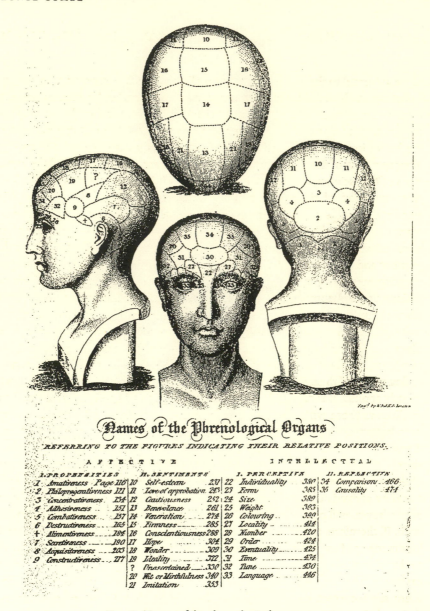

FIG. 5. Names of the phrenological organs

MAN CONSIDERED AS AN ANIMAL, MORAL, AND INTELLECTUAL BEING

I have adverted to the bodily constitution of man, which is essentially animal; but I observe, in the third place, that man, viewed in regard to his mental constitution, is an animal, moral, and intellectual being. To discover the adaptation of the mental parts of his nature to his external circumstances, we must first know what are his various animal, moral, and intellectual powers themselves. Phrenology gives us a view of them, drawn from observation; and as I have verified the inductions of that science, so as to satisfy myself that it is the most complete and correct exposition of the nature of man which has yet been given, I adopt its classification of faculties as the basis of the subsequent observations. One great advantage presented by Phrenology, is the light which it throws on the *natural* constitution of the mind. Philosophers and divines have long disputed about the number and functions of the human faculties; and while each assumed his own consciousness as the standard of nature, and occupied himself chiefly with observations on its phenomena, as his means of study, there could be no end to their discussions. But the organs of the mind can be seen and felt, and their size estimated,—and the mental manifestations also that accompany them can be observed, in an unlimited number of instances,—so that, assuming the existence of organs, it is clear that a far higher degree of certainty in regard to the *natural* endowments of the mind may be attained by these means, than by any other previously applied. It is disputed also whether man be now in possession of the same qualities as those with which he was created: but the fact of the organs having been bestowed by the Creator is not open to contradiction, if they exist at all; and if we discover their functions and their uses, and distinguish these from their abuses, we shall obviously obtain clearer views of what God has instituted, and of the extent to which man himself is chargeable with error and perversion, than could be arrived at by the means hitherto employed. Such conclusions, if correctly drawn, will possess an irresistible authority—that of the record of creation itself. If, therefore, any reader be disposed to question the existence of such qualities in man as I am about to describe, he must, to do so consistently, be prepared to deny, on reasonable grounds, that mental organs exist,—or, if he allows their existence, he must establish that the observations of phrenologists in regard to them are incorrect, or their inferences regarding their functions erroneously deduced. According to Phrenology, then, the human faculties are the following. The organs are double, each faculty having two, lying in corresponding situations of the hemispheres of the brain. Their *situations* are indicated by the engravings.

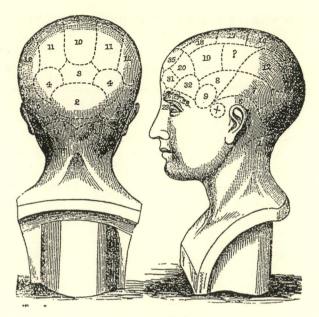

FIG. 6. Organs of feeling

ORDER I. FEELINGS

GENUS I. PROPENSITIES
common to man with the lower animals

THE LOVE OF LIFE.

APPETITE FOR FOOD.—*Uses:* Nutrition.—*Abuses:* Gluttony and drunkenness. The Organ is marked with a cross on bust.

1. AMATIVENESS—Produces sexual love.

2. PHILOPROGENITIVENESS.—*Uses:* Affection for young and tender beings.—*Abuses:* Pampering and spoiling children.

3. CONCENTRATIVENESS.—*Uses:* It gives the desire of permanence in place, and renders permanent, emotions and ideas in the mind.—*Abuses:* Aversion to move abroad; morbid dwelling on internal emotions and ideas, to the neglect of external impressions.

4. ADHESIVENESS.—*Uses:* Attachment; friendship and society result from it.—*Abuses:* Clanship for improper objects, attachment to worthless individuals. It is generally strong in women.

5. COMBATIVENESS.—*Uses:* Courage to meet danger and overcome difficulties, tendency to oppose and attack whatever requires opposition, and to resist unjust encroachments.—*Abuses:* Love of contention, and tendency to provoke and assault. This feeling obviously adapts man to a world in which danger and difficulty abound.

6. DESTRUCTIVENESS.—*Uses:* Desire to destroy noxious objects, and to kill for food. It is very discernible in carnivorous animals.—*Abuses:* Cruelty, murder, desire to torment, tendency to passion, rage, and harshness and severity in speech and writing. This feeling places man in harmony with death and destruction, which are woven into the system of sublunary creation.

7. SECRETIVENESS.—*Uses:* Tendency to restrain within the mind the various emotions and ideas that involuntarily present themselves, until the judgment has approved of giving them utterance; it is simply the propensity to conceal, and is an ingredient in prudence. *Abuses:* Cunning, deceit, duplicity, and lying.

8. ACQUISITIVENESS.—*Uses:* Desire to possess, and tendency to accumulate articles of utility, to provide against want.—*Abuses:* Inordinate desire of property, selfishness, avarice, theft.

9. CONSTRUCTIVENESS.—*Uses:* Desire to build and construct works of art.—*Abuses:* Construction of engines to injure or destroy, and fabrication of objects to deceive mankind.

GENUS II. SENTIMENTS

I. *Sentiments common to Man with the Lower Animals*

10. SELF-ESTEEM.—*Uses:* Self-respect, self-interest, love of independence, personal dignity.—*Abuses:* Pride, disdain, overweening conceit, excessive selfishess, love of dominion.

11. LOVE OF APPROBATION.—*Uses:* Desire of the esteem of others, love of praise, desire of fame or glory.—*Abuses:* Vanity, ambition, thirst for praise independently of praiseworthiness.

12. CAUTIOUSNESS.—*Uses:* It gives origin to the sentiment of fear, the desire to shun danger, and circumspection; and it is an ingredient in prudence.—*Abuses:* Excessive timidity, poltroonery, unfounded apprehensions, despondency, melancholy.

13. BENEVOLENCE.—*Uses:* Desire of the happiness of others, universal charity, mildness of disposition, and a lively sympathy with the enjoyment of all animated beings.—*Abuses:* Profusion, injurious indulgence of the appetites and fancies of others, prodigality, facility of temper.

14. VENERATION.—*Uses:* Tendency to venerate or respect whatever is great and good; gives origin to religious adoration.—*Abuses:* Senseless respect for unworthy objects consecrated by time or situation, love of antiquated customs, abject subserviency to persons in authority, superstitious awe.

15. FIRMNESS.—*Uses:* Determination, perseverance, steadiness of purpose.—*Abuses:* Stubbornness, infatuation, tenacity in evil.

16. CONSCIENTIOUSNESS.—*Uses:* It gives origin to the sentiment of justice, or respect for the rights of others, openness to conviction, the love of truth.—*Abuses:* Scrupulous adherence to noxious principles when ignorantly embraced,

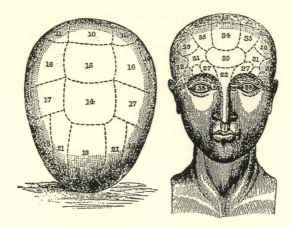

Fig. 7. Organs of feeling

excessive refinement in the views of duty and obligation, excess in remorse or self-condemnation.

17. HOPE.—*Uses:* Tendency to expect future good; it cherishes faith.—*Abuses:* Credulity with respect to the attainment of what is desired, absurd expectations of felicity not founded on reason.

18. WONDER.—*Uses:* The desire of novelty; admiration of the new, the unexpected, the grand, the wonderful, and extraordinary.—*Abuses:* Love of the marvellous, and occult; senseless astonishment; belief in false miracles, in prodigies, magic, ghosts, and other supernatural absurdities.—*Note.* Veneration, Hope, and Wonder, combined, give the tendency to religion; their abuses produce superstition.

19. IDEALITY.—*Uses:* Love of the beautiful and splendid, desire of excellence, poetic feeling.—*Abuses:* Extravagance and absurd enthusiasm, preference of the showy and glaring to the solid and useful, a tendency to dwell in the regions of fancy and to neglect the duties of life.

20. WIT—Gives the feeling of the ludicrous, and disposes to mirth.

21. IMITATION—Copies the manners, gestures, and actions of others, and appearances in nature generally.

ORDER II. INTELLECTUAL FACULTIES

GENUS I. EXTERNAL SENSES

FEELING or TOUCH. ⎫
TASTE. ⎬ *Uses:* To bring man into communication with external objects, and to enable him to enjoy

SMELL.
HEARING.
SIGHT. } them.—*Abuses:* Excessive indulgence in the pleasures arising from the senses, to the extent of impairing bodily health, and debilitating or deteriorating the mind.

GENUS II. KNOWING FACULTIES WHICH PERCEIVE THE EXISTENCE AND QUALITIES OF EXTERNAL OBJECTS

22. INDIVIDUALITY—Takes cognizance of existence and simple facts.

23. FORM—Renders man observant of form.

24. SIZE—gives the idea of space, and enables us to appreciate dimension and distance.

25. WEIGHT—Communicates the perception of momentum, weight, and resistance; and aids equilibrium.

26. COLOURING—Gives perception of colours and their harmonies.

GENUS III. KNOWING FACULTIES WHICH PERCEIVE THE RELATIONS OF EXTERNAL OBJECTS

27. LOCALITY—Gives the idea of relative position.

28. NUMBER—Gives the talent for calculation.

29. ORDER—Communicates the love of physical arrangement.

30. EVENTUALITY—Takes cognizance of occurrences or events.

31. TIME—Gives rise to the perception of duration.

32. TUNE—The sense of Melody and Harmony arises from it.

33. LANGUAGE—Gives facility in acquiring a knowledge of arbitrary signs to express thoughts, readiness in the use of them, and the power of inventing and recollecting them.

GENUS IV. REFLECTING FACULTIES, WHICH COMPARE, JUDGE, AND DISCRIMINATE

34. COMPARISON—Gives the power of discovering analogies, resemblances, and differences.

35. CAUSALITY—Traces the dependences of phenomena, and the relation of cause and effect. [. . .]

THE FACULTIES OF MAN COMPARED WITH EACH OTHER; OR THE SUPREMACY OF THE MORAL SENTIMENTS AND INTELLECT

According to the phrenological theory of human nature, the faculties are divided into Propensities common to man with the lower animals, Sentiments common to man with the lower animals, Sentiments proper to man, and Intellect. Every faculty stands in a definite relation to certain external objects: when it is internally active it desires these objects; when they are presented to it they excite it to activity, and delight it with agreeable sensations. Human happiness and misery are resolvable into the gratification, and denial of gratification, of one or more of our mental faculties, or of the feelings connected with our bodily frame. The faculties, in themselves, are mere instincts; the moral sentiments and intellect being higher instincts than the animal propensities. Every faculty is good in itself, but all are liable to abuse. Their operations are right only when they act in harmony with each other, enlightened intellect and moral sentiment holding the supremacy.

The faculties may be considered as acting in a variety of ways. First, The lower propensities may be viewed as acting by themselves, each seeking its own gratification, but without transgressing the limits prescribed by enlightened intellect and the moral sentiments: this gratification is legitimate and proper, and the fountain of much enjoyment to human beings. Secondly, The propensities may be considered as acting in opposition to the dictates of the moral sentiments and intellect: a merchant, for instance, by misrepresentation of the real qualities of his commodities, may obtain a higher price for them than if he spoke the truth; or, by depreciating unjustly the goods of a rival, he may attract that rival's customers to himself: By such conduct he would apparently benefit himself, but he would infringe the dictates of the moral sentiments and intellect; in other words, he would do an injury to the interests of his rival proportionate to the undue benefit which he attempted to secure to himself: All such manifestations of the propensities are abuses, and, when pursued systematically to their results, are seen to injure not only the individual against whom they are directed, but him also who practises them. Thirdly, The moral sentiments may be regarded as acting by themselves, each seeking its own gratification: thus Benevolence may prompt an individual to do acts of kindness, and Veneration to perform exercises of devotion. When the gratification sought by any one or more of the sentiments does not infringe the duties prescribed by all the other sentiments and enlightened intellect, the actions are proper. But any one moral sentiment, acting by itself, may run into excess—Benevolence, for instance, may instigate to generosity at the expense of justice; Veneration may prompt a person to run after sermons abroad, when he should be discharging his domestic duties, or instructing his children at home,—which actions also are abuses.

Thus there is, 1st, a wide sphere of action provided for the propensities, in which each may seek its gratification in its own way, without exceeding the limits of morality; and this is a good and proper action: 2dly, There is ample scope for the exercise of each of the moral and intellectual faculties, without infringing the dictates of any of the other faculties belonging to the same classes; and this action also is good. But, on the other hand, the propensities, and also the moral and intellectual faculties, may act singly or in groups, in opposition to the dictates of the whole moral sentiments and intellectual powers enlightened by knowledge and acting in combination; and all such actions are wrong. Hence right conduct is *that which is approved of by the whole moral and intellectual faculties, fully enlightened, and acting in harmonious combination*. This I call the supremacy of the moral sentiments and intellect. [. . .]

The head of Philip Melancthon,[1] the illustrious reformer and associate of Luther, furnishes an example of the decided predominance of the moral and intellectual regions over that of the animal propensities. The drawing is copied from a portrait by Albert Durer.

FIG. 8. Melanchthon

The following description of Melancthon's head and character is given in Dr Spurzheim's work on Phrenology in Connexion with Physiognomy.[2] 'It is the brain of an extraordinary man. The organs of the moral and religious feelings predominate greatly, and will disapprove of all violence, irreverence, and injustice. The forehead betokens a vast and comprehensive understanding; and the *ensemble* a mind the noblest, the most amiable, and the most intellectual that can be conceived.' [. . .]

With the head of Melancthon may be contrasted that of Pope Alexander VI.[3]

'This cerebral organization,' says Dr Spurzheim, 'is despicable in the eyes of a phrenologist. The animal organs compose by far its greatest portion. Such a brain is no more adequate to the manifestation of Christian virtues, than the

---

[1] (1497–1560), friend of Luther, and responsible for reorganizing the education system in Germany, and reforming and founding several universities.

[2] J. G. Spurzheim, *Phrenology in Connection with the Study of Physiognomy* (1826).

[3] (1497–1560), a Spanish pope whose notorious corruption contributed to the development of the Protestant Reformation.

FIG. 9. Pope Alexander VI

brain of an idiot from birth to the exhibition of the intellect of a Leibnitz or a Bacon. The cervical and whole basilar region of the head are particularly developed; the organs of the perceptive faculties are pretty large; but the sincipital (or coronal) region is exceedingly low, particularly at the organs of Benevolence, Veneration, and Conscientiousness. Such a head is unfit for any employment of a superior kind, and never gives birth to sentiments of humanity. The sphere of its activity does not extend beyond those enjoyments which minister to the animal portion of human nature. [. . .]

If the doctrine before expounded be true, that every faculty is good in itself, that the folly and crime which disgrace human society spring from abuses of the faculties, and that the tendency to abuse them originates in the disproportion of certain parts of the brain to each other, and in ignorance of the proper mode of manifesting them, how completely do these considerations go to the root of theology and morals! At present the influence of organization in determining the natural dispositions is altogether neglected or denied by the common school of divines, moralists, and philosophers; yet it is of an importance exceeding all other terrestrial influences and considerations.

If, under the influence of youthful passion and inexperience, an individual endowed with the splendid cerebral development of Melancthon, should unite himself for life to a female possessing a head like that of Hare,[4] Williams,[5] or Vitellius,[6] the effects could not fail to be most disastrous, with respect both to his

[4] William Hare, who, together with William Burke, was arrested in 1828 in Edinburgh for a series of murders. Burke and Hare had been murdering their victims in order to sell their bodies for medical dissection.
[5] Not traced, but probably another murderer.
[6] (AD 15–69), a Roman emperor. During the disturbances after Nero's death he was proclaimed emperor by his troops, but was subsequently murdered by them.

own happiness and to the qualities of his offspring. In the first place, after the animal feelings were gratified, and their ardour had subsided, the two minds could not by any possibility sympathize. Many marriages are unhappy in consequence of an instinctive discord between the modes of feeling and thinking of the husband and wife, the cause of which they themselves cannot explain. The mental differences will be found to arise from different configurations and qualities of brain. Thus, if the husband be deficient in the organ of Conscientiousness, and the wife possess it in a high degree, she will be secretly disgusted with the dishonesty and inherent falsehood of his character, which she will have many opportunities of observing, even when they are unknown to the world; while, on the other hand, few conditions are more lamentable than that of an intellectual and well educated man, irretrievably doomed to the society of an ignorant, jealous, narrow-minded wife. [. . .]

Until Phrenology was discovered, no natural index to mental qualities, that could be safely relied on, was possessed, and each individual, in directing his conduct, was left to the guidance of his own sagacity. But the natural law never bended one iota to accommodate itself to that state of ignorance. Men suffered from unsuitable alliances; and they will continue to do so, until they shall avail themselves of the means of judging afforded by Phrenology, and act in accordance with its dictates. [. . .]

In the whole system of the education and treatment of the labouring population, the laws of the Creator, such as I have now endeavoured to expound them, are neglected or infringed. Life with them is spent to so great an extent in labour, that their moral and intellectual powers are stinted of exercise and gratification; and mental enjoyments are chiefly those afforded by the animal propensities:— in other words, their existence is too little *rational;* they are rather organized machines than moral and intellectual beings. [. . .]

My proposition is, that after ten or twelve hours of muscular exertion a day, continued for six days in the week, the labourer is not in a fit condition for that active exercise of his moral and intellectual faculties which alone constitutes him a rational being. The exercise of these powers depends on the condition of the brain and nervous system; and these are exhausted and deadened by too much muscular exertion. [. . .]

The admirable inventions which are the boast and glory of civilized men, are believed by many persons to be at this moment adding to the misery and degradation of the people. Power-looms, steam-carriages, and steam-ships, it is asserted, have all hitherto operated directly in increasing the hours of exertion, and abridging the reward of the labourer! Can we believe that God has bestowed on us the gift of an almost creative power, solely to increase the wretchedness of the many, and minister to the luxury of the few? Impossible! The ultimate effect of mechanical inventions on human society appears to be not yet divined. I hail them as the grand instruments of civilization, by giving leisure to the great mass of the people to cultivate and enjoy their moral, intellectual, and religious powers. [. . .]

The national debt of Britain has been contracted chiefly in wars, originating in commercial jealousy and thirst for conquest; in short, under the suggestions of Combativeness, Destructiveness, Acquisitiveness, and Self-Esteem. Did not our ancestors, therefore, impede their own prosperity and happiness, by engaging in these contests? and have any consequences of them reached us, except the burden of paying nearly thirty millions of taxes annually, as the price of the gratification of the propensities of our ignorant forefathers? Would a statesman, who believed in the doctrines maintained in this work, have recommended these wars *as essential to national prosperity?* If the twentieth part of the sums had been spent in effecting objects recognised by the moral sentiments—in instituting, for example, seminaries of education and penitentiaries, and in making roads, canals, and public granaries—how different would have been the present condition of the country!

THE PROFESSOR

Charlotte Brontë, *The Professor* (1857), ed. Margaret Smith and Herbert Rosengarten (Oxford: Clarendon Press, 1987), 100–1.

The Professor was Charlotte Brontë's first novel, first submitted to publishers in 1846, but only finally published, after many rejections, two years after her death in 1857. In the selected passage the hero, William Crimsworth, is surveying his female pupils in the Belgian school he has just joined. Comparison with the Combe passage dealing with Pope Alexander VI in the previous extract suggests that Charlotte Brontë was writing with a phrenological manual open at her side. Both Charlotte and Anne Brontë used phrenological vocabulary and ideas extensively in their fiction.

Aurelia and Adèle were in the first division of the second Class, the second division was headed by a pensionnaire named Juanna Trista; this girl was of mixed Belgian and Spanish origin, her Flemish Mother was dead, her Catalonian father was a merchant, residing in the —— Isles where Juanna had been born and whence she was sent to Europe to be educated. I wonder that any one, looking at that girl's head and countenance, would have received her under their roof. She had precisely the same shape of skull as Pope Alexander the sixth; her organs of benevolence, veneration, conscientiousness, adhesiveness were singularly small, those of self-esteem, firmness, destructiveness, combativeness preposterously large; her head sloped up in the penthouse shape, was contracted about the forehead and prominent behind; she had rather good, though large and marked features; her temperament was fibrous and bilious, her complexion pale and dark, hair and eyes black, form angular and rigid but proportionate, age fifteen. Juanna was not very thin but she had a gaunt visage and her 'regard' was fierce and hungry; narrow as was her brow it presented space enough for the legible graving of two words, Mutiny and Hate; in some one of her other lineaments— I think the eye—Cowardice had also its distinct cipher.

PHRENOLOGY AND EDUCATION

George Combe, *An Address Delivered at the Anniversary of the Birth of Spurzheim, and the Organization of the Boston Phrenological Society* (Boston: Marsh, Capen, Lyon and Webb, 1840), 10–11.

Combe here outlines his principles of child education drawn from his interpretation of phrenology. Combe rejects Locke's theory of the child as tabula rasa, *incapable of experiencing adult passions. In his view, children had organs and propensities which functioned just as in the adult, only they needed more guidance in the direction of their feelings.*

My experience leads me to confess that the highest and best gift which a child can inherit, is a well formed and well constituted brain. Where a peculiar combination exists, I know of no method by which its effects can be removed; and if a feeble or diseased organization be inherited by the child, I have discovered no means by which its mental manifestations can be rendered equal to those of a brain enjoying native health and vigor. I disavow, therefore, all pretensions to the power of perfecting, by means of Phrenology, every individual child; but there are degrees of comparison: there may be good, better, best; as well as bad, worse, worst. Need I assure the members of this Society, that by teaching the functions of the different organs, and the uses and abuses of the different faculties, to children, the good have been rendered strikingly better, and the worst have become less bad? Wherever the organization has been of a high order; that is, where the quality of the brain was good, and the moral and intellectual organs predominated, the results have been truly admirable. A few brief remarks will suffice to explain the operation of this kind of instruction.

The organs exist and perform their functions in children as they do in adults. The feelings are first developed; they are strong, they are blind, and they sometimes conflict. Phrenology enables the child to understand the nature, objects, uses, and relative authority of each. It introduces light and order where darkness and chaos formerly reigned. I can well recollect the painful conflicts which I experienced in my own childhood, and the difficulty which I felt in determining which feeling was right. For example: Having a large Self-esteem, and tolerably good Combativeness and Destructiveness, I was easily offended, and I often burned to gratify my feelings of revenge; but Benevolence and Conscientiousness would whisper that this was wrong. I felt instinctively the opposition between these feelings, but I knew not their relative values. I sometimes thought that submission to aggression and forgiveness of injuries were cowardice, and indicated a want of manly spirit; and if the better principles actually prevailed, I rarely enjoyed the satisfaction of the conscious triumph of virtue. Again: Having Love of Approbation equally large with Self-esteem, I felt these two emotions constantly conflicting in my childhood. Love of Approbation prompted me to acts of vain glory and boasting, of which Self-esteem and the moral sentiments were soon heartily ashamed. I resolved to correct this fault, and put on a dogged indifference to the opinion of others, which was to me equally unnatural and unsatisfactory, and in itself unamiable. I could not adjust the balance between the two faculties. Nay, not only did this conflict annoy me in childhood, but it persecuted me far on in life, and I was constantly liable to run into an excess of complaisance, to give way to an undignified desire to cultivate favor by compliances, or to fall back on Self-esteem, and set opinion at defiance. Phrenology conferred on me the first internal peace of mind that I experienced; and although I am still conscious of defects in external manners, arising from these disadvantages of youthful training, I now know, at least, what is the character and value of the different emotions that visit me. I could give many other examples; but these will suffice to render my proposition intelligible, that a knowledge of the faculties may be rendered of the highest utility to children themselves.

OBSERVATIONS ON MENTAL DERANGEMENT

Andrew Combe, *Observations on Mental Derangement: Being an Application of the Principles of Phrenology to the Elucidation of the Causes, Symptoms, Nature, and Treatment of Insanity* (Edinburgh: John Anderson, 1831), 116–17, 120–1.

Like his brother, George, the physician Andrew Combe was also a follower of phrenology. Despite the waning of interest in phrenology from the mid-century, this text was still deemed worthy of reissue in 1887, in an abridged version, by Sir Arthur Mitchell, Commissioner in Lunacy for Scotland. Andrew Combe here draws on the phrenological emphasis on the importance of exercising the mental organs in order to criticize the current practices of female education. Such criticisms were made repeatedly in medical literature of the time. They formed one side of the debates on female education which were later to culminate in the exchange between Henry Maudsley and Elizabeth Garrett Anderson featured in Section 5.

The laws of exercise regulate the health of the brain, and the performance of its functions. If the different cerebral organs be called into daily activity, and duly stimulated, by being employed on their own objects for a length of time, proportioned to their constitutional vigour, and sufficient intervals of repose be allowed, their vital action becomes animated and enduring, and the corresponding mental powers act with a readiness, vivacity, and force, characteristic of health. But to attain this most desirable end, the feelings and moral sentiments must be daily in exercise, as well as the intellectual faculties, for they also go to constitute the mind, and their organs being parts of the same brain as those which manifest the intellect, and composed of the same kind of nervous matter, and nourished by branches from the same bloodvessels, are subject to the same laws, and consequently require the same diligent training, and the same treatment, as to action and repose, to keep them in health, and bring them to perfection. If, on the other hand, they be too strongly or too permanently excited, their vital energies are exhausted, nutrition is deteriorated, and the functions are executed with feebleness and irritation; and, lastly, if their exercise be neglected, they become feeble and indolent in their operations, and prone to morbid action from inherent debility.

Keeping these principles in view, it will excite no surprise to find, that *non-exercise* of the brain and nervous system, or, in other words, inactivity of intellect and of feeling, is a very frequent predisposing cause of insanity, and of every form of nervous disease. For demonstrative evidence of this position, we have only to look at the numerous victims to be found among females of the middle and higher ranks, who have no call to exertion to gain the means of subsistence, and no objects of interest on which to expend and exercise their mental faculties, and who consequently sink into a state of mental sloth and nervous weakness, which not only deprives them of every enjoyment, but lays them open to suffering, both of mind and body, from the slightest causes. [. . .]

The most frequent victims of this kind of predisposition are females of the middle and higher ranks, especially those of a nervous constitution, and good natural abilities; but who, from ill-directed education, possess nothing more solid than mere accomplishments, and have no materials of thought or feeling, and no regular or imperative occupations to *demand* attention, and whose brains, in short, are half asleep. Such persons have literally nothing on which to expend half the nervous energy which nature has bestowed on them for better purposes. They have nothing to excite and exercise the brain—nothing to elicit activity; their own feelings and personal relations necessarily constitute the grand objects of their contemplations; these are brooded over till the mental energies become impaired, false ideas of existence and of providence spring up in the mind, the fancy is haunted by strange impressions, and every trifle which relates to self is exaggerated into an object of immense importance. The brain having literally nothing on which to exercise itself, becomes weak, and the mental manifestations are enfeebled in proportion; so that a person of good endowments, thus treated, will often not only exhibit something of the imbecility of a fool, but gradually become irritable, peevish, and discontented, and open to the attack of every form of nervous disease and of derangement from causes which, under different circumstances, would never have disturbed them for a moment.

APPLICATIONS OF PHRENOLOGY

Anon. *Phrenology Simplified: Being an Exposition of the Principles and Applications of Phrenology to the Practical Uses of Life.* Intended as a sequel to the 'Catechism of Phrenology' by a Member of the Phrenological Society of Edinburgh (Glasgow: W. R. M'Phun, 1836), 192–4.

Taken from one of the many hundreds of popular phrenological handbooks, this extract, which deals with the hiring of servants, illustrates the ways in which phrenology was conscientiously applied to the practical details of social and domestic life. The employer is here warned to make sure not only that the servant has a good phrenological profile, but that it is also compatible with his or her own configuration of organs.

The best combination of intellectual organs for a servant is that which occurs when the lower region of the forehead is large, the middle region immediately above the nose up to the line of the hair is also large, and the upper lateral region full. The dispositions depend on the combinations of the moral and animal organs. If Acquisitiveness, Secretiveness, and Love of Approbation, be all large, and Conscientiousness deficient, the servant will be selfish and cunning, but extremely plausible, deferential, and polite; and eye service will be rendered abundantly, but conscientious discharge of duty will be wanting. If Benevolence, Conscientiousness, Firmness, Self-Esteem, Secretiveness, Love of Approbation, and Veneration moderate, there may be great fidelity and honesty, with heat of temper, unbending stiffness of deportment, and in short, an exterior manner the reverse of the former; but internal disposition and practical conduct in situations of trust far superior. The combinations also determine the fitness of the individual for particular employments; a female with small Philoprogenitiveness ought never to be employed as a nursery maid, nor one deficient in Order and Ideality as a lady's maid. A man deficient in Conscientiousness is unfit to be a butler or a steward. The varieties of combination are extremely numerous, and the effects of them can be learned only from experience. [. . .]

The relation of the natural qualities of the master or mistress to those of the servant must be attended to. If a mistress with a small brain having Conscientiousness and Benevolence moderate, and Self Esteem and Combativeness large, should hire a servant possessed of a large, active, and well proportioned brain, the latter will instantly feel that nature has made her the superior, although fortune has reversed their natural positions. The mistress will feel this too, but will maintain her command by imperiousness, captiousness or violence. In this condition the best dispositions of the servant may be outraged, and conduct produced of a discreditable nature, when contemplated by itself, apart from the provocation. A servant with a small brain, but favourable combination, would prove a treasure to a mistress possessed of similar qualities, whereas she would be felt as too feeble and inefficacious in her whole manner and mode of acting by a lady whose brain was very large, very favourably combined and very active. This principle explains why the same individual may be found to be an excellent servant in one family, and unsuitable in another.

A 'PAGE' OF PHRENOLOGY

Illustration from Paul Prendergast, 'A "page" of phrenology', *Illuminated Magazine*, 11 (Nov.–April, 1844), 17.

This humorous article portrays a naïve phrenological enthusiast who employs his servants on phrenological principles, with disastrous results. He remains, however, unshaken in his commitment to these principles.

FIG. 10. A 'page' of phrenology

THE DISPOSITIONS OF NATIONS

Anon., 'On the coincidence between the natural talents and dispositions of nations, and the development of their brains', *Phrenological Journal*, 2 (1824–5), 16–18.

As this article reveals, racial comparison was an early component of phrenology, and laid the foundations for the later excesses of craniology (see Section 5). There was by no means, however, unanimity amongst phrenological followers as to the racial implications of their theories. The writer here tones down the arguments for racial inferiority through reference to the influence of political factors on national development.

The brains of the different EUROPEAN NATIONS differ considerably from each other, but a common type characterizes them all, and distinguishes them from those now described. They are decidedly larger than the Hindoo, American Indian, and Negro heads; and this indicates superior force of mental character. The portion before the ear, connected with the intellectual faculties, and the coronal surface, or the organs of the moral sentiments, are more amply developed in proportion to the base and posterior inferior parts of the brain, the organs of the animal propensities. In short, they indicate a higher natural power of reflection, and a greater natural tendency to Justice, Benevolence, and Refinement, than the others. The three features in which the European brain in an especial degree excels are, Ideality, Conscientiousness, Causality, and Wit. The organs of these faculties are almost invariably small in the barbarous and savage tribes. The European skull belongs to the Caucasian variety of Blumenbach,[1] which he considers as the most beautiful and perfect of all the national crania in the world; and in this point he and the Phrenologists agree.

The ANCIENT EGYPTIANS appear, from the stupendous monuments of art and science left behind them, to have been a highly intelligent and civilized people; and it is a striking fact, that the skulls of ancient mummies are found almost invariably to belong to the same class as those of modern Europeans. In the Society's collection, there are casts of the skulls of five mummies, and we have seen and obtained accurate descriptions of the skulls of half a dozen more, and the full size, large development before the ear, and broad coronal surface, characterize them all.

These facts appear to indicate, that when a nation is independent, and left at liberty to follow the bent of their own judgment and dispositions, their institutions spring from the peculiar mental constitution which they have received from nature, and that this constitution is in exact accordance with the development of their brains. Climate and other external causes modify to some extent the effects of natural endowment, but the distinguishing features of each people seem to bear a more direct and uniform relation to the size and form of their brain, than to those adventitious circumstances. Where a people is subjugated by a foreign power, as the Greeks by the Turks, and the Italians by the Austrians, the national character has no adequate opportunity of unfolding its peculiarities; and hence, if this circumstance is overlooked, the same race may seem to present different characteristics at different periods of their history. The modern Greeks, it was lately said, no more resemble their ancestors than the Hindoos the Europeans; and this was urged as an insuperable objection against Phrenology. Now, however, when the Turkish yoke is loosened so as to allow the native qualities to shoot, we see the same force of character, the same deliberate and determined heroism, and the same capacity for stratagem in war, with all the fickleness and

---

[1] J. F. Blumenbach (1752–1840), noted comparative anatomist and natural historian at Göttingen University. Drawing on measurements of his own collection of craniums, he proposed one of the earliest classifications of the races, dividing men into five families: Caucasian, Mongolian, Malayan, Ethiopian, American.

proneness to dissension, the same ascendency of passion over intellect and just-ice which distinguished the Greeks in the days of Pericles, re-appearing in their descendants. Many millions of Hindoos, Africans, and American Indians, have been for ages independent of a foreign yoke, and never displayed qualities such as those exhibited by independent Europe.

3. Mesmerism

A LETTER FROM DR ELLIOTSON

W. C. Engledue, *Cerebral Physiology and Materialism: With the Result of the Application of Animal Magnetism to the Cerebral Organs. An Address, Delivered to the Phrenological Association in London June 20, 1842. With a Letter from Dr Elliotson, on Mesmeric Phrenology and Materialism* (London: H. Ballière, 1843), 33–5.

The extract is from the appended letter from the eminent physician, John Elliotson, whose mesmeric work with the O'Key sisters at University College, London, had led to his enforced resignation. Elliotson was an early enthusiastic supporter of phrenology, and in this letter describes how his mesmeric experiments have vindicated his belief in phrenology.

My dear Doctor,

[. . .] I have had for some months under my care, for dreadful fits of many years' standing, which are yielding satisfactorily to mesmerism, two charming youthful patients, of excellent cerebral development and carefully brought up, of high intelligence, and of high moral character,—beautifully illustrating the power of good training upon a well-developed brain. No poet or moralist could desire finer specimens of all that is delightful in the youthful mind. They have not known each other. They both exhibit exquisite mesmeric phenomena. Are thrown into a profound coma, which no impression on the senses will dispel, and which soon becomes sleep-waking; their limbs may then be stiffened at pleasure and endowed with enormous force, which, although not yielding to mechanical violence, gives way to contact, or to the breath, or to movements of the operator's hand, without contact, in the direction opposite to that of the limbs' position; the various muscles of the face may be made to twitch as if with electricity, and the eyes be opened or the body be drawn by movements of the fingers and hands held at a short distance; the position of each finger of the operator's hand will be minutely imitated, though the eyes be closed, and the experiment be made out of the patient's sphere of vision. Though showing all the signs of sleep in the breathing, the falling of the head, the aspect, and the exquisite positions, they may be roused to talk, but never recognize the person nor the place. Their dream, if so it may be called, is perfectly rational; but the real place, and person addressing, and even the time, are invariably fancied otherwise than is the fact.

I know to a *certainty* that both are *totally ignorant* of phrenology. Without any previous intention, I one day tried to mesmerize some of the cerebral organs in the young lady. On placing the point of a finger on the right organ of attachment, she strongly squeezed my fingers of the other hand, placed in her right hand, and fancied I was her favorite sister; on removing it to the organ of self-esteem, she let go my fingers which were in her right hand, repelled my hand, mistook me for a person she disliked, and talked in the haughtiest manner. On replacing the point of my finger on attachment, she squeezed my fingers of the other hand again, and spoke affectionately. I removed the point of my finger to destructiveness, and she let go my fingers again, repelled my hand, mistook me for some one she disliked, and fell into a passion. The finger upon benevolence silenced her instantly; and made her amiable, though not attached. I thus could alter her mood, and her conception of my person at pleasure, and play upon her head as upon a piano.

On repeating these experiments, I soon found that the same results ensued, though not so rapidly, by merely pointing the finger near the organs: and this was the more satisfactory in demonstrating the facts to others; and indeed it has been quite satisfactory to every one, for not only were the eyes closed, but stopped up by a handful of handkerchief, held firmly upon each eye, and the experiments were made on organs so situated, that, had her eyes been open, I defy her to know to what organ I was pointing. These experiments I have repeated twenty times. But a fact still more wonderful is this. The state of the organ of one side gives evidence of itself on only half of the system. For instance, if I place my fingers in her right hand, and mesmerize attachment in the *right* side, she squeezes them and mistakes me for a dear friend; if I then mesmerize self-esteem, on the *left* side, she still speaks to me kindly, and squeezes my fingers with her right as much as ever. But if I place my fingers in her left hand, she repels them, and speaks scornfully to me, mistaking me for some one whom she dislikes. If I take hold of both her hands with one of mine, I can at pleasure make her repel both, by pointing over each organ of self-esteem or destructiveness; squeeze both, by pointing over each organ of attachment; or repel one and squeeze the other, right or left, accordingly as I point over the organ of self-esteem or destructiveness on the one side and that of attachment on the other, at the same time. These simultaneous, and especially the opposite, influences on the two sides, are the most astonishing and beautiful experiments that all physiology affords; and the sight of them enraptures every person. They are the more satisfactory, because there is no necessity for me to operate;—any person, even a sceptic in both phrenology and mesmerism, may point to and mesmerize her respective cerebral organs himself, if standing behind her. Under the opposite states of the two sides of the brain, she will address the person supposed on the one side or on the other, and speak affectionately, proudly, or angrily, as attachment on the one hand, or self-esteem or destructiveness on the other, is mesmerized. The expression, the tone, to say nothing of the words or the action of her hands, are exquisitely and rapidly in character. In the youth, the organs at present can be excited by contact only of the point of the finger, or by breathing over them. Attachment, self-esteem, destructiveness, music, and color, I have excited in him, and the effects come very slowly and continue long.

It is very interesting to see the first degree and the working up of the feelings. When self-esteem begins slowly, they think others are proud, and then become haughty themselves; when destructiveness begins slowly, they think others wish to quarrel, and then they quarrel,—or they begin to find fault with the fancied person, who is beloved in the waking state, and then mistake him for one disliked in the waking state.

Oh, that Gall could have lived to see this day—these astounding proofs of the truth of phrenology—proofs by which I have at once converted irresistibly to the firmest conviction of the truth of phrenology those who could never be induced before to bestow a moment's attention upon it. I have made more persons phrenologists during the last month than in all my previous life.

MESMERIC SLEEPWAKING

Chauncy Hare Townshend, *Facts in Mesmerism, with Reasons for a Dispassionate Inquiry into it* (London: Longman, Orme, Brown, Green and Longman, 1840), 195–8, 199–201, plate p. 206.

This book was dedicated to John Elliotson. Townshend, a clergyman and Cambridge academic, was an amateur enthusiast and close friend of Dickens. The plate illustrates one of his mesmeric subjects, Anna M., mesmerizing her sister. In opposition to those critics who saw the abdication of will during mesmerism as a degrading, threatening state, Townshend advocates a religious notion of a state of higher being attained through mesmeric influence.

If common sleep, then, be so manifestly the index of a suspended will, the mesmeric slumber is not less clearly an indication of a will that is over-ruled and held in abeyance by a force that is external to itself. [. . .]

The state of things resulting from this sway on the one side and submission on the other is most remarkable. We have the phenomenon before us of an existence at once dual and single; for, when the sleepwaker's capacities are acting under the immediate direction of the mesmeriser, the latter may be considered as making up together with him the complement of one full being, whereof the mesmeriser supplies the willing and the conscious portion, and the patient the intellectual part. The one impels, the other obeys impulsion: the one designs, the other executes: the one sets in motion a machine (and what a machine! the mind of man, with all its complicated marvels!), the other is the machine itself, instinct with life, as was the fiery car of Kehama,[1] innately active, yet guided by the volition of another! [. . .]

Such a view of the state of mesmeric sleepwaking may seem unpleasing, and incompatible with its being a rise in man's condition; but, let it be remembered, we do not rob the soul of any one faculty, we only change its mode of action, and that mode of action has its own undeviating law. In order to sleep, we must abdicate our will; yet, in order to enjoy intellectual activity, it is plain that we must *substitute* a presiding will; for it is the absence of this which makes slumber a state of disorganised and inconsequent thoughts. Thus the terms are absolute. If we desire to be freed from the thrall of the senses, yet to retain the mental faculties, we must abjure our own will, yet find an intellectual substitute. [. . .]

The power which the mesmeriser has over his patient is, indeed, as great as it is undeniable, and involves, in my apprehension, an immense responsibility on the part of the former. Should he direct the patient's attention to frivolous or evil things, he might do harm, for which he would be justly answerable. But, fortunately, as I have before remarked, there is, in mesmeric sleepwaking, a natural elevation of the mind above what is base and sensual; and the powers that appertain to reason, though the subjects on which they shall exercise themselves may be much at the mesmeriser's disposal, are neither to be clouded nor controlled. Nor is this to be wondered at. The mesmeriser can hardly be expected to command in another that which he can by no means dispose of in himself. In him, in every one of us, Reason, though too often we would quench her voice, will speak as loudly as conscience, which, indeed, is but a more rapid reason; and he who takes the evil path beholds, and reluctantly approves, the better way. This shows a godlike capability in reason, apart from volition: it seems less to belong to our-

[1] The magical carriage in Robert's Southey's epic narrative poem *The Curse of Kehama* (1810), Book XXII, st. 14:

Poised on a single wheel it moved along
Instinct with motion; by what wondrous skill
Compact, no human tongue could tell,
Nor human wit devise; but on that wheel,
    Moving or still
    As if with life induced
The Car miraculous supported stood.

selves than to be heaven speaking in us; and, in proportion as we obey its dictates, we are exalted in the scale of creation. Its peculiar luminousness, then, under the mesmeric conditions, is at once a safeguard to the sleepwaker, and a clear record of the most valuable birthright of man. Many persons, as I am aware, have disliked the idea of being mesmerised, from the fear of making wrong revelations, when deprived of their usual consciousness. But this is a vain apprehension. It is true that mesmeric patients act from impulse, but then their impulses are good. They will say severe but wholesome truths to persons' faces; but their instinctive sense of right forbids them to speak ill of any one behind his back. Anna M——, with all her knowledge of circumstances relating to others, never seasoned her talk with scandalous disclosures, never uttered a word that could injure a human being; and once, being pressed to relate something which might have compromised another person, not only kept silence on that head, but reproved the curiosity of the querist.

FIG. 11. Anna M. mesmerizing her sister

THE HEALING POWER OF MESMERISM

Harriet Martineau, *Letters on Mesmerism* (1845), 2nd edn. (London: Edward Moxon, 1850), 7–9, 13–14, 60–1, 62–3.

The publication of this work by the celebrated author of Illustrations of Political Economy *(1832–4), noted for her 'unfeminine' strength of intellect, caused a public stir, and added fuel to the internal debates within the medical establishment concerning mesmeric quackery. Martineau's claims to have been cured of physical ailments triggered vigorous denials from the medical profession. Martineau, however, remained unshaken in her commitment to the healing powers of mesmerism.*

On Saturday, June 22nd, Mr. Spencer Hall[1] and my medical friend came, as arranged, at my worst hour of the day, between the expiration of one opiate and the taking of another. By an accident, the gentlemen were rather in a hurry,—a circumstance unfavourable to a first experiment. But result enough was obtained to encourage a further trial, though it was of a nature entirely unanticipated by me. I had no other idea than that I should either drop asleep or feel nothing. I did not drop asleep, and I did feel something very strange. Various passes were tried by Mr. Hall; the first that appeared effectual, and the most so for some time after, were passes over the head, made from behind,—passes from the forehead to the back of the head, and a little way down the spine. A very short time after these were tried, and twenty minutes from the beginning of the *séance*, I became sensible of an extraordinary appearance, most unexpected, and wholly unlike anything I had ever conceived of. Something seemed to diffuse itself through the atmosphere,—not like smoke, nor steam, nor haze,—but most like a clear twilight, closing in from the windows and down from the ceiling, and in which one object after another melted away, till scarcely anything was left visible before my wide-open eyes. First, the outlines of all objects were blurred; then a bust, standing on a pedestal in a strong light, melted quite away; then the opposite bust; then the table with its gay cover, then the floor, and the ceiling, till one small picture, high up on the opposite wall, only remained visible,—like a patch of phosphoric light. I feared to move my eyes, lest the singular appearance should vanish; and I cried out, 'O! deepen it! deepen it!' supposing this the precursor of the sleep. It could not be deepened, however; and when I glanced aside from the luminous point, I found that I need not fear the return of objects to their ordinary appearance while the passes were continued. The busts reappeared, ghost-like, in the dim atmosphere, like faint shadows, except that their outlines, and the parts in the highest relief, burned with the same phosphoric light. The features of one, an Isis[2] with bent head, seemed to be illuminated by a fire on the floor, though this bust has its back to the windows. Wherever I glanced, all outlines were dressed in this beautiful light; and so they have been, at every *séance*, without exception, to this day; though the appearance has rather given way to drowsiness since I left off opiates entirely. This appearance continued during the remaining twenty minutes before the gentlemen were obliged to leave me. The

[1] The foremost popularizer of the combined science of phreno-mesmerism and author of *Mesmeric Experiences* (H. Ballière: London, 1845). He was lecturing at Newcastle at the time of his visit in June 1844.

[2] An Egyptian goddess who represented the female productive force of nature.

other effects produced were, first, heat, oppression and sickness, and, for a few hours after, disordered stomach; followed, in the course of the evening, by a feeling of lightness and relief, in which I thought I could hardly be mistaken.

On occasions of a perfectly new experience, however, scepticism and self-distrust are very strong. I was aware of this beforehand, and also, of course, of the common sneer—that mesmeric effects are 'all imagination.' When the singular appearances presented themselves, I thought to myself,—'Now, shall I ever believe that this was all fancy? When it is gone, and when people laugh, shall I ever doubt having seen what is now as distinct to my waking eyes as the rolling waves of yonder sea, or the faces round my sofa?' I did a little doubt it in the course of the evening: I had some misgivings even so soon as that; and yet more the next morning, when it appeared like a dream.

Great was the comfort, therefore, of recognising the appearances on the second afternoon. 'Now,' thought I, 'can I again doubt?' I did, more faintly; but, before a week was over, I was certain of the fidelity of my own senses in regard to this, and more. [. . .]

A few days after the arrival of my kind Mesmerist,[3] I had my foot on the grass for the first time for four years and a half. I went down to the little garden under my windows. I never before was in the open air, after an illness of merely a week or two, without feeling more or less overpowered; but now, under the open sky, after four years and a half spent between bed and a sofa, I felt no faintness, exhaustion, or nervousness of any kind. I was somewhat haunted for a day or two by the stalks of the grass, which I had not seen growing for so long (for, well supplied as I had been with flowers, rich and rare, I had seen no grass, except from my windows); but at the time, I was as self-possessed as any walker in the place. In a day or two, I walked round the garden, then down the lane, then to the haven, and so on, till now, in two months, five miles are no fatigue to me. At first, the evidences of the extent of the disease were so clear as to make me think that I had never before fully understood how ill I had been. They disappeared, one by one; and now I feel nothing of them.

The same fortifying influence carried me through the greatest effort of all,— the final severance from opiates. What that struggle is, can be conceived only by those who have experienced, or watched it with solicitude in a case of desperate dependence on them for years. No previous reduction can bridge over the chasm which separates an opiated from the natural state. I see in my own experience a consoling promise for the diseased, and also for the intemperate, who may desire to regain a natural condition, but might fail through bodily suffering. Where the mesmeric sleep can be induced, the transition may be made comparatively easy. It appears, however, that opiates are a great hindrance to the production of the sleep; but even so, the mesmeric influence is an inestimable help, as I can testify.

[3] Mrs Montague Wynyard, the widow of a London clergyman, introduced to Martineau by her friend Henry Atkinson.

I gave all my opiates to my Mesmerist, desiring her not to let me have any on any entreaty; and during the day I scarcely felt the want of them. Her mesmerising kept me up; and, much more, it intercepted the distress,—obviated the accumulation of miseries under which the unaided sufferer is apt to sink. It enabled me to encounter every night afresh,—acting as it does in cases of insanity, where it is all-important to suspend the peculiar irritation—to banish the haunting idea. [. . .]

The time is past for facts of natural philosophy to be held at discretion by priesthoods; for any facts which concern all human beings to be a deposit in the hands of any social class. Instead of re-enacting the scenes of old—setting up temples with secret chambers, oracles, and miraculous ministrations—instead of reviving the factitious sin and cruel penalties of witchcraft, (all forms assumed by mesmeric powers and faculties in different times), instead of exhibiting false mysteries in an age of investigation, it is clearly our business to strip false mysteries of their falseness, in order to secure due reverence to the true, of which there will ever be no lack. Because philosophers will not study the facts of that mental *rapport* which takes place in Mesmerism, whereby the mind of the ignorant often gives out in echo the knowledge of the informed, we have claims of inspiration springing up right and left. Because medical men will not study the facts of the mesmeric trance, nor ascertain the extremest of its singularities, we have tales of Estaticas, and of sane men going into the Tyrol and elsewhere to contemplate, as a sign from heaven, what their physicians ought to be able to report of at home as natural phenomena easily producible in certain states of disease. Because physiologists and mental philosophers will not attend to facts from whose vastness they pusillanimously shrink, the infinitely delicate mechanism and organisation of brain, nerves and mind are thrown as a toy into the hands of children and other ignorant persons, and of the base. [. . .]

As for the frequent objection brought against inquiry into Mesmerism, that there should be no countenance of an influence which gives human beings such power over one another, I really think a moment's reflection, and a very slight knowledge of Mesmerism, would supply both the answers which the objection requires. First, it is too late, as I have said above; the power is abroad, and ought to be guided and controlled. Next, this is but one addition to the powers we have over one another already; and a far more slow and difficult one than many which are safely enough possessed. Every apothecary's shop is full of deadly drugs—every workshop is full of deadly weapons—wherever we go, there are plenty of people who could knock us down, rob and murder us; wherever we live, there are plenty of people who could defame and ruin us. Why do they not? Because moral considerations deter them. Then bring the same moral considerations to bear on the subject of Mesmerism. If the fear is of laying victims prostrate in trance, and exercising spells over them, the answer is, that this is done with infinitely greater ease and certainty by drugs than it can ever be by Mesmerism; by drugs which are to be had in every street. And as sensible people do not let narcotic drugs lie about in their houses, within reach of the ignorant and mischievous, so would they see that Mesmerism was not practised without witnesses and proper superintendence. It is a mistake, too, to suppose that Mesmerism can be used at will to strike down victims, helpless and unconscious, as laudanum does, except in cases of excessive susceptibility from disease; cases which are, of course, under proper ward. The concurrence of two parties is needful in the first place, which is not the case in the administration of narcotics; and then the practice is very uncertain in its results on most single occasions; and again, in the majority of instances, it appears that the intellectual and moral powers are more, and not less, vigorous than in the ordinary state.

ELECTRO-BIOLOGY

Anon., 'Electro-biology', *Westminster Review*, 55 (1851), 312.

This extract forms the opening of an article devoted to three works on mesmerism, including J. H. Bennett, The Mesmeric Mania of 1851 *which sought to give a physiological explanation of the phenomenon. The article, whilst sceptical in tone, accepts many of the occurrences as true illustrations of the laws of suggestion, but challenges the claims of clairvoyance. The article appeared during George Eliot's time as editor of the* Westminster.

The attention of the public to mesmerism, which was recently on the wane, has been suddenly revived. A new mode has been discovered of illustrating a very familiar fact,—familiar at least, to all persons in the medical profession, and to many out of it,—that the imaginative faculties, the nervous sensations and muscular motions, are not always under the control of the judgment or of the will, and that phenomena of this description may be artificially induced. The balance of the intellectual powers, it is well known, may be disturbed by many causes; and a systematic means of disturbing it, connected with mesmeric manipulations has been contrived, through which crowds of educated persons have been startled into a belief of the old and exploded doctrines of electro-nervous currents and animal magnetism.

The professors of the new art (science would be a misnomer), call themselves electro-biologists, and their success has been such in some parts of the country, especially in Scotland, as to produce a mesmeric epidemic. Mesmerism is the all-engrossing topic of conversation at every dinner or evening party in Edinburgh. In a fashionable assembly, experiments on the mental functions take the place of quadrilles. Ladies of sensitive and 'susceptible' organization, gratify a drawing-room with the exhibition of 'involuntary emotions,' instead of a fantasia on the pianoforte. Students at Universities excite them in each other till they find themselves incapacitated for attendance upon their classes; and boys at school forsake marbles to play tricks with the nervous system of their companions; from which the most serious consequences have sometimes ensued.

WHAT IS MESMERISM?

Anon. (John Eagles and J. F. Ferrier) 'What is mesmerism', *Blackwood's Edinburgh Magazine*, 70 (1851), 84–5.

The article itself is written by the editor of Blackwood's, *John Eagles, whilst the postscript, from which this extract is drawn, is written by J. F. Ferrier, Chair of Moral Philosophy at St Andrews, and frequent contributor to* Blackwood's. *The postscript is even more condemnatory than the body of the article, giving clear illustration of the reasons for the virulent hostility aroused in some quarters by the practice of mesmerism.*

It is only in the case of individuals who, without being fatuous, are hovering on the verge of fatuity, that the magnetic phenomena and the mesmeric prostration can be admitted to be in any considerable degree real. Real to a certain extent they may be; marvellous they certainly are not. Imbecility of the nervous system, a ready abandonment of the will, a facility in relinquishing every endowment which makes man *human*—these intelligible causes, eked out by a vanity and cunning which are always inherent in natures of an inferior type, are quite sufficient to account for the effects of the mesmeric manipulations on subjects of peculiar softness and pliancy. [. . .]

How, then, is the miserable nonsense to be disposed of? It can only be put a stop to by the force of public opinion, guided of course by reason and truth. Let it be announced from all authoritative quarters that the magnetic sensibility is only another name for an unsound condition of the mental and bodily functions—that it may be always accepted as an infallible index of the position which an individual occupies in the scale of humanity—that its manifestation (when real) invariably betokens a *physique* and a *morale* greatly below the average, and a character to which no respect can be attached. Let this announcement—which is the undoubted truth—be made by all respectable organs of public opinion, and by all who are in any way concerned in the diffusion of knowledge, or in the instruction of the rising generation, and the magnetic superstition will rapidly decline. Let this—the correct and scientific explanation of the phenomena—be understood and considered carefully by all young people of both sexes, and the mesmeric ranks will be speedily thinned of their recruits. Our young friends who may have been entrapped into this infatuation by want of due consideration, will be wiser for the future. If they allow themselves to be experimented upon, they will at any rate take care not to disgrace themselves by yielding to the follies to which they may be solicited both from within and from without; and we are much mistaken if, when they know what the penalty is, they will abandon themselves to a disgusting condition which is characteristic only of the most abject specimens of our species.

HYPNOTISM

James Braid, *Neurypnology; or, The Rationale of Nervous Sleep, Considered in Relation with Animal Magnetism* (London: John Churchill, 1843), 15–20, 75–6.

Braid here recounts his discovery of hypnotism, a term he created to differentiate his scientific practice from that of mesmerism. The term neurypnology, which he derived from the Greek, means the rationale, or doctrine of nervous sleep. Braid developed his ideas from watching a mesmeric performer, but the phenomena that he describes are entirely those of the nervous system. In subsequent practice he went on to use hypnotism to cure a variety of ills, including hysterical paralysis.

By the impression which hypnotism induces on the nervous system, we acquire a power of rapidly curing many functional disorders, most intractable, or altogether incurable, by ordinary remedies, and also many of those distressing affections which, as in most cases they evince no pathological change of structure, have been presumed to depend on some peculiar condition of the nervous system, and have therefore, by universal consent, been denominated '*nervous complaints;*' and as I felt satisfied it was not dependent on any special agency or emanation, passing from the body of the operator to that of the patient, as the animal magnetizers allege is the case by their process, I considered it desirable, for the sake of preventing misconception, to adopt new terms [. . .]

I was led to discover the mode I now adopt with so much success for inducing this artificial condition of the nervous system, by a course of experiments instituted with the view to determine the cause of mesmeric phenomena. From all I had read and heard of mesmerism, (such as, the phenomena being capable of being excited in so few, and these few individuals in a state of disease, or naturally of a delicate constitution, or peculiarly susceptible temperament, and from the phenomena, when induced, being said to be so exaggerated, or of such an extraordinary nature), I was fully inclined to join with those who considered the whole to be a system of collusion or delusion, or of excited imagination, sympathy, or imitation.

The first exhibition of the kind I ever had an opportunity of attending, was one of M. Lafontaine's conversazione, on the 13th November, 1841. That night I saw nothing to diminish, but rather to confirm, my previous prejudices. At the next conversazione, six nights afterwards, *one* fact, the inability of a patient to *open his eyelids*, arrested my attention. I considered that to be a *real phenomenon*, and was anxious to discover the physiological cause of it. Next night, I watched this case when again operated on, with intense interest, and before the termination of the experiment, felt assured I had discovered its cause, but considered it prudent not to announce my opinion publicly, until I had had an opportunity of testing its accuracy, by experiments and observation in private.

In two days afterwards, I developed my views to my friend Captain Brown, as I had also previously done to four other friends; and in his presence, and that of my family, and another friend, the same evening, I instituted a series of experiments to prove the correctness of my theory, namely, that the continued fixed stare, by paralyzing nervous centres in the eyes and their appendages,* and destroying the equilibrium of the nervous system, thus produced the phenomenon referred to. The experiments were varied so as to convince all present, that they fully bore out the correctness of my theoretical views.

My first object was to prove, that the inability of the patient to open his eyes was caused by paralyzing the levator muscles of the eyelids, through their continued action during the protracted fixed stare, and thus rendering it *physically* impossible for him to open them. With the view of proving this, I requested Mr Walker, a young gentleman present, to sit down, and maintain a fixed stare at the top of a wine bottle, placed so much above him as to produce a considerable strain on the eyes and eyelids, to enable him to maintain a steady view of the object. In three minutes his eyelids closed, a gush of tears ran down his cheeks, his head drooped, his face was slightly convulsed, he gave a groan, and instantly fell into profound sleep, the respiration becoming slow, deep and sibilant, the right hand and arm being agitated by slight convulsive movements. At the end of

---

* By this expression I mean the state of exhaustion which follows too long continued, or too intense action, of any organ or function.

four minutes I considered it necessary, for his safety, to put an end to the experiment. [. . .]

This experiment not only proved what I expected, but also, by calling my attention to the spasmodic state of the muscles of the face and arm, the peculiar state of the respiration, and the condition of the mind, as evinced on rousing the patient, tended to prove to my mind I had got the key to the solution of mesmerism. [. . .]

I now stated that I considered the experiments fully proved my theory; and expressed my entire conviction that the phenomena of mesmerism were to be accounted for on the principle of a derangement of the state of the cerebro-spinal centres, and of the circulatory, and respiratory, and muscular systems, induced, as I have explained, by a fixed stare, absolute repose of body, fixed attention, and suppressed respiration, concomitant with that fixity of attention. That the whole depended on the physical and psychical condition of the patient, arising from the causes referred to, and not at all on the volition, or passes of the operator, throwing out a magnetic fluid, or exciting into activity some mystical universal fluid or medium. [. . .]

When I had ascertained that Hypnotism was important as a curative power, and that the prejudices existing against it in the public mind, as to its having an immoral tendency, were erroneous; and the idea, that it was calculated to sap the foundation of the Christian creed, by suggesting that the Gospel miracles might have been wrought by this agency, was quite unfounded and absurd, I felt it to be a duty I owed to the cause of humanity, and my profession, to use my best endeavours to remove those fallacies, so that the profession generally might be at liberty to prosecute the inquiry, and apply it practically, without hazarding their personal and professional interest, by prosecuting it in opposition to popular prejudice. It appeared to me there was no mode so likely to insure this happy consummation as delivering lectures on the subject to mixed audiences. The public could thus have demonstrative proof of its practical utility; and, when it was proved to proceed from a law of the animal economy, and that the patient could only be affected *in accordance with his own free will and consent*, and not, as the animal magnetizers contend, through the irresistible power of volitions and passes of the mesmerizers, which might be done in secret and at a distance, the ground of charge as to my agency having an immoral tendency, must at once fall to the ground. I have reason to believe my labours have not been altogether unsuccessful, in removing the popular prejudices; and I hope that the more liberal of my professional brethren, now that they know my true motives of action, in giving lectures to mixed audiences, instead of confining them to the profession only, and *especially as I made no secret of my modes of operating*, will be inclined to approve rather than blame me, for the course I have taken in this respect.

WILLIAM BENJAMIN CARPENTER

MESMERISM, SCIENTIFICALLY CONSIDERED

William Benjamin Carpenter, *Mesmerism, Spiritualism etc. Historically and Scientifically Considered* (London: Longmans, Green, 1877), 15–17, 18–19.

Drawing on the work of James Braid, the eminent physiologist William Carpenter here sets the claims of mesmerism in scientific perspective, giving a physical rationale for many of the phenomena claimed, without reference to any special 'magnetic' or 'mesmeric' agency.

This 'mesmeric sleep' corresponds precisely in character with what is known in medicine as 'hysteric coma;' the insensibility being as profound, while it lasts, as in the coma of narcotic poisoning or pressure on the brain; but coming on and passing off with such suddenness as to show that it is dependent upon some transient condition of the sensorium, which, with our present knowledge, we can pretty certainly assign to a reduction in the supply of blood caused by a sort of spasmodic contraction of the blood-vessels. That there is no adequate ground for regarding it as otherwise than *real*, appears further from the discovery made not long afterwards by Mr. Braid, a surgeon practising at Manchester, that he could induce it by a very simple method, which is not only even more effective than the 'passes' of the mesmeriser, but is moreover quite independent of any other will than that of the person who subjects himself to it. He found that this state (which he designated as Hypnotism) could be induced in a large proportion of individuals of either sex, and of all ranks, ages, and temperaments, who determinately fix their gaze for several minutes consecutively on an object brought so near to their eyes, as to require a degree of convergence of their axes that is maintainable only by a strong effort.

The first state thus induced is usually one of profound comatose sleep; the 'subject' not being capable of being roused by sensory impressions of any ordinary kind, and bearing without the least indication of consciousness what would ordinarily produce intolerable uneasiness or even severe pain. But after some little time, this state very commonly passes into one of somnambulism, which again corresponds closely on the one hand with *natural*, and on the other with *mesmeric* somnambulism. In fact, it has been by the study of the Somnambulism artificially induced by Mr. Braid's process, that the essential nature of this condition has been elucidated, and that a scientific *rationale* can now be given of a large proportion of the phenomena reported by Mesmerisers as having been presented by their somnambules. [. . .]

I shall try to set before you briefly the essential characters which distinguish the state of Somnambulism (whether natural or induced), on the one hand from dreaming, and on the other from the ordinary waking condition. As in both these, the mind is in a state of activity; but, as in dreaming, its activity is free from that controlling power of the will, by which it is directed in the waking state; and is also removed from this last by the complete ignorance of all that has passed in it, which is manifested by the 'subject' when called back to his waking self,—although the events of one access of this 'second consciousness' may vividly present themselves in the next, as if they had happened only just before. Again, instead of all the senses being shut up, as in ordinary dreaming sleep, some of them are not only awake, but preternaturally impressible; so that the course of the somnambulist's thought may be completely directed by suggestions of any kind that can be conveyed from without through the sense-channels which still remain open. But further, while the mind of the ordinary dreamer can no more produce movements in his body than impressions on his sense-organs can affect his mind, that of the Somnambulist retains full direction of his body (in so far, at least, as his senses serve to guide its movements); so that he *acts* his dreams as if they were his waking thoughts. The mesmerised or hypnotised Somnambule may, in fact, be characterised as a *conscious automaton*, which, by appropriate suggestions, may be made to think, feel, say, or do almost anything that its director wills it to think, feel, say, or do; with this remarkable peculiarity, that its whole power seems concentrated upon the state of activity in which it is at each moment, so that every faculty it is capable of exerting may become extraordinarily intensified. Thus, while vision is usually suspended, the senses of hearing, smell, and touch, with the muscular sense, are often preternaturally acute; in consequence, it would seem, of the undistracted concentration of the attention on their indications. I could give you many curious instances of this, which I have myself witnessed; as also of the great exertion of muscular power by subjects of extremely feeble *physique*: but as they are all obviously referrible to this one simple principle, I need not dwell on their details.

Section II

The Unconscious Mind and the Workings of Memory

The Unconscious Mind and the Workings of Memory

THE relationship between the conscious and the unconscious mind and the significance and workings of memory were central to the debate about the nature of individual and social identity during the nineteenth century. Is it possible to know, and thus control, the unconscious mind? Is the self unified, divided, or multiple? How is a sense of personal identity formed through different patterns of memory, and what is the relationship between the individual's childhood and the collective, historical, and organic past? In asking these questions, Victorian psychologists were not raising completely new concerns—fascination with 'the obscure recesses of the mind' was part of both eighteenth-century philosophy and Romantic thought, and remained the cornerstone of German idealist tradition throughout the nineteenth century.[1] And although they did not directly prefigure Freud's work their writing was an important part of the intellectual context within which psychoanalytic theory arose. In mid-nineteenth-century Britain, the interest in what William Carpenter termed 'unconscious cerebration' was closely connected to the growing enquiry into modes of insanity and the uncertain division between 'deranged' and 'sane' states of mind. As with the specific accounts of phrenology, mesmerism, and the various forms of insanity, mid-century debates on 'latent thought' or the 'automatic action' of the mind wavered between a desire to explore and to control the self; between the impulse to establish hierarchical boundaries between the normal and the pathological, and the acknowledgement that the working of transformed states of consciousness is the key to the operation of the mind as a whole.

Mid-nineteenth-century 'mental science' adapted and modified two earlier intellectual traditions in developing specific concepts of unconscious processes. On the one hand lay phrenology, with its materialist notion of localized mental traits; on the other lay the eighteenth-century associationist tradition in philosophy. Associationism was originally based on the idea that the mind spontaneously links ideas in chains of thought—that it was the mental representations themselves which somehow recognized their affinity with each other. As Coleridge pointed out in the *Biographia Literaria*, the concept of mental association can be traced back to Aristotle, and was developed by John Locke, but it was in the eighteenth century, particularly in the work of David Hartley, that it became a fully-fledged philosophical system based on a theory of the physical working of the mind. In *Observations of Man, his Frame, Duty and Expectations* (1749) Hartley argued that the repetition of associations created a set of physical

---

[1] This culminates in 1868 with the publication of Eduard von Hartmann's massive *The Philosophy of the Unconscious*.

vibrations along a continuum between the nerves and the brain. Coleridge was strongly critical of Hartley's physiological interpretations of mental association, which he considered to be static and mechanistic; yet while he developed his argument about the active power of latent thought primarily as part of his own aesthetic theory, the example he used of the uneducated young woman who suddenly started speaking Greek and Hebrew became a key narrative in nineteenth-century discussions of the unconscious. Moreover, Coleridge's arguments closely tallied with those of the late eighteenth-century Edinburgh philosophers Dugald Stewart and Thomas Brown, whose work formed one of the important foundations of nineteenth-century psychological theory. In his *Lectures on the Philosophy of the Human Mind* (1820) Thomas Brown had stressed the dynamic and creative nature of mental association, arguing the mind is always linking associations in new combinations through an active process of *suggestion*.[2] Developing their work, William Hamilton (who succeeded Brown in the Chair of Metaphysics and Logic at Edinburgh University) argued in his lectures on metaphysics given during the 1830s and 1840s that the unconscious plays a central role in all mental activity, and that the mind continually follows a pattern of 'latent mental modification', whereby it makes apparently incongruous connections through relying on suppressed links which always remain unconscious. Hamilton's theory was taken up by many mid-century writers, particularly Eneas Sweetland Dallas who aimed, in *The Gay Science* (1866), to develop a 'science of the laws of pleasure' based on an understanding of the unconscious, or 'hidden soul'.

While E. S. Dallas aimed to base his aesthetic theory on psychological principles, more mainstream physiological psychologists, such as Alexander Bain, William Carpenter, G. H. Lewes, and Herbert Spencer wanted to develop a model of the mind that was materialist as well as dynamic. While they, too, drew on the work of the Edinburgh philosophers, they did so more critically and they emphasized that mental processes are embodied in the physical workings of the mind as an evolving organism rather than being represented in abstract images. As the extracts from Herbert Spencer, G. H. Lewes, and William Carpenter's work included here suggest, this has very different ideological implications. Spencer's writing indicates that mental physiology certainly could help shape and reinforce dominant contemporary progressivist ideas about individual and social development, but as Lewes's more subtle theories show, they also challenged these assumptions by emphasizing the complexity of the connections between past and present identity, the body and the social world. Like the phrenologists, these writers conceptualized the mind in spatial terms, while developing the associationists' metaphors of 'channels' or streams of thought, and they emphasized the transformative processes of individual growth within a social

---

[2] See R. Hoeldtke, 'The history of associationism and British medical psychology', *Medical History*, 11 (1967), 46–65.

environment. 'If there is a valid objection against the functions of the brain being investigated in the cabinets of metaphysicians, there is an equally valid objection against intellectual and moral processes being sought in the laboratory of physiologists', wrote G. H. Lewes. 'To understand the Human Mind we must study it under normal conditions, and these are social conditions.' They argued that we learn habits of thought and feeling through the earliest associations of childhood and the repetition of habitual mental gestures that carve grooves in the mind, so that our mental processes become a set of automatic responses; but these streams, too, run underground and can spring out in unexpected places. For Spencer and Carpenter the implications of these ideas have a crucial bearing on notions of individual autonomy and the power of the will. Spencer suggested that evolutionary theory challenged many of the fundamental tenets of the doctrine of free will, arguing that while we may be able to make conscious choices we may not be free to choose what we desire, while Carpenter maintained that the power of 'unconscious cerebration' meant that mental training was all the more important. Although he emphasized its power more decisively in his later work, Carpenter acknowledged that the will alone can never define or encompass the self. In the extract from *Principles of Mental Physiology* included here he uses the image of a skilful rider controlling a frisky horse to make the point that many of our actions are automatic and spontaneous even though it may be ultimately possible to control them. The implications of his arguments—in particular, the question of whether the unconscious should be seen as part of the 'self'—were energetically debated by Francis Power Cobbe in her attempt to reconcile the claims of contemporary psychology with the Christian belief in free will and moral responsibility.

Dreaming was perhaps the most obvious way in which, as John Abercrombie put it, 'ideas and images of the mind follow one another according to associations over which we have no control', and, as with debates on mesmerism, dreams were construed as demonstrating both the separateness and the connectedness of the conscious and the unconscious mind.[3] The phrenologist Robert Macnish argued in his influential *Philosophy of Sleep* (1830) that dreams represent 'a state of partial slumber' in which we tend to reorganize and replay experiences of the recent past; they transform immediate physical sensations into vivid dramas which are ultimately determined by the character of the dreamer. The 'heavy supper' theory of dreaming remained a significant element of physiological psychological interpretations in the mid-nineteenth century, but it was placed within more subtle readings of how dreams offered a means of exploring the intricate archaeology of the mind. John Addington Symonds, Henry Holland, and G. H. Lewes each emphasized that sleeping was never one but 'a series of ever-fluctuating states . . . in which different mental functions are under its

---

[3] John Abercrombie, *Inquiries Concerning the Intellectual Powers and the Investigation of Truth* (Edinburgh: Waugh and Innes, 1830), 267.

influence at the same moment in time', and they stressed the crucial connections between states of dreaming and of trance and insanity, as well as the active process of transformation which takes place in the work of dreaming. Victorian psychologists were intrigued by how dreams undercut unilinear notions of time; with how the combination of particular predispositions and long-forgotten associations made them seem prophetic. This interest in the dream as a 'revelation' of a deeper self itself undergoes significant shifts during the latter half of the century, culminating in James Sully's important essay of 1893 which Freud would cite in his own work on dreams a few years later. While dreams remain crucial clues to the individual psyche they are increasingly read as representations of the connections between individual childhood and the collective past, allied to a general human capacity of myth-making, and as the expression of a long-term process of organic and psychic change.

The notion that the dreaming and waking state might correspond to two parallel mental worlds, each separate from the other, was further explored in debates about *double consciousness* in the mid-nineteenth century. Here too the associationist position that the self was created through different strands of latent memory intersected with the physiological argument that the key to the self's division lay within the structures of the brain. MacNish had discussed cases of mental dissociation in *The Philosophy of Sleep*, in particular the bizarre case of the young American woman Mary Reynolds, who apparently manifested two parallel personalities, and the influential London physician Henry Holland (doctor to both Queen Victoria and George Eliot) mooted the idea that the brain itself was a 'double' or divided organ in an essay in a general medical textbook in 1840. Four years later a Brighton doctor, Arthur Ladbroke Wigan, took this argument to an extreme in *The Duality of the Mind*. In his 'new view of insanity' Wigan claimed that the cerebrum was not simply divided but composed of two entirely separate brains, each of which could work with or against the other, and while his work was considered extreme by his contemporaries, it indirectly contributed to the analysis of the specific place of mental properties in the brain's two hemispheres during the latter part of the century with the development of neurophysiology.[4] However 'double consciousness' continued to be discussed through the second half of the nineteenth century as an extreme state of disordered association and disrupted memory. By the 1870s the case of Mary Reynolds was set against examples of not only dual but 'multiplex' personalities—particularly the cases of Louis Vivé and Félida X—which were extensively discussed in French psychiatric journals within the context of a renewed interest in hypnotism as a means of both exploring and controlling suppressed memories in the treatment

[4] For a full account of these developments, see Robert M. Young, *Mind, Brain and Adaptation: Cerebral Localisation and its Context from Gall to Ferrier* (Oxford: Oxford University Press, 1970) and Anne Harrington, *Medicine, Mind and the Double Brain* (Princeton: Princeton University Press, 1987).

of mental disease.[5] These discussions were made available to an English audience by Frederick W. H. Myers, a leading figure in the newly founded Society for Psychical Research who closely followed developments in contemporary psychiatry in Europe, while the French psychologist T. A. Ribot, whose work had an important influence on contemporary studies of diseases of memory and personality, drew heavily on the perceptions of mid-century British physiological psychology.

'Double consciousness' formed part of a much wider discussion of hidden traces within the mind, and it is on the relationship between conscious and unconscious memory that debates on the nature of identity ultimately turned. But again they did so ambivalently. Victorian psychologists acknowledged that the sense of a continuous self depends on the awareness of the connections—on what William Carpenter termed 'consciousness of agreement' between the past and the present; that when memory breaks down, so does a coherent, directed identity. But they also knew both that our minds contain far more than they ever consciously recall and that memory itself is profoundly unreliable. They were acutely aware that, just as apparently solid rock formations are actually in a continual state of flux, so the very substance as well as the contents of the brain are undergoing constant transformation, and that a stable identity is an illusion, a fiction spun out of the narratives of the individual past. Mid-century discussions of memory developed Dugald Stewart's distinction between *recollection*—the ability to recall specific events at will—and *memory* itself—the vast storehouse of old impressions and experiences which lie beyond the sphere of consciousness. In particular, the spontaneous ability to recall languages heard in early childhood while in a state of trance fascinated many writers, providing one clue to the mind's ability to unconsciously assimilate complex structures of knowledge: Coleridge's anecdote in his *Biographia Literaria* about the illiterate German woman who spoke Greek and Hebrew is a crucial reference here.

The hidden 'place' in the mind where these lost thoughts reside was conceptualized through various metaphors, each of which implied different ideas of self-control. It could be a *palimpsest*, as for De Quincey and Lewes—a parchment on which countless inscriptions have been written and rewritten, but none entirely erased. Here memory forms a spontaneous archaeology in which the past is continually present, a hypothesis challenged by Frances Power Cobbe in her striking

---

[5] On the development of theories of the unconscious, memory, and dual and multiple personality in Britain and Europe during the second half of the nineteenth century, see Henri F. Ellenberger, *The Discovery of the Unconscious: the History and Evolution of Dynamic Psychiatry*, (New York: Basic Books, 1970); Adam Crabtree, *From Mesmer to Freud: Magnetic Sleep and the Roots of Psychological Healing* (New Haven: Yale University Press, 1993); Laura Otis, *Organic Memory: History and the Body in the Late Nineteenth and Early Twentieth Centuries* (Lincoln, Neb.: University of Nebraska Press, 1994); Janet Oppenheim, *The Other World: Spiritualism and Psychical Research in England, 1850–1914* (Cambridge: Cambridge University Press 1985); and Ian Hacking, *Rewriting the Soul: Multiple Personality and the Sciences of Memory* (Princeton: Princeton University Press, 1995).

analysis of what we would now term 'false memory syndrome'. For Winslow the metaphor of the hidden room as a storehouse—either treasure trove, or lumber-room of discarded objects—merges into the geological image of the simultaneous indestructibility and transmutability of matter. It could be a set of concentric circles, as for E. S. Dallas, in which there is a 'constant but unobserved traffic' between the 'inner ring' and the great sea which surrounds it. William Carpenter laid stress on how individual memory is overdetermined by patterns set in early childhood, emphasizing the importance of early mental training, but his concentration on the individual was gradually replaced by Spencer's collective concept of 'organic memory', in which traces of the past form channels in the mind, and patterns of bodily behaviour become increasingly automatic, *instinctive*. Individuals here are the sum not only of their own past experience but also that of their ancestors, in a drama strikingly portrayed in Samuel Butler's *Life and Habit* (1877); here the self is the embodiment and unconscious witness of the accumulated habits of the past, and the stage on which old battles are endlessly re-enacted.

1. Associationism and Physiological Psychology

A CRITIQUE OF HARTLEY'S ASSOCIATIONISM

Samuel Taylor Coleridge, *Biographia Literaria, or Biographical Sketches of my Literary Life and Opinions*, 2 vols. (London: Rest, Fenner, 1817), i. 108–16.

The critique of Hartley is developed in the fifth and sixth chapter of Biographia Literaria, *and it places a critical exploration of associationism at the centre of Coleridge's aesthetic theory. Chapter 5 briefly traces the history of 'the law of association' as a central aspect of theories of consciousness from Aristotle to David Hartley's* Observations on Man, his Frame, Duty and Expectations *(1749), dividing mental experience into three types, the active, the passive, and between them, the spontaneous. This extract is from the beginning of chapter 6.*

According to [Hartley's] system the idea or vibration *a* from the external object A becomes associable with the idea or vibration *m* from the external object M, because the oscillation *a* propagated itself so as to re-produce the oscillation *m*. But the original impression from M was essentially different from the impression A: unless therefore different causes may produce the same effect, the vibration *a* could never produce the vibration *m*: and this therefore could never be the means by which *a* and *m* are associated. To understand this, the attentive reader need only be reminded, that the ideas are themselves, in Hartley's system, nothing more than their appropriate configurative vibrations. It is a mere delusion of the fancy to conceive the pre-existence of the ideas, in any chain of association, as so many differently colored billiard-balls in contact, so that when an object, the billiard-stick, strikes the first or white ball, the same motion propagates itself through the red, green, blue, black, &c. and sets the whole in motion. No! we must suppose the very same force, which *constitutes* the white ball, to *constitute* the red or black; or the idea of a circle to *constitute* the idea of a triangle; which is impossible. [. . .]

It is fashionable to smile at Hartley's vibrations and vibratiuncles; and his work has been re-edited by Priestley,[1] with the omission of the *material* hypothesis. But Hartley was too great a man, too coherent a thinker, for this to have been done, either consistently or to any wise purpose. For all other parts of his system, as far as they are peculiar to that system, once removed from their mechanical basis, not only lose their main support, but the very motive which led to their adoption. Thus the principle of *contemporaneity*, which Aristotle had made the common *condition* of all the laws of association, Hartley was constrained to represent as being itself the sole *law*. For to what law can the action of *material* atoms be subject, but that of proximity in *place*? And to what law can their *motions* be subjected, but that of *time*? Again, from this results inevitably, that the will, the reason, the judgment, and the understanding, instead of being the determining causes of association, must needs be represented as its *creatures*, and among its mechanical *effects*. Conceive, for instance, a broad stream, winding through a mountainous country with an indefinite number of currents, varying and running into each other according as the gusts chance to blow from the opening of the mountains. The temporary union of several currents in one, so as to form the main current of the moment, would present an accurate image of Hartley's theory of the will.

Had this been really the case, the consequence would have been, that our whole life would be divided between the despotism of outward impressions, and that of senseless and passive memory. Take his law in its highest abstraction and most philosophical form, viz. that every partial representation recalls the total representation of which it was a part; and the law becomes nugatory, were it only from its universality. In practice it would indeed be mere lawlessness. Consider, how immense must be the sphere of a total impression from the top of St. Paul's church; and how rapid and continuous the series of such total impressions. If therefore we suppose the absence of all interference of the will, reason, and judgement, one or other of two consequences must result. Either the ideas (or relicts of such impression) will exactly imitate the order of the impression itself, which would be absolute *delirium*: or any one part of that impression might recall any other part, and (as from the law of continuity, there must exist in every total impression some one or more parts, which are components of some other following total impression, and so on ad infinitum) *any* part of *any* impression might recall *any* part of any *other*, without a cause present to determine *what* it should be. For to bring in the will, or reason, as causes of their own cause, that is, as at once causes and effects, can satisfy those only who in their pretended evidences of a God having first demanded organization, as the sole cause and ground of

[1] In his 1775 edition of *Observations on Man*, Joseph Priestley omitted Hartley's vibration theory.

intellect, will then coolly demand the pre-existence of intellect, as the cause and ground-work of organization. There is in truth but one state to which this theory applies at all, namely, that of complete light-headedness; and even to this it applies but partially, because the will, and reason are perhaps never wholly suspended.

A case of this kind occurred in a Catholic town in Germany a year or two before my arrival at Göttingen,[2] and had not then ceased to be a frequent subject of conversation. A young woman of four or five and twenty, who could neither read, nor write, was seized with a nervous fever; during which, according to the asseverations of all the priests and monks of the neighbourhood, she became *possessed*, and, as it appeared, by a very learned devil. She continued incessantly talking Latin, Greek, and Hebrew, in very pompous tones and with most distinct enunciation. This possession was rendered more probable by the known fact, that she was or had been an heretic. Voltaire humourously advises the devil to decline all acquaintance with medical men; and it would have been more to his reputation, if he had taken this advice in the present instance. The case had attracted the particular attention of a young physician, and by his statement many eminent physiologists and psychologists visited the town, and cross-examined the case on the spot. Sheets full of her ravings were taken down from her own mouth, and were found to consist of sentences, coherent and intelligible each for itself, but with little or no connection with each other. Of the Hebrew, a small portion only could be traced to the Bible; the remainder seemed to be in the rabinical dialect. All trick or conspiracy was out of the question. Not only had the young woman ever been an harmless, simple creature; but she was evidently labouring under a nervous fever. In the town, in which she had been resident for many years as a servant in different families, no solution presented itself. The young physician, however, determined to trace her past life step by step; for the patient herself was incapable of returning a rational answer. He at length succeeded in discovering the place, where her parents had lived: travelled thither, found *them* dead, but an uncle surviving; and from him learnt, that the patient had been charitably taken by an old protestant pastor at nine years old, and had remained with him some years, even till the old man's death. Of this pastor the uncle knew nothing, but that he was a very good man. With great difficulty, and after much search, our young medical philosopher discovered a niece of the pastor's, who had lived with him as his house-keeper, and had inherited his effects. She remembered the girl; related, that her venerable uncle had been too indulgent, and could not bear to hear the girl scolded; that she was willing to have kept her, but that after her patron's death, the girl herself refused to stay. Anxious enquiries were then, of course, made concerning the pastor's habits; and the solution of the phenomenon was soon obtained. For it appeared, that it had been

---

[2] i.e. February 1799.

the old man's custom, for years, to walk up and down a passage of his house into which the kitchen door opened, and to read to himself with a loud voice, out of his favorite books. A considerable number of these were still in the niece's possession. She added, that he was a very learned man and a great Hebraist. Among the books were found a collection of rabbinical writings, together with several of the Greek and Latin fathers; and the physician succeeded in identifying so many passages with those taken down at the young woman's bedside, that no doubt could remain in any rational mind concerning the true origin of the impressions made on her nervous system.

This authenticated case furnishes both proof and instance, that reliques of sensation may exist for an indefinite time in a latent state, in the very same order in which they were originally impressed; and as we cannot rationally suppose the feverish state of the brain to act in any other way than as a stimulus, this fact (and it would not be difficult to adduce several of the same kind) contributes to make it even probable, that all thoughts are in themselves imperishable; and, that if the intelligent faculty should be rendered more comprehensive, it would require only a different and apportioned organization, *the body celestial* instead of *the body terrestrial*, to bring before every human soul the collective experience of its whole past existence. And this, this, perchance, is the dread book of judgement, in whose mysterious hieroglyphics every idle word is recorded! Yea, in the very nature of a living spirit, it may be more possible that heaven and earth should pass away, than that a single act, a single thought, should be loosened or lost from that living chain of causes, to all whose links, conscious or unconscious, the free-will, our only absolute *self*, is co-extensive and co-present.

PHILOSOPHICAL, LOCAL, AND ARBITRARY ASSOCIATION

John Abercrombie, *Inquiries Concerning the Intellectual Powers and the Investigation of Truth* (1830), 19th edn., (London: John Murray, 1871), 80–6, 90.

Abercrombie's popular treatise, which went through four editions in as many years, provided an invaluable source of case-studies for writers throughout the nineteenth century. Writing within the associationist tradition, Abercrombie states that 'the study of the phenomenon of mind presents great interest, not to the moral philosopher only, but to everyone who has in view the cultivation of his mental powers'; noting 'the deeper interest that the philosophy of mind presents to the medical inquirer', while emphasizing that mental disease illustrates 'important points in the philosophy of the mental powers' (p. 1).

In the mental process now referred to, it is probable that the term *suggestion* is much more correct than *association*, which has often been applied to it.[1] For in the cases which belong to this class, the facts or thoughts suggest each other, not according to any connexion or association which the mind had previously formed between them, but according to some mental impression or emotion, which by a law of our constitution proves a principle of analogy or suggestion. We readily perceive how this takes place in regard to circumstances which are allied to each other by resemblance, contiguity, cause, or effect; and the suggestion of contrast must also occur to every one as by no means unnatural. Thus, the sight of a remarkably fat man may recall to us the thought of another man we had lately seen, who was equally remarkable for his leanness: the playfulness and mirth of childhood may suggest the cares and anxieties of afterlife; and an instance of conduct, which we greatly disapprove, may lead us to recollect how very differently another individual conducted himself in similar circumstances.

In a practical view, the subject of association leads us chiefly to a consideration of the manner in which facts are so associated in the mind as to be recalled by means of the connexion; in other words, the influence of association upon memory. In this view associations are distinctly referable to three classes:—

    I. Natural or philosophical association.

    II. Local or incidental association.

    III. Arbitrary or fictitious association.

A variety of mental phenomena of the most interesting kind will be found connected with the subjects referred to under these classes. The principle on which they all depend, is simply the circumstance of two or more facts, thoughts, or events, being contemplated together by the mind, though many of them have no relation to each other except this conjunction. The strength of the association is generally in proportion to the intensity of the mental emotion; and is likewise in a great measure regulated by the length of time, or the number of times, in which the facts have been contemplated in this connexion. Astonishing examples may often be met with, of facts or occurrences, which have long ceased to be objects

---

[1] As Abercrombie notes earlier, it is Thomas Brown (1778–1820) who makes this distinction in *Lectures on the Philosophy of the Human Mind* (1820). Thomas Brown (who was appointed professor of moral philosophy at Edinburgh University in 1810) argued that all mental activity proceeds through a process of assimilation, through which the mind modifies and transforms present and past sensations and impressions to produce new combinations and meanings, and he maintained that the concept of suggestion, which links the image to the emotional response, is preferable to Locke's more rationalist notion of association.

of simple memory, being brought up in this manner by association, though they had not passed through the mind for a very long time.

I. NATURAL OR PHILOSOPHICAL ASSOCIATION takes place when a fact or state-ment, on which the attention is fixed, is, by a mental process, associated with some fact previously known, to which it has a relation, or with some subject which it is calculated to illustrate. The fact so acquired is thus, to use a figurative expression, put by in its proper place in the mind, and can afterwards be recalled by means of the association.

The formation of associations in this manner, is of course influenced in a very great degree by previous mental habits, pursuits, or subjects of reflection; and, according to the nature and the variety of these pursuits or subjects of thought, facts which by some are passed by and instantly forgotten, may be fixed upon by others with eager attention, and referred to some principle which they are cal-culated to illustrate. [. . .]

This habit of attention and association ought therefore to be carefully culti-vated, as it must have a great influence on our progress in knowledge, and like-wise on the formation of intellectual character, provided the associations be made upon sound principles, or according to the true and important relations of things. [. . .]

When various facts have been associated in the mind, in the manner now referred to, they form a series which hang together and recall each other in a very remarkable manner. There are two ways in which this takes place, which may be called voluntary and spontaneous. (1.) We call up facts by a voluntary effort, by directing the mind into particular trains of thought calculated to lead to those which we are in search of. This is what we call recollecting ourselves on a particular subject. We have an impression, perhaps, that the mind is in posses-sion of information which bears upon the subject, but do not at the moment remember it; or we remember some circumstances, and wish to recall a more full and complete remembrance. We therefore commence a mental process which consists in putting in motion, to speak figuratively, a train of thoughts, or a series of associated facts, which we think calculated to lead us to the facts which we wish to recall. (2.) Associations recur spontaneously, either when par-ticular topics naturally leading to them are brought before the mind, in reading or conversation, or in that state in which the mind is left to follow, without any effort, the current of thoughts as they succeed each other. In the healthy state of the mind, we can give way to this spontaneous succession of thoughts; or we can check it at our pleasure, and direct the mind into some new train connected with the same subject, or arising out of it; or we can dismiss it altogether. While we allow it to go on, it does so, not only without effort, but often without con-sciousness; so that when the attention is, after some time, arrested by a subject of thought which is in the mind, we do not at first remember what led us to think of it, and begin to recollect ourselves by tracing the series backwards. In this state of mind, it is most interesting to observe the manner in which old associations are revived, and old recollections renewed, which seemed to have been lost or forgotten; and how facts and occurrences come into the mind which had not been thought of for many years. They are recalled, we scarcely know how, by some train of association which we can hardly trace, and which had long ceased to be the subject of any voluntary effort of attention. We shall again allude to this most interesting subject, in relation to the manner in which associations, long forgotten, are sometimes brought into the mind in dreaming, and in certain states of delirium.

The voluntary power over the succession of thoughts and associations which has now been alluded to is a subject of extreme interest. We shall have occasion to refer to it again when we come to speak of a remarkable condition in which it is lost, and in which the mind is left entirely under the influence of the series of thoughts as they happen to succeed each other, according probably to old associations, without the power of arresting or varying it. This occurs in two very interesting mental conditions to be afterwards more particularly mentioned,— dreaming and insanity.

II. LOCAL OR INCIDENTAL ASSOCIATION.—In the mental process referred to under the preceding head, facts or thoughts are associated according to certain real relations; though these, we have seen, may be various; and the particular relation which is fixed upon, in particular cases, depends upon the intellectual habits of the individual. In the class now to be mentioned, the associations are formed according to no other relations than such as are entirely local or casual. Thus, a fact, a thought, or a mental impression, is associated with the person by whom it was communicated, or the place where the communication was made; and is recalled to the mind when the place or person is seen, mentioned, or thought of. [. . .]

These mere local associations, however, often make a very deep impression upon the mind; more vivid, certainly, than simple memory of the facts or transactions connected with them. Thus, we avoid a place which is associated with some painful recollection; yet the very fact of avoiding it shows that we have a full remembrance of the circumstances, and, at the same time, a conviction that the sight of the spot would make the impression more vivid and more painful. After the death of a beloved child or a much valued friend, we may retain a lively remembrance of them, and even anxiously cherish the impression of their endearing qualities; yet, after time has in some measure blunted the acuteness of feeling, the accidental discovery of some trifling memorial, strongly associated with the lamented object of our affection, produces a freshness and intensity of emotion known only to those who have experienced it. This feeling is peculiarly strong, if the memorial has been long lost sight of, and discovered by accident,— because, as has been well remarked by Dr. Brown, it in this case presents the unmixed image of the friend with whom it is associated; whereas a memorial which has become familiar to us, is associated with other feelings not relating exclusively to him. [. . .]

III. ARBITRARY OR FICTITIOUS ASSOCIATION.—This association is generally produced by a voluntary effort of the mind; and the facts associated are not connected by any relation except what arises out of this effort. The process is exemplified in the connexion we establish between something which we wish to remember and something we are in no danger of forgetting; as in the common expedients of tying a thread about the finger, or making a knot on the pocket-handkerchief. A Roman, for the same purpose, turned the stone of his ring inwards towards the palm of his hand. There is an analogous expedient which most people probably have employed for enabling them to remember the names of persons. It consists in forming an association between the name to be remembered, and that of some intimate friend, or public character of the same name, which is familiar to us. The remarkable circumstance in these cases is, that, whatever difficulty a person may have in simply remembering a name, he never forgets who the individual was with whose name he formed the association.

THREE DEGREES OF MENTAL LATENCY

William Hamilton, *Lectures on Metaphysics and Logic* (1859), ed. H. C. Mansel and John Veith, 2nd edn., 4 vols. (Edinburgh: William Blackwood and Sons, 1861), i. 338–41, 347–9.

Professor of Logic and Metaphysics at Edinburgh University, William Hamilton was influenced by German philosophy (particularly Kant's work), and although he was criticized for his idealism, his theory of latent mental modification remained a central influence on later psychological writing. Hamilton's work, based on his biennial course of lectures given from 1836, were published posthumously, and first presented, according to the editors, in an incomplete state, although the second edition is amended and polished. This extract is from lecture 18, eighth in a set of nine lectures on consciousness.

I pass now to a question in some respects of still more proximate interest to the psychologist; for it is one which, according as it is decided, will determine the character of our explanation of many of the most important phænomena in the philosophy of mind, and, in particular, the great phænomena of Memory and Association. The question I refer to is, Whether the mind exerts energies, and is the subject of modifications, of neither of which it is conscious. This is the most general expression of a problem which has hardly been mentioned, far less mooted, in this country; and when it has attracted a passing notice, the supposition of an unconscious action or passion of the mind, has been treated as something either unintelligible, or absurd. In Germany, on the contrary, it has not only been canvassed, but the alternative which the philosophers of this country have lightly considered as ridiculous, has been gravely established as a conclusion which the phænomena not only warrant, but enforce. [. . .]

I shall first of all adduce some proof of the fact, that the mind may, and does, contain far more latent furniture than consciousness informs us it possesses. To simplify the discussion, I shall distinguish three degrees of this mental latency.

In the first place, it is to be remembered that the riches,—the possessions, of our mind, are not to be measured by its present momentary activities, but by the amount of its acquired habits. I know a science, or language, not merely while I make a temporary use of it, but inasmuch as I can apply it when and how I will. Thus the infinitely greater part of our spiritual treasures, lies always beyond the sphere of consciousness, hid in the obscure recesses of the mind. This is the first degree of latency. In regard to this, there is no difficulty, or dispute; and I only take it into account in order to obviate misconception, and because it affords a transition towards the other two degrees which it conduces to illustrate.

The second degree of latency exists when the mind contains certain systems of knowledge, or certain habits of action, which it is wholly unconscious of possessing in its ordinary state, but which are revealed to consciousness in certain extraordinary exaltations of its powers. The evidence on this point shows that the mind frequently contains whole systems of knowledge, which, though in our normal state they have faded into absolute oblivion, may, in certain abnormal states, as madness, febrile delirium, somnambulism, catalepsy, &c., flash out into luminous consciousness, and even throw into the shade of unconsciousness these other systems by which they had, for a long period, been eclipsed and even extinguished. For example, there are cases in which the extinct memory of whole languages was suddenly restored, and, what is even still more remarkable, in which the faculty was exhibited of accurately repeating, in known or unknown tongues, passages which were never within the grasp of conscious memory in the normal state. This degree,—this phænomenon of latency, is one of the most marvellous in the whole compass of philosophy, and the proof of its reality will prepare us for an enlightened consideration of the third, of which the evidence, though not less certain, is not equally obtrusive. [. . .] That in madness, in fever, in somnambulism, and other abnormal states, the mind should betray capacities and extensive systems of knowledge, of which it was at other times wholly unconscious, is a fact so remarkable that it may well demand the highest evidence to establish its truth. But of such a character is the evidence which I am now to give you. It consists of cases reported by the most intelligent and trustworthy observers,—by observers wholly ignorant of each other's testimony; and the phænomena observed were of so palpable and unambiguous a nature that they could not possibly have been mistaken or misinterpreted.[1] [. . .]

This general fact being established, I now proceed to consider the question in relation to the third class or degree of latent modifications,—a class in relation to, and on the ground of which alone, it has ever hitherto been argued by philosophers.

The problem, then, in regard to this class is,—Are there, in ordinary, mental modifications,—i.e. mental activities and passivities, of which we are unconscious, but which manifest their existence by effects of which we are conscious? [. . .]

In the question proposed, I am not only strongly inclined to the affirmative,—nay, I do not hesitate to maintain, that what we are conscious of is constructed out of what we are not conscious of,—that our whole knowledge, in fact, is made up of the unknown and the incognisable.

This at first sight may appear not only paradoxical, but contradictory. It may be objected, 1°, How can we know that to exist which lies beyond the one condition of all knowledge,—consciousness? And, 2°, How can knowledge arise out of ignorance,—consciousness out of unconsciousness,—the cognisable out of the incognisable, that is, how can one opposite proceed out of the other?

In answer to the first objection,—How can we know that of which we are unconscious, seeing that consciousness is the condition of knowledge?—it is enough to allege, that there are many things which we neither know nor can know in themselves,—that is, in their direct and immediate relation to our faculties of knowledge, but which manifest their existence indirectly through the medium of their effects. This is the case with the mental modifications in question; they are not in themselves revealed to consciousness, but as certain facts of consciousness necessarily suppose them to exist, and to exert an influence in the mental processes, we are thus constrained to admit, as modifications of mind, what are not in themselves phænomena of consciousness. The truth of this will be apparent, if, before descending to any special illustration, we consider that consciousness cannot exist independently of some peculiar modification of mind; we are only conscious as we are conscious of a determinate state. To be conscious, we must be conscious of some particular perception, or remembrance, or imagination, or feeling, &c.; we have no general consciousness. But as consciousness supposes a special mental modification as its object, it must be remembered, that this modification or state supposes a change,—a transition from some other state or modification. But as the modification must be present, before we have a consciousness of the modification, it is evident, that we can have

---

[1] Here Hamilton cites various cases of latent memory, including the case of the German servant girl described by Coleridge above.

no consciousness of its rise or awakening; for its rise or awakening is also the rise or awakening of consciousness.

But the illustration of this is contained in an answer to the second objection which asks,—How can knowledge come out of ignorance,—consciousness out of unconsciousness,—the known out of the unknown,—how can one opposite be made up of the other?

In the removal of this objection, the proof of the thesis which I support is involved. And without dealing in any general speculation, I shall at once descend to the special evidence which appears to me, not merely to warrant, but to necessitate, the conclusion, that the sphere of our conscious modifications is only a small circle in the centre of a far wider sphere of action and passion, of which we are only conscious through its effects.

ON CONSCIOUSNESS AND THE WILL

Herbert Spencer, *The Principles of Psychology* (London: Longman, Brown, Green and Longmans, 1855), 332–4, 617–20.

Spencer believed that the move from homogeneity to heterogeneity was the fundamental law of all physical and social development, and in the first edition of The Principles of Psychology *he reinterprets associationist explanations of consciousness by arguing that identity develops through a process of organic evolution. Like Hamilton, Spencer sees consciousness arising out of unconscious processes, but argues that these take the form not of mental representations so much as latent (or instinctive) adaptation to the environment; consciousness emerges in response to, and as a central part of, a process of continual development and differentiation. These extracts are taken from Part III—'General synthesis'—and Part IV—'Special synthesis'—where Spencer brings the general arguments to bear on memory, reason, feelings, and the will.*

We have seen that the condition on which only consciousness can begin to exist, is the occurrence of a change of state; and that this change of state necessarily generates the terms of a relation of unlikeness. We have seen that not simply does consciousness become nascent only by virtue of a change—by the occurrence of a state unlike the previous state; but that consciousness can continue only so long as changes continue—only so long as relations of unlikeness are being established. Hence then, consciousness can neither arise nor be maintained without the occurrence of differences in its state. It must be ever passing from some one state into a different state. In other words—there must be *a continuous differentiation* of its states.

But we have also seen that the states of consciousness successively arising, can become elements of thought, only by being known as like certain before-experienced states. If no note be taken of the different states as they occur—if they pass through consciousness simply as images pass over a mirror; there can be no intelligence, however long the process be continued. Intelligence can arise only by the organization, by the arrangement, by the classification of these states. If they are severally taken note of, it can only be as more or less like certain previous ones. They are thinkable only as such or such; that is, as like such or such before-experienced states. The act of knowing them is impossible except by classing them with others of the same nature—assimilating them to those others. Hence then, in being known, each state must become one with certain previous states—must be integrated with those previous states. Each successive act of knowing must be an act of integrating. That is to say, there must be *a continuous integration* of states of consciousness.

These, then, are the two antagonist processes by which consciousness subsists—the centrifugal and centripetal actions by which its balance is maintained. That there may be the material for thought, consciousness must every moment have its state differentiated. And for the new state hence resulting to become a thought, it must be integrated with before-experienced states. This perpetual alternation is the characteristic of all consciousness from the very lowest to the very highest. It is distinctly typified in that oscillation between two states, constituting the simplest conceivable form of consciousness; and it is illustrated in the most complex thinkings of the advanced man of science.

Nor is it only in every passing process of thought that this law is displayed: it is traceable also in the general progress of thought. These minor differentiations and integrations that are going on from moment to moment, result in those greater differentiations and integrations which constitute mental development. Every case in which an advancing intelligence distinguishes between objects, or phenomena, or laws, that were previously confounded together as of like kind, implies a differentiation of states of consciousness. And every case in which such advancing intelligence recognizes, as of the same essential nature, objects, or phenomena, or laws, that were previously thought distinct, implies an integration of states of consciousness.

Under its most general aspect therefore, all mental action whatever is definable as *the continuous differentiation and integration of states of consciousness*. [. . .]

As there are two antagonist processes by which consciousness is maintained, so there are two antagonist processes by which bodily life is maintained: and the same two antagonist processes are common to both. By the action of oxygen every tissue is being differentiated; and every tissue is integrating the materials supplied by the blood. No function can be performed without the differentiation of the tissue performing it; and no tissue is enabled to perform its function save by the integration of nutriment. In the balance of these two actions the organic life consists. By each new integration, an organ is fitted for being again differentiated: each new differentiation enables the organ again to integrate. And as with the psychical life, so with the physical—the stopping of either process is the stopping of both.

Moreover the parallel equally holds under the second aspect. Not only does this law apply to the vital processes going on throughout the body from moment to moment; it also applies to organic progress in general. Commencing, as every organism does, as a uniform mass of matter, every step in its evolution consists in the differentiation and integration of parts. On contemplating the phenomena of organization in general, as exhibited throughout creation, it will be seen that the integration of elements which perform the same function, goes on *pari passu* with the differentiation of elements which perform unlike functions. That advance from homogeneity to heterogeneity, in which all organization consists, is wholly effected by this duplex action.

Thus, in two senses, there is a continuous differentiation and integration of tissues; as, in two senses, there is a continuous differentiation and integration of states of consciousness. [. . .]

Long before reaching this point, most readers will have perceived that the doctrines developed in the last two parts of this work, are quite at variance with the current tenets respecting the freedom of the Will. That every one is at liberty to do what he desires to do (supposing there are no external hindrances), all admit; though people of confused conceptions commonly suppose this to be the thing denied. But that every one is at liberty to desire or not to desire, which is the real proposition involved in the dogma of free-will, is negatived as much by the internal perception of every one as by the contents of the preceding chapters. From the universal law that, other things equal, the cohesion of physchical states is proportionate to the frequency with which they have followed one another in experience, it is an inevitable corollary, that all actions whatever must be determined by those psychical connections which experience has generated—either in the life of the individual, or in that general antecedent life whose accumulated results are organized in his constitution.

To go at length into this long-standing controversy respecting the Will, would be alike useless and out of place. I can but briefly indicate what seems to me the nature of the current illusion, as interpreted from the point of view at which we have arrived.

Considered as an internal perception, the illusion appears chiefly to consist in supposing that at each moment the *ego* is something more than the composite state of consciousness which then exists. A man who, after being subject to an impulse consisting of a group of psychical states positive and nascent, performs a certain action, usually asserts that he determined to perform the action, and performed it under the influence of this impulse: and by speaking of himself as having been something separate from the group of psychical states constituting the impulse, he falls into the error of supposing that it was not the impulse alone which determined the action. But the entire group of psychical states which constituted the antecedent of the action, also constituted himself at that moment—constituted his psychical self, that is, as distinguished from his physical self. It is alike true that he determined the action and that the impulse determined it; seeing that during its existence the impulse constituted his then state of consciousness, that is, himself. Either the *ego* which is supposed to determine or will the action, is some state of consciousness, simple or composite, or it is not. If it is not some state of consciousness, it is something of which we are unconscious—something, therefore, that is unknown to us—something, therefore, of whose existence we neither have nor can have any evidence—something, therefore, which it is absurd to suppose existing. If the *ego* is some state of consciousness, then, as it is ever present, it can be at each moment nothing else than the state of consciousness present at that moment. And thus it follows inevitably, that when any impression received from without, makes nascent certain appropriate motor changes and various of the impressions that must accompany and follow them; and when, under the stimulus of this composite psychical state, the nascent motor changes pass in actual motor changes; this composite psychical state which forms the stimulus to the action, is at the same time the *ego* which is said to will the action. Thus it is natural enough that the subject of such psychical changes should say that he wills the action; seeing that, psychically considered, he is at that moment nothing more than the composite state of consciousness by which the action is excited. But to say that the performance of the action is, therefore, the result of his free-will, is to say that he determines the cohesions of psychical states by which the action is aroused; and as these psychical states constitute himself at that moment, this is to say that these psychical states determine their own cohesions: which is absurd. Their cohesions have been wholly determined by experiences—the greater part of them, constituting what we call his natural character, by the experiences of antecedent organisms; and the rest by his own experiences. The changes which at each moment take place in his consciousness, and, among others, those which he is said to will, are wholly determined by this infinitude of previous experiences; so far, at least, as they are not produced by immediate impressions on the senses. [. . .]

Respecting this matter I will only further say, that free-will, did it exist, would be entirely at variance with that beneficent necessity displayed in the progressive evolution of the correspondence between the organism and its environment. That gradual advance in the moulding of inner relations to outer relations, which has been delineated in the foregoing pages—that ever-extending adaptation of the cohesions of psychical states to the connections between the answering phenomena, which we have seen to result from the accumulation of experiences, would be arrested, did there exist anything which otherwise determined their cohesions. As it is, we see that the correspondence between the internal changes and the external coexistences and sequences, must become more and more complete. The continuous adjustment of the vital activities to the activities in the environment, must become more accurate and exhaustive. The life must become higher and the happiness greater—must do so because the inner relations are determined by the outer relations. But were the inner relations to any extent determined by some other agency, the harmony at any moment subsisting, and the advance to a higher harmony, would alike be interrupted to a proportionate extent: there would be an arrest of that grand progression which is now bearing Humanity onwards to perfection.

FEELING AND THINKING

George Henry Lewes, *The Physiology of Common Life*, 2 vols. (London: William Blackwood and Sons, 1859–60), ii. 58–60.

G. H. Lewes's work, an application of physiological psychology to everyday life, aims to meet the needs of both the student and the general reader unfamiliar with specialist terminology. 'In pursuance of this object', Lewes stresses in the Preface, 'I have been forced to depart very widely from the practice of other popular writers, who consider themselves bound to act as "middle men" between scientific authorities and the public, and to expound facts and doctrines as they find them.' (p. vi) Rejecting this 'easy and convenient plan', The Physiology of Common Life is both summary and critique of existing ideas and forum for Lewes's own theories of the development of the nervous system and was written while his partner, George Eliot, was working on The Mill on the Floss. This extract is from chapter 8, where Lewes draws heavily on Hamilton's work, reinterpreting it in a physiological framework.

Habits, Fixed Ideas, and what are called Automatic Actions, all depend on the tendency which a sensation has to discharge itself through the readiest channel. In learning to speak a new language, to play on a musical instrument, or to perform any unaccustomed movements, great difficulty is felt, because the channels through which each sensation has to pass have not become established; but no sooner has frequent repetition cut a pathway, than this difficulty vanishes; the actions become so automatic that they can be performed while the mind is otherwise engaged; and sometimes, if once commenced, they must continue. We have all our tricks of phrase or gesture, which no effort can prevent. We utter, as meaningless expletives, phrases which originally cost us trouble to learn. It is in vain that people laugh at us for the iteration of 'you know,' 'well then,' and similar phrases, which are often ludicrously inappropriate; they have become automatic—the paths of discharge have been established, and along these paths the sensation must discharge itself. The same thing is observable in the region of ideas. Old associations, old beliefs, are not to be displaced. A man may be thoroughly convinced to-day by the logic of his opponent, and yet to-morrow he will be heard uttering his old convictions, as if no one had ever doubted them. His mind cannot move except in the old paths. It may be noted as the peculiar characteristic of vigorous intellects, that their thoughts are ever finding new pathways instead of moving amid old associations. The vigorous thinker is one who thinks for himself; the vigorous writer is one who expresses what he means, and does not suffer one phrase automatically to determine another. If he has a manner, or mannerism, it is his own. Inferior minds think the thoughts of others, and write the phrases of others. Hence, as Goethe says, in this world there are so few voices and so many echoes.

Returning from this digression, we may now understand that although a sensation must discharge itself, and may do so in various directions, now exciting muscular contractions, and now trains of thought, we are not to suppose the sensation itself is dependent on these effects; or to suppose, as the dominant doctrine does, that, unless a train of thought be excited, no sensation at all has been excited. Sensation is simply the active state of Sensibility, which is the property of ganglionic tissue.

The mill-wheel, at first so obtrusive in its sound, ceases at length to excite any attention. The impressions on our auditory nerves continue; but although we hear them, we cease to think about them: the same reflex-feelings are no longer excited. It is held, indeed, that we cease to hear them, in ceasing to be 'conscious' that we hear them; but this is manifestly erroneous. Let the wheel suddenly stop, and there is an immediate corresponding sensational change in us; so much so, that if it occurs during sleep, we awake. Let the wheel move with a slower movement, and we shall at once be aware of it. Let it creak, and we hear it. Now, it is clear that unless we are all the while sensible of the sounds of the wheel, no alterations in the *degrees* of sound will affect us. If the sensation of sound has ceased, the *cessation* of that sound cannot awaken us. The truth seems to be that at first the sound of the wheel was *obtrusive*—excited reflex-feelings—gave determinate directions to our thoughts. It afterwards ceased to excite these feelings, and the sensations became *merged* on the general sum of sensations which make up our total Consciousness.

PSYCHOLOGICAL PRINCIPLES

George Henry Lewes, *Problems of Life and Mind*, 5 vols. (London: Trübner and Co., 1874–9); First series, 2 vols., *The Foundations of a Creed* (1874), i. 121, 123–5, 127–8, 162.

Lewes first began to develop the ideas that would lead to Problems of Life and Mind *at the very beginning of his career in 1836, when preparing a course of lectures interpreting Reid, Brown, and Stewart's philosophy of mind through physiological principles. The scheme was abandoned, then revived when Lewes started to concentrate on developing his theories of physiological psychology in the 1860s, and culminates in this, his final work. In* The Foundations of a Creed *Lewes develops the ideas discussed in* The Physiology of Common Life, *and emphasizes the centrality of social and historical as well as biological factors when analysing human consciousness and evolution, critically drawing on Auguste Comte's social theory.*

There are three Psychostatical laws.

I. *The Law of Interest.*—It has long been observed that we only *see* what interests us, only know what is sufficiently like former experiences to become, so to speak, incorporated with them—assimilated by them. The satisfaction of desire is that which both impels and quiets mental movement. Were it not for this controlling effect of the established pathways, every excitation would be indefinitely irradiated throughout the whole organism; but a pathway once established is the ready issue for any new excitation. The evolution of Mind is the establishment of definite paths: this is the mental organisation, fitting it for the reception of definite impressions, and their co-ordination with past feelings.

II. *The Law of Signature.*—Every feeling being a group of neutral units, and varying with the varying units, or varying groups of such groups, has its particular signature, or mark in Consciousness, in consequence of which it acquires its objective Localisation, *i.e.*, its place in the organism or in the cosmos.

III. *The Law of Experience.*—This is only the mental side of the laws of Heredity and Adaptation. *Experience is the registration of Feeling.* Through their registered modifications, feelings once produced are capable of reproduction; and must always be reproduced, more or less completely, whenever the new excitation is discharged along the old channels. [. . .]

This influence of the psychostatical conditions in determining the character of every psychical phenomenon suggests an important distinction which must be established between Animal Consciousness and Human Consciousness, one far greater than any other distinction to be established between Animals and Man. [. . .] Between the Cosmos and the Consciousness there is interposed a psychological medium, briefly designated by the term Experience. This applies both to animals and to man. But in man we must recognise another medium, one from which his moral and intellectual life is mainly drawn, one which separates him from all animals by the broadest line: this is the Social Medium—the collective accumulations of centuries, condensed in knowledge, beliefs, prejudices, institutions, and tendencies; and forming another kind of Psychoplasm to which the animal is a stranger. The animal feels the Cosmos, and adapts himself to it. Man feels the Cosmos, but he also *thinks* it; again he feels the Social world, and thinks it. His feelings and his thoughts of both are powerfully modified by *residua*. Hence the very Cosmos is to him greatly different from what it is to the animal; for just as what is organised in the individual becomes transmitted to offspring, and determines the mode in which the offspring will react on stimulus, so what is registered in the Social Organism determines the mode in which succeeding generations will feel and think. By Tools and Instruments, by Creeds and Institutions, by Literature, Art, and Science, the Social Organism acquires and develops its powers; and how even simple perceptions are modified by social influences will strikingly appear in a subsequent part of this work, wherein it will be shown that all perceptions are the results of slow evolution, as the organic forms are; and not only will it be shown that many thousands of years passed before even man was able to *perceive* the colour blue, for instance, (though of course he felt a difference between a blue object and a brown one) it will be shown that no animal can possibly perceive blue as we perceive it, and the reason in both cases is not to be sought in physiological processes of Vision, but in psychological processes of Thought. The possibility of this perception is due to Language; and Language exists only as a social function. [. . .]

The mental life of man has two sources: 1°, the animal organism, and 2°, the social organism. Man apart from Society is simply an animal organism; restore him to his real position as a social unit, and the problem changes. It is in the development of Civilisation that we trace the real development of Humanity. The soul of man has thus a double root, a double history. It passes quite out of the range of animal life; and no explanation of mental phenomena can be valid which does not allow for this extension of range. [. . .]

Let us suppose the student equipped with all the aid which the science of the day will supply, not only respecting the normal actions of the nervous system, but also respecting its abnormal actions, especially in Insanity, he will still need to invoke another aid, for he will only have what may be called biological data, and will still need the equally important sociological data. Having studied the Organism in relation to its Medium, he has only studied the Animal side of the problem; there still remains the Human side, and he has to study the Organism in relation to the Social Medium, in which man lives no less than in the Cosmical

Medium. If there is a valid objection against the functions of the brain being investigated in the cabinets of metaphysicians, there is an equally valid objection against intellectual and moral processes being sought in the laboratories of physiologists. To understand the Human Mind we must study it under its normal conditions, and these are social conditions. [. . .]

The mind is not a passive recipient of external impressions, but an active co-operant. It has not only its own laws of action, but brings with it that very elementary condition of Consciousness which most theorists attempt to derive *ab extra*. I mean that the sensitive mechanism is not a simple mechanism, and as such constant, but a variable mechanism, which has a *history*. What the Senses inscribe on it, are not merely the changes of the external world; but these characters are commingled with the characters of preceding inscriptions. The sensitive subject is no *tabula rasa*:[1] it is not a blank sheet of paper, but a palimpsest. The sensational school was strangely, blind to the very conditions of the results it intended to explain. It treated Thought as 'transformed Sensation,' without seeing that the presence of the grouping faculty, on which Thought depends, was necessary both for the Sensation and for the transformation. Not aware of the fact that the Organism is an evolution, bringing with it, in its structure, evolved modes of action inherited from ancestors, these writers overlooked the fact that the Organism brings with it inherited Experience, *i.e.*, a mode of reaction antecedent to all direct relation with external influences, which necessarily determines the results of individual Experience. There is thus what may be called an *a priori* condition in all Sensation, and in all Ideation. But this is *historical*, not *transcendental*: it is itself the product of Experience, though not of the individual. Our perceptions are evolutions; and, having necessarily a history at their back, it is clear that all perceptions are modified by pre-perceptions, all conceptions by pre-conceptions. Hence mental diversities.

ON IMAGINATION

Eneas Sweetland Dallas, *The Gay Science*, 2 vols. (London: Chapman and Hall, 1866), i. 193–6, 201, 207–8.

In the eclectic and exuberant The Gay Science, *Dallas argues that pleasure (rather than truth or beauty) should be the end of art; that 'a science of criticism is possible, and it must of necessity be a science of the laws of pleasure' based on a*

---

[1] A reference to John Locke's argument against the notion of innate ideas in *An Essay Concerning Human Understanding* (1690).

study of the working of the unconscious, or 'Hidden Soul'. The first volume begins with a lengthy discussion of critical debates, followed by an analysis of the imagination, 'this Proteus of the mind which defies our search' (p. 180). Imagination, Dallas argues, drawing heavily on his former teacher William Hamilton's work, should be understood not in traditionally Romantic, transcendent terms but as one aspect of 'the automatic action of the mind' that is present in all mental activity.

I propose this theory, that the imagination or fantasy is not a special faculty but that it is a special function. It is a name given to the automatic action of the mind or any of its faculties—to what may not unfitly be called the Hidden Soul. [. . .]

Now for the most part this automatic action takes place unawares; and when we come to analyse the movements of thought we find that to be quite sure of our steps we are obliged very much to identify what is involuntary with what is unconscious. We are seldom quite sure that our wills have had nought to do in producing certain actions, unless these actions have come about without our knowledge. Therefore although involuntary does not in strictness coincide with unconscious action, yet for practical purposes, and, above all, for the sake of clearness, it may be well to put out of sight altogether such involuntary action as may consist with full consciousness, and to treat of the automatic exercise of the mind as either quite unconscious or but half conscious. And if on this understanding we may substitute the one phrase for the other as very nearly coinciding, then the task before me is to show that imagination is but a name for the unknown, unconscious action of the mind—the whole mind or any of its faculties—for the Hidden Soul. [. . .]

The hidden efficacy of our thoughts, their prodigious power of working in the dark and helping us underhand, can be compared only to the stories of our folklore, and chiefly to that of the lubber-fiend who toils for us when we are asleep or when we are not looking. There is a stack of corn to be thrashed, or a house to be built, or a canal to be dug, or a mountain to be levelled, and we are affrighted at the task before us. Our backs are turned and it is done in a trice, or we awake in the morning and find that it has been wrought in the night. The lubber-fiend or some other shy creature comes to our aid. He will not lift a finger that we can see; but let us shut our eyes, or turn our heads, or put out the light, and there is nothing which the good fairy will not do for us. We have such a fairy in our thoughts, a willing but unknown and tricksy worker which commonly bears the name of Imagination, and which may be named—as I think more clearly—The Hidden Soul. [. . .]

I hope to avoid the nonsense and the jargon of those who have discoursed most on the sphere of the transcendental—that is, the sphere of our mental existence which transcends or spreads beyond our consciousness; but that consciousness is not our entire world, that the mind stretches in full play far beyond the bourne of consciousness, there will be little difficulty in proving. Outside consciousness there rolls a vast tide of life, which is, perhaps, even more important to us than the little isle of our thoughts which lies within our ken. Comparisons, however, between the two are vain, because each is necessary to the other. The thing to be firmly seized is, that we live in two concentric worlds of thought,—an inner ring, of which we are conscious, and which may be described as illuminated; an outer one, of which we are unconscious, and which may be described as in the dark. Between the outer and the inner ring, between our unconscious and our conscious existence, there is a free and a constant but unobserved traffic for ever carried on. Trains of thought are continually passing to and fro, from the light into the dark, and back from the dark into the light. When the current of thought flows from within our ken to beyond our ken, it is gone, we forget it, we know not what has become of it. After a time it comes back to us changed and grown, as if it were a new thought, and we know not whence it comes.

ON UNCONSCIOUS CEREBRATION

Frances Power Cobbe 'Unconscious cerebration' *Darwinism in Morals and Other Essays* (London: Williams and Norgate, 1872), 330–3.

Reprinted from Macmillan's Magazine *(Nov. 1870). Frances Power Cobbe aims to reconcile contemporary scientific notions of unconscious cerebration with Christian belief on the nature of the soul, determinism, and free-will, by arguing for 'the entire separability of the conscious self from its thinking organ, the physical brain' (p. 306). This extract comes after a lengthy overview of Carpenter's theory which was first outlined in the fifth edition of* Human Physiology *(1855). Carpenter directly responds to Cobbe's argument in his later development of his theory below.*

Let us be content with these ordinary and unmistakable exercises of unconscious cerebration, and leave aside all rare or questionable wonders of somnambulism and cognate states. We have got Memory, Fancy, Understanding, at all events, as faculties exercised by the Unconscious Brain. Now it is obvious that it would be an unusual definition of the word 'Thought' which should debar us from applying it to the above phenomena; or compel us to say that we can remember, fancy, and understand without 'thinking' of the things remembered, fancied, or understood. But Who, or What, then, is it that accomplishes these confessedly mental functions? Two answers are given to the query, each of them, as I venture to think, erroneous. Büchner[1] and his followers say, 'It is our physical Brains, and these Brains are ourselves.' And non-materialists say, 'It is our conscious Selves, which merely use our brains as their instruments.' We must go into this matter somewhat carefully.

In a certain loose and popular way of speaking, our brains are 'ourselves.' So also in the same way of speaking are our hearts, our limbs, and the hairs of our head. But in more accurate language the use of the pronoun 'I' applied to any part of our bodies is obviously incorrect, and even inadmissible. We say, indeed, commonly, 'I struck with my hand,' when our hand has obeyed our volition. It is, then, in fact, the will of the Self which we are describing. But if our hand has been forcibly compelled to strike by another man seizing it, or if it have shaken by palsy, we only say, 'My hand was forced,' or 'was shaken.' The limb's action is not *ours*, unless it has been done by our will. In the case of the heart, the very centre of physical life, we never dream of using such a phrase as 'I am beating slowly,' or 'I am palpitating fast.' And why do we not say so? Because, the action of our hearts being involuntary, we are sensible that the conscious 'I' is not the agent in question, albeit the mortal life of that 'I' is hanging on every pulsation. Now the problem which concerns us is this: Can we, or can we *not*, properly speak of our brains as we do of our hearts? Is it more proper to say, 'I invent my dreams,' than it is to say, 'I am beating slowly'? I venture to think the cases are precisely parallel. When our brains perform acts of unconscious cerebration (such as dreams), they act just as our hearts do, *i.e.* involuntarily; and we ought to speak of them as we always do of our hearts, as of organs of our frame, but not our Selves. When our brains obey our wills, then they act as our hands do when we voluntarily strike a blow; and then we do right to speak as if 'we' performed the act accomplished by their means.

Now to return to our point. Are the anti-Materialists right to say that the agent in unconscious cerebration is, 'We, ourselves, who merely use our brains as their instruments;' or are the Materialists right who say, 'It is our physical brains alone, and these brains are ourselves'? With regard to the first reply, I think that all the foregoing study has gone to show that 'we' are *not* remembering, *not* fancying, *not* understanding, what is being at the moment remembered, fancied, or understood. To say, then, that in such acts 'we' are 'using our brains as our instruments,' appears nothing but a servile and unmeaning adherence to the foregone conclusion that our brains are nothing else than the organs of our will. It is absurd to call them so when we are concerned with phenomena whose speciality is that the will has nothing to do with them. So far, then, as this part of the

---

[1] Ludwig Büchner: German materialist philosopher, author of *Force and Matter* (trans. 1855); *Nature and Spirit* (trans. 1857), and *The Place of Man in Nature* (trans. 1869).

argument is concerned, I think the answer of the anti-Materialists must be pronounced to be erroneous. The balance of evidence inclines to the Materialists' doctrine that the brain itself performs the mental processes in question, and, to use Vogt's[2] expression, 'secretes Thought' automatically and spontaneously.

But if this presumption be accepted provisionally, and the possibility admitted of its future physiological demonstration, have we, with it, accepted also the Materialist's ordinary conclusion that *we* and our automatically thinking brains are one and indivisible? If the brain can work by itself, have we any reason to believe it ever works *also* under the guidance of something external to itself, which we may describe as the Conscious Self? It seems to me that this is precisely what the preceding facts have likewise gone to prove—namely, that there are two kinds of action of the brain, the one Automatic, and the other subject to the will of the Conscious Self; just as the actions of a horse are some of them spontaneous and some done under the compulsion of his rider. The first order of actions tend to indicate that the brain 'secretes thought;' the second order (strongly contrasting with the first) show that, beside that automatically working brain, there is another agency in the field under whose control the brain performs a wholly different class of labours. Everywhere in the preceding pages we have traced the extraordinary *separation* which continually takes place between our Conscious Selves and the automatic action of the organ, which serves as our medium of communication with the outward world. We have seen, in a word, that we are not Centaurs, steed and rider in one, but horsemen, astride on roadsters which obey us when we guide them, and when we drop the reins, trot a little way of their own accord or canter off without our permission.

THE POWER OF THE WILL OVER MENTAL ACTION

William Benjamin Carpenter, *Principles of Mental Physiology* (1874), 2nd edn. (London: Henry S. King, 1875), 24–8, 516–17, 519–20, 539–41.

The Principles of Mental Physiology *is an expanded and developed version of the fourth and fifth editions of* Human Physiology *(1852 and 1855). This had established Carpenter as leading authority in the area, although his claim to propose the theory of 'unconscious cerebration' in the 1855 edition was challenged by Thomas Laycock, who insisted that he had developed the notion of the 'reflex*

---

[2] Carl Vogt, German psychologist, author of *Lectures on Man: His Place in Creation and in the History of the Earth* (trans. 1864).

action of the cerebrum' in his study of the effects of mesmerism on the O'Key sisters, published in the Edinburgh Medical and Surgical Journal *in 1838, and later developed in* Mind and Brain, or the Correlations of Consciousness and Organisation *(1860). Here Carpenter aims to establish a materialist analysis of the mind, developing and reinterpreting associationist theory. Carpenter gives the will a more decisive role than, say, Spencer does, and in discussing its power over mental action, he is responding to a wide range of arguments, including Frances Power Cobbe's discussions of his theory (see above), and T. H. Huxley's controversial essay, based on an address to the British Association for the Advancement of Science, 'On the Hypothesis that Animals are Automata and its History' (1874) (in* Collected Essays, *9 vols., vol. i (London: Macmillan, 1901)).*

The relation between the Automatic activity of the body, and the Volitional direction by which it is utilized and directed, may be compared to the independent locomotive power of a horse under the guidance and control of a skilful rider. It is not the rider's whip or spur that furnishes the *power*, but the nerves and muscles of the horse; and when these have been exhausted, no further action can be got out of them by the sharpest stimulation. But the rate and direction of the movement are determined by the Will of the rider, who impresses his mandates on the well-trained steed with as much readiness and certainty as if he were acting on his own limbs. Now and then, it is true, some unusual excitement calls forth the essential independence of the equine nature; the horse takes the bit between his teeth, and runs away with his master; and it is for the time uncertain whether the independent energy of the one, or the controlling power of the other, will obtain the mastery. This is just what we see in those Spasms and Convulsions which occur without loss of consciousness, and in which the muscles that we are accustomed to regard as 'voluntary' are called into violent contraction, in spite of the strongest Volitional resistance. On the other hand, the horse will quietly find his way home, whilst his rider, wrapped in a profound reverie, entirely ceases to guide him; just as our own legs carry us along a course which habit has made familiar, while our Mind is engaged only upon its own operations, and our Will is altogether in abeyance. [. . .]

Now all this will be found to be as true of the *Mind*, as it is of the body. Our Mental activity is, in the first instance, entirely *spontaneous* or *automatic*; being determined by our congenital nervous Organization, and by the conditions of its early development. It may be stated as a fundamental principle, that the Will can never *originate* any form of Mental activity. Thus, no one has ever *acquired* the creative power of Genius, or *made himself* a great Artist or a great Poet, or *gained by practice* that peculiar insight which characterises the original Discoverer; for these gifts are Mental Instincts or Intuitions which, though capable of being developed and strengthened by due cultivation, can never be generated *de novo*.

But the power of the Will is exerted in the *purposive selection*, from among those objects of consciousness which Sensations from without and the working of the internal 'Mechanism of Thought and Feeling' bring before the Ego (whether simultaneously or successively), of that which shall be determinately followed up; and in the *intensification of the force of its impression*, which seems the direct consequence of such limitation. This state is what is termed *Attention*; in regard to which it was well said by Sir William Hamilton, that its intensity is in a precisely inverse ratio to its *extensity*. And it will be the Writer's object to show, that it is solely by the Volitional *direction of the attention* that the Will exerts its domination; so that the acquirement of this power, which is within the reach of every one, should be the primary object of all Mental discipline. It is thus that each individual can perfect and utilize his natural gifts; by rigorously training them in the first instance, and then by exercising them only in the manner most fitted to expand and elevate, while restraining them from all that would limit or debase.— In regard to every kind of Mental activity that does *not* involve origination, the power of the Will, though limited to *selection*, is almost unbounded. For although it cannot directly bring objects before the consciousness which are not present to it, yet, by concentrating the Mental gaze (so to speak) upon any object that may be within its reach, it can make use of this to bring in other objects by associative Suggestion. And, moreover, it can virtually determine what shall *not* be regarded by the Mind, through its power of keeping the Attention fixed *in some other direction*; and thus it can subdue the force of violent impulse, and give to the conflict of opposing motives a result quite different from that which would ensue without its interference. This exercise of the Will, moreover, if habitually exerted in certain directions, will tend to form the Character, by establishing a set of *acquired habitudes*; which, no less than those dependent upon original constitution and circumstances, help to determine the working of the 'Mechanism of Thought and Feeling.' In so *utilising* it, the Will can also *improve* it by appropriate discipline; repressing its activities where too strong, fostering and developing them where originally feeble, directing all healthful energy into the most fitting channel for its exercise, and training the entire Mental as it does the Bodily organism to harmonious and effective working. And thus in proportion as our Will acquires domination over our Automatic tendencies, the spontaneous succession of our Ideas and the play of our Emotions show the influence of its habitual control; while our Character and Conduct in Life come to be the expression of our best Intellectual energies, directed by the Motives which we *determinately elect* as our guiding principles of action.

It is obvious that the view here taken does not in the least militate against the idea, that Mind may have an existence altogether independent of the Body which serves as its instrument. All which has been contended for is, that the connexion between Mind and Body is such, that the actions of each have, in this present state of existence (which is all of which Science can legitimately take cognizance), a definite *causal relation* to those of the other; so that the actions of our Minds, *in so far as they are carried on without any interference from our Will,* may be considered as 'Functions of the Brain.'—On the other hand, in the control which the Will can exert over the *direction* of the thoughts, and over the *motive force* exerted by the feelings, we have the evidence of a new and independent Power, which may either oppose or concur-with the automatic tendencies, and which, according as it is habitually exerted, tends to render the Ego *a free agent.* And, truly, in the existence of this Power, which is capable of thus regulating the very highest of those operations that are causally related to corporeal states, we find a better evidence than we gain from the study of any other part of our Psychical nature, that there *is* an entity wherein Man's nobility essentially consists, which does not depend for its existence on any play of Physical or Vital forces, but which makes these forces subservient to its determinations. It is, in fact, in virtue of the Will, that we are *not* mere thinking Automata, mere puppets to be pulled by suggesting-strings, capable of being played-upon by every one who shall have made himself master of our springs of action.

It may be freely admitted, however, that such thinking Automata *do* exist: for there are many individuals whose Will has never been called into due exercise, and who gradually or almost entirely lose the power of exerting it, becoming the mere creatures of habit and impulse; and there are others in whom (as we shall hereafter see) such Automatic states are of occasional occurrence, whilst in others, again, they may be artificially induced. And it is (1) by the study of those conditions in which the Will is completely in abeyance,—the course of thought being *entirely* determined by the influence of suggestions upon the Mind, whose mode of reaction upon them depends upon its original peculiarities and its subsequently-acquired habits,—and (2) by the comparison of such abnormal states with that in which the Ego, in full possession of all his faculties, and accustomed to the habitual direction of his thoughts and control of his feelings, determinately applies his judgement to the formation of a decision between contending impulses, and carries that decision into action,—that we shall obtain the most satisfactory ideas of what share the Will really takes in the operations of our Minds and in the direction of our conduct, and of what must be set down to that automatic activity of our Psychical nature, which is correlated with Cerebral changes.

Thus, then, the Psychologist may fearlessly throw himself into the deepest waters of speculative inquiry in regard to the relation between his Mind and its Bodily instrument, provided that he trusts to the inherent buoyancy of that great fact of Consciousness, that *we have within us a self-determining Power which we call Will.* And he may even find in the evidence of the intimate relation between Mental activity and Physical changes in the Brain, the most satisfactory grounds which Science can afford, for his belief that the phenomena of the Material Universe are the expressions of an Infinite Mind and Will, of which Man's is the finite representative. [. . .]

OF UNCONSCIOUS CEREBRATION

To the Writer it seems a matter of no practical consequence, whether the doctrine be stated in terms of Metaphysics, or in terms of Physiology—in terms of *mind*, or in terms of *brain*,—provided it be recognised as having a positive scientific basis. But since, in the systems of Philosophy long prevalent in this country, *consciousness* has been almost uniformly taken as the basis of all strictly *mental* activity, it seems convenient to designate as Functions of the Nervous System all those operations which lie below that level. And there is this advantage in approaching the subject from the Physiological side,—that the study of the automatic actions of other parts of the Nervous System furnishes a clue, by the guidance of which we may be led to the scientific elucidation of many phenomena that would otherwise remain obscure and meaningless. For, as we have seen, each of the Nervous centres has an independent 'reflex' activity of its own, sometimes 'primary' or 'original,' sometimes 'secondary' or 'acquired'; while our *consciousness* of its exercise depends upon the impression which it makes upon the Sensorium, which is the instrument alike of the external and of the internal senses. Looking, therefore, at all the automatic operations of the Mind in the light of 'reflex actions' of the Cerebrum, there is no more difficulty in comprehending that such reflex actions may proceed without our cognizance,—their results being evolved as *intellectual products*, when we become conscious of the impressions transmitted along the 'nerves of the internal senses' from the Cerebrum to the Sensorium,—than there is in understanding that impressions may excite muscular movements through the 'reflex' power of the Spinal Cord without the necessary intervention of sensation. In both cases, the condition of this mode of unconscious operation is, that the *receptivity* of the Sensorium shall be suspended *quoad*[1] the changes in question; either by its own functional inactivity, or through its temporary engrossment by other impressions.—It is difficult to find an appropriate term for this class of operations. They can scarcely be designated as Reasoning processes, since 'unconscious reasoning' seems a contradiction in terms. The designation *unconscious cerebration* is perhaps as unobjectionable as any other, and has been found readily intelligible. [. . .]

A very apposite example of this form of activity is afforded by a phenomenon, which, although familiar to every one who takes note of the workings of his own mind, has been scarcely recognised by Metaphysical inquirers; namely, that when we have been *trying to recollect* some name, phrase, occurrence, &c.,—and, after vainly employing all the expedients we can think of for bringing the desiderated

---

[1] As far as.

idea to our minds, have abandoned the attempt as useless,—it will often occur *spontaneously* a little while afterwards, suddenly flashing (as it were) into our consciousness, either when we are thinking of something altogether different, or on awaking out of profound sleep.—Now it is important to note, in the *first* case, that the Mind may have been entirely engrossed in the mean time by some entirely different subject of contemplation, and that we cannot detect any link of association whereby the result has been obtained, notwithstanding that the whole 'train of thought' which has passed through the mind in the interval may be most distinctly remembered; and, in the *second*, that the missing idea seems more likely to present itself when the sleep has been profound, than when it has been disturbed. The first form of the phenomenon has been thus admirably described by Miss Cobbe:—

It is an every-day occurrence to most of us to forget a particular word, or a line of poetry, and to remember it some hours later, when we have ceased consciously to seek for it. We try, perhaps anxiously, at first to recover it, well aware that it lies somewhere hidden in our memory, but unable to seize it. As the saying is, we "ransack our brains for it," but, failing to find it, we at last turn our attention to other matters. By-and-bye, when, so far as consciousness goes, our whole minds are absorbed in a different topic, we exclaim, "Eureka! the word or verse is so-and-so." So familiar is this phenomenon, that we are accustomed in similar straits to say, "Never mind: I shall think of the missing word by-and-by, when I am attending to something else"; and we deliberately turn away, not intending finally to abandon the pursuit, but precisely as if we were possessed of an obedient secretary or librarian, whom we could order to hunt up a missing document, or turn out a word in a dictionary, while we amused ourselves with something else.[2] [. . .]

The more thoroughly, then, we examine into what may be termed the Mechanism of Thought, the more clear does it become that not only an *automatic*, but an *unconscious* action enters largely into all its processes. [. . .]

It is not *intellectual* work alone, that is done in this manner; for it seems equally clear that *emotional* states, or rather states which constitute Emotions when we become conscious of them, may be developed by the same process; so that our feelings towards persons and objects may undergo most important changes, without our being in the least degree aware, until we have our attention directed to our own mental state, of the alteration which has taken place in them. [. . .]

The fact, indeed, is recognised in our ordinary language; for we continually speak of the 'feelings' which we *unconsciously* entertain towards another, and of our not becoming aware of them until some circumstance calls them into activity.

Here again, it would seem as if the material organ of these Feelings tends to *form itself* in accordance with the impressions habitually made upon it; whilst we may be as completely unaware of the changes which have taken place in it, as we

---

[2] This is a quotation from Cobbe's article on 'Unconscious cerebration' in *Macmillan's Magazine*.

are of those by which passing events have been registered in our memory, until some circumstance calls-forth the conscious manifestation, which is the 'reflex' of the new condition which the organ has acquired. And it is desirable, in this connection, to recall the fact that the Emotional state seems often to be determined by circumstances of which the individual has no Ideational consciousness, and especially by the emotional states of those by whom he is surrounded; a mode of influence which acts with peculiar potency on the minds of Children, and which is a most important element in their Moral education.

2. Dreams

THE PROPHETIC CHARACTER OF DREAMS, AND NIGHTMARE

Robert Macnish, *The Philosophy of Sleep* (Glasgow: W. R. M'Phun, 1830), 50–3, 117–18, 124–8, 136–9, 143.

This short study of the physical and mental processes at work in sleeping and dreaming became a standard reference in the nineteenth century, and is, indeed, cited by Freud in his discussion of 'The Stimulii and Source of Dreams in The Interpretation of Dreams *(The Standard Edition of the Complete Works of Sigmund Freud, trans. James Strachey, vol. iv (1900), 24). Like other popular scientific treatises, it draws on a wide range of theories and interpretations and brings together numerous case-studies, while reflecting Macnish's own strong phrenological interests.*

A suspension (almost always complete) of the judgment, and an active state of memory, imagination, &c., are the only conditions essential to ordinary dreaming; but along with them there is usually a torpor of the organs of the senses, and of the powers of voluntary motion, the same as in complete sleep. Dreaming, therefore, is a state of partial slumber, in which certain parts of the brain are asleep, or deprived of their sensorial power, while others continue awake, or possess their accustomed proportion; and whatever produces dreams has the effect of exhausting this power in one set of faculties, while it leaves it untouched in others. Dreaming, then, takes place when the repose is broken; and consists of a series of thoughts or feelings called into existence by certain powers of the mind, while the other mental powers which control these thoughts or feelings, are inactive. This theory is the only one capable of affording a satisfactory explanation of all the phenomena of dreams. It embraces every difficult point, and is so accordant with nature, that there is every reason to suppose it founded on truth. [. . .]

In dreaming, the voluntary powers are generally, but not necessarily suspended: we have a striking proof of this in somnambulism, which is a modification of dreaming. Dreams cannot take place in complete repose, for all the mental faculties are then dormant, and for a short period the person exists in a state of the most perfect oblivion. When, however, one faculty, or more than one, bursts asunder the bonds which enthralled it, while its fellows continue chained in sleep, then visions ensue, and the imagination dwells in that wide empire which separates the waking state from that of perfect sleep. It is the unequal distribution of sensorial energy which gives rise to those visionary phenomena. One faculty exerts itself vividly, without being under the control of the others. The imagination is at work, while the judgment is asleep; and thereby indulges in the maddest and most extravagant thoughts, free from the salutary check of the latter more sedate and judicious faculty. [. . .]

It is undoubtedly owing to the faculty, sometimes possessed by sleep, of renewing long-forgotten ideas, that persons have had important facts communicated to them in dreams. There have been instances, for example, where valuable documents, sums of money, &c., have been concealed, and where either the person who secreted them, or he who had the place of their concealment communicated to him, may have forgotten every thing therewith connected. He may then torture his mind in vain, during the waking state, to recollect the event; and it may be brought to his remembrance at once in a dream. In such cases, an apparition is generally the medium through which the seemingly mysterious knowledge is communicated. The imagination conjures up some phantom that discloses the secret, which circumstance, proceeding in reality from a simple operation of the mind, is straightway converted into something supernatural, and invested with all the attributes of wonder and awe. When such spectral forms appear, and communicate some fact which turns out to be founded on truth, the person is not always aware that the whole occurred in a dream, but often fancies that the apparition appeared to him when he was broad awake, and, during this state, communicated the intelligence. When we hear, therefore, of hidden treasures, wills, &c., being disclosed in such a manner, we are not always to scout the report as false. The spectre communicating the intelligence was certainly the mere chimera of the dreamer's brain, but the facts revealed, apparently by this phantom, may, from the above circumstance, be substantially true. [. . .]

NIGHT-MARE

Fantastic passions, maddening brawl,
And shame and terror over all,
Deeds to be hid, which were not hid;
Which all confused I could not know
Whether I suffered or I did;

> For all seemed guilt, remorse, or woe,
> My own, or others'; still the same
> Soul-stifling fear, heart-sickening shame.
>
> Coleridge.[1]

The following are the conditions of night-mare.

1. An active state of the memory, imagination, &c.

2. An impaired state of the respiratory functions.

3. A torpor in the power of volition. The judgment is generally more or less awake; and in this respect night-mare differs from simple dreaming, where that faculty is suspended. [. . .]

The modifications which night-mare assumes are infinite; but one passion is never absent—that of utter and incomprehensible dread. Sometimes the sufferer is buried beneath overwhelming rocks, which crush him on all sides, but still leave him with a miserable consciousness of his situation. Sometimes he is involved in the coils of a horrid, slimy monster, whose eyes have the phosphorescent glare of the sepulchre, and whose breath is poisonous as the marsh of Lerna.[2] Every thing horrible, disgusting, or terrific in the physical or moral world, is brought before him in fearful array: he is hissed at by serpents, tortured by demons, stunned by the hollow voices and cold touch of apparitions. A mighty stone is laid upon his breast, and crushes him to the ground in helpless agony: mad bulls and tigers pursue his palsied footsteps: the unearthly shrieks and gibberish of hags, witches, and fiends float around him. [. . .]

In every instance, there is a sense of oppression and helplessness; and the extent to which these are carried, varies according to the violence of the paroxysm. The individual never feels himself a free agent; on the contrary, he is spellbound by some enchantment, and remains an unresisting victim for malice to work its will upon. He can neither breathe, nor walk, nor run with his wonted facility. If pursued by any imminent danger, he can hardly drag one limb after another; if engaged in combat, his blows are utterly ineffective; if involved in the fangs of any animal, or in the grasp of an enemy, extrication is impossible. He struggles, he pants, he toils, but it is all in vain: his muscles are rebels to the will, and refuse to obey its calls. [. . .]

Much of the horror experienced in this dreadful affection will depend upon the activity of the imagination, upon the condition of the body, and upon the previous state of mental exertion before going to sleep. If, for instance, we have been engaged in the perusal of such works as 'The Monk,' 'The Mysteries of Udolpho,'

---

[1] S. T. Coleridge, 'The Pains of Sleep', (1803), st. 2.

[2] A district near Argos in Greek mythology where Hercules killed the Lernean hydra, or many-headed monster.

or 'Satan's Invisible World Discovered;'[3] and if an attack of night-mare should supervene, it will be aggravated into sevenfold horror by the spectral phantoms with which our minds have been thereby filled. We will enter into all the fearful mysteries of these writings, which, instead of being mitigated by slumber, acquire an intensity which they never could have possessed in the waking state.

During night-mare, the deepness of our slumber varies much at different times. Sometimes we are in a state closely approximating upon perfect sleep; at other times we are almost completely awake; and it will be remarked, that the more awake we are, the greater is the violence of the paroxysm. I have frequently experienced the affection stealing upon me while in perfect possession of my faculties, and have undergone the greatest tortures, being haunted by spectres, hags, and every sort of phantom—having, at the same time, a full consciousness that I was labouring under incubus, and that all the terrifying objects around me were the creations of my own brain. This shows that the judgment is often only very partially affected, and proves also that night-mare is not merely a disagreeable dream, but a painful bodily affection. Were it nothing more than the former, we could not possess a knowledge of our condition, for, in simple visions, the reasoning powers are almost uniformly abolished, and we scarcely ever for a moment doubt the reality of what we see, or hear, or feel. In night-mare, this is often, perhaps generally, the case, but we frequently meet with instances, in which, during the worst periods of the fit, we possess our consciousness almost unimpaired. [. . .]

Some people are much more prone to incubus than others. Those whose digestion is healthy, whose minds are at ease, and who go supperless to bed, will seldom be troubled with it. Those, again, who keep late hours, study hard, eat heavy suppers, and are subject to bile, acid, or hypochondria, are almost sure to be more or less its victims. There are particular kinds of food, which pretty constantly lead to the same result, such as cheese, cucumbers, almonds, and whatever is hard to be digested. [. . .]

Certain diseases, also, are apt to induce it, such as asthma, hydrothorax, angina pectoris, and other varieties of dyspnœa.[4] Men are more subject to it than women, probably from their stomachs being more frequently disordered, and their minds more intently occupied. Sailors, in particular, owing to the hard and indigestible nature of their food, are its most frequent victims; and it is a general remark that it more frequently occurs at sea than on shore. I have no doubt that much of the superstitious belief of these men, in apparitions, proceeds from the phantoms which it calls into existence. Unmarried women are more annoyed with it, than those who are married; and the latter, when pregnant, have it

[3] Matthew Lewis, *The Monk* (1796), Ann Radcliffe, *The Mysteries of Udolpho* (1794): Gothic tales of terror. *Satan's Invisible World Discovered, Detailing the Strange Pranks Played by the Devil*, a popular chapbook published in Glasgow (n.d.).

[4] *Hydrothorax*: watery fluid in the chest cavity, pleurisy; *dyspnoea*: difficult breathing.

oftener than at other times. Persons who were extremely subject to the complaint in their youth, sometimes get rid of it when they reach the age of puberty, owing, probably, to some change in the constitution which occurs at this time. [. . .]

Why are literary men, deep thinkers, and hypochondriacs peculiarly subject to night-mare? The cause is obvious. Such individuals have generally a bad digestion: their stomachs are subject to acidity, and other functional derangements, and, therefore, peculiarly prone to dispose to the complaint. The sedentary life, and habits of intellectual or melancholy reflection in which they indulge, have a tendency not merely to disturb this organ, but to act upon the whole cerebral system: hence, they are far more subject to dreams of every kind than other people, in so far as their minds are more intently employed; and when, in sleep, they are pained by any physical endurance, the activity of their mental powers will naturally associate the most horrible ideas with such suffering, and produce incubus, and all its frightful accompaniments.

ON SLEEP, AND THE RELATIONS OF DREAMING AND INSANITY

Henry Holland, *Chapters on Mental Physiology* (London: Longman, Brown, Green and Longmans, 1852), 78–9, 90–4, 113–15, 125–8.

Holland's Chapters on Mental Physiology *was revised and expanded from* Medical Notes and Reflections *(1840), and while not intended to be a coherent treatise, was one of the most influential psychological studies to be published in the mid-nineteenth century. These extracts are taken from the chapters 'On sleep' and 'On the relations of sleep, dreaming, insanity, etc.'; other chapters included 'The effects of mental attention on bodily organs', 'Mental consciousness in relation to time and succession', and 'On the memory as affected by age and disease'.*

ON SLEEP

It concerns not less the physician than the metaphysical inquirer, to learn all the conditions of this remarkable function of life, and the causes by which they are modified. Remarkable it may fitly be called; for what more singular than that nearly a third part of existence should be passed in a state thus far separate from the external world!—a state in which consciousness and sense of identity are scarcely maintained; where memory and reason are equally disturbed; and yet, with all this, where the fancy works variously and boldly, creating images and impressions which are carried forwards into waking life, and blend themselves deeply and strongly with every part of our mental existence. It is the familiarity with this great function of our nature which prevents our feeling how vast is the mystery it involves; how closely interpreting all the phenomena of mental derangement, whencesoever produced; and, yet further, how singularly shadowing forth to our conception the greater and more lasting changes the mind may undergo without loss of its individuality. [. . .]

In thus, too, following the various states and acts of sleeping, through their relation to those of waking existence, and tracing the gradations from one into the other, we obtain results of the same precise and practical kind as those derived from pursuing the natural and healthy functions of mind into the different forms of insanity and mental disorder. Each part of these topics, so considered, illustrates every other; furnishing suggestions which could not be derived from any other source.

In this manner, again, of viewing sleep—not as one, but a series of complex and ever-varying states—we find best explanations of those singular conditions of trance, mesmeric sleep, catalepsy, &c., which have served at all times to perplex the world by the strange breach they seem to make between the bodily and mental functions; by their unexpectedness in some cases; and by the peculiar agency producing them in others. The latter circumstance, especially, serves to disguise from us their real relation to other and more familiar affections of the nervous system. As respects magnetic sleep or trance, in particular, whatever its shape or degree, there is no authenticated fact making it needful to believe that any influence is received from without; beyond those impressions on the senses and imaginations, which are capable in certain persons and temperaments of exciting unwonted or disordered actions throughout every part of the nervous system, and especially in the sensorial functions. The whole scope of the question is manifestly comprised in this single point. [. . .]

All that relates to dreaming is of course subordinate to the general idea we have taken of the nature of sleep. [. . .] There is but one question to which I will allude, from its connexion with the inquiry into the physical conditions of sleep,—viz. why some dreams are well remembered, others not at all, or very imperfectly? Two causes, at least, may be conjectured here. One is, that in the former instance the sleep is really less complete in kind—that peculiar condition of brain less marked, upon which the imperfection of memory, if not also the exclusion of sensations, appears to depend. Another is, that the images and thoughts forming some dreams are actually stronger and deeper in their impression than those of others;—an expression too vague for use, were it not that we are obliged equally to apply it to the more common diversity of waking states, upon which the memory so much depends for all that regard its promptitude and completeness. The combination of these circumstances, with others perhaps less obvious, affords as much explanation as we can attain without more complete knowledge of the proximate causes of sleep. To the first probably we may look for interpretation of the old notion of the *'somnia vera'*[1] of approaching day. The physical state of sleep is then less perfect;—trains of thought suggested, follow more nearly the course of waking associations—and the memory retains them, while earlier and more confused dreams are wholly lost to the mind.

The latter, however, though lost at the moment, leave traces which, like the memory of waking acts, are capable of being restored at a more remote time by new associations. There are few who have not occasionally felt certain vague and fleeting impressions of a past state of mind, of which the recollection cannot by any effort take a firm hold, or attach it to any distinct points of time or place;— something which does not link itself to any one part of life, yet is felt to belong to the identity of the being. These are not improbably the shades of former dreams; the consciousness, from some casual association, wandering back into that strange world of thoughts and feelings in which it has existed during some antecedent time of sleep, without memory of it at the moment, or in the interval since. A fervid fancy might seek a still higher source for this phenomenon, and poetry adopt such; but the explanation is probably that just given. [. . .]

ON THE RELATIONS OF DREAMING, INSANITY, ETC.

[. . .] If it were an object to obtain a description of insanity, which might apply to the greatest number of cases of such disorder, I believe this would be found in the conditions which most associate it with dreaming; viz., the loss, partial or complete, of power to distinguish between unreal images created within the sensorium and the actual perceptions drawn from the external senses, thereby giving to the former the semblance and influence of realities—and secondly, the alteration or suspension of that faculty of mind by which we arrange and associate the perceptions and thoughts successively coming before us.

Though this general description will by no means apply to all that is termed mental derangement, particularly to the various cases of moral insanity, yet, from the extensive influence of the causes denoted in it, there is much reason for their careful consideration—and particularly as they strikingly illustrate those gradations from the sound to the unsound mind, which I have mentioned as affording the best basis for every part of this inquiry. [. . .]

Much has been written on the subject of spectral illusions; and not without reason, from their strange and almost mysterious nature—from the seeming

---

[1] True dreams.

warrant they give to the wildest tales of credulity—and yet further, from the link they form in the chain betwixt sound reason and madness. Without repeating instances which have become familiar, I may remark that these singular phenomena—while connected on the one side with dreaming, delirium, and insanity—are related on the other, by a series of gradations, with the most natural and healthy functions of the mind. From the recollected images of objects of sense, which the volition, rationally exercised, places before our consciousness for the purposes of thought, and which the reason duly separates from the realities around us; we have a gradual transition, under different states of the sensorium, to those spectral images of illusions which come unbidden into the mind; dominate alike over the senses and reason; and either by their intensity or duration, produce disorder in the intellectual functions, and in all the actions depending thereon. [. . .]

I have spoken at length on that rational theory of sleep, by which it is regarded as a series of ever-fluctuating states; varying not only in general intensity, but even more remarkably in the degree in which different mental functions are under its influence at the same moment of time. This view, which more happily than any other explains the various aspects of sleep and dreaming, is that also which we may best follow in reasoning upon their connexion with permanent states of mental disorder.

In many points, indeed, the phenomena both of dreaming and insanity find more illustration from the waking moods of mind than is generally supposed. Dreams appear inconsecutive in the series of impressions and thoughts which compose them; and are so in fact in different degrees, according to the varying condition of sleep. But let any one follow with consciousness or immediate recollection the ramblings and transitions of the waking state, when the mind is not bound down to any one subject, and no strong impressions are present to the senses—and he will often find these no less singular, abrupt, and rapid in change; though the effect of such irregularity is here subordinate to certain regulating causes, which are absent during sleep. [. . .]

Another connexion between these several states is that afforded by the curious phenomena of reverie, trance, or cataleptic ecstasy; where, with the external senses as much closed as in perfect sleep, it would seem that the intellectual and voluntary powers are sometimes exercised much more clearly and consecutively, yet not under the same relation to consciousness and memory, as in the waking state. Though the evidence as to these extraordinary cases is much obscured by fiction, there is quite enough that is authentic to give them place among the most remarkable forms of sensorial disorder. Here, however, we may still follow out the connexion with the more common phenomena of mind. Reverie, in this medical sense, is but a higher degree of that which we call such in ordinary language; or what is still more usually termed absence of mind. And this again is merely the excess of the condition, common to all and of constant occurrence; in which the consciousness is detached for a time from objects of sense actually present to the organs, concentrating itself upon trains of thought and feeling within;—a condition which belongs to and characterises man as an intellectual being.

A THEORY OF DREAMING

George Henry Lewes, *The Physiology of Common Life*, 2 vols. (London: William Blackwood and Sons, 1859–60), ii. 366–72.

This extract comes after an extended discussion of 'The mind and brain', and 'Our senses and sensation', in which Lewes, arguing against eighteenth-century sensationist philosophy, which, following Locke, suggested that all knowledge is gained through the medium of the five senses, stresses 'the strange blending of Thought in the act of Perception' (p. 343), and maintains that in addition to the five senses themselves, 'there is a vast class of sensations derived through the Muscles and Viscera, sensations not less specific, not less important, than those of the eye and ear' (p. 345). While he is drawing on existing work, Lewes is using dreaming as a crucial example in his expanded and dynamic theory of sensation.

To understand Dreaming, we must try and discover what the action of the brain would be under such conditions as are present in sleep; and we can only do so by analogies drawn from our waking experience, coupled with a correct interpretation of nervous action in general. For example, in our waking condition, we are familiar with what has been styled *subjective* sensations; that is to say, we *see* objects very vividly, where no such objects exist; we *hear* sounds of many kinds, where none of their external causes exist; we *taste* flavours in an empty mouth; we *smell* odours, where no volatile substance is present; and we *feel* prickings or pains in limbs which have been amputated. These are actual, not imaginary, sensations. They are indistinguishable from the sensations caused by actual contact of the objects with our organs. They are sometimes so intense, or accompanied by a cerebral excitement which so completely domineers over the controlling suggestions of other senses, that they produce Hallucinations. And as it is the inevitable tendency of our nature to connect every sensation with an external cause—to project it outside of us, so to speak,—we should never think of doubting that every one of these subjective sensations had a corresponding object, did not the suggestions of some *other* sense control this idea. A man feels prickings in his amputated fingers, but he sees that the fingers are not there, and, consequently, he knows that his sensation is deceptive. [. . .] In the state of cerebral excitement named Hallucination, this confrontation is *disregarded*; in the state of cerebral isolation named Dreaming, this confrontation is *impossible*: the first condition is one in which the cerebral activity completely domineers over the excitations from without; the second condition is one in which the cerebral activity, though feeble, is entirely isolated from external excitations—thus, in both cases, the cerebral reflexes are undisturbed, uncontrolled by reflexes from Sense.

It is the fact that sensations may be subjective—in other words, that they may arise from internal stimuli no less than from external stimuli, and *must* arise whenever the centres are excited: it is this fact which gives us the clue to Dreaming. The avenues of Sense are closed in Sleep, but the sensational centres may be reached from within. That Law of Sensibility, whereby every sensation discharges itself either in a reflex-action or a reflex-feeling (or in both together), and whereby every centre, once stimulated, must inevitably stimulate some other, gives us the explanation why subjective sensations may arise in sleep, or waking, and why they must stimulate cerebral action. Moreover, the external senses have not their avenues completely closed in sleep; and a sound will be heard by the sleeper, though dimly; a light will be seen, or a touch felt. These dim sensations are reflected in his dreams. The coldness of a touch will cause him perhaps to dream that he has grasped a corpse; the rattling of the windows will suggest a storm, or a battle. There is a story told of a lady who dreamt that her servant was coming to murder her; she opened her eyes in terror, and saw the servant at her bedside, knife in hand! The explanation of this is, probably, that she heard in sleep the creaking of the footsteps on the stairs, or the opening of the door; and this sensation, which might have suggested any one of a thousand different trains of thought, happened to suggest (perhaps because the idea was not unfamiliar to her mind) the idea of the servant's intention to murder her. [. . .]

If we reflect that the nervous centres must be incessantly called into activity, either through the imperfectly-closed channels of the Five Senses, or through the Systemic Senses, and that these centres, once excited, must necessarily play on each other—and if we reflect farther, that the sensational and ideational activities thus stimulated operate under very different conditions, and in very different conjunctions, during sleep, we shall be at no loss to understand both the incoherence and the coherence of dreams—the perfect congruity of certain trains of thought amid the most absurd incongruities. The coherence of dreams results from the succession of associated ideas; the train of thought follows very much the course it would follow in waking moments, at least when uncontrolled by reference to external things—as in Reverie. The incoherence results from this train being interrupted or diverted from its course by the suggestion of some other train, either arising by the laws of association, or from the stimulus of some new sensation. And because in Dreams, as in Reverie, we do not pause on certain suggestions, do not recur to them, and reflect on them, but let one rapidly succeed another, like shadows chasing each other over a cornfield, we take little or no heed of any incongruities. It is constantly said that in dreams nothing surprises us. I think this is a mistake. Nothing *arrests* us; but every incongruity surprises us, at least as much in dreams as in reveries. I am distinctly conscious of this in my own experience. If when I dream that I am in a certain place, conversing with a certain person, I am also aware that the place suddenly becomes another place, and the person has a very different appearance, a slight surprise is felt as the difference is noted, but my dream is not arrested; I accept the new facts, and go on quite content with them, just as in reverie the mind passes instantaneously from London to India, and the persons vanish to give place to very different persons, without once interrupting the imaginary story. In dreams no perception is confronted with actual objects; no ideas are confronted with present existences. The waves of sensation and of thought succeed each other, and are interrupted, broken, diverted by the fresh streams of sensation constantly pouring in from the changing states of the system. This interruption is to some extent controlled in waking moments by the presence of objects both to the senses and the mind; yet even the presence of objects, and the energetic resolution which a strong motive will give, will not prevent the most steadfast mind from continually wandering, although the mind may be recalled from its wanderings to the subject originally occupying it. [. . .] If when I am working out some plan, or thinking of some problem, the thoughts wander away, lured by some accidental association, they are soon recalled again by the suggestions of the paper, portfolio, desk, or even by the very attitude in which I am sitting, and I recommence. But, asleep, this recall would never take place. The objects are not there to suggest the requisite thoughts. The sensations I receive are carried along with my dream, each succeeding sensation or idea having a diverging influence; and thus a dream is never long, never very coherent. If the reader wishes to understand this operation of the mind, let him attend to the fluctuating stream of thought which passes through his brain as he lies awake in bed, with his eyes closed, and in perfect stillness; he will soon be aware of the influence which must be exercised by the presence of external objects in determining the direction of his thoughts.

DREAMS, AS ILLUSTRATIONS OF INVOLUNTARY CEREBRATION

Frances Power Cobbe, *Darwinism in Morals and Other Essays* (London: Williams and Norgate, 1872), 336–8, 361–2.

Cobbe starts this piece (also reprinted from Macmillan's Magazine, *April 1871) by referring back to her article on 'Unconscious cerebration' (see above), noting that 'the large number of letters and friendly criticism which my first paper called forth have . . . encouraged me to pursue the subject by showing how much interest is felt in its popular treatment' (p. 335). These extracts are taken from the first and final parts of the essay; after discussing the mythic quality of many dreams, she returns to the question she raised before, of whether dreams (where moral sense is usually absent) are expressions of our 'deeper selves'.*

Dreams are to our waking thoughts much like echoes to music; but their reverberations are so partial, so varied, so complex, that it is almost in vain we seek among the notes of consciousness for the echoes of the dream. If we could by any means ascertain on what principle our dreams for a given night are arranged, and why one idea more than another furnishes their cue, it would be comparatively easy to follow out the chain of associations by which they unroll themselves afterwards; and to note the singular ease and delicacy whereby subordinate topics, recently wafted across our minds, are seized and woven into the network of the dream. But the reason why from among the five thousand thoughts of the day, we revert at night especially to thoughts number 2, and 4, instead of to thoughts number 3, and 6, or any other in the list, is obviously impossible to conjecture. We can but observe that the echo of the one note has been caught, and of the others lost amid the obscure caverns of the memory. [. . .]

How does the brain treat its theme when it has got it? Does it drily reflect upon it, as we are wont to do awake? Or does it pursue a course wholly foreign to the laws of waking thoughts? It does, I conceive, neither one nor the other, but treats its theme, whenever it is possible to do so, according to a certain very important, though obscure, law of thought, whose action we are too apt to ignore. We have been accustomed to consider the myth-creating power of the human mind as one specially belonging to the earlier stages of growth of society and of the individual. It will throw, I think, a rather curious light on the subject if we discover that this instinct exists in every one of us, and exerts itself with more or less energy through the whole of our lives. In hours of waking consciousness, indeed, it is suppressed, or has only the narrowest range of exercise, as in the tendency, noticeable in all persons not of the very strictest veracity, to supplement an incomplete anecdote with explanatory incidents, or to throw a slightly known story into the dramatic form, with dialogues constructed out of their own consciousness. But such small play of the myth-making faculty is nothing compared to its achievements during sleep. The instant that daylight and common sense are excluded, the fairy-work begins. At the very least half our dreams (unless I greatly err) are nothing else than myths formed by unconscious cerebration on the same approved principles, whereby Greece and India and Scandinavia gave to us the stories which we were once pleased to set apart as 'mythology' proper. Have we not here, then, evidence that there is a real law of the human mind causing us constantly to compose ingenious fables explanatory of the phenomena around us,—a law which only sinks into abeyance in the waking hours of persons in whom the reason has been highly cultivated, but which resumes its sway even over their well-tutored brains when they sleep?* [. . .]

Take it how we will, I think it remains evident that in dreams (except those belonging to the class of nightmare wherein the will is partially awakened) we are in a condition of entire passivity; receiving impressions indeed from the work which is going on in our brains, but incurring no fatigue thereby, and exempted from all sense of moral responsibility as regards it. The instrument on which we are wont to play has slipped from our loosened grasp, and its secondary and almost equally wondrous powers have become manifest. It is not only a finger-organ, but a *self-acting* one; which, while we lie still and listen, goes over, more or less perfectly, and with many a quaint wrong note and variation, the airs which we performed on it yesterday, or long ago.

Is this instrument *ourselves*? Are *we* quite inseparable from this manufactory of thoughts? If it never worked except by our volition and under our control, then, indeed, it might be difficult to conceive of our consciousness apart from it. But every night a different lesson is taught us. The brain, released from its bit and rein, plays like a colt turned to pasture, or, like the horse of the miller, goes round from left to right to relieve itself from having gone round from right to left all the

---

* A correspondent has kindly sent me the following interesting remarks on the above:—'When dropping asleep some nights ago I suddenly started awake with the thought on my mind, "Why I was *making* a dream!" I had detected myself in the act of inventing a dream. Three or four impressions of scenes and events which had passed across my mind during the day were present together in my mind, and the effort was certainly being made, but not by my fully conscious will, to arrange them so as to form a continuous story. They had actually not the slightest connexion, but a process was evidently going on in my brain by which they were being united into one scheme or plot. Had I remained asleep until the plot had been matured, I presume my waking sensation would have been that I had had an ordinary dream. But perhaps through the partial failure of the unconscious effort at a plan, I woke up just in time to catch a trace of the 'unconscious cerebration' as it was vanishing before the full light of conscious life. I accordingly propounded a tentative theory to my friends, that the brain uniting upon one thread the fancies and memories present at the same time in the mind, is really what takes place in dreams—a sort of faint shadow of the mind's natural craving for and effort after system and unity. Your explanation of dreams, by reference to the "myth-making tendency," seems to be so nearly in accord with mine that I venture to write on the subject.'

day before. Watching these instinctive sports and relaxations by which we benefit but in whose direction we have no part, do we not acquire the conviction that
the dreaming brain-self is not the true self for whose moral worthiness we strive,
and for whose existence after death alone we care? 'We are of the stuff which
dreams are made of.'[1] Not wholly so, O mighty poet-philosopher! In that 'stuff'
there enters not the noblest element of our nature; that Moral Will which allies
us, not to the world of passing shadows, but to the great Eternal Will, in whose
Life it is our hope that we shall live for ever.

THE DREAM AS A REVELATION

James Sully, 'The dream as a revelation' *Fortnightly Review*, 59 (March 1893)
354–65.

---

*James Sully was one of the leading figures in the emerging field of child psychology
in the late nineteenth century. However, his early work* Sensation and Intuition:
Studies in Aesthetics and Psychology *(1874) had established his reputation
as a psychological theorist and was admired by (amongst others) George Eliot
and G. H. Lewes. Although it is just outside our time-frame, we include substantial extracts from his later article, which develops Cobbe's ideas about the
collective myth-making aspect of dreams within an explicitly evolutionary
framework, in which 'like some palimpsest, the dream discloses . . . traces of
an old and precious communication'. In* The Interpretation of Dreams
Freud *approvingly cites Sully's essay, particularly his image of the palimpsest
(*The Standard Edition of the Complete Works of Sigmund Freud, *ed.
James Strachey (London: The Hogarth Press), vol. iv (1900), 135 (note added
1909)).*

In the history of human ideas we meet with two opposite views of the
nature and significance of dreaming. The one attributes to it a degree of intelligence, of insight into things, vastly superior to that of waking cognition. The
extreme form of this idea invested the vision of the night with the awful dignity
of a supernatural revelation. The other view goes to the opposite extreme, and
dismisses dream-experiences as so much intellectual fooling, as:

[1] William Shakespeare, *The Tempest*, IV. i. 157–8. The actual quotation is 'We are such stuff/As
dreams are made on'.

> 'Children of an idle brain,
> Begot of nothing but vain phantasy.'[1]

The modern scientific theory of dreaming may be said to combine and to reconcile these antagonistic ideas. It recognises and seeks to account for the irrational
side of dream-life. At the same time it regards this life as an extension of human
experience, as a revelation of what would otherwise have never been known.

According to this theory, the form of mental activity which survives during
sleep is made what it is by the very special cerebral conditions of the sleeping
state itself. What these conditions precisely are physiology cannot as yet tell us,
though it is probable that they consist in the main in a greatly retarded circulation in the fine blood-vessels of the brain, and in a resulting increase of pressure
on the nervous substance. This new state of things excludes the perfect normal
action of the brain as a whole, and as a connected system of organs. It reduces
the complexity of this normal action to a comparative simplicity, a restricted or
isolated functioning of particular brain-tracts, which tracts happen to be stimulated during sleep, whether directly as the result of some agency supplied by a
particular local condition of the blood, or indirectly through the action of stimuli on the peripheral sense-organs.

As a result of this altered state of the 'organs of mind' we get a new pattern of
mental experience. The complicated web of thought and feeling of waking hours
becomes simplified. In place of a full reflective consciousness we have a rudimentary, fragmentary consciousness. In this respect the mental phenomena of
natural sleep are analogous to that greatly restricted pattern of consciousness
which is brought about by the hypnotic trance, as also to those truncated forms
of consciousness which result from certain varieties of brain disease, involving
the suppression of the functional activities of particular cerebral regions.

It seems natural at first to think of this transition from waking to sleeping consciousness as a degradation, as a reversion to a primitive infantile type of psy-
chosis, in which sensation and its immediate offspring, sensuous imagination,
are uncontrolled by the higher later-acquired functions—rational reflection,
moral self-control. There is, no doubt, a certain appropriateness in this way of
envisaging our dreams. There is a good deal of the *naïveté* of the child in our ways
of conceiving of things and of feeling about things during sleep. On entering
dreamland we leave much of the later and maturer intelligence behind us, and
survey the spectacle with the pristine directness, with the pure elemental emotions of little children.

Yet the change from waking to sleeping consciousness is less simple than the
figure of retrogression from mature to infantile experience would suggest. Even
the process of mental dissolution brought about by brain disease cannot, it is
said, be accurately described as a mere removal of the higher and later acquired

---

[1] William Shakespeare, *Romeo and Juliet*, I. iv. 97–8.

functions. And it is still less true of the reduction of consciousness during sleep. The dream may be a weakened mental activity, but it is a weakened activity of a mature kind, of a mind that has been formed by complex human experience. [. . .]

Still more striking than this prolongation of waking experience into our dreams is the carrying on of those habits of rational reflection and of moral self-criticism which have become so firmly woven into the mental tissue of educated men. It is often said that conscience slumbers when we dream. Yet I have in my sleep done a wrong action, recognised its wrongness, tried to excuse myself to myself, and finally rejected the excuse. Similarly the impulse to explain, to understand, frequently reappears in the dream-state. The explanation is often fanciful enough, no doubt, yet it is enough to show that the dreamer is still in a sense a 'rational animal.' [. . .]

Yet, [. . .] the dream is the outcome of a maimed consciousness. When overtaken by sleep the mechanism of mind does not work as a co-ordinated whole, but only in a disjointed fashion. The mark of the vigorous, unimpaired intelligence is ability to grasp a number of facts at one and the same moment. This power is greatly weakened during sleep. I once had an uncanny feeling in my sleep that I was clutching somebody's arm. I remembered that I was alone, and racked my brain to discover who could be in my bed. On waking, I found that I was clasping my right wrist with my left hand. I had in my sleep become aware of the sensation in the clutching hand, but was apparently unequal to giving attention at the same moment to the sensation of the clutched hand. I suspect that the common dream experience of flying illustrates the same monopoly of consciousness by single impressions. Certain sensations, possibly those connected with the stretching of an arm or leg, or even with the movements of respiration, start the idea of aerial locomotion, and the idea realises itself in its blissful fulness, unchecked by the contradictory reports of the other sensations of the moment.

It is this same limitation of the area of consciousness which gives to dreaming its aspect of absurdity. A rational view of things is the result of a complex process of reflection, which again depends upon the instantaneous reinstatement of a whole cluster of experience-products. If, for example, I happen when awake to see my image in a glass, I instantly check the impulse to take the image for my real self by a rapid mental side glance at the cause of the appearance. Not so when dreaming: the impression now calls up merely the first and most obvious suggestion. Like children, we innocently take the appearance for what it seems to be. [. . .]

Closely connected with the loss of customary lines of association, is the suppression of that co-ordinative function by which impressions are fitted into a consistent series, into what we understand by an intelligible experience. Nothing is more striking in our dreams than the kaleidoscopic transformations, the new scene having no discoverable relation to its predecessor, yet being confusedly identified with it in the jumble of the nocturnal phantasmagoria. I once dreamt of seeing an intimate friend of my youth. Moved by a childish impulse of tenderness, I put out my hand to touch his face, and, lo, I found it to be a mosaic. The impression of the cold hard surface in place of the softness and warmth of the skin, brought no shock, and, what is odd, the initial caressing feeling persisted. One may easily see that in this dream the mind had lost is hold on all that we mean by the persistence and identity of external objects.

This simplification of the mature complex pattern of consciousness is at the same time a bringing to light of forces and tendencies which, under normal circumstances, are hidden under the superincumbent mass of the later and higher acquisitions. The newest conception of the brain is of a hierarchy of organs, the higher and later evolved seeming to control, and in a measure to repress, the functional activities of the lower and earlier. Translated into psychological language, this means that what is instinctive, primitive, elemental, in our mental life, is being continually overborne by the fruit of experience, by the regulative process of reflection. By throwing the higher centres *hors de combat* you may bring back the earlier state of things in which sensation, instinct, and a rudimentary animal intelligence have it all their own way. Sleep is one means of stupefying the supreme controlling organs. Hence in sleep we have a reversion to a more primitive type of experience, an upwelling in vigorous pristine abundance of sensation and impulse.

This unveiling during sleep of the more instinctive layers of our mental life may be seen in the leaping forth into full activity of some nascent and instantly inhibited impulse of thought or feeling of the waking hours. Thus a new name through its similarity to a familiar one may happen to start a train of ideas, which we at once check as irrelevant; or the perception or imagination of a thing may rouse a momentary desire which we repress as foolish or wrong. The next night these half-formed psychical tendencies, relieved of all restraint, work themselves out to their natural issue, and we dream irrationally or immorally as the case may be. Nor need the impulse thus attaining complete fulfilment in sleep be a degrading one. Southey tells us that he dreamt again and again of killing Bonaparte. George Sand, when a girl, more girl-like, dreamt that she took the tyrant in aerial flight to the top of the cupola of the Tuileries and remonstrated with him. We may assume, perhaps, that in each case the dream was the expansion and complete development of a vague fugitive wish of the waking mind.

And now, perhaps, the reader begins to see how the dream becomes a revelation. It strips the ego of its artificial wrappings and exposes it in its rude native nudity. It brings up from the dim depths of our sub-conscious life the primal, instinctive impulses, and discloses to us a side of ourselves which connects us with the great sentient world.

I may illustrate this emergence into the full light of consciousness of the deeper and customarily veiled strata of our nature in another way. It has often been observed that dreaming stands in a very close relation to the bodily life. The sensations by means of which we apprehend the existence of the several regions of our organism and their varying condition are greatly obscured during waking life through the preponderance of the 'objective consciousness,' as it has been called, the impressions supplied by external things. In sleep, however, this organic sentience grows intense and impressive. So much is this the case that some writers would regard dreaming in general as a kind of pictorial symbolism into which the exalted organic sensibility of sleep projects itself. Thus the frequent dreams of water, of burning or freezing, of vast cavernous spaces, of preternatural forms of motion, and so forth, may be supposed to have their origin in some altered condition of the bodily organs, giving rise to a marked change of organic sensations.

Here, again, we appear to see a reversion to a primitive phenomenon. Absorption in the bodily life is the characteristic of infancy before the growing intelligence has been attracted and held by the everchanging spectacle of the external world. It is probable that a child or an animal feels its hunger with an overpowering intensity of sensation, of which grown persons know next to nothing. A slight change of temperature is for the infant a stupendous calamity. When asleep we may be said to go back to this primitive animal immersion in bodily sensation. The all-important groundwork of our life once more engages our thought. We hear the heart beat, and feel the incoming and outgoing of the breath; we rejoice with the weary limb in its repose, with the chilled extremity warmed by an effusion of generous blood, or, on the other hand, suffer with the overladen stomach or with the cramp-seized muscle. [. . .]

Our dreams, by restoring the bodily factor of consciousness to its primitive supremacy, may properly be described as revelations. By noting this aspect of our dreams, we may learn much concerning that organic substrate of our conscious personality which links us on to the animal series. [. . .]

It is probable that many of the strange faces, scenes, and occurrences of our dream-life may be handed down from a remote past, though not recognised as recollections. [. . .] I suspect that we are much less creators in our dreams than we are apt to suppose, and that the rush of apparently new imagery which sometimes threatens to whelm the spirit, is but a sudden tidal return of the swiftly receding past.

This reversion of consciousness to the remote half-forgotten past finds its explanation in a temporary disabling of that portion of brain-function which answers to our later mental acquisitions. That when asleep we do forget much of our recent experience is certain. It is quite astonishing to note how profound is the oblivescence of late events, even when dreaming of things which should, one supposes, directly remind us of them. This is clearly illustrated in our dreams of the dead, in which awareness of the fact of death wholly disappears, or reduces itself to a vague feeling of something delightfully wonderful in the restored presence. It is this temporary withdrawal of the pressure of the newer experiences which allows the overlaid strata of old experience to come to light again. If, as we have supposed, the brain is a system of parts, the functional activity of any one of which interferes to some extent with the complete vigorous activity of the others, we may say that these revivals of half-effaced memories is due to the resumption of certain forms of cerebral activity which have been obstructed by later developed forms. [. . .]

In the case of many persons, for a certain period at least, this reversion in dreaming to the experience of early life is recurrent and habitual. To this extent dreams constitute a second revived life, which intersects and interrupts our normal waking life.

Here we find the dream touching analogically another and more distinctly abnormal region of human experience. Psychology has of late occupied itself much with the curious phenomena of double or alternating personality. By this is meant the recurrent interruption of the normal state by the intrusion of a secondary state, in which the thoughts, feelings, and the whole personality become other than they were. This occasional substitution of a new for the old self is sometimes spontaneous, the result of brain-trouble; sometimes it is artificially brought about in specially susceptible persons by hypnotizing them. In the hypnotic trance it is possible to blot out from the subject's mind all that has occurred in his experience since a particular date and, in this way to restore the childish self. In the case of certain hysterical subjects, the hypnotic trance may disinter more than one abnormal personality which are buried and forgotten during the normal state. [. . .]

The proposition that the soundest of men undergo changes of personality may well strike the reader as paradoxical; yet the paradox is only on the surface. Although we talk of ourselves as single personalities, as continuing to be the same as we were, a little thought suffices to show that this is not absolutely true. Just as our bodily framework undergoes material re-formation, so the pattern of our consciousness is ever being re-formed and transformed. As the years go by old fancies, beliefs, emotions tend to drop out and new ones to take their place. I may dimly remember the fact that as a youth I felt about nature, music, religious subjects in a particular way, but I know I do not now feel in this way. Under the conditions of a happy development these changes are gradual, though most of us probably can refer a part of them to memorable crises, catastrophic shocks in our experience. However this be, when we sit down and quietly glance back over the succession of our years, we may see that by making the interval wide enough we confront what is, in a large part of its characteristic modes of consciousness, a new, a foreign personality.

Now our dreams are a means of conserving these successive personalities. When asleep we go back to the old ways of looking at things and of feeling about them, to impulses and activities which long ago dominated us, in a way which seems impossible in the waking hours, when the later self is in the ascendant. In this way the rhythmic change from wakefulness to sleep effects a recurrent reinstatement of our 'dead selves,' an overlapping of the successive personalities, the series of whose doings and transformations constitutes our history.

There is one other way in which dreams may become an unveiling of what is customarily hidden, viz., by giving freer play to individual characteristics and tendencies. It is a commonplace that our highly artificial form of social life tends greatly to restrict the sphere of individuality. Our peculiar tendencies get sadly crossed and driven back in the daily collision with our surroundings. Much that is deepest and most vital in us may in this way be repressed and atrophied. The particular personality which we have developed, which is all that our friends know of us, is a kind of selection from among many possible personalities, a selection effected by the peculiar conditions of our 'environment.'

Now these undeveloped, rudimentary selves belong to the hidden substrata of our mental being. Hence, according to what has been said above, they are very apt to disclose themselves when sleep has stupefied the dominant personality. A friend of mine tells me, and I believe him, that he is perfectly matter-of-fact and unimaginative during the waking state, but that when asleep he indulges in the wildest flights of fancy. Thus he once dreamt of visiting the Crystal Palace with some friends, of their all leaving their bodies outside, and of his finding, on going out, that somebody had gone off with his body. In another dream he met a stranger to whom he felt strongly attracted, and was afterwards told that the interesting person was himself as he was to be three years hence. Such quaint freaks of phantasy in one habitually unimaginative seem to point to the existence of germs of faculty which have never in this limited world of ours found their external developing conditions, their proper nutritive soil. [. . .]

It would seem then, after all, that dreams are not the utter nonsense they have been said to be by such authorities as Chaucer, Shakespeare, and Milton. The chaotic aggregations of our night-fancy have a significance and communicate new knowledge. Like some letter in cipher, the dream-inscription when scrutinised closely loses its first look of balderdash and takes on the aspect of a serious, intelligible message. Or, to vary the figure slightly, we may say that, like some palimpsest, the dream discloses beneath its worthless surface-characters traces of an old and precious communication.

I am well aware that most of this unveiling of the self is unpleasant and humiliating, and I am not surprised that sober-minded men should dismiss dreams from their mind as quickly as possible. Yet our slight study of the phenomena suggests that this is by no means necessary. If now and again we catch ourselves when asleep supinely obeying some gross instinct we light at other times on worthier selves. We do better things as well as worse things in our dreams than we are wont to do in the waking state. The stripping off of life's artificial swathings, if it sometimes gives too lively play to appetite, will also give free bound to some nobler impulse, as the perfect candour, the unstinting generosity of youth.

Whatever the moral dignity of these dream-disclosures may be, there is no doubt as to their having at their best a high hedonic and æsthetic value. In the revival of young experience, the delicious fulness of childish sensation, the dreamer may be said to enjoy a prolongation of life's golden prime. He sees things with the glad dilated eyes of the child artist, and feels once more the masterful spell of earth's beauty. [. . .]

The pessimist tells us that the world is growing sadder and sadder as it sees through its happy illusions. This announcement sounds so doleful just because the author has omitted to add that men may go on drawing comfort and refreshment from illusions after they have been recognised. We can still get a delicious thrill out of a good story or a fine dramatic show, even though we abandoned the simple belief in their full reality with our first years. In our dreams we attain to a more perfect state of illusion than when we half lose ourselves over a novel or before the stage of a theatre. Indeed, from a philosophical point of view, it is difficult to say in what respect a dream is less a direct apprehension of the real than a perception of waking life. This being so, what does it matter that when we are illumined by the cold, penetrating light of day we see our dreams to be pretty unsubstantial bubbles, the creations of a sportive-brain? Such intervals of scientific disillusion need not deter the wise man from repairing to the nocturnal phantasmagoria as a source of preternatural delight, as an outlet from the narrow and somewhat gloomy enclosure of the matter-of-fact world, giving swift transition into the large and luminous spaces of the imagination.

3. Double Consciousness

THE CASE OF MARY REYNOLDS

Robert Macnish, *The Philosophy of Sleep* (1830), 3rd edn. (Glasgow, W. R. M'Phun: 1836), 187–8.

The case of the young American woman Mary Reynolds became one of the most famous instances of double or divided consciousness during the nineteenth century. Macnish's extended quotation of S. L. Mitchell's description of 'A double consciousness, or a duality of person in the same individual' (Medical Repository, 3 (Feb. 1816), 185–6) was widely cited in later discussions. These actively reinterpreted the case, arguing that Mary awoke to her 'second state' possessed of a mature consciousness, and emphasizing the dramatic difference in the personalities of the two Marys: the first quiet and sober, the second loquacious, witty, and fond of practical jokes. See, for example, W. S. Plumer, 'Mary Reynolds: A Case of Double Consciousness' in the American journal Harper's New Monthly Magazine, 20 (1860), 807–12.

A case was published in the Medical Repository, by Dr. Mitchell, who received the particulars of it from Major Ellicot, Professor of Mathematics in the United States Military Academy at West Point. The subject was a young lady, of a good constitution, excellent capacity, and well educated. 'Her memory was capacious and well stored with a copious stock of ideas. Unexpectedly, and without any forewarning, she fell into a profound sleep, which continued several hours beyond the ordinary term. On waking, she was discovered to have lost every trait of acquired knowledge. Her memory was *tabula rasa*[1]—all vestiges, both of words and things were obliterated and gone. It was found necessary for her to learn every thing again. She even acquired, by new efforts, the art of spelling, reading, writing, and calculating, and gradually became acquainted with the persons and objects around, like a being for the first time brought into

[1] A reference to Locke's famous description of the new-born infant's mind as a blank sheet of paper.

the world. In these exercises she made considerable proficiency. But after a few months, another fit of somnolency invaded her. On rousing from it, she found herself restored to the state she was in before the first paroxysm; but was wholly ignorant of every event and occurrence that had befallen her afterwards. The former condition of her existence she now calls the Old State, and the latter the New State; and she is as unconscious of her double character as two distinct persons are of their respective natures. For example, in her old state, she possesses all the original knowledge; in her new state, only what she acquired since. If a lady or gentleman be introduced to her in the old state, and *vice versa*, (and so of all other matters) to know them satisfactorily, she must learn them in both states. In the old state, she possesses fine powers of penmanship, while in the new, she writes a poor, awkward hand, having not had time or means to become expert. During four years and upwards, she has had periodical transitions from one of these states to the other. The alterations are always consequent upon a long and sound sleep. Both the lady and her family are now capable of conducting the affair without embarrassment. By simply knowing whether she is in the old or new state, they regulate the intercourse, and govern themselves accordingly.'

THE DUALITY OF THE MIND

Arthur Ladbroke Wigan, *A New View of Insanity: The Duality of the Mind proved by the Structure, Function and Diseases of the Brain, and by the Phenomena of Mental Derangement, and Shewn to be Essential to Moral Responsibility* (London: Longman, Brown, Green and Longman, 1844), 26–31.

Wigan's Duality of the Mind *was dedicated to Henry Holland, whose essay 'The brain as a double organ' first appeared in* Medical Notes and Reflections *in 1840. Wigan takes Holland's description to an extreme here in arguing for 'two distinct and separate cerebra'. However, as its full title implies, his argument through the book as a whole is to stress the possibilities of moral management. Describing how he was prompted to write the book on reading John Barlow's 'highly interesting little work',* On Man's Power over himself to Prevent or Control Insanity *(see Section IV on Insanity, below), he aims to reconcile physiological and moral interpretations of insanity within an overall Christian framework by stressing the ability of the dominant, moral brain to contain and control its potentially wayward other. In this extract he outlines his basic argument.*

I believe myself able to prove—

1. That each cerebrum is a distinct and perfect whole, as an organ of thought.
2. That a separate and distinct process of thinking or ratiocination may be carried on in each cerebrum simultaneously.
3. That each cerebrum is capable of a distinct and separate volition, and that these are very often opposing volitions.
4. That, in the healthy brain, one of the cerebra is almost always superior in power to the other, and capable of exercising control over the volitions of its fellow, and of preventing them from passing into acts, or from being manifested to others.
5. That when one of these cerebra becomes the subject of functional disorder, or of positive change of structure, of such a kind as to vitiate mind or induce insanity, the healthy organ can still, up to a certain point, control the morbid volitions of its fellow.
6. That this point depends partly on the extent of the disease or disorder, and partly on the degree of cultivation of the general brain in the art of self-government.
7. That when the disease or disorder of one cerebrum becomes sufficiently aggravated to defy the control of the other, the case is then one of the commonest forms of mental derangement or insanity; and that a lesser degree of discrepancy between the functions of the two cerebra constitutes the state of conscious delusion.
8. That in the insane, it is almost always possible to trace the intermixture of two synchronous trains of thought, and that it is the irregularly alternate utterance of portions of these two trains of thought which constitutes incoherence.
9. That of the two distinct simultaneous trains of thought, one may be rational and the other irrational, or both may be irrational; but that, in either case, the effect is the same, to deprive the discourse of coherence or congruity.

Even in furious mania, this double process may be generally perceived; often it takes the form of a colloquy between the diseased mind and the healthy one, and sometimes even resembles the steady continuous argument or narrative of a sane man, more or less frequently interrupted by a madman; but persevering with tenacity of purpose in the endeavour to overpower the intruder.

10. That when both cerebra are the subjects of disease, which is not of remittent periodicity, there are no lucid intervals, no attempt at self-control, and no means of promoting the cure; and that a spontaneous cure is rarely to be expected in such cases.

125

11. That however, where such mental derangement depends on inflammation, fever, gout, impoverished or diseased blood, or manifest bodily disease, it may often be cured by curing the malady which gave rise to it.

12. That in cases of insanity, not depending on structural injury, in which the patients retain the partial use of reason (from one of the cerebra remaining healthy or only slightly affected), the only mode in which the medical art can promote the cure beyond the means alluded to is by presenting motives of encouragement to the sound brain to exercise and strengthen its control over the unsound brain.

13. That the power of the higher organs of the intellect to coerce the mere instincts and propensities, as well as the power of one cerebrum to control the volitions of the other, may be indefinitely increased by exercise and moral cultivation; may be partially or wholly lost by desuetude or neglect; or, from depraved habits and criminal indulgence in childhood, and a general vicious education in a polluted moral atmosphere, may never have been acquired.

14. That one cerebrum may be entirely destroyed by disease, cancer, softening, atrophy, or absorption; may be *annihilated*, and in its place a yawning chasm; yet the mind remain complete and capable of exercising its functions in the same manner and to the same extent that one eye is capable of exercising the faculty of vision when its fellow is injured or destroyed; although there are some exercises of the brain, as of the eye, which are better performed with two organs than one. In the case of vision, the power of measuring distances for example, and in the case of the brain, the power of concentrating the thoughts upon one subject, deep consideration, hard study; but in this latter case, it is difficult to decide how far the diminished power depends on diminution of general vigour from formidable and necessarily fatal disease.

15. That a lesion or injury of both cerebra is incompatible with such an exercise of the intellectual functions, as the common sense of mankind would designate *sound mind*.

16. That from the apparent division of each cerebrum into three lobes, it is a natural and reasonable presumption that the three portions have distinct offices, and highly probable that the three great divisions of the mental functions laid down by phrenologists, are founded in nature; whether these distinctions correspond with the natural divisions is a different question, but the fact of different portions of the brain executing different functions, is too well established to admit of denial from any physiologist.

17. That it is an error to suppose the two sides of the cranium to be always alike, that on the contrary, it is rarely found that the two halves of the exterior surface exactly correspond; that indeed, in the insane, there is often a

notable difference—still more frequent in idiots, and especially in congenital idiots.

18. That the object and effect of a well-managed education are to establish and confirm the power of concentrating the energies of both brains on the same subject at the same time; that is, to make both cerebra carry on the same train of thought together, as the object of moral discipline is to strengthen the power of self-control; not merely the power of both intellectual organs to govern the animal propensities and passions, but the intellectual antagonism of the two brains, each (so to speak) a sentinel and security for the other while both are healthy; and the healthy one to correct and control the erroneous judgments of its fellow when disordered.

19. That it is the exercise of this power of compeling the combined attention of both brains to the same object, till it becomes easy and habitual, that constitutes the great superiority of the disciplined scholar over the self-educated man; the latter may perhaps possess a greater stock of useful knowledge, but set him to study a new subject, and he is soon outstripped by the other, who has acquired the very difficult accomplishment of *thinking of only one thing at a time*; that is, of concentrating the action of both brains on the same subject.

20. That every man is, in his own person, conscious of two volitions, and very often conflicting volitions, quite distinct from the government of the passions by the intellect; a consciousness so universal, that it enters into all figurative language on the moral feelings and sentiments, has been enlisted into the service of every religion, and forms the basis of some of them, as the Manichæan.

While the structure of the brain is considered as the structure of one organ only, there is not much hope of any improvement in our physiology. We know so little of the respective uses of parts in so complicated an organization, that we can form opinions of its functions only by observing the consequences of morbid changes of structure, and the connexion between changes of partial organs and changes of function; but while we consider the integrity of the whole mass of both cerebra as essential to the performance of offices which are proper to each, it is vain to expect that we shall make advance in the knowledge of the separate uses of separate parts. Had we treated the eye in the same manner, we should have contended that opacity of the crystalline lens could not impede vision, because we saw that vision remained when one lobe or hemisphere (or whatever we might call it) of THE EYE was obliterated. How much stronger would have been this illustration had the organs of vision (the two lobes of the eye we will suppose) been concealed from our view by a bony covering, their axes directed to one aperture, and cataract only to be recognised on dissection, after other morbid changes had taken place tending to mystify and obscure the judgment. I can fancy some teacher of anatomy holding up to ridicule the doctrine that transparency of the lens was necessary to vision, and shewing, in refutation of so absurd an assertion, one *lobe* of the eye completely opaque, yet the vision perfect to the last, when every one knew that the integrity of both lobes was essential to the performance of that function, and consequently no impediment to vision.

ON THE BRAIN AS A DOUBLE ORGAN

Henry Holland, *Chapters on Mental Physiology* (London: Longman, Brown, Green and Longmans, 1852), 185–9.

Holland first discussed mental duality as primarily a problem of disordered association and memory in his essay 'The brain as a double organ' in Medical Notes and Reflections *(see note on Wigan, above). This extract is taken from the more developed analysis in* Chapters in Mental Physiology, *which takes account of Wigan's work.*

It has been a familiar remark that in certain states of mental derangement, as well as in some cases of hysteria which border closely upon it, there appear, as it were, two minds; one tending to correct by more just perceptions, feelings, and volitions, the aberrations of the other; and the relative power of these influences varying at different times. Cases of this singular kind cannot fail to be in the recollection of every medical man. I have myself seen many such, in which there occurred great disorder of mind from this sort of double-dealing with itself. In some cases there would seem to be a double series of sensations; the real and unreal objects of sense impressing the individual so far simultaneously that the judgment and acts of mind are disordered by their concurrence. In other instances the incongruity is chiefly marked in the moral feelings,—an opposition far more striking than that of incongruous perceptions, and forming one of the most painful studies to the observer of mental disease. We have often occasion to witness acts of personal violence committed by those who have at the very time a keen sense of the wrong, and remorse in committing it; and revolting language used by persons whose natural purity of taste and feeling are shown in the horror they feel and express of the sort of compulsion under which they are labouring.

Admitting the truth of this description, as attested by experience, the fact may be explained in some cases, as we have seen, by the presence to the mind of real and unreal objects of sense, each successively the subject of belief,—this phenomenon itself possibly depending on the doubleness of the brain and of the parts ministering to perception, though we cannot obtain any certain proof that such is the case. But this explanation will not adequately apply to the instances where complete trains of thought are perverted and deranged, while others are preserved in sufficiently natural course to become a sort of watch upon the former. Here we have no conjecture to hazard other than that of supposing the two states of mind to be never strictly coincident in time;—a view in some sort sanctioned by what observation tells us of the inconceivable rapidity with which the mind actually shifts its state from one train of thought or feeling to another. [I have] shown our inability to measure by time these momentary passages of mental existence; crowding upon each other, and withal so interwoven into one chain, that consciousness, while it makes us aware of unceasing change, tells of no breach of continuity.

If the latter explanation be admitted, then the cases just mentioned come under the description of what has been termed *double consciousness*; where the mind passes by alternation from one state to another, each having the perception of external impressions and appropriate trains of thought, but not linked together by the ordinary gradations, or by mutual memory. I have seen one or two singular examples of this kind, but none so extraordinary as have been recorded by other authors. Their relations to the phenomena of sleep, of somnambulism, reverie, and insanity, abound in conclusions, of the deepest interest to every part of the mental history of man.

Even admitting, however, that these curiously contrasted states of mind are never strictly simultaneous, it is still a question whence their close concurrence is derived. And, in the absence of any certainty on this very obscure subject, we may reasonably, perhaps, look to that part of our constitution in which manifest provision is made for unity of result from parts double in structure and function. This provision we know in many cases to be disturbed by accident, disease, or other less obvious cause; and though we cannot so well show this in regard to the higher faculties of mind, as in the instance of the senses and voluntary power, yet it is conceivable that there are cases where the two sides of the brain minister differently to these functions, so as to produce incongruity, where there should be identity or individuality of result.*

---

* It may be fitting to mention here a work of the late Dr. Wigan, published in 1844, entitled the 'Duality of the Mind,' and dedicated to me, in reference to the subject of this chapter. In this volume, the ingenious author has adopted, as the foundation of his reasoning, the various facts here stated; and has added numerous instances to the same effect. But he is much bolder in his inference from them; and plunges at once, as the title of his work implies, into the theory of a real *doubleness* or duality of mind; expressing it as a discovery which I might have reached had I ventured a little further in the same track. I can see no foundation for such doctrine. I believe that the suggestions offered above, though falling far short of an explanation of this obscure subject, yet come nearer to it than the opinion just alluded to. Surrounded as we are by mysteries, many of them insuperable by human reason, it is right to seek for, and record, whatever we can authenticate as facts; but unwise and injurious to push speculation beyond the closest induction from such observations.

It is not easy to carry the argument beyond this form of simple question, without relinquishing that strict rule of inquiry which alone can be rightly pursued. But there are other points connected with this topic, of much interest to the physiology of man, and giving greater scope to research. For example, we have cause to suppose that there is in infancy a progressive education of the organs of sense, correcting the original perceptions they afford, defining the relations of the several senses, and giving unity of effect to impressions made on double organs. Instances in proof of this are familiar to observation. In like manner the education of the voluntary powers may be said not merely to extend the influence of the will to new muscular movements, but also to concentrate and individualise the powers of the mind in acts of volition, separating them more entirely from the involuntary actions of the same parts. And carrying the argument further, we may suppose that the faculties of memory and combination are subject to the like education, tending always to give more proper and perfect unity to these functions than belongs to them in the outset of life, and thereby to establish more completely the conscious individuality of the being.

DREAMS AND DOUBLE CONSCIOUSNESS

John Addington Symonds, *Sleep and Dreams* (London: Longman, Brown, 1851), 23, 25–8.

In this pamphlet, based on two lectures given to the Bristol Literary and Philosophical Institution, Symonds echoes many of his contemporaries by explaining double consciousness as primarily a disorder of association and disrupted memory, rather than as having an organic cause.

I now return to the consideration of double consciousness. We have seen that the apparatus of speech may awake and act in correspondence with the ideas of the dream only, or with those suggested by sounds, the sense of hearing being also awake; and also that the locomotive apparatus may be in action without the sense of vision, as in the case of the somnambulist who comes in contact with outward objects; or with a complete power of vision. This latter state abuts immediately on the present topic. The person sees, hears, walks, has, in fact, the ordinary attributes of the waking state, and yet is not awake. He may pass from that condition into ordinary slumber, and then wake up like other people; or the transition may be from the morbid condition to the ordinary waking state without intermediate sleep. This is double consciousness. [. . .]

The healthy waking of the mind is the resumption of the form of consciousness which existed previously to sleep. The objects before the eyes have the same aspect and the same associations; the thoughts return to the same channel; the occupations of the previous day, and those projected for the ensuing day, are remembered, and there is no confusion of personal identity. But a man may awake up to the outward world, and that world is all changed to him. His eyes are open, and his ears catch every sound, and he can feel and handle. But, alas! how delicate and fragile a thing is perception! All has gone wrong. He is awake, and he looks around his chamber in which he has every day, for years, hailed the morning sunshine. It has once more lighted up his household gods; and dear familiar faces are anxiously bent on those eyes which look, and yet have no speculation in them; and gentle voices hail, and condole, and soothe, and number up many a word and name, which but the day before would have been key-notes to his heart's sweetest harmonies; but all is now jarred and 'jangled out of tune.'[1] He looks out on a new world projected from his own inner being. By a melancholy power, a fatal gift, of appropriating and assimilating the real objects perceived by his senses, he takes possession of them, nay, disembodies them, and fuses them into his imaginary creation. And as for those beloved beings who fondly think themselves linked with all his strongest and most tender memories, he takes no more note of them than as they swell that strange fantastic pageant which floats before his bewildered fancy; they are mere *dramatis personæ* in the mad farce or tragedy which his poor brain is weaving. They are all shadows; no more the dear flesh-and-blood realities of his heart; they are metamorphosed into the unsubstantial figments of a distempered imagination.

What is the explanation of all this? It is, that all things relatively to the percipient mind *are* as they *seem*:—

'Nothing *is*; but all things *seem*.'

For to seem, is to be seen in a certain relation. No outward sensation is perfectly isolated; it is always connected with some other, past or present, from which it may take, or to which it may impart its hue, and tone, and character. Perception, as distinguished by metaphysicians from sensation, is resolvable into this. The individual we have been describing is awake, but awake with a new consciousness. In the morbid state of his brain, ideas (using this word as representative of the results of internal operations of the mind, as distinguished from those received from without,) have so undue a vivacity and preponderance, that outward objects are no longer viewed in their former associations; they are made subordinate, and mere appendages, as it were, to the internal changes. It is a

---

[1] William Shakespeare, *Hamlet*, III. i. 158.

frightful excess of what, to a certain extent, is often taking place in healthy but powerful minds, which impress their own individuality on the external world. [. . .]

From these and like considerations, we can better understand the phenomena of double consciousness. In this unusual state, the individual, though awake, perceives objects only in relation to the new phase of the mind, which has lost its habitual memories, and emotions, and sentiments, and is the temporary subject of a different group,—so different, that they change for the time the mental identity; for identity is the *me*,—the *ego*, around which remembered objects and ideas are clustered, while they are at the same time interpenetrated with an infinite variety of emotions and sentiments, and harmoniously mingled with present perceptions.

What, then, is the test of healthy waking or consciousness? To the individual himself, one state is as healthy as the other; but we, observing him, take a different view. Our test is the correspondence of his perceptions with our own, or with those which ordinary people receive from the external world. Common opinion is the necessary standard. [. . .]

The double consciousness, then, is only the alternation of healthy and morbid conditions of mind (lucid and insane oscillations), even though in the morbid state there may be achievements of memory and the other mental faculties not attained to in the waking condition.

MULTIPLEX PERSONALITY

Frederick W. H. Myers, *Nineteenth Century*, 20 (Nov. 1886), 648–56.

Frederick Myers's theory of the 'Subliminal Consciousness' was developed in a series of articles in the Proceeding of the Society for Psychical Research *during the 1890s and finally published posthumously in* Human Personality and its Survival of Bodily Death *(1903). Myers closely followed developments in French psychiatry and his account here makes two of the most famous cases of divided and multiple personality in the late nineteenth century available to an English readership. The French psychiatrist Eugène Azam, who helped to introduce Braid's theory and practice of hypnotism in France, started to observe 'Félida X' in 1856, and wrote several reports on the case in the* Revue Scientifique *during the 1870s. Like Mary Reynolds (see Macnish, above), Félida X oscillated between two alternating personalities, and in using hypnotism to treat her, Azam significantly developed the existing idea that the doubling of the self was created through the splitting of strands of memory. Assuming some knowledge of this case, Myers here describes the case of Louis Vivé, who was first discussed by Charcot's student Jules Voisin, a prominent doctor at the Bicêtre.* Variations de la Personalité, *H. Bourru and P. Burot's important full-length study mentioned in Myers's note, was published in 1888. In the second half of the article, Myers goes on to advocate the use of hypnotism.*

My theme is the multiplex and mutable character of that which we know as the Personality of man, and the practical advantage which we may gain by discerning and working upon this as yet unrecognised modifiability. I shall begin by citing a few examples of hysterical transfer, of morbid disintegration; I shall then show that these spontaneous readjustments of man's being are not all of them pathological or retrogressive; nay, that the familiar changes of sleep and waking contain the hint of further alternations which may be beneficially acquired. And, lastly, I shall point out that we can already by artificial means induce and regulate some central nervous changes which effect physical and moral good; changes which may be more restorative than sleep, more rapid than education. Here, I shall urge, is an avenue open at once to scientific and to philanthropic endeavour, a hope which hangs neither on fable nor on fancy, but is based on actual experience and consists with rational conceptions of the genesis and evolution of man.

I begin, then, with one or two examples of the pitch to which the dissociation of memories, faculties, sensibilities may be carried, without resulting in mere insane chaos, mere demented oblivion. These cases as yet are few in number. It is only of late years—and it is mainly in France—that *savants* have recorded with due care those psychical lessons, deeper than any art of our own can teach us, which natural anomalies and aberrant instances afford.

Pre-eminent among the priceless living documents which nature thus offers to our study stand the singular personages known as Louis V. and Félida X. Félida's name at least is probably familiar to most of my readers; but Louis V.'s case is little known, and although some account of it has already been given in English,* it will be needful to recall certain particulars in order to introduce the speculations which follow.

Louis V. began life (in 1863) as the neglected child of a turbulent mother. He was sent to a reformatory at ten years old, and there showed himself, as he has always done when his organisation has given him a chance, quiet, well-behaved, and obedient. Then at fourteen years old he had a great fright from a viper—a fright which threw him off his balance and started the series of psychical oscillations on which he has been tossed ever since. At first the symptoms were only

---

* *Journal of Mental Science* for January 1886. *Proceedings of the Society for Psychical Research*, part x. 1886 (Trübner & Co.).

physical, epilepsy and hysterical paralysis of the legs; and at the asylum of Bonneval, whither he was next sent, he worked at tailoring steadily for a couple of months. Then suddenly he had a hystero-epileptic attack—fifty hours of convulsions and ecstasy—and when he awoke from it he was no longer paralysed, no longer acquainted with tailoring, and no longer virtuous. His memory was set back, so to say, to the moment of the viper's appearance, and he could remember nothing since. His character had become violent, greedy, and quarrelsome, and his tastes were radically changed. For instance, though he had before the attack been a total abstainer, he now not only drank his own wine but stole the wine of the other patients. He escaped from Bonneval, and after a few turbulent years, tracked by his occasional relapses into hospital or madhouse, he turned up once more at the Rochefort asylum in the character of a private of marines, convicted of theft but considered to be of unsound mind. And at Rochefort and La Rochelle, by great good fortune, he fell into the hands of three physicians—Professors Bourru and Burot, and Dr. Mabille—able and willing to continue and extend the observations which Dr. Camuset at Bonneval and Dr. Jules Voisin at Bicêtre had already made on this most precious of *mauvais sujets* at earlier points in his chequered career.*

He is now no longer at Rochefort, and Dr. Burot informs me that his health has much improved, and that his peculiarities have in great part disappeared. I must, however, for clearness' sake, use the present tense in briefly describing his condition at the time when the long series of experiments were made.

The state into which he has gravitated is a very unpleasing one. There is paralysis and insensibility of the right side, and (as is often the case in right hemiplegia)[1] the speech is indistinct and difficult. Nevertheless he is constantly haranguing any one who will listen to him, abusing his physicians, or preaching, with a monkey-like impudence rather than with reasoned clearness, radicalism in politics and atheism in religion. He makes bad jokes, and if any one pleases him he endeavours to caress him. He remembers recent events during his residence at the Rochefort asylum, but only two scraps of his life before that date—namely, his vicious period at Bonneval and a part of his stay at Bicêtre. [. . .]

Is there, then, the reader may ask, any assignable law which governs these strange revolutions? any reason why Louis V. should at one moment seem a mere lunatic or savage, at another moment should rise into decorous manhood, at another should recover his physical soundness, but sink backward in mind into the child? Briefly, and with many reserves and technicalities perforce omitted, the

---

* For Dr. Camuset's account see *Annales Médico-Pyschologiques*, 1882, p. 75; for Dr. Voisin's, *Archives de Néurologie*, Sept. 1885. The observations at Rochefort have been carefully recorded by Dr. Berjon, *La Grande Hystérie chez l'Homme*, Paris, 1886. The subject was again discussed at the recent meeting (Nancy, Aug. 1886) of the French Association for the Advancement of Science, when professor Burot promised a longer treatise on the subject.

[1] Paralysis of one side.

view of the doctors who have watched him is somewhat as follows: A sudden shock, falling on an unstable organisation, has effected in this boy a profounder severance between the functions of the right and left hemispheres of the brain than has perhaps ever been observed before. We are accustomed, of course, to see the right side of the body paralysed and insensible in consequence of injury to the left hemisphere, which governs it, and *vice versâ*. And we are accustomed in hysterical cases—cases where there is no actual traceable injury to either hemisphere—to see the defects in sensation and motility shift rapidly—shift, as I may say, at a touch—from one side of the body to the other. But we cannot usually trace any corresponding change in the mode of functioning of what we assume as the 'highest centres,' the centres which determine those manifestations of intelligence, character, memory, on which our *identity* mainly depends. Yet in some cases of *aphasia* and of other forms of *asemia* (the loss of power over *signs*, spoken or written words and the like) phenomena have occurred which have somewhat prepared us to find that the loss of power to use the left—which certainly is in some ways the more developed—hemisphere may bring with it a retrogression in the higher characteristics of human life. And the singular phenomenon of *automatic writing* (as I have tried elsewhere to show*) seems often to depend on an obscure action of the less-used hemisphere. Those who have followed these lines of observation may be somewhat prepared to think it possible that in Louis V.'s case the alternate predominance of right or left hemisphere affects memory and character as well as motor and sensory innervation. Inhibit his left brain (and right side) and he becomes, as one may say, not only left-handed but *sinister*; he manifests himself through nervous arrangements which have reached a lower degree of evolution. And he can represent in memory those periods only when his personality had assumed the same attitude, when he had crystallised about the same point.

Inhibit his right brain, and the higher qualities of character remain, like the power of speech, intact. There is self-control; there is modesty; there is the sense of duty—the qualities which man has developed as he has risen from the savage level. But nevertheless he is only half himself. Besides the hemiplegia, which is a matter of course, memory is truncated too, and he can summon up only such fragments of the past as chance to have been linked with this one abnormal state, leaving unrecalled not only the period of sinister inward ascendency, but the normal period of childhood, before his *Wesen*[2] was thus cloven in twain. And now if by some art we can restore the equipoise of the two hemispheres again, if we can throw him into a state in which no physical trace is left of the severance which has become for him a second nature, what may we expect to find as the physical concomitant of this restored integrity? What we *do* find is a change in the patient

---

* *Proceedings of the Society for Psychical Research*, vol. iii. (Trübner & Co.).

---

[2] Being, or essence.

which, in the glimpse of psychical possibilities which it offers us, is among the most interesting of all. He is, if I may so say, born again; he becomes as a little child; he is set back in memory, character, knowledge, powers, to the days before this trouble came upon him or his worse self assumed its sway.

I have begun with the description of an extreme case, a case which to many of my readers may seem incredible in its *bizarrerie*. But though it is extreme it is not really isolated; it is approached from different sides by cases already known. The mere resumption of life at an earlier moment, for instance, is of course only an exaggeration of a phenomenon which frequently appears after cerebral injury. The trainer, stunned by the kick of a horse, completes his order to loosen the girths the moment that trepanning has been successfully performed. The old lady struck down at a card party, and restored to consciousness after long insensibility, surprises her weeping family by the inquiry, 'What are trumps?' But in these common cases there is but a morsel cut out of life; the personality reawakens as from sleep and is the same as of old. With Louis V. it is not thus; the memories of the successive stages are not lost but juxtaposed, as it were, in separate compartments; nor can one say what epochs are in truth intercalary, or in what central channel the stream of his being flows.

Self-severances profound as Louis V.'s are naturally to be sought mainly in the lunatic asylum.* There indeed we find duplicated individuality in its grotesquer forms. We have the man who has always lost himself and insists on looking for himself under the bed. We have the man who maintains that there are two of him, and sends his plate a second time, remarking, 'I have had plenty, but the other fellow has not.' We have the man who maintains that he is himself and his brother too, and when asked how he can possibly be both at once, replies, 'Oh, by a different mother.' [. . .]

These instances have shown us the *retrogressive* change of personality, the dissolution into incoordinate elements of the polity of our being. We have seen the state of man like a city blockaded, like a great empire dying at the core. And of course a spontaneous, unguided disturbance in a machinery so complete is likely to alter it more often for the worse than for the better. Yet here we reach the very point which I most desire to urge in this paper. I mean that even these spontaneous, these unguided disturbances do sometimes effect a change which is a marked improvement. Apart from all direct experiment they show us that we are in fact capable of being reconstituted after an improved pattern, that we may be fused and recrystallised into greater clarity; or, let us say more modestly, that the shifting sand-heap of our being will sometimes suddenly settle itself into a new attitude of more assured equilibrium.

Among cases of this kind which have thus far been recorded, none is more striking than that of Dr. Azam's often quoted patient, Félida X.

* The cases cited here come mainly from Krishaber's *Néuropathie Cérébro-cardiaque*. Several of them will be found cited in Ribot's admirable monograph *Maladies de la Personnalité*.

Many of my readers will remember that in her case the somnambulic life has become the normal life; the 'second state,' which appeared at first only in short, dream-like accesses, has gradually replaced the 'first state,' which now recurs but for a few hours at long intervals. But the point on which I wish to dwell is this: that Félida's second state is altogether *superior* to the first—physically superior, since the nervous pains which had troubled her from childhood have disappeared; and morally superior, inasmuch as her morose, self-centred disposition is exchanged for a cheerful activity which enables her to attend to her children and her shop much more effectively than when she was in the 'état bête,' as she now calls what was once the only personality that she knew. In this case, then, which is now of nearly thirty years' standing, the spontaneous readjustment of nervous activities—the second state, no memory of which remains in the first state—has resulted in an improvement profounder than could have been anticipated from any moral or medical treatment that we know. The case shows us how often the word 'normal' means nothing more than 'what happens to exist.' For Félida's *normal* state was in fact her *morbid* state; and the new condition, which seemed at first a mere hysterical abnormality, has brought her to a life of bodily and mental sanity which makes her fully the equal of average women of her class.

Now, before we go further, let us ask ourselves whether this result, which sounds so odd and paradoxical, ought in reality to surprise us. Had we any reason for supposing that changes as profound as Félida's need always be for the worse, that the phase of personality in which we happen to find ourselves is the phase in which, given our innate capacities, it is always best for us to be?

To make this question more intelligible, I must have recourse to a metaphor. Let us picture the human brain as a vast manufactory, in which thousands of looms, of complex and differing patterns, are habitually at work. These looms are used in varying combinations; but the main driving-bands, which connect them severally or collectively with the motive power, remain for the most part unaltered.

Now, how do I come to have my looms and driving-gear arranged in this particular way? Not, certainly, through any deliberate choice of my own. My ancestor the ascidian, in fact, inherited the business when it consisted of little more than a single spindle. Since his day my nearer ancestors have added loom after loom. Some of their looms have fallen to pieces unheeded; others have been kept in repair because they suited the style of order which the firm had at that time to meet. But the class of orders received has changed very rapidly during the last few hundred years. I have now to try to turn out altruistic emotions and intelligent reasoning with machinery adapted to self-preserving fierceness or manual toil. And in my efforts to readjust and reorganise I am hindered not only by the old-fashioned type of the looms, but by the inconvenient disposition of the driving gear. I cannot start one useful loom without starting a dozen others that are merely in the way. And I cannot shift the driving gear to suit myself, for I cannot get at much of it without stopping the engines, and if I stopped my engines I should not know how to set them going again. In this perplexity I watch what happens in certain factories—Félida's, for instance—where the hidden part of the machinery is subject to certain dangerous jerks or dislocations, after which the gearings shift of themselves and whole groups of looms are connected and disconnected in a novel manner. From hence I get at least a hint as to the concealed attachments; and if I see that new arrangement working well I have an object to aim at; I can try to produce a similar change, though a smaller one, among my own looms and by my own manipulation.

PERIODIC AMNESIA

Théodule A. Ribot, *Diseases of Memory: An Essay in the Positive Psychology* (London: Kegan Paul, Trench & Co., 1882), 105–8, 110.

In Diseases of Memory T. A. Ribot provides a summary and overview of existing theories of memory, particularly those based in physiological psychology. Here he outlines his conclusions on the role of memory in shaping identity based on his discussion of specific cases of double consciousness, citing Macnish's description of Mary Reynolds and Azam's account of Félida X.

On examining the general characteristics of periodic amnesia as illustrated in the cases given, we find, first, *an evolution of two memories*. In extreme cases (Macnish) the two memories are independent of one another; when one appears, the other disappears. Each is self-supporting; each utilizes, so to speak, its own material. The organized memory employed in speaking, reading, and writing is not a common basis of the two states. In each there is a distinct recollection of words, graphic signs, and the movements necessary to record them. In modified cases (Azam, Dufay,[1] somnambulism) a partial memory alternates with the normal memory. The latter embraces the totality of conscious states; the former, a limited group of states which, by a natural process of selection, separate from the others, and form in the life of the individual a series of connected fragments. But they retain a common basis in the less stable and less conscious forms of memory which enter indifferently into either group.

[1] Earlier Ribot cites R. Dufay's, 'La Notion de la personalité', *Revue scientifique* (15 July 1876).
[2] severance.

As a result of this discerption[2] of memory, the individual appears—at least to others—to be living a double life. The illusion is natural, the *Ego* depending (or appearing to depend) upon the possibility of association of present states with those that are reanimated or localized in the past, according to laws already formulated. There are here two distinct centers of association and attraction. Each draws to itself certain groups, and is without influence upon others. It is evident that this formation of two memories, entirely or partly independent of one another, is not a primitive cause; it is the symptom of a morbid process, the psychical expression of a disorder yet to be analyzed. And this leads to a great subject, much to our regret, since we must treat it as a side issue: we refer to the conditions of personality.

Let us first reject the idea of an *Ego* conceived as a distinct entity of conscious states. Such an hypothesis is useless and contradictory; it is a conception worthy of a psychology in its infancy, content to accept superficial observations as the whole of truth and to theorize where it can not explain. I avow allegiance to contemporary science which sees in conscious personality a compound resultant of very complex states.

The *Ego* subjectively considered consists of a sum of conscious states. There is a central group surrounded by secondary states which tend to supplant it, and these in turn are encompassed in a similar manner with other less conscious states. The highest state, after a more or less extended period of vitality, succumbs, and is replaced by another, about which the remaining states group themselves as before. The mechanism of consciousness is comparable to that of vision. Here we have a visual point in which alone perception is clear and precise; about it is the visual field in which perception is progressively less clear and precise as we advance from center to circumference. The *Ego*, its present perpetually renewed, is for the most part nourished by the memory; that is to say, the present state is associated with others which, thrown back and localized in the past, constitute at each moment what we regard as our personality. In brief, the *Ego* may be considered in two ways: either in its actual form, and then it is the sum of existing conscious states; or, in its continuity with the past, and then it is formed by the memory according to the process outlined above.

It would seem, according to this view, that the identity of the *Ego* depended entirely upon the memory. But such a conception is only partial. Beneath the unstable compound phenomenon in all its protean phases of growth, degeneration, and reproduction, there is a something that remains: and this something is the undefined consciousness, the product of all the vital processes, constituting bodily perception. [. . .]

The unity of the *Ego* is, then, not that of a mathematical point, but that of a very complicated mechanism. It is a consensus of vital processes, co-ordinated first by the nervous system—the chief regulator in the bodily economy—and finally by consciousness whose natural form is unity. It is, in fact, inherent in the nature of psychical states that they can co-exist only in a very limited number, grouped about a center which alone represents consciousness in the plenitude of its powers.

4. Memory

OF MEMORY

Dugald Stewart, *Elements of the Philosophy of the Human Mind* (1792), 6th edn., 2 vols. (London: T. Cadell & W. Davies, 1818), i. 403–7.

Dugald Stewart's work in the philosophy of mind profoundly influenced nine-teenth-century psychology. In particular, his discussion of memory in Elements of the Philosophy of the Human Mind *set up the basic terms of all subsequent discussion. This extract is from the beginning of chapter 6.*

The word Memory is not employed uniformly in the same precise sense; but it always expresses some modification of that faculty, which enables us to trea-sure up, and preserve for future use, the knowledge we acquire; a faculty which is obviously the great foundation of all intellectual improvement, and without which, no advantage could be derived from the most enlarged experience. This faculty implies two things: a capacity of retaining knowledge; and a power of recalling it to our thoughts when we have occasion to apply it to use. The word Memory is sometimes employed to express the capacity, and sometimes the power. When we speak of a retentive memory, we use it in the former sense; when, of a ready memory, in the latter.

The various particulars which compose our stock of knowledge are, from time to time, recalled to our thoughts, in one of two ways: sometimes they recur to us spontaneously, or at least, without any interference on our part; in other cases, they are recalled, in consequence of an effort of our will. For the former operation of the mind, we have no appropriated name in our language, distinct from Memory. The latter, too, is often called by the same name, but is more properly distinguished by the word Recollection. [. . .]

It is evident, that when I think of an event, in which any object of sense was concerned, my recollection of the event must necessarily involve an act of Conception. Thus, when I think of a dramatic representation which I have recently seen, my recollection of what I saw, necessarily involves a conception of the different actors by whom it was performed. But every act of recollection which relates to events, is accompanied with a belief of their past existence. How then are we to reconcile this conclusion with the doctrine formerly maintained concerning Conception, according to which every exertion of that power is accompanied with a belief, that its object exists before us at the present moment?

The only way that occurs to me of removing this difficulty, is by supposing, that the remembrance of a past event is not a simple act of the mind; but that the mind first forms a conception of the event, and then judges from circumstances, of the period of time to which it is to be referred: a supposition which is by no means a gratuitous one, invented to answer a particular purpose; but which, as far as I am able to judge, is agreeable to fact: for if we have the power, as will not be disputed, of conceiving a past event without any reference to time, it follows, that there is nothing in the ideas or notions which Memory presents to us, which is necessarily accompanied with a belief of past existence, in a way analogous to that in which our perceptions are accompanied with a belief of the present existence of their objects; and therefore, that the reference of the event to the particular period at which it happened, is a judgment founded on concomitant circumstances. So long as we are occupied with the conception of any particular object connected with the event, we believe the present existence of the object; but this belief, which, in most cases, is only momentary, is instantly corrected by habits of judging acquired by experience; and as soon as the mind is disengaged from such a belief, it is left at liberty to refer the event to the period at which it actually happened. Nor will the apparent instantaneousness of such judgments be considered as an unsurmountable objection to the doctrine now advanced, by those who have reflected on the perception of distance obtained by sight, which, although it seems to be as immediate as any perception of touch, has been shewn by philosophers to be the result of a judgment founded on experience and observation. The reference we make of past events to the particular points of time at which they took place, will, I am inclined to think, the more we consider the subject, be found the more strikingly analogous to the estimates of distance we learn to form by the eye.

THE PALIMPSEST

Thomas De Quincey, *Suspiria de Profundis*, *Blackwood's Edinburgh Magazine*, 57 (June 1845), 742–3.

As a psychological study, De Quincey's Confessions of an English Opium-Eater *was widely cited in medical accounts of the effects of opium. De Quincey had published articles in* Blackwood's, *which had a long tradition of publishing psychological studies and stories (including Macnish's 'The metempsychosis'), since the 1820s.* Suspiria de Profundis *was advertised here as a sequel to the* Confessions, *and in the final section, 'The palimpsest', De Quincey develops an enduring metaphor of the working of hidden memory which reverberates through the century. (See also the extract from Lewes's* Foundations of a Creed *and Sully's 'The dream as a revelation', above.) The article starts with a description of the palimpsest for the benefit of the 'female reader': 'a membrane or roll cleansed of its manuscript by reiterated successions' (p. 739), but where the ghostly traces of former writings still remain.*

What else than a natural and mighty palimpsest is the human brain? Such a palimpsest is my brain; such a palimpsest, O reader! is yours. Everlasting layers of ideas, images, feelings, have fallen upon your brain softly as light. Each succession has seemed to bury all that went before. And yet in reality not one has been extinguished. And if, in the vellum palimpsest, lying amongst the other *diplomata*[1] of human archives or libraries, there is any thing fantastic or which moves to laughter, as oftentimes there is in the grotesque collisions of those successive themes, having no natural connexion, which by pure accident have consecutively occupied the roll, yet, in our own heaven-created palimpsest, the deep memorial palimpsest of the brain, there are not and cannot be such incoherences. The fleeting accidents of a man's life, and its external shows, may indeed be irrelate and incongruous; but the organizing principles which fuse into harmony, and gather about fixed predetermined centres, whatever heterogeneous elements life may have accumulated from without, will not permit the grandeur of human unity greatly to be violated, or its ultimate repose to be troubled in the retrospect from dying moments, or from other great convulsions.

Such a convulsion is the struggle of gradual suffocation, as in drowning; and, in the original Opium Confessions, I mentioned a case of that nature communicated to me by a lady from her own childish experience. The lady is still living, though now of unusually great age; and I may mention—that amongst her faults

[1] Letters, pieces of paper.

143

never was numbered any levity of principle, or carelessness of the most scrupulous veracity; but, on the contrary, such faults as arise from austerity, too harsh perhaps, and gloomy—indulgent neither to others nor herself. And, at the time of relating this incident, when already very old, she had become religious to asceticism. According to my present belief, she had completed her ninth year, when playing by the side of a solitary brook, she fell into one of its deepest pools. Eventually, but after what lapse of time nobody ever knew, she was saved from death by a farmer, who, riding in some distant lane, had seen her rise to the surface; but not until she had descended within the abyss of death, and looked into its secrets, as far, perhaps, as ever human eye *can* have looked that had permission to return. At a certain stage of this descent, a blow seemed to strike her—phosphoric radiance sprang forth from her eyeballs; and immediately a mighty theatre expanded within her brain. In a moment, in the twinkling of an eye, every act—every design of her past life lived again—arraying themselves not as a succession, but as parts of a coexistence. Such a light fell upon the whole path of her life backwards into the shades of infancy, as the light perhaps which wrapt the destined apostle on his road to Damascus.[2] Yet that light blinded for a season; but hers poured celestial vision upon the brain, so that her consciousness became omnipresent at one moment to every feature in the infinite review.

This anecdote was treated sceptically at the time by some critics. But besides that it has since been confirmed by other experiences essentially the same, reported by other parties in the same circumstances who had never heard of each other; the true point for astonishment is not the *simultaneity* of arrangement under which the past events of life—though in fact successive—had formed their dread line of revelation. This was but a secondary phenomenon; the deeper lay in the resurrection itself, and the possibility of resurrection, for what had so long slept in the dust. A pall, deep as oblivion, had been thrown by life over every trace of these experiences; and yet suddenly, at a silent command, at the signal of a blazing rocket sent up from the brain, the pall draws up, and the whole depths of the theatre are exposed. Here was the greater mystery: now this mystery is liable to no doubt; for it is repeated, and ten thousand times repeated by opium, for those who are its martyrs.

Yes, reader, countless are the mysterious handwritings of grief or joy which have inscribed themselves successively upon the palimpsest of your brain; and, like the annual leaves of aboriginal forests, or the undissolving snows on the Himalaya, or light falling upon light, the endless strata have covered up each other in forgetfulness. But by the hour of death, but by fever, but by the searchings of opium, all these can revive in strength. They are not dead, but sleeping. In the illustration imagined by myself, from the case of some individual palimpsest, the Grecian tragedy had seemed to be displaced, but was *not* dis-

---

[2] A reference to St Paul's sudden and dramatic conversion.

placed, by the monkish legend; and the monkish legend had seemed to be displaced, but was *not* displaced, by the knightly romance. In some potent convulsion of the system, all wheels back into its earliest elementary stage. The bewildering romance, light tarnished with darkness, the semi-fabulous legend, truth celestial mixed with human falsehoods, these fade even of themselves as life advances. The romance has perished that the young man adored. The legend has gone that deluded the boy. But the deep deep tragedies of infancy, as when the child's hands were unlinked for ever from his mother's neck, or his lips for ever from his sister's kisses, these remain lurking below all and these lurk to the last.*

THE PSYCHOLOGY AND PATHOLOGY OF MEMORY

Forbes Benignus Winslow, *On Obscure Diseases of the Brain and Disorders of the Mind* (1860), 4th edn. (London: John Churchill, 1868), 277–9, 286–7, 291, 293.

Forbes Winslow believed that most forms of mental derangement were the result of cerebral disease and considered that recognizing symptoms in their early stages offered the best possibilities of cure. On Obscure Diseases of the Brain *is a long and extremely detailed study, written 'with the view of exciting a deeper interest in and awakening a profounder and more philosophical attention to this subject' (preface to 3rd edition). The following comes in the last of a series of six chapters on memory, which cover its acute disorders and chronic affections, the perversion and the exaltation of memory, the memory of the insane and the psychology and pathology of memory. 'What is memory?' Winslow opens the series by asking, domesticating De Quincey's image: 'Where is situated the vesicular mental repository and cerebral treasure-house destined to garner, preserve and protect from injury the myriads of ideas that obtain an entrance to the mind through the media of the senses?' (p. 234) This extract comes immediately after a discussion of various cases of disordered association and double consciousness.*

---

* This, it may be said, requires a corresponding duration of experience; but, as an argument for this mysterious power lurking in our nature, I may remind the reader of one phenomenon open to the notice of every body, viz. the tendency of very aged persons to throw back and concentrate the light of their memory upon scenes of early childhood, as to which they recall many traces that had faded even to *themselves* in middle life, whilst they often forget altogether the whole intermediate stages of their experience. This shows that naturally, and without violent agencies, the human brain is by tendency a palimpsest.

Perversion of memory.—There is a curious modification of the memory connected with a sudden or gradual loss of the remembrance of everything, save one object in the morbid contemplation of which the mind is exclusively absorbed. Andral[1] refers to a very singular perversion of the memory which consists in the patient remembering everything except himself. He has, as it were, forgotten his own existence, and when he speaks of himself, it is in the third person, the words I or ME not being in his vocabulary. A woman when speaking of herself, always said, 'la personne de moi-même.'[2]

An old soldier who was in the asylum of Saint Yon, believed that he was killed at the battle of Austerlitz.[3] When he spoke of himself, he was in the habit of saying, 'This machine, which they thought to make like me, is very badly manufactured.' When he spoke of himself he did not use the personal pronoun I, but the demonstrative pronoun THAT, as if speaking of some inanimate object.

A man seventy years of age was suddenly seized with lock-jaw, and formication over the surface of the body. This was succeeded by vertigo and a strange alteration in his language. He spoke with ease and fluency, but often made use of odd words which nobody understood. He appeared to have coined new phrases in the place of others which he had forgotten. Occasionally he mixed numbers instead of words in his conversation, and in this respect the memory appeared to have been altered in its mode of action.

John Hunter[4] refers to a singular case of perversion of the memory succeeding an attack of acute disease of the brain. A gentleman, who, besides referring the circumstances of his early life to the present period, had to such an extent lost all idea of the connexion between the *past* and the *present*, that although his mind could direct him as to what was to be done in consequence of certain impressions, and would direct him rightly as to the part of the body affected by them, was in the habit (having apparently lost all notion of his own identity) of constantly referring his own sensations to those immediately about him. Thus, he would tell his nurse and the bystanders that he was certain that *they* were hungry or thirsty; but on offering him food or drink, it was evident by his eagerness that the absurd idea had been suggested by a sense of hunger and thirst, and that the word *they* referred to himself and not to others.

He was subject to a violent cough, and after each paroxysm he would, in very appropriate and sympathetic terms, resume the subject on which he had been previously conversing, expressing, however, his feelings of distress from having witnessed the sufferings of his friend, adding, 'I am sorry to see that *you* have so troublesome and harassing a cough.'

[1] G. Andral, French psychiatrist, author of *Clinique médicale: Choix d'observations recueillies à l'Hôpital de la Chanté*, 3rd edn. (Paris, 1834).

[2] 'The figure of myself'.

[3] Napoleon's most celebrated victory over the Germans and Russians, on 2 Dec. 1803.

[4] (1728–93), surgeon to George III who wrote widely on physical and mental disease, and whose papers were edited and published posthumously by Richard Owen in 1861.

A gentleman who was in the habit of indulging in 'potations, pottle deep,'[5] whenever he became intoxicated invariably referred his own perverted sensations in a similar way to those immediately about him. Hence, upon going home, he, imagining all the family to be in the lamentable state to which he had reduced himself, would insist on undressing and putting them to bed, declaring that they were all too drunk to do so for themselves. [. . .]

It is difficult to suggest a physiological or metaphysical hypothesis which satisfactorily explains those remarkable conditions of mental paralysis, singular manifestations, and aberrations of memory [. . .] as preceding, accompanying, and following acute and chronic affections of the brain, unless we espouse the doctrine of the indestructibility of ideas, and subscribe to the notion that no impression made upon the mind is ever destroyed.

If we accept this as an established philosophical theory, we can easily understand how subtle microscopic changes in the delicate nerve vesicle[6] (grey matter of the brain) may cause great eccentricity and singular irregularity in the exercise of memory, and occasionally in certain morbid as well as healthy conditions of cerebral exaltation, awaken into active consciousness ideas imagined either to have no existence, or long since supposed to be buried in oblivion.

Annihilation exists but in the fancy. It is an illusion of the imagination, dream of the poet, the wild and frigid phantasy of the sceptic. Nothing obvious to sense admits of destruction. This is a well-established axiom in physics. It is not in the power of man to destroy the slightest particle of matter. What is termed destruction, as applied to material substances, is nothing but a change in their elementary composition or an alteration of their constituent atoms. God has not delegated to poor puny man the power of destroying any portion of the physical universe by which he is surrounded, and which ministers so bountifully and mercifully to his every necessity. He may, by the aid of chemical science, alter and rearrange the existing combinations of organic matter, but, when disintegrated by such means, the particles so dissipated, and apparently destroyed, enter into new and different forms, and assume other types or compounds, but are never in their *original* nature and elements annihilated. [. . .]

What is true with regard to material holds good, *à fortiori*, respecting psychical phenomena. Hence the tonic, permanent, and indestructible character of the impressions made upon the cerebrum, and received and registered in the mind during infancy and childhood, as well as in adult age, as established by their resuscitation at all periods of life during certain normal and abnormal conditions of the vesicular brain structure and cerebral circulation.

I use the phrase *'received'* advisedly, for it must be admitted that there are many impressions which impinge themselves transiently on the mind—ideas that are evanescent in character, and therefore obtain no settled hold upon the

---

[5] William Shakespeare, *Othello*, II. iii. 57.   [6] Brain cells or tissue.

consciousness—which cannot philosophically be deemed as *received* and *registered* in the memorial archives. Such are the fugitive notions which do not become objects of *perception*, that so frequently float upon and pass like shadows over the surface of the mind, in early as well as matured life, when the brain is not anatomically and physiologically organised or fitted for the facile perception, reception, and registration of ideas. There can be no doubt that the defective memory which so often accompanies old age is mainly dependent upon certain (as yet unexplained) modifications in the physical nutrition or chemical constitution of the brain interfering with that *vital, organic,* and I may add *psychical sensibility,* so essentially necessary for its ready adaptation to mental impressions. It may be that the ideas are in reality received, but that the faculty of *reminiscence* being either originally defective or enfeebled by age or disease, it ceases to obey the commands of the will. [. . .]

How can we explain the growth, expansion, and discipline which the mind undergoes as the effect of a system of educational training? by what physiological and psychical processes are the memory, attention, and reasoning faculties developed and invigorated by exercise? What is the rationale of the judgment being improved by judicious and careful cultivation, the moral sense elevated, the taste disciplined and chastened, or the volitional power increased? Are not these various conditions of mind the result of an inexplicable law regulating the action of nerve-matter? Is it possible to suppose that changes similar to those previously referred to, in the thinking principle, can be consequent upon any alteration in the mind *per se?* May not these developments and modifications in the psychical attributes of the cerebrum and gradual unfoldings of the intellect which we perceive through the various epochs of life be connected with and dependent upon either the growth, waste, and repair of cerebral brain-matter or some modifications in its chemical composition?

THE HIDDEN SOUL

Eneas Sweetland Dallas, *The Gay Science,* 2 vols. (London: Chapman and Hall, 1866), 209–11, 213, 216–17, 220–1.

Dallas continues his discussion of the 'hidden soul' by arguing that three faculties—memory, reason, and feeling—in their own way display the workings of the unconscious in all aspects of mental life. Like Winslow he believes that no thought is entirely lost, but he sees this hidden knowledge as active and dynamic, rejecting passive physiological explanations.

In memory we encounter the oftest-noted marvel of hidden thought. It is a power that belongs even more to the unconscious than to the conscious mind. How and where we hide our knowledge so that it seems dead and buried; and how in a moment we can bring it to life again, finding it in the dark where it lies unheeded amid our innumerable boards, is a mystery over which every one capable of thinking has puzzled. The miracle here is most evident and most interesting when memory halts a little. Then we become aware that we are seeking for something which we know not; and there arises the strange contradiction of a faculty knowing what it searches for, and yet making the search because it does not know. [. . .]

The clue, but only a clue, to this perpetual magic of reminiscence lies in the theory of our hidden life. I do not attempt to follow out the explanation, since at best it only throws the riddle but a step or two backwards, and for the present inquiry it is enough that I should barely state the facts which indicate the reality and the intensity of our covert life. Strictly speaking the mind never forgets: what it once seizes, it holds to the death, and cannot let go. We may not know it, but we are greater than we know, and the mind, faithful to its trust, keeps a secret watch on whatever we give to it. Thus beams upon us the strange phenomenon of knowledge, possessed, enjoyed, and used by us, of which nevertheless we are ignorant—ignorant not only at times, but also in some cases during our whole lives. [. . .]

That understanding is not essential to memory we see in children who learn by heart what has no meaning to them. The meaning comes long years afterwards. But it would seem as if the process which we have all observed on such a small scale goes on continually on a much larger scale. Absolute as a photograph, the mind refuses nought. An impression once made upon the sense, even unwittingly, abides for evermore.[1] [. . .] The memory grips and appropriates what it does not understand—appropriates it mechanically, like a magpie stealing a silver spoon, without knowing what it is, or what to do with it. The memory cannot help itself. It is a kleptomaniac and lets nothing go by.

Nor must we have mean ideas as to the nature of the existence in the mind of things preserved beyond our knowledge and without our understanding. This is the second point aforesaid which calls for attention. When we think of something preserved in the mind, but lost and wellnigh irrecoverable, we are apt to imagine it as dormant; when we know that it was unintelligible we are apt to imagine it as dead. On the contrary, the mind is an organic whole and lives in every part, even though we know it not. Aldebaran was once the grandest star in the firmament, and Sirius had a companion star once the brightest in heaven, and now one of the feeblest. Because they are now dim to us, are we to conclude that they are going out and becoming nought? The stars are overhead, though in the

---

[1] Here Dallas cites various examples of unconscious memory, including Coleridge's anecdote, of the German servant who spoke Greek and Hebrew, from the *Biographia Literaria*.

blaze of day they are unseen; they are not only overhead, but also all their influences are unchanged. So there is knowledge active within us of which we see nothing, know nothing, think nothing. Thus, in the sequence of thought, the mind, busied with the first link in a chain of ideas, may dart to the third or fourth, the intermediate link or links being utterly unknown to it. They may be irrecoverable, they may even be unintelligible, but they are there, and they are there in force. [. . .]

So much then for memory, in so far as it represents the immense involuntary life which we lead out of consciousness. If the facts I have brought together do not account for all, certainly they account for much of what we understand by the word imagination. They account for much even of what is most mysterious in the processes called imaginative. In the mechanical accuracy with which memory all unknown to us registers the flitting impressions of our daily life, and in the faithfulness with which at times and in ways of its own choosing, it surrenders to consciousness these impressions, we have a glimpse of what is meant by the creativeness of imagination. It is true, that the theory of unconscious memory does not explain all the creative work of fantasy. There is in the mind, as I shall afterwards have to show, a genuine creative process, over and above the seeming creativeness of unconscious memory. Still, it is difficult to exaggerate the importance of mere memory—involuntary and secret—as a worker of miracles, as a discoverer of things unknown, and as contributing to invest all objects of thought with a halo of mystery, which is but the faint reflection of forgotten knowledge. The Platonic theory of pre-existence is but the exaggeration of a truth. Our powers of memory are prodigious; our powers of invention are very limited. The same fables, the same comparisons, the same jests are produced and reproduced like the tunes of a barrel-organ in successive ages and in different countries.

THE FALLACIES OF MEMORY

Frances Power Cobbe, 'The fallacies of memory' *Hours of Work and Play* (London: N. Trübner & Co., 1867), 103–8, 111–13.

First published in the American magazine the Galaxy *in May 1866 and reprinted in a popular edition of her essays, Cobbe's account of the unreliability of memory challenges prevailing notions of the mind as a palimpsest or storehouse of latent impressions. Here she maintains that the individual remembers the reconstruction of events rather than the truth itself and develops Dugald Stewart's point about the essentially fictive nature of all reconstruction.*

Memory is for ever likened by poets and rhetoricians to an engraved tablet, treasured in the recesses of mind, and liable only to obliteration by the slow abrasion of time, or the dissolving heat of madness. We venture to affirm that such a simile is not in the remotest degree applicable to the real phenomena of the case, and that memory is neither an impression made, once for all, like an engraving on a tablet, nor yet safe for an hour from obliteration or modification, after being formed. Rather is memory a finger-mark traced on shifting sand, ever exposed to obliteration when left unrenewed; and if renewed, then modified, and made, not the same, but a fresh and different mark. Beyond the first time of recalling a place or event, it is rare to remember again actually the place or the event. We remember, not the things themselves, but the first recollection of them, and then the second and the third, always the latest recollection of them. A proof that this is so may be found by anybody who will carefully study the processes of his own mind, after he has once detailed at length, in words, any scene he has previously witnessed. He will find himself constantly going over *precisely what he has narrated*, and no more. To proceed beyond this and recall from oblivion a single incident of which he had not spoken will require a distinct effort, perceptibly different and more difficult than the recollection of those facts of which he has spoken, and after a certain lapse of time or repetition of his narrative *minus* the excluded incidents, this effort will become nearly impracticable. In other words, it is easy to go back over the impression we have renewed with a fresh mark, but to descend beneath and clear up the original impression is extremely difficult. Thus, as in accordance with various laws of mind, each fresh trace varies a little from the trace beneath, sometimes magnifying and beautifying it, through the natural bias of the soul to grandeur and beauty; sometimes contracting it through languid imagination; sometimes distorting it through passion or prejudice; in all and every case the original mark is ere long essentially changed. We find, indeed, in our minds something which we call a remembrance, and which appertains in truth to the faculty of memory; but it reproduces, not the event it assumes to record, but that idea of it which, after twenty modifying repetitions, has left for the moment the uppermost trace in our minds.

The more this view of memory is considered the more, we venture to affirm, it will be found to correspond with the actual phenomena of the case. By adopting it we account for the great fact we have signalized above, that the main portion of our past lives is a blank in memory, with only a few marks of remembered hours. Why is it a blank? Simply because we have not thought of it, brought it up for fresh remembrance, marked it afresh on the sand. Sometimes the most trifling scenes are passed on from childhood, remembered and renewed again and again. Why are these retained and others lost? Only because from some chance we have thought, or talked, or written of them, and have let the rest pass away without the fixing process of revision.

Again, by this theory of memory, we obtain an available hypothesis, to account for the notorious but marvellous fact, that liars come in time to believe their own falsehoods. The warping of the original trace of the story, albeit voluntary and conscious, has, equally with unconscious dereliction, effected the end of obliterating the primary mark, and substituting a false one, which has assumed the place of a remembrance. Without conscious falsehood, the same thing happens also occasionally when we realize strongly by imagination some circumstance which never happened, or happened to another person. A most truthful woman asserted, in our hearing, that a certain adventure had befallen her. It had really befallen her child, but the child repeating it often to her, she had realized it so vividly that it seemed her own experience. [. . .] A very common way in which the same mendacious effect is produced, is by the habit of speculating on what *would have* happened had certain contingencies been otherwise than they were. We begin by saying: 'It might have happened so and so,' till having realized in fancy that hypothetical case more vividly than we remember the real one, we suddenly and unconsciously substitute the fancy for the fact. [. . .]

If it be granted that the simile now suggested to describe the action of memory be a just one, and that by using it we can in some degree figure to ourselves the mode in which the familiar phenomena of error and forgetfulness are produced, it will follow that our chief practical concern must be to study the laws of mind, whereby the successive traces of memory are liable to be warped and distorted, and, so far as it may prove possible, guard ourselves against the causes of error. These causes seem chiefly to be the following:

1st. Wilful falsehood, leading to unconscious self-deception.

2nd. Allowing ourselves to dwell on imaginary contingencies till they become realities in our imagination.

3rd. Diverging from literal truth, with the honest purpose of conveying a true meaning. This is a form of unveracity to which little attention is ever paid, and yet it is one of the most common of all, and whose constant practice tends very peculiarly to warp the memory. So strong is the dramatic element in us all that few ever detail a narrative without completing it by some touches not actually true, though conscientiously believed to *explain* the truth; to supply the genuine reason for this speech or the other action, or to bring into relief the real feelings of the actors. The fact is, we can never witness any transaction without making some theory of the motives, sentiments, and purposes of the agents; and, in telling the history thereof, we inevitably work out this theory in our description. Sketching on one occasion in the great temple at Baalbec,[1] it occurred to the

---

[1] Phoenician temple to the god Baal, in what is now Syria.

writer, in striving to give some idea of the splendid ruin, to endeavour to define where a certain arch had once extended. Every stone of the arch had fallen; only the marks on the walls revealed where it had been, and these marks, copied in a poor, hasty sketch, would have utterly failed to convey any impression of the fact. Quite unconsciously, a stone or two (fallen, doubtless, a thousand years ago) were replaced in the sketch; just enough, and no more, to convey the desired idea of the original arch. Then came the reflection, 'Here is precisely what we do every day in our stories. We just add a stone, just darken a shadow, just double a line, to show what we very honestly believe to be true!' How large might be the falsehoods thus originated, how soon our theory would take in our memories the place of fact, there is no need to tell.

The form of memory most safe from such distortions is unquestionably the verbal memory, where the words to be remembered are arranged either in regular verse or in that special kind of rhythmical prose which answers the same purpose of keeping them in close phalanx. The reason why such words are remembered is plain. The trace they make in the memory each time they are repeated is marked precisely in the same furrow. Any divergence is not (as in the case of other errors of memory) an exaggeration or distortion, but a positive transformation, which the rhythm usually disowns, or which, if permitted by the rhythm, yet jars upon ear to sense. After the curious process of committing verses to memory has been achieved, we do not very often find ourselves betrayed by such unconscious transformation. We may lose the trace altogether, or find it broken here and there, but we rarely find a wrong word established in our minds in the place of a right one, as we find a wrong circumstance of an event or feature of a scene. The real nature of this kind of memory remains, after all efforts to elucidate it, one of the most marvellous of all the mysteries of our nature. The law of association of ideas is surely here developed to the uttermost. After the lapse of twenty years, a few leading words will suggest to us line after line, perhaps hundreds of lines together, till we seem to draw out an endless coil of golden chain which has lain hidden in the deepest treasury of our minds. [. . .]

The conclusions to which this brief review of the failures and weaknesses of memory must lead us are undoubtedly painful. To be deceived a hundred times, and misled even in important matters, by a wrong estimate of our powers, seems less sad than to be compelled to admit that the powers themselves are untrustworthy. 'To be weak is to be miserable,'[2] in this as in all other things; but to find Memory weak is to be not only feeble in the present, but to lose our grasp of the past. That dear Past! the past by whose grave we are standing all our later life, is doubly lost to us if we must cover it up in dust and oblivion. To know that what we deem we recall so vividly is but a poor, shifting reflex—hardly of the thing itself, only of our earlier remembrance of the thing—this is sad and mournful.

[2] John Milton, *Paradise Lost*, I, 157. The quotation is inaccurate: 'To be weak is to be miserable' should read 'To be weak is miserable'.

Almost more terrible it seems to confess the fallaciousness of the great traditions of History, and in the waste of waters, over which we are drifting, to behold the barks of past centuries no longer stretching their sails in our wake, but growing hazy and spectral in the mist of doubt, till some we deemed the richest galleons in that mighty fleet fade from our eyes, and are lost for ever in impenetrable cloud. These things cannot be evaded or averted. On our generation of mankind has come the knowledge of an isolation, such as younger races never felt, and perhaps could less have borne. [. . .] Must we be content to know, that only the outlines of the ancestral pictures of our house are true, and all the colours which make them beautiful, retouched and falsified? Perchance it must be so. Perchance the loneliness of human nature must needs be more impressed on us as science advances in the field of historical criticism, as in the fields of mythology and physiology. The past is becoming like a twilight scene in a mountain land, where the valleys are all filled with mist, and wood and waterfall and village spire are dimly shadowed. Only some snowy Alp, whose huge outline we recognize, towers into the upper air; while the lights gleam here and there, from hearth and cloister and student's cell, the rays of genius shining through the night of time. We are a thousand millions of men and women and babes living now upon earth; but of those who are gone before on whose dust we tread; and of those who may be dwelling now in the stars which glitter in our wintry sky, we know almost as much,—and that is not knowledge, but conjecture.

OF MEMORY

William Benjamin Carpenter, *Principles of Mental Physiology* (1874), 2nd edn. (London: Henry S. King, 1875), 436–7, 453–7.

Here Carpenter, like Dallas, invokes the image of a photograph to describe the storing of mental representations, while developing the physiological account of memory favoured by Winslow. Carpenter's analysis, however, is far more subtle than Winslow's, for he argues that there has to be a subjective recognition of the past, or 'consciousness of agreement' for remembrance to take place, and here he directly refers to Frances Power Cobbe's point (see above), that we construct our memories as much as simply recognize them.

Now there is very strong Physiological reason to believe that this 'storing-up of ideas' in the Memory is the psychological expression of physical changes in the

Cerebrum, by which ideational states are permanently registered or recorded; so that any 'trace' left by them, although remaining so long outside the 'sphere of consciousness' as to have *seemed* non-existent, may be revived again in full vividness under certain special conditions,—just as the invisible impression left upon the sensitive paper of the Photographer, is developed into a picture by the application of particular chemical re-agents. For in no other way does it seem possible to account for the fact of very frequent occurrence, that the presence of a fever-poison in the blood,—perverting the normal activity of the Cerebrum, so as to produce *Delirium*—brings within the 'sphere of consciousness' the 'traces' of mental experiences long since past, of which, in the ordinary condition, there was no remembrance whatever. Thus, the revival, in the delirium of fever, of the remembrance of a Language once familiarly known, but long forgotten, has been often noticed.[1] [. . .]

It seems perfectly clear, then, that under what we cannot but term purely *physical* conditions, strictly *mental* phenomena present themselves. It is common to the whole series of cases, that the automatic action of the 'Mechanism of Thought' does that which Volition is unable to effect. Whether it be the *toxic* condition of the blood, or the simple excitement of the cerebral circulation generally, or the special direction of blood to a particular part of the brain, it is beyond our present power to tell; but as *all* Brain-change is (like the action of any other mechanism) the expression of Force, the production of these *unusual* mental phenomena by the instrumentality of an unusual reaction between the blood and the brain-substance is no more difficult of comprehension, than that of those *ordinary* forms of Psychical activity, which we have seen reason to regard as the results of the translation (so to speak) of one form of Force into another. [. . .]

It seems, [however], to admit of question, whether *everything* that passes through our Minds thus leaves its impression on their material instrument; and whether a somewhat too extensive generalization has not been erected on a rather limited basis. For the doctrine of the indelibility of Memory rests on the spontaneous revival, under circumstances indicative of some change in the physical condition of the Brain, of the long dormant 'traces' left by such former impressions as are referable to one or other of the three following categories:— (1) States of Consciousness as to places, persons, languages, &c., which are *habitual* in early life, and which are, therefore, likely to have directed the *growth* of the Brain; (2) Modes of Thought in which the formation of Associations largely participates, and which are likely to have modified the course of its *maintenance* by Nutrition after the attainment of maturity; or (3) Single experiences of peculiar force and vividness, such as are likely to have left very decided 'traces,' although the circumstances of their formation were so unusual as to keep them out of ordinary Associational remembrance. [. . .]

[1] Here again Carpenter cites Coleridge's anecdote from the *Biographia Literaria*.

This Reproduction, however, is not all that constitutes Memory; for there must be, in addition, a *recognition* of the reproduced state of Consciousness as one which has been formerly experienced; and this involves a distinct Mental state, which has been termed the 'consciousness of agreement.' Without this recognition, we should live in the present alone; for the reproduction of past states of Consciousness would affect us only like the succession of fantasies presented to us in the play of the Imagination. We should only be conscious of them as *present* to us at the time of their recurrence, and should not in any way connect them with the past. Hence this Consciousness of Agreement between our present and our past Mental experiences, constitutes the basis of our feeling of *personal identity*; for, if it were entirely extinguished, there would be nothing to carry on that feeling of identity from one moment to another. I am satisfied that *I* am the person to whom such and such experiences happened yesterday or a month, or a year, or twenty years ago; because I am not only conscious at this moment of the ideas which represent those experiences, but because I recognize them as the revived representations of my past experiences. But I may be told by others that things have happened to me in the past, of which I can call up no remembrance whatever, even when they mention circumstances likely to revive their traces by Association. And in *this* case, I cannot recognize my own identity with the subject of these experiences, save as I do so *indirectly* by reliance on the testimony of those who relate them. Sometimes, indeed, we come so completely to *realise* such forgotten experiences, by repeatedly *picturing* them to ourselves, that the ideas of them attain a force and vividness which equals or even exceeds that which the actual memory of them would afford. In like manner, when the Imagination has been exercised in a sustained and determinate manner,—as in the composition of a work of fiction,—its ideal creations may be reproduced with the force of actual experiences; and the sense of personal identity may be projected backwards (so to speak) into the characters which the Author has 'evolved out of the depths of his own consciousness,'—as Dickens states to have been continually the case with himself. And something of the same kind has happened to most persons, however unimaginative they may be, in the reproduction of ideas which have previously only passed through the mind in Dreams; for almost every one has had occasion, at some time or other, to say 'Did this really happen to me, or did I dream it?'—the past *mental* experience having been as complete in the one case as in the other. [. . .]

Though we are accustomed to speak of Memory as if it consisted in an *exact* reproduction of past states of Consciousness, yet experience is continually showing us that this reproduction is very often *inexact*, through the modification which the 'trace' has undergone in the interval. Sometimes the trace has been partially obliterated; and what remains may serve to give a very erroneous (because imperfect) view of the occurrence. And where it is one in which our own Feelings are interested, we are extremely apt to lose sight of what goes against them, so that the representation given by Memory is altogether one-sided. This is continually demonstrated by the entire dissimilarity of the accounts of the same occurrence or conversation, which shall be given by two or more parties concerned in it, even when the matter is fresh in their minds, and they are honestly desirous of telling the truth. And this diversity will usually become still more pronounced with the lapse of time: the trace becoming gradually but unconsciously modified by the habitual course of thought and feeling; so that when it is so acted on after a lengthened interval as to bring up a reminiscence of the original occurrence, that reminiscence really represents, *not* the actual occurrence, but the modified trace of it. And this is the source of an enormous number of 'fallacies of testimony,' which recent experiences of Mesmerism and Spiritualism have brought into strong light. [. . .] Miss Cobbe, has specially directed attention to these 'Fallacies of Memory'.[2]

ORGANIC MEMORY

Herbert Spencer, *The Principles of Psychology* (1855), 2nd edn., 2 vols. (London: Williams and Norgate, 1870–2), i. 444–5, 450–2.

'Words are somewhat strained in their meanings by calling that a Second Edition, of which the new portion greatly exceeds the old portion in amount', wrote Spencer in the Preface of the revised and much extended Principles of Psychology. *The new edition, written when evolutionary theory had gained greater public recognition, elaborates Spencer's earlier work rather than radically departing from it. This account of 'organic memory' develops the physiological account of memory discussed in the extracts above within an evolutionary perspective. Spencer's general analyses of the role of acquired habits and reflex actions were central to late nineteenth-century ideas of unconscious inheritance. The section on memory comes immediately after chapters on 'reflex action' and 'instinct'.*

While, in any instinctive act, we see an entire process of bringing internal relations into harmony with external relations, Memory, taken alone, exhibits relations in consciousness which do not include any active adjustment of the organism to relations in the environment. Though those successions of ideas which constitute Memory, nearly all represent past experiences of the outer

---

[2] Carpenter here quotes from Cobbe's article above.

world; yet, as many if not most of them stand for past experiences of the outer world that are fortuitously combined, it is clear that, even considered as fragments of correspondences, they cannot be held to have as marked a harmony with the environment as have the homologous parts of automatic actions. True, each act of recollection is the establishment of an inner relation answering to *some* outer relation; but as that outer relation is often a transitory one, the inner relation established in the act of recollection is often one answering to no relation now existing or ever likely to exist again; and in that sense is not a correspondence. The correspondence here becomes evanescent.

From this it will probably be inferred that a satisfactory account of Memory, as viewed from our present stand-point, is impracticable. The doctrine that all psychical changes are interpretable as incidents of the correspondence between the organism and its environment, seems to be at fault. Besides the fact that part of the psychical changes constituting Memory have reference to no existing outer relations, there is the further fact that many trains of thought have apparently little or nothing to do with adjusting the conduct to the requirements. But though the position of Memory in the psychological system here sketched out, may not be at once understood, we need only pursue the synthesis a step further to see how Memory results from that same process of development by which Instinct, becoming more and more complicated, finally merges into the higher forms of psychical action.

Some clue will be gained on observing that while, on the one hand, Instinct may be regarded as a kind of organized memory; on the other hand, Memory may be regarded as a kind of incipient instinct. The automatic actions of a bee building one of its wax cells, answer to outer relations so constantly experienced that they are, as it were, organically remembered. Conversely, an ordinary recollection implies a cohesion of psychical states which becomes stronger by repetition, and so approximates more and more to the indissoluble, the automatic, or instinctive cohesions. [. . .]

This truth, that Memory comes into existence when the involved connexions among psychical states render their successions imperfectly automatic, is in harmony with the obverse truth, that as fast as those connexions among psychical states which we form in Memory, grow by constant repetition automatic, they cease to be part of Memory. We do not speak of ourselves as recollecting relations which have become organically registered. We recollect those relations only of which the registration is incomplete. No one remembers that the object at which he looks has an opposite side; or that a certain modification of the visual impression implies a certain distance; or that the thing he sees moving about is a live animal. To ask a man whether he remembers that the sun shines, that fire burns, that iron is hard, would be a misuse of language. Even the almost fortuitous connexions among our experiences, cease to be classed as memories when they have become thoroughly familiar. Though, on hearing the voice of some unseen person slightly known to us, we say we recollect to whom the voice belongs, we do not use the same expression respecting the voices of those with whom we live. The meanings of words which in childhood have to be consciously recalled, seem in adult life to be immediately present. But the clearest instance of the gradual lapse of memory into automatic coherence, is yielded by the musician. Originally, he was taught that each mark on the paper has a certain name, and implies that a particular key on the piano is to be struck; and during his first lessons, each recurrence of this mark was accompanied with a distinct process of recollecting which key on the piano he must strike. By long-continued practice, however, the series of psychical changes that occur between seeing this mark and striking this key, have been reduced into one almost automatic change. The visual perception of the crotchet or quaver; the perception of its position on the lines of the stave, and of its relation to the beginning of the bar; the consciousness of the place on the piano where the answering key lies; the consciousness of the muscular adjustments required to bring the arm, hand, and finger, into the attitudes requisite for touching that key; the consciousness of the muscular impulse which will give a blow of the due strength, and of the time during which the muscles must be kept contracted to produce the right length of note—all these mental states, which were at first so many separate recollections, ultimately constitute a succession so rapid that the whole of them pass in an instant. As fast as they cease to be distinct states of mind—as fast as they cease to fill appreciable places in consciousness, so fast do they become automatic. The two things are two sides of the same thing. And thus it happens that the practised pianist can play while conversing with those around—while his memory is occupied with quite other ideas than the meanings of the signs before him.

Now the fact that in ourselves psychical states which are originally connected by the process we call recollection, become, by perpetual repetition, connected automatically or instinctively, is manifestly the obverse of the fact that as, in the development of the instincts, the psychical states grow into more involved groups that are less frequently repeated, there occur among them connexions that are not automatic, and memory commences. Our inductive knowledge of the one fact confirms our deduction of the other.

Memory, then, pertains to that class of psychical states which are in process of being organized. It continues so long as the organizing of them continues, and disappears when the organization of them is complete. In the advance of the correspondence, each more complex cluster of attributes and relations which a creature acquires the power of recognizing, is responded to at first irregularly and uncertainly; and there is then a weak remembrance. By multiplication of experiences this remembrance is made stronger—the internal cohesions are better adjusted to the external persistences; and the response is rendered more appropriate. By further multiplication of experiences, the internal relations are at last structurally registered in harmony with the external ones; and so, conscious memory passes into unconscious or organic memory. At the same time, a new and still more complex order of experiences is rendered appreciable. The relations that occur between these groups of phenomena that have thus been severally integrated in consciousness, occupy Memory in place of the relations between the components of each group. These become gradually organized; and, like the previous ones, are succeeded by others more complex still.

LIFE AND HABIT

Samuel Butler, *Life and Habit* (1877), 2nd edn. (London: Trübner and Co., 1878), 52–4.

Butler was not a professional physiologist, and Life and Habit *was not taken entirely seriously by the scientific establishment. However, his argument that each individual contains the accumulated memories of their ancestors strikingly dramatizes late nineteenth-century notions of inheritance. Here Butler approvingly cites Darwin, though later, in* Unconscious Memory, *he rejects Darwin's theory of chance selection in favour of Lamarck's notion of the inheritance of acquired characteristics. (See also Section V below.)*

It is one against legion when a creature tries to differ from his own past selves. He must yield or die if he wants to differ widely, so as to lack natural instincts, such as hunger or thirst, or not to gratify them. [. . .] 'Do this, this, this, which we too have done, and found our profit in it,' cry the souls of his forefathers within him. Faint are the far ones, coming and going as the sound of bells wafted on to a high mountain; loud and clear are the near ones, urgent as an alarm of fire. 'Withhold,' cry some. 'Go on boldly,' cry others. 'Me, me, me, revert hitherward, my descendant,' shouts one as it were from some high vantage-ground over the heads of the clamorous multitude. 'Nay, but me, me, me,' echoes another; and our former selves fight within us and wrangle for our possession. Have we not here what is commonly called an *internal tumult*, when dead pleasures and pains tug within us hither and thither? Then may the battle be decided by what people are pleased to call our own experience. Our own indeed! What is our own save by mere courtesy of speech? A matter of fashion. Sanction sanctifieth and fashion fashioneth. And so with death—the most inexorable of all conventions.

However this may be, we may assume it as an axiom with regard to actions acquired after birth, that we never do them automatically save as the result of long practice, and after having thus acquired perfect mastery over the action in question.

But given the practice or experience, and the intricacy of the process to be performed appears to matter very little. There is hardly anything conceivable as being done by man, which a certain amount of familiarity will not enable him to do, as it were mechanically and without conscious effort. 'The most complex and difficult movements,' writes Mr. Darwin, 'can in time be performed without the least effort or consciousness.' All the main business of life is done thus unconsciously or semi-unconsciously. For what is the main business of life? We work that we may eat and digest, rather than eat and digest that we may work; this, at any rate, is the normal state of things: the more important business then is that which is carried on unconsciously. So again the action of the brain, which goes on prior to our realising the idea in which it results, is not perceived by the individual. So also all the deeper springs of action and conviction. The residuum with which we fret and worry ourselves is a mere matter of detail, as the higgling and haggling of the market, which is not over the bulk of the price, but over the last halfpenny.

Section III
The Sexual Body

The Sexual Body

The contorted attitudes towards female sexuality in the Victorian era are clearly illustrated in J. G. Millingen's assertion that 'Woman, with her exalted spiritualism, is more under the control of matter'. The simple virgin–whore distinction does not begin to explain the complexities and contradictions operative in an era when all women were seen, increasingly, to be under the tyrannical command of what was termed their 'uterine economy'. In the hierarchy of being, man was assigned the central place of rationality, and woman came to inhabit the two poles of difference, the body and spirituality. Discussions of womanhood oscillate wildly between these poles, moving, as in 'Woman in her Psychological Relations', between extravagant praise of the spiritual beauties of womanhood and zestful accounts of female cannibalism and monomaniacal cunning stimulated by uterine disorders.

The nineteenth century witnessed the growing professionalization of the medical profession, and, within that, the development of a new specialist area in gynaecological medicine. The female bodily economy, subject from puberty to the strains of menstruation and pregnancy, was seen to be far more liable to disorder than the male. In the intertwined systems of bodily and mental health, any slight disruption of the uterine functions would be reflected in the state of the nerves. As Millingen observes, in woman, 'a hysteric predisposition is incessantly predominating from the dawn of puberty'. Menstruation was seen to hold the key to female health, acting, as George Man Burrows notes, as 'the moral and physical barometer of the female constitution'. Damming up of the menstrual flow could lead, it was believed, to nervous diseases and possible insanity: the eminent French physician, Esquirol, always noted the relationship between menstrual flow and mental health in the inmates of his asylum. According to the Victorian medical profession, the female body was almost permanently in a state of pathology. There was a multiplication of the pathological states attached to menstruation and a correlative increase in the importance of the doctor's role in monitoring the discharge to make sure it passed the tests of quality and quantity, here defined by Locock, and repeated in Chavasse's popular domestic manual. If no discharge at all appeared, some physicians believed it was necessary to draw blood from elsewhere to stop this 'excess' polluting the rest of the bodily economy. Far from living in ignorance of their bodily functions, middle-class and upper-class women were constantly exhorted to pay minute attention to the workings of their reproductive systems.

The obsession with the menstrual flow at this period can be partly explained by the prevalent belief, here defined by Locock, that the catamenia (menstruation) in women was equivalent to sexual heat in animals, and hence the outward sign of sexual excitement. Although the basic principles of human ovulation were more or less understood by the 1860s, these associations clearly lingered on. The belief that women were subjected to the forces of their reproductive system, with all its capacity for threatening excesses of sexual energy, existed, however, side by side with claims for female purity, passionlessness, and sexual anaesthesia. We include here the classic statement by Acton on female sexual indifference, but it is important to notice the context: Acton is trying to reassure men that women will not be as sexually demanding as they fear. Like all Victorian statements on female sexuality, his arguments are riddled with contradictions. Nor was his voice the dominant one in Victorian medicine.

Fears about unrestrained female sexual energy led to concerns, here expressed by Thomas Laycock, that private schools, and the current practices of education, would lead girls into the 'vicious' practice of masturbation, thus unfitting them for marriage (although boys are the primary cultural targets of these fears). Laycock, one of the most influential medical commentators on female nervous diseases, sought to explain female pathology by placing woman in the context of the reproductive cycles of animal and plant life, laying the foundations, thirty years before Darwin's *Descent of Man*, for a form of socio-biology. His vision of womanhood emphasizes her powerlessness to control her own sexual urges: it is also a highly normative vision, drawing on work on brain size to prove woman's inferior position within the social hierarchy, and emphasizing her maternal role. 'Old maids' and women past the 'climacteric', or menopause, fare badly in the medical literature of the time. Life itself was frequently deemed to be at risk with the ending of woman's reproductive usefulness, whilst, for those sufferers of 'arid virginity', the old maids, the penalties could be a withering away of organs that rendered them female and a consequent development of masculine traits, as depicted here in 'Woman in her Psychological Relations'.

The term 'hysteria' is ever-present in these discussions of female sexuality and nervous disorders. Although hysteria was no longer regarded as a uniquely female affliction, linked to the wandering of the womb, commentators throughout the period were nonetheless united in their belief that one of the dominant causes was repressed sexual, or uterine, energy. Long before Freud, physicians such as Georget (here cited by Conolly), Carter, and Donkin were discussing hysteria in terms of sexual repression and, more radically, drawing attention to the ways in which the cultural role assigned to women exacerbated these problems. It was frequently noted (as here by Millingen), that it was the women who were outwardly the most pure and self-controlled who were liable to suffer the worst attacks of hysteria and other consequences of sexual repression. Many of the medical writers quoted in these extracts seem to adopt a very sympathetic stance to women, highlighting the social practices which make sexual suppression a necessity for them. Yet it is worthwhile remembering that this sympathy held its origins in their prior belief that women were in fact prisoners of their own bodies.

Religion features in these discussions only as a form of displacement for sexual energy. Maudsley, who makes the first systematic attempt to define the psychological features of puberty, indeed goes so far as to suggest that St Theresa (model for George Eliot's Dorothea Brooke in *Middlemarch*) was simply suffering from 'the influence of excited sexual organs on the mind'. With the work of Skey in the 1860s, the role of mimicry in hysteria, first noted by Sir Benjamin Brodie in the 1830s, began to play a more central role in analysis, although the dominant organizing metaphors are still those of pressure systems, where energies need channels of release (Carter) or 'safety valves' (Donkin).

Strong class biases are operative throughout these medical discussions of womanhood. The highly-strung hysteric women of the upper classes were blamed for their condition and directed to look at the bouncing health of the lower classes who did not subject themselves to the idle, artificial lives of society women. Clearly, fears of the decline of upper-class dominance fuelled this unrealistic picture of working-class health. Laycock's suggestion that 'healthy mothers of healthy children lie at the root of all national greatness' outlines the assumptions underpinning most of the intertwined discussions of female education and mental health. Yet amidst all the clamour about the increase in female pathology one could still find dissenting voices, as in Clifford Allbutt's attack, printed here, on the 'gynaecological tyranny' of doctors who would fasten all female ailments on the uterus, thereby creating for the woman 'morbid chains' of physical introspection: 'Arraign the uterus, and you fix in the woman the arrow of hypochondria, it may be for life'.

If discussions of female sexuality were riddled with contradictions, the notion of male sexuality—from childhood through to old age—was also deeply problematic. While women's entire bodies were pathologized, concern with the male body focused almost exclusively on the genitals, and on explicitly sexual behaviour. At its simplest, masculine sexuality was seen as a potentially self-destructive drive that had to be kept within its proper channels of adult heterosexual intercourse, if it was not to become diseased and morbid. In many of these extracts the control of sexuality is literally the sign of control over the self—its breakdown is both cause and symptom of insanity. This occurs most clearly in debates on masturbation ('a nameless vice, and one we blush even to allude to', Ritchie remarks), seen by several writers here as one of the primary causes of insanity in young men. The penis, like the uterus, is the worrying site of mental and physical decay.

Acton, and Ritchie in particular, see masturbation as a simultaneously perverse and ubiquitous habit, a universal tendency in youth which nonetheless is learnt primarily by example, paradoxically in the very institutions designed to shape rational male subjectivity—the private schools. It is middle- and upper-class youth that are most at risk, most in need of continual surveillance. These writers saw the habit as leading to certain decline, both mental and physical; the self-abuser, marked by his sweaty palms, his shifty eyes, his solitary, studious demeanour, progressing through the inevitable mental stages of monomania and dementia, and concluding in many cases in suicide or self-mutilation. Physically, 'self-abuse' led to impotence, and the complete extinction of desire. It also resulted in 'involuntary seminal emissions', usually dissociated from sexual pleasure, and the foremost symptom of *spermatorrhea*. 'Spermatorrhea' was first conceived in France by Claude Lallemand in the early 1840s but it was in England that the notion of the disease was most fully elaborated. Action cites Lallemand as the absolute authority on the condition, and follows his method of 'curing' spermatorrhea by cauterization, a treatment which parallels that meted out to women in attempts to cure 'unhealthy' vaginal discharges.

But this view of masculine sexuality was not universally accepted, and it is too easy to accept Acton's view as typical in turn. James Paget saw spermatorrhea not as a morbid physical condition which caused insanity, but as a form of 'sexual hypochondriasis', a male equivalent to hysteria. The ignorance and silence surrounding sexuality, he suggested, created this obsession with the genitals and their functioning. He argued, too, that one could not draw a line between healthy and pathological sexuality; as far as the body was concerned there was absolutely no difference between 'spending' in masturbation or in sexual intercourse. The radical George Drysdale went even further in his critique of mainstream attitudes. In his anonymously published *Physical, Sexual and Natural Religion* he stressed the need for wider education on the body and sexuality for both men and women. He argued against involuntary abstinence for women as well as men, and for the need of both sexes to understand and explore their sexuality. Drysdale explicitly linked sexual and social health: 'It is always a sign of imperfection in an individual, or in society, if the normal requirements of all their members be not duly provided for'. It remains a question of debate how far Drysdale was straying from common orthodoxy, or merely developing the implied arguments against continence to be found in many of the texts on hysteria. Whatever their perspective, however, in all these texts the control of the body, subjectivity and sexuality, is intimately bound up, whether explicitly or implicitly, with questions of social regulation and control.

1. Defining Womanhood

THE PASSIONS, OR MIND AND MATTER

John Gideon Millingen, *The Passions; or Mind and Matter* (London: J. and D. Darling, 1848), 157–9.

Millingen, who also wrote literary works, clearly designed this text for both a general and specialist audience. In this passage he seeks to supply a physiological explanation for the two, seemingly conflicting, Victorian images of womanhood: why woman, generally regarded as more spiritual than man, should also be seen as in thrall to the workings of her reproductive body. Millingen also outlines a version of the mid-Victorian understanding of sexual repression. The image of smouldering fires recurs across a range of medical texts at this period.

If corporeal agency is thus powerful in man, its tyrannic influence will more frequently cause the misery of the gentler sex. Woman, with her exalted spiritualism, is more forcibly under the control of matter; her sensations are more vivid and acute, her sympathies more irresistible. She is less under the influence of the brain than the uterine system, the plexi of abdominal nerves, and irritation of the spinal cord; in her, a hysteric predisposition is incessantly predominating from the dawn of puberty. Therefore is she subject to all the aberrations of love and religion; ecstatic under the impression of both, the latter becomes a resource when the excitement of the former is exhausted by disappointment, infidelity, and age—when, no longer attractive, she is left by the ebb of fond emotions on the bleak shore of despondency; where, like a lost wanderer in the desert, without an oasis upon earth on which to fix her straining eyes, she turns them to heaven, as her last consolation and retreat.

In woman, the concentration of her feelings (a concentration that her social position renders indispensable) adds to their intensity; and like a smouldering fire that has at last got vent, her passions, when no longer trammelled by conventional propriety, burst forth in unquenchable violence. Insanity frequently offers a sad proof of this fact; for it is invariably observed that those females who have been educated with the greatest care and precaution, are the most obscene and disgusting in their language and conduct, when labouring under mental aberration. The reason of this apparently extraordinary fact is to be attributed to that very concentration and imprisonment of the mind to which I have alluded. In females who move in the lower and humbler spheres, there does not exist that necessity for concealing the thoughts that come uppermost in the mind. Their ears have become accustomed to the foul language that is constantly uttered around them, and when under the influence of passion, they will freely indulge in a similar phraseology: not so in higher grades, when nature casts off the shackles of artificial life. It is owing to this strange compound of anomalous emotions that poor Woman has been exposed to the bitter and unjust invectives of many of our poets and satirists—even of our Shakespeare. [. . .]

'frailty, thy name is woman!'[1]

seems to have been his ruling notion

But alas! if women are frail, and may occasionally deserve the harsh epithets bestowed upon them, to what are we to attribute their sad destiny? Simply *to their organization, their education, and our injustice*. What is dishonour in them, is the boast and pride of man; and their fall constitutes his triumph.

WOMAN IN HER PSYCHOLOGICAL RELATIONS

Anon., 'Woman in her psychological relations', *Journal of Psychological Medicine and Mental Pathology*, 4 (1851), 18, 21, 23, 24–5, 30–5.

The author draws heavily on the work of Thomas Laycock in this piece, both his articles on hysteria, published in the Edinburgh Medical and Surgical Journal, *1838–9, and his reworking of that material in* A Treatise on the Nervous Diseases of Women *(1840). Although some of the passages include summary and direct quotation, we have chosen to use this source since the author develops and embellishes the points in his own way, as in his reflections on why women are attracted to soldiers, or the features of the 'old maid'. In its movement from lyrical praise of the glories of womanhood to depictions of female insane cunning, the text, like that of Millingen, illustrates the fundamental conflicts in Victorian medical responses to womanhood.*

[1] *Hamlet*, I. ii. 146

The relations of woman are twofold; material and spiritual—corporeal and moral. By her corporeal nature she is the type and model of Beauty; by her spiritual, of Grace, by her moral, of Love. A perfect woman is indeed the most exalted of terrestrial creatures—physically, mentally, morally. The most profound philosophy, and the most universal instincts of the popular mind concur in this doctrine, each in their own way. [. . .]

It cannot be denied, however, that rarely, if ever, is the ideal perfection of the Divine mind attained; here or there some imperfection mars the grand design; the mind of woman, or the body, or both suffer deformity. Yet we cannot but think that the most beautiful and perfect, physically, are the most excellent and perfect mentally; and that, when the two excellencies fail to be combined in the same person, the failure arises from some morbid reaction of the corporeal organs on the nervous system, or from some bias in the formative effort of the whole. It is in this respect, indeed,—the psychological imperfections in their relation to corporeal disorder and defect—that woman presents the most interesting problems for inquiry and solution; and it is only by a wide and comprehensively philosophical inquiry in the two directions indicated, that anything like a satisfactory comprehension of the problems can be acquired, or the problems themselves adequately solved. [. . .]

To assist us in comprehending the psychological relations of woman, we will here observe that, although there is doubtless a general difference in the constitution of the two sexes, many of the more *special* characteristics are either dependent upon the influence of the reproductive organs, or are *general* characteristics rendered more marked or exaggerated by the same influence. The development of these organs in man and animals generally corresponds very closely to the flowering of plants; and numerous interesting analogies may be traced between the adult life of flowering plants and the adult life of man. [. . .] The *blooming maiden* [. . .] is well compared to those brilliant flowers, the reproductive organs of which, when fully developed, are surrounded with the most gorgeous tissues—for what reason we know not. [. . .] The colour, composition, and form, of the numerous cutaneous appendages of animals are often exclusively connected with these fundamental functions of the reproductive organs; and there cannot be a doubt that the appearance of these appendages to the opposite sex, exercises an important influence upon the sexual instinct. Usually, the male is more brilliant and more beautiful than the female; and this is particularly striking in butterflies and birds, in which (as in many flowers) the Divine Idea has lavishly displayed every possible combination of the beautiful in colour and form. [. . .]

Woman, in virtue of that mysterious chain which binds creation together in one common bond of vitality, is not exempt from this influence of colour and form. Often, indeed, it is not recognised, or if recognised, its true nature and bearings are not understood; but many a scene of domestic anguish might have been averted, and many an irrevocable sacrifice prevented—the sacrifice of home, reputation, friends, conscience—to the gratification of an irresistible passion, if this secret influence of external form and colour on the mere instinct had been met and counterbalanced. The soldier is *par excellence* the most attractive to the sex; his warlike profession, his manly moustache, the scarlet and gold, the nodding plume, the burnished helm of his uniform, his glittering arms, and the tout-ensemble of his accoutrements, often, where there is a special susceptibility to the sexual influence of form and colour, awake strange mysterious emotions in the young female just bursting into womanhood, that quickly shape themselves into a longing desire, the object of which she scarcely comprehends. Different in its origin, but analogous in its nature, is the preference so often given by the more susceptible portion of the sex to the manly sensualist. The vigorous bold front, the ample beard and luxuriant hair, the broad chest, the firm port, and an eye flashing passion and admiration, too often carry away an amorous female; and she yields to the tempter, against her better judgment, in spite of the earnest entreaties of her friends, and to the utter rupture of the dearest ties—not even excepting the maternal. This *enchantment*—which it literally is—this infatuation, is often due to the unrecognised reaction of the physical appearance of the tempter upon the mind of his victim, untrained to self-control, predisposed to the allurement by an excess of reproductive energy, and irresistibly impelled forward to the gratification of the obscure, deep-felt longings he excites by an over-stimulated nervous system. [. . .]

MORBID APPETITES

The modifications of the *appetite* necessary in the females of lower animals, for the proper nutrition and development of the ovum or fœtus, are occasionally reproduced in the pregnant human female as *morbid* appetites; but perhaps they, like other similar modifications of the instincts, occur more frequently, *proportionally*, in the young unmarried female. [. . .]

The things desired in this ovarian perversion of the appetite are sometimes very extraordinary, and outrageously absurd. Dr. Laycock quotes Dr. Elliotson as mentioning in his lectures that a 'patient has longed for raw flesh' (the carnivorous appetite) 'and even for live flesh, so that some have eaten live kittens and rats.' Langius, a German writer, tells a story of a woman who lived near Cologne, who had such a cannibalish longing for the flesh of her husband, that she killed him, ate as much of him as she could while still fresh, and pickled the remainder. Another longed for a bite out of a baker's arm! [. . .]

There are other alterations in the mental character of woman belonging to this class of perverted instincts, which are of greater importance, because they involve the social and moral relations. The hysterical *cunning* of the young female is traced by Dr. Laycock to the same ovarian source. Referring to the development of certain instincts in the female at the period of procreation, and when the care of offspring is the great end of life, he compares the artfulness of lower animals with this hysterical cunning, and attributes it to the influence of the ovaria on the nervous system. [. . .] When the young female suffers from irregular action of the ovaria on the system, the natural astuteness and quickness of perception degenerates into mere artfulness or monomaniacal cunning; and it is to this morbid influence of the ovaria on the organ of mind, that Dr. Laycock attributes the extraordinary instances of monomaniacal cunning in females, on record. He observes, on this head, 'of all animals, woman has the most acute faculties; and when we consider how much these may be exalted by the influence of the reproductive organs, there is not much ground for surprise at the grotesque forms which cunning assumes in the hysterical female, although they have caused much speculation and astonishment. Insane cunning is usually exhibited in attempts at deception, but occasionally in a propensity to steal, or rather to steal slily. It may be remarked, that when it occurs, it may be as much a symptom of hysteria as any corporeal affection whatever. It is a true monomania, and is most likely to occur in the female who is hysterical from excess of sexual development—*one possessing the utmost modesty of deportment, and grace of figure and movement, for the modesty itself springs out of that feminine timidity to which I have just alluded.* Sly stealing, however, is most frequently observed in pregnant women.' The italics in the above quotation are our own, as we wish to direct the reader's special attention to the important principle pointed out by Dr. Laycock. The propensity, in such case, is dependent solely on the excitement of the nervous system by the ovaria; hence it is, that when, in consequence of an active condition of those structures, the graces peculiar to the feminine character are peculiarly developed, and gentleness, modesty, and timidity, are prominent characteristics, often in those identical cases it is, that there is this morbid excitation of the instinct of artfulness or cunning; and it is these endowments which explain the influence that hysterical girls have upon all that come near them, and which is, as Dr. Laycock observes, really 'astonishing: parents, women, physicians, all yield to them.' It is also the marked excitation of this sexual artfulness which renders nugatory all the experiments and labours of those mesmerists, whose principal subjects are young females or youths about the age of puberty. Psychologists, practically acquainted with this subject, can place no reliance upon the statements of the hysterical females upon whom mesmerists experiment, however well educated, gentle, good, and truth-loving they may be naturally, and really *are* in all other matters. Physicians have recorded numerous instances of strange and motiveless deceptions, thefts, and crimes practised by young women, even by ladies of unexceptionable morals, excellent education, and high rank. Fasting women, *ecstatica*, sly poisoners, pilfering lady-thieves, &c., present examples of this kind; particular instances we need not mention, as they may be found in most works on hysteria, and often occupy a niche in the newspapers. When *cunning* is combined with a morbid excitation of the propensity to destroy, such as is manifested in the females of brutes, the effect is sometimes dreadful, and is seen in the perpetration of *secret* murders by wholesale poisoning, or in secret incendiarism; and if other natural instincts be perverted, the objects of woman's warmest and most disinterested affections may perish by her hand. It is a singular fact, in natural history, and remarkably illustrative of our views, the parturient domestic animals sometimes suffer from the same morbid condition of the nervous system as the human mother, and they also destroy their offspring. Thus cats, sows, and bitches, have been known to *eat* their litter; cows to butt their calves to death, hens chase their chickens, &c. When cunning is combined with a morbid state of *the temper*, the misery inflicted upon domestic peace is inexpressible. The ingenuity in malice and falsehood displayed by the patient is most extraordinary; so extraordinary, indeed, that it is never credited until it is experienced. Cases are by no means infrequent in which the sufferer from this sad derangement is the most intellectual and most amiable of the family; beloved by all, respected, almost worshipped. Hence, when, after numerous struggles to repress them, the propensities, excited into such fearful and almost supernatural activity, by the ovarian irritation, burst forth beyond all control, and the pet of the family is seen to be the opposite, morally, in every respect to what she had been—irreligious, selfish, slanderous, false, malicious, devoid of affection, thievish in a thousand petty ways, bold—may be erotic, self-willed, and quarrelsome—the shock to the family circle and friends is intense; and if the case be not rightly understood, great, and often irreparable mischief is done to correct what seems to be *vice*, but is really *moral insanity*. Dr. Laycock, we are happy to learn, has been able to treat cases of this kind with perfect success, by a course of galvanism directed through the ovaria, and by suitable medication and moral and hygienic treatment.

Perhaps in the whole range of psychology there is no subject so deeply interesting as this; for it is in moral insanity that man's spiritual and moral nature is the most awfully and most distressingly subjected to his corporeal frame. It is a disease undoubtedly much more frequent in the sex than in man; and if the warning voice we shall here raise against all those methods of education, and mental and physical training—all those conventional customs and social habits—all those *fashions* in dress and social intercourse, which stimulate the nervous system generally of the sex, and the sexual system in particular—be at all successful in placing woman in greater safety from this sad clouding of her intellect—this lamentable spoliation of her greatest charms, we shall feel that we have done good services to society and the state.

Shall we omit the consideration of the psychology of 'Old Maids?' Our gallantry forbids us; for, although their 'single blessedness' may have left them to pass through the world 'in maiden meditation fancy free,'[1] the non-fulfilment of

---

[1] Shakespeare, *A Midsummer Night's Dream*, II. ii. 164.

their duties as *women* involves its punishment, or its penalty. Celibacy is more frequent in the middle and higher classes of society than in the lower, with whom prudential considerations have less weight; hence it is that the 'Old Maid' is seldom to be found in that class. It is not difficult to trace the gradual development of the mental and corporeal peculiarities of the woman who has passed middle life in celibacy. A great void in her nature has been left unfilled, except occasionally. At first, the future victim of Society's conventionalism is 'as scornful as scornful can be' in the flush of youth and beauty. She expects to see 'wit and wisdom and gold' at her feet, and hardly understands how it is that year after year glides away, and she is still unmarried, until she discovers, when it is too late, that pride and haughtiness mar woman's charms, however charming; and that anyhow they repel the timid lover. Then, when the climacteric period is dawning upon her, she possibly makes a foolish match, in sheer desperation, with her junior in age, her inferior in station, and her unequal companion in every respect. Or, if prudence still guides her, she lavishes the love with which her nature is instinct on nephews and nieces, or some pet family. Or the love that would have found its natural outpouring on a husband or children, may be directed by religious feelings to suffering humanity, and she may become warmly charitable; or if the intellect be contracted and selfish, it may find vent in domestic or tame animals. Hence the cat, the parrot, and the poodle, are connected popularly with arid virginity.

With the shrinking of the ovaria and the consequent cessation of the reproductive nisus, there is a corresponding change in the outer form. The subcutaneous fat is no longer deposited, and consequently the form becomes angular, the body lean, the skin wrinkled. The hair changes in colour and loses its luxuriancy; the skin is less transparent and soft, and the chin and upper lip become downy. Sometimes, indeed, the male characteristics are in part developed (a change which has been observed in lower animals to occur concurrently with a change in the ovaries) and a hoarser voice accompanies a slight development of the beard. With this change in the person there is an analogous change in the mind, temper, and feelings. The woman approximates in fact to a man, or in one word, she is a *virago*. She becomes strong-minded; is masculine in her pursuits, severe in her temper, bold and unfeminine in her manners. This unwomanly condition undoubtedly renders her repulsive to man, while her envious, overbearing temper, renders her offensive to her own sex. If there be such a change in the ovaria that the temper is modified in the way we have described, the 'Old Maid' is the pest and scourge of the circle in which she moves; and in extreme cases—verging upon, if not actually the subject of—worse insanity, she is little less than a she-fiend. Her whole life is devoted to an ingenious system of mischief-making; she delights in tormenting—corporeally and mentally—all that she dare to practise upon. She is intrusive, insolent, regardless of the ordinary rules of politeness; ever feeling insults where none were intended; ungrateful, treacherous, and revengeful—not sparing even her oldest and truest friends. Add to these mental characteristics, a quaint untidy dress, a shrivelled skin, a lean figure, a bearded lip, shattered teeth, harsh grating voice, and manly stride, and the *typical* 'Old Maid' is complete.

MIND AND BRAIN

Thomas Laycock, *Mind and Brain: or, The Correlations of Consciousness and Organisation: Systematically Investigated and Applied to Philosophy, Mental Science and Practice* (1860), 2nd edn. 2 vols. (London: Simpkin, Marshall, and Co., 1869), ii. 481–8, 490.

In this chapter of Mind and Brain, *Laycock draws together many of his previous reflections on womanhood from* A Treatise on the Nervous Diseases of Women *(1840), and co-ordinates them with recent studies on brain size, and anthropology. His earlier, pre-Darwinian work had carefully sought to understand woman in relation to the workings of the plant and animal kingdom, and these forms of analysis are further developed here; female patterns of behaviour are referred back to the workings of animal instincts.*

MANHOOD AND WOMANHOOD

The mental organology and the corresponding endowments of the sexes differ in regard to both the size and qualities of the encephalon in general, and of particular portions of it. According to Tiedemann's researches, the female brain is smaller from birth than the male. An adult male's brain is heavier than an adult female's by one tenth, or in other words, man's brain is in proportion by weight to woman's as 100 to 90.* [. . .] Milton's affirmation that man's 'fair large front and eye sublime declare absolute rule,'[1] does not apply to the smaller frontal development of a woman, in whom a large forehead derogates from beauty of form and expression. Experience shows that woman has less capability than man for dealing with the abstract in philosophy, science, and art, and this fact is in accordance with the less development of the frontal convolutions. It has been plausibly alleged (chiefly, however, by those who have not looked at the physio-

---

* *On the Weight of the Brain and on the Circumstances affecting it,* by John Thurnam, M.D.; *Journal of Mental Science,* April 1866.

[1] *Paradise Lost,* Book IV, ll. 300–1.

logical side of the question), that the difference is owing to the defective education of woman as compared with man, and that if she had the same advantages of a training in logic, metaphysics, and the exact sciences, she would be the equal of man in these qualities of mind. But many men have risen to eminence in these departments who have had no better educational advantages than women—in some instances, even fewer. One fact seems to be conclusive as to this point. A much greater number of women than of men are educated in music, and many have attained to eminence as musical artists; but, so far as I know, all the great musical composers are men. This is equally true of the other æsthetic arts, as painting, sculpture, poetry, and literature. [. . .] A few women have manifested the masculine faculties which lead to eminence in the physical sciences, but these have been quite as rare as bearded women. [. . .] Woman's excellence over man is not, in truth, in the manifestation of force of intellect and energy of will, but in the sphere of wisdom, and love, and moral power.

The natural history of man is in accordance with these scientific data. The less intellectual and physical energy of woman has determined her social position in all ages and all races. [. . .]

So low down in the scale of creation as we can go, wherever there is a discoverable distinction of sex, we find that maternity is the first and most fundamental duty of the female. [. . .]

The females of both solitary and social animals manifest constructive instincts in the formation of homes and clothing for their young, and in the collection and use of textile and other materials to this end. Feminine skill in the textile and constructive arts is but an evolution of this fundamental part of the maternal instinct. Therewith are evolved the faculty of judging of the materials and the desire to attain them, so often morbidly manifested in women as kleptomania. [. . .]

The differences in the affective relations and sentiments of the sexes arise equally out of fundamental laws and instincts. [. . .] In fully developed domestic animals the male animal desires and seeks the society of the female; the female desires, allures, but does not seek the male. This relation of the sexes in man is well shown, as to the male, by those primitive marriage customs in which the man carries off the woman by force. It is out of this primordial law of sexual relation that the sentiment of feminine modesty is evolved, and which is sometimes markedly developed in hysteria. Modesty being thus one of the sexual characteristics of the perfect woman, is manifested in its most attractive form at puberty. When a woman has lost her modesty, her fitness to procreate offspring of high moral excellence is probably lost too. Certainly, she is no longer either a suitable companion or a solace for her husband, or a fit teacher and trainer for her children. To a man of high moral purity an immodest woman, however attractive corporeally and sensually, is an object of repugnance—even a masculine woman repels a man of refined taste.

It is, in fact, in the manifestation of reciprocal fitness for the duties of life that the attractions proper to each sex in regard to the other consist. These are both corporeal and moral; but the moral qualities, being the latest and most highly evolved, are the least regarded. The corporeal signs of healthy vigour and of reproductive fitness are those which render individuals of the two sexes especially attractive to each other in man, in common with lower animals. In woman, the breadth of the hips or pelvis, the glow of health on the cheeks and lips, the purity of the teeth, the luxuriant hair, the elastic step, the graceful easy carriage, indicate the mere corporeal qualities; the 'heaving bosom,' the open brow, the sympathising smile, the gentle emotional voice, indicate her social and moral qualities. It is to her bosom woman clasps all that she loves, and it is by a sort of instinctive outness that she seeks solace and protection, when needed, on the firm and unyielding breast of her husband.

The social duties of the sexes are regulated in man, as in all other social animals, by the fundamental law of the genesis of society, whereby there is a division of labour for the common good [. . .] In man, the most highly evolved domestic and social animal, the Monogamous family is the unit of the community; polygamy belongs rather to the gregarious mammals. But in both these forms the fundamental relations of the sexes to society are the same. The female widens the sphere of her sympathies to the inclusion of the males generally and of the offspring of other females, and thus maternal affection evolves into the feminine social sympathies. Every man who has suffered much knows how instinctively woman is 'a ministering angel.' That it is an instinctive quality is proved by facts of natural history. The hinds of a herd have been seen to caress and solace a wounded and dying stag, and the female elephant nurses the wounded male. [. . .] On the other hand, the males are the warriors and defenders of the community, and fight, when it is attacked, in battle-array under a leader; in these conflicts the females rarely take part. Since the masculine qualities of energy and vigour are equally as necessary for the continued perfection of the species as for the defence of the community, those corporeal characteristics which indicate that a man is endowed with these qualities and with masculine sympathy for the sex, are those which attract a woman's eye, and lead her to prefer him. Hence arise the mystic sympathies of the true woman with virile strength, fortitude, and courage of the chivalrous kind, and her contempt for what is effeminate, base, and cowardly in man. [. . .]

Various means have been recommended for the redress of woman's grievances. The higher education of woman has been chiefly advocated in this country, partly with a view to fit her for the better performance of the duties of wife and mother, and so diminish that disinclination to marry which in a luxurious state of civilisation men manifest, and partly with a view to breadwinning as a self-supporter. Whatever enlightens the understanding of a woman, and teaches her that the domestic virtues and acquirements are her best recommendation, and the true sources of her power, must advance her position. It is not too much to say that to a woman the knowledge of the things that lie before her in daily life is her prime wisdom, and the most solid basis for her welfare and the welfare of society, which are in truth identical. Healthy mothers of healthy children lie at the root of all national greatness, of whatever kind.

WANT OF SEXUAL FEELING IN THE FEMALE

William Acton, *The Functions and Disorders of the Reproductive Organs in Childhood, Youth, Adult Age, and Advanced Life Considered in their Physiological, Social and Moral Relations* (1857), 4th edn. (London: John Churchill, 1865), 133–7.

This text has frequently been used to define Victorian attitudes to sexuality. 'The majority of women', Acton observes, 'are not very much troubled by sexual feeling'. It is important to note the context of these remarks, however. The chapter is entitled 'False Impotence' and Acton is trying to reassure males that marriage will not be too terrifying an ordeal. As the other texts in this section show, passionlessness was not the only, or even the dominant, medical notion of female sexuality in the Victorian era. The conflicts in Acton's own position are made clear by his attack on women who fail to show sufficient sexual interest in their husbands. Lack of interest is also traced to a prior addiction to the vice of masturbation.

Want of Sexual Feeling in the Female a Cause of Impotence.—We have already mentioned lack of sexual feeling in the female as not an uncommon cause of apparent or temporary impotence in the male. There is so much ignorance on the subject, and so many false ideas are current as to women's sexual condition, and are so productive of mischief, that I need offer no apology for giving here, before we proceed, the true state of the case.

I have taken pains to obtain and compare abundant evidence on this subject, and the result of my inquiries I may briefly epitomise as follows:—I should say that the majority of women (happily for them) are not very much troubled with sexual feeling of any kind. What men are habitually, women are only exceptionally. It is too true, I admit, as the divorce courts show, that there are some few women who have sexual desires so strong that they surpass those of men, and shock public feeling by their exhibition. I admit, of course, the existence of sexual excitement terminating even in nymphomania, a form of insanity that those accustomed to visit lunatic asylums must be fully conversant with; but, with these sad exceptions, there can be no doubt that sexual feeling in the female is in the majority of cases in abeyance, and that it requires positive and considerable excitement to be roused at all; and even if roused (which in many instances it never can be) is very moderate compared with that of the male. Many men, and particularly young men, form their ideas of women's feelings from what they notice early in life among loose or, at least, low and vulgar women. There is always a certain number of females who, though not ostensibly in the rank of prostitutes, make a kind of trade of a pretty face. They are fond of admiration, they like to attract the attention of those immediately above them. Any susceptible boy is easily led to believe, whether he is altogether overcome by the syren or not, that she, and therefore all women, must have at least as strong passions as himself. Such women however give a very false idea of the condition of female sexual feeling in general. Association with the loose women of London streets, in casinos, and other immoral haunts (who, if they have not sexual feeling, counterfeit it so well that the novice does not suspect but that it is genuine), all seem to corroborate such an impression, and as I have stated above, it is from these erroneous notions that so many young men think that the marital duties they will have to undertake are beyond their exhausted strength, and from this reason dread and avoid marriage.

Married men—medical men—or married women themselves, would, if appealed to, tell a very different tale, and vindicate female nature from the vile aspersions cast on it by the abandoned conduct and ungoverned lusts of a few of its worst examples.

There are many females who never feel any sexual excitement whatever. Others, again, immediately after each period, do become, to a limited degree, capable of experiencing it; but this capacity is often temporary, and will cease entirely till the next menstrual period. The best mothers, wives, and managers of households, know little or nothing of sexual indulgences. Love of home, children, and domestic duties are the only passions they feel.*

As a general rule, a modest woman seldom desires any sexual gratification for herself. She submits to her husband, but only to please him; and, but for the desire of maternity, would far rather be relieved from his attentions. No nervous or feeble young man need, therefore, be deterred from marriage by any exaggerated notion of the duties required from him. The married woman has no wish to be treated on the footing of a mistress.

* The physiologist will not be surprised that the human female should in these respects differ but little from the female among animals. We well know it, as a fact, that the dog or stallion is not allowed to approach to the female except at particular seasons. In the human female, indeed, I believe it is rather from the wish of pleasing or gratifying the husband than from any strong sexual feeling, that cohabitation is so habitually allowed. Certainly, it is so during the months of gestation. I have known instances where the female has during gestation evinced positive loathing for any marital familiarity whatever. In some of these instances, indeed, feeling has been sacrificed to duty, and the wife has endured, with all the self-martyrdom of womanhood, what was almost worse than death.

One instance may better illustrate the real state of the case than much description.

In —, 185 , a barrister, about thirty years of age, came to me on account of sexual debility. On cross-examination, I found he had been married a twelve-month, and that connection had taken place but once since the commencement of the year, and that there was some doubt as to the completion of the act then. He brought his wife with him, as she was, he said, desirous of having some conversation with me.

I found the lady a refined but highly sensitive person. Speaking with a freedom equally removed from assurance, or *mauvaise honte*, she told me she thought it her duty to consult me. She neither blushed nor faltered in telling her story, and I regret that my words must fail to convey the delicacy with which her avowal was made.

Her husband and herself, she said, had been acquainted since childhood, had grown up together, become mutually attached, and married. She believed him debilitated, but—as she was fully convinced—from no indiscreet acts on his part. She believed it was his natural condition. She was dotingly attached to him, and would not have determined to consult me but that she wished, for his sake, to have a family, as it would, she hoped, conduce to their mutual happiness. She assured me that she felt no sexual passions whatever; that if she was capable of them, they were dormant. Her passion for her husband was of a Platonic kind, and far from wishing to stimulate his frigid feelings, she doubted whether it would be right or not. She loved him as he was and would not desire him to be otherwise except for the hope of having a child.

I believe this lady is a perfect ideal of an English wife and mother, kind, considerate, self-sacrificing, and sensible, so pure-hearted as to be utterly ignorant of and averse to any sensual indulgence, but so unselfishly attached to the man she loves, as to be willing to give up her own wishes and feelings for his sake.

A great contrast to the unselfish sacrifices such married woman make of their feelings in allowing cohabitation is offered by others, who, either from ignorance or utter want of sympathy, although they are model wives in every other respect, not only evince no sexual feeling, but, on the contrary, scruple not to declare their aversion to the least manifestation of it. Doubtless this may, and often does, depend upon disease, and if so, the sooner the suffering female is treated the better. Much more frequently, however, it depends upon apathy, selfish indifference to please, or unwillingness to overcome the natural repugnance which such females feel for cohabitation.

Perversion of Sexual Feeling.—Where, in addition to indisposition to cohabitation which many modest women feel, we find a persistent aversion to it, so strong as to be invincible by habit or by any amount of kindness on the husband's part, a very painful suspicion may sometimes arise as to the origin of so unconquerable a frigidity.

The following is a case in which these suspicions seems to be justified by the facts:—A gentleman came to ask my opinion on the cause of want of sexual feeling in his wife. He told me he had been married four years. His wife was about his own age (twenty-seven), and had had four children, but she evinced no sexual feeling, although a lively, healthy lady, living in the country. I suggested several causes, when he at last asked me if it was possible that a woman might lose sexual feeling from the same causes as man. 'I have read your former edition, Mr. Acton,' said he, 'and though you only allude to the subject incidentally, yet, from what I have learned since my marriage, I am led to think that my wife's want of sexual feeling may arise, if such a thing is possible, from self-abuse. She has confessed to me that at a boarding-school, in perfect ignorance of any injurious effects, she early acquired the habit. This practice still gives her gratification; not so connection, which she views with positive aversion, although it gives her no pain.' I told him that medical men, who are consulted about female complaints, have not unfrequently observed cases like that of his wife. It appears, that at last, nothing but the morbid excitement produced by the baneful practice can give any sexual gratification, and that the natural stimulus fails to cause any pleasure whatever. A similar phenomenon occurs in men, and this state of things never ceases as long as self-abuse is practised. I feared, therefore, that his surmises were correct, and that the lady practised self-abuse more frequently than she was willing to admit. So ruinous is the practice of solitary vice, both in the one and other sex, that it is carried on even in married life, where no excuse can be devised, and comes to be actually preferred to the natural excitement. Venereal excesses engender satiety just as certainly as any other indulgences, and satiety is followed by indifference and disgust. If the unnatural excesses of masturbation take place early in life, before the subjects who commit them have arrived at maturity, it is not surprising that we meet with women whose sexual feelings, if they ever existed, become prematurely worn out. Doubtless sexual feeling differs largely in different women. Although it is not my object to treat otherwise than incidentally of the sexual economy in women, yet I may here say that the same causes which in early life induce abnormal sexual excitement in boys have similar effects in girls. This tendency may be checked in girls, as in boys, by careful moral education in early life. But no doubt can exist that hereditary predisposition has much to do with this, besides education and early associations. There are well-known families, for instance, in which chastity among the females is not the characteristic feature. We offer, I think, no apology for light conduct when we admit that there are some *few* women who, like men, in consequence of hereditary predisposition or ill-directed moral education, find it difficult to restrain their passions, while their more fortunate sisters have never been tempted, and have, therefore, never fallen. This, however, does not alter the fact which I would venture again to impress on the reader, that, in general women do *not* feel any great sexual tendencies. The unfortunately large numbers whose lives would seem to prove the contrary are to be accounted for on much more mercenary motives. Vanity, giddiness, greediness, love of dress, distress, hunger, make women prostitutes, but do not induce female profligacy so largely as has been supposed.

2. The Uterine Economy

(a) Hysteria

HYSTERIA

John Conolly, in John Forbes, Alexander Tweedie, and John Conolly (eds.), *The Cyclopaedia of Practical Medicine: Comprising the Nature and Treatment of Diseases, Materia Medica and Therapeutics, Medical Jurisprudence*, 4 vols. (London: Sherwood, Gilbert and Piper, 1833–5), ii. 568–9, 572–3, 575–6.

Conolly, one of the pioneers of moral management in the treatment of the insane, here draws on developments in French psychiatry to argue that hysteria was caused by an undue excitement of the nervous system. He rejects the ancients' theory that hysteria was the product of a wandering womb, since the various forms of the disorder clearly suggested various causes, and men as well as women could suffer. Nonetheless, he believes that women are the primary sufferers due to stresses placed on the uterine economy; such stresses were not merely physiological in origin, but were also caused by the social requirements for emotional repression in women. E. J. Georget, the author of the article on which Conolly draws quite largely, was a pupil of the eminent French psychiatrist, J. E. D. Esquirol (see Section IV).

That certain states of the uterus, causing peculiar sympathies in different parts of the frame, are the causes of hysteria, is an opinion of great antiquity, and has been supported by nearly every observer from the time of Hippocrates, who has often been quoted as saying that a woman's best remedy in this disorder is to marry and bear children. Whoever considers the sympathies excited by the changes which the uterine system undergoes at puberty and during pregnancy, and at the cessation of the catamenia; the altered form and character of the young female; the capricious wishes and taste, or *longings* of the state of utero-gestation; and the morbid actions of what is called the 'change of life;' will without difficulty admit that the hysterical phenomena, bodily and mental, may very probably be called forth by peculiar conditions of the same dominating system in the female economy. Extensive experience confirms such an opinion; and the occurrence of hysteria in early life, or after marriage, or at a later period, is so often observed in individuals in whom there are evident signs of the activity of the uterine system, as to connect the two circumstances together in the firmest manner. Precocious development and disappointed hopes on the one hand, and excessive indulgence, or marriages immature or physically disproportionate on the other, are causes of hysteria of which every practitioner finds illustrations within the circle of his own practice; as well as of the disappearance of hysteria after a long-desired marriage, or when means are taken to prevent hurtful excesses. In some females hysteria supervenes on puberty, continues to be more or less troublesome until the period of cessation, and then disappears. [. . .] In a susceptible female temperament, and in the unmarried state, the system of reproduction, every change in which involves many other changes, acts strongly on the system at large, and in certain circumstances disorders all the functions of the body and the mind; the digestion of food, the circulation of the blood, the judgment, the affections, and the temper; and in many of these cases all the mischief is removed by marriage, which, by awakening the natural functions and normal sympathies, allays the whole series of irritations or morbid actions. There can, therefore, be no reasonable doubt entertained that in a great many cases—perhaps we might say in the majority of cases—the cause of hysteria is some more or less discoverable irritation existing in some part of the uterine system, exercising its wide influence on the susceptibilities of a nervous system by nature too easily affected by all impressions. [. . .]

The influence of sex and of education is generally admitted. Medical philosophers declaim, and will long declaim in vain, against a system of education which, apparently solely directed to securing an advantageous establishment to young females, leaves them at once artificial and ignorant; full of the terms of many kinds of knowledge, but wearied or disgusted with all; trained to subdue the feelings only so far as to form alliances from selfish motives, but unprepared to be the companions of intellectual men, or to bear the neglect which their insipidity, or motives as selfish as their own, too often entail upon them. The predominance of the uterine system, although much less marked in the generality of cases in this country than in those in which the observations of some of the continental writers have been made, is yet sometimes sufficiently declared; and the disappointments of females who begin to feel that they are no longer young, and yet who have not become wives, have in many cases effects sufficiently observable. English practitioners pay, perhaps, too little attention to these circumstances; and, exercising their profession in a country where the passions and emotions have but a limited external manifestation, and where the female character is less intensely expressed, sometimes seem to forget their silent operation on the frame, and are inclined to charge the medical writers of other countries with being somewhat fanciful and extravagant.

'The social position of women,' observes M. Georget,[1] 'renders the sex, already subjected to peculiar ills from their organisation, the victims of the most acute and painful moral affections. Their moral existence is entirely opposed to their faculties; they possess a will, and are constantly oppressed by the yoke of prejudices and social arrangements in their infancy and early life; of a husband in their youth; and of indifference in old age. Sensible and loving, they must only love when the master orders them: they are for ever constrained to concentrate within themselves the most powerful passions and the gentlest inclinations; to dissemble their desires; to feign a calmness and indifference when an inward fire devours them, and their whole organization is in tumult; and to sacrifice to a sense of duty, or rather for the happiness of others, the happiness and tranquillity of a whole life.' [...]

The causes acting through the mind which have now been mentioned, are occasionally exciting causes, but much more frequently only predisposing. Mental impressions of a more sudden and transient character may act as causes immediately exciting a paroxysm; such as anger, grief, terror, or great surprise. [...] Generally, however, the severer shocks lead to a reaction, which is violent without being fatal; and after the feeling of faintness or depression, or sometimes almost without time being afforded for that feeling, the muscles are thrown into disordered and energetic motions, and all the vascular and nervous actions become irregular or tumultuous, and assume the form of hysteria or of epilepsy. Even the mimic representation of the more agitating passions will sometimes produce these effects; and hysteria has converted the cries and screams of the actress into reality, whilst the female part of the spectators have been similarly affected. Dr. Gregory used to relate, that when Mrs. Siddons first appeared in Edinburgh, these effects upon the audience were so common, that it became quite the fashion for the young men of the place to attend the theatre to carry off those affected; a service which was termed 'carrying off the dead.'[2] [...]

PATHOLOGY OF HYSTERIA

The malady chiefly affects women, or men of a peculiar temperament, or whose constitutions have become enfeebled by intemperance, or by excessive study, or other causes capable of debilitating the nervous system, and of rendering its power of enduring impressions less than in the natural state. A nervous system thus susceptible by original constitution, or thus enfeebled, feels impressions more keenly, and responds to them more forcibly than is seen in firmer organi-

---

[1] E. J. Georget, 'Hystérie', *Dictionnaire des sciences médicales* (1812–22), i. 193.

[2] Sarah Siddons (1755–1831), the daughter of the travelling actors Roger and Sarah Kemble, who was introduced to the stage as an infant phenomenon and became the most celebrated actress of her time.

zations, or in a state of perfect health, and, thus prepared, may be excited to disordered actions by numerous accidental causes. In the female system the exciting cause is very often an irritable or morbid condition of the uterine system. [...]

The existence of an original susceptibility in excess in the nervous system of hysterical patients, is an assumption warranted, we conceive, by all observation. The natural or congenital constitution of the nervous system, and even of different portions of it, is most plainly discerned to be different in different individuals. From the very cradle may be observed a different degree of susceptibility to impressions; and even a different countenance, impressed by the hand of nature herself, before human feelings have written their deeper lines upon it; a countenance indicative of a distinct and individual character, which is associated with an individual mode of receiving and being affected by external circumstances, and of exercising the internal faculties upon the impressions received. As the individual being grows up, the results of the original organization, modified but not changed by education and various accidents, are observed in all the varieties between stupid insensibility on the one hand, and morbid or too ready excitement and activity on the other. The excitement and activity are in different individuals more conspicuously manifested in different parts of the mixed system of body and mind. Thus, some are seen to be endowed with almost inexhaustible muscular energies, and some with vast powers of intellectual perception and combination; whilst in some the functions of the mind are feeble or disturbed, and in others divers other functions are debilitated or disordered. In the hysterical patient we may observe the most intense development of susceptibility, connected with a singular proneness to irregular actions, often arising from slight causes; the natural proportion designed to exist between the impressions of the external world and the sentient human system being in them not preserved.

EARLY MARRIAGES OF EXCELLENT TENDENCY

Thomas John Graham, *On the Management and Disorders of Infancy and Childhood* (London: Simpkin, Marshall and Co., 1853), 40–1.

This popular domestic manual reiterates the advice to be found in Conolly, that sexual desire, if thwarted, will lead to hysteria. Graham reinforces for his women readers the importance of exercising the 'appetite for love'.

There are certain years of manhood and womanhood when it is as prejudicial—nay, more so—to suppress by violence of any kind the propensity of nature to physical love, as it is to gratify it before the proper period. No power in us must remain unexpanded; each requires to be exercised in moderation. The appetite of love is seated in the cerebellum, at the base of the brain; and when excited by any cause, it does, under certain circumstances, if not indulged, become greater and greater, until it induces derangement of various functions, and hence hypochondriasis, convulsions, hysteria, and even insanity may be the result. Hysteria, in nine cases out of ten, arises from continence; and it is admitted by all discerning professional men that marriage removes a vast number of diseases incidental to both sexes. Hippocrates, Hoffmann, Boerhaave, Esquirol, Elliotson,[1] and many other physicians, state that it is the best cure for hysteria; and medical practice daily proves that it cures *amenorrhœa*, or retention of the menses; and *chlorosis*, or green-sickness, when all other remedies have failed. One of its excellent effects is pregnancy, which often produces the happiest changes in women, because this accomplishment of the law of nature being attended with considerable determination of blood to the uterus, suspends, as if almost by enchantment, a variety of uncomfortable feelings and diseases, by the concentration of vascular and nervous actions, which arrest irritation and morbid actions in remote organs. It is well known to arrest consumption and hypochondriasis, to exempt the woman from contagious diseases, and sometimes, as we have already hinted, to cure chronic affections, such as hysteria, St. Vitus's dance,[2] epilepsy, convulsions, &c. Married women, although exposed to many dangers in parturition, generally live longer than those who remain unmarried.

THE NERVOUS DISEASES OF WOMEN

Thomas Laycock, *A Treatise on the Nervous Diseases of Women: Comprising an Inquiry into the Nature, Causes, and Treatment of Spinal and Hysterical Disorders* (London: Longman, Orme, Brown, Green, and Longmans, 1840), 126, 140–2.

See also the notes for 'Woman in her Psychological Relations' and Laycock above. Laycock here relates the development of hysteria to the forms of education and life-style followed by a middle-class female.

---

[1] An eclectic list of medical authorities, ranging from the ancient Greek Hippocrates, to the contemporary figures of Esquirol and Elliotson (see biographical notes).

[2] Otherwise known as chorea, a form of convulsive fit characterized by the involuntary contraction of muscles.

When we reflect upon [. . .] the multiplicity of agencies by which the nervous system may be influenced, and the natural susceptibility of that of woman increased; upon the numerous connexions of the reproductive organs in each individual organism, extending directly or indirectly to every important structure; and upon the equally extensive relations of these organs to the general scheme of vital development, there is little room left for surprise at the infinite variety of evanescent forms, which, when occurring more particularly in women, the diseases of the nervous system assume. Ever essentially the same, they are continually differing in their distinguishing characters. The alternate gloom and gaiety, and mutable love and hatred of the hysterical woman, are really not less remarkable than the rapid transition from robust health to death-like trance—from acute bronchitis to peritonitis or hepatitis,—from active effort to helpless paralysis, observed in these diseases. They are all evidences of the same state of the nervous system, variously developed as the causes vary. [. . .]

The relations of hysteria to the present modes of education are of great importance. The anxiety to render a young lady accomplished, at all hazards, has originated a system of forced mental training, which greatly increases the irritability of the brain: sedentary employments, as drawing, embroidery &c., are followed frequently as amusements, to the exclusion of active exercise out of doors. The slow but powerful influences of music, dancing, vivid colours, and odours, on the nervous system, but especially on the reproductive system, is quite overlooked [. . .] The baleful effects of musical studies on the mind and passions is certainly not suspected at all by many excellent mothers.

Young females of the same age, and influenced by the same novel feelings towards the opposite sex, cannot associate together in public schools without serious risk of exciting the passions, and of being led to indulge in practices injurious to both body and mind. [. . .]

The consequence of all this is, that the young female returns from school to her home a hysterical, wayward, capricious girl; imbecile in mind, habits, and pursuits; prone to hysteric paroxysms upon any unusual mental excitement, and yielding to them, until at last she will 'die twenty times on the poorest moment,' and, like Cleopatra,* has acquired 'a facility in dying.'

The robust unmarried female, in easy circumstances, may escape many of these evils: but after the age of eighteen the reproductive organs are fully—probably largely—developed, and strong passions, indolence, and luxury, fail not to produce their effects on the system, and to develope the sthenic[1] form of hysteria. It is to such that marriage [. . .] is so useful; although doubtless the asthenic[2] forms are sometimes benefited by this procedure; the ovaria being excited to the performance of their proper function, and the cares of life dispelling the 'vapours' so apt to congregate about the idle and well-fed.

---

* *Antony and Cleopatra*, Act I, Scene ii. The quotation is inaccurate: 'facility' should read 'celerity'.
[1] Characterized by excessive nervous energy.   [2] Characterized by low nervous energy.

After the young female has returned home, and is introduced into mixed society, she is more than ever exposed to influences acting injuriously on the nervous system: The excitement and competition of social life, excited love, ungratified desire, disappointed vanity as well as affection, late hours, long and late indulgence in sleep, and the excessive use of stimulants, as wines, liqueurs, coffee, tea, &c., all act with more or less of combined energy upon the unfortunate young lady in fashionable life. Nor ought the effect of dress to be overlooked; for the waist (in despite of all warnings) is frequently compressed into the most preposterously diminutive proportions, and the circulation through all the important viscera retarded. Even free muscular action is impeded, and each elevation of the arm endangers the rupture of some of the bands, or laces, or straps which maintain her slender elegance of form. The mammæ are compressed (if beyond the fashionable magnitude) and irritated, and re-act upon the ovaria and uterus; while these last are further stimulated by the heat caused by the masses of padding appended to the loins. When we remember that both the reproductive and general systems are nearly at their climax of development, the injurious effects of such agencies can be easily conceived.

PATHOLOGY AND TREATMENT OF HYSTERIA

Robert Brudenell Carter, *On the Pathology and Treatment of Hysteria* (London: John Churchill, 1853), 33–7.

Carter here develops the lines of argument offered by Conolly twenty years earlier. Hysteria is not an exclusively female disease, but women are more prone since they are more likely than men to feel, rather than think, and also are forced socially to restrain expression of their sexual desires. Men, however, have 'facilities' for gratifying their sexual desires (a euphemism, one assumes, for mistresses and prostitutes) and are not therefore subject to the ill-consequences of restraint. Continent men form the one exception to this rule. Carter's arguments have edged one step further than Conolly's away from a somatic base: Carter dismisses the notion of irritation of the uterus as a cause, but then suggests that the mental impact created by uterine disorders is one of the chief agencies of hysteria.

If the relative power of emotion against the sexes be compared in the present day, even without including the erotic passion, it is seen to be considerably greater in the woman than in the man, partly from that natural conformation which causes the former to feel, under circumstances where the latter thinks; and partly because the woman is more often under the necessity of endeavouring to conceal her feelings. But when sexual desire is taken into account, it will add immensely to the forces bearing upon the female, who is often much under its dominion; and who, if unmarried and chaste, is compelled to restrain every manifestation of its sway. Man, on the contrary, has such facilities for its gratification, that as a source of disease it is almost inert against him, and when powerfully excited, it is pretty sure to be speedily exhausted through the proper channel. It may, however, be remarked, that in many cases of hysteria in the male, the sufferers are recorded to have been 'continent,' a circumstance which may have assimilated the effects of amativeness upon them to those which are constantly witnessed in the female. In others, some emotional cause is assigned to the attack, and the Emperor Napoleon is said to have had a paroxysm in his boyhood, as a consequence of wounded pride. On the whole, it appears reasonable to ascribe the comparative immunity of man, not so much to the failure of emotion, when excited, in producing its legitimate effects; as to the fact that in him strong emotion is a matter of comparatively rare occurrence, scarcely called forth except to demand immediate and energetic action of some other kind.

Having thus been able to assign a satisfactory reason for the greater proclivity of the female sex to hysteria, and also for the absolute rarity of its occurrence in man, the next question which arises will have reference to the especial proneness of some individuals among women, and to the great and striking difference which exists in this respect. [. . .] For while the advance of civilisation and the ever-increasing complications of social intercourse tend to call forth new feelings, and by their means throw amativeness somewhat into the shade, as one powerful emotion among many others, still its absolute intensity is in no way lessened, and from the modern necessity for its entire concealment, it is likely to produce hysteria in a larger number of the women subject to its influence, than it would do if the state of society permitted its free expression. It may, therefore, be inferred, as a matter of reasoning, that the sexual emotions are those most concerned in the production of the disease, as it is seen among the poor and ignorant; but that in the higher classes there are many other kinds of feeling, which, in the aggregate, are able to dispute for the pre-eminence.

The greatest difficulty which has hitherto presented itself to writers on the disease under consideration, has depended upon its distinct association, in the majority of cases, with the sexual propensities of the female, and with derangements of her sexual organs, while, at the same time, it cannot be connected with any one kind of derangement rather than with others, or with desire rather than with loathing, except in the usual numerical proportion which exists between the different states. Hence many endeavours have been made to discover a common action exerted by them all, and (without regard to the cases in which none of them are apparent,) the phenomena have been accounted for by the employment of a word which is useful to express ignorance rather than know-ledge; that is, they have been referred to *irritation* of the uterus and ovaria. But it is hardly necessary to say, that the existence of many well-authenticated instances of masculine hysteria renders this explanation utterly untenable, while, at the same time, the emotional doctrine affords an easy and complete solution of the difficulty, on the ground that the disorder is very frequently connected with the sexual feelings, because they are both more universal and more constantly con-cealed than any others.

The word 'hysteria,' the hypothesis of irritation, and the universal consent of the medical profession, may all safely be appealed to, as bearing out, by actual experience, the theoretical conclusions arrived at in a foregoing paragraph, namely, that the sexual passion is more concerned than any other single emotion, and, perhaps, as much as all others put together, in the production of the hysteric paroxysm.

This being so, it is evident that any circumstances which direct attention to the reproductive system, will tend to increase materially the proclivity of the persons exposed to them, and to establish trains of thought of the kind most likely to originate the disease. Such conditions are furnished by all morbid conditions of the uterus, whether they only excite sensations, or whether they are fixed upon the mind of the patient in consequence of medical treatment. Faulty menstrua-tion, whether local or constitutional, will have a similar effect; and it will be found that, although affections of this kind often arise consecutively to hysteria, still that women suffering from them are more liable than others, *cæteris paribus*,[1] to be the subjects of that disorder.

Women of strong passions, who are separated from their husbands, either per-manently or for a time, are especially liable to hysterical attacks. This is well instanced by the wives of sailors, or other men, who are constantly taken from home by their occupation.

Next to the reproductive instincts as a cause of the disease, may be arranged various states of constitutional debility, which, by weakening the body, greatly diminish the power of resisting emotional influences. In this way anæmia, chlorosis,[2] any morbid diathesis,[3] convalescence from acute illness, or the cachexia[4] resulting from neglect of sanitary regulations, may all be regarded as increasing the proclivity to hysteria, whatever be the kind of feeling immediately concerned in its production.

There are, therefore, two distinct classes of agencies by which an individual may be subjugated to a given amount of emotional influence more completely

[1] Other things being equal.
[2] A disorder associated with puberty, and also known as 'green sickness', caused by anaemia and irregular or suppressed menstruation.
[3] A permanent condition of the body rendering it liable to particular diseases or disorders.
[4] Overall disorder of the bodily system.

than would be possible without their operation. By the first of them, as illustrated in uterine or menstrual disorders, the emotion is rendered permanent and engrossing, being continually recalled to the mind by sensations or accidental associations, when, of its own force, it would probably have passed by and have been forgotten. By the second, the emotion is neither strengthened nor retained, but the body itself is so weakened as to offer no resistance to its effects, either by directing or by absolutely counteracting them.

Hence, it may be concluded, that the power which an emotion will exercise, in producing an hysteric fit, depends upon circumstances, which are themselves liable to vary, both in the same and in different individuals. They are chiefly, the intensity of the emotion itself, and the concentration or diffusion of its action, as opposed to various degrees of susceptibility or resisting power; and it is evident that these forces are of a character to place peculiar difficulties in the way of their exact estimation. [. . .] There is probably no woman, not past middle age, in whom a paroxysm could not be produced by purely moral influences, without any previous derangement of her health, and without the necessity for any excitement of her sexual organs.

THE MIMICRY OF HYSTERIA

F. C. Skey, *Hysteria: Six Lectures* (London: Longman, Green, Reader, and Dyer, 1867), 43–6, 51, 58–9.

Skey here develops his theory of hysteria as a form of mimicry. He draws on Benjamin Brodie's Lectures Illustrative of Certain Local Nervous Affections *(1837), which outlined for the first time a distinction between diseases caused by 'organic affections' and those caused by emotional and psychological factors. According to Brodie, 'among the higher classes of society, at least four-fifths of the female patients who are commonly supposed to labour under diseases of the joints, labour under Hysteria, and nothing else'. Skey enlarged this definition to include 'a large proportion' of the lower class as well. Nonetheless, he makes his diagnosis an opportunity for attacking the idle life of the rich, who unlike the poor, fail to make an effort and shake off their fancied suffering.*

It may be asserted with truth, that *every part of the body may become*, under provocation, *the seat of an apparent disease that in reality does not exist*—that it may and often does assume all the attributes of reality with an exactness of imitation which nothing short of careful and accurate diagnosis can distinguish from the real disease. You think this impossible. Surely you know a diseased knee-joint, you reply, when you see it. You find severe pain, aggravated by the slightest movement. The temperature of the joint may be raised, and it is slightly swelled. You leech, you blister, you employ an iodine liniment (few cases escape it), you may even resort to issues, but the evil remains in spite of all your remedies, which have been applied to the wrong 'system.' It is the nervous, not the vascular,[1] that is involved, but the nervous has imitated the vascular and deluded you, and led to the employment of false remedies, which have failed to reduce the pain or give mobility to the joint, and the general influence of which on the health of the patient cannot be said to have proved eminently serviceable!

The case, on more perfect investigation, proves to be one of local nervous irritation, or Hysteria. You think you will not be again deceived, but you are mistaken. A single error, corrected by the experience of another, will not teach you Hysteria. You are consulted by a lady in reference to a daughter of 18 or 20 years of age, who has exhibited failing health for some time, and now complains of her inability to walk in consequence of a pain in her back. You examine her, and discover that she suffers extremely on pressure over two or three of the lower dorsal vertebræ, or on any other of the twenty-four. You repeat the examination with the same result, and you make a report to the mother that her daughter has *'spinal disease'*. The result of your opinion is two or more years' confinement to her couch, coupled with the usual concomitants of restricted diet, alternative and other depletive medicines, leeches, blisters, and issues. Suppose these structures which you have declared to be the seat of organic disease to be examined under a microscope, what would you discover? Nothing. There is no disease whatever. As the nature of this malady dawns upon you, now awakening to a conviction of its frequency, you resolve to be more wary in your future diagnosis.

You are now consulted by another young female patient on account of a tendency in one or more fingers to close in flexion. In the attempt to straighten them you cause intense pain, and if persisted in the consequences may be serious. Your patient appears in fair average health, and all her functions are regular and healthy; while the hand, for all ordinary purposes, is useless. Under the idea that she may have some chronic inflammation of the theca or of the palmar fascia, you treat it with the usual remedies. But your remedies produce no impression on the finger, which continues obstinately flexed as before; you adopt another principle of treatment founded upon a more correct diagnosis, and your patient recovers. These cases sound strange to your limited experience. You think they are rare, and brought forward from a distance, and with an effort. By no means. *They are cases of daily occurrence.* If you could suddenly throw off that nebulous vision of vascular disease which years of bad pathology have impressed

---

[1] i.e. blood vessels, lymph glands, etc.

upon your judgment, you would see them in their true light. You may deem them to be exceptional. I assure you they constitute the rule of disease, and not the exception. *Real disease is the exception.* Speaking of one variety, and they have all characters in common, Sir B. Brodie,[2] a man who rarely committed an error in diagnosis, says: 'I do not hesitate to declare that, among the higher classes of society, at least four-fifths of the female patients who are commonly supposed to labour under diseases of the joints, labour under Hysteria and nothing else.' I would venture to enlarge this statement as regards the 'upper classes,' by including a large proportion of the lower; for much of my own experience of Hysteria has been obtained from the wards of St. Bartholomew's Hospital, and in reference to spinal affections in young persons, I unhesitatingly assert that real disease is not found in a greater proportion than one case in twenty, and even this is a liberal allotment.

Have you never experienced the difficulty of discovering an object floating in the air, such as a bird singing overhead, or an early star in the evening? When once the object becomes visible, the eye is readily adjusted to it, and when you look again in the right direction, it is the first object that strikes the eye.

And so with this class of diseases. They are not seen, because they are not looked for. If you will so focus your mental vision and endeavour to distinguish the minute texture of your cases, and, as I have said, look into and not at them, you will acknowledge the truth of the description, and you will adopt a sound principle of treatment that meets disease face to face with a direct instead of an oblique force, which far too generally claims the credit of a success for which Nature alone is responsible. [...]

Thirty or forty years since these cases were, happily for our time, far more common than at present. At that date, and for how many years anterior I know not, all the sea-side towns were crowded with young ladies between 17 and 25 years of age and beyond it, who were confined to the horizontal posture, and were wheeled about on the shore in Bath chairs, on the supposition that they were the subjects of spinal disease. They were placed under much medical and dietetic discipline, not of the most invigorating character, and the large majority carried a pair of handsome issues in the back! Brighton, Worthing, Hastings, and other places on the South Coast were largely tenanted by these unfortunate females, to which a moderate sprinkling of young gentlemen was added. What has become of all these cases? They appear to have vanished just in proportion as the eyes of the Surgeon have opened to the absurdity of inferring that pain alone which locates itself with remarkable precision in Hysteria on a given vertebra, can indicate the presence of organic disease of the body of the bone without collateral evidence in its favour. When the spinal column is really diseased the case

---

[2] Sir Benjamin Brodie (1783–1862), one of the most eminent medical men of his day, physician to Queen Victoria, and President of the Royal Society of the Royal College of Surgeons. The text is quoted from *Lectures Illustrative of Certain Local Nervous Affections* (1837)

is obvious at a glance; the health is degenerate, and the whole system proclaims to the eye of the Surgeon the presence of a great evil. These examples are but a miserable mockery of the reality, and a fraud on the judgment of the ignorant. [. . .]

It is curious to observe the influence which the nervous system exerts on the daily condition of us all. When unstrung it preys upon ourselves. It is not in the varying force of our pulse, for that gauge is not sufficiently fine to detect the variations of health, that we can refer a consciousness of strength and vigour on one day that fails us on another. It is that our nervous system is more or less relaxed. There is a real illness and a factitious illness, and in this we observe the remarkable influence of mind in exercising a controlling power over the body. People without compulsory occupation, who lead a life of both bodily and mental inactivity—people whose means are sufficiently ample to indulge in, and who can purchase, the luxury of illness, the daily visit of the Physician and, not the least, the sympathy of friends—these real comforts come home to the hearts of those ornamental members of society who are living examples of an intense sensibility, whether morbid or genuine, who can afford to be ill, and will not make the effort to be well. They are, in truth, well or ill, as you choose to take it, and they are only ill because they fail in mental effort, that mental resolution which is sufficiently powerful to rouse the dormant energies of the body and throw off the sensations of lassitude, of unreal fatigue and weariness of body and mind. A poor man cannot afford this indulgence, and so he throws the sensations aside by mental resolution. How often does a sense of weariness and fatigue succumb to active and vigorous muscular exertion?

HYSTERIA

Horatio Bryan Donkin, in Daniel Hack Tuke (ed.), *A Dictionary of Psychological Medicine*, 2 vols. (London: J. and A. Churchill, 1892), i. 619–21.

Donkin was involved in London progressive circles and had treated Eleanor Marx and Olive Schreiner. He develops the idea, found sixty years earlier in Conolly's article, that female hysteria is in large part due to social restrictions and prohibitions: ' "Thou shall not" meets a girl at almost every turn.' Sexuality, although one of the primary agencies, is not the only one; all forms of repressed desire can lead to hysteria. He notes, however, that education and employment can offer women the same form of 'safety valve' already enjoyed by men. Despite the sympathy evident in this presentation, Donkin is nonetheless highly judgemental of the sufferer, defining the hysteric as an 'individualist, an unsocial unit' with a passion for notoriety and sympathy. Hysteria ranges from a mere giving way, to outright imposture, with behaviour that arouses 'our contempt and aversion'.

The subjects of hysteria are, in a very large proportion, of the female sex, the symptoms most often appearing at or soon after puberty. Children, however, even when quite young, may suffer from it, the sexual distribution being much less unequal in the earlier years; and marked cases occur not infrequently in men. The typical subject of hysteria, however, is the young woman; in her organism and her social conditions the potential factors of hysteria are present in a notable degree. Apart from whatever fundamental difference of nerve-stability there may be between the sexes, and this is probably very great, the girl usually meets with far more obstacles to uniform development and consequent nervous control than the youth. The stress of puberty, marked in both sexes by a great increase in and complexity and activity of the organism, is more sudden and intense in the female; the sexual organs which undergo these great changes are of relatively greater importance in her physical economy, and consequently involve a larger area of central innervation than in the male. The nervous balance is thus in especially unstable equilibrium. With this greater internal stress on the nervous organism there are in the surroundings and general training of most girls many hindrances to the retention or restoration of a due stability, and but few channels of outlet for her new activities. It is not only in the educational repression and ignorance as regards sexual matters of which the girl is the subject that this difference is manifest, but all kinds of other barriers to the free play of her powers are set up by ordinary social and ethical customs. 'Thou shall not' meets a girl at almost every turn. The exceptions to this rule are found in those instances where girls and women of all conditions, owing to the influence of good education or necessity, or both, have regular work and definite pursuits. The comparative freedom and the various and necessary occupations of the youth offer many safety valves for his comparatively minor nervous tension. In proportion as the energies are in some way satisfied, the nervous control is retained. Among the activities thus artificially repressed in girls, it must be recognised that the sexual play an important part, and, indeed, the frequent evidence given of dammed-up sexual emotions by both the special act of masturbation and numerous extraordinary vagaries of conduct, have led many to regard unsatisfied sexual desire as one of the leading causes of hysteria. It may be briefly said in this context that this is but one cause, or rather, occasion, for hysterical display. The most severe form of this affection may be seen in both men, women, and children, where there is no disorder, inability, or repression as regards the sexual organs or function; but enforced abstinence from the gratification of any of the inherent and primitive desires, in the absence of other outlets for the activities of the natural organism, must have untoward results, and in certain cases, when this special desire is in excess, may, even when other conditions are favourable, be in itself an adequate exciting cause of morbid display. There are clearly other stresses which render women especially liable to hysteria. The periodical disturbance of menstruation, the times of pregnancy and parturition, and the numerous and multiform anxieties of home life, have their influence in contributing to the number of sufferers. There are, perhaps, as many or more instances of neurotic women commencing hysterics after marriage, as there are of hysterical girls showing greater nervous stability with the same change of condition.

Mental Characteristics of Hysteria.—The cardinal fact in the psychopathy of hysteria is an exaggerated self-consciousness dependent on undue prominence of feelings uncontrolled by intellect—that is to say, on the physical side, an undue preponderance of general widely diffused, undirected nervous discharges, and an undue lack of determination of such discharges into definite channels. Thus the hysteric is pre-eminently an individualist, an unsocial unit, and fails in adaptation to organic surroundings. This predominant disorder in the sphere of feeling is generally accompanied by more or less evidence of intellectual disturbance, as shown in the multiform vagaries of conduct which are so prominent among hysterical symptoms; but in the majority of cases intellectual disorder is not conspicuous, and mental abnormality is mainly evidenced by exaggerated impressionability or tumultuous emotion on apparently slight provocation. It is difficult or impossible in some few cases to draw a hard-and-fast line between insanity and hysteria, and we may find all grades of temporarily disordered thought; but as a rule the hysteric recognises the impropriety or outrageousness of those actions which spring from this cause, and shows that, if she has lost control or 'will power,' she at least admits the want of it. Hysterics are deficient in energy, or in appropriate direction of energy; some become inert, others actively mischievous. Her abnormal action or inaction is the result of the passion for sympathy or notoriety, and instances of this range from mere giving way to or exaggeration of suffering, to wilful imposture, simulation of all kinds of diseases, and even to actual crimes. The steps from the lowest to the highest grade of hysteria are imperceptible, and the intermixture of imposture is often hard to recognise or duly appreciate. This difficulty has given rise to the common error of regarding hysterical disorder as deliberate sham, and thus limiting its sphere to the extent of rendering the subject unintelligible. The most obvious cases of hysteria in both men and women where certain disorders of sensation and motion are demonstrably outside voluntary control, may also be marked by conduct which is the outcome of the subtlest craft; and the most typical of the physical affections of hysteria may be seen as well in those who are powerless to help themselves and rightly excite our pity, as in those whose actions occasion our contempt and aversion.

(b) Menstruation and Puberty

MENSTRUATION AND THE FEMALE CONSTITUTION

George Man Burrows, *Commentaries on the Causes, Forms, Symptoms, and Treatment, Moral and Medical, of Insanity* (London: Thomas and George Underwood, 1828), 146–8.

In this major work on insanity at the start of our period, Burrows points to the centrality of menstruation in medical understanding of the female mind and body: 'it is the moral and physical barometer of the female constitution'. Doctors were divided as to whether obstructed or irregular menstruation was a cause or symptom of insanity, but, following Esquirol, the state of the catamenia (as it was known) was usually recorded in medical case-notes on female inmates of asylums. Mental stability was also at risk, Burrows points out, at the 'critical period', or menopause (also known as the climacteric).

MENSTRUAL DISCHARGE

Every body of the least experience must be sensible of the influence of menstruation on the operations of the mind. In truth, it is the moral and physical barometer of the female constitution. Both the accession and subsequent regularity of the menses depend on the due equilibrium of the vascular and nervous systems. If the balance be disturbed, so likewise will be the uterine action and periodical discharge; though it does not follow that the mind always sympathises with its irregularities so as to disturb the cerebral functions. Yet the functions of the brain are so intimately connected with the uterine system, that the interruption of any one process which the latter has to perform in the human economy may implicate the former.

Whether this evacuation be delayed beyond the period when it ought to appear, or be obstructed after being once established, or a female be arrived at the critical age when it ceases entirely; or whether the state of utero-gestation, or parturition, or lactation, be going on, they are all conditions in which the vascular system is involved.

When the menses are stopped, a sudden or gradual plethora sometimes follows in a system long accustomed to the discharge, and a consecutive local determination to some other part often ensues.

Ere the system accommodates itself to this innovation, the seeds of various disorders are sown; and especially where any predisposition obtains, the hazard of insanity is imminent.

The state of utero-gestation is a state of local determination, from which the general system seeks relief by uterine hæmorrhage. Or sometimes this local determination influences the nervous system, and superinduces those phantasies called longings, which are decided perversions or aberrations of the judgment, though perhaps the simplest modifications of intellectual derangement. These anomalous feelings have been referred to uterine irritation from mere gravitation, and so they may be; but they first induce a greater determination of blood to the uterus and its contents, and then to the brain, through the reciprocal connexion and action existing between the two organs.

Amenorrhœa or obstruction of the menstrual flux is, however, by no means so frequent a cause of insanity as is supposed. I am quite convinced that amenorrhœa is oftener a consequence of cerebral disturbance; for in numerous cases, derangement of the mind precedes the menstrual obstruction, and the discharge returns as the functions of the brain and other organs return to a healthy state. Emmenagogues,[1] therefore, and other remedies given in insanity (vulgarly) to force the menses, may do a great deal of mischief.

Before any remedy is prescribed with this view, it behoves us to ascertain whether the amenorrhœa should be considered as a cause or an effect of the mental derangement. That it is often a cause there can be no doubt; because terror, the sudden application of cold, &c., have occasioned the instant cessation of the menses, upon which severe cerebral affections, or instant insanity, has supervened; and the senses have been restored with the discharge.

The critical period, as it is called, when menstruation ceases, is certainly a period favourable to the development of mental aberration. The whole economy of the constitution at that epoch again undergoes a revolution. The moral character, at the age when the menses naturally cease, is much changed to what it was on their first access; and every care or anxiety produces a more depressing and permanent impression on the mind. There is neither so much vital nor mental energy to resist the effects of the various adverse circumstances which it is the lot of most to meet with in the interval between puberty and the critical period.

Besides, as an author has observed, the age of pleasing in all females is then past, though in many the desire to please is not the less lively. The exterior alone loses its attractions, but vanity preserves its pretensions. It is now especially that jealousy exerts its empire, and becomes very often a cause of delirium. Many,

---

[1] Medicine given to induce the menstrual flow.

too, at this epoch imbibe very enthusiastic religious notions; but more have recourse to the stimulus of strong cordials to allay the uneasy and nervous sensations peculiar to this time of life, and thus produce a degree of excitation equally dangerous to the equanimity of the moral feelings and mental faculties.

THE PATHOLOGY OF MENSTRUATION

Charles Locock, in John Forbes, Alexander Tweedie, and John Conolly (eds.), *The Cyclopaedia of Practical Medicine: Comprising the Nature and Treatment of Diseases, Materia Medica and Therapeutics, Medical Jurisprudence*, 4 vols. (London: Sherwood, Gilbert and Piper, 1833–5), iii. 110–12.

Locock here outlines the predominant view of the era that menstruation is equivalent to the state of sexual heat in animals. This view was still unchanged with the issue of the revised version of the Cyclopaedia *in 1854. A woman menstruating was compared to a rabbit 'during the state of genital excitement called the time of heat'. Nonetheless, Locock later notes the cases of insanity provoked by sexual intercourse, 'either by accident or criminal impatience', during menstruation. Locock's text aptly illustrates some of the many confusions surrounding medical attitudes to menstruation during this era. Although not strictly an article on female mental health, it clearly shows the centrality of menstruation to all medical interpretations of the female mind and body.*

MENSTRUATION, PATHOLOGY OF

We consider the menstrual discharge to be the consequence of a peculiar periodical condition of the blood-vessels of the uterus, fitting it for impregnation, which condition is analogous to that of 'heat' in the inferior animals. [. . .]

The function of menstruation lasts, upon the average, for about thirty years of the life of woman, beginning at puberty, and ending somewhere between forty and fifty years of age, unless interrupted by disease, by pregnancy, or by suckling. During this large proportion of female life, there is a great liability to derangements, of one form or another, in the menstrual process; and to which much importance is attributed, though from some remains of the old doctrine that the menses were the outlets of 'peccant humours' more anxiety is generally expressed in cases of diminished or suspended discharge than in those where it is unnaturally profuse. Women have also been always in the habit of considering the time of the first appearance of the catamenia, and of their final cessation, as requiring particular caution and management, and as tending to the development of a healthy or diseased condition for a long period of life. The actual flow of the menstrual discharge itself is also looked upon as a time of great delicacy, and as demanding particular attention; so that very few diseases can exist, and very few plans of treatment be recommended, without the presence of the menses in some way influencing the nature of the symptoms or the remedies to be applied. It is in this especially that the character of the female constitution in disease is manifested; for before puberty, and after the cessation of menstruation, the female differs but little from the male in the character of disease, unless in those points which may be considered as accidental, such as organic diseases of the sexual organs. [. . .]

During the menstrual period, when quite regularly and properly performed, no medical treatment is required; but it should never be lost sight of either by the patient herself or by her medical attendant, in case of any accidental illness, or any general plan of management of the health. Women expect this carefulness, from the great importance they habitually attach to the proper performance of the function; and therefore, in prescribing for females, it is always right to enquire as to the expected time, as well as the regularity of the periods, to guide us as to the propriety of continuing or remitting any part of the remedial measures. [. . .]

The Jews, and even more modern nations, believed that there was something deleterious and contaminating in the menstrual discharge itself; and hence various directions and regulations as to seclusion and cleanliness of person. It is not necessary now to controvert these doctrines; but it were well, perhaps, if more strict attention were to be paid to some part of the regulations even in the present times. Either by accident or by criminal impatience, sexual intercourse has sometimes been permitted during the period of menstruation; and, although not constantly, yet such conduct has been frequently followed by the most serious effects—generally by profuse hemorrhage; at other times by a sudden suppression of the discharge; to which have succeeded fever, delirium, obstinate hysteria, confirmed mania, and even catalepsy.

When the function of menstruation has been once fairly established, it may become disordered in several ways, each forming distinct classes of diseases. Menstruation may be faulty in respect to the quantity of the discharge, the quality of the discharge, the regularity of its appearance, the time of its duration, and the degree of pain with which the process is accompanied. When the discharge has been in any way suppressed in a peculiar condition of health, what has been called *vicarious menstruation* has sometimes periodically occurred from other parts of the body, the stomach, the lungs, the bowels, &c. For a minute account of these several forms of disordered menstruation, the reader is referred to the articles AMENORRHŒA,[1] DYSMENORRHŒA,[2] and MENORRHAGIA.[3]

ADVICE TO A WIFE

Pye Henry Chavasse, *Advice to a Wife on the Management of her own Health; and on the Treatment of some of the Complaints Incidental to Pregnancy, Labour and Suckling* (1839), 6th edn. (London: J. Churchill, 1864), 38–9, 10–11.

Chavasse published various works on domestic medicine and childcare, many of which were still being reprinted at the beginning of the twentieth century. We include these passages to show the ways in which the advice offered by Locock as to the necessary quality and quantity of the menstrual discharge, and the various medical strictures against luxurious living, found their way into popular domestic medicine.

When a lady is not 'regular,' and provided that she be not pregnant, she must immediately apply to a Medical man; as, she may depend upon it, that there is something wrong about her, and that she is not likely to become *enceinte* until menstruation is properly established.

When a woman is said to be 'regular,' it is understood,—that she is regular as to *quality*, and *quantity*, and *time*. If she is only 'regular' as to the *time*, and the *quantity* is deficient or in excess, or if she is regular as to the *time*, and the *quality* is bad—either too pale or too dark—she cannot be well; and the sooner means are adopted to rectify the evil, the better will it be for her health and happiness.

As soon as a lady ceases to menstruate, it is said, that she has 'a change of life,' and, if she does not take care, she will have 'a change of health' which, probably, will be for the worse.—It is important, in such a case, that she should consult a Medical man on the subject, as he may, with judicious treatment, be able to ward off many serious illnesses, to which she would otherwise be liable. [. . .]

Hot and close rooms, soft cushions, and luxurious couches, should be eschewed.—I have somewhere read, that if a fine, healthy whelp, of the bull-dog species, were fed upon chicken, rice, and delicacies, and made to lie upon soft cushions, and if he were shut up in a close room for some months, that when he grew up, he would become unhealthy, weak, and spiritless.—So it is with a young

[1] Retention, or suppression of the menses.   [2] Acute pain during menstruation.
[3] Morbidly profuse menstruation.

married woman; the more she indulges, the more unhealthy, weak, and inanimate she becomes—unfit to perform the duties of a wife, and the offices of a
mother.

Rich and luxurious ladies are less likely to be blessed with a family than poor
and hard-worked women.—'Hippocrates,' says Dr. Tanner,[1] in his recent, valuable work, 'did not leave unnoticed the fact, however, that the labour and privation of the lowest sphere of life was as favourable to fertility as the indolence and
affluence of the highest was adverse to it: and it still remains true, that the poorest and most industrious part of mankind are the most fruitful.'—Riches, in such
a case, is an evil and a curse, rather than a good and a blessing.

INSANITY OF PUBESCENCE

Henry Maudsley, *Body and Mind: An Inquiry into their Connection and Mutual
Influence, Specially in Reference to Mental Disorders* (London: Macmillan, 1870),
83–8.

---

*The essays in this work formed the Gulstonian Lectures for 1870, delivered at the
Royal College of Physicians. Under the heading 'Insanity of Pubescence', Maudsley
offers one of the first attempts at defining what would later come to be known as
the period of adolescence. Throughout this period, medical writers had pointed to a
correlation between female sexual disappointment and religious enthusiasm.
Maudsley pushes this association even further to suggest that even the religious
visions of St Theresa or St Catherine were due 'though they knew it not, [to] the
influence of excited sexual organs on the mind'.*

INSANITY OF PUBESCENCE

The great mental revolution which occurs at puberty may go beyond its physiological limits, in some instances and become pathological. The vague feelings,
blind longings, and obscure impulses which then arise in the mind attest the
awakening of an impulse which knows not at first its aim or the means of its gratification; a kind of vague and yearning melancholy is engendered, which leads to
an abandonment to poetry of a gloomy Byronic kind, or to indulgence in indefinite religious feelings and aspirations. There is a want of some object to fill the
void in the feelings, to satisfy the undefined yearning—a need of something to

---

[1] Thomas Hawkes Tanner, *On the Signs and Diseases of Pregnancy* (1860).

adore; consequently, where there is no visible object of worship the invisible is adored. The time of this mental revolution is, at best, a trying period for youth; and where there is an inherited infirmity of nervous organization, the natural disturbance of the mental balance may easily pass into actual destruction of it.

The form of derangement connected with this period of life I believe to be either a fanciful and quasi-hysterical melancholia, which is not very serious when it is properly treated; or an acute mania, which is apt to be recurrent, and is much more serious. The former occurs especially in girls, if it be not peculiar to them: there are periods of depression and paroxysms of apparently causeless weeping, alternating with times of undue excitability, more especially at the menstrual periods; a disinclination is evinced to work, to rational amusement, to exertion of any kind; the behaviour is capricious, and soon becomes perverse and wilful; the natural affections seem to be blunted or abolished, the patient taking pleasure in distressing those whose feelings she would most consider when in health; and, although there are no fixed delusions, there are unfounded suspicions or fears and changing morbid fancies. The anxious sympathies of those most dear are apt to foster the morbid self-feeling which craves them, and thus to aggravate the disease: what such patients need to learn is, not the indulgence but a forgetfulness of their feelings, not the observation but the renunciation of self, not introspection but useful action. In some of these cases, where the disease has become chronic, delusions of sexual origin occur, and the patient whose virginity is intact imagines that she is pregnant or has had a baby.

The morbid self-feeling that has its root in the sexual system is not unapt to take on a religious guise. We observe examples of this in certain members of those latter-day religious sects which profess to commingle religion and love, and which especially abound in America. No physiologist can well doubt that the holy kiss of love in such cases owes all its warmth to the sexual feeling which consciously or unconsciously inspires it, or that the mystical union of the sexes lies very close to a union that is nowise mystical, when it does not lead to madness. A similar intimate connection between fanatical religious exaltation and sexual excitement is exemplified by the lives of such religious enthusiasts as St. Theresa and St. Catherine de Sienne, whose nightly trances and visions, in which they believed themselves received as veritable spouses into the bosom of Christ and transported into an unspeakable ecstasy by the touch of His sacred lips, attested, though they knew it not, the influence of excited sexual organs on the mind. More extreme examples of a like pathological action are afforded by those insane women who believe themselves to be visited by lovers or ravished by persecutors during the night. Sexual hallucinations, betraying an ovarian or uterine excitement, might almost be described as the characteristic feature of the insanity of old maids; the false visions of unreal indulgence being engendered probably in the same way as visions of banquets occur in the dreams of a starving person, or as visions of cooling streams to one who is perishing of thirst. It seems to be the fact that, although women bear sexual excesses better than men, they suffer more than men do from the entire deprivation of sexual intercourse. [. . .]

PERIODIC INSANITY

The monthly activity of the ovaries which marks the advent of puberty in women has a notable effect upon the mind and body; wherefore it may become an important cause of mental and physical derangement. Most women at that time are susceptible, irritable, and capricious, any cause of vexation affecting them more seriously than usual; and some who have the insane neurosis exhibit a disturbance of mind which amounts almost to disease. A sudden suppression of the menses has produced a direct explosion of insanity; or, occurring some time before an outbreak, it may be an important link in its causation. It is a matter also of common experience in asylums, that exacerbations of insanity often take place at the menstrual periods; but whether there is a particular variety of mental derangement connected with disordered menstruation, and, if so, what are its special features, we are not yet in a position to say positively.

GYNAECOLOGICAL TYRANNY

Clifford Allbutt, *On Visceral Neuroses: Being the Gulstonian Lectures on Neuralgia of the Stomach and Allied Disorders* (Philadelphia: P. Blakiston, 1884), 15–17.

In this forthright lecture, Allbutt attacks his gynaecological colleagues who have sought to defend their area of specialism against all intruders. Allbutt attacks both their methods, such as the weekly application of carbolic acid to the lining of the uterus, and also their assumption that all female ill-health is to be traced to the workings of the uterine economy. Female pain is either set aside as mere hysteria, or traced to the reproductive system. In his approach, Allbutt offers a healthy corrective to his colleagues' undue preoccupation with uterine disorder, and also points out the probable effects on the female psyche of such obsessive concern.

THE UTERUS

How intimately this organ, or this system, is associated with the nervous system is well known; but, unfortunately, the weight of our knowledge all leans one way—it leans to a curious and busy search for every local ill which may arise in the female pelvis, while blind oblivion scatters the poppy over every outer evil which in its turn might hurt the uterus; nay, more, a resolute prejudice would deny that in the woman any distress can arise which owes not its origin to these mischievous parts. *L'utérus c'est la femme* is a proverb which has received a new development in these days; for if by courtesy, rather than by conviction, woman be granted the possession of a few subsidiary organs, these, at best, have no prerogative nor any order of their own.

The uterus has its maladies of local causation, its maladies of nervous causation, and its maladies of mixed causation, as other organs have; and to assume, as is constantly assumed, that all uterine neuroses, or even all general neuroses in women, are due to coarse changes in the womb itself, is as dull as to suppose that the stomach can never be the seat of pain except it be the seat of some local affection, or that the face can never be the seat of tic-douloureux unless there be decayed teeth in the jaw. All mucous membranes, indeed, seem readily to betray nervous suffering by relaxation or changed secretion; and I make no doubt whatever that a very large number of uterine disorders which are elevated to the place and name of diseases of the uterine system are but manifestations of neurosis. All neuroses are commoner in women than in men. Facial neuralgia is commoner in them, migraine is commoner; so is gastralgia,[1] again, and the pseudo-angina. Not only so, but in the uterus they possess one organ the more, with its own rich nervous connections, and its own chapter of added diseases and neuroses; but to say that all these maladies are due primarily to uterine vagaries, is to talk wide of all analogies. Again, some men as brave as others feel equal sums of pain far more acutely than the others; women, speaking generally, feel pain more than men do; patient as they are, they seem to have less reserve of force and less resistance, more susceptibility, and resentment, and less capacity. Yet there is no standard of pain, nor of men, by which you shall say this patient is a coward and his outcry exaggerated. Men and women are variously organized in respect of resistance to pain, and their fortitude or their despair must be tested, not by their cries, but by the other features of their characters. What right have we to say that a man writing in the pangs of a toothache is a great sufferer, while, in the same breath, we hint that a woman complaining of a pain in the abdomen is hysterical? The pain is equally invisible, equally unmeasured in the two cases, and the degree of credit to be given to the complaints is to be gauged by other probabilities. A neuralgic woman seems thus to be peculiarly unfortunate. However bitter and repeated may be her visceral neuralgias, she is either told she is hysterical or that it is all uterus. In the first place she is comparatively fortunate, for she is only slighted; in the second case she is entangled in the net of the gynæcologist, who finds her uterus, like her nose, is a little on one side, or again, like that organ,

---

[1] Neuralgia of the stomach.

is running a little, or it is as flabby as her biceps, so that the unhappy viscus is impaled upon a stem, or perched upon a prop, or is painted with carbolic acid every week in the year except during the long vacation when the gynæcologist is grouse-shooting, or salmon-catching, or leading the fashion in the Upper Engadine. Her mind thus fastened to a more or less nasty mystery becomes newly apprehensive and physically introspective, and the morbid chains are riveted more strongly than ever. Arraign the uterus, and you fix in the woman the arrow of hypochondria, it may be for life.

3. Masculinity and the Control of Sexuality

DISORDERS IN CHILDHOOD AND YOUTH

William Acton, *The Functions and Disorders of the Reproductive Organs in Childhood, Youth, Adult Age, and Advanced Life Considered in their Physiological, Social and Moral Relations* (1857), 4th edn. (London: John Churchill, 1865), 1–3, 7–8, 9, 25–6, 28–9, 183–4.

This much reprinted work is primarily devoted to a study of male sexuality. Despite Acton's opening remarks, it soon becomes clear that he fears that very few children remain in the state of sexual innocence he deems so desirable. In his fears about the dire effects of masturbation, Acton follows a line of thought made popular by Tissot at the end of the eighteenth century, and revitalized in England in the 1840s by the publication of the work of the French doctor, Claude François Lallemand, A Practical Treatise on the Causes, Symptoms, and Treatment of Spermatorrhoea *(1847). Spermatorrhoea, a condition of enervation caused by loss of semen, was taken up by quack doctors who made a thriving trade out of male sexual fears. Acton, whilst indignant at the quacks, nonetheless regarded spermatorrhoea as a real condition, caused predominantly by masturbation, but also by other forms of excessive drains on the body's resources, as illustrated in the final case-study offered here. Acton argued throughout for continence, an economic hoarding of energy rather than reckless, undirected spending.*

NORMAL FUNCTIONS

In a state of health no sexual idea should ever enter a child's mind. All its vital energy should be employed in building up the growing body, and in storing up external impressions and educating the brain to receive them. During a well-regulated childhood, and in the case of ordinary temperaments, there is no temptation to infringe this primary law of nature. The sexes, it is true, in English

homes, are allowed most unrestricted companionship. Experience shows, however, that this intimacy is not only unattended with evil results, but is productive,
in the immense majority of instance, of great benefit. At a very early age the pas-
times of the boy and girl diverge. The boy takes to more boisterous amusements,
and affects the society of boys older than himself, simply because they make
rougher, or, in his opinion, manlier playfellows, while the little girls' quieter
games are despised, and their society, to a considerable extent, deserted. This tendency, often stigmatised as rudeness, and lamented over by anxious parents, may
almost be regarded as a provision of nature against possible danger. At any rate,
in healthy subjects, and especially in children brought up in the pure air, and
amid the simple amusements of the country, perfect freedom from, and indeed
total ignorance of, any sexual affection is, as it should always be, the rule. The
first and only feeling exhibited between the sexes in the young should be that
pure fraternal and sisterly affection, which it is the glory and blessing of our
simple English home-life to create and foster with all its softening influences on
the after life.

Education, of course, still further separates children, as they grow into boys
and girls—and the instructive and powerful check of natural modesty is an additional safeguard. Thus it happens that with most healthy and well-brought up
children, no sexual notion or feeling has ever entered their heads, even in the way
of speculation. I believe that healthy children's curiosity is hardly ever excited on
sexual subjects except in cases when such questions are purposely suggested, or
where bad example has demoralised them. [. . .]

DISORDERS IN CHILDHOOD

It were well if the child's reproductive organs always remained in this quiescent
state till puberty. This is unfortunately not the case.

CHAPT. I. SEXUAL PRECOCITY

In many instances, either from hereditary predispositions, bad companionship,
or other evil influences, sexual feelings are excited at a very early age, and too
often with the most deplorable consequences. Slight signs are sufficient to indicate when a boy has this unfortunate predisposition. He shows marked preferences. You will see him single out one girl, and evidently derive an unusual
pleasure, for a boy, in her society. His penchant does not take the ordinary form
of a boy's good nature, but little attentions that are generally reserved for a later
period prove that his feeling is different, and sadly premature. He may be quite
healthy, and fond of playing with other boys, still there are slight, but ominous
indications of propensities fraught with danger to himself. His play with the girl

210

is different from his play with his brothers. His kindness to her is a little too ardent. He follows her and he does not know why. He fondles her with a tenderness painfully suggestive of a vague dawning of passion. No one can find fault with him. He does nothing wrong. Parents and friends are delighted at his gentleness and politeness, and not a little amused at the early flirtation. But if they were wise they would rather feel profound anxiety; and he would be an unfaithful or unwise medical friend who did not, if an opportunity occurred, warn them that the boy, unsuspicious and innocent as he is, should be carefully watched, and removed from every influence that could possibly excite his slumbering tendencies. [. . .]

MASTURBATION IN CHILDHOOD

[. . .] This practice in a young child may arise in a variety of ways. The commonest is of course the bad example of other children. In other cases again, vicious or foolish female servants suggest the idea. [. . .] On the whole, I am disposed to think that in most *public* schools, the feeling is strongly against these vile practices. [. . .] In *private* schools, however, which are to a great extent free from the control of that healthy public opinion that, even among boys, has so salutary an effect, there is too much reason to fear that this scourge of our youth prevails to an extent which will not be known, with any certainty, till years hence the sufferers from early vice are seeking medical relief, too often, alas, in vain. It is for us now to consider what preventive steps can be taken to lessen if not remove the evil; that it exists among children, even now, to a frightful extent, I have only too abundant reason to know. And that schools are still subject to it is pretty evident from much information I have had [. . .]

The symptoms which mark the commencement of the practice are too clear for an experienced eye to be deceived. As Lallemand[1] remarks: 'However young the children may be, they get thin, pale, or irritable, and their features become haggard. We notice the sunken eye, the long, cadaverous looking countenance, the downcast look which seems to arise from a consciousness that their habits are suspected, and, at a later period, that their virility is lost. It may depend upon timidity acquired or inherited. I wish by no means to assert that every boy unable to look another in the face, is or has been a masturbator, but I believe this vice is a very frequent cause of timidity. These boys have a dank, moist, cold hand, very characteristic of great vital exhaustion; their sleep is short, and most complete marasmus[2] comes on; they may die if their evil passion is not got the better of; nervous symptoms set in, such as spasmodic contraction, or partial or entire

---

[1] Claude François Lallemand, *A Practical Treatise on the Causes, Symptoms, and Treatment of Spermatorrhoea*, trans. and ed. Henry J. McDougall (1847). Lallemand's work was first published in France, 1836–42.

[2] A wasting away of the body.

convulsive movements, together with epilepsy, eclampsy,[3] and a species of paralysis accompanied with contractions of the limbs.' [. . .]

PREVENTIVE TREATMENT.—I cannot but think that much of this evil could be prevented, by wisely watching children in early life; and where a sexual temperament,—a suspicion of the practice having been begun,—or other circumstances rendered it desirable, by pointing out the dreadful evils that result from it, kindly but solemnly warning them against it. [. . .]

PUBERTY

And now begins the trial which every healthy boy must encounter, and come out of victorious if he is to be all that he can and ought to be. The child should know nothing of this trial, and ought never to be disturbed with one sexual feeling or thought. But with puberty a very different state of things arises. A new *power* is present to be exercised, a new *want* to be satisfied. It is, I take it, of vital importance that boys and young men should know, not only the guilt of an illicit indulgence of their dawning passions, but also the danger of straining an immature power, and the solemn truth that the *want* will be an irresistible tyrant only to those who have lent it strength by yielding; that the only true safety lies in keeping even the thought pure. And nothing, I feel convinced, but a frank statement of the truth will persuade them that these new feelings, powers, and delights, must not be indulged in.

Now, it is very well known to medical men that the healthy secretion of semen has a direct effect upon the whole physical and mental conformation of the man. A series of phenomena attend the natural action of the testicles which influence the whole system; gradually, in fact, forming the character itself. A function so important, which does, in truth, to a great extent determine, according as it is dealt with, the happiness or misery of a life, is surely one of the last, if not the very last, to be abused.

But what, too often, are the facts? The youth, finding himself in possession of these sexual feelings and powers, utterly ignorant of their importance or even of their nature, except from the ribald conversation of the worst of his companions, and knowing absolutely nothing of the consequences of giving way to them, fancies, as he, with many compunctions, begins a career of depravity, that he is obeying nature's dictates. Every fresh indulgence helps to forge the chains of habit, and, too late, the truth dawns on him that he is, more or less, ruined for this world, that he can never be what he might have been, and that it can only be by a struggle as for life or death that he can hope for any recovery. Alas, in too many there is no strength left for any such struggle, and, hopelessly and helplessly, they drift on into irremediable ruin, tied and bound in the chain of a sin with the commencement of which ignorance had as much to do as vice. [. . .]

[3] A form of seizure.

THE ADVANTAGES OF CONTINENCE.—If a healthy, well-disposed boy has been properly educated, by the time he arrives at the age of fourteen or sixteen he possesses a frame approaching its full vigour. His conscience is unburdened, his intellect clear, his address frank and candid, his memory good, his spirits are buoyant, his complexion bright. Every function of the body is well performed, and no fatigue is felt after moderate exertion. The youth evinces that elasticity of body and that happy control of himself and his feelings which are indicative of that robust health and absence of care which should accompany youth. His whole time is given up to his studies and his amusements, and as he feels his stature increase and his intellect enlarge, he gladly prepares for his coming struggle with the world. The case is very different where a boy has been incontinent, especially in that most vicious of all ways, masturbation.

In extreme cases the outward signs of debasement are only too obvious. The frame is stunted and weak, the muscles undeveloped, the eye is sunken and heavy, the complexion is sallow, pasty, or covered with spots of acne, the hands are damp and cold, and the skin moist. The boy shuns the society of others, creeps about alone, joins with repugnance in the amusements of his schoolfellows. He cannot look any one in the face, and becomes careless in dress and uncleanly in person. His intellect is often of the lowest class, and if his evil habits are persisted in, he may end in becoming a drivelling idiot or a peevish valetudinarian. Such boys are to be seen in all the stages of degeneration. What we have described is but the result towards which *all* incontinent boys are tending.

The cause of the difference between these cases is very simple. The continent boy has not expended that vital fluid, semen, and his youthful vigour has been employed for its legitimate purpose, namely, in building up his growing frame. On the other hand, the incessant excitement of sexual thoughts and the large expenditure of semen has exhausted the vital force of the incontinent, and has reduced the immature frame to a pitiable wreck. [. . .]

SPERMATORRHŒA

[. . .] It is to the interested exaggeration of quack writers (professional as well as extra-professional) of the symptoms of spermatorrhœa that we must, I imagine, attribute the fact of medical writers of eminence denying that such a disease exists at all. Great exaggeration has doubtless been indulged in by many of those who have written on the complaint, and from obvious and infamous motives. But I am convinced, as I have already stated, that many of the most obstinate complaints which the medical man meets with arise from loss of semen—hypochondriasis, the various forms of indigestion, debility, and nervous affections, with loss of sleep, are often only the effects of spermatorrhœa; and in such cases the best, and indeed the only treatment, is that which removes the *cause,* and is not confined to combating the symptoms. The best evidence of this is, that such radical treatment alone relieves the symptoms when all other remedies have failed. The condition or ailment which we here characterise as *Spermatorrhœa*, then, as we shall use the word, is a state of enervation produced, at least primarily, by the loss of semen. [. . .]

From the painful stigma which its existence casts on the past life of the patient, and the secrecy he would naturally desire, as well as from the somewhat doubtful nature of the symptoms to an inexperienced eye, this disease has been and is used by unprincipled practitioners as a means of imposition to a very great extent. Every disease or fancied ailment which their unfortunate victim can be persuaded into believing Spermatorrhœa, is called Spermatorrhœa forthwith; and, in his agony of terror and humiliation, the wretched, and often innocent patient, becomes a fit subject for the wickedest cruelty, and, I need hardly add, the most extravagant extortion. [. . .]

Perhaps a knowledge of the truth may save some reader from the perils to which his ignorance, judiciously played on by an unscrupulous quack, would leave him exposed.

CAUSES OF SPERMATORRHŒA.—*Hard study* I have already mentioned more than once as able to produce, or predispose to, this condition. The following is a sample of the cases to be met with in which over-exertion of the brain has had this effect. A patient called on me in June, 1860, complaining that he was labouring under spermatorrhœa. He stated that he had recently been studying hard at the University, and admitted also having had connection about four times in a month, without feeling any great desire, and without experiencing any great pleasure; erection and emission had, however, taken place. I found he was engaged, but from pecuniary circumstances the marriage was postponed. He had nearly all the symptoms which constitute spermatorrhœa, and was naturally alarmed at his state; this I could and did assure him was temporary. After contrasting the conditions of the continent and incontinent man, I think I succeeded in convincing him that the only danger he had to dread arose from continuing venereal excess; that, if he remained continent, the mere temporary result of vigorous mental exertion would pass away, leaving him none the worse; but that the double strain on both the brain and the generative system, against which nature herself cried out, would most certainly deteriorate if not ruin both.

A FREQUENT CAUSE OF INSANITY IN YOUNG MEN

Robert P. Ritchie, *An Inquiry into a Frequent Cause of Insanity in Young Men* (London: Henry Renshaw, 1961), 5, 7, 8, 12, 23–4, 26–7.

This was first published as a series of articles in the Lancet *during February and March 1861, and reprinted as a pamphlet. Ritchie offers an analysis of asylum records and various treatises on insanity to further his argument that masturbation as a cause in itself of insanity has not received sufficient recognition. He concludes that, despite problems of record keeping, men of the middle classes are twice as likely to suffer insanity from this cause than either lower or upper-class males. In discussion of the 'maniacal form' of this derangement he moves away from a physical cause to locate the disorder's origin in the patient's own 'disgust' at his 'criminal conduct'.*

On entering an asylum for the insane, especially if it be one receiving patients from the middle as well as from the lower class of society, there is one group of inmates which may arrest the attention of the visitor from the contrast presented to the excited persons around him, on the one hand, and to those who are convalescent on the other. Engaged in no social diversion, the patients of this group live alone in the midst of many. In their exercise they choose the quietest and most unfrequented parts of the airing-grounds. They join in no social conversation, nor enter with others into any amusement. They walk alone, or they sit alone. If engaged in reading, they talk not to others of what they may have read; their desire apparently is, in the midst of numbers, to be in solitude. They seek no social joys, nor is the wish for fellowship evinced.

In some asylums these patients form a considerable proportion of the male inmates; but, for reasons to be presently alluded, it is not very remarkable that the cause of this kind of mental alienation, and its existence as a distinct form of disease, have by some been doubted. It is, however, remarkable that writers on mental maladies pass over this class of mental affection with scarcely an allusion to the occasion of it. It is surprising that those who undertake to treat of a whole subject should refer to so important a section in a most cursory and unsatisfactory manner. [. . .]

Let us not ignore so powerful a cause of mental disease merely because it is a nameless vice, and one we blush even to allude to. It is of too frequent occurrence, and is too serious in its results, to be passed over lightly. [. . .]

Frequency as a cause of insanity.—It is especially desirable to ascertain the frequency of cases of insanity arising from masturbation—a word which in future shall be alluded to rather than expressed.

There are considerable difficulties in obtaining definite and certain information on this head, because, as has been already remarked, some alienist physicians do not recognize mental disease to be produced by this cause, and they are satisfied with the cause being stated to be 'unknown,' or receive as correct some other than the true one. [. . .] It would appear that the middle classes are more the subjects of insanity thus occasioned than either the class above, or that below them in social grade. This result is just that which might have been expected from the consideration of the inducements to the habit, having regard to morality (whether due to religious feeling or self-imposed), to occupation, recreation, social intercourse, and facilities for marriage.

Sex.—A few remarks on the sex of the patients may not be quite out of place. The object of this paper being to show the frequency of one of the causes of insanity in young men, it has not been considered necessary to make any comparison with the female insane, and I shall only remark that there appears to be great similarity in the mental symptoms presented by the sexes, with this addition, that in the female a hysterical condition is manifested which in the male does not appear. Although there is reason to believe that indulgence in this vicious propensity is by no means infrequent among females, it does not appear that insanity is so commonly produced thereby in them as in males. [. . .]

It is sad that, under the guise of a strictly moral life, a vicious indulgence, and one, too, of most aggravated character and baneful results, may be practised in solitude. It is to be deplored that the finest qualities of our nature may frequently but cloak the hidden evil, and that the apparently well conducted, studious youth may be but too certainly preparing a manhood of misery and uselessness. How earnestly do those who know what the future will bring to such a one repeat these feeling words of Ellis[1]—'Would that I could take its melancholy victims with me in my daily rounds (at Hanwell Asylum), and could point out to them the awful consequences which they do but little suspect to be the result of its indulgence. I could show them those gifted by nature with high talents, and fitted to be an ornament and a benefit to society, sunk into such a state of physical and moral degradation as wrings the heart to witness, and still preserving, with the last remnant of a mind gradually sinking into fatuity, the consciousness that their hopeless wretchedness is the just reward of their own misconduct.' [. . .]

THE MANIACAL FORM

The system, being reduced both physically and mentally, is but little able to stand against any mental emotion of a violent character. The intensity exerted by the

---

[1] William Ellis, *Treatise on Insanity* (1838)

exciting emotion of course varies in proportion to the previous deteriorating effect of the predisposing cause, and whilst, in one case, but a slight increase of mental exertion upsets the mind, in another a more severe or more prolonged continuance of the exciting cause is necessary.

Although it will be found that various supposed causes may be alleged, still I believe that in the greater proportion of such cases the immediate exciting cause is the feeling of disgust at, combined with alarm for the consequences of, the patient's criminal conduct. Hence it is that feelings of their own unworthiness arise in such patients, and, under the impression that they have committed the unpardonable sin—have sinned against the Holy Ghost—and that a future world presents no hope of joy or happiness for them, as they are excluded from it by their past conduct, they frequently make attempts to terminate their own existence.

THE EVILS OF ABSTINENCE AND EXCESS

George Drysdale, *Elements of Social Science, or, Physical, Sexual and Natural Religion* (1854), 13th edn. (London: Truelove, 1873), 30–3, 84–5, 87–90.

Drysdale was a maverick figure in mid-nineteenth century medicine, openly arguing for the benefits of sexual intercourse outside marriage and for the use of birth control. Many of his arguments, however, mirrored those of the medical establishment: his strictures, for example, against the evils of sexual excess, or the evils of self-abuse. Where he differed was in his depiction of the 'evils of abstinence': he was the only British writer to take up Lallemand's suggestion that spermatorrhoea could be caused by continence. His arguments, however, are only a logical following through of the firmly held medical view that male hysteria, for example, could be caused by continence. In his advice to exercise the sexual organs, he differs little in medical grounds from Graham's decorous On the Management and Disorders of Infancy and Childhood. *Unlike his contemporaries, however, he openly advocated sexual exercise outside the bounds of marriage.*

EVILS OF ABSTINENCE

It is most unwise to suppose that our chief duty with regard to our appetites and passions is to exercise self-denial. This quality is far from being at all times a virtue; it is quite as often a vice; and it should by no means be unconditionally praised. Every natural passion, like every organ of the body, was intended to have normal exercise and gratification; and this it is to which every individual and society at large should aspire. It is always a sign of imperfection in an individual, or in society, if the normal requirements of all their members be not duly provided for. At present, in this country, abstinence or self-denial in the matter of sexual love is much more frequently a natural vice than a virtue; and instead of deserving praise, merits condemnation, as we may learn from the mode in which all-just nature punishes it. Wherever we see disease following any line of conduct, we may be certain it has been erroneous and sinful; for nature is unerring. Sexual abstinence is frequently attended by consequences not one whit less serious than sexual excess, and far more insidious and dangerous, as they are not so generally recognised. While every moralist can paint in all its horrors the evils of excess, how few are aware that the reverse of the picture is just as deplorable to the impartial and instructed eye!

The young man enters on the period of puberty with an imagination glowing with the ideas of love and romance he has read of, or conceived in his own visions of happiness, and all these receive ten-fold intensity from the stimulus of the new bodily development. If this have no natural outlet, the consequences may be most fearful and deplorable. Thrown upon himself by the asceticism of our morality, he is very liable to contract the habit of solitary indulgence, the baneful effects of which I shall describe under the head of the *abuse* of the sexual organs. If he do not: if, persuaded by the theoretically received, but by no means generally practised, views on moral subjects which surround him, he abstains from all sexual gratifications, he is exposed to the following evils, of which, if we look around us, we may see too many examples. Haunted by amatory ideas, and tormented by frequent erections of the sexual organ, the spirited youth wars manfully for the citadel of his chastity; he takes refuge in study, in severe bodily exercise, in platonics, the unhappy one! and reasons on love instead of feeling it; and perhaps at last is so unfortunately successful, that the strong sexual passions and erections vanish together. But not with impunity, do we triumph over any part of our nature. He now becomes restless and dissatisfied, he loses his serenity and active vigour of mind, he is distracted by nervous irritability and probably dyspepsia, that frequent attendant on mental anxiety; weak and exhausted, he cannot fix his attention on the objects he would wish to study; his intellect, formerly vivid and elastic, has become turbid and sluggish, and instead of the objective and impetuous passions of youth, he becomes morbidly shy and bashful, wrapping himself in subjective speculations, so that the very thought of woman's society is often distasteful to him. Poor fellow! is this the result of his imagined good conduct? Nay, but the penalty for a youth unphysiologically spent. If we examine into the cause of this train of evils, we shall find it to be the enfeeblement of the genital organs from *disuse*, besides the exceedingly pernicious effect, that a powerful natural passion has when repressed upon all the rest of the mind.

Subject to the frequent excitement of erotic ideas, the genital organs have been denied all normal exercise, and the effects of this are now manifest. The penis may be shrunk and flabby, the testicles soft, and even, in extreme cases, greatly atrophied; the erections which, when vigorous, are a sign of power in the organ, have in great part disappeared, and perhaps involuntary discharges of the seminal fluid have been established. These discharges, when they occur unfrequently and in a healthy person, have often but little bad effect on the health, although perhaps they should always, when proceeding from abstinence, be considered as a warning that sexual exercise is required; they occur generally at the time of puberty, as a sign of the maturity of the organs; but when they are frequent, proceeding from irritability and enfeeblement, and acquire a morbid habit of recurrence, they form one of the most miserable diseases to which man is liable, and which I shall describe more fully under the head of spermatorrhœa.

If this disease be established, the young man sinks gradually into a gloomy hypochondria, an invariable attendant in a greater or less degree, on any seminal weakness; he begins perhaps a system of mental analysis, which may lead, according to his disposition, to a hopeless scepticism, or to a religious melancholy; society is a burden to him, and the love of his friends an annoyance. His health becomes much impaired, all the symptoms marking nervous weakness, for such is always the effect of loss of the seminal fluid. Night brings no consolation after the gloomy day, for he lives in constant dread of nocturnal discharges of semen, which weaken him so much, that in the morning he feels as if bound down by a weight to his couch. He goes from one physician to another, but is probably rather injured than benefited, for all but the natural remedy, namely, sexual connexion, can do little good, and may do much evil. [. . .]

We must acknowledge, that every man, who has not a due amount of sexual exercise, lives a life of natural imperfection and sin; and he can never be certain how far nature's punishment for this will proceed in his case. I am well aware how intricate and difficult are many of the social questions, which are involved in these relations of the sexes; but such questions are incapable of solution without reference to the physical laws of the generative organs; and nothing but confusion and misery can arise from the mysterious way in which these subjects are at present viewed. The youth of both sexes are at present almost uniformly suffering to a greater or less degree from the evils caused by this ignorance; the female sex especially, as is seen in the matter of prostitution, are placed in the most appalling and heart-rending position of degradation and misery, in which any class of human beings, not even excepting the slaves, have been placed in the world's history; and such evils are more than sufficient to show the inadequacy of our present moral views, and to make us strive in every possible manner to gain more insight into so important a subject.

EVILS OF EXCESS

The evil effects of excessive venereal indulgence are not so often met with among us as those of abstinence or abuse. The reason is, that there are many natural checks on excessive sexual intercourse which do not exist in solitary indulgence. Besides this, any abnormal gratification of the sexual passions is much more dangerous, both physically and morally, than the natural one.

Venereal excesses arise in many cases more from ignorance and imprudence than from confirmed sensuality. There is nothing, perhaps, in which constitutions differ more than in the amount of sexual exercise they can severally bear. Among men we shall find every degree of difference in this respect, from those of exceedingly erotic temperament and powerful frame, like the extreme case of a Greek mentioned in M. Lallemand's work on spermatorrhœa, who for years indulged in sexual connection several times a day, to those who are injured by indulging oftener than once, or at most twice, a week. The cause of this difference lies, first, in the nervous temperament; those who are of an erotic disposition being *caeteris paribus*, more capable of, and less injured by immoderate venereal indulgences than the more lymphatic; also in the strength on weakness of the muscular development; and also to a great degree on men's habits of life. Those who take plenty of exercise in the country air and live well, are less subject to injury from frequent venereal indulgence than the studious or indolent. Nothing seems to have greater influence in weakening sexual power than overwork of the brain. The student is therefore liable to suffer from slight excesses, which would be unfelt by one of more healthy pursuits. In this matter, as in all other physical gratifications, we must sedulously bear in mind that a greater indulgence demands from us greater exertions to maintain the balance of the constitution. Thus if a man drink, smoke, or exercise his brain, or his sexual organs, to a great extent, he will infallibly become exhausted and diseased, unless he at the same time take plenty of exercise in the open air, and live otherwise a healthy life.

Although it is difficult to give any general rule in a matter in which different constitutions vary so much, yet it may perhaps be said that about twice a week is the average amount of sexual intercourse of which the majority of those who live in towns are permanently capable without injury; while for the delicate, once a week, or even less, may often be sufficient. But each individual should be guided by his own sensations; and whenever he feels at all exhausted or enervated by sexual indulgences, he should recognise that he has exceeded his natural powers, and practise greater moderation. Excesses are often committed from ignorance of the amount of sexual intercourse which the constitution can bear; as well as from the desire to please, and not to appear deficient in what is justly regarded as a proof of manly vigour; but no man should allow himself to be tempted to exceed his true powers by such feelings, nor should any woman permit so dangerous an error. A great deal of mischief is done by two persons of unequal constitutions being matched together, as is so frequently seen in married life. Here the wife either exhausts the husband, or the husband the wife, the weaker party being constantly tempted to exceed their strength. This shows us, that in all sexual relations, as in the other relations of life, we should have a careful consideration for the health and happiness of others, as well as of ourselves, and never allow our partner to overtask his or her energies for our own gratification. It is not so much from selfishness that such a mistake is made, as from ignorance, and still more from the lamentable morbid delicacy, which prevails of sexual matters, and which prevents all open and rational conversation on them, even between those who have the most intimate knowledge of each other.

EVILS OF ABUSE

I come now to consider one of the most serious and frequent causes of disease in youth; one which ruins more constitutions than enters into the conception of the uninstructed. Any one who reads M. Lallemand's work will see, that by far the majority of the worst cases of seminal weakness are owing to this cause. Its evil effects are confined to the one class, but are found in all ranks of society; and there are few rocks, on which the health of more individuals is wrecked. The unfortunate habit of solitary indulgence or masturbation, is frequently contracted at schools or elsewhere, and often adopted more out of sport or ignorance of the consequences it may lead to, than from any more serious purpose. However, the habit grows on the young man, and if he be not diverted from it, may gradually master his powers of mind and become almost irresistible. Some of the cases given by M. Lallemand show the surprising extent to which this practice may be carried; some of his patients owned, that they had been in the habit of exciting seminal emissions from ten to twenty times daily, and this during a long period of time. In others, a far more moderate indulgence soon brought on the worst results; for in this, as in the case of venereal excesses, different constitutions will be very differently effected. Hence, of those who acquire the habit, some may escape with little injury, while others may bring on the most intractable seminal disease, which will prostrate their powers. Those who are most likely to suffer, are young men of a shy and retiring disposition, whose bashfulness prevents them from stepping across the gulph, which in this country separates the sexes. Others of a more forward character, though they may for a while indulge in the practice (which, were the truth known, probably few men have not done more or less) yet soon relinquish it, for the more natural and infinitely more desirable sexual intercourse, and thus any injury they may have done themselves is soon corrected. [. . .]

It is a disgrace to medicine and mankind, that so important a class of diseases, as those of the genital organs, have become the trade and speculation of unscientific men, because forsooth they are looked upon unfavourably by society, and even by some of our own profession. Until this class of diseases receive due respect from all, and till no greater blame attach to them, than to any other violation of natural laws and consequent disease, so long shall we be disgusted by the degrading advertisements of 'silent friends,' 'cures for certain diseases,' &c., in reading which one's breast glows with indignation and sorrow, or, if he be a sufferer from these miserable diseases, sinks to the dust in humiliation. The very existence of these degrading advertisements shows the erroneous mode in which the sexual organs and their diseases are regarded; and it is not the empiric on whom the real blame for them should rest, but the spurious delicacy which makes a mystery of all these subjects, and thus inevitably consigns them to the destructive and mercenary treatment of this body of men. [. . .]

The true and only preventive means for this most ruinous habit, is to instruct youth in the laws of the genital organs, and to alter the strictness of the moral code; of which subject I shall speak more fully hereafter. As long as the present rigorous sexual code continues, so long will the whole of our youth of both sexes be liable to this disease, along with the other genital and venereal complaints. Masturbation is practised only because the natural sexual intercourse cannot be attained, or because its attainment is difficult and dangerous. Were it readily attainable without the danger of disease and the degradation of illicit intercourse, masturbation would rarely if ever be resorted to, and one of the most fearful and prevalent causes of disease, moral and physical, eradicated.

SEXUAL HYPOCHONDRIASIS

James Paget, 'Sexual hypochondriasis', *Clinical Lectures and Essays*, ed. H. Marsh (London: Longman, Green, 1875), 47–50.

Paget here tries to counter some of the anxieties created by fears of spermatorrhoea. The state of sexual hypochondriasis he defines is pre-eminently a mental condition. Although masturbation receives the full weight of his moral disapproval, in physiological terms he deems it to be no worse in its effects than normal intercourse. He does not, however, follow what he deems to be a fairly common medical practice of recommending 'fornication'. Instead he offers a fierce moral defence of the values of sexual chastity.

You may observe that, in speaking of sexual hypochondriasis, I have spoken of three different classes of men or boys in whom functional disorders of the sexual organs may need to be treated. There are, first, the merely ignorant or misinformed; next, those with over-sensitive or too irritable nervous systems; and lastly, the hypochondriacs. The conditions respectively characteristic of each may be mingled in various degrees, but they are worth keeping in mind as guides to treatment. The patients of the second class alone need medicinal help, and what this may be I said just now: the others must be mentally helped.

With careful and very positive teaching you will cure the ignorant, and do good to all but those whose hypochondriasis is near to complete insanity. But on some subjects of your teaching you will have to be very clear as to matters of fact; especially, for instance, as to the practice of masturbation, to which many of your patients will ascribe their chief distresses.

Now, I believe you may teach positively that masturbation does neither more nor less harm than sexual intercourse practised with the same frequency in the same conditions of general health and age and circumstance. Practised frequently by the very young, that is, at any time before or at the beginning of puberty, masturbation is very likely to produce exhaustion, effeminacy, over-sensitiveness and nervousness; just as equally frequent copulation at the same age would probably produce them. Or, practised every day, or many times a day, at any age, either masturbation or copulation is likely to produce similar mischiefs or greater. And the mischiefs are especially likely or nearly sure to happen, and to be greatest, if the excesses are practised by those who, by inheritance or circumstances, are liable to any nervous disease,—to 'spinal irritation,' epilepsy, insanity, or any other. But the mischiefs are due to the quantity, not to the method, of the excesses; and the quantity is to be estimated in relation to age and the power of the nervous system. I have seen as numerous and as great evils consequent on excessive sexual intercourse as on excessive masturbation: but I have not seen or heard anything to make me believe that occasional masturbation has any other effects on one who practises it than has occasional sexual intercourse, nor anything justifying the dread with which sexual hypochondriacs regard the having occasionally practised it. I wish that I could say something worse of so nasty a practice; an uncleanliness, a filthiness forbidden by God, an unmanliness despised by men.

Another point on which you may have to teach is that of dreams associated with nocturnal seminal emissions. Men of scrupulous conscience are deeply distressed with the thought that these emissions are due to sexual feelings which they ought to be able to suppress even in their dreams; they look on them as tokens of a prevalent impurity of mind which they must cure. Well, you may tell them that, according to all we know of dreams, it is not the dream that excites the emission, but the natural and involuntary erection and emission that determine the dream, and that over the erection and emission that may occur in sleep or on just waking it is impossible that any man should exercise direct control; he might as well try to control while asleep the tone of his snoring or the posture of his limbs. Some indirect control a man may have on all these things, and of the sexual part of them it may be held that the more the mind while awake is occupied in other than sexual matters, and so occupied that it is not even necessary to use any effort for the suppression or exclusion of sexual thoughts, the less will be the secretion of semen and the sensibility of the sexual organs, and therefore the less frequent the excitements and emissions during sleep. But, in some persons and, as I believe, in the great majority of those who are chaste, nocturnal emissions and the associated unclean dreams are simply irrepressible: they are due to a natural secretion of semen which we have no means of suppressing and no right to suppress. Therefore, to men with healthy nervous systems you must tell that their nocturnal emissions are evidences of health rather than of disease. And to those in whom too frequent emissions are connected with a too irritable state of the spinal marrow, you may tell that they cannot and ought not to be wholly suppressed; but that they may be remedied by marriage and may, very probably, be diminished by means that will improve the condition of the spinal marrow.

To all alike you may try to teach a virtuous and judicious carelessness about these things; a state of mind which would be an inestimable blessing to many besides these sexual hypochondriacs.

Many of your patients will ask you about sexual intercourse and some will expect you to prescribe fornication. I would just as soon prescribe theft or lying or anything else that God has forbidden. If men will practise fornication or uncleanness it must be of their own choice and on their sole responsibility. We are not to advise that which is morally wrong, even if we have some reason to think that a patient's health would be better for the wrong-doing. But in the cases before us, and I can imagine none in which I should think differently, there is not ground enough for so much as raising a question about wrong-doing. Chastity does no harm to mind or body; its discipline is excellent: marriage can safely be waited for; and among the many nervous and hypochondriacal patients who have talked to me about fornication, I have never heard one say that he was better or happier after it; several have said that they were worse: and many, having failed, have been made much worse.

Section IV

Insanity and
Nervous Disorders

Insanity and Nervous Disorders

In 1793 the French physician Philippe Pinel struck off the chains of his patients in the Bicêtre asylum in the name of Liberté, Egalité, Fraternité. Simultaneously in England, the Quaker William Tuke, appalled at the current treatment of the insane in asylums, was raising money to fund the Retreat in York, an institution for insane persons of the Society of Friends which admitted its first patients in 1796. The Retreat was the first institution founded specifically on non-restraint principles, and ushered in in England the new humanitarian system of treatment known as moral management which underpinned the rise of psychological medicine in the nineteenth century. Tuke's aim, as his grandson Samuel makes clear in his *Description of the Retreat* (1813), was to create more of a home than a prison, where inmates were to be governed more by the moral force of 'desire of esteem' than by physical control. The famous tea-parties, where female patients were encouraged to conform to middle-class notions of 'politeness and propriety' were copied in asylums across the land.

Tuke's text also sparked off widespread public concern about the conditions in non-reformed asylums, and was one of the factors contributing to the setting-up of the 1815 parliamentary committee on the regulation of madhouses. Although no actual legislation was passed for another thirteen years, the plight of lunatics now became a cause for public concern, and a general movement for reform was under way, culminating, in 1845, with the Lunacy Acts, which called for the mandatory construction of public, county asylums, and set up a national Lunacy Commission to regulate and inspect all asylums, both public and private.

Medical reformers and social commentators on asylums now published numerous accounts emphasizing the miracles of transformation that had occurred. Scenes of cosy domesticity were set against images of the bestial confinement which had earlier reigned. Seductive as such portraits are, they should be treated with considerable scepticism. The treatment of the insane in the eighteenth century was not so universally horrific as these accounts suggest, nor were nineteenth-century methods entirely those of the 'ministering angel', as Andrew Wynter would have us believe. Michel Foucault's influential work has shown how the discourse of moral management and the regime of surveillance adopted within asylums, led to an internalization of social controls.[1] As the material on sexuality has also shown, medical psychology played a crucial role in policing the boundaries of social acceptability.

---

[1] Michel Foucault, *Madness and Civilisation: A History of Insanity in the Age of Reason*, trans. Richard Howard (London: Tavistock, 1967); and *Discipline and Punish: The Birth of the Prison*, trans. Alan Sheridan (Penguin: Harmondsworth, 1979).

The texts of these early psychiatrists further reveal an emergent profession eager to consolidate its own power base. According to John Conolly, one of the foremost proponents of moral management, only the watchful eye of the physician could save the greater part of the English nation from becoming 'helpless and miserable' under the pressures of nervous disease. Conolly's own role was to come under scrutiny, however, in the late 1840s with the rise of several highly publicized cases focusing on wrongful confinement, where Conolly gave testimony supporting confinement.[2] Public alarm was raised regarding the power of the doctors, and newspapers and journals carried numerous editorials and articles on issues surrounding the detection and treatment of insanity. John Perceval, whose narrative of the horrors of his own confinement is featured here, was active in founding the Alleged Lunatics' Friend Society, and gave evidence to the 1859 Select Committee on the Care and Treatment of Lunatics and their Property.

The major shift in attitudes to the insane in the nineteenth century came in the belief that they could be cured: no longer were they to be set apart as irredeemable, but treated as sufferers who could be restored to humanity. As Esquirol, the highly influential heir to Pinel observes, in the house of the insane one finds the same ideas and passions as in the outer world, only here they are revealed in all their nakedness, without dissimulation. In a sense, insanity thus expresses a heightened state of normality. This blurring of the boundaries between sanity and insanity proved peculiarly unsettling. If the insane could no longer be set apart from the sane, then how did one know whether one had crossed the border? The obverse of the belief that all could be cured was the belief that all could also succumb. In his popular work, *Man's Power over Himself to Prevent or Control Insanity* (1843), the Reverend John Barlow calls upon the 'soi-disant sane' to consider carefully their position. We all experience thoughts and feelings that are as frightful as those of any madman: the only difference between the sane and insane is that the sane man exerts a greater degree of self-control, and represses his desires.

Barlow's text clearly highlights the ways in which ideas of moral management were intricately linked to the economic ideologies of the Victorian age. In an age of bewildering, mass social change, ideas of self-help and self-control firmly placed responsibility for success at the door of the individual. Phrenological theories, which were very influential in early asylum practice, also brought together the two strands of psychological and economic thought: individuals were to focus on controlling their undesirable propensities, and developing their positive faculties. Cures could be effected through the development of the right forms of self-control.

---

[2] In the celebrated case in 1849 of Eliza Nottridge, an heiress who had joined a millenial sect and had been confined against her will by her mother and brother-in-law, Conolly argued for the necessity of confinement. Conolly was parodied as Dr Wycherley in Charles Reade's novel, *Hard Cash* (1863), which focused on the scandal of wrongful confinement.

Madness was no longer an absolute term. As Conolly argued, a man was mad only for as long as passion overturned his reason; sanity returned as soon as he was able once more to exercise comparative judgement. Theories of monomania, popularized by Esquirol in France, were quickly brought into currency in England and twinned with Prichard's theories of moral insanity. Moral insanity was thought to be a perversion of moral feelings which left the mental faculties unaffected, and monomania a form of insanity attached only to particular strains of thought in the mind. Both were theories of partial insanity which stressed that an individual could live in a family and community for many years whilst harbouring a strain of insanity unsuspected by all around. Physiognomical analysis thus became a crucial tool of the skilled physician who claimed by this means to unmask the secrets of even the most arch dissembler. Morison's before and after sketches were among the first attempts to delineate the transformations in features and dress wrought by insanity.[3] Erotomania, depicted here, was a favourite with nineteenth-century physicians: female patients could be depicted as simultaneously subject to sexual excess, but also thoroughly chaste. The varieties of monomania, Esquirol suggests, function as a physical map of our developing civilization, each new stress producing a new form of monomania. Even children, in his eyes, were subject to some of the most extreme forms of mental aberration such as homicidal monomania.

Ideas of partial insanity made the legal issue of responsibility quite fraught, particularly when the view was taken that insanity could be transient, lasting only as long as judgement was overturned. For Bucknill the issue related not to a simple question of knowledge of right or wrong, but to whether the individual had the power to follow that knowledge. From the 1860s, the question of inheritance came to play a greater role in insanity debates. According to Maudsley's famous formulation, 'lunatics and criminals are as much manufactured articles as are steam-engines and calico-printing machines' created alike by inheritance and education. Responsibility for their actions lay outside their own hands, therefore. Maudsley was not, however, endorsing an extreme version of biological determinism. Like Barlow in the 1840s, he too wanted to stress the importance of self-control, but in this case control was to be exerted to combat inherited traits, not merely the wayward passions of the individual mind.

The moral, reforming zeal of the early psychiatrists survived through into the second half of the century, even though the belief in the possibility of curing many forms of insanity was now sadly dinted. The populace of England still needed to be saved from themselves, as Andrew Wynter's stern address to the 'sherry drinking ladies of this generation' clearly shows. The rhetoric sustaining these invocations to the reader remains largely unchanged: true human potential

---

[3] The first atlas of the insane was published by Pinel's pupil, J. E. D. Esquirol, as an appendix to his 1838 work, *Des maladies mentales*. See Sander Gilman, *Seeing the Insane* (New York: John Wiley, 1982), 90–100.

is turned to mere waste. Humanitarian concern is here yoked to economics. Barlow's attack on the inadequacies of female education is matched by later writers, including Maudsley, who also includes the single-minded business man on his list of social groups who waste their human potential (see also Section V).

Stylistically these texts make very interesting reading. Whether designed for a general or specialist audience, they are still nonetheless accessible to the lay reader; medical psychology has not yet moved into an era of scientized language. No sense of scientific decorum restrained the purple prose of Forbes Winslow, for example, and one finds throughout these texts stirring calls to the readers to change their behaviour before it is too late. The case-histories are themselves literary narratives, and at least one practitioner, Mackenzie Bacon, took serious note of the insane's own writings. Medical examples are as likely to be drawn from literature as from life, with Ophelia and Hamlet providing two of the most popular stereotypes for diagnosis. Literary and cultural expectations exerted strong pressure on the formulation of medical categories and diagnoses, which then in turn influenced the development of cultural interpretations of insanity.

1. Moral Management and the Rise of the Psychiatrist

MORAL TREATMENT AT THE RETREAT

Samuel Tuke, *A Description of the Retreat, an Institution Near York, for Insane Persons of the Society of Friends* (York: Alexander, 1813), 157–8, 178.

Samuel Tuke's description of the mild, humane system of management followed at the asylum founded by his grandfather, William Tuke, had an immediate, widespread social impact. By exciting public interest in the plight of the insane, it brought about the exposure of maltreatment at both the rival York Asylum and the famous Bethlem Hospital in London, which in turn led to the setting-up in 1815 of the parliamentary Committee to consider the regulation of madhouses.

In an early part of this chapter, it is stated, that the patients are considered capable of rational and honourable inducement; and though we allowed *fear* a considerable place in the production of that restraint, which the patient generally exerts on his entrance into a new situation; yet the *desire of esteem* is considered, at the Retreat, as operating, in general, still more powerfully. This principle in the human mind, which doubtless influences, in a great degree, though often secretly, our general manners; and which operates with peculiar force on our introduction into a new circle of acquaintance, is found to have great influence, even over the conduct of the insane. Though it has obviously not been sufficiently powerful, to enable them entirely to resist the strong irregular tendencies of their disease; yet when properly cultivated, it leads many to struggle to conceal and overcome their morbid propensities; and, at least, materially assists them in confining their deviations, within such bounds, as do not make them obnoxious to the family.

This struggle is highly beneficial to the patient, by strengthening his mind, and conducing to a salutary habit of self-restraint; an object which experience points out as of the greatest importance, in the cure of insanity, by moral means. [. . .]

The comfort of the patients is [. . .] considered of the highest importance, in a curative point of view. The study of the superintendents to promote it with all the assiduity of parental, but judicious attention, has been, in numerous instances, rewarded by an almost filial attachment. In their conversation with the patients, they adapt themselves to their particular weaknesses; but, at the same time, endeavour to draw them insensibly from the sorrow, or the error, which marks the disease.

The female superintendent, who possesses an uncommon share of benevolent activity, and who has the chief management of the female patients, as well as of the domestic department, occasionally gives a general invitation to the patients, to a tea-party. All who attend, dress in their best clothes, and vie with each other in politeness and propriety. The best fare is provided, and the visiters are treated with all the attention of strangers. The evening generally passes in the greatest harmony and enjoyment. It rarely happens that any unpleasant circumstance occurs; the patients control, in a wonderful degree, their different propensities; and the scene is at once curious, and affectingly gratifying.

LUNATIC ASYLUMS

Andrew Wynter (unsigned), 'Lunatic asylums', *Quarterly Review*, 101 (Apr. 1857), 358-60.

This popular account, by the physician Wynter, of the gulf dividing the brutal regime which previously reigned in insane asylums from current humane practices illustrates the moral managers' views of their achievements. Similar accounts were also to be found in medical textbooks.

Supposed to be degraded to the level of beasts, as wild beasts they were treated. Like them they were shut up in dens littered with straw, exhibited for money, and made to growl and roar for the diversion of the spectators who had paid their fee. No wonder that Bedlam should have become a word of fear—no wonder that in popular estimation the bad odour of centuries should still cling to its walls—and that the stranger, tempted by curiosity to pass beneath the shadow of its dome, should enter with sickening trepidation. But now, instead of the howling madhouse his imagination may have painted it, he sees prim galleries filled with orderly persons. Scenes of cheerfulness and content meet the eye of the visitor as he is conducted along well-lit corridors, from which the bars and gratings of old have vanished. He stops, surprised and delighted, to look at the engravings of Landseer's pictures on the walls, or to admire the busts upon the brackets; he beholds tranquil persons walking around him, or watches them feeding the birds which abound in the aviaries fitted up in the depths of the ample windows. Indeed the pet animals, such as rabbits, squirrels, &c., with the verdant ferneries, render the convalescent wards of this hospital more cheerful than any we have seen in similar institutions. At intervals the monotony of the long-drawn corridors is broken by ample-sized rooms carpeted and furnished like the better class of dwellings. If we pass along the female side of the hospital, we find the apartments occupied by a score of busy workers, the majority of whom appear to be gentlewomen. Every conceivable kind of needlework is dividing their attention with the young lady who reads aloud 'David Copperfield,' or 'Dred;'[1] while beside the fire, perhaps, an old lady with silver locks gives a touch of domesticity to the scene, which we should little have expected to meet within these walls. In traversing the male side, instead of the workroom we find a library, in which the patients, reclining upon the sofas or lolling in arm-chairs round the fire, beguile the hours with books or the 'Illustrated News.' Many a scholar, the silver chord of whose brain gingles for the moment out of tune, here finds a congenial atmosphere, and such materials for study as he often could not obtain out-of-doors; and here many an artist, clergyman, officer, and broken-down gentleman, meets with social converse, which the world does not dream could exist in Bedlam. [. . .] When we contrast the condition of the Bethlehem of fifty years ago with the Bethlehem of to-day, we see at a glance what a gulf has been leaped in half a century—a gulf on one side of which we see man like a demon torturing his unfortunate fellows, on the other like a ministering angel carrying out the all-powerful law of love.

MENTAL MALADIES

Jean Étienne Esquirol, *Mental Maladies: A Treatise on Insanity*, trans, E. J. Hunt (Philadelphia: Lea and Blanchard, 1845), 19–21.

Although this translation of Esquirol's 1838 work was not published until 1845, he had long exerted a profound influence over the development of English psychiatry. Many eminent English physicians had visited him at the Salpêtrière and

---

[1] A novel by Harriet Beecher Stowe (1756), dealing with the plight of the slaves in America.

Charenton and studied his work there. Two of his papers had also been published in English by William Liddell in 1833: Observations on the Illusions of the Insane, and on the Medico-Legal Question of their Confinement. *These passages come from the opening of the text.*

What reflections engage the mind of the philosopher, who, turning aside from the tumult of the world, makes the circuit of a House for the insane! He finds there the same ideas, the same errors, the same passions, the same misfortunes, that elsewhere prevail. It is the same world; but its distinctive characters are more noticeable, its features more marked, its colors more vivid, its effects more striking, because man there displays himself in all his nakedness; dissimulating not his thoughts, nor concealing his defects; lending not to his passions seductive charms, nor to his vices deceitful appearances.

Every House for the insane has its gods, its priests, its faithful, its fanatics. It has its emperors, its kings, its ministers, its courtiers, its opulent, its generals, its soldiers, and a people who obey. [. . .]

In a House for the insane, one can hear at the same time, the shouts of gladness mingled with sentiments of sorrow; expressions of joy, in connection with the groans of despair. He may see contentment in some, and tears flowing from the eyes of others.

In these establishments, the social bonds are broken; habits are changed; friendships cease; confidence is destroyed. Their inmates do good without benevolence; injure without dislike, and obey through fear. Each has his own ideas, affections, and language. With no community of thoughts, each lives alone, and for himself. Egotism isolates all. Their language is extravagant, and disordered, like the thoughts and passions which it expresses. An asylum of this character is not exempt from crime. They denounce, calumniate, conspire. They give themselves up to brutish libertinism; ravish, rob, assassinate. The son curses his father, the mother strangles her children. [. . .] In this assemblage of enemies, who know only how to shun, or injure each other; what application, what devotion to duty, what zeal are necessary, to unfold the cause, and seat of so many disorders; to restore to reason its perverted powers; to control so many diverse passions, to conciliate so many opposing interests; in fine, to restore man to himself! We must correct and restrain one; animate and sustain another: attract the attention of a third, touch the feelings of a fourth. One may be controlled by fear, another by mildness; all by hope. For this untiring devotion, an approving conscience must be our chief reward. For what can a physician hope, who is always considered wrong when he does not succeed, who rarely secures confidence when successful; and who is followed by prejudices, even in the good which has been obtained.

THE NON-RESTRAINT SYSTEM

John Conolly, *The Treatment of the Insane without Mechanical Restraints*
(London: Smith, Elder and Co., 1856), 35, 148–51.

---

*Within months of his appointment to the Middlesex County Lunatic Asylum,
Hanwell, in 1839 Conolly had abolished all the forms of personal restraint previously in use, from strait-jackets to leg irons. Both as a practical reformer and
author he was one of the main influences on the development of English nineteenth-century psychiatry. These extracts define his understanding of the non-
restraint system and demonstrate his case that treatment in a residential asylum is
infinitely preferable to the patient remaining at home by reference to the example of
a wildly deranged lunatic lady who shatters the peace of her family home.*

As the restraint system comprehended every possible evil of bad treatment,
every fault of commission and omission, so the watchful, preventive, almost
parental superintendence included in the term non-restraint, creates guards
against them all. For such is its real character, if properly understood and practised. It is, indeed, above all, important to remember, and it is the principal object
of this work to explain, that the mere abolition of fetters and restraints constitutes only a part of what is properly called the non-restraint system. Accepted in
its full and true sense, it is a complete system of management of insane patients,
of which the operation begins the moment a patient is admitted over the threshold of an asylum. [. . .] The great medicine [. . .] in numerous cases, is the separation of the patient from all the circumstances which surrounded him when he
became insane, and placing him in the centre of new and salutary influences.

The state of the mind of the insane often makes them, indeed, more satisfied
with the new life they lead in the asylum than with the old life they led at home,
for which a morbid restlessness had long unfitted them; and they enjoy the companionship and occupations of their new abode so completely as to prevent their
regretting the absence of old friends, and the entire suspension of all their ordinary employments and pursuits. Certain harassing trains of thought appear to be
interrupted by the change, with relief to the distressed mind; whilst numerous
unsalutary associations are put an end to by the presence of new scenes and new
people.

As respects lady-patients, so long as they remain at home, all domestic influences usually cease to benefit them; they live in an insane reverie. Religious
ecstacy, or deep-despondency, occupies them: voices from heaven have enjoined
abstinence from food, or the abandonment of all their domestic duties; sometimes they have been declared, as they believe, to be the bride of Christ, and

counselled to suicide as a means of joining their heavenly bridegroom. From all their relatives they have been quite estranged; all their conduct has been fierce and unnatural; life itself, perhaps, in constant jeopardy. In the meantime, the habitation of the family has been full of anxiety or terror. The remotest parts of it have been rendered awful, by the presence of a deranged creature under the same roof: her voice; her sudden and violent efforts to destroy things or persons; her vehement rushings to fire and window; her very tread and stamp in her dark and disordered and remote chamber, have seemed to penetrate the whole house; and, assailed by her wild energy, the very walls and roof have appeared unsafe, and capable of partial demolition. To all these sources of alarm, removal to a good asylum puts an immediate end. The malady remains, but the terror is gone; and whilst by the patient's being removed to an asylum, the friends are thus relieved from disturbance and dread, the situation of the patient herself undergoes no less happy a change. The strait-waistcoat, and all the ingenious bonds resorted to by frightened servants and nurses at home, are at once removed; and if she continues excited and violent she is placed in a secure room, not darkened, but having the fire-place and windows protected; and presenting no very ready means of offensive measures being successful. An interval is allowed for the supervention of calmness, or of some approach to it. The case is medically examined; and all that course of mingled kindness and caution is commenced and persevered in of which the many details have been already described. The wider range of moral causes affecting educated persons receives due attention; and attempts to soothe the mind are made without rashness, and only as favourable times occur for such attempts. All the conversation addressed to them is discreet. The physical condition is diligently inquired into; and functions manifestly disordered are rectified by appropriate remedies. The real cause of the malady is sought for either in these bodily derangements, or in the previous habits of the patient, or in circumstances which may have suddenly or slowly disturbed the brain. The tendency of long-continued irritation to produce structural change is remembered; and the frail tenure of life in recent and violent mania is not forgotten. As immediate consequences, all excitement of mind, and all bodily irritation, all foolish indulgence, and all exciting topics of discussion, are carefully avoided. To tranquillise and to cure, and not merely to subdue, being the object, nothing in the treatment is at variance with the great system of non-restraint prevailing throughout the establishment.

A CURIOUS DANCE ROUND A CURIOUS TREE

Charles Dickens (unsigned), *Household Words*, 4 (17 Jan. 1852), 387–8.

The article describes a visit Charles Dickens made on Boxing Day, 1851, to St Luke's Hospital for the insane, London. The 'curious tree' of the title is the Christmas tree, and the article describes Dickens's responses to the dance organized for the inmates. In a subsequent visit in 1858, Dickens noted in the visitors' book that he was delighted with the improvements that had been made.

As I was looking at the marks in the walls of the galleries, of the posts to which the patients were formerly chained, sounds of music were heard from a distance. The ball had begun, and we hurried off in the direction of the music. [. . .]

There were the patients usually to be found in all such asylums, among the dancers. There was the brisk, vain, pippin-faced little old lady, in a fantastic cap— proud of her foot and ankle; there was the old-young woman with the dishevelled long light hair, spare figure, and weird gentility; there was the vacantly-laughing girl, requiring now and then a warning finger to admonish her; there was the quiet young woman, almost well, and soon going out. For partners, there were the sturdy bull-necked thick-set little fellow who had tried to get away last week; the wry-faced tailor, formerly suicidal, but much improved; the suspicious patient with a countenance of gloom, wandering round and round strangers, furtively eyeing them behind from head to foot, and not indisposed to resent their intrusion. There was the man of happy silliness, pleased with everything. But the only chain that made any clatter was Ladies' Chain, and there was no straiter waistcoat in company than the polka-garment of the old-young woman with the weird gentility, which was of a faded black satin, and languished through the dance with a lovelorn affability and condescension to the force of circumstances, in itself a faint reflection of all Bedlam.

Among those seated on the forms, the usual loss of social habits and the usual solitude in society, were again to be observed. It was very remarkable to see how they huddled together without communicating; how some watched the dancing with lack-lustre eyes, scarcely seeming to know what they watched; how others rested weary heads on hands, and moped; how others had the air of eternally expecting some miraculous visitor who never came, and looking out for some deliverances that never happened. The last figure of the set danced out, the women-dancers instantly returned to their station at one end of the gallery, the men-dancers repaired to *their* station at the other; and all were shut up within themselves in a moment. [. . .]

To one coming freshly from outer life, unused to such scenes, it was a very sad and touching spectacle, when the patients were admitted in a line, to pass round the lighted tree, and admire. I could not but remember with what happy, hope-fully-flushed faces, the brilliant toy was associated in my usual knowledge of it, and compare them with the worn cheek, the listless stare, the dull eye raised for a moment and then confusedly dropped, the restless eagerness, the moody sur-prise, so different from the sweet expectancy and astonishment of children, that came in melancholy array before me. And when the sorrowful procession was closed by 'Tommy,' the favourite of the house, the harmless old man, with a gig-gle and a chuckle and a nod for every one, I think I would have rather that Tommy had charged at the tree like a Bull, than that Tommy had been, at once so childish and so dreadfully un-childlike.

THE CURE OF SICK MINDS

Anon., 'The cure of sick minds,' *Household Words*, 19 (2 Apr. 1859), 415–17.

Offering a general account of the review written by John Bucknill in the Journal of Mental Science *of the reports by English, Scottish, Irish, and East Indian Lunatic Asylums published over the previous two years, this article (probably by Henry Morley) highlights the interdependence of body and mind in cases of insanity, and gives graphic warning of the dangers of letting the onset of madness pass untreated.*

There are few household calamities so utterly deplorable as loss of reason in a husband, wife, or child; and there is, perhaps, no household calamity for the lightening of which so much can be done or left undone by the friends of the afflicted, according to their knowledge or their ignorance of certain leading truths.

The development of this kind of knowledge has been the work of science in our own day, and its diffusion is the duty of all journals such as ours. For that reason we have, from time to time, dwelt upon points relating to insanity in England, and we now found, upon the latest reports of our county Lunatic Asylums, a few more notes of profitable information. [. . .]

Taking for granted the first principle of the treatment of insane persons, with-out harsh restraint, a principle which is now recognised almost universally in England, we pass to two main facts which have been more recently established, and which should have as general a recognition. One is, that insanity is a disease of bodily weakness, not of strength,—a disease commonly arising from defect of nourishment and physical depression. The other is, that in its first stages, insanity is generally curable; that on its appearance help against it should be sought without even a putting off until to-morrow, since every day's delay adds to the difficulty of cure, and after the delay of two or three months, relief—perhaps a long relief—may indeed be obtained, but cure has become nearly impossible.

Most important is it that a proper understanding of these facts should be impressed on all who are concerned in the administration of our workhouse system. Throughout the curable stage of their disease insane paupers very frequently indeed are retained in the workhouses to save the expense of their maintenance in the county asylum. While so detained they are receiving neither the right medical treatment nor the right supply of nourishment. Rightly to treat a pauper lunatic in a workhouse would, for want of the organised system and all the appliances belonging to an establishment built and maintained with the sole view to such a purpose, cost more than the charge payable to a county asylum for the care of him. Patients retained thus in the workhouse during the first weeks of lunacy do not recover, but becoming worse, are sent when the possibility of perfect cure is at an end, to the asylum, and become for the rest of their lives a permanent or an occasional charge upon the rates. [. . .]

Cases of lunacy will be multiplied five fold throughout the country whenever the whole public has been made alive to the necessity of seeking instant remedy. In the last report of the Derbyshire Asylum there is mention of an interesting case. A young woman, liable to returns of insanity, and living fourteen miles away, left her home at four o'clock one wet morning, and taking the railway as her guide, hurried to the asylum; she passed through several tunnels on her road, and arrived wet and exhausted. She said, 'she dreaded being ill at home, for they treated her badly when mad. She knew the asylum was her best place, and she came as fast as she could, to get help in time; she did not let her friends know of her intention, for she had asked them to bring her, and they were unwilling to do so.' A little medicine and repose tranquillised the rising nervous agitation. In two or three days she returned home to her friends, and has remained with them ever since. This instant hurry to secure relief was a half mad act, founded on the soundest judgment. At the very first symptom of disease in the mind let remedy be sought. Let there be no avoidable postponement of the search for efficient help,—not even for an hour.

Moreover, if the sufferer be in want through poverty, or through the not uncommon error that induces some people to starve the body—keep it under— for advantage of the mind, let there be immediate recognition of the truth, that there is often better mental food in a beafsteak than in a book—that the mind partakes of the body's health or sickness—that whatever weakens one weakens the other, whatever strengthens one strengthens the other. The main root of insanity is defect of nutrition, often a transmitted weakness, often a depression caused by personal privation; it never is a strength of fury added to good health: its wildest paroxysm is, so to speak, the agony of a mind upon which its house of the flesh falls torturing and crushing, after its foundations have been loosened. Insanity is not the immaterial disease of an immaterial essence, but the perverted action of the mind caused by a defect in its instrument. Whatever helps to put the body into good physical condition does something towards the repair of the defective instrument.

PASSION AND REASON

John Conolly, *An Inquiry Concerning the Indications of Insanity, with Suggestions for the Better Protection and Care of the Insane* (London: John Taylor, 1830), 224–5, 227–8, 374–5, 377–80, 494–6.

This text, Conolly's first book on the treatment of the insane, remains a classic of nineteenth-century psychiatry. Although Conolly was not to have first-hand experience of running an asylum until 1839, with his appointment to the Middlesex County Asylum in Hanwell, he had long shown an interest in the subject of insanity, writing his thesis on it in 1821, and lecturing in this area at University College, London, 1827–31. In these passages he defines madness as a state that endures only whilst passion overturns reason, and outlines the physiognomical skills required by the physician trained to spot lurking insanity. The final extract comes from the close of the book where Conolly highlights the increase of insanity which follows social advancement, and makes a case for the crucial role of the physician in preserving the nation's mental health.

If the ordinary impressions acting upon us are the gentle gales, which bear us along the course of life with variable swiftness, the stronger feelings are the tempests, before which we are driven, and by which we run a constant risk of wreck. Until the age of passion, the child is secure from the more violent forms of intellectual disorder; and when the age of passion is past, men fall into imbecility rather than madness. [. . .] Poetry, eloquence, invention, persevering labour, have each, in different examples, sprung from these passions. How often these same passions, when unrestrained, have ruined the mind, the wards of every lunatic asylum teach us but too well. It has been said that anger is a short madness; and it has been said, as truly, that no man can at once be in love and be wise: and, in like manner, we may observe each passion and emotion in excess disturbing the mind by a direct impairment of the comparing power, and, consequently, the judgment. Until the tyranny of the passion is past, the attention is forcibly withheld from all objects which would correct the false decision. [. . .]

It is only when the passion so impairs one or more faculties of the mind as to prevent the exercise of comparison, that the reason is overturned; and then the man is mad. He is mad only whilst this state continues; but whilst it continues, whether for a short or a long time, he is mad on the subject of his fear. He ceases to be mad when he can correct the erroneous judgment of his excited state; and not before. We see many madmen whose malady consists in their peculiar excitability to anger, and in the impossibility of correcting the judgments of their angry state: seeming to have become tranquil, the renewal of the subject of their anger renews the passion; and as they are never able to reason upon it, to compare and to judge, they continue to be mad on that subject. The commencement of the correction of their angry judgment is the commencement of convalescence. Until they can do this, however reasonable they may be on all other subjects, on this they are mad. When they can do it, they are mad no longer. [. . .]

The practitioner is generally deeply impressed with an idea of the difficulty of detecting madness, if the madman does not choose that he should see it. The reluctance of a patient to allow opportunities for ascertaining the actual state of his mind, is certainly often greatest when the disorder most requires attention; and if a man, knowing himself to be suspected of insanity, evades those who endeavour to see and converse with him, although it would not be right to set him down as insane, on account of such conduct, the previous suspicion of his insanity would be not a little confirmed by it; and the suspicion is alone sufficient to justify watching. [. . .]

Among the attributes of a perfect mind, has been enumerated the power of perfectly regulating the expression of the thoughts and affections. The manifestation of this power is so easily observed in speech and gesture, that its varieties and impairments are among those things which we most familiarly observe. But what is merely matter of common observation and passing remark among unprofessional persons, is often, to the medical observer, a source of very important information. There is certainly something more in physiognomy than the mere result of habitual muscular actions. The external parts of the face derive from the original constitution of each individual a peculiarity of character, independent, in the first instance, of habitual affections or of features. It would seem as if each individual were but a physical organization, animated by a nervous constitution of a distinct quality, influencing all the expression and all the character. The affections, also, associated with the same constitution of nervous system, the susceptibility to impressions or emotions, the passions of each individual, soon render the physiognomical expression more intense; and when speech is acquired, the combined power of gesture and words gives to each

character that strong external manifestation, concerning which, if it is sufficiently attended to, it is almost impossible to be deceived. [. . .] Those who have
the care of lunatics well know, though they cannot define, certain characters of
the lunatics' countenance, which the most masterly dissembling cannot conceal
from one who has known the same face when that peculiar look was not yet
acquired; and I have repeatedly observed, in persons disposed to maniacal paroxysms, a warning of the attack, in the altered tone of the voice or manner of speaking; and in patients easily excited to delirium by fever, I have found the same
circumstances continue to indicate the lingering of the malady, when other
symptoms would have supported the belief of the disorder being at an end. The
dress also of a lunatic is almost always odd and peculiar; and there are singularities of mind which manifest themselves chiefly by some eccentricity in this particular. The very mode of wearing the hat will differ in the same man, in his sane
and in his insane state. It prepares us for the application of this kind of knowledge, to remark the diversity of countenance, of modes of speaking, of tones of
voice, of gesture, and of dress, in men of different measures of intellectual power.
Habit, and systematic effort, may have led to a control of all these indications in
ordinary circumstances, but agitation, excitement, a great occasion of exertion,
cause all that is the result of mere art to be thrown off; and under such circumstances no man can appear to be what he is not. The most guarded countenance,
the most measured voice, the most restrained gesture, yields to strong and real
emotion; and the tones, and the manner, and the person, and the face, speak a
language in which there is no deception. Nor can any art or care prevent the
more ordinary revelation of what is really most habitual to the mind, under circumstances even of a trifling kind: something is always occurring to them to
throw the most cautious dissembler off his guard. [. . .]

Improved habits of life, and an enlightened system of medicine, are daily
decreasing the number of the disorders which primarily affect the corporeal fabric; but as communities advance in zeal for intellectual acquirement, in refinement, and in all the means and appliances of luxury, the human frame, not
destined for perfection, is seen to become exposed to the operation of new causes
of disorder; and, in a particular manner, the susceptibility of its nervous structure
becomes increased as respects all ordinary influences. From hence arise new irritations, various in their character and intensity, but all, by duration or excess,
passing into disorder and disease; disturbing the actions of the body and mind,
and altering even the physical characters of the organs in which those actions are
performed. The physician finds the result in almost every case that he is called
upon to investigate; and observes, in his daily practice, the widening empire of
causes which, almost undeveloped in new societies, modify the symptoms of disease in a large majority of those whose minds are exercised by the complicated
excitement and anxieties of communities which have reached a high degree of
cultivation. He neglects half the history of half the cases concerning which he is

consulted, if he overlooks the inward influence of the restless mind. He is unprepared for the duties required by the age in which he practises, if he forgets the slow processes of change which the advance of man, from the savage state to a state of the utmost refinement, has effected, or is effecting. In various parts of the world, and in various stations of life, all the steps of this long and predestined process are visible at once; but in no country are all the causes connected with high civilization and intellectual culture more spread over the constitution of society than in our own, and in none, consequently, are their effects more developed, or more deserving of attention.*

Without the aid of medicine, the ordinary influences to which men are subjected, and the various accidents to which they are exposed, would soon render the greater part of mankind helpless and miserable. But if to prevent such wide calamity be the chief glory of our art, certainly its most brilliant achievements are performed when, by averting the disturbances of bodily disorder on mental processes, and by counteracting the increased tendencies to mental susceptibility, it preserves to the individual, in times and in societies of men in which the gifts of the understanding exceed all other possessions in value, the power of controlling his emotions, of commanding his expressions, of regulating his affections, to exercising and directing all the faculties of his mind, and of governing all the parts of his conduct.

THE POWER OF SELF-CONTROL

John Barlow, *On Man's Power over Himself to Prevent or Control Insanity* (London: William Pickering, 1843), 12–15, 43–5, 49–50.

The text is drawn from a lecture delivered by the Reverend Barlow to members of the Royal Institution, 20 May 1843. It was then published in a cheap, accessible edition for a general readership (Small Books on Great Subjects, no. 31). Barlow, who was not a physician, drew heavily on Conolly for his arguments, but gave them his own emphases. Like Conolly, he suggests there is no firm dividing line between the sane and the insane: for Barlow the only distinction lies in the exercise of self-control. Barlow's suggestion here that women have proportionately larger 'organs of thought' than men runs counter to the dominant view at that time, although his subsequent insistence on the need for improvements in female

---

* Sir Andrew Halliday states, that the number of the insane in England has 'become more than tripled during the last twenty years.'—*Letter to Lord Robert Seymour*. The increased prevalence of what are called *Nervous* disorders, many of which are produced by irregularities of the circulation in different portions of the nervous system, is established by common observation.

education is in harmony with the advice of many of his medical contemporaries.
The concluding alarmist passage on the recent increase in insanity illustrates the
level of contemporary concern on this issue.

Nothing then but an extent of disease which destroys at once all possibility of reasoning, by annihilating, or entirely changing the structure of the organ, can make a man necessarily mad. In all other cases, the being sane or otherwise, notwithstanding considerable disease of brain, depends on the individual himself. He who has given a proper direction to the intellectual force, and thus obtained an early command over the bodily organ by habituating it to processes of calm reasoning, remains sane amid all the vagaries of sense; while he who has been the slave, rather than the master of his animal nature, listens to its dictates without question even when distorted by disease,—and is mad. A fearful result of an uncultivated childhood!

If I am right in what I have advanced, a man may labour under a mental delusion, and yet be a responsible agent: and if sanity or insanity be in a great many instances the consequences of a greater or less resolution in exerting the power of reasoning still possessed, the same kind of motives which influence a man in common life, are still available, though they may require to be somewhat heightened. It is on this principle that the treatment of lunatics has been generally conducted. Fear, one of the lowest, but also one of the most general of instinctive emotions, has been called in to balance the delusions of sense, and, excepting in cases where the structural disease is so extensive as to deprive the man of all power of connecting cause and effect, it has been found sufficient to curb violence, and enforce a certain degree of peaceable demeanour towards the attendants. And in this the insane person differs not from the cultivated man who is left at liberty, whose self-control rarely amounts to more than the avoiding actions which would have unpleasant consequences to himself. Suppose an irascible man, incensed by a false report; which, however, he believes to be true; he seeks his supposed enemy, and he horsewhips or knocks him down: he does not assassinate, because he fears for his own life if he does; for it is clear that no feeling of duty has held his hand, or he would not have transgressed the laws both of God and man by thus revenging himself.

The madman has the false report from his own senses; wherein do the two differ? Neither has employed means within his power to ascertain the truth, and both are aware that such vengeance is forbidden. I can see no distinction between them, save that the delusion of sense has, as a chemist would say, decomposed the character, and shown how much of the individual's previous conduct was rational, and how much the result of mere animal instinct. It would be well for the world if the soi-disant sane were sometimes to ask themselves how far their sanity would bear this test; and endeavour to acquire that rational self-command which nothing but the last extremity of cerebral disease could unseat. We do not descend from our high rank with impugnity;—and as, when matter has become organized, if the process of change, occasioned by the vital forces, be impeded or arrested, the plant pines away and perishes:—as, after the organs of locomotion have been superadded, the animal debarred from the use of them, languishes and becomes diseased; so man, if he give not full scope to the intellectual force, becomes subject to evils greater than animals ever know, because his nature is of a higher order. [. . .]

But if this be the case as regards the male sex, how much more fearfully then is it of the female! Here the Drawing-room but perpetuates the inertness of the Nursery,—and woman, so largely endowed by nature, is degraded by social prejudice, and the frivolous education consequent upon it, till she is left at the mercy of events, the creature of impulse and of instinct. Yet physiologists have demonstrated that the organs of thought are proportionably larger in woman than in man: and many a bright example has shewn how well they *can* be employed. One plain statistical fact shows that no terms that I can use in the reprobation of this cruel system can be too strong. The registers of Lunatic Asylums show the number of female patients to exceed that of males by nearly one third.—We have the assurance of professional men well experienced in the treatment of the insane, that nothing is more rare than to find among them a person of a judiciously cultivated mind; and yet, with this fact staring us in the face, we systematically consign the mothers of the rising generation to a species of training which leaves them and their families a prey to one of the worst ills that flesh is heir to. We need not ask what woman's destination is—nature has written it in characters too clear to be mistaken: the large development of the intellectual organs, and the feeble muscular power, mark her for the high-minded purifier of society—her strength must be that of knowledge:—yet, we refuse the kind of culture which such an organization requires, hide the victim of mis-management in a madhouse—and then talk proudly about an enlightened age!

Should my position, that the difference between sanity and insanity consists in the degree of self-control exercised, appear paradoxical to any one, let him note for a short time the thoughts that pass through his mind, and the feelings that agitate him: and he will find that, were they all expressed and indulged, they would be as wild, and perhaps as frightful in their consequences as those of any madman. But the man of strong mind represses them, and seeks fresh impressions from without if he finds that aid needful: the man of weak mind yields to them, and then he is insane. [. . .]

The cases of insanity, we are told, have nearly tripled within the last twenty years!—a fearful increase even after allowing to the utmost for a larger population!—of these cases it is calculated that less than three hundred in one thousand are the result of disease, or of unavoidable circumstances, thus leaving above seven hundred resulting from bodily excess or mental misgovernment.—On the heads then of legislators, of teachers, and of parents, like the heavy charge of having in all these instances, left those godlike faculties uncultivated, which, if duly used, might make earth the ante-room of heaven, and man the fit Vice-gerent of the Deity in this fair world. What man *is* generally, and what the world is in consequence, I need not detail.—We all know and feel it. Would to heaven we all knew what man *can* be, and had felt what the world might be were he such!

THE TREATMENT OF A GENTLEMAN IN A STATE OF MENTAL DERANGEMENT

John Perceval, *A Narrative of the Treatment Experienced by a Gentleman, During a State of Mental Derangement; Designed to Explain the Causes and the Nature of Insanity, and to Expose the Injudicious Conduct Pursued towards Many Unfortunate Sufferers under that Calamity*, 2 vols. (London: Effingham Wilson, 1838–40), i. 1–2, 144–7.

In this account of his incarceration in two lunatic asylums, and his dealings with various other doctors, John Perceval challenges the reader to say whether he is mad to have resented his mode of treatment. He does not deny his own madness, and indeed his accounts of his various visions and hallucinations confirm for the reader Perceval's sense of his own madness. The text is at once an account of the forms of thought operating during a period of madness and a strong attack on the forms of treatment he received, including confinement against his own will. The second passage relates to his time at Edward Long Fox's asylum at Brislington, but even Ticehurst, the reformed asylum where he was subsequently placed and cured, is portrayed in an uncomplimentary light.

In the year 1830, I was unfortunately deprived of the use of reason. This calamity befel me about Christmas. I was then in Dublin. The Almighty allowed my mind to become a ruin under sickness—delusions of a religious nature, and treatment contrary to nature. My soul survived that ruin. As I was a victim at first, in part to the ignorance or want of thought of my physician, so I was consigned afterwards to the control of other medical men, whose habitual cruelty, and worse than ignorance—*charlatanism*—became the severest part of my most severe scourge. I suffered great cruelties, accompanied with much wrong and insult; first, during my confinement, when in a state of childish imbecility in the year 1831; secondly, during my recovery from that state, between November,

1831, and May, 1832; thirdly, during the remainder of the year 1832, and the year 1833, when I considered myself to be of sane mind. Having been under the care of four lunatic doctors, whose systems of treatment differ widely from each other—having conversed with two others, and having lived in company with Lunatics, observing their manners, and reflecting on my own, I deem that alone sufficient excuse for setting forth my griefs and theirs, before men of understanding, to whom I desire to be supposed addressing myself, and for obtruding upon them more of my personal history than might otherwise be prudent or becoming. Because I wish to stir up an intelligent and active sympathy, in behalf of the most wretched, the most oppressed, the only helpless of mankind, by proving with how much needless tyranny they are treated—and this in mockery—by men who pretend indeed their cure, but who are, in reality, their tormentors and destroyers.

I open my mouth for the dumb; and let it be recollected, that I write in defence of youth and old age, of female delicacy, modesty, and tenderness, not only of man and of manhood—surrendered up in weakness to indecent exposure, disgusting outrage, or uncalled for violence—that I write for the few who are objects of suspicion and alarm,—to society, who too much engrossed in business or in pleasure to exercise reflection, are equally capable of treating these objects of their dread and insolence, with lunatic cruelty, and the insanest mismanagement; being deprived, like them, of understanding, by exaggerated and unreasonable fear, but not like them by illness, of the guilt of their misconduct. The subject to which I direct attention, is also one on which, my readers, according to man's wont, the wisest of you are hasty to decide in action, or to hazard an opinion in proportion even to your ignorance.

In the name of humanity, then, in the name of modesty, in the name of wisdom, I intreat you to place yourselves in the position of those whose sufferings I describe, before you attempt to discuss what course is to be pursued towards them. Feel for them; try to defend them. Be their friends,—argue not hostilely. Feeling the ignorance to be in one sense real, which all of you confess on your lips, listen to one who can instruct you. Bring the ears and the minds of children, children as you are, or pretend to be, in knowledge—not believing without questioning, but questioning that you may believe. [. . .]

If the insulting and degrading treatment I have described, was indeed designed to mortify and probe the feelings, it was preposterous, without explanation, expostulation, or remonstrance; and impolitic, without a thorough knowledge of the temper and humor of the individual to whom it was applied. Why was I confined? Because I was a lunatic. And what is a lunatic, but one whose reasoning cannot be depended upon; one of imperfect and deranged understanding, and of a diseased imagination? What, then, was the natural consequence of my being placed in the most extraordinary, difficult, and unreasonable circumstances, without explanation, but that I should, as I did, attribute that insult which was heaped upon me to the most absurd causes; to the non-performance of the very acts, which in a sane mind I might have condemned; or to the performance of those which I might have applauded. With me, conscience was entirely confounded—judgment perverted. That which others called sin, I deemed virtue; that which men called folly, I called wisdom. What can be said, when I struck, kicked, wrestled, endangered my own security and that of others, as the acts most pleasing to them witness, most dutiful for me to attempt? The reader now, perhaps, wonders at treatment like this being possible; but if he does now resent it, in nine cases out of ten it is not without my having been obliged to reason with him as with a child; so rooted is the prejudice, *that lunacy cannot be subdued, except by harsh treatment.* If he asks why these things are so, I will tell him why: *because it is the interest of the lunatic doctors.* That is the end. And the cause lies in the servile folly of mankind, of which these lunatic doctors make their profit.

But such treatment is impolitic, not in the lunatic doctor, but in the conduct of such as, in good faith, desire a patient's cure; because, if discovered or suspected, it may work, as it did in me, a deadly hate towards those dealing with me, and a resolution to endure any thing, rather than bow a haughty and stubborn spirit to their cunning, address, or cruelty. In return for their insolent severity, the mind mocks at their care and vigilance, their respect and their benevolence. The question, then, lies between the power of the patient to endure, and the power of the quack to break his spirit. The latter is shamefully uncontrolled by law, in consequence of the very generous, legitimate, and simple confidence placed by chancellors, magistrates and law-officers of the crown in the humane, and tender, and scrupulous doctor. I have proved that the power of the patient is equal to that of the oppressor. But in this contest, when the patience and fortitude of the first is exhausted, look to it if the stamina of the constitution—if those foundations of sound health, are not undermined or broken through, on which, with respectful and natural treatment, cure, *perfect cure*, might have been established, and good citizens assured to the state; not those patched up pieces of work called healed patients, now returned to the world. And again, besides the danger thus incurred, through the sullen and obstinate resentment of the patient, I have proved how, through his very disease, through his very delusions, the power of the spirit of evil mocks at such endeavours to subdue his empire over our conduct and our imaginations, without the will of the individual working malignantly with him.

THE WRITING OF THE INSANE

G. Mackenzie Bacon, *On the Writing of the Insane* (London: John Churchill, 1870), i, 15–17.

Patients' writings and drawings did not draw much attention from the psychiatrists of the pre-Freudian era. Where they are considered, it is generally, as here, as a form of physiognomy, a way of recognizing the insanity concealed within. Little attention is paid, however, to the actual substance of the writing. Letters or drawings are cited as examples of madness, but not analysed.

The letters of the insane are worth study—as the most reliable evidence of the state of the patient's mind for the time being; they are a sort of involuntary photograph, and for this reason it is often useful to make patients write, as well as to converse with them when investigating cases of lunacy. [. . .]

In ordinary cases of mania the patients' letters are odd and grotesque, exhibiting the same want of balance that their actions do. These productions are of little value in diagnosis, but are curious illustrations of the topsy-turvy condition of the writer's mind. This is well illustrated in the following case:—The patient was a respectable artisan of considerable intelligence, and was sent to the Cambridgeshire Asylum after being nearly three years in a melancholy mood. As this passed off, he showed a good deal of pride and self-esteem, and gradually recovered, so that at the end of two years more he was able to be discharged. During the greater part of these two years he spent much of his time in writing—sometimes verses, at others long letters of the most rambling character, and in drawing extraordinary diagrams [. . .] It would require no little ingenuity to conceive, and perseverance to execute, such a diagram, and the curious feature in the case is, that a man with such disordered ideas should concentrate his efforts sufficiently for such an undertaking. [. . .] On looking at it one is strikingly reminded of the lines in Pope's Essay on Man—

> 'A mighty maze! but not without a plan,
> A wild, where weeds and flowers promiscuous shoot;'

although it may not be easy to find the key to this plan, whatever it might have been, not to distinguish which are the weeds and which the flowers in so tangled a 'wild'.

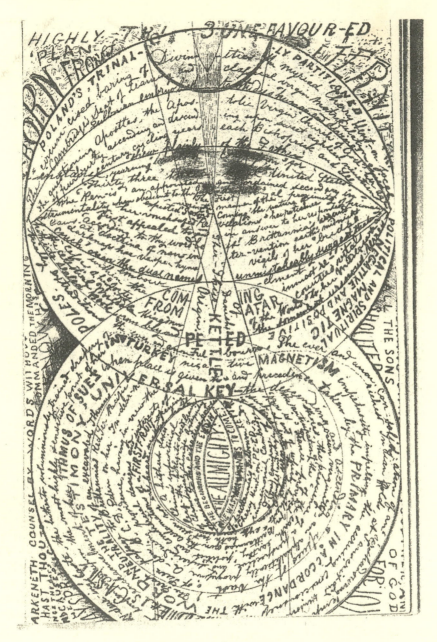

FIG. 12. Writing by an inmate

2. Monomania, Moral Insanity, and Moral Responsibility

FORMS OF INSANITY

James Cowles Prichard, *A Treatise on Insanity and Other Disorders Affecting the Mind* (London: Sherwood, Gilbert, and Piper, 1835), 3–7, 12–14, 18–19, 30, 35–6.

This work, which was dedicated to Esquirol, became the standard textbook for the next twenty years. Prichard here defined his theory of moral insanity, which envisaged for the first time a form of insanity where the sufferer does not experience delusions or hallucinations and the reasoning powers remain unaffected. The extracts offer Prichard's definitions of moral insanity and monomania, with general examples and one case-study.

It has generally been supposed that the chief, if not the sole disorder of persons labouring under insanity consists in some particular false conviction, or in some erroneous notion indelibly impressed upon the belief. Mr. Locke made a remark which has often been cited, that 'madmen do not appear to have lost the faculty of reasoning; but having joined together some ideas very wrongly, they mistake them for truths, and they err, as men do that argue right from wrong principles.'[1] From Mr. Locke's time it has been customary to observe that insane persons reason correctly from erroneous premises; and some instance of illusion, or some particular erroneous impression has been looked for as the characteristic of the disease, or an essential circumstance in it. [. . .]

An attentive consideration of the phenomena which present themselves in different cases of insanity, enables us to observe several forms or varieties, which are

[1] John Locke, *An Essay Concerning Human Understanding* (1690). This still remained the touchstone for definitions of insanity in the early part of the nineteenth century.

distinguishable from each other by well-marked lines. To one division of cases,— namely, to those which are referable to the form of madness termed *melancholia, monomania,* or *partial insanity,*—the preceding remarks of Mr. Locke are alone applicable. These are instances in which the illusion of the understanding is connected with some particular subject, and leaves the judgement comparatively clear in other respects. The phenomena of such cases are very different from those of *mania* or *raving madness,* in which the mind is totally deranged, and the individual affected talks nonsense, or expresses himself wildly and absurdly on every subject. There is, in the third place, a class of persons generally reckoned among lunatics, but consisting chiefly, though not entirely, of individuals whose disorder has already reached an advanced or protracted stage. In these the condition of the faculties is such as to preclude the possibility of any mental effort or voluntary direction of thought. The most striking characteristics in this state are the rapid succession of ideas, and the unconnected manner in which they enter into the mind, without order or coherence, or, at least, without following their ordinary and natural arrangement and association. *Incoherence* is the characteristic of this morbid condition.

The modifications of insanity already mentioned are affections of the understanding or rational powers, but there is likewise a form of mental derangement in which the intellectual faculties appear to have sustained little or no injury, while the disorder is manifested principally or alone, in the state of the feelings, temper, or habits. In cases of this description the moral and active principles of the kind are strangely perverted and depraved; the power of self-government is lost or greatly impaired; and the individual is found to be incapable, not of talking or reasoning upon any subject proposed to him, for this he will often do with great shrewdness and volubility, but of conducting himself with decency and propriety in the business of life. His wishes and inclinations, his attachments, his likings and dislikings have all undergone a morbid change, and this change appears to be the originating cause, or to lie at the foundation of any disturbance which the understanding itself may seem to have sustained, and even in some instances to form throughout the sole manifestation of the disease. [. . .]

If the preceding observations are well founded, we shall be enabled to distinguish the principal forms or varieties of insanity under the following terms:

1. *Moral Insanity,* or madness consisting in a morbid perversion of the natural feelings, affections, inclinations, temper, habits, moral dispositions, and natural impulses, without any remarkable disorder or defect of the intellect or knowing and reasoning faculties, and particularly without any insane illusion or hallucination.

The three following modifications of the disease may be termed *Intellectual Insanity* in contradistinction to the preceding form. They are severally:—

2. *Monomania,* or partial insanity, in which the understanding is partially disordered or under the influence of some particular illusion, referring to one sub-

ject, and involving one train of ideas, while the intellectual powers appear, when exercised on other subjects, to be in a great measure unimpaired.

3. *Mania*, or raving madness, in which the understanding is generally deranged; the reasoning faculty, if not lost, is confused and disturbed in its exercise; the mind is in a state of morbid excitement, and the individual talks absurdly on every subject to which his thoughts are momentarily directed.

4. *Incoherence*, or dementia. By some persons it may be thought scarcely correct to term this a form of insanity, as it has been generally considered as a result and sequel of that disease. In some instances, however, mental derangement has nearly this character from the commencement, or at least assumes it at a very early period. I am therefore justified in stating it, after Pinel, to be a fourth and distinct form of madness. It is thus characterised by that justly celebrated writer:—'Rapid succession or uninterrupted alternation of insulated ideas, and evanescent and unconnected emotions; continually repeated acts of extravagance; complete forgetfulness of every previous state; diminished sensibility to external impressions; abolition of the faculty of judgement; perpetual activity.'[2]

If I am correct in assuming that all the varieties of madness may find their place under one of the descriptions thus marked out, a short nosography of the disease, which will answer many of the purposes of a definition, will be furnished by summing up the characteristics of the different forms. We may, then, describe insanity as a chronic disease, manifested by deviations from the healthy and natural state of the mind, such deviations consisting either in a *moral perversion*, or a disorder of the feelings, affections, and habits of the individual, or in *intellectual derangement*, which last is sometimes partial, namely, in *monomania*, affecting the understanding only in particular trains of thought; or general, and accompanied with excitement, namely, in *mania*, or *raving madness*; or, lastly, confounding or destroying the connections or associations of ideas, and producing a state of *incoherence*. [. . .]

MORAL INSANITY

[. . .] There are many individuals living at large, and not entirely separated from society, who are affected in a certain degree with this modification of insanity. They are reputed persons of a singular, wayward, and eccentric character. An attentive observer will often recognize something remarkable in their manners and habits, which may lead him to entertain doubts as to their entire sanity [. . .]

Persons labouring under this disorder are capable of reasoning or supporting an argument upon any subject within their sphere of knowledge that may be

---

[2] The great French reformer, Phillipe Pinel, *Traité médico-philosophique sur l'aliénation mentale, ou la manie* (1801). Prichard cites the second 1809 edition in his text. The work was translated into English as *A Treatise on Insanity* in 1806 by D. D. Davies.

presented to them; and they often display great ingenuity in giving reasons for the eccentricities of their conduct, and in accounting for and justifying the state of moral feeling under which they appear to exist. In one sense, indeed, their intellectual faculties may be termed unsound; they think and act under the influence of strongly-excited feelings, and persons accounted sane are, under such circumstances, proverbially liable to error both in judgement and conduct. [. . .]

A considerable proportion among the most striking instances of moral insanity are those in which a tendency to gloom or sorrow is the predominant feature. When this habitude of mind is natural to the individual and comparatively slight, it does not constitute madness; and it is perhaps impossible to determine the line which marks a transition from predisposition to disease; but there is a degree of this affection which certainly constitutes disease of mind, and that disease exists without any illusion impressed upon the understanding. [. . .] In some cases it appears in persons whose temperament is the very reverse of the state described; and in such examples it is so much the more striking. In this form of moral derangement the disordered condition of the mind displays itself in a want of self-government, in continual excitement, an unusual expression of strong feelings, in thoughtless and extravagant conduct. A female modest and circumspect becomes violent and abrupt in her manners, loquacious, impetuous, talks loudly and abusively against her relations and guardians, before perfect strangers. Sometimes she uses indecent expressions, and betrays without reserve unbecoming feelings and trains of thought. Not unfrequently persons affected with this form of disease become drunkards; they have an incontrollable desire for intoxicating liquors, and a debauch is followed by a period of raving madness, during which it becomes absolutely necessary to keep them in confinement. Individuals are occasionally seen in lunatic asylums who under such circumstances have been placed under control. After the raving fit has passed off, they demand their release; and when they obtain it, at the first opportunity to resort to their former excesses, though perfectly aware of the consequences which await them. [. . .]

MONOMANIA

Medical writers have distributed the forms of monomania into many classes or divisions. The subdivisions would be endless if we were to constitute as many different kinds as there are modes and varieties of hallucination; but the most proper and useful distribution is founded on the prevailing passions or feelings which give origin and impart their peculiar character to the disease.

Mental dejection or melancholy, which extinguishes hope and gives the mind up to fear and the anticipation of evils, lays the foundation for many kinds or varieties of monomania. The most numerous and the worst instances are those in which the thoughts are directed towards the evils of a future life. The unseen state opens the most ample scope to the dark and gloomy anticipations of melancholy and remorse, and hence it is selected by the desponding monomaniac as field for the exercise of his self-torturing imagination. If the habits of his mind lead him to fix by preference on scenes connected with the present life, he still finds imaginary objects of terror and disquietude. [. . .]

CASES EXEMPLIFYING THE DESCRIPTION OF MORAL INSANITY AND THAT OF MONOMANIA, OR ILLUSTRATING THE RELATION BETWEEN THESE FORMS OF DISEASE, AND THE TRANSITION FROM ONE INTO THE OTHER

[. . .] *Case* 1.—A. B., a gentleman remarkable for the warmth of his affections, and the amiable simplicity of his character, possessed of great intellectual capacity, strong powers of reasoning, and a lively imagination, married a lady of high mental endowments, and who was long well known in the literary world. He was devotedly attached to her, but entertained the greatest jealousy lest the world should suppose that, in consequence of her talents, she exercised an undue influence over his judgement, or dictated his compositions. He accordingly set out with a determination of never consulting her, or yielding to her influence, and was always careful, when engaged in writing, that she should be ignorant of the subject which occupied his thoughts. His wife has been often heard to lament that want of sympathy and union of mind which are so desirable in married life. This peculiarity, however, in the husband so much increased, that in after years the most trifling proposition on her part was canvassed and discussed by every kind of argument. In the meantime he acquired strange peculiarities of habits. His love of order, or placing things in what he considered order or regularity, was remarkable. He was continually putting chairs, &c. in their places; and if articles of ladies' work or books were left upon a table, he would take an opportunity unobserved of putting them in order, generally spreading the work smooth, and putting the other articles in rows. He would steal into rooms belonging to other persons for the purpose of arranging the various articles. So much time did he consume in trifles, placing and replacing, and running from one room to another, that he was rarely dressed by dinner-time, and often apologised for dining in his dressing-gown, when it was well known that he had done nothing the whole morning but dress. And he would often take a walk in a winter's evening with a lanthorn, because he had not been able to get ready earlier in the day. He would run up and down the garden a certain number of times, rinsing his mouth with water, and spitting alternately on one side and then on the other in regular succession. He employed a good deal of time in rolling up little pieces of writing-paper which he used for cleaning his nose. In short his peculiarities were innumerable, but he concealed them as much as possible from the observation of his wife, whom he knew to be vexed at his habits, and to whom he always behaved with the most respectful and affectionate attention, although she could not influence him in the slightest degree. He would, however, occasionally break through these habits; as on Sundays, though he rose early for the purpose, he was always ready to perform service at a chapel a mile and a half distant from his house. It was a mystery to his intimate friends when and how he prepared these services. It did not at all surprise those who were best acquainted with his peculiarities, to hear that in a short time he became notoriously insane. He fancied his wife's affections were alienated from him, continually affirming that it was quite impossible she could have any regard for a person who had rendered himself so contemptible. He committed several acts of violence, argued vehemently in favour of suicide, and was shortly afterwards found drowned in a canal near his house. It must not be omitted that this individual derived a predisposition to madness by hereditary transmission: his father had been insane.

MONOMANIA

Jean Étienne Esquirol, *Mental Maladies: A Treatise on Insanity*, trans. E. K. Hunt (Philadelphia: Lea and Blanchard, 1845), 200–1, 335–7, 371–2.

Esquirol here outlines his theory of monomania, as a form of malady, a 'disease of the sensibility', which changes in accordance with the prevailing forms of society. The extracts include a case-study of erotomania, a form of illness which combines chastity with 'excessive sexual passion', and a description of homicidal monomania in a child. Esquirol was unusual in including examples of child insanity in his work.

Monomania is of all maladies, that which presents to the observer, phenomena the most strange and varied, and which offers, for our consideration, subjects the most numerous and profound. It embraces all the mysterious anomalies of sensibility, all the phenomena of the human understanding, all the consequences of the perversion of our natural inclinations, and all the errors of our passions. He who is profoundly versed in whatever relates to monomania, cannot be a stranger to that knowledge which relates to the progress and course of the human mind. It is also, in direct relation in point of frequency, with the development of the intellectual faculties. The more the understanding is developed, and the more active the brain becomes, the more is monomania to be feared. There has been no advancement in the sciences, no invention in the arts, nor any important innovation, which has not served as a cause of monomania, or lent to it, its peculiar character. The same is true of the prevailing notions, general errors, and universal convictions, whether true or false, which impress a peculiar feature upon each period of social life. Monomania is essentially a disease of the sensibility. It reposes altogether upon the affections, and its study is inseparable from a knowledge of the passions. Its seat is in the heart of man, and it is there that we must search for it, in order to possess ourselves of all its peculiarities. How many are the cases of monomania, caused by thwarted love, by fear, vanity, wounded self-love, or disappointed ambition! This malady presents all the signs which characterize the passions. The delirium of monomaniacs is exclusive, fixed and permanent, like the ideas of a passionate man. Like the passions, monomania now manifests itself by joy, contentment, gayety, exaltation of the faculties, boldness, and transports of feeling; now, it is concentrated, sad, silent, timid and fearful; but always exclusive and obstinate.

It has long been said, that insanity is a disease of civilization; it would have been more correct to have said this respecting monomania. Monomania is indeed frequent in proportion to the advancement of civilization. It borrows its character, and finds again the causes which produce it, in the different periods of society. It is superstitious and erotic in the infancy of society, as it is also, in the countries and regions where civilization and its excesses have made little progress; whilst in an advanced state of society, its cause and character manifest themselves in, and depend upon, pride, scepticism, ambition, the passion for gaming, despair and suicide. There has been no social epoch, which has not been remarkable, in consequence of some indications which monomania furnishes, of the intellectual and moral character of each.

The state of modern society has modified the causes and character of monomania, and this malady now reveals itself under new forms. With the weakening of religious convictions, demonomania, and forms of insanity depending upon superstition, have also disappeared. The influence of religion over the conduct of people being lessened, governments, in order to maintain authority over men, have had recourse to a *police*. Since that period, it is the police that troubles feeble imaginations, and establishments for the insane are peopled with monomaniacs who, fearing this authority, are delirious respecting the influence which it exercises, and by which they think themselves pursued. This monomaniac, who would formerly have been delirious with respect to magic, sorcery and the infernal regions; is now delirious, thinking himself threatened, pursued, and ready to be incarcerated by the agents of the police. Our political convulsions, in France, have been the occasion of much monomania, which has been provoked and characterized by events which have signalized each epoch of our revolution. [. . .]

257

EROTIC MONOMANIA

Erotomania is not that languor, which pervades the heart and soul of him who experiences the first impulses of a desire to love, nor that soft revery, which has such charms for youth, and which lead him who has once felt its influence, to seek again for solitude, the better to taste at leisure, the luxury of a sentiment, which was before unknown to him. This is not a disease; it is melancholy. Erotomania comes within the province of medicine, is a chronic cerebral affection, and is characterized by an excessive sexual passion; now, for a known object; now, for one unknown. In this disorder, there is a lesion of the imagination only. There is likewise an error of the understanding. It is a mental affection, in which the amorous sentiments are fixed and dominant, like religious ideas in theomania, or in religious lypemania. Erotomania differs essentially from nymphomania, and satyriasis. In the latter, the evil originates in the organs of reproduction, whose irritation reacts upon the brain. In erotomania, the sentiment which characterizes it, is in the head. The nymphomaniac, as well as the victim to satyriasis, is the subject of a physical disorder. The erotomaniac is, on the contrary, the sport of his imagination. Erotomania is to nymphomania and satyriasis, what the ardent affections of the heart, when chaste and honorable are, in comparison with frightful libertinism; while proposals the most obscene, and actions the most shameful and humiliating, betray both nymphomania and satyriasis. The erotomaniac neither desires, nor dreams even, of the favors to which he might aspire from the object of his insane tenderness; his love, sometimes, having for its object, things inanimate. [. . .] In erotomania, the eyes are lively and animated, the look passionate, the discourse tender, and the actions expansive; but the subjects of it never pass the limits of propriety. They, in some sort, forget themselves; vow a pure, and often secret devotion to the object of their love; make themselves slaves to it; execute its orders with a fidelity often puerile; and obey also the caprices that are connected with it. While contemplating its often imaginary perfections, they are thrown into ecstasies. Despairing in its absence, the look of this class of patients is dejected: their complexion becomes pale; their features change; sleep and appetite are lost. They are restless, thoughtful, greatly depressed in mind, agitated, irritable and passionate. The return of the object beloved, intoxicates them with joy. Their extreme happiness is apparent throughout their whole frame, and spreads to every thing that surrounds them. Their augmented muscular activity is convulsive in its character. These patients are ordinarily exceedingly loquacious, and always speaking of their love. During sleep, they have dreams which give birth to *succubi* and *incubi*.

Like all monomaniacs, those suffering from erotomania, are pursued both night and day, by the same thoughts and affections, which are the more disordered as they are concentrated or exasperated by opposition. Fear, hope, jealousy, joy and fury, seem unitedly to concur, or in turn, to render more cruel the

(handwritten annotations at top:)
★ social class issues
★ well educated
★ physical appearance
★ health, activity, deportment

(handwritten in left margin, vertical:) physiognomy

torment of these wretched beings. They neglect, abandon, and then fly both their relatives and friends. They disdain fortune, and despising social customs, are capable of the most extraordinary, difficult, painful and strange actions.

The following case is the more interesting as it presents the characteristics of erotic delirium without complication. A lady thirty-two years of age, tall, of a strong constitution and nervous temperament, having blue eyes, a light complexion, and chestnut colored hair, had received her education at a school in which the most brilliant future, and the highest pretensions were presented in perspective, to those young persons who went from this institution. Some time after her marriage, she saw a young man of a higher rank than her husband, and immediately becomes strongly impressed in his favor, though she had never spoken to him. She begins by complaining of her position, and speaking with contempt of her husband. She murmurs at being obliged to live with him, and at length conceives an aversion for him, as well as her nearest relatives, who endeavor, in vain, to recall her from her error. The evil increases, and it becomes necessary to separate her from her husband. She goes into the family of her father, discourses constantly of the object of her passion, and becomes difficult, capricious and choleric. She also suffers from nervous pains. She escapes from the house of her relatives to pursue *him.* She sees him every where, and addresses him in passionate songs. He is the handsomest, the greatest, the most humorous, amiable and perfect of men. She never had any other husband. It is him who lives in her heart, controls its pulsations, governs her thoughts and actions, animates and adorns her existence. She is sometimes surprised in a kind of ecstasy, and ravished with delight. She is then motionless; her look is fixed, and a smile is upon her lips. She frequently writes letters and verses copying them several times, with much care; and though they express the most vehement passion, are proof of the most virtuous sentiments. When she walks, she moves with sprightliness, and with the air of one engrossed in thought; or else her step is slow and haughty. She avoids men whom she disdains, and places far below her idol. However, she is not always indifferent to those marks of interest that are shown her; while every expression, that is not altogether respectful, offends her. To proofs of affection and devotion, she opposes the name, merit, and perfections of him whom she adores.

During both day and night, she often converses by herself; now, in a high, and now, in a low tone. She is now, gay and full of laughter; now, melancholic, and weeps; and is now angry, in her solitary conversations. If any one refers to these, she assures him that she is constrained to speak. Most frequently it is her *lover who converses with her, by means known to himself alone.* She sometimes believes, that jealous persons endeavor to oppose her good fortune, by disturbing their conversation, and striking her. (I have seen her ready to break out into a violent paroxysm of fury, after having uttered a loud cry, assuring me that she has just been struck). Under other circumstances, her face is flushed, and her eyes

259

sparkling. She rages against every one, utters cries, and no longer recognizes the persons with whom she lives. She is furious, and utters the most threatening language. This state, which is usually temporary, sometimes persists for two and three days, after which the patient experiences violent pains at the epigastrium and heart. These pains, which are confined to the precordial region, and *which she could not endure without aid furnished by her lover, are caused by her relatives and friends, although they may be several leagues distant from her, or by persons who are about her*. The appearance of force, and words spoken with decision, restrain her. She then grows pale, and trembles; tears flow, and terminate the paroxysm.

This lady, who is rational in every other respect, labors, and carefully superintends the objects, which are adapted to her convenience and use. She does justice to the merit of her husband, and the tenderness of her relatives, but can neither see the former, nor live with the latter. The menses are regular and abundant; the paroxysms of excitement ordinarily taking place at the menstrual period, though not always. Her appetite is capricious, and her actions, like her language, are subordinate to the whims of her delirious passion. She sleeps little, and her rest is troubled by dreams, and even nightmare. She has long seasons of watchfulness, and when she does not sleep, walks about, talking to herself or singing. This disease was of several years' duration, when she was committed to my care. A systematic treatment for a year, isolation, tepid, cold and shower baths, antispadmodics externally and internally employed, none of them succeed in restoring to the use of her reason, this interesting patient. [. . .]

On the 7th June, 1835, I was consulted in behalf of a little girl, seven and a half years of age, of ordinary stature, having a pale skin, an abundant and thick growth of hair, of a blond color, her eyes of a deep blue, and the upper lip slightly tumefied, but presenting no symptom of scurvy. Her physiognomy has an expression of deceit; and her eyes are often turned towards the internal angle of the orbit, which gives to her countenance, otherwise pale, a convulsive aspect. Her understanding is well developed, and although the daughter of a laborer, she has learned to read and write. She was trying to read the title of a book, lying upon my desk, while her mother-in-law was giving me the following account; for at first, the little one would neither speak to me, nor reply to my questions. She listened to the statement of her mother with the most perfect indifference; as if it had reference to another individual. 'I married my husband as his second wife, when this little girl was two years of age. We sent her to live with her grand-parents who were much displeased at my marriage with their son, and often expressed their dissatisfaction in presence of their grand-daughter. The child was five years old, when my husband and myself went to visit his parents. They received me kindly; but the child, who testified great satisfaction on seeing her father, almost refused my caresses, and would not embrace me. Nevertheless, she returned with us to Paris. Every time an opportunity offered, however, she was accustomed to scratch and strike me, saying: I hope you will die. When she was five years and three months old, I was pregnant, and she kicked me in the abdomen; at the same time expressing a like wish. We sent her back to her grand-parents, where she remained for two years more. On returning to us, at the age of seven years and four months, she began again to abuse me, and is incessantly repeating, that she heartily wishes that I may die, as well as her little brother, who was nursed abroad, and whom she had never seen. Not a day passes, on which she does not strike me. If I stoop down before the fire place, she strikes me in the back, in order to cause me to fall into the fire. She beats me with her fist, some-times seizes the scissors, knives, or other instrument that may fall in her way, always accompanying her abusive treatment with the same remark; I wish I could kill you. Her father has often corrected her, and I have not unfrequently opposed him, but the child has never expressed a willingness to abandon her design. Her father once threatened to have her imprisoned. That, she replied, will not save my mother and little brother from death, nor prevent me from destroying them. After this account, which the child heard with coldness, I addressed her the following questions. Her replies were made without bitterness or anger; and with composure and indifference. Why do you wish to kill you mother? Because I do not love her. Why do you not love her? I do not know. Has she treated you ill? No. Is she kind to you? Does she take care of you? Yes. Why do you beat her? In order to kill her. How! In order to kill her? Yes, I desire that she may die. Your blows cannot kill her; you are too young for that. I know it. One must suffer, to die. I wish to make her sick, so that she may suffer and die, as I am too small to kill her at a blow. When she is dead, who will take care of you? I do not know. You will be poorly taken care of, and poorly clothed, unhappy child! That is all one with me; I will kill her; I wish her dead. If you were large enough, would you kill your mother? Yes. Would you kill your grand-mother, (she is the mother of the young woman, and is present at the consulta-tion)? No. And why would you not kill her? I do not know. Do you love your father? Yes. Do you wish to kill him? No. Notwithstanding he punishes you? That is all the same, I will not kill him. Although your father scolds and beats you, will you still love him? Yes. Have you a little brother? Yes. He has been sent abroad to nurse, have you ever seen him? Yes. Do you love him? No. Do you wish that he may die? Yes. Do you want to kill him? Yes. I have asked father to bring him home from his nurse, in order to kill him. Why do you not love your mother? I know nothing about it. I hope she will die. Where did you get such dreadful thoughts? My grand-parents and aunt, were accustomed often to say, *that my mother and little brother must die.* But is that possible? Yes, Yes. I wish to say no more about my plans. I will take care of them, until I am grown up.

This conversation lasted an hour and a half. The coolness, composure and indifference of the child, excited in my mind the most painful emotions. The step-mother of this little girl is young, her physiognomy mild, and her tone and manners are agreeable. She dwells in the neighborhood of the Garden of Plants, and enjoys a good reputation, as well as her husband. By my advice, this child was sent into the country, to the residence of some nuns, where she passed three months. Her grand-parents have again taken her.

This case is remarkable in more than one respect.

1. For the fixedness of the desire to destroy her step-mother, on the part of a little girl, eight years of age, who had nothing to complain of, according to her own confession.

2. On account of the age, at which this deplorable disposition was developed. The grand-parents of this little girl, dissatisfied with the marriage of their son, express their displeasure by violent language, without foreseeing the effect, which these sentiments may produce upon the mind of a little child, from two to five years old. What a lesson to parents, who know not how to restrain themselves, either in their language or actions, in the presence of their children, whose minds and hearts they corrupt from their earliest infancy.

nature vs. nurture

THE PHYSIOGNOMY OF MENTAL DISEASES

Alexander Morison, *The Physiognomy of Mental Diseases* (1838), 2nd edn. (London: Longman and Co., 1840), 1, 83–5.

This was the first English atlas of the physiognomy of the insane. Morison was heavily influenced by Esquirol, whom he had visited in Paris in 1817. The second edition of Morison's Outlines of Lectures on Mental Diseases *(1825: 2nd edn. 1826), had included thirteen engravings based on drawings commissioned by Esquirol. Morison, however, was to develop his own impressionistic style for catching fleeting aspects of expression.[1] The examples given here are of a case of erotomania, following Esquirol, before and after treatment. See also Section I.*

There is no class of diseases in which the study of Physiognomy is so necessary as that of Mental diseases. It not only enables us to distinguish the characteristic features of different varieties, but it gives us warning of the approach of the disease in those in whom there is a predisposition to it, as well as confirms our opinion of convalescence in those in whom it is subsiding.

The appearance of the face is intimately connected with and dependant upon the state of the mind; the repetition of the same ideas and emotions, and the consequent repetition of the same movements of the muscles of the eyes and of the

[1] See Sander Gilman, *Seeing the Insane* (New York: John Wiley, 1982).

face give a peculiar expression, which, in the insane state, is a combination of wildness, abstraction, or vacancy, and of those ideas and emotions characterising different varieties of mental disorder, as pride, anger, suspicion, mirth, love, fear, grief, &c.

EXPLANATION OF PLATE XXIX

EROTOMANIA

M. S. P. aged 22, an unmarried female, educated as a governess—had an hereditary tendency to insanity.

FIG. 13. Erotomania

She was naturally of a very chaste and modest disposition; her Catamenia had been obstructed for six months, about three years ago, and she became insane. Her insanity assumed a religious character, she conceived herself to be 'the Virgin Mary; that she had received spiritual birth on a certain day, for she then felt joy by the Holy Ghost;' she was quite cured after the disease had existed about a year, and she remained well for two years and a half.

She now labours under a second attack, and has been two months insane; she expresses her love for the clergyman whom she had attended; her eyes are red and brilliant, her face is flushed and her ideas are amatory, for she expresses a

263

wish to be kissed—talks of being pregnant with something holy, and of marriage; but she does not farther transgress the bonds of decency in looks or discourse.

EXPLANATION OF PLATE XXX

PORTRAIT OF NO. XXIX CURED

This case was cured in about five months.

Her head was shaved and leeches were several times applied to it, laxatives were employed, and small doses of tartarized antimony, morphine, and camphor, were given, and the douche and the shower bath were employed.

This patient expressed great relief from the cold douche applied to the back of her head.

Fig. 14. Portrait of No. XXIX cured

THE PROGRESS OF MONOMANIA

William Benjamin Carpenter, *Principles of Mental Physiology, with their Application's to the Training and Discipline of the Mind, and the Study of its Morbid Conditions* (London: Henry S. King, 1874), 672–5.

Carpenter was a major figure in the development of mental physiology, and his comments on mental disorder emerge from that tradition, rather than from the practice of medical psychiatry. Here he integrates his theories of the reflex functions of the brain with a strong moral sense to produce, in the 1870s, an interpretation of the workings of mental disorder which harks back to Barlow's arguments in the 1840s. The concept of the Will played a far stronger role in Carpenter's work than in that of his fellow mental physiologists.

It is singular how closely the ordinary history of the access of *Monomania* corresponds with that of intoxication by Hachisch. A man who has been for some time under the strain of severe mental labour, perhaps with the addition of emotional excitement, breaks down in mental and bodily health; and becomes subject to morbid ideas, of whose abnormal character he is in the first instance quite aware. He may see spectral illusions, but he knows that they are illusive. He may hear imaginary conversations, but is conscious that they are empty words. He feels an extreme depression of spirits, but is willing to attribute this to some physical cause. He exhibits an excessive irritability of temper, but is conscious of his irascibility and endeavours to restrain it. [. . .] It is in this stage that a change of scene, the withdrawal from painful associations, the invigoration of the bodily health, and the direction of the Mental activity towards any subject that has a healthful attraction for it, exert a most beneficial influence; and there can be no doubt that many a man has been saved from an attack of Insanity, by the resolute determination of his Will *not* to yield to his morbid tendencies.—But if he should give way to these tendencies, and should dwell upon his morbid ideas instead of endeavouring to escape from them, they come at last to acquire a complete mastery over him; and his Will, his Common sense, and his Moral sense, at last succumb to their domination. [. . .] No conception can be too obviously fallacious or absurd, as judged by the sound intellect, to command his assent and govern his actions; for when the directing power of the Will is altogether lost, he is as incapable as a Biologized or Hypnotized subject, of testing his ideas by their conformity to the general result of his previous experience or of keeping his emotions under due control.

But, it may be said, if Insanity be the expression of disordered *physical* action of the Cerebrum, it is inconsistent to expect that a man can control this by any

265

effort of his own; or that *moral* treatment can have any efficacy in the restoration of mental health. Those, however, who have followed the course of the argument expounded in this Treatise, will have no difficulty in reconciling the two orders of facts. For whilst the disordered physical action of the Cerebrum, *when once established*, puts the automatic action of his mind altogether beyond the control of the Ego, there is frequently a stage in which he has the power of so directing and controlling that action, as *to prevent the establishment of the disorder*; just as, in the state of perfect health, he has the power of forming habits of Mental action, to which the nutrition of the Brain responds, so as ultimately to render them automatic. And so, the judicious Physician, in the treatment of an insane patient, whilst doing everything he can to invigorate the bodily health, to ward off sources of mental disturbance, and to divert the current of thought and feeling from a morbid into a healthful channel, will sedulously watch for every opportunity of fostering the power of self-control, will seek out the motives most likely to act upon the individual, will bring these into play upon every suitable occasion, will approve and reward its successful exercise, will sympathize with failure even when having recourse to the restraint which it has rendered necessary, will encourage every renewed exertion, and will thus give every aid he can to the reacquirement of that Volitional direction, which, as the bodily malady abates, it alone needed to prevent the recurrence of the disordered mental action. It is when the patient has so far recovered, as to be capable of being made to feel that he *can* do what he *ought*, if he will only *try*, that moral treatment becomes efficacious. And thus the judicious Physician, when endeavouring either to ward-off or to cure Mental disorder, brings to bear upon his patient exactly the same power as that which is exerted by an Educator of the highest type. Each has the high prerogative of calling into exercise that element in Man's nature which is the noblest gift of his Creator, enabling him to turn to the best account whatever mental endowments he may possess, 'for the glory of God, and the good of Man's estate.'

A CASE OF MORAL INSANITY

Henry Maudsley, *The Physiology and Pathology of Mind* (London: Macmillan, 1867), 313–16.

Maudsley, the most pre-eminent figure in medical psychiatry of the late century, here gives a case-study of female moral insanity. The peculiarly ambiguous nature of this disorder is highlighted by the explicit connections Maudsley draws between

*diagnosis and social class: behaviour appropriate for a lower social order is
evidence of moral insanity if it is enacted by a member of a higher social class.*

When compelled to give an opinion upon a particular case of suspected moral insanity, it is of some importance to bear in mind that the individual is a *social* element, and to have regard therefore to his social relations. That which would scarcely be offensive or unnatural in a person belonging to the lowest strata of society—and certainly nowise inconsistent with his relations there— would be most offensive and unnatural in one holding a good position in society, and entirely inconsistent with his relations in it: words which, used in the latter case, would betoken grave mental disorder, may be familiar terms of address amongst the lowest classes. Between individuals, as elements in the social organism, there is in this regard a difference not unlike that which there is between the different kinds of organic elements in the bodily organism; it is important, therefore, that we have in remembrance the individual's social relations when dealing with moral insanity, as we regard the very different relations of an epithelial[1] cell and a nerve cell when dealing with structures so far apart in the scale of life. As it is chiefly in the degeneration of the social sentiments that the symptoms of moral insanity declare themselves, it is plain that the most typical forms of the disease can only be met with in those who have had some social cultivation.

The following case, which came under my observation and treatment, may stand here as an example of a mental perversion which it would seem impossible to describe as other than moral insanity:— [. . .]

Miss C. D. æt. forty-five, was a cousin of the above patient,[2] and also of good social position. Her appearance was anything but attractive; she was withered, sallow, blear-eyed, with an eminently unsteady and untrustworthy eye. So improper and immoral was her conduct, that she was obliged to live apart from her family in lodgings; for she seemed incapable, in certain regards, of any control over her propensities. Whenever she was able, she left her lodgings to spend days together at a brothel with a common fellow, whom she supplied with money, frequently pawning her clothes for that purpose. When at home, she generally lay in bed for most of the day. No appeal was of any avail to induce her to alter her mode of life. She was prone to burn little articles, impulsively throwing them into the fire, saying that she could not help it, and then cutting and pricking her own flesh by way of penance. Now and then she would all of a sudden pirouette on one leg, and throw her arms about; and, with like sudden impulsiveness, would not unfrequently break a pane of glass. When reasoned or remonstrated with about her foolish tricks, she professed to feel them to be very absurd, expressed great regret, and talked with exceeding plausibility about

[1] Outer membrane.   [2] Case included in omitted passage.

them, as though she were not responsible for them, but were an angel in diffi-culties, which she could not overcome. It was of no use whatever speaking earnestly with her, for she admitted her folly to a greater extent than accusation painted it, and spoke of it with a resigned air of an innocent victim. Her habits were unwomanly, and often offensive. The more sensible of the other patients amongst whom she was, used to get very angry with her, because they thought that she could behave better if she would. 'One can bear with Miss ——, because, poor girl, she does not know what she does, and cannot help it; but Miss —— knows quite well what she is about, and I am quite sure she can help it if she likes,' was the style of complaint made against her. And there could be no doubt that she did know perfectly well what she was about, but her unconscious vicious nature, ever prompting, surprised and overpowered conscious reflection, which was only occasional. [. . .]

It is quite certain that these women, so lost to all sense of the obligations of their position, could not restrain their immoral extravagances and perverse acts for any length of time; punishment had no effect, except in so far as it was a restraint for the time being. All of them knew quite well the difference between right and wrong, but no motive could be excited in their minds to induce them to pursue the right and eschew the wrong; their conduct revealed the tyranny of an unhappy organization; the world's wrong was their right. The ruling planets by which one of them, in her angry moods, professed to be guided was not, therefore, an absolute fiction, for therein was expressed the fate made for her by a vicious organization. For a like reason such patients feel no shame, regret, nor remorse for their conduct, however flagrantly unbecoming and immoral it may have been, never think that they are to blame, and consider themselves ill-treated by their relatives when they are interfered with. They are examples illustrating the retrograde metamorphosis of mind. The moral feeling has been slowly acquired in the course of human cultivation through generations as the highest effort of mental evolution; and in the course of family degeneration, we find its loss mark a stage in the downward course. The victims of such vice or defect of nature cannot be fitted for social intercourse. Friends may remonstrate, entreat, and blame, and punishment may be allowed to take its due course, but in the end both friends and all who know them recognise the hopelessness of improvement, and acknowledge that they must be sent to an asylum.

THE MYSTERIES OF THE INNER LIFE

Forbes Benignus Winslow, *On Obscure Diseases of the Brain, and Disorders of the Mind* (1860), 4th edn. (London: John Churchill, 1868), 141–3, 145–6, 153–5, 156–7, 568–70.

An aura of scientific detachment did not form an essential element of nineteenth-century psychiatric writing, and Forbes Winslow, editor of the Journal of Psychological Medicine and Mental Pathology, *provided some of the most emotionally charged prose in the profession. Here he charges readers to examine the darkest corners of their minds and to acknowledge their kinship with the insane. Like many other alienists (including John Bucknill) he takes the figure of Ophelia as an exemplum of chastity, overwhelmed by 'a morbidly exalted state of the reproductive instincts'. He also attempts to answer that vexed question of where these chaste sufferers could have acquired the obscene vocabulary they employ during their illness.*

Were we to scrutinise the mysteries of the inner mental life, and analyse the nature of those terrible conceptions that occasionally throw their phantasmal shade across the anxious and troubled mind, what a melancholy, degrading, and profoundly humiliating revelation most men would have to make of the dark corners, secret recesses, and hidden crevices of the human heart. If this self-examination were faithfully and honestly executed, it would cause the best and fairest of God's creatures to shrink back from the contemplation of their own most secret thoughts.

Philosophers intimately acquainted with the anatomy of the human mind have often asked, Who has not occasionally had a demon pursuing with remorseless impetuosity his every footstep, suggesting to his ever-active and often morbidly-disturbed and perverted imagination the commission of some dark deed of crime, from the conception of which he has at the time recoiled with horror? Is there any mind, pure and untainted, which has not yielded, when the reason and moral sense have been transiently paralysed and God's grace ceases to exercise an influence over the heart, to the seduction of impure thought, lingered with apparent pleasure on the contemplation of physically unchaste images, or delighted in a fascinating dalliance with criminal thoughts? [. . .] Is not every bosom polluted by a dark, leprous spot, corroding ulcer, or portion of moral gangrene? Does there not cling to every mind some melancholy reminiscence of the past, which throws at times a sombre tinge over the chequered path of life? We may flatter our pharisaical vanity and human pride by affirming that we are exempt from these melancholy conditions of moral suffering and sad states of mental infirmity; but, alas! we should be closing our eyes to the truth if we were to ignore the existence of such, thank God, perhaps only temporary, paroxysmal, and evanescent conditions of unhealthy thought, and phases of passion which occasionally have been known to cast their withering influence and death-like shadow over mind, blighting, saddening, and often crushing the best, kindest, and noblest of human natures. [. . .]

In the incipient stage of insanity the patient is fully sensible of entertaining exaggerated and unnatural impressions; is acutely conscious of the mind dwelling morbidly and sometimes irresistibly upon certain trains of absurd, unhealthy, and it may be very *impure* thought; he painfully recognises the fact that insane conceptions are struggling to master his reason, obtain an ascendancy over his judgment, an abnormal influence and control over his passions and the subjugation of his instincts. In some cases (and this is a distressing and dangerous type of insanity) he is impelled (why and wherefore he knows not) to commit suicide, sacrifice the lives of those related to him by the closest ties of relationship, and give utterance to blasphemous, revolting, and impure expressions. He finds it occasionally extremely difficult and almost impossible to dismiss from the mind and keep in subjection these morbid impulses to acts of homicidal and suicidal violence, or to conquer the insane desire to clothe in grossly obscene language conceptions from the contemplation of which his delicate and sensitive nature would, when unclouded by disease, have instinctively shrunk with horror, loathing, and disgust. [. . .]

In some women the insanity (particularly if it be of the puerperal type) is characterised by a singularly distressing perversion of thought, connected with and caused by a morbidly-exalted state of the reproductive instincts. The conversation is, in these cases, occasionally tinctured with expressions from the utterance of which the unhappy sufferer would, when in health, like a sensitive plant, have recoiled. The gentlest of the sex, the purest of feminine minds, and most pious, refined, and cultivated moral natures, are often the first to exhibit, when suffering from a particular phase of mental derangement, this painful moral and mental degeneration. [. . .]

In this malady the emotions, sensations, and appetites are unhappily in a melancholy state of degradation, perversion, and alienation, and, as a general rule, the conversation and conduct of those so afflicted reflect and are in unison with this derangement of the intellect and disordered state of the instincts. The reason is dethroned and taken forcibly captive by the animal impulses, and these, when in a state of supremacy, exercise an undisputed and tyrannical sovereignty over the judgment, conscience, and the will.

Shakspeare, in one of the most touchingly affecting creations of his transcendent genius, threw a poetic charm, a brilliant flood of fancy, round the character of Ophelia—

'Sweet as spring-time flowers,'

so redolent of feminine gentleness, purity, and grace; but ever true to nature, this great magician and all but inspired poet, could not sacrifice truth to fiction, fancy to fact, and he therefore makes this love-sick girl, during her insane warblings, give utterance to conceptions that never could have suggested themselves to her exquisitely chaste and delicate mind before it was prostrated and perverted by disease. [. . .]

We may hence account pathologically for the development of natural physical tendencies usually developed at or after the age of puberty, but it does not explain the actual knowledge and use of prurient words and obscene expressions. This phase of mental alienation can only result from the patients having heard the identical words used by persons with whom they have unfortunately associated, or from having seen them in print, or heard them publicly or privately uttered.

There are, however, in operation other sources of moral contamination and mental deterioration from which the most vigilant parents are not always able to guard their children. I refer to the pernicious example and wicked suggestions of depraved, irreligious, and profligate servants (a frightful cause of moral pollution as well as of mental idiocy in early life), occasionally smuggled into the bosom of families by false characters, to a perusal of vicious books, sensational novels, sight of indecent prints surreptitiously taken into the nursery, and reading the details of gross acts of immorality, made matters of judicial investigation so faithfully, and, it is to be regretted, minutely reported in the ordinary channels of daily communication. These frightful records of vice and crime so palpably exposed, elaborately and artistically developed, are fearfully and fatally destructive to the pure and unsophisticated minds of young persons. [. . .]

Like the historian and antiquarian wandering with a sad heart over ground made classical and memorable in the story of great men, and in the annals of heroic deeds, surveying with painful interest the ruins of ancient temples, viewing with vivid emotion the sad wreck of proud imperial cities, consecrated by the genius of men renowned in the world's history as statesmen, scholars, artists, philosophers, and poets, so it is the duty of the mental physician to wander through the ruins of still greater temples than any raised in ancient days to the honour of imaginary deities. It is his distressing province to witness great and good intellects, proud and elevated understandings levelled to the earth, and there crumbling, like dust in the balance, under the crushing influence of disease.

Survey that old man crouched in the corner of the room, with his face buried in his hands. He is indifferent to all that is passing around him; he heeds not the voice of man nor woman; he delights not in the carolling of birds nor in the sweet music of the rippling brooks. The gentle wind of heaven, playing its sweetest melody as it rushes through the greenwood, awakens in his mind no consciousness of nature's charms. Speak to him in terms of endearment and affection; bring before him the glowing and impassioned images of the past. He elevates himself, gazes listlessly and mechanically at you, 'makes no sign,' and, dropping his poor head, buries it in his bosom, and sinks into his former state of melancholy abstraction. This man's oratory charmed the senate; the magic of his eloquence held thousands in a state of breathless admiration; his influence was commanding, his sagacity eminently acute, and his judgment profound. View him as he is fallen from his high and honourable estate.

Listen to the sweet and gentle voice of yonder woman, upon whose head scarcely eighteen summers have shed their genial warmth and influence. How merrily she dances over the green sward; how touchingly she warbles in her delirium sweet snatches of song! What a pitiful spectacle she presents of a noble mind lying in beautiful fragments before us! Look! she has decked herself with a spring garland. Now she holds herself perfectly erect, and walks with queenly majesty. Approach and accost her. She exclaims, 'Yes, he will come; he promised to be here; where are the guests? where is the ring? where my wedding robe— my orange-blossoms?' Suddenly her mind is overshadowed; her face assumes an expression of deep, choking, and bitter anguish—she alternately sobs and laughs, is gay and sad, cheerful and melancholy—

> 'Thought and affliction, passion, hell itself,
> She turns to favour and to prettiness.'[1]

Speak again to her, and another change takes place in the spirit of her dream. Like her sad prototype, Ophelia, the purest creation of Shakspeare's immortal genius, she plaintively sings—

> 'He is dead and gone, lady,
> He is dead and gone;
> At his head a green grass turf,
> At his heels a stone.'[2]

Her history is soon told. Deep and absorbing passion, elevated hopes, bright, sunny, and fanciful dreams of the future—death with all its factitious trappings, sad and solemn mockery of woe—seared affections, a broken heart, and a disordered brain.

The two illustrations I have cited are truthful outlines of a type of lunacy that frequently comes under the notice of those engaged in the treatment of the insane. How keenly such cases tear the heartstrings asunder, and call into active operation all the loving sympathies of man's noble nature!

---

[1] *Hamlet*, IV. v. 187–8.   [2] *Hamlet*, IV. v. 29–32.

INSANITY AND CRIMINAL RESPONSIBILITY

John Charles Bucknill, *Unsoundness of Mind in Relation to Criminal Acts* (1854), 2nd edn. (London: Longman, Brown, Green, Longman and Roberts, 1857), 2–3, 4–6, 58–60.

In this text Bucknill tackles the highly-charged issue of the relationship between the absolute legal judgment of criminal responsibility and psychiatric notions of insanity as a variable state, not easily divided from sanity. Ideas of partial insanity, such as moral insanity and monomania, had provoked long debates in legal and medical circles on the issue of responsibility. Bucknill suggests the legal impasse could be solved by acknowledging a distinction between knowledge of right and wrong, and the power to act upon that knowledge. Bucknill argues that the successes of moral treatment in the asylums have shown that the feeling of right and wrong is an innate principle of the human mind.

Insanity is a condition of the human mind ranging from the slightest aberration from positive health to the wildest incoherence of mania, or the lowest degradations of cretinism. Insanity is a term applied to conditions measurable by all the degrees included between these widely separated poles, and to all the variations which are capable of being produced by partial or total affection of the many faculties into which the mind can be analysed.

There is no quality of anything cognizable to our senses or to our understanding, more variable in its degrees or its combinations than insanity. But legal responsibility is strictly defined. It is bounded by a line, a Rubicon, on one side of which Cæsar is the servant of the state, on the other a traitor and a rebel. It is also uniform, it admits not of degrees of greater or smaller, of more or less. If this uniformity is unreal and inconsistent with the actualities to be found in nature, and if the boundary line is capable of being moved to and fro, these circumstances will increase the difficulty of making the characteristics of insanity correspond with the common law essence of irresponsibility. It is no doubt of importance that under all possible circumstances the administrators of our laws should have landmarks erected for their guidance; for the smaller the latitude of private opinion which is permitted to the executive, the surer will be the guarantees of liberty and of the impartial administration of justice. Fixed points therefore are rightly decided upon whenever it is possible to do so. [. . .]

To measure degrees of responsibility and adapt them to the variable conditions of disordered mind is a problem, upon the solution of which the whole medico-legal question of insanity rests. But how can responsibility be measured? Extension in time and place can be measured by duration and by substance;

[. . .] but in what practical balance shall the responsibility of man for his actions be estimated? As the weight of a body is measured by the power it overcomes, so degrees of responsibility must be measured by the degrees of mental disorder, and by the amount of inflection they produce from the standard of health.

A man having the knowledge of right and wrong, and in the possession of the power of choosing the one and refusing the other, is rightly held to be responsible for his conduct to his God, to his neighbours, and to himself. A man knowing and capable of discharging his duties to his God, to his neighbours, and to himself, is a sane man. A man who from any mental imperfection or infirmity is incapable of discharging these duties cannot be considered to be in a state of mental sanity, and cannot with justice be held responsible to do that which he is morally unable to do.

It will be hereafter seen, that the neglect of this distinction between *knowledge* and *power* forms one of the fundamental difficulties of the question. [. . .]

The sense of duty, the feeling of right and wrong, is an innate principle of the human mind implanted by the Almighty, and serving as a sure foundation for the responsibility of man for his actions; which is thus not left to chance developement, but is rendered an essential and necessary part of human nature. It seems needful to enquire to what extent this absolute and necessary part of human nature becomes capable of being perverted or destroyed under the influence of cerebro-mental disease. It may be taken as an axiom, that *the innate and essential principles of mind are ever present where mind exists*. It may also be asserted as the result of observation and experience, that in all lunatics, and even in the most degraded idiots, whenever manifestations of any mental action can be educed, the feeling of right and wrong may be proved to exist. The education of idiots and cretins has proved that there is no zero in the human mind; and the success of the *moral treatment* prevailing in lunatic asylums has demonstrated, that insanity does not neutralize the influences by which the moral government of the world is effected. But if insanity does not remove these innate principles, does it on that account leave persons under their influence wholly responsible for their actions? Certainly not: *Responsibility depends upon power, not upon knowledge, still less upon feeling. A man is responsible to do that which he can do, not that which he feels or knows it right to do.* If a man is reduced under thraldom to passion by disease of the brain, he loses moral freedom and responsibility, although his knowledge of right and wrong may remain intact.

THE MANUFACTURE OF LUNATICS AND CRIMINALS

Henry Maudsley, *Responsibility in Mental Disease* (London: Henry S. King, 1874), 3–4, 28–9, 34–5, 268–9, 272–3, 275–7, 295–6.

One can see in these extracts the ways in which Maudsley is differentiating himself from the work of the moral managers who preceded him. The power of the will is acknowledged, but only within limits set down by a character's past history. The lunatic, like the criminal, is a 'manufactured article' and science must study the 'fixed and unchanging laws' which govern that process. Maudsley emphasizes the determining role played by inheritance, and sounds an early eugenic note in his reflections on unwise marriages. Like the phrenologists in the earlier part of the century, he stresses the importance of mental culture, singling out the narrow-minded business man as a prime target for mental decay and insanity.

Much of the success of the modern humane treatment of insanity rests upon the recognition of two principles: first, that the insane have like passions with those who are not insane, and are restrained from doing wrong, and constrained to do right, by the same motives which have the same effects in sane persons; secondly, that these motives are only effective within limits, and that beyond these limits they become powerless, the hope of reward being of no avail, and the expectation or infliction of punishment actually provoking more unreason and violence. By the skilful combination of these principles in practice it has come to pass that asylums are now, for the most part, quiet and orderly institutions, instead of being, as in olden times, dens of disorder and violence, and that the curious sight-seer, who visits an asylum as he would visit a menagerie, sees nothing extraordinary, and comes away disappointed. [. . .]

Not until comparatively lately has much attention been given to the way in which criminals are produced. It was with them much as it was at one time with lunatics: to say of the former that they were wicked, and of the latter that they were mad, was thought to render any further explanation unnecessary and any further inquiry superfluous. It is certain, however, that lunatics and criminals are as much manufactured articles as are steam-engines and calico-printing machines, only the processes of the organic manufactory are so complex that we are not able to follow them. They are neither accidents nor anomalies in the universe, but come by law and testify to causality; and it is the business of science to find out what the causes are and by what laws they work. There is nothing accidental, nothing supernatural, in the impulse to do right or in the impulse to do wrong; both come by inheritance or by education; and science can no more rest content with the explanation which attributes one to the grace of Heaven and the other to the malice of the devil, than it could rest content with the explanation of insanity as a possession by the devil.

The few and imperfect investigations of the personal and family histories of criminals which have yet been made are sufficient to excite some serious reflections. One fact which is brought strongly out by these inquiries is that crime is often hereditary; that just as a man may inherit the stamp of the bodily features and characters of his parents, so he may also inherit the impress of their evil passions and propensities: of the true thief as of the true poet it may be indeed said that he is born, not made. This is what observation of the phenomena of hereditary action would lead us to expect; and although certain theologians, who are prone to square the order of nature to their notions of what it should be, may repel such a doctrine as the heritage of an *immoral* in place of a *moral* sense, they will in the end find it impossible in this matter, as they have done in other matters, to contend against facts. To add to their misfortunes, many criminals are not only begotten, and conceived, and bred in crime, but they are instructed in it from their youth upwards, so that their original criminal instincts acquire a power which no subsequent efforts to produce reformation will ever counteract. [. . .]

There is a borderland between crime and insanity, near one boundary of which we meet with something of madness but more of sin, and near the other boundary of which something of sin but more of madness. A just estimate of the moral responsibility of the unhappy people inhabiting this borderland will assuredly not be made until we get rid of the metaphysical measure of responsibility as well as of the theological notion that vices and crimes are due to the instigation of the devil, and proceed by way of observation and induction to sound generalizations concerning the origin of the moral sentiments, the laws of their development, and the causes, course and varieties of moral degeneracy. Here as in other departments of nature our aim should be the discovery of natural laws by patient interrogation of nature, not the invention of theories by invoking our own minds to utter oracles to us. It must be received as a scientific axiom that there is no study to which the inductive method of research is not applicable; every attempt to prohibit such research by authority of any kind must be withstood and repelled with the utmost energy as a deadly attack upon the fundamental principle of scientific inquiry. With a better knowledge of crime, we may not come to the practice of treating criminals as we now treat insane persons, but it is probable that we shall come to other and more tolerant sentiments, and that a less hostile feeling towards them, derived from a better knowledge of defective organization, will beget an indulgence at any rate towards all doubtful cases inhabiting the borderland between insanity and crime; in like manner as within living memory the feelings of mankind with regard to the insane have been entirely revolutionized by an inductive method of study. [. . .]

Most persons who have suffered from the malady of thought must at one period or other of their lives have had a feeling that it would not be a hard matter to become insane, that in fact something of an effort was required to preserve their sanity. To those in whose blood a tendency to insanity runs this effort must without doubt be a sustained and severe one, being no less in some instances than a continual struggle to oppose the strong bent of their being. How far then is a man responsible for going mad? This is a question which has not been much considered; yet it is one well worthy of deep consideration; for it is certain that a man has, or might have, some power over himself to prevent insanity.* However it be brought about, it is the dethronement of will, the loss of the power of co-ordinating the ideas and feelings; and in the wise development of the control of will over the thoughts and feelings there is a power in ourselves which makes strongly for sanity. From time to time we may see two persons who have had the same faulty heritage, and who, so far as we can judge, have not differed much in the degree of their predisposition to insanity, go very different ways in life—one perhaps to reputation and success, the other to suicide or madness. A great purpose earnestly pursued through life, a purpose to the achievement of which the energies of the individual have been definitely bent, and which has, therefore, involved much renunciation and discipline of self, has perhaps been a saving labour to the one, while the absence of such a life-aim, whether great in itself or great to the individual in the self-discipline which its pursuit entailed, may have left the other without a sufficiently powerful motive to self-government, and so have opened the door to the perturbed streams of thought and feeling which make for madness.

It would be quite useless to inculcate rules for self-formation upon one whose character had taken a certain mould of development; for character is a slow and gradual growth through action in relation to the circumstances of life; it cannot be fashioned suddenly and through reflection only. A man can no more will than he can speak without having learned to do so, nor can he be taught volition any more than he can be taught speech except by practice. It was a pregnant saying, that the history of a man is his character; to which one might add that whosoever would transform a character must undo a life history. The fixed and unchanging laws by which events come to pass hold sway in the domain of mind as in every other domain of nature.

A striking illustration of the difficulty of realising the reign of law in the development of character and in the events of human life is afforded by the criticisms

---

* More than twenty years ago, a small volume, entitled 'Man's Power over Himself to prevent or control Insanity,' was published. It contained the substance of two lectures given at the Royal Institution, by the late Reverend John Barlow, and was one of a series of Small Books on Great Subjects. Though excellent of its kind, the author regards the subject entirely from a moral point of view, and certainly in some respects overrates the power of control.

of those who have blamed Goethe because he made Werter[1] commit suicide, instead of making him attain to clearer insight, calmer feeling, and a tranquil life after his sorrows; had they reflected well they must have perceived that suicide was the natural and inevitable termination of the morbid sorrows of such a nature. It was the final explosion of a train of antecedent preparations, an event which was as certain to come as the death of the flower with a canker at its heart. Suicide or madness is the natural end of a morbidly sensitive nature, with a feeble will, unable to contend with the hard experiences of life. You might as well, in truth, preach moderation to the hurricane as talk philosophy to one whose antecedent life has conducted him to the edge of madness.

I cannot but think that moral philosophers have sometimes exaggerated greatly the direct power of the will, as an abstract entity, over the thoughts and feelings, without at the same time having taken sufficient account of the slow and gradual way in which the concrete will itself must be formed. The culminating effort of mental development, the final blossom of human evolution, it betokens a physiological development as real, though not as apparent, as that which distinguishes the nervous system of man from that of one of the lower animals. Time and systematic exercise are necessary to the gradual organisation of the structure which shall manifest it in full function. No one can resolve successfully by a mere effort of will to think in a certain way, or to feel in a certain way, or even, which is easier, to act always in accordance with certain rules; but he can, by acting upon the circumstances which will in turn act upon him, imperceptibly modify his character: he can thus, by calling external circumstances to his aid, learn to withdraw his mind from one train of thought and feeling, the activity of which will thereupon subside, and can direct it to another train of thought and feeling, which will thereupon become active, and so by constant watchfulness over himself and by habitual exercise of will in the required direction, bring about insensibly the formation of such a habit of thought, feeling and action as he may wish to attain unto. He can make his character grow by degrees to the ideal which he sets before himself. [. . .]

If there is one conviction which a widening experience brings home to the practical physician, it is a conviction of the large part which hereditary predisposition in some form or other plays in the causation of insanity: it would scarcely be an exaggeration to say that few persons go mad, save from palpable physical causes, who do not show more or less plainly by their gait, manner, gestures, habits of thought, feeling and action, that they have a sort of predestination to madness. The inherited liability may be strong or weak; it may be so weak as hardly to peril sanity amidst the most adverse circumstances of life, or so strong as to issue an outbreak of madness amidst the most favourable external circumstances. Now it is certain that if we were interested in the breeding of a variety of

---

[1] *The Sorrows of Werter* by Goethe (1774).

animals, we should not think of breeding from a stock which was wanting in those qualities that were the highest characteristics of the species: we should not willingly select for breeding purposes a hound that was deficient in scent, or a greyhound that was deficient in speed, or a racehorse that could neither stay well nor gallop fast. Is it right then to sanction propaganda of his kind by an individual who is wanting in that which is the highest attribute of man—a sound and stable mental constitution? I note this as a question to be seriously faced and sincerely answered, although not expecting that mankind, in the present state of their development, will either seriously face it or sincerely answer it.

When one considers the reckless way in which persons, whatever the defects of their mental and bodily constitution, often get married, without sense of responsibility for the miseries which they entail upon those who will be the heirs of their infirmities, without regard, in fact, to anything but their own present gratification, one is driven to think either that man is not the pre-eminently reasoning and moral animal which he claims to be, or that there is in him an instinct which is deeper than knowledge. He has persuaded himself, rightly or wrongly, that in his case there is in the feeling of love between the sexes something of so sacred and mysterious a character as to justify disregard to consequences in marriage. We have only to look at the large part which love fills in novels, poetry and painting, and to consider what a justification of unreason in life it is held to be, to realise what a hold it has on him in his present state of development, and what a repugnance there would be to quench its glow by cold words of reason. At bottom, however, there is nothing particularly holy about it; on the contrary, it is a passion which man shares with other animals; and when its essential nature and function are regarded, we shall nowhere find stronger evidence of a community of nature between man and animals. [. . .]

The full development of the resources of the mental nature can be achieved only by a deliberate culture and sustained activity of the mind as an aim in itself. [. . .] It is no exaggeration to say that a great many persons never exercise any real mental activity, never undergo any real development, after they have become skilled in the special work of their lives. Their thoughts run in a groove so well worn that the difficulty is to get out of it. The higher faculties being unused undergo decay, if not degeneration; real mental application becomes first difficult and then impossible; and when a calamity occurs they are without internal resources to enable them to bear up against its strain. When they are taken from the routine of their labours they have no interests, they can turn to no intellectual work, are a torment to themselves and to others, as they go through the tedious process of a decay of mind. The matter is worse when a person has made success in business the one aim of his life, when he has by long concentration of desire and energy upon such an aim so completely grown to it as to have made it the main part of his inner life—that to which all his thoughts, feelings, and actions are directed; then if some error of his own, or some misfortune beyond his control, shatters his hopes, destroys the pride of his previous accomplishments, lays low the fabric which he has been building with all the eagerness and energy of an intense egoism, he is left naked and defenceless against his afflictions, sinks into melancholy, and from melancholy into madness. To neglect the continued culture and exercise of the intellectual and moral faculties is to leave the mind at the mercy of external circumstances: with it as with the body, to cease to strive is to begin to die.

THE BORDERLANDS OF INSANITY

Andrew Wynter, *The Borderlands of Insanity and other Allied Papers* (London: Robert Hardwicke, 1875), 50–3, 71–3.

These essays, first published in the Quarterly *and* Edinburgh Reviews, *helped to popularize the notion of a Borderland of Insanity, a 'vast army of undiscovered lunatics' in the population, who never quite cross the frontiers into open insanity. Wynter follows Maudsley and others in arguing that a mother is more likely to transmit mental disease than a father, and that transmission normally occurs from mother to daughter, and father to son. Drunkenness, a crucial area of concern in both the social and medical literature of the time, is here defined as a form of moral insanity.*

The unprofessional world, especially the lawyers, cannot understand that what they consider to be certain forms of vice should be explained away and removed from the denunciations of the moralists and the punishment of the law by a new-fangled theory of 'mad doctors,' which they ascribe to undoubted brain disease. That an individual should in all other matters appear to be of sound mind, but that at certain seasons he should be seized with an irrepressible desire to commit theft, arson, or to reduce himself below the level of a beast by means of drink, seems to the unprofessional understanding quite incomprehensible; and the common view—taking this bare aspect of the case—is the right one. There is indeed no such thing as simple thirst-madness, or fire-madness, or thieving madness, or homicidal madness. Those who have watched such cases with professional knowledge and experience, observe that the whole moral tone of the individuals so afflicted is, so to speak, below par. They suffer from a paralysis of the moral sense; invariably they are untruthful, very commonly full of impure thoughts, and always eccentric both in thought and action. They have long belonged to the Borderland of Insanity, in the opinion of those who know them best; but it is only the last supreme act which, in the eyes of the world, takes them over the frontier into the domain of the insane. There are thousands who, lacking the opportunity or the power of will, never indeed do cross the frontier, but remain and swell the vast army of undiscovered lunatics which leavens unsuspectedly the sane population.

It may be as well, in view of a more ready discrimination of the probability of the symptoms of a person being those of incipient insanity, to remember what experience teaches us as to the relative powers of the father and mother to transmit the insane neurosis to their children. It is agreed by all alienist physicians, that girls are far more likely to inherit insanity from their mothers than from the other parent, and that the same rule obtains as regards the sons. The tendency of the mother to transmit her mental disease is, however, in all cases stronger than the father's; some physicians have, indeed, insisted that it is twice as strong. In judging of the chances of an individual inheriting mental disease, or, indeed, of the insane temperament, it may not be unadvisable to study the general likeness and character. If the daughter of an insane mother very much resembles her in feature and in temperament, the chances are that she is more likely to inherit the disease than other daughters who are not so like. [. . .] Let us trust that the warning voice, which all alienist physicians have raised with reference to this vice, may be listened to by the sherry-drinking ladies of this generation, lest the tippling inheritance so many of them have more or less received, unknown to themselves, be strengthened, and transformed into a more permanent and terrible form of insanity in their posterity. It is true that Nature, wearied, as it were, by repeated offences against her laws, sometimes—out of mercy to the race—takes the matter into her own hands in a very summary manner by extinguishing the posterity of the habitual drunkard. There is nothing more clearly ascertained in psychological medicine, than that children conceived in conditions of drunkenness of either parents, are liable to become idiots unable to prolong their race. There is not a physician of experience in these low forms of moral insanity, brought about by persistent drinking, who cannot point to the downfall in one generation of the most intellectual parents to the most abject offspring not possessing any claim to humanity. A more terrible example of the swift manufacture of a perfectly waste material out of what might have been an honour to humanity, the mind cannot conceive. In old Rome the bestial vices of the slaves used to be paraded as an example before the children of their masters, as a warning and terror to them. Oh that dipsomaniacs could be so utilized! But unfortunately, as regards their children, the tyranny of their sad inheritance would only render the example a mockery, a delusion, and a snare, into which, with a fatal certainty, they would be drawn and destroyed. So cruel at first sight would appear to be the law of nature, as regards the individual; but so merciful when we consider the welfare of the race.

MORAL INSANITY

George Henry Savage, 'Moral insanity', *Journal of Mental Science*, 27 (July 1881), 147–9, 150–2.

Savage here takes ideas of inherited insanity to their logical conclusion, and considers the ways in which moral insanity can reveal itself even in young children. Two of his patients at Bethlem give birth to babies who 'were saturated with insanity while still in the womb'. Ideas of moral insanity have now become detached from their origins in moral management, and form part of the pessimistic discourse of degeneration of the closing decades of the century. See also Section V. 3.

In attempting to define moral insanity it is easier to describe what it is not than to come to a comprehensive definition which will include all the cases falling into this group, and no others; and, by way of clearing up the condition, I would say that I look upon the moral relationships, so called, of the individual, as among the highest of his mental possessions, that long after the evolution of the mere organic lower parts, the moral side of man developed; that the recognition of property and of right in property developed with the appreciation of the value of human life, so that the control of one's passions, and of one's desires for possession, and of one's passion for power developed quite late in man, and, as might be expected, the last and highest acquisitions are those which are lost most readily. It is frequently noticed that in cases in which slow progressive nervous change takes place the moral relationships are the first, or among the first, to be affected [. . .] From this point we shall have to notice moral insanity, it being in many cases a state or stage of mental disease, and not a fixed or permanent condition itself; so that in very many, if not in all, acute cases of insanity there is a period of moral perversion, just as in nearly all such cases there is a period of mental depression. [. . .] The cases of moral insanity are best considered under the heads of 'primary' or 'secondary,' and when speaking of 'primary' I would refer to those cases which, from the first development, have some peculiarity or eccentricity of character exhibited purely on their social side. Such cases may be divided into the morally eccentric and the truly insane. The eccentric person who neglects his relationship to his fellow men and to the society and social position into which he was born must be looked upon as morally insane. Other cases seem from infancy prone to wickedness, and I would most emphatically state my belief that very many so-called spoiled children are nothing more nor less than children who are morally of unsound mind, and that the spoiled child owes quite as much to his inheritance as to his education. In many cases, doubtless, the parent who begets a nervous child is very likely to further spoil such child by bad or

unsuitable education. In considering these latter cases—those that from childhood show some peculiarity of temper and character—it is all-important to
remember that inheritance of neurosis plays a very prominent part indeed—that,
in fact, the inheritance of neurosis may mean that the children are naturally
unstable and unfitted to control their lower natures; that they come into the
world unfitted to suit themselves to their surroundings; and, but for the conventional states of society, would soon lose their places and become exterminated.
[. . .]

   As seen in children, the primary moral insanity may be due almost entirely to
inheritance of neurosis, or it may be due to some physical disease. It has probably
been associated in some cases with a condition that has ended in tubercular disease either in the brain or lungs; in fact, the patients are to be considered unstable from birth. Undoubtedly injury or bad treatment may have had something to
do with their condition. In cases of this kind it is not very uncommon to find
some genius, or, at all events, some precocity, and in some morally insane children one is disgusted to find not only precocity in some lines of intellectual life,
but a precocity of the animal passions also. Sexual desires are developed at an
unusually early—in fact, sometimes at an infantine—age. The moral insanity
may show itself before five years of age, though this is rare. In my experience it
is seen to come on in these cases between five and ten. I have seen two cases,
born of patients who were in Bethlem while they were pregnant, so that the children were saturated with insanity while still in the womb. The mothers told me
that these infants seemed to be perfect little devils from birth. In both cases the
mothers had had other children, and were well acquainted with the ordinary
troubles of maternity, but the children which they bore after they themselves had
been insane were the most fretful, the most exacting, and the most restless that
they had ever had any experience of. The prospect of life in these children was,
however, so small that there was a speedy issue to the terrible troubles that I
believe might be considered as the earliest examples of moral insanity. I may be
thought to be going rather far in attributing morality to infants, but I think that
as a complete investigation of these cases is required, it is better to record such
facts as the above, putting my own interpretation upon them, and allowing my
readers the same privilege, so they may agree with me these infants were suffering from moral perversion or not, as they please. The morally insane child generally begins to evidence the fact by persistent lying, and I have seen one or two
instructive cases in which the power of romancing as a genius and the power or
habit of lying was scarcely to be distinguished. In one case I was consulted by a
father, a most honest and straightforward man, who was almost heartbroken
because his only daughter—he having four healthy and normal-minded sons—
could not, as he expressed it, tell the truth; but when, on investigation, I enquired
whether she told lies to her own advantage or to the advantage of other
people, I found that nothing of the sort was the case, but that she had a habit of

romancing, and on every available occasion would tell her parents the most extraordinary tales of her adventures, and of the people whom she had met, and what they said to her, without malice and without truth. In other cases the lying is of a lower order, so that the child lies either to damage those who are injurious to him or against whom he has a spite, or he lies on every occasion to cover his faults or to escape well-merited punishment. These, of course, are very natural failings of all children, but the morally insane child does it persistently, and with such wonderful power that he lies like truth. At the same time that the child takes to lying he probably takes also to stealing. These two are the most common, and one is associated with the other in so far that the child steals, and lies to conceal his thefts. Another class of patients take to cruelty, and become not only bullies but unmitigated brutes, torturing anything in their power, beginning with the smaller animals and birds, and gradually, as they gain confidence, torturing their school-fellows. This last type of boy not uncommonly develops further—into the masturbator, and in this capacity works endless harm in schools, taking all sorts of advantages over smaller and weaker children. In some cases I have seen the children develop so-called pyromania, and one boy, whose case I knew, set fire to every house that he was sent to after he had been there for a short time. In other cases the same thing has happened, and without rhyme or reason, and often for the mere love of seeing a blaze. These people will set light to house, church, or haystack. In the more truly morally insane it seems to be done out of spite or malice, and not absolutely wantonly, but no amount of teaching, training, or threatening seems sufficient to prevent these patients following out their evil ways. To my mind, one of the most marked characteristics of this state is the fact that experience of punishment does not seem to affect them; so that the boy punished to-day will repeat his crime to-morrow, and if he learns anything, it is only to be more deeply cunning or more completely brutal. In tracing the development of these symptoms I have noticed the relative periods at which they appear. At puberty, often, children who have been morally insane before, but controllable, become quite uncontrollable; and I have seen several cases in which such patients had to be secluded shortly after the age of puberty in consequence of their disgusting and lascivious conduct. In one or more cases I have seen education, home life, and careful discipline work a slight improvement in young cases, and by punishing and watching some good has been done up to the time of puberty, but then, as it were, the whole thing was started afresh, and the result was disastrous. The chief characteristic of the moral insanity of pubescence is the uncontrolled sexual passion exhibiting itself in self-abuse, unrestrained sexual intercourse, even with near relations, and bestiality of the lowest description.

Section V
Heredity, Degeneration, and Modern Life

Heredity, Degeneration, and Modern Life

> Heredity, indeed, is a specific memory: it is to the species what memory is
> to the individual.

T. H. Ribot, *Heredity* (1875)

During the second half of the nineteenth century accounts of mental instability
and concepts of individual identity were recast within the contentious arena of
post-Darwinian theory. The earlier optimistic beliefs in the benefits of progress
gave way to fears about the crises it brought in its wake, and these worries
encompassed all aspects of social change, all forms of psychological and cultural
development. These anxieties were widespread in France, Germany, and Italy as
well as in Britain, and as existing concerns about the hereditary transmission of
physical and mental traits and fears of the long-term decline of families and civilizations took on a new significance, the concept of *degeneration* took hold as a
widespread explanation of social and cultural divisions.[1] It had long been claimed
that 'civilization' was only gained at the cost of nervous exhaustion and premature mental collapse. George Cheyne's warning in *The English Malady* in 1733
that the English were peculiarly susceptible to insanity was reinforced by
Thomas Trotter in *A View of the Nervous Temperament* (1807), where he compared
the 'chaste, temperate and abstemious' 'savage tribes' of the New World with the
moral and physical decay that threatened to engulf modern society. In the late
nineteenth century, however, these anxieties took new and distinct forms. For
the middle classes the main danger was of nervous depletion or 'neurasthenia' (a
term used widely in America and to a lesser extent in Britain); the body only contained a limited amount of 'nervous force' which could be prematurely drained
by excessive brain work or other kinds of mental strain.[2] The decline in the therapeutic practice of moral management for the ever-increasing pauper population
of the now vast state asylums contributed to and was reinforced by a growing
sense that chronic insanity was an inevitable by-product of industrial society.
This assumption is questioned here in the extract from Andrew Wynter's article;
but both middle- and working-class patients now posed a threat not only to
themselves and contemporary society but also to the future, as 'the acquired ill
of the parent becomes the inborn infirmity of the offspring' (so Maudsley put it);
the self is seen not as an individual so much as a link in a long-term genealogy.

---

[1] For a full account of the impact of theories of degeneration on late nineteenth-century culture,
see William Greenslade, *Culture, Degeneration and the Novel* (Cambridge: Cambridge University
Press, 1994), and Daniel Pick, *Faces of Degeneration: A European Disorder c.1849–c.1918* (Cambridge:
Cambridge University Press, 1989).

[2] See Janet Oppenheim, *'Shattered Nerves': Doctors, Patients and Depression in Victorian England*
(Oxford: Oxford University Press, 1991).

Late nineteenth-century theories of mental degeneration drew on and adapted different sources in stressing the overwhelming power of inheritance, and in them heredity itself takes on a range of complex meanings. One important influence was contemporary French psychiatry, which had started to emphasize the hereditary aspects of insanity in the 1850s, and this reinforced the existing view in Britain that madness could be transmitted between generations. As the extracts in the previous section have suggested, Henry Maudsley (one of the most prominent late nineteenth-century psychiatrists) did not completely abandon the possibility of curing the insane, but he was critical of his predecessors' optimism, and his gloomy pronouncements on 'the tyranny of organisation' were based not only on his own particular reading of Darwin, but more decisively on the work of the French psychologist B. A. Morel. In *Traité des dégénérescences physiques, intellectuelles et morales de l'espèce humaine* (1857), Morel had argued that the 'morbid deviation' of degeneration had become endemic in modern civilization, working its way through the generations of suspect families through the stages of nervousness, eccentricity, insanity, idiocy, and finally extinction, and T. A. Ribot gave this family pathology a wider dimension in his description of the decline of nations and civilizations. But the existence of these 'degenerate' types also suggested that some groups may not become extinct—they might flourish as a lower form of life, and this involved various kinds of reinterpretation and adaptation of evolutionary theory.

In England it was the biologist Edwin Ray Lankester who argued most explicitly that Darwin's theory of natural selection called for reassessment. *Degeneration: A Chapter in Darwinism* (1880) maintained that while most species progressed from simpler to more complex form of life, not all did. Some species—certain kinds of crustaceans for example—represented a form of arrested development in which they became adapted to *less* complex environments, he claimed. Lankester's fears that a similar fate to that of the barnacles may befall humanity may have been extreme, but they were widely discussed (their impact can be seen on H. G. Wells's story *The Time Machine* of 1895 for example) and they formed a strand in a cluster of contentious ideas that permeated late Victorian intellectual culture and spanned the political spectrum. The long-term changes that Lankester feared were premissed on the argument, set out most fully by Ernst Haeckel, that *ontogeny* recapitulates *phylogeny*—that the development of the individual from embryo to adult was a performance in miniature of the evolution of the species as a whole.[3] The concept of hereditary degeneration also involved questioning Darwin's stress on the role of chance in *The Origin of Species*, and returning to the earlier theory proposed by Lamarck that characteristics acquired by the parent are passed on to the next generation. Moreover, Darwin himself became increasingly 'Lamarckian' in his later writ-

[3] For a full account, see Stephen Jay Gould, *Ontogeny and Phylogeny* (Cambridge, Mass.: Harvard University Press, 1977).

ings. The argument that environmental factors played an important role in heredity did not necessarily lead to pessimistic fatalism—it could be forcefully deployed to argue for the urgent need to improve the appalling conditions of the casual poor as the spectre of urban degeneration fostered fears of a pauperized underclass flourishing in city slums, their criminal tendencies passed on, with interest, to their children.[4] It was the German biologist August Weismann who challenged this view, and his proposition that environmental adaptation was relatively insignificant and that characteristics were passed from parents to children through the 'germ plasm' could be used in turn to strengthen arguments for the all-powerful influence of heredity.[5] Writers extrapolated from arguments based in biological theory to argue for and against a wide range of social and political policies, and while some of them—most notably T. H. Huxley—objected to such crude analogies, the paradigm remained virtually inescapable.

This stress on inheritance and the transmission of acquired traits from parents to children contributed to the growing centrality of childhood in late nineteenth-century discussion of individual and social development.[6] The idea that the child's growth should be carefully guarded and controlled was nothing new. Manuals on the moral management of middle-class children and their particular susceptibility to nervous complaints were popular throughout the nineteenth century, and as we have seen in the debates on memory, mental physiologists such as Carpenter argued that the moral education of children was important precisely because early impressions never entirely disappeared but remained latent. The concern over the plight of factory children and child 'savages' running wild in the cities in the early and middle part of the century had been based on fears for the future health of society as well as the welfare of the individual child. But now these anxieties took on a new urgency in the context of degenerative discourse. For here the child was perceived as facing both backwards and forwards, recalling an earlier stage of human development and representing the legacy of the present to be transmitted to future generations, and this consciousness permeated the analysis of children's physical and mental health in educational and psychological theory.

The inverse side of the fear that the slum child's degeneracy would become endemic was the alarm that working- and middle-class children alike would be rushed through the process of evolution with unseemly haste, their minds

---

[4] We do not have space to include material on 'urban degeneration' in this anthology; see Gareth Stedman Jones, *Outcast London: A Study of the Relationship between the Classes in Victorian London* (Oxford: Clarendon Press, 1971).

[5] See G. R. Moore, *The Post-Darwinian Controversies: A Study of the Protestant Struggle to Come to Terms with Darwin in Great Britain and America, 1870–1900* (Cambridge: Cambridge University Press, 1979).

[6] See Carolyn Steedman, *Childhood, Culture and Class in Britain: Margaret Macmillan, 1860–1931* (London: Virago, 1990), and Carolyn Steedman, *Strange Dislocations: Childhood and the Idea of Human Interiority 1780–1930* (London: Virago, 1995).

collapsing under the burden of too much knowledge. Herbert Spencer had argued that the child's mind needs to be allowed to grow at its natural pace in his influential essays on education in 1861, and the anxieties about 'brain forcing' expressed here by James Crichton-Browne were part of the wider concern about nervous collapse accompanying the pressures of modern life. However, they also contributed to the discussions about existing educational methods that were thrown into sharp relief by the introduction of compulsory universal elementary education that followed the Education Acts of 1870, 1876, and 1880. At the same time writers in the growing field of child psychology were intrigued by the growing consciousness and abilities of the child. In evolutionary terms, they suggested, children were both the culmination of hereditary influences in the present and the living memory of a primitive past—'diamond editions of remote ancestors, full of savage whims and impulses' as James Crichton-Browne put it. In 1877 the newly established journal *Mind* carried two formative articles on the growth of consciousness in the infant, one by the eminent French writer Hippolyte Taine, the other by Darwin (based on his own observations), and already by 1881 the influential child psychologist James Sully is jokingly describing the spectacle of the male scientist invading the female realm of the nursery and examining the infant as a new kind of specimen. As the extracts here from James Sully and George Romanes's work suggest, this 'primitive' stage in the development of the mind, always present beneath adult consciousness, was at once the clue to the emergence of human consciousness and the trace of its early origins; the playfulness and spontaneity of children were the key to understanding the process of human development as well as to their own future health.

The idea that the 'savagery' of childhood must be both acknowledged and controlled depended on and contributed to ideas about 'race' and racial difference that had become almost completely dominant by the 1870s. Racial theory in nineteenth-century ethnography and anthropology adapted and reinterpreted the debate between contrasting eighteenth-century explanations of physical and cultural difference and human origin. On the one hand the *monogenists* supported the Christian argument that humanity was descended from a common ancestor; on the other was the *polygenic* view that different human races were in fact different species.[7] Here we include a sample of the most significant participants, first James Cowles Prichard (whose ethnographic work was known before his writings on mental disease), who maintained that notions of human variety should be based as much on ethnography and philology as physiological comparisons. Prichard argued that it was through shared cultural practices that one could recognize humanity's underlying unity—and it is in this essentially moral

7 For overviews of Victorian theories of race and the development of anthropological theory, see Nancy Stepan, *The Idea of Race in Science: Great Britain 1800–1960* (London: Macmillan, 1982), Robert J. C. Young, *Colonial Desire: Hybridity in Theory, Culture and Race* (London: Routledge, 1995) and George Stocking, *Victorian Anthropology* (New York: Free Press, 1987).

concept of identity that the connections between his ethnographic and psychological writings emerge. Acknowledging the instability of the concept of 'race', Prichard made a clear distinction between *species*, *races*, and *varieties* in order to argue through analogy that there is far less variation between human types (such as Chinese and Europeans) than within other species; that there was no such thing as a 'pure' race. The growing obsession with measuring and classifying physical characteristics played a key part in the re-emergence of the polygenist preoccupation with difference and type, reframed within evolutionary theories of descent, turning, and crucially, on the concept of *hybridity*.

Do different races form stable types which cannot ultimately mix with one another? Nineteenth-century theories of race (in the broad and narrow sense) hinged on this question. Earlier in the century the eminent French scientist Georges Cuvier had argued that while humanity might have a common origin, three distinct racial types, each developing in isolation, could be identified, and within these parameters he proposed a hierarchy of racial varieties which he based on a hypothetical correlation between brain size and intelligence. Cuvier was critical of phrenology, but his concept of the relationship between the shape of the brain and mental capacity was in tune with the ways in which phrenology, for all its acknowledgement of the possibility of adaptability and self-control, contributed to static and deterministic theories of race in the early nineteenth century, and would contribute to the obsession with brain size and weight in later years. It helped to shape the intellectual climate within which polygenic ideas would re-emerge, as ethnography increasingly gave way to an anthropology rooted in the idea of biological difference during the second part of the century. The polygenic case had been aggressively made in Britain by Robert Knox in *The Races of Men* (1850), which extrapolated from Cuvier's work to argue that each race would work out their own destiny, that intermarriage was doomed to fail, and that each group needed to stay in its own native climate as it could never thrive in a foreign environment—an argument which led him to a kind of separatist anti-colonialism. The polygenic argument gained increasing intellectual respectability, however, with the publication of Paul Broca's *On the Phenomena of Hybridity in the Genus Homo* ten years later, which argued that the crossing of 'close' races might be both possible and beneficial, but not 'distant ones'. Darwin drew on Broca's work, and though he ultimately refuted notions of racial purity in *The Descent of Man*, his model of development nonetheless contributed to the claim that 'lower' races are trapped in a state of perpetual childhood. Conversely, the co-founder of evolutionary theory, A. R. Wallace, completely inverted these arguments about 'brain size' in order to stress that the craniums of 'primitive' races were far larger than was strictly necessary, that all races contained infinite and undeveloped potential—though this, of course, did nothing to challenge the idea that different groups were at different stages of development.

The diverse strands of these debates converged around the controversial question of women's education in the late nineteenth century, as the earlier discussions of the relationship between women's minds and bodies are both reasserted and challenged with the emergence of an articulate and forceful women's movement. As these extracts on 'sex in mind and in education' suggest, concepts of degeneration could be used by those arguing both for and against women's access to higher education. Both sides based their arguments on women's higher moral role and guardian of the future health of the race.[8] Herbert Spencer and T. H. Huxley present the two sides of the case for 'natural' sexual difference— Spencer disturbed by the image of the spinsterish bluestocking, Huxley drawn to the 'sweet girl graduate'; note too how Huxley bases his arguments for women to be given the opportunity to develop their 'natural' ability on an even more fundamental notion of race. We include Maudsley's infamous attack on women's higher education here and Elizabeth Garrett Anderson's trenchant rebuttal; it is significant that Maudsley is modifying his own argument in *The Physiology and Pathology of Mind*, where he stresses that women's 'constitutional weakness' has been created by the restrictions of their education and lives. In the concluding piece George Romanes both applies Darwin's analysis of natural selection to contemporary women and demonstrates the inconsistencies of Darwin's arguments, concluding with a qualified defence of feminism. These ambivalent arguments would be extended with the development of sexology in the 1890s, when the homosexual, or 'invert' is constructed as a specific biological type; seen, on the one hand, as the expression of the degeneracy and sterility of modern culture, on the other as another human variation rather than moral deviant, one whose 'inversion' is inherited, beyond individual control. The discourse of degeneration may have been ubiquitous in the last part of the nineteenth century, but it could take very different forms and have widely divergent cultural and political meanings.

[8] On debates on women's higher education and feminists' use of evolutionary theory, see for example, Lucy Bland, *Banishing the Beast: English Feminism and Sexual Morality 1885–1914* (Harmondsworth: Penguin, 1995), Carol Dyhouse, *Girls Growing up in Late Victorian and Edwardian England* (London: Routledge and Kegan Paul, 1981), Lorna Duffin, 'Prisoners of progress: women and evolution', in Sara Delamont and Lorna Duffin (eds.), *The Nineteenth-Century Woman: Her Cultural and Physical World* (London: Croom Helm, 1978).

1. Nervous Economies: Morbidity and Modernity

MERCHANTS AND MASTER MANUFACTURERS

Charles Turner Thackrah, *The Effects of Arts, Trades and Professions, and of Civic States and Habits of Living: With Suggestions for the Removal of Many of the Agents which Produce Disease, and Shorten the Duration of Life* (1831), 2nd edn. (London: Longman, Rees, Orme, Brown, Green and Longman, 1832), 164–7.

In the first major systematic attempt to study the psychological effects of various industrial occupations, Thackrah divides the population into five classes: operatives; dealers; master-manufacturers and merchants; independent man and professional men. The following describes the dangers facing 'merchants and master manufacturers'.

Of the causes of disease, anxiety of mind is one of the most frequent and important. When we walk the streets of large commercial towns, we can scarcely fail to remark the hurried gait and care-worn features of the well-dressed passengers. Some young men, indeed, we may see, with countenances possessing natural cheerfulness and colour; but these appearances rarely survive the age of manhood. *Cuvier*[1] closes an eloquent description of animal existence and change, with the conclusion that 'Life is a state of Force.' What he would urge in a physical view, we may more strongly urge in a moral. Civilization has changed our

[1] Georges Cuvier (1769–1832); pioneer in the field of comparative anatomy, Professor of Natural History at the Collège de France from 1799 and three years later at the Jardin des Plantes. Author of *Tableaux élémentaires de l'histoire naturelle des animaux* (1798) and *Le Règne animal* (1817). See also Introduction to this section.

character of mind as well as of body. We live in a state of unnatural excitement;—unnatural, because it is partial, irregular, and excessive. Our muscles waste for *want* of action: our nervous system is worn out by *excess* of action. Vital energy is drawn from the operations for which nature designed it, and devoted to operations which nature never contemplated. [. . .] The various disorders, generally known under the name of indigestion, disorders dependent on a want of circulation of blood through the bowels, biliary derangements, constipation, and headache, are well known to be the general attendants on trade, closely pursued. Indeed in almost every individual, this absorbing principle produces one or other of the various maladies to which I have alluded. More marked is the effect, when anxiety is added. This greatly reduces the functions of the stomach; it produces flatulency, and often diarrhœa; it sometimes affects even the kidneys; it almost always, when long-continued, produces permanent disease of the liver. Scirrhus of the stomach moreover, medullary and fungoid tumours,[2] and other malignant diseases, occur most frequently among the victims of mental depression and care.

The physical evils of commercial life would be considerably reduced, if men reflected that the success of business may be prevented by the very means used to promote it. Excessive application and anxiety, by disordering the animal economy, weaken the mental powers. Our opinions are affected by states of the body, and our judgment often perverted. If a clear head be required in commercial transactions, a healthy state of the body is of the first importance; and a healthy state of body is incompatible with excessive application of mind,—the want of exercise and of fresh air. But subjects like this find no entry in the books of our merchants. Intent on their avocations, they strangely overlook the means necessary for pursuing them with success. They find, too late, that they have sacrificed the body to the mind.

And why this perversion of nature? Why do we think and toil? To obtain wealth, and thus increase our means of happiness. But will wealth compensate for the evils which attend it? Its acquisition produces—will its possession remove, functional or structural maladies? Will it banish those thousand nervous and hypochrondriacal feelings which produce more misery than even organic disease? And when we have sacrificed health and abbreviated life for the acquisition of property, what happiness have we got in exchange? Every moralist tells us, or rather reminds us, of the insufficiency, the vanity of riches. The subject is trite and hacknied: the truth is admitted, approved, and forgotten.

[2] *Scirrus* Hard tumour as early stage of cancer; *medullary tumours*: bone marrow cancer.

LUNACY ON THE INCREASE?

Andrew Wynter (unsigned), 'Lunatic asylums', *Quarterly Review*, 101 (Apr. 1857), 390–3.

This comes towards the end of Wynter's detailed overview of the current state of asylums, where he responds to the fear of a national 'epidemic' of insanity that accompanied the rapid growth of state asylums during the second half of the century. See also the extract in Section IV. 1.

It has been asserted by some psychologists that lunacy is on the increase, and that its rapid development of late years has been consequent upon the increased activity of the national mind. This statement is certainly startling, and calculated to arrest the attention of all thoughtful men. Is it true that civilisation has called to life a monster such as that which appalled Frankenstein? Is it a necessity of progress that it shall ever be accompanied by that fearful black rider which, like Despair, sits behind it? Does mental development mean increased mental decay? If these questions were truly answered in the affirmative, we might indeed sigh for the golden time when

'Wild in woods the noble savage ran',[1]

for it would be clear that the nearer humanity strove to attain towards divine perfection, the more it was retrograding towards a state inferior to that of the brute creation. A patient examination, however, of the question entirely negatives such a conclusion. [. . .]

Such is the burthen of the story of all those psychologists who believe that insanity is fast gaining upon us; but if 'in the ever-widening circle of objects calculated to influence desire and impel to effort we find so many additional agencies for tasking the mental energies, and thereby deranging the healthy equilibrium which binds the faculties together,' it should appear that those classes of society which are in the van of civilisation should be the chief sufferers. Bankers, great speculators, merchants, engineers, statesmen, philosophers, and men of letters—those who work with the brain rather than with their hands, should afford the largest proportion to the alleged increase of insanity. How does the matter really stand? In the Report of the Commissioners in Lunacy for the year 1847 we find the total number of private patients of the middle and upper classes, then under confinement in private asylums, amounted to 4649. Now, if we skip eight years, and refer to the Report of 1855, we find that there were only

---

[1] John Dryden, *The Conquest of Granada*, Part 1, i. iii.

"in asylums"

4557 patients under confinement, or about 96 less, notwithstanding the increase of population during that period. If we compare the number of pauper lunatics under confinement at these two different periods we shall find a widely-different state of things; for in 1847 there were 9654 in our public and private asylums, whilst in 1855 they numbered 15,822. In other words, our pauper lunatics would *appear* to have increased 6170 in eight years, or upwards of 64 per cent. It is this extraordinary increase of pauper lunatics in the county asylums which has frightened some psychologists from their propriety, and led them to believe that insanity is running a winning race with the healthy intellect. But these figures, if they mean anything, prove that it is not the intellect of the country that breeds insanity, but its ignorance, as it cannot be for one moment contended that the great movements now taking place in the world originate with the labouring classes. We shall be told, we know, that there is a constant descent of patients from private asylums to the public asylums; that the professional man and the tradesman, after expending the means of his friends and family for a year or two in the vain hope of a speedy cure, becomes necessarily in the end a pauper lunatic, and that this stream aids to swell the numbers in the county institution. Allowing its due weight to this explanation—and those who know public asylums are well aware how small, comparatively speaking, is the educated element—yet as the same disturbing element in the calculation obtained at both periods, we may safely conclude that the figures are not thereby essentially altered.

A still more convincing proof that mental ruin springs rather from mental torpidity than from mental stimulation, is to be found by comparing the proportion of lunatics to the population in the rural and the manufacturing districts. [. . .] The Hodges of England, who know nothing of the march of intellect, who are entirely guiltless of speculations of any kind, contribute far more inmates to the public lunatic asylums than the toil-worn artisans of Manchester or Liverpool, who live in the great eye of the world and keep step with the march of civilisation, even if they do but bring up its rear. Isolation is a greater cause of mental ruin than aggregation—our English fields can afford cretins as plentifully as the upland valleys of the mountain range seldom visited by the foot of the traveller; whilst, on the other hand, in the workshop and the public assembly, 'As iron weareth iron, so man sharpeneth the face of his friend.'[2]

If we required further proof of the groundless nature of the alarm that mental activity was destroying the national mind, we should find it in the well-ascertained fact that the proportion of lunatics is greater among females than males. It may also be urged that Quakers, who pride themselves on the sedateness of their conduct, furnish much more than their share; but for this singular result their system of intermarriage is doubtless much to blame. Still the fact remains that within a period of eight years, extending from 1847 to 1855, an increase of

[2] Proverbs 27: 17.

64 per cent, took place in our pauper lunatic asylums. These figures, however, afford no more proof of the increase of pauper lunatics, than the increase of criminal convictions since the introduction of a milder code of laws and the appointment of the new police, afford a proof of increased crime. As the Commissioners very justly observe, medical practitioners of late years have taken a far more comprehensive as well as scientific view of insanity than formerly; and many forms of the disease now fall under their care, that were previously overlooked, when no man was considered mad unless he raved, or was an idiot. But the great cause of the increase of lunatics in our asylums is to be ascribed to the erection of the asylums themselves. With the exception of three or four Welsh counties, and two or three in the north of England, there is not a shire in England which does not possess some palatial building. These establishments, in which restraint, speaking in the ordinary acceptance of the term, is unknown, and in which the inmates are always treated with humanity, have drained the land of a lunatic population which before was scattered among villages or workhouses, amounting, according to the computation of the Commissioners, to upwards of 10,500—just as the deep wells of the metropolitan brewers have drained for miles around the shallow wells of the neighbourhood in which they are situated. For the same reason the number of lunatic paupers has declined in registered hospitals since 1847 from 384 to 185, and in 'licensed houses' from 3996 to 2313. Upon the whole we may safely predict that when these disturbing causes have ceased to act, the annual returns of the Commissioners will show, that, as the treatment of insanity is every day better understood, so the pauper lunatics in our public asylums, instead of increasing in a ratio far beyond that of the general population, show a diminished proportion.

ON THE CAUSES OF INSANITY

Henry Maudsley, *The Physiology and Pathology of Mind* (London: Macmillan, 1867), 202–6.

In his first full-length study Maudsley aims 'first to treat of mental phenomena from a physiological rather than metaphysical point of view; and secondly, to bring the manifold instructive instances presented by the unsound mind to bear upon the interpretation of the obscure problems of mental science' (Preface, p. v). The first part, focusing on physiology, draws heavily on Bain, Spencer, Laycock, and Carpenter's work; this extract is taken from the first chapter of Part 2, which aims to explore the 'relation of sound and unsound mind'.

If we admit such an increase of insanity with our present civilization, we shall be at no loss to indicate causes for it. Some would no doubt easily find in over-population the prolific parent of this as of numerous other ills to mankind. In the fierce and active struggle for existence which there necessarily is where the claimants are many and the supplies are limited, the weakest must suffer, and some of them break down into madness. As it is the distinctly manifested aim of mental development to bring man into more intimate, special, and complex relations with the rest of nature by means of patient investigations of physical laws, and a corresponding internal adaptation to external relations, it is no marvel, it appears indeed inevitable, that those who, either from inherited weakness or some other debilitating causes, have been rendered unequal to the struggle of life should be ruthlessly crushed out as abortive beings in nature. They are the waste thrown up by the silent but strong current of progress; they are the weak crushed out by the strong in the mortal struggle for development; they are examples of decaying reason thrown off by vigorous mental growth, the energy of which they testify. Everywhere and always 'to be weak is to be miserable.'[1]

If we want a striking illustration of the operation of this hard law, we may see it in the appropriation by man, the stronger sex, of all the means of subsistence by labour, to the almost entire exclusion of women, the feebler sex. Because, however, women are necessary to the gratification of man's passions, indispensable to the comfort of his life, they are not crushed out of existence, they are only kept in a state of subjection and dependence. The woman who can find no opening for her honourable energies in the present social system, is yet willingly permitted to gain a precarious livelihood by selling the charms of her person to gratify the lusts of her lord and master. Under the institution of marriage she has the position of a subordinate, herself debarred from the noble aims and activities of life, and ministering, in a silent manner, to the comfort and greatness of him who appropriates the labour and enjoys the rewards. Practically, then, woman has no honourable outlook but marriage in our present social system: if that aim is missed, all else is missed. Through generations her character has been formed with that chief aim; it has been made feeble by long habit of dependence; by the circumstances of her position the sexual life has been undesignedly developed at the expense of the intellectual. Now, therefore, when the luxuries thought necessary in social life are so many and costly that marriage is much avoided by men, there is a cruel stress laid upon many a gentle nature. In this disappointment of their life-aim, and the long train of consequences, physical and moral, which it unconsciously draws after it, there is, I believe, a fertile source of insanity among women. [. . .]

Another way in which over-population leads to deterioration of the health of a community is by the overcrowding and the insanitary condition of dwelling-

[1] John Milton, *Paradise Lost*, I, 157. See p. 153, n. 2.

houses which it occasions in towns. Not fevers only, but scrofula, perhaps phthisis, and certainly general deterioration of nutrition, are thus generated and transmitted as evil heritages to future generations: the acquired ill of the parent becomes the inborn infirmity of the offspring. It is not that the child necessarily inherits the particular disease of the parent, for diseases unquestionably undergo transformation through generations; but it does often inherit a constitution in which there is a certain inherent aptitude to some kind of morbid degeneration, or a constitution destitute of that reserve power necessary to meet the trying occasions of life. [. . .]

Perhaps one, and certainly not the least, of the ill effects which come from some of the conditions of our present civilization is seen in the general dread and disdain of poverty, in the eager passion to become rich. The practical gospel of the age, testified everywhere by faith and works, is that of money-getting; men are estimated mainly by the amount of their wealth, take social rank accordingly, and consequently bend all their energies to acquire that which gains them esteem and influence. The result is that in the higher departments of trade and commerce speculations of all sorts are eagerly entered on, and that many people are kept in a continued state of excitement and anxiety by the fluctuations of the money market. In the lower branches of trade there is the same eager desire for petty gains; and the continued absorption of the mind in these small acquisitions generates a littleness of mind and meanness of spirit, where it does not lead to actual dishonesty, which are nowhere displayed in a more pitiable form that in certain petty tradesmen. The occupation which a man is entirely engaged in does not fail to modify his character, and the reaction upon the individual's nature of a life which is being spent with the sole aim of becoming rich, is most baneful. It is not that the fluctuations of excitement unhinge the merchant's mind and lead to maniacal outbreaks, although that does sometimes happen; it is not that failure in the paroxysm of some crisis prostrates his energies and makes him melancholic, although that also is occasionally witnessed; but it is that the exclusiveness of his life-aim and occupation too often saps the moral or altruistic element in his nature, makes him become egoistic, formal, and unsympathetic, and in his person deteriorates the nature of humanity. What is the result? If one conviction has been fixed in my mind more distinctly than another by observation of instances, it is that it is extremely unlikely such a man will beget healthy children; that, in fact, it is extremely likely that the deterioration of nature, which he has acquired, will be transmitted as an evil heritage to his children. In several instances in which the father has toiled upwards from poverty to vast wealth, with the aim and hope of founding a family, I have witnessed the results in a degeneracy, mental and physical, of his offspring, which has sometimes gone as far as extinction of the family in the third or fourth generation. When the evil is not so extreme as madness or ruinous vice, the savour of a mother's influence perhaps having been present, it may still be manifest in an instinctive cunning and duplicity, and an extreme selfishness of nature—a nature not having the capacity of a true moral conception or altruistic feeling. Whatever opinion other more experienced observers may hold, I cannot but think, after what I have seen, that the extreme passion for getting rich, absorbing the whole energies of a life, does predispose to mental degeneration in the offspring—either to moral defect, or to moral and intellectual deficiency, or to outbreaks of positive insanity under the conditions of life.

OVERWORK

Charles Henry Felix Routh, *On Overwork and Premature Mental Decay: Its Treatment* (1876), 3rd edn. (London: Baillière, Tindall and Cox, 1878), 4–5, 15–17, 19–20.

Routh's study started life as a lecture to the Medical Society of London, then as an 'unpretending pamphlet'. One of a spate of similar books on the dangers of overwork leading to the draining of 'nervous force' from the body's internal economy, it aimed to be a popular book sounding 'a warning note' about the effects on modern life on both male and female constitutions (Preface to 3rd edn.). For Routh the danger is still primarily to the individual body; increasingly though, as it is for Maudsley, the threat becomes inheritable, leading to race degeneration.

Let me first define then what I mean by premature mental decay. This latter expression in its simple meaning is clearly a disintegration of, a defective condition, a loss of, mental powers previously known to be good and sound.

In the common course of things, it occurs after a considerable amount of wear and tear of every man's brain. It is the normal goal of old age. But it is said to be premature mental decay when it occurs in a man before the time at which his intellectual vigour should have normally deteriorated. A mind thus weakened is no longer in equilibrium. It is, in fact, bordering on insanity, but which has come on prematurely. For clearly, if we understand by insanity an unsoundness of mind which is the result of functional or organic disease, or rather of a particular class of such diseases which are known to impair, weaken, or pervert the mental faculties in various ways and in different degrees, then premature mental decay is, after all, only a progress towards, if not an allied form of, a pending although unmatured insanity. Call it eccentricity, early old age, weak-mindedness, impaired reasoning power—in each and every such case the mind after all is unsound, and premature mental decay comes only to be a minor degree of, or a special form of, insanity. At any rate, none will be disposed to deny that the phenomena of premature mental decay constitute the long links of a chain, or the several steps of a ladder, which terminate, if undetected, sooner or later, in insanity. This admission is, after all, a very important one, because as kindred causes will be found productive of the two forms of disease, so we are through a full consideration of these, enabled to make not only an earlier diagnosis, but also to adopt earlier remedial measures, and thus obtain a better chance of success. [. . .]

Let us now consider what are the evidences of premature mental decay from overwork. They are, in fact, the general symptoms of exhausted nervous power; viz., general debility of the body, inability to walk even short distances without fatigue, general feeling of languor, unwillingness to any active exertion; great tendency to sweat, specially at night, but induced during the day by the slightest exertion; generally an unsteady gait. The heart's action is weak, often irregular, accompanied with palpitation, and not unfrequently with symptoms of general indigestion.

A change is gradually observed to come over the *man's mind*; and generally some peculiarity develops itself in the character, not previously noticeable in the affected person. It is not unusual in such cases to find an undue exaltation of some peculiar talent or property of the mind in a different direction, or one totally opposed to former hobbies, and what strikes one more than anything in these changes is the suddenness with which these hobbies spring up.

A man may become intensely selfish and garrulous, who was formerly generous and reticent. He takes, without any apparent reason, likes and dislikes to those with whom he is associated, often his nearest relatives, whose motives he invariably misunderstands. He becomes subject to uncontrollable fits of moroseness or bad temper. A previously careful man becomes unusually liberal, even extravagant; a remarkably modest and prudent man puts off all reserve, and becomes intensely disagreeable in genteel society; a dull man becomes a poet; a deep, far-sighted politician will become a religious controversialist; a man who, perhaps, never turned a note of music correctly, becomes a devotee to music. Sometimes the very *morale* of the mind is changed. For instance, there is an alternation in his manner of acting—one moment intensely joyous and excited, now greatly depressed—one moment friendly, the next hostile. Sometimes obstinacy develops itself to an intense degree, and nothing will move his determination; at another time he can be led as a child. Sometimes it is indecision of character, or in his opinions, which forms the prominent symptom, often the more remarkable because occurring in one heretofore known to be every ready and resolute. Frequently there is an utter inability to fix the attention on any one subject. In reading, the thread of the story or argument cannot be long followed. Again, sometimes not only is there an entire inability to arrange ideas in order, but the judgment is strangely perverted. This is clearly not from wicked intentions, as it often seems, but really from conviction. A few years ago, a London physician of great note contended that all cases of epilepsy were curable by tracheotomy. Later, another surgeon of great eminence believed that this and allied forms of nervous disease were curable by clitoridectomy.[1] These opinions gave great offence to the profession at the time, and rightly so, because they were erroneous. But here was no malice prepense, but disease, and the individuals were more deserving of pity than of persecution. And so far, in the second case, the *post mortem* appearances gave full evidence of the fact. [. . .]

It is remarkable that synchronously with this gradual deterioration of nervous power, two symptoms are observed to be almost invariably present. Want of sleep and loss of virile power. Both come on gradually, but very certainly, and their conjunction with loss of memory is always a very serious circumstance. In the first of these effects, if the case goes on it assumes more melancholy characters. Want of sleep brings its concomitants. The patient becomes extremely depressed and unhappy about himself. Very little makes him sob and weep.

Indeed, it is precisely in these cases that we find hysterical symptoms presenting themselves in the man previously strong-minded and of powerful intellect. It would seem as if he became effeminate in many of his mental emotions, and the tears and sobs are only the common evidences of his weakened powers. Hypochrondriacal to a degree, life is a perfect burden, and frequently the disease terminates in suicide. The case of a remarkably great man, a judge, who of late perished by his own hand, in which most of these symptoms were marked, will be at once recalled to the memory—an instructive, but a very sad example of overwork. The equilibrium of what was once a mighty brain no longer existed, and its function no longer regularly performed, culminated in insanity.

---

[1] Possibly a reference to Dr Isaac Baker Brown, who widely advocated and practised the removal of the clitoris as a 'cure' for female insanity. Brown was expelled from the Obstetrical Society in 1867; Routh, however, had noted with approval his use of the operation in the *British Medical Journal* in 1866. See Elaine Showalter, *The Female Malady: Women, Madness and English Culture 1830–1980* (London: Virago, 1987), 75–9.

2. Concepts of Descent and Degeneration

COMPARISON OF THE MENTAL POWERS OF MAN AND ANIMALS

Charles Darwin, *The Descent of Man, and Selection in Relation to Sex* (1871), 2nd edn. (London: John Murray, 1883), 67–8, 71, 75.

The Origin of Species by Means of Natural Selection (1859) did not explicitly deal with the human species, though Darwin concluded by suggesting that it would 'throw light' on 'the origin of man and his history'. By the time he came to prepare The Descent of Man, *many of the arguments about the interconnection of species had been accepted by naturalists, and here Darwin aimed 'to see how far the general conclusions arrived at in my former works were applicable to man'. Its aims, he stated in the Introduction, were to consider, first, 'whether man, like every other species, is descended from some other pre-existing form; secondly, the manner of his development; and thirdly, the value of the differences between the so-called races of man' (p. 2). These extracts are from chapter 3, and the discussion of Spencer's ideas with which Darwin opens refers to the account of 'organic memory' in the 1870 edition of* The Principles of Psychology. *(See section II. 4 above.)*

Although the first dawnings of intelligence, according to Mr. Herbert Spencer,* have been developed through the multiplication and co-ordination of reflex actions, and although many of the simpler instincts graduate into reflex actions, and can hardly be distinguished from them, as in the case of young animals sucking, yet the more complex instincts seem to have originated independently of intelligence. I am, however, very far from wishing to deny that instinctive actions may lose their fixed and untaught character, and be replaced

* 'The Principles of Psychology', 2nd edit. 1870, pp. 418–443.

by others performed by the aid of the free will. On the other hand, some intelligent actions, after being performed during several generations, become converted into instincts and are inherited, as when birds on oceanic islands learn to avoid man. These actions may then be said to be degraded in character, for they are no longer performed through reason or from experience. But the greater number of the more complex instincts appear to have been gained in a wholly different manner, through the natural selection of variations of simpler instinctive actions. Such variations appear to arise from the same unknown causes acting on the cerebral organisation, which induce slight variations or individual differences in other parts of the body; and those variations, owing to our ignorance, are often said to arise spontaneously. We can, I think, come to no other conclusion with respect to the origin of the more complex instincts, when we reflect on the marvellous instincts of sterile worker-ants and bees, which leave no offspring to inherit the effects of experience and of modified habits.

Although, as we learn from the above-mentioned insects and the beaver, a high degree of intelligence is certainly compatible with complex instincts, and although actions, at first learnt voluntarily can soon through habit be performed with the quickness and certainty of a reflex action, yet it is not improbable that there is a certain amount of interference between the development of free intelligence and of instinct,—which latter implies some inherited modification of the brain. Little is known about the functions of the brain, but we can perceive that as the intellectual powers become highly developed, the various parts of the brain must be connected by very intricate channels of the freest intercommunication; and as a consequence, each separate part would perhaps tend to be less well fitted to answer to particular sensations or associations in a definite and inherited—that is instinctive—manner. There seems even to exist some relation between a low degree of intelligence and a strong tendency to the formation of fixed, though not inherited habits; for as a sagacious physician remarked to me, persons who are slightly imbecile tend to act in everything by routine or habit; and they are rendered much happier if this is encouraged.

I have thought this digression worth giving, because we may easily underrate the mental powers of the higher animals, and especially of man, when we compare their actions founded on the memory of past events, on foresight, reason, and imagination, with exactly similar actions instinctively performed by the lower animals; in this latter case the capacity of performing such actions has been gained, step by step, through the variability of the mental organs and natural selection, without any conscious intelligence on the part of the animal during each successive generation. [. . .]

Most of the more complex emotions are common to the higher animals and ourselves. Every one has seen how jealous a dog is of his master's affection, if lavished on any other creature; and I have observed the same fact with monkeys. This shews that animals not only love, but have desire to be loved. Animals manifestly feel emulation. They love approbation or praise; and a dog carrying a basket for his master exhibits in a high degree self-complacency or pride. There can, I think, be no doubt that a dog feels shame, as distinct from fear, and something very like modesty when begging too often for food. A great dog scorns the snarling of a little dog, and this may be called magnanimity. Several observers have stated that monkeys certainly dislike being laughed at; and they sometimes invent imaginary offences. In the Zoological Gardens I saw a baboon who always got into a furious rage when his keeper took out a letter or book and read it aloud to him; and his rage was so violent that, as I witnessed on one occasion, he bit his own leg till the blood flowed. Dogs show what may be fairly called a sense of humour, as distinct from here play; if a bit of stick or other such object be thrown to one, he will often carry it away for a short distance; and then squatting down with it on the ground close before him, will wait until his master comes quite close to take it away. The dog will then seize it and rush away in triumph, repeating the same manœuvre, and evidently enjoying the practical joke. [. . .]

Of all the faculties of the human mind, it will, I presume, be admitted that *Reason* stands at the summit. Only a few persons now dispute that animals possess some power of reasoning. Animals may constantly be seen to pause, deliberate, and resolve. It is a significant fact, that the more the habits of any particular animal are studied by a naturalist, the more he attributes to reason and the less to unlearnt instincts. In future chapters we shall see that some animals extremely low in the scale apparently display a certain amount of reason. No doubt it is often difficult to distinguish between the power of reason and that of instinct. For instance, Dr. Hayes, in his work on 'The Open Polar Sea,' repeatedly remarks that his dogs, instead of continuing to draw the sledges in a compact body, diverged and separated when they came to thin ice, so that their weight might be more evenly distributed. This was often the first warning which the travellers received that the ice was becoming thin and dangerous. Now, did the dogs act thus from the experience of each individual, or from the example of the older and wiser dogs, or from an inherited habit, that is from instinct? This instinct, may possibly have arisen since the time, long ago, when dogs were first employed by the natives in drawing their sledges; or the Arctic wolves, the parent-stock of the Esquimaux dog, may have acquired an instinct, impelling them not to attack their prey in a close pack, when on thin ice.

We can only judge by the circumstances under which actions are performed, whether they are due to instinct, or to reason, or to the mere association of ideas: this latter principle, however, is intimately connected with reason.

HEREDITY AND THE LAW OF EVOLUTION

Théodule A. Ribot, *Heredity: A Psychological Study of its Phenomena, Laws, Causes and Consequences* (1873), 2nd edn. (London: Henry S. King, 1875), 303–5.

Ribot begins this study by defining heredity as 'the biological law by which things endowed with life tend to repeat themselves in their descendants' (Introduction, p. 10). The first part discusses 'Physiological heredity' as a form of 'organic memory' (see Section II. 4 above); the second discusses the concept of heredity as a natural 'law' and the third considers the relationship between physical and moral, and psychological and physiological inheritance. This extract is from the fourth part ('Consequences'), and forms part of chapter 1.

Considered as an indirect cause of decline, heredity acts by way of accumulation. Every family, every people, every race brings into the world at their birth a certain amount of vitality, and of physical and moral aptitudes, which in course of time will become manifest. This evolution has for its causes the continual action and reaction between the being and its surroundings. It goes on until the family, people, or race has fulfilled its destiny, brilliant for some, distinguished for others, obscure for the majority. When this sum of vitality and of aptitudes begins to fail, decay commences. This process of decay may at first be of no moment, but heredity transmits it to the next generation, from that to the following one, and so on till the period of utter extinction, if no external cause interferes to stay the decay. Here, then, heredity is only an indirect cause of degeneration, the direct cause being the action of the environment, by which term we understand all action from without—not only climate and mode of life, but also manners, customs, religious ideas, institutions, and laws, which often are very influential in determining the degeneration of a race. In the east, the harem, with its life of absolute ignorance and complete indolence, has, through physical and moral heredity, led to the rapid decay of various nations. 'We have no harem in France,' says a naturalist, 'but there are other causes, quite different in their origin, which tend ultimately to lower the race. In our day, paternal affection, with the assistance of medical science, more certain, and possessed of more resources, makes more and more certain the future of children, by saving the lives of countless weak, deformed, or otherwise ill-constituted creatures that would surely have died in a savage race, or in our own a century or two ago. These children become men, they marry, and by heredity transmit to their descendants at least a predisposition to imperfections like their own. Sometimes both husband and wife bring each a share to this heritage. The descendants go on degenerating, and the result for the community is debasement, and, finally, the disappearance of certain groups.'*

The only way of getting a clear idea of a case of psychological and moral decay, hereditarily transmitted, is by finding for it some organic cause. The physiology and anatomy of the brain are not yet sufficiently advanced to explain it; we cannot say to what change in the brain such and such a decay of intellect, or such and such a perversion of the will, is to be attributed. But cerebral phenomena and psychical phenomena are so closely connected that a variation of the one implies a variation of the other.

This being assumed, let us take a man of average organization, physically and morally. Let us suppose that, in consequence of disease, outward circumstances, influences coming from his surroundings or from his own will, his mind is impaired, to only a trifling extent it may be, but yet permanently. Clearly heredity has nothing to do with this decay; but then, if it is transmitted to the next generation, and if, further, the same causes go on acting in the same direction, it is equally clear that heredity in turn becomes a cause of decay. And if this slow action goes on with each new generation it may end in total extinction of intellect.

These remarks also apply in every respect to nations and races: all that is required is that the destructive influences should bear, not on an isolated individual, but upon a mass of individuals. The mechanism of decay is identical in the two cases; and we are justified in the conclusion that the causes which, in the narrow world of the individual and the family, produce a considerable diminution of the intellectual forces, must produce the like effect in that agglomeration of individuals which constitutes a society.

Historians usually explain the decline of nations by their manners, institutions, and character, and in a certain sense the explanation is correct. These reasons, however, are rather vague, and, as we see, there exists a more profound, an ultimate cause—an organic cause, which can act only through heredity, but which is altogether overlooked. These organic causes will probably be ignored for some time to come, but our ignoring them will not do away with them. As for ourselves, who have, for purposes of our own, attempted to study the decay of the Lower Empire—the most amazing instance of decay presented by history—tracing step by step this degeneration through a thousand years: seeing, in their works of art, the plastic talent of the Greeks fade away by degrees, and result in the stiff drawing, and in the feeble, motionless figures of the Paleology;[1] seeing the imagination of the Greeks wither up and become reduced to a few platitudes of description; seeing their lively wit change to empty babbling and senile dotage; seeing all the characters of mind so disappear that the great men of their latter period would

---

* *Revue des Cours Scientifiques*, vol. vi, p. 690.

[1] Byzantine; after Paleologus, Byzantine family of eleventh and twelfth centuries.

elsewhere pass only for mediocrities—it appears to us that beneath these visible, palpable facts—the only facts on which historians dwell—we discern the slow, blind, unconscious working of nature in the millions of human beings who were decayed, though they knew it not, and who transmitted to their descendants a germ of death, each generation adding to it somewhat of its own.

Thus, in every people, whether it be rising or falling, there exists always, as the groundwork of every change, a secret working of the mind, and consequently of a part of the organism, and this of necessity comes under the law of heredity.

ONTOGENY AND PHYLOGENY

Ernst Haeckel, *The Evolution of Man: A Popular Exposition of the Principal Points of Human Ontology and Phylogeny*, 2 vols. (London: C. Kegan Paul, 1879), i. 6–9.

Haeckel had first proposed the theory that the history of the individual recapitulates that of the species in The General Morphology of Organisms *(1866). Here his aim is not only to 'render the facts of human germ-history accessible to a wider circle of educated people' (Preface to the first edition), but also to provide a history of the concepts of ontology and phylogeny from Aristotle to Darwin. This extract is from chapter 1, 'The fundamental law of the evolution of organisms'.*

These two divisions of our science, Ontogeny, or the history of the germ, Phylogeny, or the history of the tribe, are most intimately connected, and the one cannot be understood without the other. The close intertwining of both branches, the increased proportions which germ-history and tribal history lend to each other, alone raise Biogeny (or the history of organic evolution, in the widest sense) to the rank of a philosophic natural science. The connection between the two is not external and superficial, but deeply internal and causal. Our knowledge of this connection has been but very recently obtained; it is most clearly and accurately expressed in the comprehensive statement which I call 'the fundamental law of organic evolution,' or more briefly, 'the first principle of Biogeny.'

This fundamental law, to which we shall recur again and again, and on the recognition of which depends the thorough understanding of the history of evolution, is briefly expressed in the proposition: that the History of the Germ is an epitome of the History of the Descent; or, in other words: that Ontogeny is a recapitulation of Phylogeny; or, somewhat more explicitly: that the series of

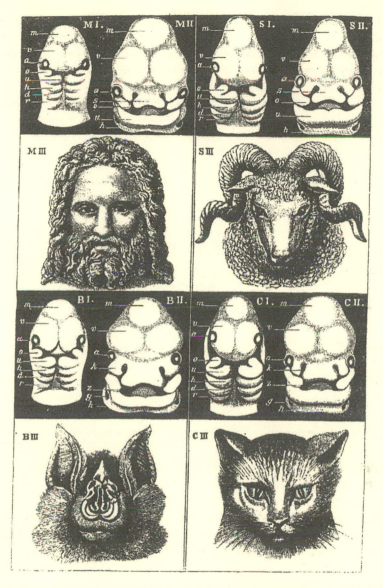

Note: M = Man; B = bat; S = sheep; C = cat.

FIG. 15. Development of the face (third stage)

forms through which the Individual Organism passes during its progress from the egg cell to its fully developed state, is a brief, compressed reproduction of the long series of forms through which the animal ancestors of that organism (or the ancestral forms of its species) have passed from the earliest periods of so-called organic creation down to the present time.

The causal nature of the relation which connects the History of the Germ (Embryology, or Ontogeny) with that of the tribe (Phylogeny) is dependent on the phenomena of Heredity and Adaptation. When these are properly understood, and their fundamental importance in determining the forms of organisms recognized, we may go a step further, and say: Phylogenesis is the mechanical cause of Ontogenesis. The Evolution of the Tribe, which is dependent on the laws of Heredity and Adaptation, effects all the events which take place in the course of the Evolution of the Germ or Embryo.

The chain of different animal forms which, according to the Theory of Descent, constitutes the series of ancestors, or chain of forefathers of every higher organism, and hence also of man, always forms a connected whole. This unbroken succession of forms may be represented by the letters of the Alphabet A, B, C, D, E, etc., down to Z, in their alphabetical order. In apparent contradiction to this, the history of the individual evolution, or the Ontogeny of most organisms show us only a fragment of this series of forms, so that the interrupted chain of embryonic forms would be represented by something like: A, B, F, H, I, K, L, etc.; or, in other cases, thus: B, D, H, L, M, N, etc. Several evolutionary forms have, therefore, usually dropped out of the originally unbroken chain of forms. In many cases also (retaining the figure of the repeated alphabet) one or more letters, representing ancestral forms, are replaced in the corresponding places among the embryonic forms by equivalent letters of another alphabet. Thus, for example, in place of the Latin B or D, a Greek B or Δ is often found. Here, therefore, the text of the biogenetic first principle is vitiated, while in the former case it was epitomized. This gives more importance to the fact that, notwithstanding this, the sequence remains the same, so that we are enabled to recognize its original order.

Indeed, there is always a complete parallelism between the two series of evolution. This is, however, vitiated by the fact that in most cases many forms which formerly existed and actually lived in the phylogenetic series are now wanting, and have been lost from the ontogenetic series of evolution. If the parallelism between the two series were perfect, and if this great fundamental law of the causal connection between Ontogeny and Phylogeny, in the strict sense of the word, had full and unconditional sway, we should only have to ascertain, with the aid of microscope and scalpel, the series of forms through which the fertilized human egg passes before it attains its complete development. Such an examination would at once give us a complete picture of the remarkable series of forms through which the animal ancestors of the human race have passed, from the beginning of organic creation to the first appearance of man. But this reproduction of the Phylogeny in the Ontogeny is complete only in rare instances, and seldom corresponds to the entire series of the letters of the alphabet. In fact, in most cases the epitome is very incomplete, and greatly altered and perverted by causes which we shall investigate hereafter. Hence we are seldom able to determine directly, by means of its Ontogeny, the different forms through which the ancestry of each organism has passed; on the contrary, we commonly find,—and not less so in the Phylogeny of man,—a number of gaps. We are, however, able to bridge over the greater part of these gaps satisfactorily by the help of Comparative Anatomy, though not to fill them up directly by ontogenetic research. It is therefore all the more important that we are acquainted with a considerable number of lower animal forms which still find place in the history of the individual evolution of man. In such cases, from the nature of the transient individual form, we may quite safely infer the nature of the ancestral animal form.

DEGENERATION, A CHAPTER IN DARWINISM

Edwin Ray Lankester, *Degeneration: A Chapter in Darwinism* (London: Macmillan, 1880), 24–9, 30, 32–3, 58–60.

This short book was based on a lecture given to the British Association for the Advancement of Science in Sheffield on 22 August 1879. Lankester starts by stressing the essentially speculative and hypothetical nature of his argument, the implications of which, however, he doesn't hesitate to apply to human society. In the 1890s Lankester became friendly with H. G. Wells and it is probable that this essay influenced both The Time Machine *(1895) and Wells's essay 'Zoological Retrogression'* (Gentlemen's Magazine, 271 (Sept. 1891), 246–53).

In attempting to reconstruct the pedigree of the animal kingdom and so to exhibit correctly the genetic relationships of all existing forms of animals, naturalists have hitherto assumed that the process of natural selection and survival of the fittest has invariably acted so as either to improve and elaborate the structure of *all* the organisms subject to it, or else has left them unchanged, exactly fitted to their conditions, maintained as it were in a state of *balance*. It has been held that there have been some six or seven great lines of descent—main branches of the pedigree—such as that of the Vertebrates, that of the Molluscs, that of the

311

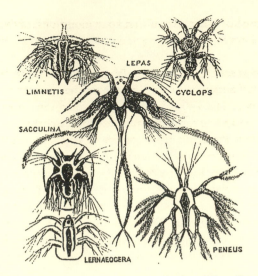

FIG. 16. Nauplius larval form of various Crustacea (Shrimps, Water-fleas, Barnacles, etc.)

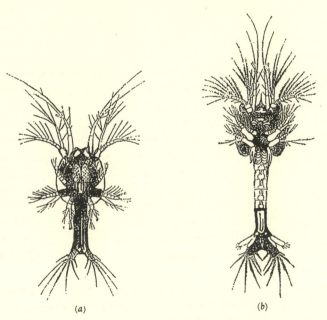

(a)   (b)

FIG. 17. (a) Larva of the Shrimp Peneus
(b) More advanced larva of the Shrimp Peneus

Insects, that of the Starfish, and so on; and that along each of these lines there has been always and continuously a progress—a change in the direction of greater elaboration.

Each of these great branches of the family-tree is held to be independent—they all branch off nearly simultaneously from the main trunk like the leading branches of an oak. The animal forms constituting the series in each of these branches are supposed to gradually increase in elaboration of structure as we pass upwards from the main trunk of origin and climb further and further towards the youngest, most recent twigs. New organs have, it is supposed, been gradually developed in each series, giving their possessors greater powers, enabling them to cope more successfully with others in that struggle for existence in virtue of which these new organs have been little by little called into being. At the same time *here and there* along the line of march, certain forms have been supposed to have 'fallen out,' to have ceased to improve, and being happily fitted to the conditions of life in which they were long ago existing, have continued down to the present day to exist in the same low, imperfect condition. It is in this way that the lowest forms of animal life at present existing are usually explained, such as the microscopic animalcules, Amœbæ and Infusoria.[1] It is in this way that the lower or more simply-made families of higher groups have been generally regarded. The simpler living Mollusca or shellfish have been supposed necessarily to represent the original forms of the great race of Mollusca. The simpler Vertebrates have been supposed necessarily to represent the original Vertebrates. The simpler Worms have been supposed necessarily to be the stereotyped representatives of very ancient Worms.

That this is, to a certain extent, a true explanation of the existence at the present day of *low* forms of animals is proved by the fact that we find in very ancient strata fossil remains of animals which differ, ever so little, from particular animals existing at the present day; for instance, the Brachiopods (lamp-shells), Lingula and Terebratula,[2] the King-crabs, and the Pearly Nautilus are found living at the present day, and are also found with no appreciable difference in very ancient strata of the earth's crust; strata deposited so long ago that most of the forms of life at present inhabiting the earth's surface had not then been brought into existence, whilst other most strange and varied forms occupied their place, and have now for long ages been extinct.

Whilst we are thus justified by the direct testimony of fossil remains in accounting for *some* living forms on the hypothesis that their peculiar conditions of life have been such as to maintain them for an immense period of time *in statu quo* unchanged, *we have no reason for applying this hypothesis, and this only*, to the explanation of all the more imperfectly organised forms of animal or plant-life.

---

[1] Form of protozoa found in infusions of decaying animal or vegetable matter.
[2] Forms of very primitive molluscs.

It is clearly enough possible for a set of forces such as we sum up under the head 'natural selection' to so act on the structure of an organism as to produce one of three results, namely these; to keep it *in statu quo*; to increase the complexity of its structure; or lastly, to diminish the complexity of its structure. We have as possibilities either BALANCE, or ELABORATION, or DEGENERATION. [. . .]

The statement that the hypothesis of Degeneration has not been recognised by naturalists generally as an explanation of animal forms, requires to be corrected by the exception of certain kinds of animals, namely, those that are parasitic or quasi-parasitic. With regard to parasites, naturalists have long recognised what is called *retrogressive metamorphosis*; and parasitic animals are as a rule admitted to be instances of Degeneration. It is the more remarkable whilst the possibility of a degeneration—a loss of organisation making the descendant far *simpler* or *lower* in structure than its ancestor—has been admitted for a few exceptional animals, that the same hypothesis should not have been applied to the explanation of other simple forms of animals. The hypothesis of Degeneration will, I believe, be found to render most valuable service in pointing out the true relationships of animals which are a puzzle and a mystery when we use only and exclusively the hypothesis of Balance, or the hypothesis of Elaboration. It will, as a true scientific hypothesis, help us to discover causes. [. . .]

Degeneration may be defined as a gradual change of the structure in which the organism becomes adapted to *less* varied and *less* complex conditions of life; whilst Elaboration is a gradual change of structure in which the organism becomes adapted to more and more varied and complex conditions of existence. In Elaboration there is a new *expression* of form, corresponding to new perfection of work in the animal machine. In Degeneration there is *suppression* of form, corresponding to the cessation of work. Elaboration of some one organ *may* be a necessary accompaniment of Degeneration in all the others; in fact, this is very generally the case; and it is only when the total result of the Elaboration of some organs, and the Degeneration of others, is such as to leave the whole animal in a *lower* condition, that is, fitted to less complex action and reaction in regard to its surroundings, than was the ancestral form with which we are comparing it (either actually or in imagination) that we speak of that animal as an instance of Degeneration.

Any new set of conditions occurring to an animal which render its food and safety very easily attained, seem to lead as a rule to Degeneration; just as an active healthy man sometimes degenerates when he becomes suddenly possessed of a fortune; or as Rome degenerated when possessed of the riches of the ancient world. The habit of parasitism clearly acts upon animal organisation in this way. Let the parasitic life once be secured, and away go legs, jaws, eyes, and ears; the active, highly-gifted crab, insect, or annelid[3] may become a mere sac, absorbing nourishment and laying eggs. [. . .]

[3] Type of red-blooded worm.

The traditional history of mankind furnishes us with notable examples of degeneration. High states of civilisation have decayed and given place to low and degenerate states. At one time it was a favourite doctrine that the savage races of mankind were degenerate descendants of the higher and civilised races. This general and sweeping application of the doctrine of degeneration has been proved to be erroneous by careful study of the habits, arts, and beliefs of savages; at the same time there is no doubt that many savage races as we at present see them are actually degenerate and are descended from ancestors possessed of a relatively elaborate civilisation. As such we may cite some of the Indians of Central America, the modern Egyptians, and even the heirs of the great oriental monarchies of præ-Christian times. Whilst the hypothesis of universal degeneration as an explanation of savage races has been justly discarded, it yet appears that degeneration has a very large share in the explanation of the condition of the most barbarous races, such as the Fuegians, the Bushmen, and even the Australians. They exhibit evidence of being descended from ancestors more cultivated than themselves.

With regard to ourselves, the white races of Europe, the possibility of degeneration seems to be worth some consideration. In accordance with a tacit assumption of universal progress—an unreasoning optimism—we are accustomed to regard ourselves as necessarily progressing, as necessarily having arrived at a higher and more elaborated condition than that which our ancestors reached, and as destined to progress still further. On the other hand, it is well to remember that we are subject to the general laws of evolution, and are as likely to degenerate as to progress. As compared with the immediate forefathers of our civilisation—the ancient Greeks—we do not appear to have improved so far as our bodily structure is concerned, nor assuredly so far as some of our mental capacities are concerned. Our powers of perceiving and expressing beauty of form have certainly *not* increased since the days of the Parthenon and Aphrodite of Melos.[4] In matters of the reason, in the development of intellect, we may seriously inquire how the case stands. Does the reason of the average man of civilised Europe stand out clearly as an evidence of progress when compared with that of the men of bygone ages? Are all the inventions and figments of human superstition and folly, the self-inflicted torturing of mind, the reiterated substitution of wrong for right, and of falsehood for truth, which disfigure our modern civilisation—are these evidences of progress? In such respects we have at least reason to fear that we may be degenerate. Possibly we are all drifting, tending to the condition of intellectual Barnacles or Ascidians.[5]

---

[4] The Melos Venus (*c.*150 BC), now in the Louvre in Paris, was one of the central emblems of feminine beauty in the nineteenth century.

[5] A form of mollusc considered by evolutionists to be an important link in the development of the vertebrates.

ON HEREDITY

August Weismann, 'On heredity' (1883), *Essays upon Heredity and Kindred Biological Problems*, authorized translation edited by E. B. Poulton, Selmar Schönland and A. E. Shipley (Oxford: Clarendon Press, 1889), 90–3, 95–6, 98.

English translations of Weismann's lectures on heredity appeared from 1883, and this collection was produced in response to the great interest shown in his work. The Fortnightly Review *published a series of articles debating his theory of the continuity of the 'germ-plasm' (including three by George Romanes and five from Spencer) between August 1889 and October 1894. Here the editors thank E. Ray Lankester, Francis Galton, and A. R. Wallace for their editorial suggestions.*

The suspension of the preserving influence of natural selection may be termed *Panmixia*,[1] for all individuals can reproduce themselves and thus stamp their characters upon the series, and not only those which are in all respects, or in respect to some single organ, the fittest. In my opinion, the greater number of those variations which are usually attributed to the direct influence of external conditions of life, are to be ascribed to panmixia. For example, the great variability of most domesticated animals essentially depends upon this principle.

A goose or a duck must possess strong powers of flight in the natural state, but such powers are no longer necessary for obtaining food when it is brought into the poultry-yard, so that a rigid selection of individuals with well-developed wings, at once ceases among its descendants. Hence in the course of generations, a deterioration of the organs of flight must necessarily ensue, and the other members and organs of the bird will be similarly affected.

This example very clearly indicates that the degeneration of an organ does not depend upon its disuse; for although our domestic poultry very rarely make use of their wings, the muscles of flight have not disappeared, and, at any rate in the goose, do not seem to have undergone any marked degeneration. [. . .]

It is usually considered that the origin and variation of instincts are also dependent upon the exercise of certain groups of muscles and nerves during a single life-time; and that the gradual improvement which is thus caused by practice, is accumulated by hereditary transmission. I believe that this is an entirely erroneous view, and I hold that all instinct is entirely due to the operation of natural selection, and has its foundation, not upon inherited experiences, but upon the variations of the germ.

---

[1] Literally, 'universal or general mingling'.

Why, for instance, should not the instinct to fly from enemies have arisen by the survival of those individuals which are naturally timid and easily startled, together with the extermination of those which are unwary? It may be urged in opposition to this explanation that the birds of uninhabited islands which are not at first shy of man, acquire in a few generations an instinctive dread of him, an instinct which cannot have arisen in so short a time by means of natural selection. But in this case are we really dealing with the origin of a new instinct, or only with the addition of one new perception of the same kind as those which incite to the instinct of flight—an instinct which had been previously developed in past ages but had never been called forth by man? Again, has any one ascertained whether the young birds of the second or third generation are frightened by man? May it not be that the experience of a single life-time plays a great part in the origin of the habit? For my part, I am inclined to believe that the habit of flying from man is developed in the first generation which encounters him as a foe. We see how wary and cautious a flock of birds become as soon as a few shots have been fired at them, and yet shortly before this occurrence they were perhaps playing carelessly close to the sportsmen. Intelligence plays a considerable part in the life of birds, and it by no means follows that the transmission of individual habits explains the above-mentioned phenomena. The long-continued operation of natural selection may very well have been necessary before the perception of man could awake the instinct to flee in young, inexperienced birds. Unfortunately the observations upon these points are far too indefinite to enable us to draw conclusions.

There is again the frequently-quoted instance of the young pointer, 'which, untrained, and without any example which might have been imitated, pointed at a lizard in a subtropical jungle, just as many of its forefathers had pointed at partridges on the plain of St. Denis,' and which, without knowing the effect of a shot, sprang forward barking, at the first discharge, to bring in the game. This conduct must not be attributed to the inheritance of any mental picture, such as the effect of a shot, but to the inheritance of a certain reflex mechanism. The young pointer does not spring forward at the shot because he has inherited from his forefathers a certain association of ideas,—shot and game,—but because he has inherited a reflex mechanism, which impels him to start forward on hearing a report. We cannot yet determine without more experiments how such an impulse due to perception has arisen; but, in my opinion, it is almost inconceivable that artificial breeding has had nothing to do with it; and that we are here concerned—not with the inheritance of the effects of training—but with some pre-disposition on the part of the germ, which has been increased by artificial selection. [. . .]

It may be objected that, in man, in addition to the instincts inherent in every individual, special individual predispositions are also found, of such a nature that it is impossible that they can have arisen by individual variations of the germ. On the other hand, these predisposition—which we call talents—cannot have arisen through natural selection, because life is in no way dependent upon their presence, and there seems to be no way of explaining their origin except by an assumption of the summation of the skill attained by exercise in the course of each single life. In this case, therefore, we seem at first sight to be compelled to accept the transmission of acquired characters.

Now it cannot be denied that all predispositions may be improved by practice during the course of a life-time,—and, in truth, very remarkably improved. If we could explain the existence of great talent, such as, for example, a gift for music, painting, sculpture, or mathematics, as due to the presence or absence of a special organ in the brain, it follows that we could only understand its origin and increase (natural selection being excluded) by accumulation, due to the transmission of the results of practice through a series of generations. But talents are not dependent upon the possession of special organs in the brain. They are not simple mental dispositions, but combinations of many dispositions, and often of a most complex nature: they depend upon a certain degree of irritability, and a power of readily transmitting impulses along the nerve-tracts of the brain, as well as upon the especial development of single parts of the brain. In my opinion, there is absolutely no trustworthy proof that talents have been improved by their exercise through the course of a long series of generations. The Bach family shows that musical talent, and the Bernoulli[2] family that mathematical power, can be transmitted from generation to generation, but this teaches us nothing as to the origin of such talents. In both families the high-water mark of talent lies, not at the end of the series of generations, as it should do if the results of practice are transmitted, but in the middle. Again, talents frequently appear in some single member of a family which has not been previously distinguished. [. . .]

Talents do not appear to depend upon the improvement of any special mental quality by continued practice, but they are the expression, and to a certain extent the bye-product, of the human mind, which is so highly developed in all directions.

But if any one asks whether this high mental development, acquired in the course of innumerable generations of men, is not dependent upon the hereditary effects of use, I would remind him that human intelligence in general is the chief means and the chief weapon which has served and still serves the human species in the struggle for existence. Even in the present state of civilization—distorted as it is by numerous artificial encroachments and unnatural conditions—the degree of intelligence possessed by the individual chiefly decides between destruction and life; and in a natural state, or still better in a state of low civilization, this result is even more striking.

---

[2] Eighteenth-century Swiss family of mathematicians running through three generations.

EVOLUTION AND ETHICS

T. H. Huxley, *Evolution and Ethics* (London: Macmillan, 1893), 33–7.

This extract forms part of the concluding section of Evolution and Ethics, *first presented as the Romanes Lecture on 18 May 1893, which in many ways represents the culminating statement of Huxley's scientific and ethical beliefs. Unlike Spencer and Lankester, Huxley insists that it is impossible to explain human culture by extrapolating from biological processes.*

As I have already urged, the practice of that which is ethically best—what we call goodness or virtue—involves a course of conduct which, in all respect, is opposed to that which leads to success in the cosmic struggle for existence. In place of ruthless self-assertion it demands self-restraint; in place of thrusting aside, or treading down, all competitors, it requires that the individual shall not merely respect, but shall help his fellows; its influence is directed, not so much to the survival of the fittest, as to the fitting of as many as possible to survive. It repudiates the gladiatorial theory of existence. It demands that each man who enters into the enjoyment of the advantages of a policy shall be mindful of his debt to those who have laboriously constructed it; and shall take heed that no act of his weakens the fabric in which he has been permitted to live. Laws and moral precepts are directed to the end of curbing the cosmic process and reminding the individual of his duty to the community, to the protection and influence of which he owes, if not existence itself, at least the life of something better than a brutal savage.

It is from neglect of these plain considerations that the fanatical individualism of our time attempts to apply the analogy of cosmic nature to society. Once more we have a misapplication of the stoical injunction to follow nature; the duties of the individual to the state are forgotten and his tendencies to self-assertion are dignified by the name of rights. It is seriously debated whether the members of a community are justified in using their combined strength to constrain one of their number to contribute his share to the maintenance of it; or even to prevent him from doing his best to destroy it. The struggle for existence, which has done such admirable work in cosmic nature, must, it appears, be equally beneficent in the ethical sphere. Yet, if that which I have insisted upon is true; if the cosmic process has no sort of relation to moral ends; if the imitation of it by man is inconsistent with the first principles of ethics; what becomes of this surprising theory?

Let us understand, once for all, that the ethical progress of society depends, not on imitating the cosmic process, still less in running away from it, but in combating it. It may seem an audacious proposal thus to pit the microcosm against the macrocosm and to set man to subdue nature to his higher ends; but, I venture to think that the great intellectual difference between the ancient times with which we have been occupied and our day, lies in the solid foundation we have acquired for the hope that such an enterprise may meet with a certain measure of success.

The history of civilization details the steps by which men have succeeded in building up an artificial world within the cosmos. Fragile reed, as he may be, man, as Pascal says, is a thinking reed:* there lies within him a fund of energy, operating intelligently and so far akin to that which pervades the universe, that it is competent to influence and modify the cosmic process. In virtue of his intelligence, the dwarf bends the Titan to his will. In every family, in every polity that has been established, the cosmic process in man has been restrained and otherwise modified by law and custom; in surrounding nature, it has been similarly influenced by the art of the shepherd, the agriculturist, the artisan. As civilization has advanced, so has the extent of this interference increased; until the organized and highly developed sciences and arts of the present day have endowed man with a command over the course of non-human nature greater than that once attributed to the magicians. The most impressive, I might say startling, of these changes have been brought about in the course of the last two centuries; while a right comprehension of the process of life and of the means of influencing its manifestations is only just dawning upon us. We do not yet see our way beyond generalities; and we are befogged by the obtrusion of false analogies and crude anticipations. But Astronomy, Physics, Chemistry, have all had to pass through similar phases, before they reached the stage at which their influence became an important factor in human affairs. Physiology, Psychology, Ethics, Political Science, must submit to the same ordeal. Yet it seems to me irrational to doubt that, at no distant period, they will work as great a revolution in the sphere of practice.

The theory of evolution encourages no millennial anticipations. If, for millions of years, our globe has taken the upward road, yet, sometime, the summit will be reached and the downward route will be commenced. The most daring imagination will hardly venture upon the suggestion that the power and the intelligence of man can ever arrest the procession of the great year.

Moreover the cosmic nature born with us and, to a large extent, necessary for our maintenance, is the outcome of millions of years of severe training, and it would be folly to imagine that a few centuries will suffice to subdue its masterfulness to purely ethical ends. Ethical nature may count upon having to reckon with a tenacious and powerful enemy as long as the world lasts. But, on the other hand, I see no limit to the extent to which intelligence and will, guided by sound

* *Pensées*, Chapter II. x.

principles of investigation, and organized in common effort, may modify the conditions of existence, for a period longer than that now covered by history. And much may be done to change the nature of man himself. The intelligence which has converted the brother of the wolf into the faithful guardian of the flock ought to be able to do something towards curbing the instincts of savagery in civilized men.

3. Inherited Legacies: Idiocy and Criminality

IDIOTS AGAIN

Anon., 'Idiots again', *Household Words*, 9 (15 Apr. 1854), 197–200.

Dickens had surveyed development in the treatment of idiocy in an earlier article, written in collaboration with W. H. Wills, where he approvingly describes the new method of Dr Guggenbühl's mountain clinic in Switzerland, which produced extraordinary improvements in 'idiot' children, transforming them from 'stunted withered skeletons' to children moving 'rapidly towards perfect development' ('Idiots', Household Words *(4 June 1853), 315). The author of this unsigned article (probably Harriet Martineau) also emphasizes the role of moral management and education, but lays more stress on inherited factors.*

It used to be thought a very religious and beautiful thing (it certainly was the easiest thing) to say that it pleased God to send idiots, and other defective or diseased children, to try and discipline their parents by affliction, and so on; but religious physicians now tell us (showing reason for what they say) that there is something very like blasphemy in talking so,—in imputing to Providence the sufferings which we bring upon ourselves, precisely by disobedience to the great natural laws which it is the best piety to obey. It is a common saying, that families who intermarry too often, die out; but no account is taken of the miseries which precede that dying out. Those miseries of disease of body and mind are ascribed to Providence, as if Providence had not given us abundant warning to avoid them! Dr. Howe, the wise and benevolent teacher of Laura Bridgman,[1] says, in his Report on Idiotcy in

[1] A deaf mute child whose remarkable mental development was widely discussed through the second half of the nineteenth century.

Massachusetts, that 'the law against the marriage of relatives is made out as clearly as though it were written on tables of stone.'[2] He gives his reasons for saying so; and of those reasons, the following sample will, we think, be enough. When the tables of health and disease were compiled for Massachusetts, a few years ago, the following was found to be the state of seventeen families, where the father and mother were related by blood. Some of the parents were unhealthy, and some were intemperate— but to set against this disadvantage to begin with, there is the fact, that the evil consequences of such intermarriage very often do not appear until the second generation, or even later. However in these seventeen households there were ninety-five children. What were these children like? Imagine a school of ninety-five children, of all ages, or the children of a hamlet at play, and think what the little crowd would look like; and then read this! Of these ninety-five children, one was a dwarf. Well, that might easily be. One was deaf. Well, no great wonder in that. Twelve were scrofulous. That is a large number, certainly; but scrofula is sadly common, and especially in unhealthy situations. Well, but FORTY-FOUR were IDIOTS.

Of all the long and weary pains of mind to which the unselfish can be subject, we know of none so terrible as that of the mother attaining the certainty that her child is an idiot. [. . .] Time goes on; and the singularity is apparent that the baby makes *no response* to anything. He is not deaf. Very distant street music probably causes a kind of quiver through his whole frame. He sees very well. He certainly is aware of the flies which are performing minuets and reels between him and the ceiling. As for his other senses, there never was anything like his keenness of smell and taste. He is ravenous for food—even already unpleasantly so; but excessively difficult to please. The terrible thing is his still taking no notice. His mother longs to feel the clasp of his arms round her neck; but her fondlings receive no return. His arm hangs lax over her shoulder. She longs for a look from him, and lays him back on her lap, hoping that they may look into each other's eyes; but he looks at nobody. All his life long nobody will ever meet his eyes; and neither in that way nor any other way will his mind expressly meet that of anybody else. [. . .]

The wearing uncertainty of many years succeeds the infancy. The ignorant notions of idiotcy that prevailed before we knew even the little that we yet know of the brain, prevent the parents recognising the real state of the case. The old legal accounts of idiotcy, and the old suppositions of what it is, are very unlike what they see. The child ought not, according to legal definition, to know his own name, but he certainly does; for when his own plate or cup is declared to be ready, he rushes to it. He ought not to be able, by law, 'to know letters;' yet he can read, and even write, perhaps, although nobody can tell how he learned, for he never seemed to attend when taught. it was just as if his fingers and tongue went of themselves, while his mind was in the moon. Again, the law declared

---

[2] Saul Gridley Howe, *On the Causes of Idiocy: The Supplement to a Report by Commissioners Appointed by the Governors of Massachusetts to Inquire into the Condition of Idiots in the Colony* (1848).

anybody an idiot 'who could not count twenty pence;' whereas, this body seems, in some unaccountable way, to know more about sums (of money and of everything else) than anybody in the family. He does not want to learn figures, his arithmetic is strong without them, and always instantaneously ready. Of course we do not mean that every idiot has these particular powers. Many cannot speak; more cannot read. But almost every one of the thousands of idiots in England has some power that the legal definition declares him not to have, and that popular prejudice will not believe. Thus does the mother go on from year to year, hardly admitting that her boy is 'deficient,' and quite sure that he is not an idiot—there being some things in which he is so very clever!

The great improvement in the treatment of idiots and lunatics since science began to throw light on the separate organisation of the human faculties, is one of the most striking instances in all human experience of the practical blessedness induced by knowledge. In a former paper of this journal an account was given of the way in which, by beneficent training, the apparent faculties of idiots are made to bring out the latent ones, and the strong powers to exercise the weaker, until the whole class are found to be capable of a cultivation never dreamed of in the old days when the name IDIOT swallowed up all the rights and all the chances of the unfortunate creature who was so described. In those days the mother might well deny the description, and refuse the term. She would point to the wonderful faculty her child had in some one direction, and admit no more than that he was 'not like other children.' Well, this is enough. She need not be driven further. If her Harry is 'not like other children,' that is enough for his own training, and that of the rest of the household.

A training it may be truly called for them all, from the father to the kitchenmaid. The house that has an idiot in it can never be like any other. The discipline is very painful, but, when well conducted and borne, it is wonderfully beautiful. [. . .] He must do precisely the same thing at precisely the same moment every day: must have always the same chair, wailing or pushing in great distress if anybody else is using it: and must wear the same clothes, so that it is a serious trouble to get any new clothes put on. However carefully they may be changed while he is asleep, there is no getting him dressed in the morning without sad distress. [. . .]

As for the discipline of Harry himself, it must be discipline; for every consideration of humanity, and, of course, of parental affection, points out the sin of spoiling him. To humour, in the sense of spoiling, an idiot, is to level him with the brutes at once. One might as well do with him what used to be done with such beings,—consign him to the stye, to sleep with the pigs, or chain him up like the dog, as indulge the animal part of a being who does not possess the faculties that counteract animality in other people. Most idiots have a remarkable tendency to imitation: and this is an admirable means of domestic training,—for both the defective child and the rest. The youngest will smother its sobs at the soap in its eye, if appealed to, to let poor Harry see how cheerfully everybody ought to be washed every morning. The youngest will take the hint not to ask for more pudding, because Harry must take what is given him, and not see anybody cry for more. Crying is conquered—self-conquered—throughout the house, because Harry imitates everything; and it would be very sad if he got a habit of crying, because he could not be comforted like other people. As the other children learn self-conquest from motive, in this way Harry will be learning it from imitation. [. . .] The strong faculty of imitation usually existing among the class, seems (as we said just now, in reference to the faculties of idiots in general,) a sort of miracle before the nature of the brain-organisation was truly conceived of. How many elderly people now remember how aghast they were, as children, at the story of the idiot youth, not being able to do without the mother, who had never left him while she lived: and how, when everybody supposed him asleep, and the neighbours were themselves asleep, he went out and got the body, and set it up in the fireside chair, and made a roaring fire, and heated some broth, and was found, restlessly moaning with distress, while trying to feed the corpse. [. . .] What could we, in childhood, and the rest of the world in the ignorance of that day, make of such facts, but that they must be miraculous? [. . .]

It is for us to act upon the medium view sanctioned alike by science and morals—neither to cast out our idiots, like the savages who leave their helpless ones to perish; nor to worship them, as the pious Egyptians did, and other nations who believed that the gods dwelt in them, more or less, and made oracles of them;—a perfectly natural belief in the case of beings who manifest a very few faculties in extraordinary perfection, in the apparent absence of all others. Our business is, in the first place, to reduce the number of idiots to the utmost of our power, by attending to the conditions of sound life and health; and especially by discountenancing, as a crime, the marriage of blood-relations; and, in the next place, by trying to make the most and the best of such faculties as these imperfect beings possess. It is not enough to repeat the celebrated epitaph on an idiot, and to hope that his privations here will be made up to him hereafter. We must lessen those privations to the utmost, by the careful application of science in understanding his case; and of skill, and inexhaustible patience and love, in treating it. Happily, there are now institutions, by aiding which any of us may do something towards raising the lowest, and blessing the most afflicted, members of our race.

IDIOCY

Henry Maudsley, *Body and Mind: An Inquiry into their Connection and Mutual Influence, Specially in Reference to Mental Disorders* (London: Macmillan, 1870), 43–7, 51–3.

The first part of Body and Mind, *in which Maudsley develops his theory of mental and physical degeneracy, drawing heavily on the mid-century work of B. A. Morel, was based on three lectures given to the Royal College of Physicians in 1870, on 'The physical condition of mental function in health'; 'On certain causes of degeneracy of mind, their causation and their relation to other disorders of the nervous system'; and 'On the relations of morbid bodily states to disordered mental functions'. The second part of the book is based on two articles (in* Journal of Mental Science, *70 (1868), and* British and Foreign Medico-Chirurgical Review, *64 (1863)), on 'The Limits of Philosophical Inquiry' and 'The Theory of Vitality'. This extract appears at the beginning of the second lecture.*

For Maudsley on the inheritance of criminal traits, see the extracts from Responsibility in Mental Disease *in Section IV. 2.*

Perhaps of all the erroneous notions concerning mind which metaphysics has engendered or abetted, there is none more false than that which tacitly assumes or explicitly declares that men are born with equal original mental capacity, opportunities and education determining the differences of subsequent development. The opinion is as cruel as it is false. What man can by taking thought add one cubit either to his mental or to his bodily stature? Multitudes of human beings come into the world weighted with a destiny against which they have neither the will nor the power to contend; they are the step-children of nature, and groan under the worst of all tyrannies—the tyranny of a bad organization. Men differ, indeed, in the fundamental characters of their minds, as they do in the features of their countenances, or in the habits of their bodies; and between those who are born with the potentiality of a full and complete mental development, under favourable circumstances, and those who are born with an innate incapacity of mental development, under any circumstances, there exists every gradation. What teaching could ever raise the congenital idiot to the common level of human intelligence? What teaching could ever keep the inspired mind of the man of genius at that level?

The congenital idiot is deprived of his human birthright; for he is born with such a defect of brain that he cannot display any, or can only display very feeble and imperfect mental functions. From no fault of his own is he thus afflicted, seeing that he must be held innocent of all offence but the offence of his share of original sin; but it is nowise so clear that it is not from some fault of his parents. It is all too true that, in many cases, there has observably been a neglect or disregard of the laws which govern the progress of human development through the ages. Idiocy is, indeed, a manufactured article; and although we are not always able to tell how it is manufactured, still its important causes are known and are within control. Many cases are distinctly traceable to parental intemperance and excess. Out of 300 idiots in Massachusetts, Dr. Howe[1] found as many as 145 to be the offspring of intemperate parents; and there are numerous scattered observations which prove that chronic alcoholism in the parent may directly occasion idiocy in the child. I think, too, that there is no reasonable question of the ill effects of marriages of consanguinity: that their tendency is to produce degeneracy of the race, and idiocy as the extremest form of such degeneracy. I do not say that *all* the children of such marriages may not sometimes be healthy, and *some* of them quite healthy at other times; but the general and ultimate result of breeding in and in is to produce barrenness and sterility, children of a low degree of viability and of imperfect mental and physical development, deaf-mutism, and actual imbecility or idiocy. Again, insanity in the parent may issue in idiocy in the offspring, which is, so to speak, the natural term of mental degeneracy when it goes on unchecked through generations. It may be affirmed with no little confidence, that if the experiment of intermarrying insane persons for two or three generations were tried, the result would be sterile idiocy and extinction of the family. Certain unfavourable conditions of life tend unquestionably to produce degeneracy of the individual; the morbid predisposition so generated is then transmitted to the next generation, and, if the unfavourable conditions continue, is aggravated in it; and thus is formed a morbid variety of the human kind, which is incapable of being a link in the line of progress of humanity. Nature puts it under the ban of sterility, and thus prevents the permanent degradation of the race. Morel[2] has traced through four generations the family history of a youth who was admitted into the asylum at Rouen in a state of stupidity and semi-idiocy; the summary of which may fitly illustrate the natural course of degeneracy when it goes on through generations.

First generation: Immortality, depravity, alcoholic excess and moral degradation, in the great-grandfather, who was killed in a tavern brawl.

Second generation: Hereditary drunkenness, maniacal attacks, ending in general paralysis, in the grandfather.

Third generation: Sobriety, but hypochrondriacal tendencies, delusions of persecutions, and homicidal tendencies in the father.

---

[1] See n. 1 on 'Idiots again', above.

[2] Benedict August Morel (1809–73), the French psychiatrist whose *Traité des dégénérescences physiques, intellectuelles et morales de l'éspèce humaine et des causes qui produisent ces variétés maladives* was a crucial influence on Maudsley's work.

Fourth generation: Defective intelligence. First attack of mania at sixteen; stupidity, and transition to complete idiocy. Furthermore probable extinction of the family; for the generative functions were as little developed as those of a child of twelve years of age. He had two sisters who were both defective physically and morally, and were classed as imbeciles. To complete the proof of heredity in this case Morel adds, that the mother had a child while the father was confined in the asylum, and that this adulterous child showed no signs of degeneracy.

When epilepsy in young children leads to idiocy, as it often does, we must generally look for the deep root of the mischief in the family neurosis.

No one can well dispute that in the case of such an extreme morbid variety as a congenital idiot is, we have to do with a defective nervous organization. We are still, however, without more than a very few exact descriptions of the brains of idiots. Mr. Marshall[3] has recently examined and described the brains of two idiots of European descent. He found the convolutions to be fewer in number, individually less complex, broader and smoother than in the apes: 'in this respect,' he says, 'the idiots' brains are even more simple than that of the gibbon, and approach that of the baboon.' The condition was the result neither of atrophy nor of mere arrest of growth, but consisted essentially in an imperfect evolution of the cerebral hemispheres or their parts, dependent on an arrest of development. The proportion of the weight of brain to that of body was extraordinarily diminished. We learn, then, that when man is born with a brain no higher—indeed lower—than that of an ape, he may have the convolutions fewer in number, and individually less complex, than they are in the brain of a chimpanzee and an orang; the human brain may revert to, or fall below, that type of development from which, if the theory of Darwin be true, it has gradually ascended by evolution through the ages.

With the defect of organ there is a corresponding defect of function. But there is sometimes more than a simple defect. A curious and interesting fact, which has by no means yet received the consideration which it deserves, is that, with the appearance of this animal type of brain in idiocy, there do sometimes appear or reappear remarkable animal traits and instincts. There is a class of idiots which may justly be designed *theroid*,[4] so like brutes are the members of it. The old stories of so-called wild men, such as Peter the wild boy, and the young savage of Aveyron, who ran wild in the woods and lived on acorns and whatever else they could pick up there, were certainly exaggerated at the time. These degraded beings were evidently idiots, who exhibited a somewhat striking aptitude and capacity for a wild animal life. Dr. Carpenter, however, quotes the case of an idiot girl, who was seduced by some miscreant, and who, when she was delivered, gnawed through the umbilical cord as some of the lower animals do. [. . .]

---

[3] John Marshall, author of *Outlines of Physiology* (1867).   [4] Beast-like.

It is a natural question, Whence come these animal traits and instincts in man? Whence was derived the instinct which taught the idiot woman to gnaw through the umbilical cord? Was it really the reappearance of a primitive instinct of animal nature—a faint echo from a far distant past, testifying to a kinship which man has almost outgrown, or has grown too proud to acknowledge? No doubt such animal traits are marks of extreme human degeneracy, but it is no explanation to call them so; degenerations come by law, and are as natural as natural law can make them. Instead of passing them by as abnormal, or, worse still, stigmatizing them as unnatural, it behoves us to seek for the scientific interpretation which they must certainly have. When we reflect that every human brain does, in the course of its development, pass through the same stages as the brains of other vertebrate animals, and that its transitional states, resemble the permanent forms of their brains; and when we reflect further, that the stages of its development in the womb may be considered the abstract and brief chronicle of a series of developments that have gone on through countless ages in nature, it does not seem so wonderful, as at the first blush it might do, that it should; when in a condition of arrested development, sometimes display animal instincts. Summing up, as it were, in itself the leading forms of the vertebrate type, there is truly a brute brain within the man's; and when the latter stops short of its characteristic development as *human*—when it remains arrested at or below the level of an orang's brain, it may be presumed that it will manifest its most primitive functions, and no higher functions.

I am not aware of any other considerations than those just adduced which offer even the glimpse of an explanation of the origin of these animal traits in man. We need not, however, confine our attention to idiots only. Whence come the savage snarl, the destructive disposition, the obscene language, the wild howl, the offensive habits, displayed by some of the insane? Why should a human being deprived of his reason ever become so brutal in character as some do, unless he has the brute nature within him? In most large asylums there is one, or more than one, example of a demented person who truly ruminates: bolting his food rapidly, he retires afterwards to a corner, where at his leisure he quietly brings it up again into the mouth and masticates it as the cow does. I should take up a long time if I were to enumerate the various brute-like characteristics that are at times witnessed among the insane; enough to say that some very strong facts and arguments in support of Mr. Darwin's views might be drawn from the field of morbid psychology. We may, without much difficulty, trace savagery in civilization, as we can trace animalism in savagery; and in the degeneration of insanity, in the *unkinding*,[5] so to say, of the human kind, there are exhibited marks denoting the elementary instincts of its composition.

---

[5] Dehumanizing.

CRIMINALS AND THE INSANE

Francis Galton, *Inquiries into Human Faculty and Its Development* (London: Macmillan, 1883), 61–5.

In this eclectic collection, published fourteen years after the influential Hereditary Genius, *Galton aimed to set forth his 'science' of eugenics; discussing 'the practicability of supplanting inefficient human stock by better strains and [considering] whether it might not be our duty to do so by such efforts as may be reasonable, thus exerting to further the ends of evolution more rapidly . . . than if events were left to their own course' (Preface, p. 2).*

Criminality, though not very various in its development, is extremely complex in its origin; nevertheless certain general conclusions are arrived at by the best writers on the subject, among whom Prosper Despine is one of the most instructive.[1] The ideal criminal has marked peculiarities of character: his conscience is almost deficient, his instincts are vicious, his power of self-control is very weak, and he usually detests continuous labour. The absence of self-control is due to ungovernable temper, to passion, or to mere imbecility, and the conditions that determine the particular description of crime are the character of the instincts and of the temperament.

The deficiency of conscience in criminals, as shown by the absence of genuine remorse for their guilt, astonishes all who first become familiar with the details of prison life. Scenes of heartrending despair are hardly ever witnessed among prisoners; their sleep is broken by no uneasy dreams—on the contrary, it is easy and sound; they have also excellent appetites. But hypocrisy is a very common vice; and all my information agrees as to the utter untruthfulness of criminals, however plausible their statements may be.

We must guard ourselves against looking upon vicious instincts as perversions, inasmuch as they may be strictly in accordance with the healthy nature of the man, and, being transmissable by inheritance, may become the normal characteristics of a healthy race, just as the sheep-dog, the retriever, the pointer, and the bull-dog, have their several instincts. There can be no greater popular error than the supposition that natural instinct is a perfectly trustworthy guide, for there are striking contradictions to such an opinion in individuals of every description of animal. The most that we are entitled to say in any case is, that the prevalent instincts of each race are trustworthy, not those of every individual. But even this is saying too much, because when the conditions under which the race

[1] Author of *Psychologie naturelle: Étude sur les facultés intellectuelles et morales dans leur état normal et dans leur manifestations anormales chez les aliénés et chez les criminales* (1868).

is living have recently been changed, some instincts which were adapted to the old state of things are sure to be fallacious guides to conduct in the new one. A man who is counted as an atrocious criminal in England, and is punished as such by English law in social self-defence, may nevertheless have acted in strict accordance with instincts that are laudable in less civilised societies. The ideal criminal is, unhappily for him, deficient in qualities that are capable of restraining his unkindly or inconvenient instincts; he has neither sympathy for others nor the sense of duty, both of which lie at the base of conscience; nor has he sufficient self-control to accommodate himself to the society in which he has to live, and so to promote his own selfish interests in the long run. He cannot be preserved from criminal misadventure, either by altruistic sentiments or by intelligently egoistic ones.

The perpetuation of the criminal class by heredity is a question difficult to grapple with on many accounts. Their vagrant habits, their illegitimate unions, and extreme untruthfulness, are among the difficulties of the investigation. It is, however, easy to show that the criminal nature tends to be inherited; while, on the other hand, it is impossible that women who spend a large portion of the best years of their life in prison can contribute many children to the population. The true state of the case appears to be that the criminal population receives steady accessions from those who, without having strongly marked criminal natures, do nevertheless belong to a type of humanity that is exceedingly ill suited to play a respectable part in our modern civilisation, though it is well suited to flourish under half-savage conditions, being naturally both healthy and prolific. These persons are apt to go to the bad; their daughters consort with criminals and become the parents of criminals. An extraordinary example of this is afforded by the history of the infamous Jukes family in America, whose pedigree has been made out, with extraordinary care, during no less than seven generations, and is the subject of an elaborate memoir printed in the Thirty-first Annual Report of the Prison Association of New York, 1876.[2] It includes no less than 540 individuals of Jukes blood, of whom a frightful number degraded into criminality, pauperism, or disease.

It is difficult to summarise the results in a few plain figures, but I will state those respecting the fifth generation, through the eldest of the five prolific daughters of the man who is the common ancestor of the race. The total number of these was 123, of whom thirty-eight came through an illegitimate granddaughter, and eighty-five through legitimate grandchildren. Out of the thirty-eight, sixteen have been in jail, six of them for heinous offences, one of these having been committed no less than nine times; eleven others led openly disreputable lives or were paupers; four were notoriously intemperate; the history of three had not been traced, and only four are known to have done well.

---

[2] R. L. Dugdale, *'The Jukes': A Study in Crime, Pauperism, Disease and Heredity* (1877).

The great majority of the women consorted with criminals. As to the eighty-five legitimate descendants, they were less flagrantly bad, for only five of them had been in jail, and only thirteen others had been paupers. Now the ancestor of all this mischief, who was born about the year 1730, is described as having been a jolly companionable man, a hunter, and a fisher, averse to steady labour, but working hard and idling by turns, and who had numerous illegitimate children, whose issue has not been traced. He was, in fact, a somewhat good specimen of a half-savage, without any seriously criminal instincts. The girls were apparently attractive, marrying early and sometimes not badly; but the gipsy-like character of the race was unsuited to success in a civilised country. So the descendants went to the bad, and such hereditary moral weaknesses as they may have had, rose to the surface and worked their mischief without check. Cohabiting with criminals, and being extremely prolific, the result was the production of a stock exceeding 500 in number, of a prevalent criminal type. Through disease and intemperance the breed is now rapidly diminishing; the infant mortality has of late been horrible, but fortunately the women of the present generation bear usually but few children, and many of them are altogether childless.

CRIMINAL HEREDITY

Havelock Ellis, *The Criminal* (London: Walter Scott, 1890), 91–2, 216–18.

Ellis's primary aim in The Criminal *was to inform an English audience of European developments in criminal anthropology, particularly those in Italy. In this first edition of the book he uncritically draws on the work of the Italian criminologist Cesare Lombroso; in later editions, however, he is more critical of Lombroso's work.*

There are two factors, it must be remembered, in criminal heredity, as we commonly use the expression. There is the element of innate disposition, and there is the element of contagion from social environment. Both these factors clearly had their part in Sbro . . . who is regarded by Lombroso[1] as the classical type of 'moral insanity.' His grandfather had committed murder from jealousy; his father, condemned for rape, had killed a woman to test a gun. He in his turn

[1] Cesare Lombroso (1836–1909), Professor of Psychiatry and Criminal Anthropology at Turin University and author of *L'uomo delinquente; studiato in reporto alla anthropologia, alla medicina legale ed alle discipline carcerarie* (1876).

killed his father and his brother. Practically, it is not always possible to disentangle these two factors; a bad home will usually mean something bad in the heredity in the strict sense. Frequently the one element alone, whether the heredity or the contagion, is not sufficient to determine the child in the direction of crime. A case given by Prosper Lucas[2] seems to show this: 'In November 1845 the Assize Court of the Seine condemned three members out of five of a family of thieves, the Robert family. This case presented a circumstance worthy of remark. The father had not found among all his children the disposition that he would have desired; he had to use force with his wife and the two younger children, who up to the last were rebellious to his infamous orders. The eldest daughter, on the other hand, followed, as if by instinct, her father's example, and was as ardent and violent as he in attempting to bend the family to his odious tastes. But in one part of the family the instinct was lacking; they inherited from their mother.'

The influence of heredity, even in the strict sense of the word, in the production of criminals, does not always lie in the passing on of developed proclivities. Sometimes a generation of criminals is merely one stage in the progressive degeneration of a family. Sometimes crime seems to be the method by which the degenerating organism seeks to escape from an insane taint in the parents. [. . .]

It is worth while to enumerate briefly the probable causes of the sexual variation in criminality. There are perhaps five special causes acting on women: (1) physical weakness, (2) sexual selection, (3) domestic seclusion, (4) prostitution, (5) maternity.

There are firstly the physical and psychical traditions of the race embodied in the organisation of men and women. The extreme but rather spasmodic energy of men favours outbursts of violence, while the activities of women are at a lower but more even level, and their avocations have tended to develop the conservative rather than the destructive instincts. Apart from this, even if women were trained in violence, the superior strength of men would still make crimes of violence in women very hazardous and dangerous. Under existing circumstances, when a woman wants a crime committed, she can usually find a man to do it for her.

I have already frequently had occasion to note the approximation of criminal women in physical character to ordinary men. This has always been more or less carefully recorded, both in popular proverbs and in the records of criminal trials. Thus Sarah Chesham, a notorious wholesale poisoner, who killed several children, including her own, as well as her husband, was described as 'a woman of masculine proportions;' and a girl called Bouhours, who was executed at Paris at the age of twenty-two, for murdering and robbing several men who had been her lovers, is described as of agreeable appearance, and of sweet and feminine

[2] Author of *Traité philosophique et physiologique de l'hérédité naturelle dans les états de santé et de maladie du système nerveux* (1847–50), which became a contemporary classic.

manners, but of remarkable muscular strength; she dressed as a man; her chief pleasure was to wrestle with men, and her favourite weapon was the hammer.

Marro[3] has recently suggested that sexual selection has exerted a marked influence in diminishing the criminality of women. Masculine, unsexed, ugly, abnormal women—the women, that is, most strongly marked with the signs of degeneration, and therefore the tendency to criminality—would be to a large extent passed by in the choice of a mate, and would tend to be eliminated. It seems likely that this selection may have, at all events to some extent, existed, and exerted influence; it is, however, not universally accepted.

The domestic seclusion of women is an undoubted factor in the determination of the amount of women's criminality. In the Baltic provinces of Russia, where the women share the occupations of the men, the level of feminine criminality is very high. In Spain, the most backward of the large countries of Europe, where the education of women is at a very low level, and the women lead a very domesticated life, the level of feminine criminality is extremely low; the same is true, to a less extent, of Italy. In England, on the other hand, which has taken the lead in enlarging the sphere of women's work, the level of feminine criminality has for half a century been rising. Reference may perhaps also here be made to the fact that there is much more criminality among Irishwomen in England than among Irishwomen at home who lead a more domestic life. It is a very significant fact that Marro found among his women criminals, in marked contrast to the men, a very large proportion (35 out of 41) who possessed some more or less honourable occupation; a large proportion of the women also were possessed of some property. It may not be out of place to observe that the growing criminality of women is but the inevitable accident of a beneficial transition. Criminality, we must remember, is a natural element of life, regulated by natural laws, and as women come to touch life at more various points and to feel more of its stress, they will naturally develop the same tendency to criminality as exists among men, just as they are developing the same diseases, such as general paralysis. Our efforts must be directed, not to the vain attempt to repress the energies of women, but to the larger task of improving the conditions of life, and so diminishing the tendency to criminality among both sexes alike.

[3] Antonio Marro, *I caratteri dei delinquente: studio anthropologico-sociologico* (1887).

4. Childhood

PSYCHICAL DISEASES OF EARLY LIFE

James Crichton-Browne, 'Psychical diseases of early life', *Journal of Mental Science*, 6 (Apr. 1860), 285–7, 289–91, 303.

A leading figure in the growing area of child psychiatry during the last part of the century, James Crichton-Browne gave the paper on which this article is based to the Royal Medical Society in December 1859, aged 19, as a third-year medical student at Edinburgh University. He proposes ideas here that would be central to his later work; stressing that childhood is a vulnerable time both for hereditary and environmental reasons—children not only inherit their parents' weaknesses but are particularly susceptible to external conditions and stimulii.

When we know that the spermatozoid and the ovum convey to the progeny, in a manner as yet eluding all research, the physical and psychical qualities, not merely of the parents, but of the parents' parents for generations back, we shall easily see how necessary it is for us to consider and weigh well the characteristics and pursuits of past generations, and the influences brought to bear upon them. And here we should recollect that the spermatozoid and the ovum, not only, respectively, bear the impress of the form, gait and manners, internal qualities and construction of the respective parents, but that these microscopic bodies also transmit and communicate to the offspring the acquired tendencies and liabilities to particular forms of disease which the parents possess; we should recollect that they transmit not only general adaptations to healthy or diseased actions, not only comprehensive tendencies in certain directions, but minute and particular peculiarities and eccentricities, mental and bodily, which characterise the parents. These tendencies and liabilities, those predispositions may remain latent and concealed, but, when placed in circumstances favourable for their maturation, they may develope and become actual disease. It cannot be doubted that these may become developed, and ripened, and unfolded, as well in the womb and in the cradle, as in the strength of manhood and the second childishness of age; as well in the fœtus, the suckling, and the child, as in the stripling, the adult, and the aged.

One of the essential characteristics of a living being, is its capability of undergoing 'certain derangements from which it may recover, constituting disease;'* whilst the simplest and the most complex forms of organization are equally liable to disease. The nervous system then, even in its most rudimentary state, is liable to organic lesion, or functional derangement; in other words, to disease; and it is now my endeavour to direct attention to a certain class of nervous diseases, namely, mental disorders, as manifested in infancy and childhood—in utero, post partum; and up to puberty. Enough has already been said to point out the vast moment of the study of such diseases. For, if the mental training of children in general be of such importance, how important also is the training of those predisposed to mental disease, or actually suffering from it; how important, not only to the sufferers themselves, not only to those immediately interested in them, and solicitous regarding them, but to the community at large. [. . .]

Unfortunately, I shall be enabled to demonstrate to you that insanity does occur in utero, in infancy, and childhood, and that it is by no means so uncommon as supposed. Infantile insanity is still, however, comparatively rare, and it is so, firstly, because infancy is not exposed to many of those predisposing and existing causes which operate at other periods of life, and which go on increasing until maturity is passed; secondly, because fewer faculties of mind being then developed, fewer are liable to be assailed by disease; and, thirdly, because the delicacy of the infant brain is such that it is unable to undergo severe morbid action without perilling life. Diseases of the nervous centre in infancy and childhood are generally acute in their nature, rapid in their progress, and more frequently appear as hydrocephalus[1] and convulsions than as insanity. But with the above we should also remember the extreme susceptibility of the infant and childish mind; its high impressionability, and the readiness with which it admits of being bent aside from that perfect rectitude constituting health. Great and almost insurmountable difficulties exist in the way of arriving at a true knowledge of the mental condition of infants, and thus departures from the standard of mental health may exist in them, unknown and unobserved. Among certain class of young children, also, little or no attention is, as yet, paid to the workings and operations of the immortal mind; and in them those incoherent speeches, or odd remarks, which are attributed to childish unmeaning babbling and folly, may sometimes be in reality the result of delusions, illusions, and hallucinations. In other children those eccentricities and peculiarities of conduct, feeling and temper, those unnatural aversions and desires, which are traced by parents and guardians to wilful perversity may be but the exposition of morbid changes going on in the brain.

---

* Bennett's Outlines of Physiology, p. 11.

---

[1] Water on the brain.

With those considerations before us, and seeing an entire moral revolution and conversion may take place at the early age of four years, we have reason to believe that infants and children suffer more frequently from psycopathies than has hitherto been believed. [. . .]

Our last division of the influences, connected with the past history of the parents, exerted at conception, treats of the previous habits and modes of life of the progenitors. Those who, having been born with a good constitution, have lived in accordance with, and in obedience to, natural laws, may expect to produce children free from infirmity; but those who have violated natural laws, may expect that punishment, proportional to the offence, will inevitably be visited upon them and their descendants. Those who have perpetrated self-abuse, who have given themselves up to licentiousness, lust, and passion, to the vice of intemperance, to the pleasures of the table, or to any nervous excitement in excess, must suffer themselves from their want of self control, and must entail upon their progeny numerous and grievous ills—none more numerous and grievous than psychical disorders. The intemperate parent will transmit to his children a heritage of disease, and will inflict upon them ills innumerable. [. . .]

We have found cases recorded, of children addicted to stimulants, indeed drunkards, at and before the age of twelve; and we have ourselves observed a keen relish and liking for alcohol, in its various forms, at a much earlier age. The children of drunkards are often marked by vicious and depraved tastes, by sensual and criminal habits. [. . .] Excessive mental exertion on the part of the father is often productive of mental weakness in the child. Thus the children of the great and the eminent are frequently below mediocrity, and a race of distinguished men is quite exceptional. A liability to mental disease is oftimes the legacy left by a genius to his family. Excessive mental idleness and inactivity on the part of the father may be reproduced in his son in a morbid form; and excessive use of any faculty, or series of faculties, to the exclusion of others, in the father, may exert a baneful influence upon his progeny. In short, any departure, during the past lives of the parents, from the strict and immutable code of natural laws, may at conception, and during utero gestation, hurtfully affect their offspring.

So is it with the condition of the parents at the moment of conception. The state of the parents at this time apparently exercises a gigantic influence over the whole existence of the being conceived, no matter whether that state be permanent or transitory and accidental. [. . .]

Monomania, or delusional insanity, we believe to be more common during infancy and childhood than at any other period of life. It consists in an exaltation, or undue predominance, of some one faculty, is characterized by 'some particular illusion or erroneous conviction, impressed upon the understanding,' and implies an unhealthy state of the mind as a whole. Delusions and hallucinations are its exponents. We generally find that the delusions of the monomaniac bear distinct reference to his ordinary mode of thought and life, and are but diseased distortions, or exaggerations of his ordinary ideas. Thus, in childhood, they are frequently induced by castle building, and we would here take an opportunity of denouncing that most pleasant but pernicious practice. Impressions, created by the ever fertile imagination of a child; it may be whilst 'glow'ring at the fuffing low,'[2] are soon believed in as realities, and become a part of the child's psychical existence. They become, in fact, actual delusions. Such delusions are formed with facility, but eradicated with difficulty, and much mental derangement in mature life, we believe, is attributable to these reveries indulged in during childhood. It should not be forgotten that the 'disposition is builded up by the fashionings of first impressions.' Infantile and childish minds ought to be engaged with active, natural, and simple pursuits carried out into objectivity, and ought to be allowed little opportunity to 'Give to airy nothings a local habitation and a name.'[3]

BRAIN-FORCING

James Crichton-Browne, 'Education and the Nervous System', in M. A. Morris (ed.), *The Book of Health* (London: Cassell, 1883), 350–2, 379–80.

Anxieties about 'brain-forcing' took on a new urgency in the wake of the 1880 Education Act—and indeed were deployed to oppose the extension of universal state education. Immediately after the publication of this article, in 1884, Crichton-Browne was asked by the Department of Education to investigate the education methods in several London schools. Crichton-Browne produced a critical report which reiterates many of the points made here; though note that it is the fictional private establishment of Dr Blimber's in Dickens's Dombey and Son *that he uses as a key example.*

The evils of brain forcing may arise at any stage, and in connection with any branch of education; but they are most likely to show themselves under a system of 'cram' or spurt teaching, with a view to a specific examination, or of learning by rote and by rule, without any real understanding of what is being learnt. They are particularly apt to occur after the imposition of heavy tasks upon the memory, which in these modern times is not, perhaps, equal to the achievements that

[2] Staring at the spitting fire.
[3] William Shakespeare, *A Midsummer Night's Dream*, v. i. 16–17.

it performed in the past. The prodigies of memory which were not uncommon in Europe a few centuries ago are not now to be looked for. At the revival of literature, a man who had read a few manuscripts, and could repeat them, might travel from place to place and live by his learning; and the scholar had far more inducement to engrave the words of others on his memory, than to exercise his own judgment and invention. But in later times the case is greatly changed, and we must now go to India or China, where poems and scientific works are and have been for centuries transmitted orally from one generation to another, for such marvellous feats of memory. With us the ready access which all classes of the community now have to books and writing materials has undoubtedly a tendency to weaken the powers of memory, by superseding the necessity for its more extraordinary exertions. It was on this principle that the Druids (as we are informed by Cæsar in his Commentaries), although they knew the Greek letters, abstained from the use of writing for recording their theological and philosophical doctrines, lest by leaning upon a crutch they should weaken the limbs. We, with our pocket-books, calling-lists, encyclopædias, directories, and libraries, depend much less than our grandfathers did on the tablets of the brain. We do not inquire within for everything, but trust in large measure to external aids to memory. Conscious that lost knowledge can be easily recovered, we disburden ourselves of whatever we can commit to writing, or refer to in an index, and consequently we do not require of memory those arduous labours by which our ancestors used to brace its sinews. Some decay of mere verbal memory is, therefore, perhaps going on, though it is to be hoped that a better and classificatory memory is contemporaneously gaining strength and vigour. But the diminished power of verbal memory must make it more and more difficult for modern children to commit to its safe keeping heavy word tasks, and hence it is not surprising to find that, in them, it sometimes fails altogether when over-loaded, and goaded into fatiguing efforts. It is the memory itself that often gives way under such a discipline, becoming incapable of even ordinary exertions, or suddenly losing any extraordinary powers which it may have inherited or acquired. [. . .] Charles Dickens; with his quick insight and sympathy with the right, noticed the crippling effects of the cramming and forcing of memory, and happily hit them off in his description of Dr. Blimber's establishment.

'Whenever a young gentleman was taken in hand by Dr. Blimber, he might consider himself sure of a pretty tight squeeze. The Doctor only took the charge of ten young gentlemen; but he had always ready a supply of learning for a hundred on the lowest estimate; and it was at once the business and delight of his life to gorge the unhappy ten with it.

'In fact, Dr. Blimber's establishment was a great hot-house, in which there was a forcing apparatus constantly at work. All the boys blew before their time. Mental green peas were produced at Christmas, and intellectual asparagus all the year round. Every description of Greek and Latin vegetable was got off the driest twigs of boys under the frostiest circumstances. Nature was of no consequence at all. No matter what a young gentleman was intended to bear, Dr. Blimber made him bear to order somehow or other. This was very pleasant and ingenious, but the system of forcing was attended with its usual disadvantages: there was not a right taste about the premature productions, and they didn't keep well. Moreover, one young gentleman with a swollen nose and an excessively large head (the eldest of the ten), who had gone through everything, suddenly left off blowing one day, and remained in the establishment a mere stock. And people did say that the Doctor had rather overdone it with young Toots, who, when he began to have whiskers, left off having brains.' [. . .]

And besides general enfeeblement of mind, a loss of mental balance is seen as a consequence of injudicious forcing in education. Children previously bright and vigorous pass from time to time into what is called a brown study or absence of mind, or become eccentric in manner and conduct; this latter state being most often seen in those who have an inherited tendency to insanity, and in whom it often foreshadows, or leads up to, an outburst of madness.

But the evils of memory-stuffing and brain-forcing as carried on in schools, and sometimes under home-tuition, by tutors and governesses with more zeal than judgment, are not confined to mental failure and disorder and the frustration of all the hopes with which they were undertaken; they include a whole train of physical diseases, some of which fill with pain and bitterness what should be the bright days of childhood, radiant with joys such as the dim later years can never yield, and some of which place life in jeopardy. And it is not wonderful that they should do this, when the nature of their physiological effects on the brain and nervous apparatus is considered. [. . .]

In employing and directing the various agencies of moral culture that are at command, judgment must be used in bringing them into operation at the proper time. Favourable opportunities of forming character must not be lost, but premature endeavours after an impossible perfection must be avoided; for there is such a thing as moral precocity, and moral, like intellectual precocity, maybe a manifestation of disease, or may eventuate in weakness. Little saints, like little prodigies, often die of acute hydrocephalus,[2] and what is called 'early piety' not rarely ends in late imbecility. Parents should remember that children are not little nineteenth-century men and women, but diamond editions of very remote ancestors, full of savage whims and impulses, and savage rudiments of virtue. They should not, therefore, be disheartened by inveterately mischievous propensities, nor even by serious delinquencies now and then, which growth and good management will correct; nor should they try to put a mask of propriety on the wanton features of youthful animalism. Let them attend to the weightier matters of the law, and leave the mint and anise and cummin alone. Only when grave

---

[1] *Dombey and Son*, Ch. 11.   [2] Water on the brain.

offences succeed each other with great frequency, and are not amenable to the ordinary methods of correction, should their apprehensions be excited, and then they should at once consult their medical man, for there is such a thing as moral insanity dependent on a disordered state of the nervous system. It is all very well to laugh at kleptomania, but when a previously well-conducted school-boy, under severe educational pressure, suddenly takes to stealing all kinds of useless articles, and goes on stealing after exposure and punishment, and while at the same time he exhibits convulsive movements of the eyeballs known as nystagmus,[2] these movements and the stealing both ceasing at the same time under medical treatment, it would be preposterous to doubt that the propensity to theft is a symptom of a morbid state. When, therefore, an abrupt change of character is noticed in any child, or when precocious and singular depravity displays itself, medical aid should be invoked. Moral insanity most frequently occurs at the age of puberty—in the female, in connexion with hysteria; and then we have fasting girls and ecstatics, and the simulation of disease; but moral imbecility, as it is called, is generally recognised at a much earlier age. Don Carlos[3] who appears to have been a moral imbecile, was remarkable for falsehood, ferocity, and cruelty, when a mere child. His delight was to cut the throats of hares and other animals, and gloat over their dying struggles. He frequently roasted them alive. He once received the present of a very large snake from some person who seemed to know how to please this vile young prince. After a time, however, the favourite reptile bit its master's fingers, whereupon he retaliated by biting off its head. He was prematurely and grossly licentious. In such a case, even medical assistance is not likely to be of much avail; but it will be more efficacious than mere moral discipline, and will, at least, conduct to a just appreciation of the monstrosity.

BABIES AND SCIENCE

James Sully, 'Babies and science', *The Cornhill*, 43 (Jan.–June 1881), 543–5.

James Sully was a key figure in the emergence of child psychology at the end of the century whose major works, Outlines of Psychology *(1884),* The Human Mind *(1892), and* Studies of Childhood *(1895), argued that the study of infant development was crucial to the understanding of adult consciousness. In this early popular article he introduces many of the arguments that he would develop in his*

[2] Form of eye disease signalled by the uncontrollable rolling of the eyeballs.

[3] (1545–68), son of Philip II of Spain, he was the heir to the thrones of Castile and Aragon, but became increasingly mentally unstable and was placed under restraint after a plot to assassinate his father.

later work, while poking fun at the new class of 'scientific fathers'. In the first part of the article Sully stresses the difference between animal and human infancy, developing the argument that the helplessness of human babyhood plays a crucial part in developing family structures and social institutions.

This, then, is the utterance of science. She bids all male scoffers at the trivialities of babyhood recognise in this seemingly insignificant phenomenon one of the main sources of human greatness. She says to them, this state of infantile frailty and imbecility is causally connected with all the blessings of social life. It is these babes and sucklings which first touched the adamantine heart of mankind, making it vibrate in pulsations of tenderness. Had there been no babies there would have been no higher intellectual development, no sacred ties of kinship, friendship, and co-patriotism. Nay, more, but for the appearance of the infantile condition which you rash ingrates are wont to ridicule as molluscous, gelatinous, and so on, there would have been no human race at all: and you would not have been here to criticise nature and her ways as glibly as you do.

In this way science has come to the aid of mothers and nurses by stopping the mouth of the male blasphemer of nature. She has found a *raison d'être* for infancy, redeeming the whole class of babies from the charge of being perfectly useless incumbrances. She has compelled proud man to bow in deference to the views of the other sex, and to recognise in the phenomenon of babyhood something profoundly significant, a necessary link in the chain of cosmic events. [. . .]

Yes, the baby has become an important object of scientific scrutiny, and in this way. The modern psychologist, sharing in the spirit of positive science, feels that he must begin at the beginning, study mind in its simplest forms before attempting to explain its more complex and intricate manifestations. This impulse to study the elementary modes of mental activity has led the psychologist to greatly extend the range of his observation. Instead of confining himself to looking into his own consciousness, he carries his eye far afield to the phenomena of savage life, with its simple ideas, crude sentiments, and naïve habits. Again he devotes special attention to the mental life of the lower animals, seeking in its phenomena the dim foreshadowings of our own perceptions, emotions, &c. Finally he directs his attention to the mental phenomena of infancy, as fitted to throw most light on the later developments of the human mind. He sees here the first beginnings of that work of construction by which all mental growth takes place. It is during the twelve months or so of infancy that the blurred mass of sensation begins to take form and to resolve itself into definite, distinguishable impressions; that these impressions begin to leave a trace or after effect in the shape of a mental image, which enters into combination with impressions in that mental state which we call perception, and which appears in a detached form as an expectation, a recollection, or a pure fancy. And it is during this same period that the foundations of the emotional structure are laid; that the simple feelings of pleasure and pain connected with the action of the vital organs and of the senses begin to combine in the forms of fear and love, anger and hope, and so on. And, finally, it is now that the activities of will first come into play, beginning to wear those tracks which will become later on the habitual lines of action of the developed will. If, then, the psychologist could only ascertain what goes on in the mind of the infant, he would be in a position to solve many a knotty question in his science.

Infancy has a peculiar interest to the psychologist for another reason. My readers are probably aware that it has long been a matter of dispute whether the mind comes into the world like a blank sheet of paper on which experience has to write, or whether it brings with it innate dispositions, as they are called, a kind of invisible writing which contact with experience will make legible but not create. For example, it has long been asked whether the child is born with an instinctive moral tendency to distinguish right and wrong actions, or whether this distinction is wholly impressed on it from without, by help of the experiences of punishment, &c., connected with the discipline of early life. Now it seems obvious that, if there are such innate dispositions, intellectual and moral, they ought to be observable in a germinal form in the first stage of life. And since we can only be certain of the existence of any innate or inherited element by discovering that something appears in the course of mental development which cannot be accounted for by the individual's own previous experience, it follows that it is of the utmost consequence to the psychologist to note and record the first phases of mental history. To give an example, if the baby smiles in response to a smile long before experience and reflection can have taught it the practical value of winning people's smiles, there is clearly an argument for those who would say that we are born with an instinctive germ of sociality and sympathy.

If the psychologist is an evolutionist, and interested in studying the history of human development as a whole, the infant will attract his regards in another way. It is a doctrine of biology that the development of the individual roughly epitomises that of the race; that is to say, exhibits the main phases of this development on a small scale. If this is so, the study of infant life may be well fitted to suggest by what steps of intellectual and moral progress our race has passed into its present state. The attentive eye may thus find in seemingly meaningless little infantile ways hints of remote habits and customs of the human race.

Science having thus declared the infant to be a valuable phenomenon for observation, there has of late grown up among the class of scientific fathers the habit of noting and recording the various proceedings of the infant. Men who previously never thought of meddling with the affairs of the nursery have been impelled to make periodic visits thither in the hope of eliciting important psychological facts. The tiny occupant of the cradle has had to bear the piercing glance of the scientific eye. The psychological papa has acquired a new

343

proprietary right in his offspring; he has appropriated it as a biological specimen. This new zeal for psychological knowledge has taken possession of a number of my acquaintance. These are mostly young married men to whom the phenomenon of babyhood has all the charm of newness, and who import a youthful enthusiasm into their scientific pursuits. Their minds are very much taken up with their new line of study. If you happen to call on one of them expecting to find him free for a chat, you may, to your amazement, catch him occupied in the nursery with trying to discover the preferences of the three-months' fledgling in the matter of colours, or watching the impression which is first made on the infant mind by the image of its own face in the glass. And, even when not actually employed in his researches, it will be found that his mind tends to revert to his engrossing study; and so all your attempts to engage him in conversation on matters of ordinary interest are apt to be frustrated.

CHILDHOOD AND EVOLUTION

James Sully, Introduction to Bernard Perez, *The First Three Years of Childhood* (London: Swan Sönnenschein, 1885), pp. v –ix.

Sully discussed the development of self-consciousness and language in children in his Outlines of Psychology *and he expresses his own theory of childhood in his Introduction to the influential French child psychologist Bernard Perez's work. Here he takes up the analogy between childhood and 'primitive' societies that he suggested in 'Babies and science' and will develop in* Studies of Childhood, *which draws on the work of the cultural anthropologist E. B. Tyler and the archaeologist A. H. Pitt-Rivers as well as authorities on child development such as Bernard Perez.*

Some of the gravest questions relating to man's nature and destiny carry us back to the observation of infancy. Take, for instance, the warmly-discussed question, whether conscience is an innate faculty—each man's possession anterior to and independently of all the external human influences, authority, discipline, moral education, which go to shape it; or whether, on the contrary, it is a mere outgrowth from the impressions received in the course of this training. Nothing seems so likely to throw light on this burning question as a painstaking observation of the first years of life.

This, however, is not the whole of the significance of infancy to the modern psychologist. We are learning to connect the individual life with that of the race, and this again with the collective life of all sentient creatures. The doctrine of evolution bids us view the unfolding of a human intelligence to-day as conditioned and prepared by long ages of human experience, and still longer cycles of animal experience. The civilized individual is thus a memento, a kind of short-hand record of nature's far-receding work of organizing, or building up living conscious structures. And according to this view the successive stages of the mental life of the individual roughly answer to the periods of this extensive process of organization—vegetal, animal, human, civilized life. This being so, the first years of the child are of a peculiar antiquarian interest.

Here we may note the points of contact of man's proud reason with the lowly intelligence of the brutes. In the most ordinary child we may see a new dramatic representation of the great cosmic action, the laborious emergence of intelligence out of its shell of animal sense and appetite.

Yet it must not be supposed that the interest here is wholly historical or archæological. For in thus detecting in the developmental processes of the child's mind an epitome of human and animal evolution, we learn the better to understand those processes. We are able to see in such a simple phenomenon as an infant's responsive smile a product of far-reaching activities lying outside the individual existence. In the light of the new doctrine of evolution, the early period of individual development, which is pre-eminently the domain of instinct,—that is to say, of tendencies and impulses which cannot be referred to the action of the preceding circumstances of the individual,—is seen to be the region which bears the clearest testimony to this preparatory work of the race. It is in infancy that we are least indebted to our individual exertions, mental as well as bodily, and that our debt to our progenitors seem heaviest. In the rapidity with which the infant co-ordinates external impressions and movements, as in learning to follow a light with the eyes, or stretch out the hand to seize an object, and with which feelings of fear, anger, etc., attach themselves to objects and persons, we can plainly trace the play of heredity—that law by which each new individual starts on his life course enriched by a legacy of ancestral experience.

Viewed in this light, infant psychology is seen to be closely related to other departments of the science. To begin with, it has obvious points of contact with what is known as the psychology of race (Völkerpsychologie). The first years of the child answer indeed to the earliest known stages of human history. How curiously do the naïve conceptions of nature, the fanciful animistic ideas of things, and the rude emotions of awe and terror, which there is good reason to attribute to our earliest human ancestors, reflect themselves in the language of the child! It is probably indeed that inquiries into the beginnings of human culture, the origin of language, of primitive ideas and institutions, might derive much more help than they have yet done from a close scrutiny of the events of childhood.

Again, it is evident that the psychology of the infant borders on animal psychology. The child's love of animals points to a special facility in understanding their ways; and this, again, indicates a certain community of nature. The intelligence of children and of animals has this in common, that each is simple and direct, unencumbered with the fruit of wide comparison and abstract reflection, keen and incisive within its own narrow compass. Both the child and the brute are exposed by their ignorance to similar risks of danger and deception; both show the same instincts of attachment and trustfulness. And so a study of the one helps the understanding of the other. The man or woman who sees most clearly into the workings of a child's mind will, other things being equal, be the best understander of animal ways, and *vice versa*.

THE GROWTH OF SELF-CONSCIOUSNESS

George Romanes, *Mental Evolution in Man: Origin of Human Faculty* (London: Kegan Paul, Trench & Co., 1888), 200–6.

George Romanes's Animal Intelligence *(1882) and* Mental Evolution in Animals *(1883), the first significant works of animal psychology, applied Darwin's theories of physical evolution in animals to their mental development. In* Mental Evolution in Man, *Romanes stresses that his aim is to analyse the origin rather than the development of specifically human characteristics by reinterpreting associationist ideas within evolutionary theory. Romanes's discussion here of the growth of self-consciousness in the child draws heavily on Sully's studies of infant consciousness and emphasizes the role of social interaction in human development. Romanes's argument hangs on his theory of the 'logic of recepts': a recept or generic idea differs from a concept in that it is 'received, not conceived'. However, a recept is more than simply a reflexive physical response; it is 'that kind of idea the constituent parts of which . . . unite spontaneously as soon as they are brought together' through a process of unconscious memory (p. 49). Developing the associationist model, Romanes thus replaces the familiar division between feeling and thinking with the 'logic of recepts' and the 'logic of concepts', and in this passage on the child's growth of self-consciousness he develops the notion of the 'ejective' (similar to projected) perception of the world, which precedes, but is crucial to, the development of language.*

I take it, then, as established that true or conceptual self-consciousness consists in paying the same kind of attention to inward psychical processes as is habitually paid to outward physical processes; that in the mind of animals and infants there is a world of images standing as signs of outward objects, although we may concede that for the most part they only admit of being revived by sensuous association; that at this stage of mental evolution the logic of recepts comprises an ejective as well as an objective world; and that here we also have the recognition of individuality, so far as this is dependent on what has been termed an outward self-consciousness, or the consciousness of self as a feeling and an active agent, without the consciousness of self as an object of thought, and, therefore, as a *subject*.

Such being the mental conditions precedent to the rise of true self-consciousness, we may next turn to the growing child for evidence of subsequent stages in the gradual evolution of this faculty. All observers are agreed that for a considerable time after a child is able to use words as expressive of ideas, there is no vestige of true self-consciousness. But, to begin our survey before this period, at a year old even its own organism is not known to the child as part of the self, or, more correctly, as anything specially related to feelings. [. . .]

Later on, when the outward self-consciousness already explained has begun to be developed, we find that the child, like the animal, has learnt to associate its own organism with its own mental states, in such wise that it recognizes its body as belonging in a peculiar manner to the self, so far as the self is recognizable by the logic of recepts. This is the stage that we meet with in animals. Next the child begins to talk, and, as we might expect, this first translation of the logic of recepts reveals the fact that as yet there is no *inward* self-consciousness, but only outward: as yet the child has paid no *attention* to his own mental states, further than to feel that he feels them; and in the result we find that the child speaks to himself as an object, *i.e.* by his proper name or in the third person. That is to say, 'the child does not as yet set himself in opposition to all outer objects, including all other persons, but regards himself as one among many objects.'* The change of a child's phraseology from speaking of self as an object to speaking of self as a subject does not take place—or but rarely so—till the third year. When it has taken place we have definite evidence of true self-consciousness, though still in a rudimentary stage. And it is doubtful whether this change would take place even at so early an age as the third year, were it not promoted by the 'social environment.' For, as Mr. Sully observes, 'the relation of self and not self, including that between the I and the You, is continually being pressed on the child's attention by the language of others.'† But, taking this great change during the time of life when it is actually observed to be in progress, let us endeavour to trace the phases of its development.

It will no doubt be on all hands freely conceded, that at least up to the time when a child begins to speak it has no beginning of any true or introspective

* Sully, Outline of Psychology (1884), p. 376.   † *Loc. cit.*, p. 377.

consciousness of self; and it will further be conceded that when this consciousness begins to dawn, the use of language by a child may be taken as a fair exponent of all its subsequent progress. Now we have already seen that, long before any words are used indicative of even a dawning consciousness of self as self, the child has already advanced so far in its use of language as to frame implicit propositions. [. . .]

We have now before us unquestionable evidence that in the growing child there is a power, not only of forming, but of expressing a pre-conceptual judgment, long before there is any evidence of the child presenting the faintest rudiment of internal, conceptual, or true self-consciousness. In other words, it must be admitted that long before a human mind is sufficiently developed to perceive relations as related, or to state a truth as true, it is able to perceive relations and to state a truth: the logic of recepts is here concerned with those higher receptual judgments which I have called pre-conceptual, and is able to express such judgments in verbal signs without the intervention of true (*i.e.* introspective) self-consciousness. [. . .]

First, then, let it be observed that in these rudimentary judgments we already have a considerable advance upon those which we have considered as occurring in animals. For in a child between the second and third years we have these rudimentary judgments, not only formed by the logic of recepts, but expressed by a logic of pre-concepts in a manner which is indistinguishable from predication, except by the absence of self-consciousness. 'Dit dow ga' is a proposition in every respect, save in the absence of the copula; which, as I have previously shown, is a matter of no psychological moment. The child here perceives a certain fact, and states the perception in words, *in order to communicate information of the fact to other minds*—just as an animal, under similar circumstances, will use a gesture or a vocal sign; but the child is no more able than the animal designedly to make to its own mind the statement which it makes to another. Nevertheless, as the child has now at its disposal a much more efficient system of sign-making than has the animal, and moreover enjoys the double advantage of inheriting a strong propensity to communicate perceptions by signs, and of being surrounded by the medium of speech; we can scarcely wonder that its practical judgments (although still unattended by self-consciousness) should be more habitually expressed by signs than are the practical judgments of animals. Nor need we wonder, in view of the same considerations, that the predicative phrases are used by a child at this age show the great advance upon similar phrases as used by a parrot, in that subjects and predicates are no longer bound together in particular phrases—or, to revert to a previous simile, are no longer stereotyped in such particular phrases, but admit of being used as movable types, in order to construct, by different combinations, a variety of different phrases. To a talking bird a phrase, as we have seen, is no more in point of signification than a single word; while to the child, at the stage which we are considering, it is very much more than this: it is the separately constructed vehicle for the conveyance of a particular meaning, which may never have been conveyed by that or by any other phrase before. But while we thus attach due importance to so great an advance towards the faculty of true predication, we must notice, on the one hand, that as yet it is *not* true predication in the sense of being the expression of a true or conceptual judgment; and, on the other hand, we must notice that the power of thus using words as movable types does not deserve to be regarded as any wonderful or unaccountable advance in the faculty of sign-making, when we pay due regard to the several considerations above stated. The really important point to notice is that, notwithstanding this great *advance* towards the faculty of predication, this faculty *has not yet been reached*: the propositions which are made are still unattended by self-consciousness: they are not conceptual, but pre-conceptual.

Given, then, this stage of mental evolution, and what follows? Be it remembered I am not endeavouring to solve the impossible problem as to the intrinsic nature of self-consciousness, or how it is that such a thing is possible. I am merely accepting its existence (and therefore its possibility) as a fact; and upon the basis of this fact I shall now endeavour to show how, in my opinion, self-consciousness may be seen to follow upon the stage of mental evolution which we have here reached.

The child, like the animal, is supplied by its logic of recepts with a world of images, standing as signs of outward objects; with an ejective knowledge of other minds; and with that kind of recognition of self as an active, suffering and accountable agent which, following Mr. Chauncey Wright,[1] I have called 'outward self-consciousness.' But, over and above the animal, the child has at its command, as we have just seen, the more improved machinery of sign-making which enables it to signify to other minds (ejectively known) the contents of its receptual knowledge. Now, among these contents is the child's perception of the mental states of others as expressed in their gestures, tones, and words. These severally receive their appropriate names, and so gain clearness and precision as ejective images of the corresponding states experienced by the child itself. 'Mama pleased to Dodo' would have no meaning as spoken by a child, unless the child knew from his own feelings what is the state of mind which he thus ejectively attributes to another. Therefore we cannot be surprised to find that at the same stage of mental evolution the child will say, 'Dodo pleased to mama.' Yet it is evident that we here approach the very borders of true self-consciousness. 'Dodo' is no doubt still speaking of himself in objective terminology; but he has advanced so far in the interpretation of his own states of mind as to name them no less clearly than he names any external objects of sense perception. Thus he is enabled to fix these states before his mental vision as things which admit of being *denoted* by verbal signs, albeit he is not yet able to *denominate*.

[1] 'The Evolution of Self-Consciousness', *Philosophical Discussions* (1877).

The step from this to recognizing 'Dodo' as not only the object, but also the subject of mental changes, is not a large step. The mere act of attaching verbal signs to inward mental states has the effect of focussing attention upon those states; and, when attention is thus focussed habitually, there is supplied the only further condition required to enable the mind, through its memory of previous states, to compare its past with its present, and so to reach that apprehension of continuity among its own states wherein the full introspective consciousness of self consists.

THE CHILD AS CRIMINAL

Havelock Ellis, *The Criminal* (London: Walter Scott, 1890), 211–14.

Here Ellis is drawing both on Lombroso's work and that of Gregor Mendel and George Savage in arguing that the 'arrested development' of the criminal is echoed in the inherent 'criminality' of childhood. Cf. the extract from George Savage's articles on 'Moral insanity' in Section IV.

There is a certain form of criminality almost peculiar to children, a form to which the term 'moral insanity' may very fairly be ascribed. This has been described by Krafft-Ebing, Mendel, Savage, and others,[1] and is characterised by a certain eccentricity of character, a dislike of family habits, an incapacity for education, a tendency to lying, together with astuteness and extraordinary cynicism, bad sexual habits, and cruelty towards animals and companions. It shows itself between the ages of five and eleven, and is sometimes united with precocious intellectual qualities. There can be no doubt that many of these develop into instinctive criminals. Sometimes these characters only appear at puberty, together with exaggerated sexual tendencies, in children who have previously been remarkable only for their mental precocity, but whose energy seems now to be thrown into a new channel.

It is a very significant fact that these characters are but an exaggeration of the characters which in a less degree mark nearly all the children. The child is naturally, by his organisation, nearer to the animal, to the savage, to the criminal, than

[1] Richard von Krafft-Ebing (1840–1902), best known for his *Psychopathia Sexualis* (1886), translated into English in the 1890s, but also the author of *Die Melancholie* (1874) and *Lehrbuch der Gerichtlichen Psychopathologie* (1875). Gregor Mendel (1822–84), German biologist who developed work on heredity during the 1860s which was 'rediscovered' in 1900 and contributed both to eugenic theory and to the development of genetics; George Savage, see Notes on Authors.

the adult. Although this has frequently been noted in a fragmentary manner, it is only of recent years that the study of childhood, a subject of the gravest import-ance, has been seriously taken up by Perez[2] and others.

The child lives in the present; the emotion or the desire of the moment is large enough to blot out for him the whole world; he has no foresight, and is the easier given up to his instincts and passions; our passions, as Hobbes said, bring us near to children. Children are naturally egoists; they will commit all enormities, sometimes, to enlarge their egoistic satisfaction. They are cruel and inflict suf-fering on animals out of curiosity, enjoying the manifestations of pain. They are thieves for the gratification of their appetites, especially the chief, gluttony, and they are unscrupulous and often cunning liars, not hesitating to put the blame on the innocent when their misdeeds are discovered. The charm of childhood for those who are not children lies largely in these qualities of frank egotism and reckless obedience to impulse.

Most people who can recollect their own childhood—an ability which does not, however, appear to be very common—can remember how they have some-times yielded to overmastering impulses which, although of a trivial character, were distinctly criminal. The trifling, or even normal character of such acts in childhood is too often forgotten by those who have to deal with children. [. . .]

In many persons the impulses of childhood persist in a more or less subdued form in adult age. The impulses are not yielded to so readily, or at all, but they are still felt. The examples have often been quoted of the distinguished alienist, Morel, who, as he narrates himself, seeing a workman leaning over one of the Seine bridges, felt so strong an impulse to throw the man into the river, that he had to rush away from the spot; and of Humboldt's nurse[3] who, at the sight and touch of the new-born child's rosy flesh, felt the temptation to kill it, and was obliged to entrust it to some one else. These morbid impulses are perhaps more closely related to insanity than to criminality, but it is on a borderland that is com-mon to both. Both child and criminal are subject to such impulses.

In the criminal, we may often take it, there is an arrest of development. The criminal is an individual who, to some extent, remains a child his life long—a child of larger growth and with greater capacity for evil. This is part of the atavism of criminals. Mental acuteness is often observed among criminal chil-dren; it is rare among criminal adults. There is evidently arrest of development at a very early age, probably a precocious union of the cranial bones. Among sav-ages, also, the young children are bright, but development stops at a very early age. All who have come very intimately in contact with criminals have noted their resemblance to children.

[2] Bernard Perez, author of the influential *The First Three Years of Childhood* (1885). See also Sully's introduction to Perez's work, above.

[3] Friedrich Heinrich Alexander von Humboldt (1769–1859), German botanist and geologist who wrote extensively of his explorations in South America.

5. Race and Hybridity

SPECIES AND VARIETIES

James Cowles Prichard, *Researches into the Physical History of Mankind* (1813),
4th edn., 4 vols. (London: Sherwood, Gilbert and Piper, 1837–41), i. 105,
108–9, 147–8, 175–6, 180–3.

Prichard's Researches into the Physical History of Mankind *(developed in* The
Natural History of Man *(1845)) set the terms for the debate on 'race' that would
continue through the nineteenth century. It is dedicated to the famous German
natural historian J. F. Blumenbach (1752–1840), who classified human races into
five families (Caucasian, Mongolian, Malayan, Ethiopian, and American) but who
subscribed to the traditionally Christian monogenist view that all mankind had a
common origin. Prichard defends monogenic ideas by analogical reasoning—drawing comparisons between animal and human variation. The first volume of*
Researches *considers 'whether each species in the animal or vegetable world exists
only as the progeny of one race, or has sprung originally from several different
sources'. These extracts are from the beginning of volume* i, *starting with the problematic definition of 'race' itself, then linking it with the crucial question of hybridity. The examples of the 'Bushmen', and the 'Griqua, or Bastard Hottentot race'
recur throughout nineteenth-century discussion of racial difference and origin.*

MEANING ATTACHED TO THE TERMS SPECIES—GENERA—
VARIETIES—PERMANENT VARIETIES—RACES

The meaning attached to the term *species* in natural history is very definite and
intelligible. It includes only the following conditions, namely, separate origin and
distinctness of race, evinced by the constant transmission of some characteristic
peculiarity of organization. A race of animals or of plants marked by any peculiar character which it has ever constantly displayed, is termed a species; and two
races are considered as specifically different, if they are distinguished from each
other by some characteristic which the one cannot be supposed to have acquired,

or the other to have lost through any known operation of physical causes; for we are, hence, led to conclude, that the tribes thus distinguished have not descended from the same original stock.

This is the purport of the word species, as it has long been understood by writers on different departments of natural history. They agree essentially as to the sense which they appropriate to this term, though they have expressed themselves differently according as they have blended more or less of hypothesis with their conceptions of its meaning. [. . .]

Varieties, in natural history, are such diversities in individuals and their progeny as are observed to take place within the limits of species. Varieties are modifications produced in races of animals and of plants by the agency of external causes; they are congenital: that deviation from the character of a parent-stock which is occasioned by mixture of breed, has been regarded as a kind of variety; but varieties are quite as well known in the animal kingdom as the mere result of agencies, often little understood, on the breed, independently of such mixture. Varieties are hereditary, or transmitted to offspring with greater or less degrees of constancy.

Varieties are distinguished from species by the circumstance that they are not original or primordial, but have arisen, within the limits of a particular stock or race. *Permanent varieties* are those which having once taken place, continue to be propagated in the breed in perpetuity. The fact of their origination must be known by observation or inference, since the proof of this fact being defective it is more philosophical to consider characters which are perpetually inherited as specific or original. The term permanent variety, would otherwise express the meaning which properly belongs to species. The properties of species are two, viz. original difference of characters and the perpetuity of their transmission, of which only the latter can belong to permanent varieties.

The instances are so many in which it is doubtful whether a particular tribe is to be considered as a distinct species, or only as a variety of some other tribe, that it has been found by naturalists convenient to have a designation applicable in either case. Hence the late introduction of the term *race* in this indefinite sense. Races are properly successions of individuals propagated from any given stock; and the term should be used without any involved meaning that such a progeny or stock has always possessed a particular character. The real import of the term has often been overlooked, and the word race has been used as if it implied a distinction in the physical character of the whole series of individuals. By writers on anthropology, who adopt this term, it is often tacitly assumed that such distinctions were primordial, and that their successive transmission has been unbroken. If such were the fact, a race so characterized would be a species in the strict meaning of the word, and it ought to be so termed. [. . .]

OF MIXED HUMAN RACES

A question now offers itself to our consideration with respect to mixed races in the human kind, whether they are, in the phenomena of their propagation, analogous to hybrid productions, or to the blended offspring of tribes which are merely varieties of the same species.

Now the undoubted fact is, that all mixed races of men are remarkable for their tendency to multiplication. The men of colour, or the mixed breed between the white Creoles and the Negroes, are well known in many of the West Indian isles to increase rapidly, and this chiefly by family connexions among themselves. Hence there has resulted a particular caste in many places so numerous and so rapidly gaining ground, as to give rise to serious apprehensions that they are destined to become at length the dominant tribe in the community. In other parts of the world, in almost every example to which different varieties of mankind are brought into social relations at all similar to those of the Negroes and Creoles, or offering facilities for intercourse, similar results have taken place. I shall here only point out in a brief manner some few of these instances which I shall have future occasion to investigate, when considering the ethnography of particular countries and the physical history of particular races of mankind. In Africa there are several remarkable instances of a similar description. The Griquas, or bastard Hottentots, the mixed race between the Dutch colonists and the aborigines of South Africa form on the borders of the colonial settlements a numerous and rapidly increasing race. The Griquas now occupy the banks of the Gariep or Orange river, for the space of at least seven hundred miles, where their numbers were estimated some years ago to be at least 5,000 souls. They are powerful marauders, and harass by their predatory incursions all the native tribes in their vicinity, and are frequently troublesome to the neighbouring colonists. Great numbers of the same mixed race are in other parts thriving agriculturists; and there is a large community at Griqua Town settled under the government of the Missionaries of the United Brethren, by whose means they had been converted to Christianity and have adopted the habits of civilized society. [. . .]

OF HUMAN SENTIMENTS

[. . .] If we could divest ourselves of all previous impressions respecting our nature and social state, and look at mankind and human actions with the eyes of a natural historian, or as a zoologist observes, the life and manners of beavers or of termites, we should remark nothing more striking in the habitudes of mankind, and in their manner of existence in various parts of the world, than a reference, which is everywhere more or less distinctly perceptible, to a state of existence after death, and to the influence believed both by barbarous and civilized nations to be exercised over their present condition and future destiny by invisible agents, differing in attributes according to the sentiments of different nations, but universally believed to exist. [. . .] These are among the most striking and remarkable of the psychical phenomena, if we may so apply the expression, which are peculiar to man, and if they are to be traced among races of men which differ physically from each other, it will follow that all mankind partake of a common moral nature, and are therefore, if we take into the account the law which allots a diversity of psychical properties to different species, proved, by an extensive observation of analogies in nature, to constitute a single tribe. [. . .]

OF THE PSYCHICAL CHARACTERS OF THE BUSHMAN OR HOTTENTOT RACE

[. . .] Considering the pastoral Hottentots and the Bushmen as one race, I shall make some remarks on their mental character in general, in order to furnish the ground for a comparison between this and other families of men.

We must attempt to estimate the character of the Hottentot race, not from their present degraded condition, after the cruelty and oppression which they have endured from European colonists during so many generations have broken their spirit and reduced them to bondage or exile, but from the accounts left by older writers of the condition of these tribes soon after the first settlement of the Dutch colony. The voyager Kolben has given us a full and circumstantial account of the Hottentots at this time, and many of his statements are singularly at variance with the description which late writers have drawn. The original Hottentots were a numerous people, divided into many tribes under the patriarchal government of chiefs or elders: they wandered about with flocks and herds, associated in companies of three or four hundred persons, living in kraals or movable villages of huts constructed of poles or boughs and covered with rush mats, which were taken down and carried on pack-oxen. A mantle of sewn sheep-skins was their clothing; their arms were a bow with poisoned arrows and a light javelin or assagai. They were bold and active in the chace, and although mild in their disposition were courageous in warfare, as their European invaders frequently experienced.

Kolben extols the good moral qualities of the Hottentots. They are, perhaps, the most faithful servants in the world. Though infinitely fond of wine, brandy, and tobacco, they are safely entrusted with them, and will neither themselves take, nor suffer others to diminish any such articles when committed to their trust. To this quality they add the greatest humanity and good nature. Their chastity is remarkable, and adultery, when known among them, is punished with death.' [. . .]

The internal character of the mind is best known by discovering the religious ideas and impressions. It has often been said, that the Hottentots are destitute of all belief in a Deity or a future state. Enslaved and separated from their fellows, and scarcely able, without constant toil, to support life, some may have lost the power and habit of reflection and all traces of sentiment; but Kolben assures us, that the Hottentots of his time had a firm belief in a supreme power, which they termed 'Gounya Tekquoa,' or the god of all gods, saying, that he lived beyond the moon. They paid him in adoration, but they worshipped the moon at the full and change, by sacrifices of cattle, with distorted faces and postures, shouting, swearing, singing, jumping, stamping, dancing, and making numerous prostrations, repeating an unintelligible jargon of words. [. . .]

A faithful and correct account of the conversion of these people to Christianity, would not fail to display in striking points of view many traits in their moral and intellectual history. The early endeavours that were made to induce them to receive the truths of Christianity, were met with the same obstinate resistance of which we hear so much in almost every similar instance; [. . .] This is exemplified by the account of a Hottentot boy, who was bred up by the governor Van der Stel, in the habits and religion of the Dutch, and having learnt several languages and discovering a very promising genius was sent to India and employed in public business. After his return to the Cape, he stripped off his European dress, clothed himself in a sheep-skin, and presenting himself to the governor, emphatically renounced the society of civilized men and the Christian religion, declaring, that he would live and die in the manners and customs of his forefathers.* In this we trace one characteristic trait of human nature as it exists in other races of men. A sort of instinctive and blind attachment to the earliest impressions made upon the mind is one of our strongest intellectual propensities. In the example above cited, it appears to have been equally powerful in the mind of the Hottentot so it is known to be in more cultivated nations; yet this has not prevented the spread of Christianity in the same race of people, when introduced among them under different circumstances.

THE PHYSIOLOGICAL LAWS OF RACE

Robert Knox, *The Races of Men: A Philosophical Inquiry into the Influence of Race over the Destinies of Nations* (1850), 2nd edn. (London: Henry Renshaw, 1862), 86–90, 107–8.

Beginning life as a series of provincial lectures, The Races of Men, *which had an immediate impact in Britain, articulates many of the polygenist and anti-environmentalist arguments that would be developed in Victorian debates on race. Introducing the book with an attack on Blumenbach and Prichard, Knox redefines*

---

* Kolben's Voyages and Natural History of the Cape of Good Hope (1729).

their more flexible definition: 'I, in opposition to these views, am prepared to assert that race is everything in human history; that the races of man are not the result of accident; that they are not convertible into each other by any contrivance whatsoever' (p. 8). Knox opens with an account of the Anglo-Saxon race and its essential difference from the Celtic, leading into the more general discussion of hybridity.

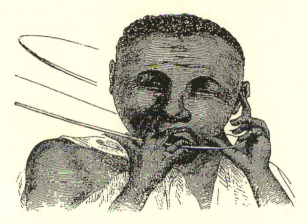

FIG. 18. Bosjeman playing on the gourah

That by mere climate, giving to the expression its utmost range of meaning, a new race of men can be established in perpetuity, is an assertion which for the present is contradicted by every well-ascertained physiological law, and by all authentic history. On the limited habitable territory of the Cape of Good Hope, shut in by deserts and by the sea, lived, when the Saxon Hollander first landed there, two races of men, as distinct from each other as can be well imagined, the Hottentot, or Bosjeman,[1] and the Amakoso Caffre.[2] To these were added a third, the Saxon Hollander. What time the Bosjeman child of the desert had hunted these desert and arid regions, for what period the Hottentot had listlessly tended his flocks of fat-tailed sheep, how long the bold Caffre had herded his droves of cattle, cannot now be ascertained: the Saxon Hollander found them there 300 years ago, as they are now in respect of physical structure and mental qualifications, inferior races, whom he drove before him, exterminating and enslaving the coloured man; destroying mercilessly the *wilde* which nature had placed there; and with the *wilde*, ultimately the coloured *man*, in harmony with all around him—antagonistic, it is true, but still in harmony to a certain extent; non-progressive; races which mysteriously had run their course, reaching the time appointed for their destruction.

[1] 'Bushman'.   [2] Later became adapted to the derogative 'Kaffir'.

357

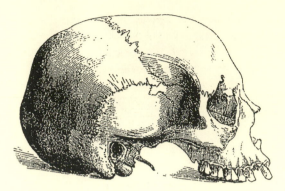

FIG. 19. Caffre skull

To assert that a race like the Bosjeman, marked by so many peculiarities, is convertible, by any process, into an Amakoso Caffre or Saxon Hollander, is at once to set all physical science at defiance. If by time, I ask what time? The influence of this element I mean to refute presently: the Dutch families who settled in Southern Africa three hundred years ago, are now as fair, and as pure in Saxon blood, as the native Hollander; the slightest change in structure or colour can at once be traced to intermarriage. By intermarriage an individual is produced, intermediate generally, and partaking of each parent; but this mulatto man or woman is a monstrosity of nature—there is no place for such a family: no such race exists on the earth, however closely affiliated the parents may be. To maintain it would require a systematic course of intermarriage, with constant draughts from the pure races whence the mixed race derives its origin. Now, such an arrangement is impossible. Since the earliest recorded times, such mixtures have been attempted and always failed; with Celt and Saxon it is the same as with Hottentot and Saxon, Caffre and Hottentot. The Slavonian race or races have been deeply intercalated for more than twice ten centuries with the South German, the pure Scandinavian, the Sarmatian, and even somewhat with the Celt, and with the Italian as conquerors: have they intermingled? Do you know of any mixed race the result of such admixture? Is it in Bohemia? or Saxony? or Prussia? or Finland?

This seems to be the law. By intermarriage a new product arises, which cannot stand its ground; 1st, By reason of the innate dislike of race to race, preventing a renewal of such intermarriages; 2nd, Because the descendants will of necessity fall back upon the stronger race, and all traces, or nearly so, of the weaker race must in time be obliterated. In what time, we shall afterwards consider. If a pure race has appeared to undergo a permanent change when transferred to a climate materially differing from their own, such changes will be found, on a closer inquiry, to be delusive. [. . .]

FIG. 20. Caffre race

Can any race of men live and thrive in any climate? Need I discuss this question seriously? Will any one venture to affirm it of man? Travel to the Antilles,
and see the European struggling with existence, a prey to fever and dysentery,
unequal to all labour, wasted and wan, finally perishing, and becoming rapidly
extinct as a race, but for the constant influx of fresh European blood. European
inhabitants of Jamaica, of Cuba, of Hispaniola, and of the Windward and
Leeward Isles, what progress have you made since your first establishment there?
Can you say you are established? Cease importing fresh European blood, and
watch the results. Labour you cannot, hence the necessity for a black population;
your pale, wan, and sickly offspring would in half a century be non-productive;
face to face with the energetic negro race, your colour must alter—first brown,
then black; look at Hayti: with a deepening colour vanishes civilization, the arts
of peace, science, literature, abstract justice; Christianity becomes a mere name,

FIG. 21. The savage Bosjemen;—Troglodytes; who build no house or hut; children of the
desert

or puts on a fetichian[3] robe—why not? The Roman robe was, and is, Pagan; the Byzantine, misnamed Greek, has an outrageous oriental look; the Protestant is a calculating, sober, drab-coloured cloak; why may not the fetiche be attached to the cloak as well as the mitre and the incense-box? Is the one superior to the other? The European, then, cannot colonize a tropical country; he cannot identify himself with it; hold it he may, with the sword, as we hold India, and as Spain once held Central America, but inhabitants of it, in the strict sense of the term, they cannot become. It never can absolutely become theirs; nature gave it not to them as an inheritance; they seized it by fraud and violence, holding it by deeds of blood and infamy, as we hold India; still it may be for a short tenure, nay, it may even be at any time measured. Withdraw from a tropical country the annual fresh influx of European blood, and in a century its European inhabitants cease to exist.

ON HYBRIDITY

Pierre Paul Broca, *On the Phenomena of Hybridity in the Genus Homo*, ed. C. Carter Blake (London: Longman, Green, Longman and Roberts, 1864), 60, 65–7, 69–71.

Broca's controversial study was promoted in Britain by the Anthropological Society, whose president in the mid-nineteenth century was James Hunt, a follower of Robert Knox and author of the extreme polygenist The Negro's Place in Nature *(1863). The society also promoted other studies, such as Carl Vogt's* Lectures on Man: His Place in Nature and in the History of the Earth *(1863), which aimed to unite polygenic and evolutionary theory and which Hunt translated. Here we include Broca's brief concluding summary and his arguments about the implications of his theory, where (at the height of the Abolitionist campaign in America, and against the more liberal ethnographic tradition), he disingenuously argues that both monogenic and polygenic perspectives can be used to support or refute slavery.*

From the whole of our researches on the hybridity of the human race we obtain the following results:–

---

[3] Fetishistic.

1. That certain intermixtures are perfectly eugenesic.[1]

2. That other intermixtures are in their results notably inferior to those of eugenesic hybridity.

3. That Mulattoes of the first degree, issued from the union of the Germanic (Anglo-Saxon) race with the African Negroes, appear inferior in fecundity and longevity to individuals of the pure races.

4. That it is at least doubtful, whether these Mulattoes, in their alliances between themselves, are capable of indefinitely perpetuating their race, and that they are less prolific in their direct alliances than in their re-crossing with the parent stocks, as is observed in paragenesic[2] hybridity.

5. That alliances between the Germanic race (Anglo-Saxon) with the Melanesian races (Australians and Tasmanians) are but little prolific.

6. That the Mulattoes sprung from such intercourse are too rare to have enabled us to obtain exact particulars as to their viability and fecundity.

7. That several degrees of hybridity, which have been observed in the cross-breeds of animals of different species, seem also to occur in the various crossings of men of different races.

8. That the lowest degree of human hybridity in which the homœogenesis[3] is so feeble as to render the fecundity of the first crossing uncertain, is exhibited in the most disparate crossings between one of the most elevated and the two lowest races of humanity. [. . .]

We recognised at the outset that the monogenists, considering their axiom as self-evident, have made no efforts to establish its correctness, so that, strictly speaking, we might have discarded it. When, contrary to the opinion of several modern authors, we wished to establish that there were really eugenesic inter-mixtures in the human genus, we found in science assertions without proofs, and we believe that our investigations concerning the mixed populations of France have, in this respect, the merit of novelty. We may be mistaken as to the value of our demonstration; but we venture to assert, that this demonstration is the first that has been attempted.

---

[1] 'Mongrels of the first generation entirely fertile. *a.* They are fertile *inter se*, and their direct descendants are equally so. *b.* They breed easily and indiscriminately with the two parent species; the mongrels of the second generation, in turn are, themselves and their descendants, indefinitely fertile, both *inter se* and with the mongrels of all kinds which result from the mixture of the two parent species.'

[2] 'Mongrels of the first generation having a partial fecundity. *a.* They are hardly fertile or infertile *inter se*, and when they produce direct descendants, these have merely a decreasing fertility, tending to necessary extinction at the end of some generations. *b.* They breed easily with at least one of the two parent species. The mongrels of the second generation, issued from this second breeding, are themselves and their descendants fertile *inter se*, and with the mongrels of the first generation, with the nearest allied pure species, and with the intermediate mongrels arising from these various crossings.' (C. Carter Blake's Glossarial Note to the English edition.)

[3] Degree of similarity of the races from which individuals are descended.

After having rendered, if not quite certain, at least extremely probable, that *certain* human crossings are eugenesic, we have inquired whether *all* human crossings are in the same condition.

From the documents collected it results, that *certain* human crossings yield results notably inferior to such as constitute in animals eugenesic hybridity. The whole of the known facts permit us to consider as very probable, that certain human races taken two by two are less homœogenesic; as, for instance, the species of the dog and the wolf. If we are to make any reservation, and leave some doubts upon this conclusion, it is that we cannot admit, without numerous verifications, a fact which definitively demonstrates the plurality of human species; a fact, by the presence of which, all other discussion is rendered superfluous; a fact, finally, of which the political and social consequences would be immense.

We cannot too much insist upon drawing the attention of observers upon this subject. But whatever be the result of ulterior researches on human hybridity, it remains well attested that animals of different species may produce an eugenesic progeny, and that consequently we cannot, from the fecundity of human intermixtures, however disparate the races may be, draw a physiological argument in favour of the unity of species, even if the fecundity were as certain as it is doubtful.

The great problem we have investigated in this essay is one of those which have caused great agitation, and most difficult to approach with a mind unbiassed by any extra-scientific preconception. This was almost inevitable; but science must keep aloof from anything not within its province. There is no faith, however respectable, no interest, however legitimate, which must not accommodate itself to the progress of human knowledge and bend before truth, if that truth be demonstrated. Hence it is always hazardous to mix up theological arguments with discussions of this kind, and to stigmatise in the name of religion any scientific opinion, since, if that opinion, sooner or later gains ground, religion has been uselessly compromised. [. . .]

The intervention of political and social considerations has not been less injurious to Anthropology than the religious element. When generous philanthropists claimed, with indefatigable constancy, the liberty of the blacks, the partisans of the old system, threatened in their dearest interests, were enchanted to hear that Negroes were scarcely human beings, but rather domestic animals, more intelligent and productive than the rest. At that time the scientific question became a question of sentiment, and whoever wished for the abolition of slavery, thought himself bound to admit that Negroes were Caucasians blackened and frizzled by the sun. Now that France and England, the two most civilised nations, have definitively emancipated their slaves, science may claim its rights without caring for the sophisms of slaveholders.

Many honest men think that the moment to speak freely is not yet come, as the emancipation struggle is far from being at an end in the United States of

America, and that we should avoid furnishing the slaveholders with arguments. But is it true that the polygenist doctrine, which is scarcely a century old, is any degree responsible for an order of things which has existed from time immemorial, and which has developed and perpetuated itself during a long series of centuries, under the shade of the doctrine of monogenists, which remained so long uncontested? And can we believe that the slave-owners are much embarrassed to find arguments in the Bible? The Rev. John Bachmann, a fervent monogenist of South Carolina, has acquired in the Southern States much popularity by demonstrating, with great unction, that slavery is a divine institution. It is not from the writings of polygenists, but from the Bible, that the representatives of the Slave States have drawn their arguments; and Mr. Bachmann tells us that the Abolitionists of Congress have been struck dumb by such an irrefragable authority! It must, therefore, not be believed that there is any connexion between the scientific and the political question. The difference of origin by no means implicates the subordination of races. It, on the contrary, implicates the idea that each race of men has originated in a determined region, as it were, as the crown of the fauna of that region; and if it were permitted to guess at the intention of nature, we might be led to suppose that she has assigned a distinct inheritance to each race, because, despite of all that has been said of the cosmopolitism of man, the inviolability of the domain of certain races is determined by their climate.

Let this mode of viewing the question be compared with that of the monogenists, and let it be asked which of the two modes is more apt to please the defenders of slavery. If all men are descendants of one couple,—if the inequality of races has been the result of a curse more or less merited,—or again, if the one have degraded themselves, and have allowed the torch of their primitive intelligence to become extinct, whilst the other have carefully guarded the precious gift of the Creator,—in other words, if there be cursed and blessed races,—races which have obeyed the voice of nature and races which have disobeyed it,—then the Rev. John Bachmann is right to say that slavery is a Divine right; that it is a providential punishment; and that it is just, to a certain point, that those races who have degraded themselves should be placed under the *protection* of others,— to borrow an ingenious euphemism from the language of the defenders of slavery.* But if the Ethiopian is king of Soudan by the same right as the Caucasian is king of Europe, what right has he to impose laws upon the former, unless by the right of might? In the first case, slavery presents itself with a certain appearance of legitimacy which might render it excusable in the eyes of certain theoricians; in the second case, it is a fact of pure violence, protested against by all who derive no benefit from it.

From another point of view, it might be said that the polygenist doctrine assigns to the inferior races of humanity a more honourable place than in the

* See, for many valuable hints on this subject, *Savage Africa*, by W. Winwood Reade, Svo, London, 1864.—EDITOR.

opposite doctrine. To be inferior to another man either in intelligence, vigour, or beauty, is not a humiliating condition. On the contrary, one might be ashamed to have undergone a physical or moral degradation, to have descended the scale of beings, and to have lost rank in creation.

CEREBRAL DEVELOPMENT

Henry Maudsley, *Body and Mind: An Inquiry into their Connection and Mutual Influence, Specially in Reference to Mendal Disorders* (London: Macmillan, 1870), 53–7.

This extract follows the passage from Body and Mind *on 'idiocy' (see above). Maudsley is drawing loosely on a range of secondary material on brain size and shape (in men and women as well as different races) that pervaded anthropological debates during the late nineteenth century, in the wake of the American craniologist Samuel George Morton's* Crania America *(1839) to reinforce his general argument about the 'tyranny of organisation'.*

It behoves us, as scientific inquirers, to realize distinctly the physical mean-ing of the progress of human intelligence from generation to generation. What structural differences in the brain are implied by it? That an increasing purpose runs through the ages, and that 'the thoughts of men are widened with the process of the suns,'[1] no one will call in question; and that this progress has been accompanied by a progressive development of the cerebral hemispheres, the convolutions of which have increased in size, number, and complexity, will hardly now be disputed. Whether the fragments of ancient human crania which have been discovered in Europe do or do not testify to the existence of a bar-barous race that disappeared before historical time, they certainly mark a race not higher than the lowest surviving human variety. Dr. Pritchard's comparison of the skulls of the same nation at different periods of its history[2] led him to the conclusion that the present inhabitants of Britain, 'either as the result of many ages of great intellectual cultivation or from some other cause, have much more capacious brain-cases than their forefathers.' Yet stronger evidence of a growth

---

[1] Alfred Tennyson, *Locksley Hall*, l. 138.

[2] Either a reference to J. C. Pritchard, whose *Researches into the Physical History of Mankind* includes a section on 'the natural forms of the skull', or to W. T. Pritchard's *Polynesian Reminiscences* (1866) which also engages in craniological comparisons.

of brain with the growth of intelligence is furnished by an examination of the brains of existing savages. Gratiolet[3] has figured and described the brain of the Hottentot Venus,[4] who was nowise an idiot. He found a striking simplicity and a regular arrangement of the convolution of the frontal lobes, which presented an almost perfect symmetry in the two hemispheres, involuntarily recalling the regularity and symmetry of the cerebral convolutions in the lower animals. The brain was palpably inferior to that of a normally developed white woman, and could only be compared with the brain of a white idiotic from arrest of cerebral development. [. . .] Among Europeans the average weight of the brain is greater in educated than in uneducated persons; its size—other circumstances being equal—bearing a general relation to the mental power of the individual. Dr. Thurnam[5] concludes, from a series of carefully-compiled tables, that while the average weight of the brain in ordinary Europeans is 49 oz., it was 54.7 oz. in ten distinguished men*; Thus, then, while we take it to be well established that the

* The following table is compiled from Dr. Thurnam's paper 'On the Weight of the Human Brain' (*Journal of Mental Science*, April 1866):–

BRAIN-WEIGHTS OF DISTINGUISHED MEN

	Ages.	Oz.
1. Cuvier, *Naturalist*	63	64.5
2. Abercrombie, *Physician*	64	63
3. Spurzheim, *Physician*	56	55.06
4. Dirichlet, *Mathematician*	54	55.6
5. De Morny, *Statesman and Courtier*	50	53.6
6. Daniel Webster, *Statesman*	70	53.5
7. Campbell, *Lord Chancellor*	80	53.5
8. Chalmers, *celebrated Preacher*	67	53
9. Fuchs, *Pathologist*	52	52.9
10. Gauss, *Mathematician*	78	52.6
Average of ten distinguished men	50–70	54.7
Brain-weights of average European men	20–60	49
	50–70	47.1
Average brain-weight of male negroes		44.3
Average brain-weight of 14 congenital idiots (males)		42
Average brain-weight of 8 congenital idiots (females)		41.2
Estimated brain-weight of Microcephalic idiocy (males)		37.5
Estimated brain-weight of Microcephalic idiocy (females)		32.5

It may be proper to add that the average weight of the adult male brain is 10 per cent. greater than that of the female—100 : 90. The brains of the Hottentot, Bushman, and Australian are, so far as observation goes, of less weight than those of negroes.

[3] French psychologist, author of *Anatomie compareé du système nerveux considéré dans ses rapports avec l'intelligence* (Paris 1839–57).

[4] The name given to Saartjie Baartman, a southern African woman brought to Europe in 1810 and displayed as a freakish specimen of racial 'otherness'.

[5] John Thurnam (1810–73), the medical superintendent of the York Retreat during the 1840s, who became increasingly interested in craniology and historical ethnography, and wrote, with J. B. Davis, a British version of Morton's *Crania Americana* (1839): *Crania Britannica: Delineations and Descriptions of the Skulls of the Aboriginal Inhabitants of the British Isles* (1865).

convolutions of the human brain have undergone a considerable development through the ages, we may no less justly conclude that its larger, more numerous, and complex convolutions reproduce the higher and more varied mental activity to the progressive evolution of which their progressive increase has answered—that they manifest the kind of function which has determined the structure. The vesicular neurine[4] has increased in quantity and in quality, and the function of the increased and more highly-endowed structure is to display that intelligence which it unconsciously embodies. The native Australian, who is one of the lowest existing savages, has no words in his language to express such exalted ideas as justice, love, virtue, mercy; he has no such ideas in his mind, and cannot comprehend them. The vesicular neurine which should embody them in its constitution and manifest them in its function, has not been developed in his convolutions; he is as incapable therefore of the higher mental displays of abstract reasoning and moral feeling as an idiot is, and for a like reason. Indeed, were we to imagine a person born in this country, at this time, with a brain of no higher development than the brain of an Australian savage or a Bushman, it is perfectly certain that he would be more or less of an imbecile. And the only way, I suppose, in which beings of so low an order of development could be raised to a civilized level of feeling and thought would be by cultivation continued through several generations; they would have to undergo a gradual process of humanization before they could attain to the capacity of civilization.

THE RACES OF MAN

Charles Darwin, *The Descent of Man, and Selection in Relation to Sex* (1871), 2nd edn. (London: John Murray, 1883), 171–4, 178–80.

Darwin devoted a chapter of Origin of Species *to 'hybridism' in animals, and here he develops his arguments in relation to humanity. While he cites Broca, Darwin reinterprets his theories within a monogenist framework, and emphasizes the indeterminacy of racial difference within an evolutionary context. However, Darwin's theory of the development of racial characteristics is based on his arguments about sexual selection.*

Even if it should hereafter be proved that all the races of men were perfectly fertile together, he who was inclined from other reasons to rank them as distinct

---

[4] Cerebral nerve tissue.

species, might with justice argue that fertility and sterility are not safe criterions of specific distinctness. We know that these qualities are easily affected by changed conditions of life, or by close inter-breeding, and that they are governed by highly complex laws, for instance, that of the unequal fertility of converse crosses between the same two species. With forms which must be ranked as undoubted species, a perfect series exists from those which are absolutely sterile when crossed, to those which are almost or completely fertile. The degrees of sterility do not coincide strictly with the degrees of difference between the parents in external structure or habits of life. Man in many respects may be compared with those animals which have long been domesticated, and a large body of evidence can be advanced in favour of the Pallasian doctrine,* that domestication tends to eliminate the sterility which is so general a result of the crossing of species in a state of nature.[1] From these several considerations, it may be justly urged that the perfect fertility of the intercrossed races of man, if established, would not absolutely preclude us from ranking them as distinct species.

Independently of fertility, the characters presented by the offspring from a cross have been thought to indicate whether or not the parent-forms ought to be ranked as species or varieties; but after carefully studying the evidence, I have come to the conclusion that no general rules of this kind can be trusted. The ordinary result of a cross is the production of a blended or intermediate form; but in certain cases some of the offspring take closely after one parent-form, and some after the other. This is especially apt to occur when the parents differ in characters which first appeared as sudden variations or monstrosities. [. . .]

We have now seen that a naturalist might feel himself fully justified in ranking the races of man as distinct species; for he has found that they are distinguished by many differences in structure and constitution, some being of importance. These differences have, also, remained nearly constant for very long periods of time. Our naturalist will have been in some degree influenced by the enormous range of man, which is a great anomaly in the class of mammals, if mankind be viewed as a single species. He will have been struck with the distribution of the several so-called races, which accords with that of other undoubtedly distinct species of mammals. Finally, he might urge that the mutual fertility of all the races has not as yet been fully proved, and even if proved would not be an absolute proof of their specific identity.

On the other side of the question, if our supposed naturalist were to enquire whether the forms of man keep distinct like ordinary species, when mingled together in large numbers in the same country, he would immediately discover

---

* 'The Variation of Animals and Plants under Domestication,' vol. ii. p. 109.

[1] *Pallasian doctrine*: after P. S. Pallas, the eighteenth-century German naturalist and geologist who questioned both Buffon's argument that food and climate influenced species variation and Linnaeus's theory of hybridization.

that this was by no means the case. In Brazil he would behold an immense mongrel population of Negroes and Portuguese; in Chiloe, and other parts of South America, he would behold the whole population consisting of Indians and Spaniards blended in various degrees. In many parts of the same continent he would meet with the most complex crosses between Negroes, Indians, and Europeans; and judging from the vegetable kingdom, such triple crosses afford the severest test of the mutual fertility of the parent-forms. In one island of the Pacific he would find a small population of mingled Polynesian and English blood; and in the Fiji Archipelago a population of Polynesian and Negritos crossed in all degrees. Many analogous cases could be added; for instance, in Africa. Hence the races of man are not sufficiently distinct to inhabit the same country without fusion; and the absence of fusion affords the usual and best test of specific distinctness.

Our naturalist would likewise be much disturbed as soon as he perceived that the distinctive characters of all the races were highly variable. This fact strikes every one on first beholding the negro slaves in Brazil, who have been imported from all parts of Africa. The same remark holds good with the Polynesians, and with many other races. It may be doubted whether any character can be named which is distinctive of a race and is constant. Savages, even within the limits of the same tribe, are not nearly so uniform in character, as has been often asserted. Hottentot women offer certain peculiarities, more strongly marked than those occurring in any other race, but these are known not to be of constant occurrence. In the several American tribes, colour and hairiness differ considerably; as does colour to a certain degree, and the shape of the features greatly, in the Negroes of Africa. The shape of the skull varies much in some races; and so it is with every other character. Now all naturalists have learnt by dearly-bought experience, how rash it is to attempt to define species by the aid of inconstant characters.

But the most weighty of all the arguments against treating the races of man as distinct species, is that they graduate into each other, independently in many cases, as far as we can judge, of their having intercrossed. [. . .]

Although the existing races of man differ in many respects, as in colour, hair, shape of skull, proportions of the body, &c., yet if their whole structure be taken into consideration they are found to resemble each other closely in a multitude of points. Many of these are of so unimportant or of so singular a nature, that it is extremely improbable that they should have been independently acquired by aboriginally distinct species or races. The same remark holds good with equal or greater force with respect to the numerous points of mental similarity between the most distinct races of man. The American aborigines, Negroes and Europeans are as different from each other in mind as any three races that can be named; yet I was incessantly struck, whilst living with the Fuegians on board the 'Beagle,' with the many little traits of character, shewing how similar their minds were to ours; and so it was with a full-blooded negro with whom I happened once to be intimate. [. . .]

Now when naturalists observe a close agreement in numerous small details of habits, tastes, and dispositions between two or more domestic races, or between nearly-allied natural forms, they use this fact as an argument that they are descended from a common progenitor who was thus endowed; and consequently that all should be classed under the same species. The same argument may be applied with much force to the races of man.

As it is improbable that the numerous and unimportant points of resemblance between the several races of man in bodily structure and mental faculties (I do not here refer to similar customs) should all have been independently acquired, they must have been inherited from progenitors who had these same characters. We thus gain some insight into the early state of man, before he had spread step by step over the face of the earth. The spreading of man to regions widely separated by the sea, no doubt, preceded any great amount of divergence of character in the several races; for otherwise we should sometimes meet with the same race in distinct continents; and this is never the case. Sir J. Lubbock,[2] after comparing the arts now practised by savages in all parts of the world, specifies those which man could not have known, when he first wandered from his original birth-place; for if once learnt they would never have been forgotten. He thus shews that 'the spear, which is but a development of the knife-point, and the club, which is but a long hammer, are the only things left.' He admits, however, that the art of making fire probably had been already discovered, for it is common to all the races now existing, and was known to the ancient cave-inhabitants of Europe. [. . .]

From the fundamental differences between certain languages, some philologists have inferred that when man first became widely diffused, he was not a speaking animal; but it may be suspected that languages, far less perfect than any now spoken, aided by gestures, might have been used, and yet have left no traces on subsequent and more highly-developed tongues. Without the use of some language, however imperfect, it appears doubtful whether man's intellect could have risen to the standard implied by his dominant position at an early period.

Whether primeval man, when he possessed but few arts, and those of the rudest kind, and when his power of language was extremely imperfect, would have deserved to be called man, must depend on the definition which we employ. In a series of forms graduating insensibly from some ape-like creature to man as he now exists, it would be impossible to fix on any definite point when the term 'man' ought to be used. But this is a matter of very little importance. So again, it is almost a matter of indifference whether the so-called races of man are thus designated, or are ranked as species or sub-species; but the latter term appears the more appropriate. Finally, we may conclude that when the principle of evolution is generally accepted, as it surely will be before long, the dispute between the monogenists and the polygenists will die a silent and unobserved death.

[2] Influential cultural anthropologist, author of *Prehistoric Times* (1865).

THE LIMITS OF NATURAL SELECTION

Alfred Russel Wallace, 'The limits of natural selection as applied to man', *Contributions to the Theory of Natural Selection* (London: Macmillan, 1870), 335–41.

This discussion is a development of 'Geological Time and the Origin of Species', first published in the Quarterly Review *in April 1869. Wallace starts by empha-sizing the importance of the theory of natural selection, but stresses the limitations of this model when applied to human culture: 'as soon as the human intellect became developed above a certain low stage, man's body would cease to be materi-ally affected by natural selection, because the development of his mental faculties would render important modifications of its form and structure unnecessary' (p. 332). Here he discusses similar evidence to Maudsley (above), but while he too ultimately subscribes to a racial hierarchy, he draws rather different conclusions.*

THE BRAIN OF THE SAVAGE SHOWN TO BE LARGER THAN HE NEEDS IT TO BE

Size of Brain an important Element of Mental Power.—The brain is universally admit-ted to be the organ of the mind; and it is almost as universally admitted, that size of brain is one of the most important of the elements which determine mental power or capacity. There seems to be no doubt that brains differ considerably in quality, as indicated by greater or less complexity of the convolutions, quantity of grey matter, and perhaps unknown peculiarities of organization; but this dif-ference of quality seems merely to increase or diminish the influence of quantity, not to neutralize it. Thus, all the most eminent modern writers see an intimate connection between the diminished size of the brain in the lower races of mankind, and their intellectual inferiority. The collections of Dr. J. B. Davis and Dr. Morton[1] give the following as the average internal capacity of the cranium in the chief races:– Teutonic family, 94 cubic inches; Esquimaux, 91 cubic inches; Negroes, 85 cubic inches; Australians and Tasmanians, 82 cubic inches; Bushmen, 77 cubic inches. These last numbers, however, are deduced from com-paratively few specimens, and may be below the average, just as a small number of Finns and Cossacks give 98 cubic inches, or considerably more than that of the German races. It is evident, therefore, that the absolute bulk of the brain is not

---

[1] J. B. Davis, author, with J. Thurnam, of *Crania Britannica. Delineation and Descriptions of the Skulls of the Aboriginal of the British Isles* (1865). This is based on S. G. Morton's *Crania America; or a Comparative View of the Skulls of Various Aboriginal Nations of North and South America: To which is Prefixed an Essay on the Varieties of the Human Species* (1839). Here Morton first developed the method establishing 'brain weight' by filling the skull with shot and then weighting it.

necessarily much less in savage than in civilised man, for Esquimaux skulls are known with a capacity of 113 inches, or hardly less than the largest among Europeans. But what is still more extraordinary, the few remains yet known of pre-historic man do not indicate any material diminution in the size of the brain case. A Swiss skull of the stone age, found in the lake dwelling of Meilen, corresponded exactly to that of a Swiss youth of the present day. The celebrated Neanderthal skull had a larger circumference than the average, and its capacity, indicating actual mass of brain, is estimated to have been no less than 75 cubic inches, or nearly the average of existing Australian crania. [. . .]

These facts might almost make us doubt whether the size of the brain is in any direct way an index of mental power, had we not the most conclusive evidence that it is so, in the fact that, whenever an adult male European has a skull less than nineteen inches in circumference, or has less than sixty-five cubic inches of brain, he is invariably idiotic. When we join with this the equally undisputed fact, that great men—those who combine acute perception with great reflective power, strong passions, and general energy of character, such as Napoleon, Cuvier, and O'Connell,[2] have always heads far above the average size, we must feel satisfied that volume of brain is one, and perhaps the most important, measure of intellect; and this being the case, we cannot fail to be struck with the apparent anomaly, that many of the lowest savages should have as much brains as average Europeans. The idea is suggested of a surplusage of power; of an instrument beyond the needs of its possessor. [. . .]

Range of intellectual power in Man.—First, let us consider what this wonderful instrument, the brain, is capable of in its higher developments. In Mr. Galton's interesting work on 'Hereditary Genius,'[3] he remarks on the enormous difference between the intellectual power and grasp of the well-trained mathematician or man of science, and the average Englishman. The number of marks obtained by high wranglers, is often more than thirty times as great as that of the men at the bottom of the honour list, who are still of fair mathematical ability; and it is the opinion of skilled examiners, that even this does not represent the full difference of intellectual power. If, now, we descend to those savage tribes who only count to three or five, and who find it impossible to comprehend the addition of two and three without having the objects actually before them, we feel that the chasm between them and the good mathematician is so vast, that a thousand to one will probably not fully express it. Yet we know that the mass of brain might be nearly the same in both, or might not differ in a greater proportion than as 5 to 6; whence we may fairly infer that the savage possesses a brain

[2] Daniel O'Connell, 'The Liberator' (1775–1847); campaigner for Irish independence in the early nineteenth century.
[3] Francis Galton's reputation in theories of heredity was first established with *Hereditary Genius* (1869).

capable, if cultivated and developed, of performing work of a kind and degree far beyond what he ever requires it to do.

Again, let us consider the power of the higher or even the average civilized man, of forming abstract ideas, and carrying on more or less complex trains of reasoning. Our languages are full of terms to express abstract conceptions. Our business and our pleasures involve the continual foresight of many contingencies. Our law, our government, and our science, continually require us to reason through a variety of complicated phenomena to the expected result. Even our games, such as chess, compel us to exercise all these faculties in a remarkable degree. Compare this with the savage languages, which contain no words for abstract conceptions; the utter want of foresight of the savage man beyond his simplest necessities; his inability to combine, or to compare, or to reason on any general subject that does not immediately appeal to his senses. So, in his moral and æsthetic faculties, the savage has none of those wide sympathies with all nature, those conceptions of the infinite, of the good, of the sublime and beautiful, which are so largely developed in civilized man. Any considerable development of these would, in fact, be useless or even hurtful to him, since they would to some extent interfere with the supremacy of those perceptive and animal faculties on which his very existence often depends, in the severe struggle he has to carry on against nature and his fellow-man. Yet the rudiments of all these powers and feelings undoubtedly exist in him, since one or other of them frequently manifest themselves in exceptional cases, or when some special circumstances call them forth. Some tribes, such as the Santals, are remarkable for as pure a love of truth as the most moral among civilized men. The Hindoo and the Polynesian have a high artistic feeling, the first traces of which are clearly visible in the rude drawings of the palæolithic men who were the contemporaries in France of the Reindeer and the Mammoth. Instances of unselfish love, of true gratitude, and of deep religious feeling, sometimes occur among most savage races.

On the whole, then, we may conclude, that the general moral and intellectual development of the savage, is not less removed from that of civilized man than has been shown to be the case in the one department of mathematics; and from the fact that all the moral and intellectual faculties do occasionally manifest themselves, we may fairly conclude that they are always latent, and that the large brain of the savage man is much beyond his actual requirements in the savage state.

6. Sex in Mind and Education

ELEMENTS OF FEMININE ATTRACTION

Herbert Spencer, *Education, Intellectual, Moral and Physical* (London: Williams and Norgate, 1861), 186–8.

First published in the Quarterly Review *in April 1859, Spencer applies the case against 'brain forcing' to young women within an explicitly degenerative framework here. In arguing that excessive education threatens women's reproductive chances as much as their individual health by draining their nervous energy, he is taking part in a controversy that will carry on through the rest of the century.*

On women the effects of this forcing system are, if possible, even more injurious than on men. Being in great measure debarred from those vigorous and enjoyable exercises of body by which boys mitigate the evils of excessive study, girls feel these evils in their full intensity. Hence, the much smaller proportion of them who grow up well-made and healthy. In the pale, angular, flat-chested young ladies, so abundant in London drawing-rooms, we see the effect of merciless application, unrelieved by youthful sports; and this physical degeneracy hinders their welfare far more than their many accomplishments aid it. Mammas anxious to make their daughters attractive, could scarcely choose a course more fatal than this, which sacrifices the body to the mind. Either they disregard the tastes of the opposite sex, or else their conception of those tastes is erroneous. Men care little for erudition in women; but very much for physical beauty, good nature, and sound sense. How many conquests does the blue-stocking make through her extensive knowledge of history? What man ever fell in love with a woman because she understood Italian? Where is the Edwin who was brought to Angelina's feet by her German? But rosy cheeks and laughing eyes are great attractions. A finely rounded figure draws admiring glances. The liveliness and good humour that overflowing health produces, go a great way towards establishing attachments. Every one knows cases where bodily perfections, in the absence of all other recommendations, have incited a passion that carried all before it; but scarcely any one can point to a case where intellectual acquirements, apart from moral or physical attributes, have aroused such a feeling. The truth is that, out of the many elements uniting in various proportions to produce in a man's breast the complex emotion we call love, the strongest are those produced by physical attractions; the next in order of strength are those produced by moral attractions; the weakest are those produced by intellectual attractions; and even these are dependent less on acquired knowledge than on natural faculty—quickness, wit, insight. [. . .]

When we remember that one of Nature's ends, or rather her supreme end, is the welfare of posterity; further that, in so far as posterity are concerned, a cultivated intelligence based on a bad *physique* is of little worth, since its descendants will die out in a generation or two; and conversely that a good *physique*, however poor the accompanying mental endowments, is worth preserving, because, throughout future generations, the mental endowments may be indefinitely developed; we perceive how important is the balance of instincts above described. But, advantage apart, the instincts being thus balanced, it is folly to persist in a system which undermines a girl's constitution that it may overload her memory. Educate as highly as possible—the higher the better—providing no bodily injury is entailed (and we may remark, in passing, that a sufficiently high standard might be reached were the parrot-faculty cultivated less, and the human faculty more, and were the discipline extended over that now wasted period between leaving school and being married). But to educate in such manner, or to such extent, as to produce physical degeneracy, is to defeat the chief end for which the toil and cost and anxiety are submitted to. By subjecting their daughters to this high-pressure system, parents frequently ruin their prospects in life. Besides inflicting on them enfeebled health, with all its pains and disabilities and gloom; they not unfrequently doom them to celibacy.

EMANCIPATION—BLACK AND WHITE

T. H. Huxley, 'Emancipation: Black and White' (1865), *Collected Essays*, 9 vols., iii: *Science and Education* (London: Macmillan, 1893), 66–9, 70–3.

First published in the Reader *(20 May 1865). Huxley is committed to the development of women's higher education, but like most of his contemporaries he still demonstrates his belief in a 'natural' racial and sexual hierarchy, both in drawing an analogy between the position of women and of slaves in America, and suggesting its limitations.*

It may be quite true that some negroes are better than some white men; but no rational man, cognisant of the facts, believes that the average negro is the equal, still less the superior, of the average white man. And, if this be true, it is simply incredible that, when all his disabilities are removed, and our prognathous relative has a fair field and no favour, as well as no oppressor, he will be able to compete successfully with his bigger-brained and smaller-jawed rival, in a contest which is to be carried on by thoughts and not by bites. The highest places in the hierarchy of civilisation will assuredly not be within the reach of our dusky cousins, though it is by no means necessary that they should be restricted to the lowest. But whatever the position of stable equilibrium into which the laws of social gravitation may bring the negro, all responsibility for the result will henceforward lie between Nature and him. The white man may wash his hands of it, and the Caucasian conscience be void of reproach for evermore. And this, if we look to the bottom of the matter, is the real justification for the abolition policy.

The doctrine of equal natural rights may be an illogical delusion; emancipation may convert the slave from a well-fed animal into a pauperised man; mankind may even have to do without cotton shirts; but all these evils must be faced if the moral law, that no human being can arbitrarily dominate over another without grievous damage to his own nature, be, as many think, as readily demonstrable by experiment as any physical truth. If this be true, no slavery can be abolished without a double emancipation, and the master will benefit by freedom more than the freed-man.

The like considerations apply to all the other questions of emancipation which are at present stirring the world—the multifarious demands that classes of mankind shall be relieved from restrictions imposed by the artifice of man, and not by the necessities of Nature. One of the most important, if not the most important, of all these, is that which daily threatens to become the 'irrepressible' woman question. What social and political rights have women? What ought they to be allowed, or not allowed, to do, be, and suffer? And, as involved in, and underlying all these questions, how ought they to be educated?

There are philogynists as fanatical as any 'misogynists' who, reversing our antiquated notions, bid the man look upon the woman as the higher type of humanity; who ask us to regard the female intellect as the clearer and the quicker, if not the stronger; who desire us to look up to the feminine moral sense as the purer and the nobler; and bid man abdicate his usurped sovereignty over Nature in favour of the female line. On the other hand, there are persons not to be outdone in all loyalty and just respect for womankind, but by nature hard of head and haters of delusion, however charming, who not only repudiate the new woman-worship which so many sentimentalists and some philosophers are desirous of setting up, but, carrying their audacity further, deny even the natural equality of the sexes. They assert, on the contrary, that in every excellent character, whether mental or physical, the average woman is inferior to the average man, in the sense of having that character less in quantity and lower in quality. Tell these persons of the rapid perceptions and the instinctive intellectual insight of women, and they reply that the feminine mental peculiarities, which pass under these names, are merely the outcome of a greater impressibility to the superficial aspects of things, and of the absence of that restraint upon expression which, in men, is imposed by reflection and a sense of responsibility. [. . .]

Supposing, however, that all these arguments have a certain foundation; admitting, for a moment, that they are comparable to those by which the inferiority of the negro to the white man may be demonstrated, are they of any value as against woman-emancipation? Do they afford us the smallest ground for refusing to educate women as well as men—to give women the same civil and political rights as men? No mistake is so commonly made by clever people as that of assuming a cause to be bad because the arguments of its supporters are, to a great extent, nonsensical. And we conceive that those who may laugh at the arguments of the extreme philogynists, may yet feel bound to work heart and soul towards the attainment of their practical ends.

As regards education, for example. Granting the alleged defects of women, is it not somewhat absurd to sanction and maintain a system of education which would seem to have been specially contrived to exaggerate all these defects?

Naturally not so firmly strung, nor so well balanced as boys, girls are in great measure debarred from the sports and physical exercises which are justly thought absolutely necessary for the full development of the vigour of the more favoured sex. Women are, by nature, more excitable than men—prone to be swept by tides of emotion, proceeding from hidden and inward, as well as from obvious and external causes; and female education does its best to weaken every physical counterpoise to this nervous mobility—tends in all ways to stimulate the emotional part of the mind and stunt the rest. We find girls naturally timid, inclined to dependence, born conservatives; and we teach them that independence is unladylike; that blind faith is the right frame of mind; and that whatever we may be permitted, and indeed encouraged, to do to our brother, our sister is to be left to the tyranny of authority and tradition. With few insignificant exceptions, girls have been educated either to be drudges, or toys, beneath man; or a sort of angels above him; the highest ideal aimed at oscillating between Clärchen and Beatrice.[1] The possibility that the ideal of womanhood lies neither in the fair saint, nor in the fair sinner; that the female type of character is neither better nor worse than the male, but only weaker; that women are meant neither to be men's guides nor their play-things,

[1] Clärchen was the working-class heroine of J. W. Goethe's *Egmont* (1788) who inspires political revolt but is finally driven to suicide; Beatrice (Portinari): Dante's idealized and unattainable love.

but their comrades, their fellows, and their equals, so far as Nature puts no bar to that equality, does not seem to have entered into the minds of those who have had the conduct of the education of girls.

If the present system of female education stands self-condemned, as inherently absurd; and if that which we have just indicated is the true position of woman, what is the first step towards a better state of things? We reply, emancipate girls. Recognise the fact that they share the senses, perceptions, feelings, reasoning powers, emotions, of boys, and that the mind of the average girl is less different from that of the average boy, than the mind of one boy is from that of another; so that whatever argument justifies a given education for all boys, justifies its application to girls as well. So far from imposing artificial restrictions upon the acquirement of knowledge by women, throw every facility in their way. [. . .] Let us have 'sweet girl graduates' by all means. They will be none the less sweet for a little wisdom; and the 'golden hair' will not curl less gracefully outside the head by reason of there being brains within. Nay, if obvious practical difficulties can be overcome, let those women who feel inclined to do so descend into the gladia-torial arena of life, not merely in the guise of *retiariæ*, as heretofore, but as bold *sicariæ*, breasting the open fray.[2] Let them, if they so please, become merchants, barristers, politicians. Let them have a fair field, but let them understand, as the necessary correlative, that they are to have no favour. Let Nature alone sit high above the lists, 'rain influence and judge the prize.'[3]

DIFFERENCE IN THE MENTAL POWERS OF THE TWO SEXES

Charles Darwin, *The Descent of Man, and Selection in Relation to Sex* (1871), 2nd edn. (London: John Murray, 1883), 564–6.

This extract comes towards the end of the study of sexual selection which forms the second part of The Descent of Man. *The majority of the discussion here is on sex-ual selection in animals; only at the end, in Part III, does Darwin turn his attention to 'Sexual selection in relation to man'. In arguing that men and women are as they are because of a mixture of natural and sexual selection, Darwin is now following a more Larmarckian model of development: acquired sexual characteristics are transmitted to children, by fathers to sons and by mothers to daughters. Darwin's*

[2] *retiariae, sicariae*: holding back and going forward.
[3] From Milton's *L'Allegro* (l. 121): 'Store of ladies, whose bright eyes | Rain influence and judge the prize.'

arguments, which reflected popular notions, were frequently cited to reinforce the
case of natural inequality (see the extract from Romanes, below).

Amongst the half-human progenitors of man, and amongst savages, there have been struggles between the males during many generations for the possession of the females. But mere bodily strength and size would do little for victory, unless associated with courage, perseverance, and determined energy. With social animals, the young males have to pass through many a contest before they win a female, and the older males have to retain their females by renewed battles. They have, also, in the case of mankind, to defend their females, as well as their young, from enemies of all kinds, and to hunt for their joint subsistence. But to avoid enemies or to attack them with success, to capture wild animals, and to fashion weapons, requires the aid of the higher mental faculties, namely, observation; reason, invention, or imagination. These various faculties will thus have been continually put to the test and selected during manhood; they will, moreover, have been strengthened by use during this same period of life. Consequently, in accordance with the principle often alluded to, we might expect that they would at least tend to be transmitted chiefly to the male offspring at the corresponding period of manhood.

Now, when two men are put into competition, or a man with a woman, both possessed of every mental quality in equal perfection, save that one has higher energy, perseverance, and courage, the latter will generally become more eminent in every pursuit, and will gain the ascendancy. He may be said to possess genius—for genius has been declared by a great authority to be patience; and patience, in this sense, means unflinching, undaunted perseverance. But this view of genius is perhaps deficient; for without the higher powers of the imagination and reason, no eminent success can be gained in many subjects. These latter faculties, as well as the former, will have been developed in man, partly through sexual selection,—that is, through the contest of rival males, and partly through natural selection,—that is, from success in the general struggle for life; and as in both cases the struggle will have been during maturity, the characters gained will have been transmitted more fully to the male than to the female offspring. It accords in a striking manner with this view of the modification and reinforcement of many of our mental faculties by sexual selection, that, firstly, they notoriously undergo a considerable change at puberty,* and, secondly, that eunuchs remain throughout life inferior in these same qualities. Thus man has ultimately become superior to woman. It is, indeed, fortunate that the law of the equal transmission of characters to both sexes prevails with mammals; otherwise

* Maudsley, 'Mind and Body,' p. 31.

it is probable that man would have become as superior in mental endowment to woman, as the peacock is in ornamental plumage to the peahen.

It must be borne in mind that the tendency in character acquired by either sex late in life, to be transmitted to the same sex at the same age, and of early acquired characters to be transmitted to both sexes, are rules which, though general, do not always hold. If they always held good, we might conclude (but I here exceed my proper bounds) that the inherited effects of the early education of boys and girls would be transmitted equally to both sexes; so that the present inequality in mental power between the sexes would not be effaced by a similar course of early training; nor can it have been caused by their dissimilar early training. In order that woman should reach the same standard as man, she ought, when nearly adult, to be trained to energy and perseverance, and to have her reason and imagination exercised to the highest point; and then she would probably transmit these qualities chiefly to her adult daughters. All woman, however, could not be thus raised, unless during many generations those who excelled in the above robust virtues were married, and produced offspring in larger numbers than other women. As before remarked of bodily strength, although men do not now fight for their wives, and this form of selection has passed away, yet during manhood, they generally undergo a severe struggle in order to maintain themselves and their families; and this will tend to keep up or even increase their mental powers, and, as a consequence, the present inequality between the sexes.

SEX IN MIND AND IN EDUCATION

Henry Maudsley, 'Sex in Mind and in Education', *Fortnightly Review*, NS 15 (Apr. 1874), 468–9;
Elizabeth Garrett Anderson, 'Sex in Mind and Education: A Reply', *Fortnightly Review*, NS 15 (June 1874), 583–5, 588–90.

Maudsley's pronouncements on the dangers of female 'brain-forcing' echo Spencer's here, and they immediately drew fire from Elizabeth Garrett Anderson, feminist and campaigner for women's access to the medical profession. Anderson argues that Maudsley is simply reiterating the ideas of Edward Clarke, former professor at Harvard, whose Sex in Education had appeared in 1873. Although she opposes Maudsley here Anderson is echoing Maudsley's own earlier point in the Physiology and Pathology of Mind; both warn of the dangers of nurturing feminine passivity and imply that women are the moral and physiological guardians of future generations.

SEX IN MIND AND IN EDUCATION

When we thus look the matter honestly in the fact, it would seem plain that women are marked out by nature for very different offices in life from those of men, and that the healthy performance of her special functions renders it improbable she will succeed, and unwise for her to persevere, in running over the same course at the same pace with him. For such a race she is certainly weighted unfairly. Nor is it a sufficient reply to this argument to allege, as is sometimes done, that there are many women who have not the opportunity of getting married, or who do not aspire to bear children; for whether they care to be mothers or not, they cannot dispense with those physiological functions of their nature that have reference to that aim, however much they might wish it, and they cannot disregard them in the labour of life without injury to their health. They cannot choose but to be women; cannot rebel successfully against the tyranny of their organization, the complete development and function whereof must take place after its kind. This is not the expression of prejudice nor of false sentiment; it is the plain statement of a physiological fact. Surely, then, it is unwise to pass it by; first or last it must have its due weight in the determination of the problem of woman's education and mission; it is best to recognise it plainly, however we may conclude finally to deal with it.

It is sometimes said, however, that sexual difference ought not to have any place in the culture of mind, and one hears it affirmed with an air of triumphant satisfaction that there is no sex in mental culture. This is a rash statement, which argues want of thought or insincerity of thought in those who make it. There is sex in mind as distinctly as there is sex in body; and if the mind is to receive the best culture of which its nature is capable, regard must be had to the mental qualities which correlate differences of sex. To aim, by means of education and pursuits in life, to assimilate the female to the male mind, might well be pronounced as unwise and fruitless a labour as it would be to strive to assimilate the female to the male body by means of the same kind of physical training and by the adoption of the same pursuits. Without doubt there have been some striking instances of extraordinary women who have shown great mental power, and these may fairly be quoted as evidence in support of the right of women to the best mental culture; but it is another matter when they are adduced in support of the assertion that there is no sex in mind, and that a system of female education should be laid down on the same lines, follow the same method, and have the same ends in view, as a system of education for men.

Let me pause here to reflect briefly upon the influence of sex upon mind. In its physiological sense, with which we are concerned here, mind is the sum of those functions of the brain which are commonly known as thought, feeling, and will. Now the brain is one among a number of organs in the commonwealth of the body; with these organs it is in the closest physiological sympathy by definite paths of nervous communication, has special correspondence with them by internuncial nerve-fibres; so that its functions habitually feel and declare the influence of the different organs. There is an intimate consensus of functions. Though it is the highest organ of the body, the co-ordinating centre to which impressions to and from which responses are sent, the nature and functions of the inferior organs with which it lives in unity, affect essentially its nature as the organ of mental functions. It is not merely that disorder of a particular organ hinders or oppresses these functions, but it affects them in a particular way; and we have good reason to believe that this special pathological effect is a consequence of the specific physiological effect which each organ exerts naturally upon the constitution and function of mind.

ANDERSON

[. . .] The position Dr. Maudsley has undertaken to defend is this, that the attempt now being made in various directions to assimilate the mental training of men and women is opposed to the teachings of physiology, and more especially, that women's health is likely to be seriously injured if they are allowed or encouraged to pursue a system of education laid down on the same lines, following the same method, and having the same ends in view, as a system of education for men. [. . .]

We have here two distinct assertions to weigh and verify: 1st, that the physiological functions started in girls between the ages of fourteen and sixteen are likely to be interfered with or interrupted by pursuing the same course of study as boys, and by being subjected to the same examinations; and, 2nd, that even when these functions are in good working order and the woman has arrived at maturity, the facts of her organization interfere periodically to such an extent with steady and serious labour of mind or body that she can never hope to compete successfully with men in any career requiring sustained energy. Both with girls and women, however, it is the assimilation of their education and the equality of their aim with those of boys and men which, in Dr. Maudsley's eyes, call for special condemnation. And in each case he grounds his objection on the fact that physiologically important differences are found in the two sexes. [. . .]

But surely this argument contains a *non sequitur*. The question depends upon the nature of the course and the quickness of the pace, and upon the fitness of both for women; not at all on the amount of likeness or unlikeness between men and women. So far as education is concerned it is conceivable, and indeed probably that, were they ten times as unlike as they are, many things would be equally good for both. If girls were less like boys than the anthropomorphic apes, nothing but experience would prove that they would not benefit by having the best methods and the best tests applied to their mental training. And if the course of study which Dr. Maudsley is criticising be one as likely to strengthen the best powers of the mind as good food is to strengthen the body, if it tend to develope habits as valuable to women as to men, and if the pace is moderate, there would seem to be no good reason why the special physiological functions of women should prevent them from running it, any more than these same functions prevent them from eating beef and bread with as much benefit as men. The question is not settled by proving that both in mind and body girls are different from boys. [. . .]

With regard to adults. Is it true, or is it a great exaggeration, to say that the physiological difference between men and women seriously interferes with the chances of success a woman would otherwise possess? We believe it to be very far indeed from the truth. When we are told that in the labour of life women cannot disregard their special physiological functions without danger to health, it is difficult to understand what is meant, considering that in adult life healthy women do as a rule disregard them almost completely. It is, we are convinced, a great exaggeration to imply that women of average health are periodically incapacitated from serious work by the facts of their organization. Among poor women, where all the available strength is spent upon manual labour, the daily work goes on without intermission, and, as a rule, without ill effects. For example, do domestic servants, either as young girls or in mature life, show by experience that a marked change in the amount of work expected from them must be made at these times unless their health is to be injured? It is well known that they do not.

With regard to mental work it is within the experience of many women that that which Dr. Maudsley speaks of as an occasion of weakness, if not of temporary prostration, is either not felt to be such or is even recognised as an aid, the nervous and mental power being in many cases greater at those times than at any other. This is confirmed by what is observed when this function is prematurely shocked, or comes naturally to an end. In either case its absence usually gives rise to a condition of nervous weakness unknown while the regularity of the function was maintained. It is surely unreasonable to assume that the same function in persons of good health can be a cause of weakness when present, and also when absent. If its performance made women weak and ill, its absence would be a gain, which it is not. [. . .]

It must not be overlooked, that the difficulties which attend the period of rapid functional development are not confined to women, though they are expressed differently in the two sexes. Analogous changes take place in the constitution and organization of young men, and the period of immature manhood is frequently one of weakness, and one during which any severe strain upon the mental and nervous powers is productive of more mischief than it is in later life. It is possible that the physiological demand thus made is lighter than that made upon young women at the corresponding age, but on the other hand it is certain that, in many other ways unknown to women, young men still further tax their strength, *e.g.* by drinking, smoking, unduly severe physical exercise, and frequently by late hours and dissipation generally. Whether, regard being had to all these varying influences, young men are much less hindered than young women in intellectual work by the demands made upon their physical and nervous strength during the period of development, it is probably impossible to determine. All that we wish to show is that the difficulties which attend development are not entirely confined to women, and that in point of fact great allowance ought to be made, and has already been made, for them in deciding what may reasonably be expected in the way of intellectual attainment from young men. [. . .]

Hitherto most of the women who have 'contended with men for the goal of man's ambition' have had no chance of being any the worse for being allowed to do so on equal terms. They have had all the benefit of being heavily handicapped. Over and above their assumed physical and mental inferiority, they have had to start in the race without a great part of the training men have enjoyed, or they have gained what training they have been able to obtain in an atmosphere of hostility, to remain in which has taxed their strength and endurance far more than any amount of mental work could tax it. Would, for instance, the ladies who for five years have been trying to get a medical education at Edinburgh find their task increased, or immeasurably lightened, by being allowed to contend 'on equal terms with men' for that goal? The intellectual work required from other medical students is nothing compared with what it has been made to them by obliging them to spend time and energy in contesting every step of their course, and yet in spite of this heavy additional burden they have not at present shown any signs of enfeebled health or of inadequate mental power. To all who know what it is to pursue intellectual work under such conditions as these, Dr. Maudsley's pity for the more fortunate women who may pursue it in peace and on equal terms with men sounds superfluous. [. . .]

In estimating the possible consequences of extending the time spent in education, and even those of increasing somewhat the pressure put upon girls under eighteen, it should be borne in mind that even if the risk of overwork, pure and simple, work unmixed with worry, is more serious than we are disposed to think it, it is not the only, nor even the most pressing, danger during the period of active physiological development. The newly developed functions of womanhood awaken instincts which are more apt at this age to make themselves unduly prominent than to be hidden or forgotten. Even were the dangers of continuous mental work as great as Dr. Maudsley thinks they are, the dangers of a life adapted to develope only the specially and consciously feminine side of the girl's nature would be much greater. From the purely physiological point of view, it is difficult to believe that study much more serious than that usually pursued by young men would do a girl's health as much harm as a life directly calculated to over-stimulate the emotional and sexual instincts, and to weaken the guiding and controlling forces which these instincts so imperatively need. The stimulus found in novel-reading, in the theatre and ball-room, the excitement which attends a premature entry into society, the competition of vanity and frivolity, these involve far more real dangers to the health of young women than the competition for knowledge, or for scientific or literary honours, ever has done, or is ever likely to do. And even if, in the absence of real culture, dissipation be avoided, there is another danger still more difficult to escape, of which the evil physical results are scarcely less grave, and this is dulness. It is not easy for those whose lives are full to overflowing of the interests which accumulate as life matures, to realise how insupportably dull the life of a young woman just out of the schoolroom is apt to be, nor the powerful influence for evil this dulness has upon her health and morals. There is no tonic in the pharmacopœia to be compared with happiness, and happiness worth calling such is not known where the days drag along filled with make-believe occupations and dreary sham amusements.

MENTAL DIFFERENCES BETWEEN MEN AND WOMEN

George Romanes, 'Mental difference between men and women', *Nineteenth Century*, 21 (May 1887), 654–5, 662, 664–6, 668, 672.

Here Romanes directly extrapolates from Darwin's discussion of sexual selection and the differences in mental power of the sexes in The Descent of Man *in intervening in the controversy over women's higher education. The arguments here are slightly different from those of Maudsley and Anderson. While maintaining that cultural difference is ultimately rooted in biology, Romanes recognizes the role of education in shaping femininity, and gives a cautious welcome to women's access to higher education even as he resists the logic of feminist arguments.*

Seeing that the average brain-weight of women is about five ounces less than that of men, on merely anatomical grounds we should be prepared to expect a marked inferiority of intellectual power in the former. Moreover, as the general physique of women is less robust than that of men—and therefore less able to sustain the fatigue of serious or prolonged brain action—we should also on physiological grounds be prepared to entertain a similar anticipation. In actual fact we find that the inferiority displays itself most conspicuously in a comparative absence of originality, and this more especially in the higher levels of intellectual work. In her powers of acquisition the woman certainly stands nearer to the man than she does in her powers of creative thought, although even as regards the former there is a marked difference. The difference, however, is one which does not assert itself till the period of adolescence—young girls being, indeed, usually more acquisitive than boys of the same age, as is proved by recent educational experiences both in this country and in America. But as soon as the brain, and with it the organism as a whole, reaches the stage of full development, it becomes apparent that there is a greater power of amassing knowledge on the part of the male. Whether we look to the general average or to the intellectual giants of both sexes, we are similarly met with the general fact that a woman's information is less wide and deep and thorough than that of a man. [. . .]

We see, then, that the principles of selection have thus determined greater strength, both of body and mind, on the part of male animals throughout the whole mammalian series; and it would certainly have been a most unaccountable fact if any exception to this rule had occurred in the case of mankind. For, as regards natural selection, it is in the case of mankind that the highest premium has been placed upon the mental faculties—or, in other words, it is here that natural selection has been most busy in the evolution of intelligence—and therefore, as Mr. Darwin remarks, we can only regard it as a fortunate accident of inheritance that there is not now a greater difference between the intelligence of men and of women than we actually find. Again, as regards sexual selection, it is evident that here also the psychologically segregating influences must have been exceptionally strong in the case of our own species, seeing that in all the more advanced stages of civilisation—or in the stages where mental evolution is highest, and, therefore, mental differences most pronounced—marriages are determined quite as much with reference to psychical as to physical endowments; and as men always admire in women what they regard as distinctively feminine qualities of mind, while women admire in men the distinctively masculine, sexual selection, by thus acting directly as well as indirectly on the mental qualities of both, is constantly engaged in moulding the minds of each upon a different pattern. [. . .]

There remains, so far as I can see, but one other cause which can be assigned of the mental differences between men and women. This cause is education. Using the term in its largest sense, we may say that in all stages of culture the education of women has differed widely from that of men. The state of abject slavery to which woman is consigned in the lower levels of human evolution clearly tends to dwarf her mind ab initio. And as woman gradually emerges from this her primitive and long-protracted condition of slavery, she still continues to be dominated by the man in numberless ways, which, although of a less brutal kind, are scarcely less effectual as mentally dwarfing influences. [. . .]

We see, then, that with advancing civilisation the theoretical equality of the sexes becomes more and more a matter of general recognition, but that the natural inequality continues to be forced upon the observation of the public mind; and chiefly on this account—although doubtless also on account of traditional usage—the education of women continues to be, as a general rule, widely different from that of men. And this difference is not merely in the positive direction of laying greater stress on psychological embellishment: it extends also in the negative direction of sheltering the female mind from all those influences of a striving and struggling kind, which constitute the practical schooling of the male intellect. Woman is still regarded by public opinion all the world over as a psychological plant of tender growth, which needs to be protected from the ruder blasts of social life in the conservatories of civilisation. And [. . .] it will be apparent that in this practice judgment I believe public opinion to be right. I am, of course, aware that there is a small section of the public—composed for the most part of persons who are not accustomed to the philosophical analysis of facts—which argues that the conspicuous absence of women in the field of intellectual work is due to the artificial restraints imposed upon them by all the traditional forms of education; that if we could suddenly make a leap of progress in this respect, and allow women everywhere to compete on fair and equal terms with men, then, under these altered circumstances of social life, women would prove themselves the intellectual compeers of man.

But the answer to this argument is almost painfully obvious. Although it is usually a matter of much difficulty to distinguish between nature and nurture, or between the results of inborn faculty and those of acquired knowledge, in the present instance no such difficulty obtains. [. . .]

The treatment of women in the past may have been very wrong, very shameful, and very much to be regretted by the present advocates of women's rights; but proof of the ethical quality of this fact does not get rid of the fact itself, any more than a proof of the criminal nature of assassination can avail to restore to life a murdered man. We must look the facts in the face. How long it may take the woman of the future to recover the ground which has been lost in the psychological race by the woman of the past, it is impossible to say; but we may predict with confidence that, even under the most favourable conditions as to culture, and even supposing the mind of man to remain stationary (and not, as is probable, to advance with a speed relatively accelerated by the momentum of its already acquired velocity), it must take many centuries for heredity to produce the missing five ounces of the female brain.

In conclusion, a few words may be added on the question of female education as this actually stands at the present time. Among all the features of progress which will cause the present century to be regarded by posterity as beyond comparison the most remarkable epoch in the history of our race, I believe that the inauguration of the so-called woman's movement in our own generation will be considered one of the most important. For I am persuaded that this movement is destined to grow; that with its growth the highest attributes of one half of the human race are destined to be widely influenced; that this influence will profoundly react upon the other half, not alone in the nursery and the drawing-room, but also in the study, the academy, the forum, and the senate; that this latest yet inevitable wave of mental evolution cannot be stayed until it has changed the whole aspect of civilisation. [. . .]

[However] the suspicion, not to say the active hostility, with which the so-called woman's movement has been met in many quarters springs from a not unhealthy ground of public opinion. For there can be no real doubt that these things are but an expression of the value which that feeling attaches to all which is held distinctive of feminine character as it stands. Woman, as she has been bequeathed to us by the many and complex influences of the past, is recognised as too precious an inheritance lightly to be tempered with; and the dread lest any change in the conditions which have given us this inheritance should lead, as it were, to desecration, is in itself both wise and worthy. In this feeling we have the true safeguard of womanhood; and we can hope for nothing better than that the deep strong voice of social opinion will always be raised against any innovations of culture which may tend to spoil to sweetest efflorescence of evolutions.

But, while we may hope that social opinion may ever continue opposed to the woman's movement in its most extravagant forms—or to those forms which endeavour to set up an unnatural, and therefore an impossible, rivalry with men in the struggles of practical life—we may also hope that social opinion will soon become unanimous in its encouragement of the higher education of women. Of the distinctively feminine qualities of mind which are admired as such by all, ignorance is certainly not one. Therefore learning, as learning, can never tend to deteriorate those qualities. On the contrary, it can only tend to refine the already refined, to beautify the already beautiful. [. . .]

The days are past when any enlightened man ought seriously to suppose that in now again reaching forth her hand to eat of the tree of knowledge woman is preparing for the human race a second fall. In the person of her admirable representative, Mrs. Fawcett,[1] she thus pleads: 'No one of those who care most for the woman's movement cares one jot to prove or to maintain that men's brains and women's brains are exactly alike or exactly equal. All we ask is that the social and legal status of women should be such as to foster, not to suppress, any gift for art, literature, learning, or goodness with which women may be endowed.' Then, I say, give her the apple, and see what comes of it. Unless I am greatly mistaken, the result will be that which is so philosophically as well as so poetically portrayed by the Laureate:–

> The woman's cause is man's: they rise or sink
> Together, dwarf'd or god-like, bond or free.
>
> .   .   .   .
>
> Then let her make herself her own
> To give or keep, to live and learn to be
> All that not harms distinctive womanhood.

[1] Millicent Garrett Fawcett (1847–1929), feminist and sister of Elizabeth Garrett Anderson.

For woman is not undevelopt man,
But diverse: could we make her as the man,
Sweet Love were slain: his dearest bond is this,
Not like to like, but like in difference.

Yet in the long years liker must they grow;
The man be more of women, she of man;
He gain in sweetness and in moral height,
Nor lose the wrestling thews that throw the world;
She mental breadth, nor fail in childward care,
Nor lose the child-like in the larger mind;
Till at the last she set herself to man,
Like perfect music unto noble words.

    .   .   .   .

Then comes the statelier Eden back to men:
Then reign the world's great bridals, chaste and calm:
Then springs the crowning race of human kind.
May these things be![2]

[2] Alfred Tennyson, *The Princess* (1847; enlarged and revised 1850) VII, ll. 243–79. A very popular poem telling the story of the medieval Princess Ida, who sets up a women-only university but finally marries, *The Princess* became a key test in the debate on the 'woman question'.

Notes on Authors

ABBREVIATIONS

DCL	Doctor of Civil Law
FRCS	Fellow of the Royal College of Surgeons
FRCP	Fellow of the Royal College of Physicians
FRS	Fellow of the Royal Society
LLD	Doctor of Laws
LSA	Licentiate of the Society of Apothecaries
LRCS	Licentiate of the Royal College of Surgeons
MA	Master of Arts
MB	Bachelor of Medicine
MD	Doctor of Medicine
MRCS	Member of the Royal College of Surgeons
Ph.D	Doctor of Philosophy

John Abercrombie, 1780–1844

MD, FRCP. Abercrombie was a leading physician and medical teacher in early nineteenth-century Scotland who studied in Edinburgh and Oxford. His *Inquiries Concerning the Intellectual Powers and the Investigation of Truth* (1830) went into four editions within four years, stayed in print through most of the nineteenth century, and was a crucial reference point for later writers. Abercrombie aimed to develop the philosophy of mind, following associationist principles, in the context of new methods of empirical observation and classification, while recognizing that these could never lead to absolutely provable results.

William Acton, 1813–1875

MRCS. The son of a clergyman, Acton was apprenticed to the Resident Apothecary at St Bartholomew's Hospital, London, 1831–6. He studied in Paris, specializing in genito-urinary diseases, and then returned to England, becoming a Member of the Royal College of Surgeons and beginning to practice in London in 1840. His first book, *A Practical Treatise on the Diseases of the Urinary and Generative Organs (in Both Sexes)* (1841) was expanded and developed in *The Functions and Disorders of the Reproductive Organs, in Childhood, Youth, Adult Age, and Advanced Life, Considered in their Physiological, Social and Moral Relations* (1857), which was translated into French in 1863. Acton was also involved in the wider study and reform of sexual behaviour: his 'Observations on Illegitimacy in London Parishes' appeared in the *Journal of the Royal Statistical Society* in 1857, and *Prostitution, Considered in its Moral, Social and Sanitary Aspects* (1862), contributed to the drafting of the Contagious Diseases Acts of 1866.

Sir Clifford Allbutt, 1836–1925

MD, FRCP, FRS. A leading member of the medical profession in the nineteenth century, Clifford Allbutt was the son of a clergyman and grew up in Yorkshire. He graduated in Natural Sciences at Cambridge in 1857, then studied medicine at St George's Hospital, London, gaining his MD from Cambridge. He took up the post of consulting physician at the Leeds General Infirmary, combining this with working at the Leeds Fever Hospital and the Leeds Hospital for Women and Children and building up a large private practice. While in Leeds, Allbutt developed the portable clinical thermometer and a new kind of ophthalmoscope, publishing a study on the uses of the ophthalmoscope in studying diseases of the nervous system in 1871. He stayed in Leeds until 1889, when he was appointed as a Commissioner in Lunacy in 1889, and in 1892 became Regius Professor of Physic at Cambridge. Allbutt's publications include his influential Gulstonian Lectures *On Visceral Neuroses* (1884), his edition, with W. S. Playfair, of *A System of Gynaecology* (1896), and his development of *A New System of Medicine* (1896–9), for which he wrote the sections on the history of medicine, neurosis, chlorosis, neurasthenia, and cardiac disease. He also wrote numerous articles for the medical press and published his series of lectures on *Greek Medicine in Rome* (1909–10).

Elizabeth Garrett Anderson, 1836–1917

MD. Feminist campaigner for women's access to higher education and the professions, especially medicine. Elizabeth Garrett Anderson began to study medicine privately in 1860, having been denied access to both the London and Scottish medical schools, and gained her MD in Paris in 1870. She opened the New Hospital for Women in Marylebone in 1866 where she was Senior Physician until 1892, and from 1873 to 1903 lectured at the London School of Medicine for Women.

George Mackenzie Bacon, 1836–1887

MD, MRCS. Mackenzie Bacon studied medicine at Guy's Hospital, London, receiving his MD from St Andrews. In 1864 he was appointed Deputy Superintendent of the Cambridgeshire County Asylum at Fulbourn, leaving two years later to travel in Europe and returning to 1867 to become Superintendent. In addition to *The Writing of the Insane*, which was based on his observations at Fulbourn, he published several other papers in the *Lancet* and the *Journal of Mental Science*.

John Barlow, 1799–1869

MA, FRS. Fellow of Trinity College, Cambridge. John Barlow was an Anglican clergyman and Secretary to the Royal Institution. *On Man's Power over Himself to Prevent or Control Insanity*, an account of the virtues of moral management and the power of self-control, was presented as a paper to the Royal Institution, then expanded with assistance from John Conolly and published as part of a popular self-help series, 'Small Books on Great Subjects', in 1843.

James Braid, 1795–1860

MRCS. Born in Fifeshire, Braid studied medicine at Edinburgh, and practised in Lanarkshire, Dumfries, and Manchester. He first became interested in mesmerism when he attended a popular demonstration in 1841. Initially sceptical, and rejecting mesmerism's mystical and spiritual aspects, he developed from his own experiments the concept and the practice of hypnotism, which he separated completely from animal magnetism. *Neurypnology; or, the Rationale of Nervous Sleep* (1842) stressed the therapeutic possibilities of hypnotic sleep that would be developed by Charcot, Janet, and Freud at the end of the century. Braid's views were derided at first by both mesmerists and the medical establishment, and he did not live to see the recognition of his ideas and the development of the method based on them that would transform psychotherapeutic practice. His other work included articles on hypnotism in the *Medical Times*, *Electro-Biological Phenomenon Considered Physiologically and Psychologically* (1851), and *Hypnotic Therapeutics, Illustrated by Cases* (1853).

Pierre Paul Broca, 1824–1880

MD. Broca studied medicine at the University of Paris, then spent ten years studying pathology, becoming professor of surgical pathology in the Faculty of Medicine and in the hospitals La Bicêtre, La Salpêtière, St Antoine, and La Pitié. He founded the Paris Société d'Anthropologie in 1859, which became a centre for radical and anti-clerical scientific activity, and became renowned for his anthropology and his study of the structure of the brain. Working on the theory of cerebral localization, Broca developed the argument that language ability is developed in the posterior portion of the third frontal convolution of the left-hand hemisphere of the brain. In anthropology, his work on hybridity was cited in support of polygenism, which Broca himself saw as a radical theory that could be used to argue against institutional forms of inequality, particularly slavery. His writing includes *Instructions générales pour les recherches anthropologiques* (1865), *Études sur les animaux ressuscitants* (1866), *Caracterè physique de l'homme préhistorique* (1869), and *Mémoires d'anthropologie* (1871–88).

Charlotte Brontë, 1816–1855

Charlotte Brontë showed a keen interest in phrenology throughout her work. Her novels repeatedly use phrenological terms, and dramatically foreground the act of phrenological reading, see for example, *Jane Eyre* (1847) especially chapter 14, or *Villette* (1853). Anne Brontë also turns to phrenology to offer us an analysis of the psychological inadequacies of the dissolute Arthur Huntingdon in *The Tenant of Wildfell Hall* (1848), especially chapter 23. Charlotte, herself, together with her publisher, visited a phrenologist in 1851 and was impressed by the accuracy of the character reading offered. West Yorkshire, at this era, was a thriving centre of phrenological activity, with numerous handbooks published, and frequent lectures. The Keighley Mechanics' Institute, to which the Revd. Patrick Brontë belonged, had its first phrenological lecture in 1836, and then duly acquired its own *Manual of Phrenology* and bust.

William Alexander Francis Browne, 1805–1885

MD, LRCS, FRS. A key figure in the asylum reform movement, W. A. F. Browne trained at Heidelberg and Edinburgh, where he was strongly influenced by George and Andrew Combe's work. He studied under Esquirol in France in the early 1830s before becoming medical superintendent at the Montrose Lunatic Asylum in 1834. Here he developed his lectures on the utopian potential of the curative asylum which, published in 1837 as *What Asylums Were, Are, and Ought to Be*, became the manifesto of lunacy reform in Britain. Browne was also the author of *Cottage Asylums* (1861), and a pamphlet analysing 'endemic degeneration' in isolated communities (1861).

Sir John Charles Bucknill, 1817–1897

MD, FRCP, FRS. Bucknill studied medicine in London and was medical superintendent of the Devon County Lunatic Asylum 1844–62 and the Lord Chancellor's Visitor in Lunacy 1862–76. An influential figure in the development of mid-century psychiatry, his publications included *Unsoundness of Mind in Relation to Criminal Acts* (1854), (with D. H. Tuke) *A Manual of Psychological Medicine* (1858), and his important study of insanity in Shakespeare, *The Psychology of Shakespeare* (1859), amended to *Mad Folk in Shakespeare* in later editions. He edited the *Asylum Journal of Mental Science* 1853–62, became president of the Medico-Psychological Association in 1860, and, with Hughlings Jackson, was co-founder and co-editor of *The Brain: A Journal of Neurology*, 1878.

George Man Burrows, 1771–1846

MRCS, LSA, MD, FRCP. Burrows was a GP in Bloomsbury who specialized in the treatment of insanity. He closely followed developments in psychiatric treatment in both Britain and France, becoming a key figure in establishing a nosology of insanity based on the close reading of psychopathological symptoms. He was the proprietor of a private asylum in Chelsea from 1814, and of the Retreat in Clapham 1823–43, and author of *An Enquiry into Certain Errors Relative to Insanity* (1820) and *Commentaries on the Causes, Forms, Symptoms and Treatment, Moral and Medical, of Insanity* (1828).

Samuel Butler, 1835–1902

Late nineteenth-century writer and painter. The son of a clergyman, Butler graduated from Cambridge in 1858. Initially drawn to religion, he became a lay reader at St James's church Piccadilly, but soon left with grave religious doubts. He emigrated to New Zealand in 1859 after falling out with his father, and became a successful sheep-breeder, doubling his investment and returning to England in 1865. Thereafter he became a moderately successful painter (exhibiting at the Royal Academy) and published *Erewhon* (a satirical Swiftian anti-utopia in which the moral and social institutions of nineteenth-century England are inverted) in 1872. He rejected Darwin's theory of natural selection in favour of his own interpretation of Lamarck's doctrine of the inheritance of acquired characteristics; these ideas are developed in *Life and Habit* (1877), *Evolution Old and New* (1879), *Unconscious Memory* (1880), and *Luck or Cunning?* (1886). *Erewhon Revisited* appeared in 1901 and his autobiographical novel *The Way of All Flesh*, Butler's powerful attack on the nineteenth-century patriarchal family, was published posthumously in 1905.

William Benjamin Carpenter, 1813–1885

MD, MRCS, LLD, FRS. Carpenter was a key figure in the development of mental physiology during the second part of the nineteenth century. He grew up in Bristol and came from a staunchly Unitarian family—his father was a Unitarian divine and his sister was Mary Carpenter the social reformer. His medical studies began in the Bristol Medical School and continued at University College, London (where he received his Surgeons and Apothecaries Diploma in 1833), then Edinburgh University, where he gained his MD and started to publish papers on physiology and the nervous system from the mid-1830s. These fed into *Principles of General and Comparative Physiology* (1839), a popular and influential textbook which went into many editions. Carpenter became the Fullerian Professor of Physiology at the Royal Institution in 1844, then Professor of Forensic Medicine at University College, London, and Registrar of London University in 1856. He edited the *British and Foreign Medico-Chirurgical Review* from 1847 until 1852. In addition to his work on mental physiology he wrote extensively on zoology, marine physics, and general physiology, including *The Popular Cyclopaedia of Natural Science* (1843), *Zoology* and *Animal Physiology* (1848), *Vegetable Physiology and Systematic Botany* (1865). His theory of unconscious cerebration was first developed in the fifth edition of *Principles of Human Physiology* (1855) and was expanded and developed in *Principles of Mental Physiology* (1874). Carpenter combined psychological materialism with a commitment to Unitarianism throughout his life, and in 1877 published his critique of mesmerism, *Mesmerism, Spiritualism etc., Historically and Scientifically Considered. Nature and Man; Essays Scientific and Philosophical* appeared posthumously in 1888.

Robert Brudenell Carter, 1828–1918

LSA. The son of a major in the Royal Marines, Carter started his medical career as an apprentice to a general practitioner before training in London. He worked as an army surgeon during the Crimean War and then as a general practitioner in a country practice until the age of 40, when he was appointed to the staff of the Royal South London Hospital, and then as ophthalmic surgeon in St George's Hospital. He wrote *On the Pathology and Treatment of Hysteria* (1853) and *The Influences of Education and Training in Preventing Diseases of the Nervous System* (1855) early in his career, later becoming known as an eye specialist. He was the author of *A Practical Treatise on Diseases of the Eye* (1875), and *Sight and Hearing in Childhood* (1903).

Pye Henry Chavasse, 1810–1879

LSA, FRCS. Doctor and President of Queen College Medico-Chirurgical Society, Birmingham. Chavasse was the author of a wide range of popular medical self-help manuals covering various aspects of gynaecology and child care, including *Advice to a Wife on the Management of her own Health* (1839), which was still in print in 1939, and *Advice to a Mother on the Care and Management of her Children* (1843).

Frances Power Cobbe, 1822–1904

A feminist and social campaigner, Frances Power Cobbe was born in Dublin, inheriting a substantial private income on her father's death. In addition to her writings on science and religion, she was involved in the movement for working-class education, working with Mary Carpenter (William's sister) at the latter's 'ragged school' in Bristol 1858–9, and reporting on social conditions for the *Echo* from 1868 to 1872. She helped initiate the campaign against vivisection, founding the Anti-Vivisection Society in 1875 and editing the *Zoophilist* until 1884—*The Modern Rack: Papers on Vivisection* appeared in 1889. She first presented a paper arguing for women's access to the universities to the Social Science Congress in 1862, supported women's suffrage and campaigned against the legal condonement of domestic violence and for the Matrimonial Causes Act of 1878.

Samuel Taylor Coleridge, 1772–1834

Poet and most significant theorist of the English Romantic movement, Coleridge was the son of a Devon clergyman and studied at Cambridge, though he never completed his degree. A supporter of the ideals of the French Revolution in his youth, he published *Poems on Various Subjects* in 1796 and the same year met William Wordsworth, collaborating with him on *The Lyrical Ballads* (1798). Coleridge visited Germany in the same year, becoming profoundly influenced by the philosophy of Schlegel and Kant, and from 1800 to 1804 lived in Keswick, near William and Dorothy Wordsworth, then intermittently in London, where he gave a series of public lectures and founded the periodical the *Friend* in 1809. Coleridge's major work of aesthetic theory and analysis of the imagination, *Biographia Literaria*, appeared in 1817; it had been planned and drafted over many years, but completion and publication was delayed—in part by Coleridge's own insecure situation and ill health, particularly his opium addiction. Although the discussion of associationism, particularly the critique of Hartley, played a crucial part in psychological debates in the nineteenth century, the *Biographia Literaria* had a generally hostile reception when it first appeared, and was not reprinted during Coleridge's own lifetime.

Andrew Combe, 1797–1847

MD, FRCP. The son of an Edinburgh brewer and younger brother of George Combe, Andrew studied medicine in Paris under Spurzheim and then in Edinburgh. He was the co-founder of the *Phrenological Journal* and the Edinburgh Phrenological Society, and, with his brother, was one of the foremost advocates of phrenology in Britain. He contracted tuberculosis in 1819 and had to spend some years abroad, but returned to Scotland and opened a successful medical practice in Edinburgh in 1823. His works include *Observations on Mental Derangement* (1831), *The Principles of Phrenology Simplified* (1836), *A Treatise on the Physical and Moral Aspects of Infancy* (1846), and numerous articles in the *Phrenological Journal*, including some on the diagnosis and treatment of criminals.

George Combe, 1788–1858

The principal promoter of phrenology in Britain, George Combe was born in Edinburgh to staunchly Calvinist parents and trained as a lawyer. Initially sceptical of phrenology, he was converted on hearing Spurzheim lecture in 1816 and became an ardent disciple, and co-founder (with Andrew) of the Edinburgh Phrenological Society. George Combe's outstandingly successful book was *The Constitution of Man Considered in Relation to External Objects* (1828), but his other books, including *Elements of Phrenology* (1824), *A System of*

Phrenology (1825), and *Phrenology Applied to Painting and Sculpture* (1836) were also immensely popular. Combe competed unsuccessfully with William Hamilton for the Chair of Logic and Metaphysics at Edinburgh University in 1836, and was the friend of other radical intellectuals such as Robert Chambers, Richard Cobden, and the Drysdale family. He also campaigned for a national system of secular education, publishing *Lectures on Popular Education* in 1835.

John Conolly, 1794–1866

MD, FRCP, Hon. DCL. Conolly was the most influential advocate of the non-restraint system in the treatment of insanity, and the hero of mid-nineteenth-century lunacy reform. *The Construction and Government of Lunatic Asylums and Hospitals for the Insane* (1847) and *The Treatment of the Insane without Mechanical Restraints* (1856) were crucial reference points in mid-century discussion of the treatment of insanity. Conolly studied medicine at Edinburgh and was the first Professor of the Practice of Medicine at London University 1827–31, developing his study of the connections between 'normal' and pathological behaviour which is outlined in his first book, *An Inquiry Concerning the Indications of Insanity* (1830). He was appointed superintendent of the Middlesex County Lunatic Asylum at Hanwell in 1839, and it was under his five-year management that Hanwell became a 'showpiece' institution, frequently represented as proof of the effectiveness of the non-restraint system in a large state asylum. Conolly was also Chairman of the Association of Medical Officers of Asylums in 1843 and 1851 and President of the Medico-Psychological Association in 1858. Although he warned against the dangers of widespread confinement at the beginning of his career, Conolly later set up two private establishments of his own: Lawn House, an asylum for women in 1845, and Hayes Park in 1850; he was often also called as an expert witness for the prosecution in legal cases where the insanity plea was made.

Sir James Crichton-Browne, 1835–1938

MD, LLD, LRCS, FRS. James Crichton-Browne was the eldest son of W. A. F. Browne (see above) who took the name of his godmother, Elizabeth Crichton, the wife of Sir Alexander Crichton (1763–1856), the influential alienist of his father's generation. Like his father, he studied in Paris after receiving his MD from Edinburgh in the early 1860s, and from 1866 to 1876 was medical director of the West Riding Lunatic Asylum in Wakefield. It was here that he developed the practice of photography in the classification of forms of insanity, corresponding with Darwin, who drew heavily on Crichton-Browne's work in *The Expression of the Emotions in Man and Animals* (1872), as well as conducting research on neurological disease. From 1876 to 1922 Crichton-Browne was the Lord Chancellor's Medical Visitor in Lunacy; he also helped to found *The Brain* in 1878, and engaged in extensive private practice. He specialized in the nervous diseases of children and wrote numerous articles, but no major medical treatise or monograph. His publications include *The Standard Family Physician* (1908–9) and several collections of popular essays, such as *Stray Leaves from a Physician's Portfolio* (1927).

Eneas Sweetland Dallas, 1828–1879

Born in Jamaica to Scottish parents and brought to England aged 4, E. S. Dallas studied philosophy under William Hamilton at Edinburgh University in the mid-1840s (though he failed to get a degree). He moved to London, and in 1952 published *Poetics*, his first attempt to create a 'science of poetry'; this was developed in *The Gay Science* (1866), his ambitious analysis of the role of the unconscious in shaping all forms of pleasure in art, which he argued had a strongly ethical dimension. Dallas became the leading *Times* literary critic in 1855; through the late 1850s and 1860s he was best known for his unsigned reviews of contemporary fiction, and as a member of the London literary intelligentsia whose friends included Dickens, George Eliot, Christina Rossetti, and Dante Gabriel Rossetti.

Charles Robert Darwin, 1809–1882

FRS. The grandson of the naturalist and poet Erasmus Darwin, Charles Darwin grew up in Shrewsbury and was educated at Edinburgh University and Christ's College Cambridge. His career as a naturalist began when he was engaged as the Captain's companion on the voyage of *The Beagle* to South America and the Galapagos Islands in 1831; this enabled him to study the development of species within an isolated environment, and, returning to England in 1836, he published the *Journal of Researches into the Geology and Natural History of the Various Countries Visited by H.M.S. Beagle* in 1839. Darwin first drafted his theory of natural selection in 1844, but delayed writing up his research until 1856, when he was persuaded by his friend the geologist Charles Lyell to prepare it for publication. Two years later he received a manuscript from Alfred Russel Wallace outlining a theory of evolution almost identical to his own; he published Wallace's essay with his response in a joint paper to the Linnaean Society in 1858, and his own *Origin of Species by Means of Natural Selection* in 1859. He developed his theory in *The Variation of Animals and Plants under Domestication* in 1868, extending it to humanity in *The Descent of Man, and Selection in Relation to Sex* (1871) and *The Expression of the Emotions in Man and Animals* (1872).

Thomas De Quincey, 1785–1859

Thomas De Quincey's father was a merchant who died while he was a child; his mother was an associate of the Evangelical Clapham Sect and friend of Hannah More. He grew up in Greenhay, near Manchester, and was educated at Bath and Manchester Grammar Schools, running away from the latter aged 17, and after a period of vagrancy went up to Oxford in 1803, where he first began to take opium. He met Coleridge in 1807 (giving him some financial help), and moved to Grasmere in 1809, becoming friends of both Coleridge and Wordsworth. Increasingly addicted to opium, De Quincey took up the editorship of the *Westmorland Gazette* in 1819, moving to London and beginning to contribute to the *London Magazine* in 1821. The first chapters of *The Confessions of an English Opium-Eater* appeared in the *London Magazine* in 1821 and the book was published in 1822. Substantially revised in the second edition of 1856, *The Confessions* was widely cited in medical works during the nineteenth century as a psychological study of the effects of opium. De Quincey started to write for *Blackwood's Edinburgh Magazine* and *Tait's Magazine* in the late 1820s, moving to Edinburgh in 1830, and remaining there for the rest of his life. *Suspiria de Profundis*, his study of fantasy and the workings of the unconscious, appeared as a series of articles in *Blackwood's* in 1845, and his other writings include *The Logic of Political Economy* (1841), 'Levana' and 'Our Lady of the Sorrows' (1845), 'Murder Considered as a Fine Art' (1827), and 'The English Mail-Coach' (1849).

Charles Dickens, 1812–1870

Dickens was actively interested both in mesmerism and asylum and lunacy reform. He met John Elliotson and started to attend his demonstrations of mesmerism in 1838; Elliotson introduced him to Chauncy Hare Townshend two years later, and he remained close friends with both for the rest of his life. Dickens also knew John Conolly. *Household Words*, which he 'conducted' from 1850 until 1859, aimed to provide popular instruction on a range of contemporary issues to a predominantly lower-middle-class readership. The journal frequently carried articles on lunacy reform and the treatment of insanity, usually written by the editor Henry Morley. Dickens reported his own visit to St Luke's Hospital in 1852 in 'A curious dance round a curious tree' (January 1852) and wrote the first of the articles on 'Idiots' (June 1853). Other unsigned articles on insanity carried in the journal are 'The treatment of the insane' (probably Richard Oliver, September 1851); 'Idiots again' (Harriet Martineau, April 1854), and a series by Henry Morley: 'Grand jury powers' (May 1857), 'The star of Bethlehem' (August 1857); 'Things within Dr Conolly's remembrance' (1857), and 'The cure of sick minds' (April 1859).

Horatio Bryan Donkin, 1845–1929

MA, MD, MRCS, FRCP. The son of a civil engineer, Donkin studied Classics at Oxford, then medicine at St Thomas's Hospital, London, qualifying in 1873. He then became Assistant Physician at the Westminster Hospital, and was soon after appointed physician at the East London Children's Hospital, consulting physician at the New Hospital for Women, and Lecturer in Medicine at the London School of Medicine for Women. The doctor and friend of Karl Marx's family and a supporter of feminism, Bryan Donkin was an active member of the radical Men and Women's Club, founded by Karl Pearson in 1885, which discussed a range of contemporary questions about sexuality, gender roles, and social development. It was in this context that he developed the argument, expanded in the article on hysteria in D. H. Tuke's *Dictionary of Psychological Medicine* of 1892, that hysteria in women is exacerbated by sexual restraint. In the latter part of his career Bryan Donkin became increasingly involved in the development of government policy on crime as well as insanity. He was made a Prison Commissioner in 1898 and in 1904 was appointed to the Royal Commission into the Care and Control of the Feeble Minded (which led to the Mental Deficiency Act of 1913). He served on various other departmental committees set up by the Home Office and was knighted in 1911. As well as his article on hysteria he wrote various articles in medical and general journals, *Diseases of Childhood* (1893), and the Harveian oration, 'The inheritance of mental characteristics', in 1910.

George Drysdale, d. 1904

MD. George Drysdale and his brother Charles (1829–1907) were the two youngest sons of Sir William Drysdale, a prominent Edinburgh citizen and City Treasurer. The family formed part of the intellectual élite of Edinburgh, and were the friends of George and Andrew Combe. After studying medicine at Edinburgh, George and Charles Drysdale established a joint practice in Southampton Row, London, where they shared consulting rooms all their professional lives. A radical Malthusian strongly influenced by J. S. Mill, George Drysdale anonymously published *Physical, Sexual and Natural Religion*, his controversial 'exposition of the three primary social evils: poverty, prostitution and celibacy', which included an account of his own experience as a case-study, in 1855. Prefixed with the title *Elements of Social Science* in the second edition, *Physical, Sexual and Natural Religion* was published by Edward Truelove, a Freethought, Owenite publisher who also supported birth control campaigners such as Charles Bradlaugh. It went into 35 editions, sold over 90,000 copies, and was widely translated. During 1856 and 1857 George Drysdale single-handedly produced the *Political Economist and Journal of Social Science*, and continued to publish, anonymously, a range of work on social, economic, and medical topics, including *Population Fallacies: A Defence of the Malthusian, or True Theory of Society* (1860), *The Land Question* (1863), *Logic and Utility* (1866), and *The Evils of an Hereditary Aristocracy* (1869).

John Elliotson, 1791–1868

MD, FRCP. One of the main advocates of mesmerism in England and a close friend of Charles Dickens, John Elliotson was the son of a prosperous Southwark chemist who studied in Edinburgh between 1805 and 1810 then in Cambridge until 1813. He translated J. F. Blumenbach's *Elements of Physiology* in 1828. Elliotson was one of the founders of and physician to University College Hospital and was appointed Professor of the Practice of Medicine at University College, London in 1831, but was forced to resign his chair in 1838 as a result of his advocacy of mesmerism. He founded and was president of the Phrenological Society of London in 1824 and founded and edited the *Zoist: A Journal of Cerebral Physiology and Mesmerism and their Application to Human Welfare*, 1843–56. Elliotson's influential textbook *Human Physiology* (1835) went into numerous editions, and was amended in the 1840 edition to include a defence of mesmerism. His pamphlets on mesmerism include *Numerous Cases of Surgical Operations Performed without Pain in the Mesmeric State* (1843), and *The Cure of True Cancer in the Female Breast with Mesmerism* (1848). Elliotson set up the London Mesmeric Infirmary in 1849, and became increasingly attracted to spiritualism in the 1860s.

Henry Havelock Ellis, 1859–1939

MB. Ellis was the son of a merchant sea captain, whose mother, a devout Evangelical, played a crucial role in his early life and education. When he was 16 his father took him to Australia, where he became a schoolteacher, returning to Britain in 1880 and studying medicine at St Thomas's Hospital, London. Ellis is best known as a key figure in the sexual radical movement and the development of sexology during the late 1880s and 1890s. A sexual radical during the 1880s, he became a founder member of the Fellowship of the New Life and started to collaborate with John Addington Symonds (the son of the eminent physician) on a study of homosexuality. *Studies in Sexual Inversion* appeared in England in 1897 but was bought up by Symonds's estate (Symonds having died in 1893), and thereafter Ellis published all seven volumes of *The Psychology of Sex* in the United States. The first edition of *The Criminal*, one of his earliest publications, is basically a paraphrase of the Italian criminologist Cesare Lombroso's work—a position Ellis completely revised in later editions of the book. Ellis's many other works included *The New Spirit* (1889), *Man and Woman: A Study of Secondary and Tertiary Sexual Characteristics* (1894), *The Problem of Race Regeneration* (1911), and *The Dance of Life* (1923).

W. C. Engledue, 1813–1858

MD, LRCS, LSA. Engledue studied medicine in Edinburgh, then practised in Portsmouth from 1835 until his death. He was co-editor of the *Zoist* with Elliotson, and a supporter of mesmerism, publishing *Celebral Physiology and Materialism* in 1842 as well as articles in the *Zoist*.

Jean Étienne Dominique Esquirol, 1772–1840

MD. Esquirol studied under Pinel in Paris, becoming physician to the Salpêtrière in 1811, and chief physician to the Royal Asylum at Charenton in 1825. His collected articles and papers were published in 1838 as *Des maladies mentales considerées sous les rapports médical, hygénique et médico-légal*, translated by E. D. Hunt as *Mental Maladies: A Treatise on Insanity* in 1845. Esquirol's theories of insanity, particularly his methods of classification and observation (it was he who developed the term 'monomania'), strongly influenced the perception and treatment of insanity in England, particularly in Burrows's and Prichard's work.

Franz Joseph Gall, 1758–1828

The founder of phrenology, Gall was born in Baden and studied medicine in Strasbourg from 1777 until 1785, when he moved to Vienna. His lectures on the new theory of the brain were proscribed by Emperor Francis I on the grounds of materialism. Together with his pupil and collaborator Spurzheim he toured Europe before arriving, six years later, in Paris, where he remained until his death. Gall and Spurzheim's four-volume *Anatomie et physiologie du système nerveux en général, et du cerveau en particulier* appeared in 1810. Gall's *Sur les fonctions du cerveau*, which became the defining text of phrenology, was published in six volumes in Paris 1822–5 and a full translation was published in Boston in 1835. Although parts of this work were translated and published in England in 1844, a full version never appeared.

Sir Francis Galton, 1822–1911

MD. Best known as the coiner of the term 'eugenics' for selective human breeding, Darwin's cousin Francis Galton, whose maternal grandfather was also Erasmus Darwin, studied medicine at London and Cambridge. He was General Secretary of the British Association, 1863–7, working mainly on meteorology, and from 1865 concentrated on developing theories of measurement and classification, and introduced both the modern form of statistical analysis and the practice of finger-printing as a mode of identification. Galton helped to form several 'eugenic societies', and on his death bequeathed a Chair in Eugenics at University College, London, financed from his estate, that was initially occupied by Karl Pearson. His books include *Hereditary Genius* (1869), *Inquiries into Human Faculty and its Development* (1883), *Natural Inheritance* (1889), *Finger Prints* (1892), and *Essays in Eugenics* (1909).

Thomas John Graham, 1795?–1876

MD, MRCS, FRCP. Graham was a well-known writer on popular medicine; Patrick Brönte owned a copy of his *Popular Domestic Medicine* (1826). He also published *Practical Observations on the Cure of Cancer* (1824), *On the Management and Disorders of Infancy and Childhood* (2nd edn., 1865), and *On the Diseases of Females* (1834).

Ernst Haeckel, 1834–1919

MD. Ernst Haeckel was the son of a lawyer and German government official. He studied medicine in Berlin, completed his dissertation in Zoology in 1861, and was appointed Professor of Zoology at Jena University in 1862. Haeckel popularized and extended Darwin's theory of descent, often in opposition to the scientific establishment, and produced the clearest early exposition of the argument that ontogeny recapitulates phylogeny—or that the stages of individual growth mirror that of the species. His works include *The Evolution of Man* (1879), *The Last Link: Our Present Knowledge of the Descent of Man* (1898), *The Riddles of the Universe at the Close of the Nineteenth Century* (translated in 1900) and *The Wonders of Life: A Popular Study of Biological Philosophy* (translated in 1904).

Sir William Hamilton, 1788–1856

MA, Ph.D. Born in Glasgow, where his father and grandfather both held the chairs of Anatomy and Physiology, Hamilton studied in Oxford and was called to the Scottish bar. Unsuccessful in his first application to the chair of Moral Philosophy at Edinburgh, he was appointed Professor of Logic and Metaphysics at that university in 1836. William Hamilton developed the principles of associationist psychology from Thomas Brown and Dugald Stewart in the light of German idealist philosophy. Opposing the phrenological concept of cerebral localization developed by his contemporaries at Edinburgh (George Combe was the rival applicant for his chair) he developed the theory of 'latent mental modification' in his lectures, published posthumously in 1859 as the four-volume *Lectures on Metaphysics and Logic*, which would have a lasting impact through the nineteenth century.

Sir Henry Holland, 1788–1873

MD, FRCP, FRS. Born in Cheshire, the son of a doctor and cousin to the novelist Elizabeth Gaskell, Holland began work as an articled clerk, then studied medicine in Glasgow, at Guy's and St Thomas's Hospitals in London, receiving his MD from Edinburgh. After travelling in Europe 1812–13, he set up what would become an extremely successful practice in London. As well as being George Eliot's doctor and friend he was physician to both William IV and Queen Victoria and president of the Royal Institution. Holland was one of the most significant writers on mental science in the mid-nineteenth century. His *Medical Notes and Reflections* (1839) went into many editions, and the material on psychology was expanded and published as *Chapters on Mental Physiology* in 1852 and was widely cited. His *Fragmentary Papers on Science and Other Subjects* was published posthumously in 1875.

Thomas Henry Huxley, 1825–1895

MB, FRS. T. H. Huxley was the son of a schoolmaster and studied medicine at Charing Cross Hospital, receiving his MB in 1845. He then joined the navy and in 1846 was appointed as assistant surgeon on HMS *Rattlesnake*, embarking on a four-year surveying cruise of the Great Barrier Reef. His career as a biologist began when he gave a set of scientific papers to the Linnaean Society based on his research on marine animals carried out on the *Rattlesnake*; his two studies of ascidians and morphological types appeared in 1851. Huxley left the navy in 1854 and the same year was appointed Lecturer in Natural History at the Royal School of Mines, and was naturalist to the school's geological survey of 1855. By then he had published more than thirty papers and had developed a method of teaching biology that would be widely emulated; from 1864 to 1867 he was the Fullerian Professor of the Royal Institution. Well established as a leading biologist by the time *The Origin of Species* appeared in 1859, Huxley became one of the most influential advocates of Darwin's theories during the second half of the nineteenth century, becoming Secretary to the Royal Society in 1871. His biological theories were reinforced by his anthropological studies which appeared in *Zoological Evidences as to Man's Place in Nature* in 1863, and his collected essays, bringing together work published throughout his career, appeared in nine volumes 1893–4. From the 1870s he also served on various parliamentary commissions, including the Commission on the Administration and Operation of the Contagious Diseases Acts (1870–1); the Commission on Scientific Instruction and the Advancement of Science (1870–3); and the Commission on the Practice of Subjecting Live Animals for Experiments for Scientific Purposes (1876).

Robert Knox, 1791–1863

MD, FRCS. Knox studied medicine in Edinburgh and became assistant surgeon in the army in 1817. He was sent to the Cape of Good Hope, where his early ethnological and medical observations formed the basis of much of his later career. In 1821 he studied in Paris under Cuvier and de Blainville, and from 1825 to 1831 was conservator of the Museum of Comparative Anatomy and Pathology set up by the Edinburgh College of Surgeons. Knox came under suspicion during the Burke and Hare trials of 1829 over his means of obtaining bodies for dissection, and although cleared, he later again fell into disrepute over a charge of plagiarism. He was finally appointed as the pathological anatomist to the Cancer Hospital in Brompton in 1856. His 1845 lectures on *The Races of Men*, arguing that different races form different species, were popular and widely cited to support the polygenic theory of race. Knox also wrote *A Manual of Comparative Anatomy* (1852).

Edwin Ray Lankester, 1847–1929

FRS. The son of Edwin Lankester, the progressive physician and Coroner for Central Middlesex, Lankester studied natural sciences at Oxford and marine zoology at the

Stazione Zoologica in Naples 1871–2. He held the Chair in Zoology at University College, London, 1874–91 and in 1898 was appointed director of the natural history departments at the British Museum. He was awarded the Darwin-Wallace medal of the Linnaean Society in 1908. Lankester was a leading authority on zoology in the late nineteenth century, and was known both for his specialist work on the embryology of the mollusc, and as a popularizer of contemporary scientific theories. In addition to *Degeneration: A Chapter in Darwinism* his publications include *The Primitive Cell-Layers of the Embryo* (1873), *Extinct Animals* (1905), and *Science from an Easy Chair* (1910).

Johann Caspar Lavater, 1741–1801

Born in Zurich and ordained as a pastor in 1763, Lavater was first known as a preacher and polemicist, author of *Prospects into Eternity* (1768). He began to develop his system of physiognomy in 1772, and, drawing heavily on the work of other contributors (including the physician J. G. Zimmermann, Goethe, and Herder), produced *Physiognomic Fragments for the Promotion of the Knowledge and Love of Mankind* between 1775 and 1777. This formed the basis of his system of physiognomy and was developed and translated into French between 1781 and 1803; it was the French edition which was translated into English by the radical publisher Thomas Holcroft in 1789. In the 1790s there were at least twelve different versions of Lavater's work.

Thomas Laycock, 1812–1876

MD, FRCP, FRS. Thomas Laycock was appointed Lecturer in Clinical Medicine at the York School of Medicine in 1846, and Lecturer in Mental Physiology at Edinburgh University, 1855–76. It was Laycock who first developed the theory of the 'reflex action of the cerebrum' in his work on hysteria in the 1830s and 1840s, anticipating some aspects of William Carpenter's theory of 'unconscious cerebration' developed in the 1850s. His *Treatise on the Nervous Diseases of Women* (1840) argued that the brain acted as a 'reflex centre' in 'hysterical' patients, a hypothesis developed in *Mind and Brain: or, The Correlations of Consciousness and Organisation* in 1860.

George Henry Lewes, 1817–1878

The grandson of the actor Charles Lee Lewes, Lewes, who was one of the most formidable intellectuals of the nineteenth century, received a desultory formal education and was largely self-taught. After considering and rejecting a medical career, he first worked as a professional actor and playwright, then took up literary journalism. He wrote chiefly on drama and aesthetic theory in the major journals and met contemporary writers such as Carlyle, Thackeray, and Mill. His first major work, the four-volume *Biographical History of Philosophy*, was published in 1846, and he became the editor of the radical journal the *Leader* in 1850. In 1854 he left his wife to live with Marian Evans (George Eliot), with whom he formed a mutually supportive lifelong partnership. Lewes published *The Life of Goethe* in 1856, then concentrated on developing his interest in science and physiological psychology. *Seaside Studies* appeared in 1856, followed by *The Physiology of Common Life* (1859) and *Animal Life* (1862), which argued for the basic homology of all nervous structures. Lewes became editor of the *Fortnightly Review* in 1865 and continued his theoretical work, developing his long-term project of the five-volume *Problems of Life and Mind* (1873–9), a highly ambitious work which sought to ground philosophy on scientific principles, and to extend physiological psychology into a framework of social and psychological evolution. The last two volumes of this work were completed by George Eliot after Lewes's death.

Sir Charles Locock, 1799–1875

MD, FRS, FRCP. Charles Locock received his MD from Edinburgh in 1821, then set up in London as an obstetrician, building up a successful and fashionable practice—he became Queen Victoria's physician-accoucher and attended the birth of all her children. From 1834 to 1835 he lectured at St Bartholomew's Hospital and was for many years physician in the Westminster lying-in hospital. Apart from his various articles in the *Cyclopaedia of Practical Medicine* and the *Library of Medicine* his only published work was his inaugural thesis on heart disease.

Robert Macnish, 1802–1837

MD. Macnish studied under Broussais in Paris, where he met F. J. Gall, and received his MD from Glasgow. *The Anatomy of Drunkenness* (1827), based on his medical thesis, went into several editions. He also wrote poetry and 'psychological Gothic' fiction—the best example is his *Blackwood's* story of 1826, 'The metempsychosis'. However, *The Philosophy of Sleep* (1830), which was expanded and revised in later editions, was his best-known work.

Harriet Martineau, 1802–1876

Harriet Martineau was born in Norwich to Huguenot parents and brought up to earn her own living; her youth was marked by illness and increasing deafness. A staunch Unitarian, her first article, 'Observations of Practical Divinity' appeared in the *Monthly Repository* in 1821, and was followed by *Devotional Exercises for the Use of Young Persons* (1823). She started to support herself by writing for the *Monthly Repository* following the bankruptcy of her father in 1829, success and recognition following the appearance of her social reformist tales, *Illustrations of Political Economy* (1832–4). Becoming increasingly interested in politics and economics, she travelled to America in 1834 and *Society in America* (which supported the Abolitionist cause) appeared in 1837. This was followed by a novel, *Deerbrook* (1839), her translation of Comte's *Positive Philosophy* (1853), and her posthumously published *Autobiography*. Martineau suffered from ill health throughout her life and was an enthusiastic supporter of mesmerism. *Letters in Mesmerism* followed her treatment by one of its famous advocates, Spencer Timothy Hall, while he was lecturing near her home in Newcastle in 1844.

Henry Maudsley, 1835–1918

MD. The son of a Yorkshire farmer and a staunchly religious mother (who died when he was a child) Maudsley studied medicine at University College, London. After briefly working at Wakefield and Brentwood asylums, he was appointed medical superintendent of the Cheadle Royal Hospital for the Insane in Manchester, 1859–62, resigning the post to become editor of the *Journal of Mental Science*, which he edited until 1878. He assisted John Conolly at Lawn House Asylum, and in 1866 married Conolly's youngest daughter, Anne, just before Conolly died. He wrote several articles in the 1860s (including a study of Edgar Allen Poe in the *Journal of Mental Science* in 1860) and his first full-length study, *The Physiology and Pathology of Mind* (1867) fully established his reputation. Maudsley became one of the most influential psychiatrists of the late nineteenth century. Usually associated with psychiatric pessimism and biological determinism, he did not completely dispense with all belief in individual autonomy, but was critical of his father-in-law John Conolly's confidence in the power of moral management, stressing 'the tyranny of organisation' in *Body and Mind* (1870) and *Responsibility in Mental Disease* (1874). His other work includes *Body and Will* (1883), *Natural Causes and Supernatural Seemings* (1897), and *Life in Mind and Conduct: Studies of the Organic in Human Nature* (1902).

John Gideon Millingen, 1782–1862

MD. A physician and popular playwright, Millingen was born in London and taken to Paris at the age of 8. He studied at the École de Médicin in Paris, returned to England, and in 1807 became an assistant surgeon in the army, serving at the Battle of Waterloo. He left the army in 1823 and became physician of the Military Lunatic Asylum at Chatham. In 1837 he was appointed physician-superintendent of Middlesex County Lunatic Asylum at Hanwell, where he stayed for two years—later he became part-owner of the private asylum, York House, Battersea. Millingen was author of *Aphorisms on the Treatment and Management of the Insane* (1840) and *The Passions, or Mind and Matter* (1848), but was also known for his musical farces, including *The Bee Hive* (1811), *Borrowed Feathers* (1825), *The Illustrious Stranger*, and *Ladies at Home, or Gentlemen, We Can Do without You* (1850).

Sir Alexander Morison, 1779–1866

MD, FRCP. Morison studied medicine in Edinburgh and was the inspecting physician of the private madhouses in Surrey. He was also consulting physician to Middlesex County Asylum at Hanwell, 1832–5, to Bethlem Hospital, 1835–53, and to the Surrey County Asylum from 1841. He was one of the first doctors to argue for a specialist training in psychiatric treatment and instituted the first sets of formal lectures on psychiatry in London and Edinburgh, published as *Outlines of Lectures on Mental Diseases* in 1825. This was followed by the textbook *Cases of Mental Diseases, with Practical Observations on their Medical Treatment* (1828); *The Physiognomy of Mental Diseases* appeared in 1838. He also founded the Society for the Improvement of the Conditions of the Insane in 1842.

Frederick William Henry Myers, 1843–1901

MA. The son of an Anglican clergyman, Frederick Myers studied Classics at Cambridge, where he was privately tutored by Henry Sidgwick, Professor of Moral Philosophy, in 1860. He became a Fellow of Trinity College and College Lecturer in Classics, then took up the post of school inspector for the Education Department in the early 1870s. Moving from intense religiosity to sceptical agnosticism, Myers began to see spiritualism as a means of reconciling religion and materialism, and in 1874 urged Sidgwick to form the group that would be the basis of the Society for Psychical Research, set up in 1882. During the 1880s and 1890s Myers aimed (with Edmund Gurney) to bring the study of psychic phenomena into the realm of experimental psychology, and his development of the theory of the 'subliminal self' emerged out of a detailed analysis of contemporary psychological theory and practice in both Britain and France. During his career Myers became acquainted with the French psychiatrists Jean Charcot, Alfred Binet, and Charles Féré, studied the work of Azam, attended experiments at the Salpêtrière, and collaborated with Pierre Janet. He also became a close friend of William James. Myers's many contributions to the *Proceedings of the Society for Psychical Research* were based on carefully annotated case studies and detailed citations, and made many French and German writings on psychiatry available to an English readership. His theory of the 'subliminal self', developed fully in the posthumously published *Human Personality and its Survival of Bodily Death* (2 vols., 1902), argued that the concept of the submerged, or subconscious personality, formed the basis of a theory of the self that encompassed all aspects of psychic life, including 'morbid' and 'healthy', normal and paranormal phenomena.

Sir James Paget, 1814–1899

LLD, Hon. DLC, MRCS, Hon. MD. The son of a brewer and ship owner, James Paget was born in Great Yarmouth, Norfolk and started his career by being apprenticed to a local surgeon. He studied briefly in Paris, then at St Bartholomew's Hospital, became a member of the Royal College of Surgeons in 1836, was Lecturer in General Anatomy and Physiology 1843–51, and member of the General Council of the Royal College of Surgeons 1865–89. Appointed 'surgeon extraordinary' to Queen Victoria, he was at various times chair of the Clinical Society, the Royal Medical and Chirurgical Society, and the Pathological Society. He became Vice-Chancellor of London University towards the end of his career, from 1884 to 1895. Paget was one of the most successful London surgeons during the mid-nineteenth century. His *Clinical Lectures and Essays* (1875) contained discussions of 'Nervous mimicry' and 'On stammering with other organs than those of speech' as well as the essay on 'Sexual hypochondriasis', which was first given as a lecture in 1870. His other works included *Theology and Science* (1880), and *Studies of Old Case-Books* (1891).

John Perceval, 1803–1876

John Perceval was the fifth son of Spencer Perceval, the only British Prime Minister to be assassinated (in the House of Commons in 1812). Entering the army, he became obsessed with religious anxieties and resigned his commission in 1830, becoming involved with the Irvingites, an extreme Evangelical sect, and started to hear voices and see visions. On his brother's intervention he was placed in Fox's private asylum at Brislington near Bristol in 1831, then moved to Ticehurst, a reformed asylum in Sussex, where he stayed from 1832 to 1834. Perceval's extraordinary account of his insanity and treatment, *A Narrative of the Treatment Experienced by a Gentleman During a State of Mental Derangement; Designed to Explain the Causes and the Nature of Insanity, and to Expose the Injudicious Conduct Pursued towards Many Unfortunate Sufferers under the Calamity*, was published in two parts, in 1838 and 1840. Perceval remained involved in campaigns for lunacy reform; in 1859 he gave evidence to the Parliamentary Select Committee on the Care and Treatment of Lunatics and their Property on behalf of the Alleged Lunatic Friends Society.

James Cowles Prichard, 1786–1848

MD, FRS. Born in Herefordshire and raised in Bristol in a Quaker family, Prichard had an extraordinary double career as psychiatrist and ethnographer, and became a centrally important figure in each field. He studied medicine in Bristol, at St Thomas's Hospital, London, and at Edinburgh University, where he started his research in ethnography, receiving his MD in 1808. Prichard started to practice medicine in Bristol in 1810 while continuing his ethnographic researches, and 1813 published *Researches into the Physical History of Mankind*, the first of his ethnographic studies based on his Edinburgh thesis. This outlined his monogenic theory of the essential unity of all human culture, and was developed in later editions and in *The Natural History of Man* (1843). During the late 1840s he was President of the Ethnographic Society. Developing his medical studies into the study and treatment of mental disease, Prichard published *A Treatise on Diseases of the Nervous System* in 1822, but his most influential work in the emerging field of mental science was *A Treatise on Insanity and other Disorders Affecting the Mind* (1835), which became a standard textbook of psychological medicine in the mid-nineteenth century. In particular, *A Treatise on Insanity* developed the concept of 'moral insanity' (in contrast with monomania and dementia) from Pinel and Esquirol's nosology. Prichard's medico-legal study, *On the Different forms of Insanity in Relation to Jurisprudence* (1842) analysed the impact of his theory of moral insanity on notions of criminal responsibility, and he was the first practising psychiatrist to be appointed a Commissioner in Lunacy, from 1844 to 1848.

Théodule Armand Ribot, 1839–1916

Ph.D. Ribot trained as a philosopher rather than a physician, and received his doctorate in 1865. He then became deeply interested in English physiological psychology, publishing *La Psychologie anglaise contemporaine* in 1870 and translating Spencer's *The Principles of Psychology* into French in 1874. Ribot studied clinical and experimental psychology in Paris from 1873 until 1885, and ran a course in experimental psychology at the Sorbonne until 1895. He was then appointed Professor of Experimental and Comparative Psychology at La Collège de France, though he was not involved in experimental work himself. Théodule Ribot introduced both German and British physiological psychology to French psychiatric medicine, and his reputation was mainly based on summarizing and making available others' work. His books, widely translated into English in turn, include *Heredity: A Psychological Study of its Phenomena, Laws, Causes and Consequences* (1873, trans. 1875), *Diseases of Memory* (1881, trans. 1882), *Diseases of Will* (1883, trans. 1884), *Diseases of Personality* (1886, trans. 1887), *The Psychology of Attention* (1888, trans. 1889), and *The Evolution of General Ideas* (1898, trans. 1899).

Robert Peel Ritchie, 1835–1902

MD, FRCP. A successful gynaecologist, Ritchie studied medicine at Edinburgh University, receiving his MD in 1856. During his career he was Examiner in Midwifery and Medical Jurisprudence at the Royal College of Physicians in Edinburgh, Consultative Physician at the Royal Edinburgh Hospital for Children and the Edinburgh Dispensary for Women and Children, the physician of the Edinburgh Rescue Home, and Medical Officer of the

Royal Dispensary. He moved to London in 1856 and took up the post of Medical Officer of the Bethnall Home Asylum, which he held until 1861. In addition to his articles on masturbation and male insanity in the *Lancet*, his publications include numerous pieces in the *Edinburgh Medical Journal*, including 'On umbilical haemorrhage and tumour' (1867), 'A report on ovarian dropsy' (1870), 'On remedies used by the Caffres to prevent blood poisoning anthrax' (1887), and 'Notes on pleuro-pneumonia and tuberculosis in the United Kingdom' (1888).

George John Romanes, 1848–1894

FRS. George Romanes was born in Canada, the family returning to England when his father received an inheritance in 1848. He graduated from Cambridge in 1870 and became a friend of Charles Darwin in 1873. Romanes studied physiology at University College, London, between 1874 and 1876, and from the late 1870s worked on the nervous and locomotive systems of various species of molluscs and sea-urchins before turning to developing and popularizing Darwinian theory. During the 1880s Romanes work was particularly concerned with the relationship between animal and human intelligence, the development of the human mind from infancy to adulthood, and the effects of physical isolation on the development of species. Arguing that man and animals share a common pattern of evolution, he attempted to apply to both a single model of character and motivation. His works include *Animal Intelligence* (1881), *Mental Evolution in Animals* (1883), *Mental Evolution in Man* (1888), *Darwin and after Darwin* (1892), and *An Examination of Weismannism* (1893). He showed a sceptical interest in spiritualism in the late 1870s, publishing *A Candid Examination of Theism* under the pseudonym 'Physicus' in 1878, and attending the first meeting of the Society for Psychical Research in 1882. Romanes was the Professor of Physiology at Edinburgh from 1886 until 1890, then Fullerian Professor of Physiology at the Royal Institution; he was Zoological Secretary of the Linnaean Society and founded the annual Romanes Lecture at Oxford University (on developments in contemporary science) in 1891.

Charles Henry Felix Routh, 1822–1900

MD, MRCP, MRCS. Routh was a successful gynaecologist who held the posts of Senior Physician to the Samaritan Hospital for Women and Children and Consultant in Gynaecology at the North London Hospital. He was a Fellow of University College, London, and delivered the Lettsomian lectures on 'Midwifery and Diseases of Women' to the Medical Society of London in 1863. Routh published a wide range of gynaecological and other works, including *On the Fallacies of Homeopathy* (1852), *The History of the Medical Society of London* (1859), *Infant Feeding and its Influence on Life* (1860), *Further Remarks on the Treatment of Uterine Cancer* (1874), and *On Overwork and Premature Mental Decay* (1876).

Sir George Henry Savage, 1842–1921

MD, FRCP. Born in Brighton, George Savage studied medicine at London University. He became assistant medical officer of Bethlem Hospital in 1872 and was senior physician and superintendent for ten years from 1878, then Consulting Lecturer in Mental Disease at Guy's Hospital. Savage was also President of the Medico-Psychological Association of

Great Britain and co-editor of the *Journal of Mental Science*. A crucial figure in developing the concept of moral insanity in late nineteenth-century psychiatry, his *Insanity and Allied Neuroses* (1884) was one of the most popular late nineteenth-century textbooks on insanity which went into many editions and was widely cited. Knighted in 1912, Savage maintained a successful medical practice throughout his life. He was the doctor and friend of Leslie Stephen and his family and treated Virginia Stephen (Woolf) during her breakdown following her father's death in 1904.

Frederick Carpenter Skey, 1798–1872

MB, FRCS. Skey was a successful surgeon and Professor of Practical and Descriptive Anatomy at St Bartholomew's Hospital, London. In addition to *Hysteria: Six Lectures* (1867)—based on lectures given at St Bartholomew's—he was the author of *A Practical Treatise on Venereal Disease* (1840) and *Operative Surgery* (1850); he was also the Chairman of the Government Commission for Inquiries into the Treatment of Syphilis.

Herbert Spencer, 1820–1903

Born in Derby, Herbert Spencer started his career as an assistant schoolmaster in 1837, then worked as an engineer on the Birmingham and Gloucester Railway from 1837 until 1841. He was actively involved in radical political circles in the Midlands, moving to London in 1848 when he worked as sub-editor on *The Economist* until 1853. The friend of the radical publisher John Chapman and of George Eliot and G. H. Lewes, Spencer published his first major work, *Social Statics* in 1851. This was followed by *The Principles of Psychology* (1855), his first venture in applying evolutionary theory to associationist principles, which he radically revised in 1870 in the light of Darwin's theory. Spencer was probably the foremost sociological and psychological theorist in Britain in the mid-nineteenth century. His 'development hypothesis' (initially set out in 'Progress, its law and cause' in the *Westminster Review* in 1856) that all forms of evolution took the form of a move from simpler to more complex forms, or from homogeneity to heterogeneity, underpinned evolutionary theory during the second half of the nineteenth century. Spencer developed this paradigm of development, in which the social is modelled on the biological, and the collective on the individual, in *First Principles* (1862), *The Principles of Biology* (1864), and *The Principles of Sociology* (1876). He also published *The Data of Ethics* (1879), and *The Man Versus the State* (based on articles in the *Contemporary Review*) in 1884.

Dugald Stewart, 1753–1828

FRS. The son of the mathematician Matthew Stewart, Stewart grew up in Edinburgh and studied in Edinburgh and under Thomas Reid in Glasgow. He held the Chair in Moral Philosophy at Edinburgh University 1785–1820. Dugald Stewart (with Thomas Brown) was the late eighteenth-century Edinburgh philosopher whose development of associationist theories of consciousness and memory had the strongest bearing on the development of mid-nineteenth-century psychology. His main works were *Elements of the Philosophy of the Human Mind* (3 vols., 1792–1827), *Outlines of Moral Philosophy* (1793), *Philosophical Essays* (1810), *The Philosophy of the Active and Moral Powers* (1826), and his edition of Adam Smith's work (1811–12).

James Sully, 1842–1925

MA, LLD. The son of a Baptist businessman and political Radical, James Sully was born in Bridgwater, Somerset, and left school aged 17 to work in his father's business. In 1862 he enrolled at Regent's Park College, a Baptist college connected to London University. Transferring to read Philosophy at University College, he studied the work of Alexander Bain, Herbert Spencer, and J. S. Mill, and after graduating he studied for a year in Göttingen, returning to London to take his MA in 1867. Abandoning his plans to become a minister, Sully took up the post of lecturer in Classics at a Baptist College in Wales; but encouraged by Bain, he continued his philosophical and psychological studies and in 1869 submitted an article—a psychological study of belief in free will—to the *Fortnightly*. In 1870 the editor of the *Fortnightly* John Morley offered him the combined job of tutor and editorial assistant, and he began to write a series of articles on various aspects of psychological and aesthetic theory (including several on music) for the *Fortnightly Review* and the *Saturday Review*. Revised as *Sensation and Intuition: Essays on Psychology and Aesthetics* in 1874, this work was well received by (amongst others) Spencer, G. H. Lewes, T. Ribot, and Darwin. In 1877 Sully published *Pessimism* (a critique of Schopenhauer and von Hartmann), and *Illusions: A Psychological Study* (1881); then, failing to get an academic Chair, wrote the textbook *Outlines of Psychology*, an introduction and survey of psychological theory. In 1892 he published his major work, *The Human Mind*, and was offered the Grote Chair of Logic and Philosophy at University College, London. Sully's interest in child psychology, which began in the 1880s, was developed in *Studies of Childhood* (1895) and *Children's Ways* (1897).

John Addington Symonds, 1807–1871

MD. The son of a doctor, Symonds studied medicine at Edinburgh University and developed a successful practice in Bristol. Strongly interested in poetry and aesthetic theory as well as psychological medicine, he became a close friend of James Cowles Prichard, publishing the latter's biography the year after Prichard's death in 1849. In addition to his lectures to the Bristol Philosophical Society, published as *Sleep and Dreams* in 1851, he published a book on aesthetic theory, *The Principles of Beauty* (1857) and *Miscellanies* (1872), a posthumous collection of essays including a memoir by his son John Addington Symonds, the cultural critic who collaborated with Havelock Ellis on the study of sexual inversion in the early 1890s.

Charles Turner Thackrah, 1795–1833

MRCS, LSA. Thackrah was a medical practitioner who was responsible for the care of poor-law patients in Leeds. He helped to found the Leeds Medical School, where he taught anatomy. His compendious *The Effects of Arts, Trades and Professions, and of Civic States and Habits of Living* (1831) was the first full-length account in English of the effects of industrialization on mental and physical health. Thackrah published various studies drawing on his practical experience, including *An Inquiry into the Nature and Properties of Blood, in Health and Disease* (1819), *Lectures on Digestion and Diet* (1824), and *Cholera: Its Character and Treatment* (1824).

Chauncy Hare Townshend, 1798–1868

A man of considerable private means, Townshend was one of the most influential advocates of mesmerism in England. He was educated at Eton and Cambridge and ordained as an Anglican minister, but never practised as a clergyman. As a young man he was the friend of Hartley Coleridge, Southey, and Wordsworth and published poetry and criticism, left England to travel in Europe in 1830, and settled in Lausanne, where he lived for most of his adult life. He dedicated *Facts in Mesmerism* (1840) to his friend John Elliotson, who introduced him to Charles Dickens the year the book was published. Townshend and Dickens remained friends; Dickens was Townshend's literary executor and published his *Religious Opinions* posthumously in 1869—the year of Dickens's own death. *Facts in Mesmerism*, which attempted to reconcile mesmerism with traditional theology, played an important part in discussions of animal magnetism in the mid-nineteenth century, and was followed by *Mesmerism Proved True* (1854).

Samuel Tuke, 1784–1857

Grandson of the founder of the Retreat in York and pioneer of moral management William Tuke, Samuel Tuke was a Quaker merchant and philanthropist who had no medical training. He was the treasurer of the Retreat during the early nineteenth century and his layman's account of the institution, *A Description of the Retreat* (1813), had a profound impact on discussions of the treatment of insanity through the first half of the nineteenth century.

Daniel Hack Tuke, 1827–1895

LLD, MD, FRCP. Son of Samuel Tuke, Daniel studied law before turning to psychological medicine, studying both at St Bartholomew's Hospital and in Heidelberg. *A Manual of Psychological Medicine* (written with J. C. Bucknill) appeared in 1858 and went into four editions. He was visiting physician at the Retreat and lectured on nervous diseases at York School of Medicine, retiring because of ill health in 1859. In 1875 D. H. Tuke became a governor of Bethlem Hospital; he also lectured at Charing Cross Hospital and founded the After Care Association. He jointly edited the *Journal of Mental Science* (with George Savage) in 1880 and edited *A Dictionary of Psychological Medicine* (1892). His other work includes *Illustrations of the Influence of the Mind upon the Body* (1872), *Insanity in Ancient and Modern Life* (1878), and *Chapters on the History of the Insane in the British Isles* (1882).

Alfred Russel Wallace, 1825–1913

FRS. A. R. Wallace was born in Monmouthshire, the son of an unsuccessful writer, and at the age of 14 trained as a surveyor in London, becoming interested in astronomy and botany and attending the lectures at the working-class radical Hall of Science, where he heard Robert Owen. He became a schoolteacher in Leicester in 1844, where he read Malthus (who had a profound influence on both him and Darwin) and attended Spencer Hall's popular series of lectures on mesmerism. In the same year he met the naturalist Henry Bates and in 1848 accompanied him on a four-year collecting voyage to the Amazon basin. Two years after returning, in 1854, Wallace visited the Malay Archipelago, where he stayed for eight years and independently developed the theory of natural selection that Darwin had already drafted. Their theory of evolution was first publicly proposed in a jointly authored paper presented to the Linnaean Society in 1858 and Wallace published his own *Contributions to the Theory of Natural Selection* in 1870. His other work includes *The Malay Archipelago* (1869), *The Geographical Distribution of Animals* (1876), *Darwinism* (1889), *The Wonderful Century* (1898), and *Man's Place in the Universe* (1903). A secularist for most of his life, Wallace became an increasingly dedicated advocate of spiritualism from the mid-1860s, which he saw as the basis of a rational religion which could be reconciled with evolutionary thought.

August Friedrich Leopold Weismann, 1834–1914

MD. The son of a Classics professor at the Gymnasium in Frankfurt and Elise Lübben, a musician and painter, August Weismann studied medicine at Göttingen and practised as a doctor until 1863, when he started research on zoology. He taught comparative anatomy and zoology at Freiburg, becoming professor in 1874 and staying there for the rest of his career. Weismann was strongly influenced by Darwin's theories, but he departed from both Darwin's theory of pangenesis and Lamarck's notion of the inheritance of acquired characteristics to argue instead for the continuity of the 'germ plasm' (the 'substance of heredity', that would soon be defined as 'chromatic loops' or chromosomes) from generation to generation. Weismann argued that the germ plasm was located in the nucleus of the cell, and contained genetic material from both parents. He was the most notable of post-Darwinian biologists to argue against the theory of transmitted acquired characteristics and for the argument that both natural selection and genetic traits influenced heredity. His essays, translated and published as *Essays upon Heredity and Kindred Biological Problems* (1889), had a profound impact in England; Herbert Spencer in particular challenged his ideas, and the *Contemporary Review* published the controversy between Spencer and Weismann during 1893–4.

Arthur Ladbroke Wigan, 1785–1847

MRCS. Wigan was the son of a Staffordshire farmer who was first employed as a laboratory assistant in London at the age of 14, then trained as a doctor's assistant, becoming a member of the Royal College of Surgeons in 1807. He was then a travelling physician until 1829, when he practised in London, moving to Brighton in 1829, where he opened a dispensary for working-class patients as well as running a fee-paying practice. An admirer of Henry Holland, friend of Forbes Winslow, and acquaintance of John Conolly, he became involved in debates in lunacy reform and visited Hanwell County Asylum in 1841. Wigan's theory that the mind contains two separate cerebra, outlined in *A New View of Insanity: The Duality of the Mind* (1844), excited considerable interest, but was not taken wholly seriously by his contemporaries.

Forbes Benignus Winslow, 1810–1874

MD, MRCS. Winslow was the son of an army captain, and studied medicine at University College, London, and at Middlesex Hospital, where he was a pupil of Sir Charles Bell (author of *Essays on the Anatomy of Expressing in Painting* (1806)). He financed his medical studies by reporting on the House of Commons for *The Times* and writing manuals on practical midwifery. By the mid-nineteenth century Winslow, who opened two private asylums in Hammersmith in 1847, had become a significant figure both in the asylum reform movement and in the physiological study of mental disease, giving the Lettsomian Lectures on insanity in 1854, and editing the *Journal of Psychological Medicine and Mental Pathology* from 1848 to 1860. He also became an authority on medical jurisprudence and was frequently called as an expert witness in trials when the insanity plea was made. In addition to *On Obscure Diseases of the Brain and Disorders of the Mind* (1860) he wrote several other studies of insanity and physiology, including *The Anatomy of Suicide* (1840), *The Plea of Insanity in Criminal Cases* (1843), and *The Incubation of Insanity* (1845) (which was satirized in Charles Reade's *Hard Cash* (1863)) and *On Uncontrollable Drunkenness, Considered as a Form of Mental Disorder* (1866).

Andrew Wynter, 1819–1876

MD, MRCP. Born in Bristol, Andrew Wynter studied medicine at St Andrew's University and St George's Hospital, London, receiving his MD in 1853. He was editor of the *British Medical Journal* from 1856 until 1860 and wrote a range of articles on insanity and general topics for the *Edinburgh Review* and the *Quarterly Review*, reprinted in *Curiosities of Civilisation* (1861). His influential article on 'Lunatic Asylums', based on a survey of Colney Hatch, Hanwell, and Bethlem, in the *Quarterly Review* in 1857, and *The Borderlands of Insanity* (1875) were his main contributions to contemporary psychiatric debates; he also published *Subtle Brains and Lissom Fingers: Being some of the Chisel-Marks of our Industrial and Scientific Progress* (1863).

Select Bibliography

Primary works cited

ABERCROMBIE, JOHN, *Inquiries Concerning the Intellectual Powers and the Investigation of Truth* (1830), 19th edn. (London: John Murray, 1871).

ACTON, WILLIAM, *The Functions and Disorders of the Reproductive Organs in Childhood, Youth, Adult Age, and Advanced Life Considered in their Physiological, Social and Moral Relations* (1857), 4th edn. (London: John Churchill, 1865).

ALLBUTT, CLIFFORD, *On Visceral Neuroses: Being the Gulstonian Lectures on Neuralgia of the Stomach and Allied Disorders* (Philadelphia: P. Blakiston, 1884).

ANDERSON, ELIZABETH GARRETT, 'Sex in Mind and Education: A Reply', *Fortnightly Review*, NS 15 (June 1874), 582–95.

Anon, 'On the coincidence between the natural talents and dispositions of nations, and the development of their brains', *Phrenological Journal*, 2 (1824–5), 1–19.

—— *Phrenology Simplified: Being an Exposition of the Principles and Applications of Phrenology to the Practical Uses of Life* (Glasgow: W. R. M'Phun, 1836).

—— 'Electro-Biology', *Westminster Review*, 55 (1851), 312–28.

—— 'Woman in her psychological relations', *Journal of Psychological Medicine and Mental Pathology*, 4 (1851), 18–50.

—— [John Eagles and J. F. Ferrier] 'What is mesmerism?', *Blackwood's Edinburgh Magazine*, 70 (1851), 70–85.

—— [?Harriet Martineau] 'Idiots Again', *Household Words*, 9 (15 Apr., 1854), 197–200.

—— [?Henry Morley] 'The cure of sick minds', *Household Words*, 19 (2 Apr., 1859), 415–18.

BACON, GEORGE MACKENZIE, *On the Writing of the Insane* (London: John Churchill, 1870).

BARLOW, JOHN, *On Man's Power over Himself to Prevent or Control Insanity* (London: William Pickering, 1843).

BRAID, JAMES, *Neurypnology; or, the Rationale of Nervous Sleep, Considered in Relation with Animal Magnetism* (London: John Churchill, 1843).

BROCA, P., *On the Phenomena of Hybridity in the Genus Homo*, ed. C. Carter Blake (London: Longman, Green, Longman and Roberts, 1864).

BRONTË, CHARLOTTE, *The Professor* (1857), ed. Margaret Smith and Herbert Rosengarten (Oxford: Clarendon Press, 1987).

BUCKNILL, JOHN CHARLES *Unsoundness of Mind in Relation to Criminal Acts* (1854), 2nd edn. (London: Longman, Brown, Green, Longman and Roberts, 1857).

BURROWS, GEORGE MAN, *Commentaries on the Causes, Forms, Symptoms, and Treatment, Moral and Medical, of Insanity* (London: Thomas and George Underwood, 1828).

BUTLER, SAMUEL, *Life and Habit* (1877), 2nd edn. (London: Trübner & Co., 1878).

CARPENTER, W. B., *Principles of Mental Physiology* (1874), 2nd edn. (London: Henry S. King, 1875).

—— *Mesmerism, Spiritualism etc., Historically and Scientifically Considered* (London: Longmans, Green, 1877).

CARTER, ROBERT BRUDENELL, *On the Pathology and Treatment of Hysteria* (London: John Churchill, 1853).

CHAVASSE, PYE HENRY, *Advice to a Wife on the Management of her own Health; and on the Treatment of some of the Complaints Incidental to Pregnancy, Labour and Suckling* (1839), 6th edn. (London: J. Churchill, 1864).

COBBE, FRANCES POWER, 'Unconscious cerebration', in *Darwinism in Morals and Other Essays* (London: William and Norgate, 1872).

—— 'Dreams, as illustrations of involuntary cerebration', *Darwinism in Morals and Other Essays* (London: Williams and Norgate, 1872).

—— 'The fallacies of memory', *Hours of Work and Play* (London: N. Trübner and Co., 1867).

COLERIDGE, S. T., *Biographie Literaria, or Biographical Sketches of my Literary Life and Opinions*, 2 vols. (London: Rest, Fenner, 1817).

COMBE, ANDREW, *Observations on Mental Derangement* (Edinburgh: John Anderson, 1831).

COMBE, GEORGE, *The Constitution of Man Considered in Relation to External Objects* (1828), 5th edn. (Edinburgh: John Anderson, 1835).

—— *An Address Delivered at the Anniversary of the Birth of Spurzheim, and the Organization of the Boston Phrenological Society* (Boston: Marsh, Capen, Lyon and Webb, 1840).

—— *A System of Phrenology*, 3rd edn. (Edinburgh: John Anderson, 1830).

CONOLLY, JOHN, *An Inquiry Concerning the Indications of Insanity, with Suggestions for the Better Protection and Care of the Insane* (London: John Taylor, 1830).

—— 'Hysteria', in John Forbes, Alexander Tweedie, and John Conolly (eds.), *The Cyclopaedia of Practical Medicine*, 4 vols. (London: Sherwood, Gilbert and Piper, 1833–5).

—— *The Treatment of the Insane without Mechanical Restraints* (London: Smith, Elder and Co., 1856).

—— 'The physiognomy of insanity', *Medical Times and Gazette*, NS 16 (2 Jan. 1858), 3–4, 14.

CRICHTON-BROWNE, JAMES, 'Psychical diseases of early life', *Journal of Mental Science*, 6 (Apr. 1860), 284–320.

—— 'Education and the Nervous System', in M. A. Morris (ed.), *The Book of Health* (London: Cassell, 1883).

DALLAS, E. S., *The Gay Science*, 2 vols. (London: Chapman and Hall, 1866).

DARWIN, CHARLES, *The Descent of Man, and Selection in Relation to Sex* (1871), 2nd edn. (London: John Murray, 1883).

DE QUINCEY, THOMAS, *Suspiria de Profundis*, Blackwoods Edinburgh Magazine, 57 (June 1845), 742–7.

DICKENS, CHARLES, *Sketches by Boz: Illustrations of Every-Day Life and Every-Day People* (London: Chapman and Hall, n.d. [1836]), 58–9.

—— [unsigned], 'A curious dance round a curious tree', *Household Words*, 4 (17 Jan. 1852), 383–9.

DONKIN, HORATIO BRYAN, 'Hysteria' in Daniel Hack Tuke (ed.), *A Dictionary of Psychological Medicine*, 2 vols. (London: J. and A. Churchill, 1892).

DRYSDALE, GEORGE, ['A Doctor of Medicine'], *Elements of Social Science, or, Physical, Sexual and Natural Religion* (1854), 13th edn. (London: Truelove, 1873).

ELLIS, H. HAVELOCK, *The Criminal* (London: Walter Scott, 1890).

ENGLEDUE, W. C., *Cerebral Physiology and Materialism . . . With a letter from Dr Elliotson, on Mesmeric Phrenology and Materialism* (London: H. Ballière, 1843).

ESQUIROL, JEAN TIENNE, *Mental Maladies: A Treatise on Insanity*, trans. E. K. Hunt (Philadelphia: Lea and Blanchard, 1845).

GALL, FRANZ JOSEPH, *On the Functions of the Brain* (1822–5), trans. Winslow Lewis, 6 vols. (Boston: Marsh, Capen and Lyon, 1835).

GALTON, FRANCIS, *Inquiries into Human Faculty and its Development* (London: Macmillan, 1883).

GRAHAM, THOMAS JOHN, *On the Management and Disorders of Infancy and Childhood* (London: Simpkin, Marshall and Co., 1853).

HAECKEL, E., *The Evolution of Man: A Popular Exposition of the Principal Points of Human Ontology and Phylogeny*, 2 vols. (London: C. Kegan Paul, 1879).

HAMILTON, WILLIAM, *Lectures on Metaphysics and Logic* (1859), ed. H. C. Mansel and John Veith, 2nd edn., 4 vols. (Edinburgh: William Blackwood and Sons, 1861).

HOLLAND, HENRY, *Chapters on Mental Physiology* (London: Longman, Brown, Green and Longmans, 1852).

HUXLEY, T. H., 'Emancipation—black and white' (1865), *Collected Essays*, 9 vols., iii: *Science and Education* (London: Macmillan, 1893).

—— *Evolution and Ethics* (London: Macmillan, 1893).

KNOX, ROBERT, *The Races of Men: A Philosophical Inquiry into the Influence of Race over the Destinies of Nations* (1850), 2nd edn. (London: Henry Renshaw, 1862).

LANKESTER, E. RAY, *Degeneration: A Chapter in Darwinism* (London: Macmillan, 1880).

LAVATER, JOHN CASPAR, *Essays on Physiognomy*, trans. T. Holcroft (1789), 9th edn. (London: William Tegg, 1855).

LAYCOCK, THOMAS, *A Treatise on the Nervous Diseases of Women: Comprising an Inquiry into the Nature, Causes, and Treatment of Spinal and Hysterical Disorders* (London: Longman, Orme, Brown, Green, and Longmans, 1840).

—— *Mind and Brain: or, The Correlations of Consciousness and Organisation; Systematically Investigated and Applied to Philosophy, Mental Science and Practice* (1860), 2nd edn., 2 vols., (London: Simpkin, Marshall, and Co., 1869).

LEWES, G. H., *The Physiology of Common Life*, 2 vols. (London: William Blackwood and Sons, 1859–60).

—— *Problems of Life and Mind*, 5 vols. (London: Trübner and Co., 1874–9); First series, 2 vols., *The Foundations of a Creed* (1874).

LOCOCK, CHARLES, 'Menstruation, Pathology of', in John Forbes, Alexander Tweedie, and John Conolly (eds.), *The Cyclopaedia of Practical Medicine*, 4 vols. (London: Sherwood, Gilbert and Piper, 1833–5).

MACNISH, ROBERT, *The Philosophy of Sleep* (Glasgow: W. R. M'Phun, 1830).

—— *The Philosophy of Sleep*, 3rd edn. (Glasgow: W. R. M'Phun, 1836).

MARTINEAU, HARRIET, *Letters on Mesmerism* (1845), 2nd edn. (London: Edward Moxon, 1850).

MAUDSLEY, HENRY, *The Physiology and Pathology of Mind* (London: Macmillan, 1867).

—— *Body and Mind: An Inquiry into their Connection and Mutual Influence, Specially in Reference to Mental Disorders* (London: Macmillan, 1870).

415

MAUDSLEY, HENRY, 'Sex in Mind and in Education', *Fortnightly Review*, NS 15 (Apr., 1874), 466–83.

—— *Responsibility in Mental Disease* (London: Henry S. King, 1874).

MILLINGEN, JOHN GIDEON, *The Passions: or Mind and Matter* (London: J. and D. Darling, 1848).

MORISON, ALEXANDER, *The Physiognomy of Mental Diseases* (1838), 2nd edn. (London: Longman and Co., 1840).

MYERS, FREDERICK W. H., 'Multiplex personality', *Nineteenth Century*, 20 (Nov. 1886), 648–66.

PAGET JAMES, *Clinical Lectures and Essays*, ed. H. Marsh (London: Longman, Green, 1875).

PERCEVAL, JOHN, *A Narrative of the Treatment Experienced by a Gentleman During a State on Mental Derangement; Designed to Explain the Causes and the Nature of Insanity, and to Expose the Injudicious Conduct Pursued towards Many Unfortunate Sufferers under that Calamity*, 2 vols. (London: Effingham Wilson, 1838–40).

PRICHARD, JAMES COWLES, *Researches into the Physical History of Mankind* (1813), 4th edn., 4 vols. (London: Sherwood, Gilbert and Piper, 1837–41).

—— *A Treatise on Insanity and Other Disorders Affecting the Mind* (London: Sherwood, Gilbert and Piper, 1835).

RIBOT, T. A., *Heredity: A Psychological Study of its Phenomena, Laws, Causes and Consequences* (1873), 2nd edn. (London: Henry S. King, 1875).

—— *Diseases of Memory: An Essay in the Positive Psychology* (London: Kegan Paul, Trench and Co., 1882).

RITCHIE, ROBERT PEEL, *An Inquiry into a Frequent Cause of Insanity in Young Men* (London: Henry Renshaw, 1861).

ROMANES, GEORGE, *Mental Evolution in Man: Origin of Human Faculty* (London: Kegan Paul, Trench and Co., 1888).

—— 'Mental differences between men and women', *Nineteenth Century*, 21 (May 1887), 654–72.

ROUTH, C. H., *On Overwork and Premature Mental Decay* (1876), 3rd edn. (London: Baillière, Tindall and Cox, 1886).

SAVAGE, GEORGE HENRY, 'Moral insanity', *Journal of Mental Science*, 27 (July 1881), 147–55.

SKEY, F. C. *Hysteria Six Lectures* (London: Longman, Green, Reader, and Dyer, 1867).

SPENCER, HERBERT, *The Principles of Psychology* (London: Longman, Brown, Green and Longmans, 1855).

—— *Education, Intellectual, Moral, and Physical* (London: Williams and Norgate, 1861).

—— *The Principles of Psychology*, 2nd edn., 2 vols. (London: Williams and Norgate, 1870–2).

STEWART, DUGALD, *Elements of the Philosophy of the Human Mind* (1792), 6th edn. 2 vols. (London: T. Cadell & W. Davies, 1818).

SULLY, JAMES, 'The dream as a revelation', *Fortnightly Review*, 59 (Mar. 1893), 354–65.

—— 'Babies and science', *The Cornhill*, 43 (Jan.–June 1881), 539–54.

—— Introduction to Bernard Perez, *The First Three Years of Childhood* (London: Swan Sönnenschein, 1885).

SYMONDS, J. A., *Sleep and Dreams* (London: Longman, Brown, 1851).

THACKRAH, C. T., *The Effects of Arts, Trades and Professions, and of Civic States and Habits of*

Living: With Suggestions for the Removal of Many of the Agents which Produce Disease, and Shorten the Duration of Life (1831), 2nd edn. (London: Longman, Rees, Orme, Brown, Green and Longman, 1832).

TOWNSHEND, CHAUNCY HARE, *Facts in Mesmerism, with Reasons for a Dispassionate Inquiry into It* (London: Longman, Orme, Green, Brown and Longman, 1840).

TUKE, SAMUEL, *A Description of the Retreat, an Institution Near York, for Insane Persons of the Society of Friends* (York: Alexander, 1813).

WALLACE, A. R., *Contributions to the Theory of Natural Selection* (London: Macmillan, 1870).

WEISMANN, AUGUST, 'On heredity' (1883), *Essays upon Heredity and Kindred Biological Problems*, trans. E. B. Poulton, S. Schönland, and A. E. Shipley (Oxford: Clarendon Press, 1889).

WIGAN, A. L., *A New View of Insanity: The Duality of the Mind* (London: Longman, Brown, Green and Longman, 1844).

WINSLOW, FORBES B., *On Obscure Diseases of the Brain and Disorders of the Mind* (1860), 4th edn. (London: John Churchill, 1868).

WYNTER, ANDREW, 'Lunatic asylums', *Quarterly Review*, 101 (Apr. 1857), 353–93.

—— *The Borderlands of Insanity and other Allied Papers* (London: Robert Hardwicke, 1875).

Secondary reading

ARENS, KATHERINE, *Structures of Knowing: Psychologies of the Nineteenth Century*, Boston Studies in the Philosophy of Science 113 (Dordrecht: Kluwer, 1989).

BANNISTER, ROBERT, *Social Darwinism: Science and Myth in Anglo-American Social Thought* (Philadelphia: Temple University Press, 1980).

BANTON, MICHAEL, *Racial Theories* (Cambridge: Cambridge University Press, 1987).

BEER, GILLIAN, *Darwin's Plots: Evolutionary Narrative in Darwin, George Eliot and Nineteenth-Century Fiction* (London: Routledge and Kegan Paul, 1983).

—— 'Origins and Oblivion in Victorian Narrative', in *Arguing with the Past: Essays in Narrative Form from Sydney to Woolf* (London: Routledge, 1986).

—— 'Speaking for the others: relativism and authority in Victorian anthropological literature', in Robert Fraser (ed.), *Sir James Frazer and the Literary Imagination: Essays in Affinity and Influence* (Basingstoke: Macmillan, 1990).

BENN, MIRIAM, *Predicaments of Love* (London: Pluto Press, 1992) [study of George and Charles Drysdale].

BLAND, LUCY, *Banishing the Beast: English Feminism and Sexual Morality 1885–1914* (Harmondsworth: Penguin, 1995).

BORING, EDWIN G., *A History of Experimental Psychology*, 2nd edn. (New York: Appleton, 1950).

BOWLER, PETER L., *Evolution: The History of an Idea* (Berkeley: University of California Press, 1984).

BYNUM, W. F., *Science and the Practice of Medicine in the Nineteenth Century* (Cambridge: Cambridge University Press, 1994).

—— PORTER, ROY, and SHEPHERD, MICHAEL (eds.), *The Anatomy of Madness. Essays in the History of Psychiatry*, vol. i: *People and Ideas*; vol. ii: *Institutions and Society*, vol. iii: *The Asylum and its Psychiatry* (London: Tavistock, 1985–8).

CARLSON, ERIC T., 'The history of multiple personality in the United States: Mary

Reynolds and her subsequent reputation', *Bulletin of the History of Medicine*, 58 (1974), 72–82.

—— 'The nerve weakness of the nineteenth century', *International Journal of Psychiatry*, 9 (1970–1), 50–6.

—— and DAIN, N., 'The meaning of moral insanity', *Bulletin of the History of Medicine*, 36 (1962), 130–40.

CLARK, EDWIN, and JACYNA, STEPHEN, *Nineteenth-Century Origins of Neuro-Scientific Concepts* (Berkeley: University of California Press, 1987).

CLARKE, BASIL, *Arthur Wigan and* The Duality of the Mind (Cambridge: Cambridge University Press, 1987).

CHAMBERLIN, J. EDWARD, and GILMAN, SANDER (eds.), *Degeneration: The Dark Side of Progress* (New York: Columbia University Press, 1985).

COOTER, ROGER, *The Cultural Meaning of Popular Science: Phrenology and the Organization of Consent in Nineteenth-Century Britain* (Cambridge: Cambridge University Press, 1984).

COWLING, MARY, *The Artist as Anthropologist: The Representation of Type and Character in Victorian Art* (Cambridge: Cambridge University Press, 1989).

CRABTREE, ADAM, *From Mesmer to Freud: Magnetic Sleep and the Roots of Psychological Healing* (New Haven: Yale University Press, 1993).

—— *Animal Magnetism, Early Hypnotism and Psychical Research: An Annotated Bibliography* (New York: Kraus International Publications, 1988).

DANZINGER, KURT, *Constructing the Subject: The Historical Origins of Psychological Research* (Cambridge: Cambridge University Press, 1990).

DARNTON, ROBERT, *Mesmerism and the End of the Enlightenment in France* (Cambridge, Mass.: Harvard University Press, 1968).

DESMOND, ADRIAN, *The Politics of Evolution: Morphology, Medicine and Reform in Radical London* (Chicago: University of Chicago Press, 1989).

DONNELLY, MICHAEL, *Managing the Mind: A Study of Medical Psychology in Early Nineteenth-Century Britain* (London: Tavistock, 1983).

DRINKER, GEORGE F., *The Birth of Neurosis: Myth, Malady and the Victorians* (New York: Simon and Schuster, 1984).

DUFFIN, LORNA, 'Prisoners of progress: women and evolution', in Sara Delamont, and Lorna Duffin (eds.), *The Nineteenth-Century Woman: Her Cultural and Physical World* (London: Croom Helm, 1978).

DYHOUSE, CAROL, *Girls Growing up in Late Victorian and Edwardian England* (London: Routledge and Kegan Paul, 1981).

EISELEY, LOREN C., *Darwin's Century: Evolution and the Men Who Discovered It* (London: Victor Gollanz, 1959).

ELLENBURGER, HENRI F., *The Discovery of the Unconscious: The History and Evolution of Dynamic Psychiatry* (New York: Basic Books, 1970).

ENDER, E., *Sexing the Mind: Nineteenth-Century Fictions of Hysteria* (Ithaca, NY: Cornell University Press, 1995).

FAHNESTOCK, JEAN, 'The heroine of irregular features: physiognomy and conventions of heroine description', *Victorian Studies*, 24 (Spring 1981), 325–50.

FASS, EKBERT, *Retreat into the Mind: Victorian Poetry and the Rise of Psychiatry* (Princeton: Princeton University Press, 1988).

FOUCAULT, MICHEL, *Madness and Civilization: A History of Insanity in an Age of Reason*, trans. Richard Howard (London: Tavistock, 1967).

—— *The History of Sexuality*, vol. I: *An Introduction*, trans. Robert Hurley (Harmondsworth: Penguin, 1981).

GALLAGHER, CATHERINE, and LAQUEUR, THOMAS (eds.), *The Making of the Modern Body: Sexuality and Society in the Nineteenth Century* (Berkeley: University of California Press, 1987).

GAY, PETER, *The Bourgeois Experience: Victoria to Freud*, vol. I: *The Education of the Senses* (Oxford: Oxford University Press, 1984).

GILMAN, SANDER L., *Seeing the Insane: A Cultural History of Psychiatric Illustration* (New York: John Wiley, 1982).

—— *Difference and Pathology: Stereotypes of Sexuality, Race and Madness* (Ithaca, NY: Cornell University Press, 1985).

—— and CHAMBERLAINE, EDWARD J. (eds.), *Degeneration: The Dark Side of Progress* (New York: Colombia University Press, 1985).

GOSHEN, CHARLES E. (ed.), *A Documentary History of Psychiatry: A Source Book on Historical Principles* (London: Vision Press, 1967).

GOULD, STEPHEN JAY, *Ontogeny and Phylogeny* (Cambridge, Mass: Harvard University Press, 1977).

GRAHAM, JOHN, 'Lavater's *Physiognomy* in England', *Journal of the History of Ideas*, 22 (1961), 561–72.

GREENSLADE, WILLIAM, *Culture, Degeneration and the Novel* (Cambridge: Cambridge University Press, 1994).

GIUSTINO, D. DE, *Conquest of Mind: Phrenology and Victorian Social Thought* (London: Croom Helm, 1975).

HACKING, IAN, *Rewriting the Soul: Multiple Personality and the Sciences of Memory* (Princeton: Princeton University Press, 1995).

HALLER, JOHN S., *Outcasts from Evolution: Scientific Attitudes on Racial Inferiority 1859–1900* (Urbana: University of Illinois Press, 1871).

HARE, E. H., 'Masturbatory insanity: the history of an idea', *Journal of Mental Science*, 102 (1962), 1–25.

HARRINGTON, ANNE, *Medicine, Mind and the Double Brain* (Princeton: Princeton University Press, 1987).

HERDMAN, J., *The Double in Nineteenth-Century Fiction* (London: Macmillan, 1990).

HEARNSHAW, LESLIE S., *A Short History of British Psychology 1840–1940* (London: Methuen, 1964).

HERRENSTEIN, RICHARD J., and BORING, EDWIN G., *A Source Book in the History of Psychology* (Cambridge, Mass.: Harvard University Press, 1965).

HOELDTKE, ROBERT, 'The History of associationism and British medical psychology', *Medical History*, 11 (1967), 46–65.

HUNTER, K. M., *Doctors' Stories: The Narrative Structure of Medical Knowledge* (Princeton: Princeton University Press, 1991).

HUNTER, RICHARD, and MacALPINE, IDA, *Three Hundred Years of Psychiatry: 1535–1860* (London: Oxford University Press, 1963).

JALLAND, PAT, and HOOPER, JOHN (eds.), *Women from Birth to Death: The Female Life-Cycle in Britain 1830–1914* (Brighton: Harvester, 1985).

Jones, Gareth Stedman, *Outcast London: A Study of the Relationship between the Classes in Victorian London* (Oxford: Clarendon Press, 1971).

Jones, Greta, *Social Darwinism and English Thought* (Brighton: Harvester Press, 1980).

Jordanova, Ludmilla, *Sexual Visions: Images of Gender in Science and Medicine between the Eighteenth and Twentieth Centuries* (London: Harvester Wheatsheaf, 1989).

Kaplan, Fred, *Dickens and Mesmerism: The Hidden Springs of Fiction* (Princeton: Princeton University Press, 1975).

Keating, Peter (ed.), *Into Unknown England: The Social Explorers 1866–1913* (London: Fontana, 1976).

Kelves, Daniel J., *In the Name of Eugenics: Genetics and the Uses of Heredity* (Harmondsworth: Penguin, 1985).

Laqueur, Thomas, *Making Sex: Gender and the Body from the Greeks to Freud* (Cambridge, Mass.: Harvard University Press, 1990).

Leight, Denis, *The Historical Development of British Psychiatry*, vol. i (Oxford: Pergamon Press, 1961).

Mason, Michael, *The Making of Victorian Sexuality* (Oxford: Oxford University Press, 1994).

—— *The Making of Victorian Sexual Attitudes* (Oxford: Oxford University Press, 1995).

Micale, Mark, *Approaching Hysteria: Disease and its Interpretations* (Princeton: Princeton University Press, 1995).

Mosedale, Susan Sleeth, 'Science corrupted: Victorian biologists consider "The Woman Question" ', *Journal of the History of Biology*, 11 (Spring 1978), 261–80.

Moore, J. R., *The Post-Darwinian Controversies: A Study of the Struggle to Come to Terms with Darwin in Great Britain and America, 1870–1900* (Cambridge: Cambridge University Press, 1979).

Morss, John R., *The Biologising of Childhood. Development Psychology and the Darwinian Myth* (Hove: Laurence Erlbaum, 1990).

Mort, Frank, *Dangerous Sexualities: Medico–Moral Politics in England since 1830* (London: Routledge and Kegal Paul, 1987).

Morton, Peter, *The Vital Science: Biology and the Literary Imagination 1860–1900* (London: George Allen and Unwin, 1984).

Moscucci, Ornella, *The Science of Woman: Gynaecology and Gender in England 1800–1929* (Cambridge: Cambridge University Press, 1990).

Olender, Maurice, *The Languages of Paradise: Race, Religion and Philology in the Nineteenth Century* (Cambridge, Mass.: Harvard University Press, 1992).

Oppenheim, Janet, *The Other World: Spiritualism and Psychical Research in England, 1850–1914* (Cambridge: Cambridge University Press, 1985).

—— *'Shattered Nerves': Doctors, Patients and Depression in Victorian England* (Oxford: Oxford University Press, 1991).

Otis, Laura, *Organic Memory: History and the Body in the Late Nineteenth and Early Twentieth Century* (Lincoln, Neb.: University of Nebraska Press, 1994).

Parry-Jones, William, *The Trade in Lunacy: A Study of Private Madhouses in England in the Eighteenth and Nineteenth Centuries* (London: Routledge and Kegan Paul, 1973).

Peterson, Dale (ed.), *A Mad People's History of Madness* (Pittsburgh: Pittsburgh University Press, 1982).

PETERSON, JEANNE M., *The Medical Profession in Victorian London* (Berkeley: University of California Press, 1978).

—— 'Mr Acton's enemy: medicine, sex and society in Victorian England', *Victorian Studies*, 29 (Summer 1986), 569–90.

PICK, DANIEL, *Faces of Degeneration: A European Disorder* c. 1849–c. 1918 (Cambridge: Cambridge University Press, 1989).

PORTER, ROY, *A Social History of Madness: Stories of the Insane* (London: Weidenfeld and Nicolson, 1987).

—— (ed.), *The Faber Book of Madness* (London: Faber, 1991).

ROGERS, J. A., 'Darwinism and Social Darwinism', *Journal of the History of Ideas*, 33 (Apr.–June 1972), 265–80.

ROTH, M. S., 'Remembering forgetting: *Maladies de la memoire* in nineteenth-century France', *Representations*, 26 (1991), 49–68.

RUSSETT, CYNTHIA EAGLE, *Sexual Science: The Victorian Construction of Womanhood* (Cambridge, Mass.: Harvard University Press, 1989).

SCULL, ANDREW, *Museums of Madness: The Social Organisation of Insanity in Nineteenth-Century England* (London: Allen Lane, 1979).

—— *The Most Solitary of Afflictions: Madness and Society in Britain 1700–1900* (New Haven: Yale University Press, 1993).

—— (ed.), *Madhouses, Mad-Doctors and Madmen: The Social History of Psychology in the Victorian Era* (London: Athlone Press, 1981).

SHOWALTER, ELAINE, *The Female Malady: Women, Madness and English Culture, 1830–1980* (New York: Pantheon, 1985).

SHUTTLEWORTH, SALLY, *George Eliot and Nineteenth-Century Science: The Make-Believe of a Beginning* (Cambridge: Cambridge University Press, 1984).

—— *Charlotte Brontë and Nineteenth-Century Psychology* (Cambridge: Cambridge University Press, 1996).

SKULTANS, VIEDA, *English Madness: Ideas on Insanity 1580–1890* (London: Routledge and Kegan Paul, 1978).

—— (ed.), *Madness and Morals: Ideas on Insanity in the Nineteenth Century* (London: Routledge and Kegan Paul, 1975).

SMALL, HELEN, *Love's Madness: Medicine, the Novel and Female Insanity, 1800–1865* (Oxford: Oxford University Press, 1996).

SMITH, ROGER *Trial by Medicine: Insanity and Responsibility in Victorian Trials* (Edinburgh: Edinburgh University Press, 1881).

STEPAN, NANCY, *The Idea of Race in Science: Great Britain 1800–1960* (London: Macmillan, 1982).

STEEDMAN, CAROLYN, *Childhood, Culture and Class in Britain: Margaret Macmillan 1860–1931* (London: Virago, 1990).

STEEDMAN, CAROLYN, *Strange Dislocations: Childhood and the Idea of Human Inferiority* (London: Virago, 1995).

STOCKING, GEORGE W. JR., 'What's in a name? The origins of the Royal Anthropological Institute 1837–1871', *Man*, 6 (1971), 369–90.

—— *Race, Culture and Evolution: Essays in the History of Anthopology*, rev. edn. (Chicago: University of Chicago Press, 1982).

—— *Victorian Anthropology* (New York: Free Press, 1987).

TATAR, MARIA, *Spellbound: Studies in Mesmerism and Literature* (Princeton: Princeton University Press, 1978).

TAYLOR, JENNY BOURNE, *In the Secret Theatre of Home: Wilkie Collins, Sensation Narrative and Nineteenth-Century Psychology* (London: Routledge, 1988).

—— 'Obscure recesses: locating the Victorian unconscious', in J. B. Bullen (ed.), *Writing and Victorianism* (London: Longmans, 1997).

TYTLER, GRAEME, *Physiognomy in the European Novel: Faces and Fortunes* (Princeton: Princeton University Press, 1982).

VEITH, ILZA, *Hysteria: The History of a Disease* (Chicago: University of Chicago Press, 1965).

VRETTOS, ATHENA, *Somatic Fictions: Imagining Illness in Victorian Culture* (Stanford, Calif.: Stanford University Press, 1995).

WALKOWITZ, JUDITH R., *City of Dreadful Delight: Narratives of Sexual Danger in Late-Victorian London* (London: Virago, 1992).

WINTER, ALISON, ' "The Island of Mesmera": the politics of mesmerism in early Victorian Britain', doctoral dissertation, University of Cambridge, 1992.

WOODWARD, WILLIAM R., and ASH, MITCHELL, G., *The Problematic Science: Psychology in Nineteenth-Century Thought* (New York: Praeger Publishers, 1982).

YOUNG, ROBERT J. C., *Colonial Desire: Hybridity in Theory, Culture and Race* (London: Routledge, 1995).

YOUNG, ROBERT M., *Mind, Brain and Adaptation: Cerebral Localisation and its Context from Gall to Ferrier* (Oxford: Oxford University Press, 1970).

—— *Darwin's Metaphor: Nature's Place in Victorian Culture* (Cambridge: Cambridge University Press, 1985).

Index

Bold references denote major sections and extracts from source material.

Made in the USA
Lexington, KY
28 August 2014